SIX WIVES
The Queens of Henry VIII

By, or edited by, the same author

This Land of England
The Reign of Henry VIII: Personalities and Politics
Revolution Reassessed: Revisions in the History of
Tudor Government and Administration
The English Court from the Wars of the Roses to the Civil War
Rivals in Power: the Lives and Letters of the Great Tudor Dynasties
Henry VIII: a European Court in England
The Inventory of King Henry VIII
Elizabeth: The Struggle for the Throne

SIX WIVES

The Queens of Henry VIII

David Starkey

Chatto & Windus
LONDON

Published by Chatto & Windus 2003

2 4 6 8 10 9 7 5 3 1

First published in Great Britain in 2003 by
Chatto & Windus
Random House, 20 Vauxhall Bridge Road,
London SW1V 2SA

Random House Australia (Pty) Limited
20 Alfred Street, Milsons Point, Sydney,
New South Wales 2061, Australia

Random House New Zealand Limited
18 Poland Road, Glenfield,
Auckland 10, New Zealand

Random House (Pty) Limited
Endulini, 5A Jubilee Road, Parktown 2193, South Africa

The Random House Group Limited Reg. No. 954009
www.randomhouse.co.uk

A CIP catalogue record for this book
is available from the British Library

ISBN 0 7011 7298 3

Papers used by Random House are natural,
recyclable products made from wood grown in sustainable forests.
The manufacturing processes conform to the environmental
regulations of the country of origin

Typeset by SX Composing DTP, Rayleigh, Essex
Printed and bound in Great Britain by
Clays Ltd, Bungay

Contents

List of illustrations

Lady Margaret Beaufort, mother of Henry VII, by Roland Lockey (Reproduced by permission of the Master and Fellows of St John's College, Cambridge)

Henry VII and his wife, Elizabeth of York. Tomb effigies in Westminster Abbey (Westminster Museum © Dean and Chapter of Westminster)

'The Catholic Kings': Ferdinand of Aragon and Isabella of Castile (The Royal Collection © 2003 Her Majesty Queen Elizabeth II)

Henry, when he was Duke of York (National Portrait Gallery)

Arthur, Prince of Wales (National Portrait Galley, loan, courtesy of private collection)

Catherine of Aragon, Princess of Spain. *Portrait of an Infanta*, once thought to be Catherine's sister, Juana; modern scholarship has identified it as a likeness of Catherine by Juan de Flandes (© Museo Thyssen-Bornemisza, Madrid, Spain)

Catherine of Aragon, Queen of England. Miniature attributed to Lucas Horenbout (National Portrait Gallery)

The jousts to celebrate the birth of Prince Henry in 1511. (Royal Tournament Roll of Westminster: College of Arms)

Henry's palace at Bridewell, where Henry's marriage to Catherine of Aragon was tried. Painting by E.H. Maund, palace subsequently destroyed (Bridgeman Art Library)

The 1530 Petition to the Pope (Scala)

The Emperor Charles V and the Pope Clement VII (Scala)

Francis I, King of France, painted by Jean Clouet (Louvre/Bridgeman Art Library)

Mary Tudor, only surviving child of Catherine of Aragon and Henry VIII, painted by Hans Eworth (National Portrait Gallery)

Cardinal Wolsey. Artist unknown (National Portrait Gallery)

Stephen Gardiner, Bishop of Winchester. Artist unknown (Trinity College, Cambridge/National Trust Photographic Library/J. Whitaker)

John Fisher, Bishop of Rochester, drawing by Hans Holbein (The Royal Library, Windsor. The Royal Collection © 2003 Her Majesty Queen Elizabeth II)

Sir Thomas More, painted by his house guest, Hans Holbein, in 1527 (© The Frick Collection, New York)

Anne Boleyn. Artist unknown (National Portrait Gallery)

Henry VIII by Joos van Cleve (The Royal Collection © 2003 Her Majesty Queen Elizabeth II)

Thomas Wyatt, drawing by Hans Holbein (The Royal Collection © 2003 Her Majesty Queen Elizabeth II)

Jane Seymour, painted by Hans Holbein at about the time of her wedding in 1536 (Kuntsthistorisches Museum, Vienna, Austria/AKG London/Erich Lessing)

The Tudor Dynasty: working drawing by Hans Holbein of a life-size mural, since lost (The Royal Collection © 2003 Her Majesty Queen Elizabeth II)

Edward VI as a baby, painted by Hans Holbein, probably 1538 (Andrew W. Mellon Collection. Photograph © 2003 Board of Trustees National Gallery of Art, Washington)

Henry VIII by Hans Holbein, at about the time of his wedding in 1536 to Jane Seymour (© Museo Thyssen-Bornemisza, Madrid, Spain)

Thomas Cromwell, chief Minister, 1532–40, painted by Hans Holbein (© The Frick Collection, New York)

Anne of Cleves. Holbein's portrait was sketched hastily on parchment, and subsequently artfully mounted and painted over (The Louvre, Paris/AKG London/Erich Lessing)

Christina of Denmark, Duchess of Milan, by Hans Holbein (National Portrait Gallery)

The family of Henry VIII. Henry in the centre with his son and heir, Edward, and Edward's mother, Jane Seymour. (Jane Seymour was dead long before this family portrait was done.) Henry's daughters, Mary and Elizabeth, are on the left and right. Artist unknown, 1545 (The Royal Collection © 2003 Her Majesty Queen Elizabeth II)

Catherine Howard by Hans Holbein (The Royal Collection © 2003 Her Majesty Queen Elizabeth II)

Henry VIII. Artist unknown (National Portrait Gallery)

Catherine Parr, attributed to Master John (National Portrait Gallery)

Thomas Seymour, who became the husband of Catherine Parr after the death of Henry VIII (National Portrait Gallery)

Edward Seymour, who became Lord Protector (Bridgeman Art Library)

Elizabeth, aged about 13 (The Royal Collection © 2003 Her Majesty Queen Elizabeth II)

Thomas Howard, 3rd Duke of Norfolk, painted by Hans Holbein in 1524. Norfolk was the uncle of both Anne Boleyn and Catherine Howard (The Royal Collection © 2003 Her Majesty Queen Elizabeth II)

Cranmer, Archbishop of Canterbury, 1532–55. Painted by Gerlack Flicke (National Portrait Gallery)

Cardinal Pole (Lambeth Palace Library. Reproduced by kind permission of His Grace the Archbishop of Canterbury)

Henry VIII in old age. Engraving by Cornelius Massys (The Royal Library, Windsor. The Royal Collection © 2003 Her Majesty Queen Elizabeth II)

While the publishers have made every effort to trace the owners of copyright, any errors or omissions can be rectified in further editions.

THE HOUSES OF LANCASTER AND YORK

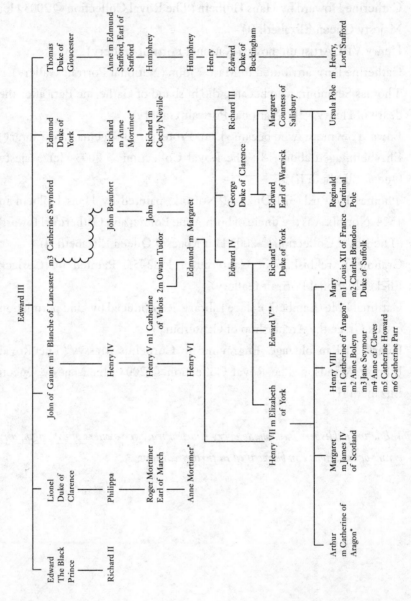

* = appears twice on this page.   ** = the 'Princes in the Tower'

THE LANCASTRIAN DESCENT

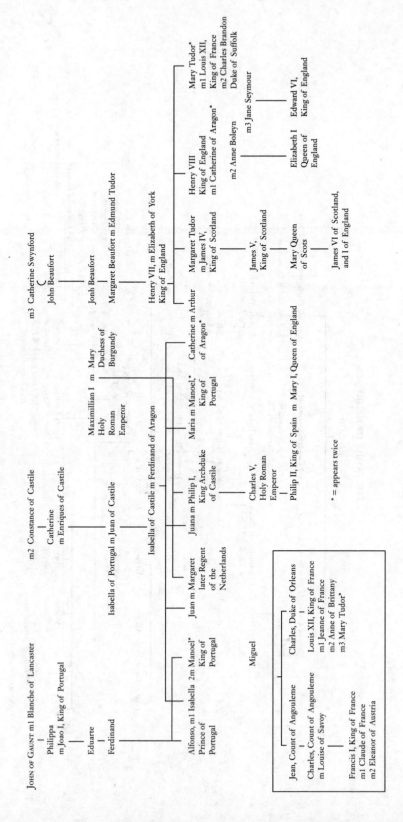

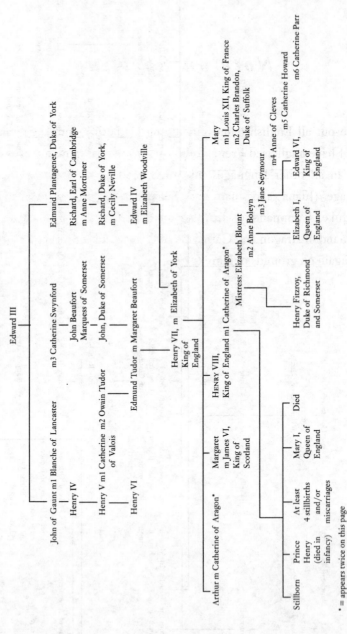

THE FAMILY OF HENRY VIII

Edward III

John of Gaunt m1 Blanche of Lancaster — m3 Catherine Swynford

Edmund Plantagenet, Duke of York

Henry IV

John Beaufort
Marquess of Somerset

Richard, Earl of Cambridge
m Anne Mortimer

Henry V m1 Catherine m2 Owain Tudor
of Valois

John, Duke of Somerset

Richard, Duke of York,
m Cecily Neville

Henry VI

Edmund Tudor m Margaret Beaufort

Edward IV
m Elizabeth Woodville

Henry VII, m Elizabeth of York
King of
England

HENRY VIII,
King of England m1 Catherine of Aragon*

Mistress: Elizabeth Blount
m2 Anne Boleyn

m3 Jane Seymour
m4 Anne of Cleves
m5 Catherine Howard
m6 Catherine Parr

Mary
m1 Louis XII, King of France
m2 Charles Brandon,
Duke of Suffolk

Elizabeth I,
Queen of
England

Edward VI,
King of
England

Henry Fitzroy,
Duke of Richmond
and Somerset

Margaret
m James VI,
King of
Scotland

Arthur m Catherine of Aragon*

Stillborn

Prince
Henry
(died in
infancy)

At least
4 stillbirths
and/or
miscarriages

Mary I,
Queen of
England

Died

* = appears twice on this page

Note on Spelling

I have put all English names, including Catherine, into their modern form. I have anglicised French ones (on grounds of familiarity) and put those in all other languages into their modern form in the relevant language (Juana and Juan and Sebastiano). Foreign titles (Duke, Archduke, Commander) are also anglicised. A few names, such as Ferdinand of Aragon and Catherine of Aragon, have breached that rule, once again on grounds of familiarity.

David Starkey

Introduction

The Six Wives of Henry VIII is one of the world's great stories: indeed, it contains a whole world of literature within itself. It is more far-fetched than any soap-opera; as sexy and violent as any tabloid; and darker and more disturbing than the legend of Bluebeard. It is both a great love story and a supreme political thriller.

It also has an incomparable cast of characters, with a male lead who begins as Prince Charming and ends as a Bloated Monster with a face like a Humpty-Dumpty of Nightmare. While, among the women (at least as conventionally told), there is almost the full range of female stereotypes: the Saint, the Schemer, the Doormat, the Dim Fat Girl, the Sexy Teenager, and the Bluestocking.

Finally, it evokes, like the best historical novels, the peculiarities of the behaviour and mind-set of another age – the quirks of sixteenth-century etiquette and love-making; the intricacies and passions of religious faith and practice; the finer points of heraldry, genealogy and precedence; the gleaming stiffness of cloth of gold and the unclean roughness of the hair shirt. But it also touches the timeless universals of love and honour and betrayal and death.

What is strangest of all, it is true.

And, being true, it is supremely important. For the reign of Henry VIII is a turning point in English history second only to the Norman conquest. When he came to the throne, Henry was the Pious Prince who ruled an England at the heart of Catholic Europe; when he died, he was the Great Schismatic, who had created a National Church and an insular politics that shaped the development of England for the next half a millennium.

Once, historians – who imagined that England was somehow 'naturally Protestant' – thought there were profound social and religious reasons for the change. It is now clear there were none. Instead, it came about only because Henry loved Anne Boleyn and could get her no other way. And he stuck to what he had done, partly because it tickled his vanity, but also because no succeeding wife was able to persuade him out of it.

It is, of course, a story that has often been told before. It was given its classic shape as long ago as the nineteenth century by Agnes Strickland in her immensely influential *Lives of the Queens of England*. Within this vast work, the number and importance of the Queens of Henry VIII made them, as Strickland herself recognized, virtually a book within a book. Strickland's historical discoveries were equally important. She used all available printed sources. She charmed (she was very pretty, especially for a scholar) her way into the national archives of both Britain and France. And, unlike the male historians of her time and long after, she realized the importance of cultural history and made effective use of buildings, paintings, literature and the history of manners.

The result was that she invented, more or less single-handedly, the female biographer as a distinctive literary figure, and established the lives of women as a proper literary subject.

It is a formidable achievement. But there is almost as great a drawback to Strickland's work. For she was undiscriminating and credulous and, as a true daughter of the Romantic Era, loved a legend – the more sentimental and doom-laden the better. Such stuff seeps through her pages like a virus. Like a virus, it risks corrupting the whole. And, like a virus again, it has proved almost impossible to get rid of – with consequences that linger to the present.

Everyone 'knows', for instance, that Catherine Parr, Henry's last Queen, acted as nurse to her increasingly lame and sickly royal husband. But there is no mention of this fact in the earlier, classic characterizations of the Queen. Herbert in the seventeenth century focuses on her age –

she had 'some maturity of years' – and Burnet in the eighteenth on her religion – she was 'a secret favourer of the Reformation'. But neither mentions her supposed nursing skills. The first to do so, indeed, seems to be Strickland herself, who paints a bold and vivid picture of Catherine as a Tudor Florence Nightingale. She was 'the most patient and skilful of nurses', Strickland claims, and she 'shrank not from any office, however humble, whereby she could afford mitigation to the sufferings of her royal husband'. 'It is recorded of her', Strickland continues, warming to her theme, 'that she would remain for hours on her knees beside him, applying fomentations and other palliatives to his ulcerated leg.'[1]

But curiously, despite the claim to evidential support, Strickland cites no sources. And, in fact, there are none. Instead, the idea of Catherine as her husband's nurse is a fiction and rests on a wholly anachronistic view of the relations of sixteenth-century Kings and Queens. Henry had male doctors, surgeons, apothecaries and body servants. There was no need for his wife to act as nurse. Indeed the notion would have been regarded as absurd, even indecent.

But that has not stopped modern historians. To a man and a woman, they have repeated Strickland, and they have sought to go one better by finding evidence. Their search has turned up the accounts of Catherine's apothecary for 1543. These indeed note innumerable 'fomentations and palliatives'. But they were all for Catherine herself or for members of her Household. Henry's name, however, despite the explicit assertion of Neville Williams, does not appear.[2]

Strickland's power is therefore considerable: it turns assertion into fact and makes respectable scholars see things.

Inevitably, the twentieth-century versions of the Six Wives have stood in Strickland's shadow. Martin Hume, *The Wives of Henry VIII* (1905), was a self-consciously 'masculine' reaction, which emphasized the political at the expense of the personal. But both Alison Weir, *The Six Wives of Henry VIII* (1991), and Antonia Fraser, *The Six Wives of Henry VIII* (1992), despite their considerable merits, reverted to Strickland's tried-and-tested formula.

The story also reached the new media and there was the notable BBC TV docu-drama of the late 1960s, *The Six Wives of Henry VIII*, to which Hester Chapman acted as historical adviser, while, some thirty years later, my own Channel Four documentary of the same title was broadcast in 2001.

The latter belonged to the new century. But it too broke only limited new ground. Nor was this book, originally conceived of as a tie-in to the Channel Four documentary, intended to be any more ambitious. I had a few new points to make. But I thought I could fit them into a short, vivid retelling of the familiar story.

It was only once I began work that I realized I had to start from scratch. For, as I wrote, the conventional story started to come apart in my hands. The result is the present book: which is both very big (which my publishers have come to love) and very late (which gave them many a headache).

My problems started quickly, with the character of Henry's first wife, Catherine of Aragon. Catherine is one of Strickland's less satisfactory lives. This is largely a question of materials. Or rather a lack of them, since the archives of Spain, unlike those of Britain and France, remained firmly closed to her. And yet there were riches there. Gaining access to them in their dusty fastness at Simancas made the name of the Victorian historian, James Anthony Froude. But it was only with the publication of the *Calendar of Letters, Despatches and State Papers . . . Preserved in the Archives at Simancas and Elsewhere* that the treasures were made generally and comprehensively available. Historians promptly fell on them and all subsequent assessment of Catherine has been based on the evidence of the *Calendar*.

But there is a *caveat*. For there is not one *Calendar* for the relevant period but two, parallel ones. For volumes I and II of the *Calendar*, published in 1862 and 1866 respectively, were followed by the *Supplement to Volume I and Volume II*, which was published two years later in 1868. The circumstances which led to the division were described by the editor, G. A. Bergenroth. When he had first been allowed into the archives at Simancas in 1860, there had been a rule that the archivist could forbid access to materials which 'might reflect dishonour on reigning families and other great personages or ... [otherwise] be unfit for publication'. Bergenroth had been assured that the rule would not be applied in his case. But he quickly discovered that it was. It took years of lobbying to get the rule lifted and to obtain free access to the entire collection.

The result, however, was worth the effort. For one of the principal lines of demarcation between what Bergenroth had been shown and what he had been forbidden turned out to lie through the material relating to Catherine of Aragon. He had been allowed to see the documents which supported the almost universally accepted view of Catherine as virgin before her second marriage to Henry and as a woman of unimpeachable honesty at all times. But he had been denied anything which cast doubt on this favourable picture. However, as he discovered on his second, unrestricted search, there was plenty on the debit side of the account.

Bergenroth reacted with typical Victorian moralism. Previously, he wrote in the Introduction to the *Supplement*, 'he had joined in the universal praise of [Catherine's] personal virtues'. But now, knowing what he did, he could only reflect, censoriously, that 'exceedingly few, if any, of the men and women who were mixed up with the public affairs of three or four hundred years ago can bear close examination without their characters being more or less lowered in our estimation'. 'Of this', he concluded, 'Queen Catherine furnishes us with new evidence.'

All of which is, no doubt, very interesting. But, it will be objected, even setting aside his Victorian moralism, is not Bergenroth's tale itself now history? After all, both the original *Calendar* and the *Supplement* have been in print for almost a hundred and fifty years. Surely that is time enough for historians and biographers to have arrived at a balanced verdict?

The answer, I fear, is that the issue is still very much alive. For historians, wedded to 'the universal praise of [Catherine's] personal virtues', have shown an extraordinary determination to ignore the clear evidence of the *Supplement*. It shows, for example, that Henry's claim that Catherine had had intercourse with her first husband, Prince Arthur, is supported by good contemporary testimony, including that of

Catherine's own tutor and confessor, Alessandro Geraldini. This does not *prove* the fact of sexual relations, of course, especially bearing in mind Catherine's own impassioned word to the contrary. But it does suggest that the matter should be left rather more open than it normally is.

I have also been able to add another piece to the jigsaw puzzle and one which eluded even Bergenroth. This is the letter from Catherine's father-in-law, Henry VII, to her parents, Ferdinand and Isabella, in which he described the decision to send Catherine to live with her husband Arthur at Ludlow and explained Geraldini's part in it. The letter had been abstracted from the Spanish archives and sent, it is supposed, as a gift from Queen Isabella II of Spain to her opposite number in France, where it formed part of 'the private cabinet of the Empress Eugénie at the Tuilleries'. The letter and a translation were printed in 1864 by William Drogo Montagu, the 7th Duke of Manchester, in his *Court and Society from Elizabeth to Anne*.

Montagu was well aware of the sensational nature of the letter, and speculated smoothly on the real reasons for its removal from the regular Spanish records. But, once again, despite its appearance in print, the letter slipped through the historians' net (which seems, it must be admitted, to have a very large mesh for anything injurious to Catherine's reputation). And I was only alerted to its existence as the result of a chance exchange at the Quincentennial Conference to mark the death of Prince Arthur, which was held at his burial place at Worcester in 2002. I should like to thank Frederick Hepburn, who drew my attention to the document and kindly supplied me with a copy of it.

Like Montagu, I was aware that any new information which appeared to cast a slur on Catherine would be controversial. But the fact was brought home by the response to the public seminar which I gave at the launch of the new Centre for the Editing of Lives and Letters (CELL) at Queen Mary College, London in November 2002.

Here I presented the other key incident from the *Supplement*, which concerns Catherine's first pregnancy. The *Calendar* itself contains only a single letter on the subject. It is from Catherine herself; is dated May 1510; and informs her father that, in the last few days, she had miscarried of a daughter. What could be more straightforward? But letters in the *Supplement* make clear that things were anything but. For the letters show beyond doubt that Catherine's miscarriage had taken place in January; that, despite the miscarriage, she had persisted in the belief that she was still pregnant; and that, fortified by this belief, she had 'taken to her chamber' (that is, undergone the formal, very public ceremony of confinement for a Queen of England) in March 1510. The result, needless to say, was a humiliating end to a 'false pregnancy', which cast doubts on Catherine's fertility and led directly to her first serious breach with her new husband.

The facts are indisputable. But not, apparently, the words in which they should be described. For when I said that Catherine had 'lied' to her father about the date of her miscarriage, I was immediately denounced by a significant section of the audience.

Was I being unfeeling? Unimaginative? Was I ignoring the Rights of Women (which seem, indeed, to have a flexibility denied to the mere Rights of Men)?

The reader must judge.

Readers must also decide whether they are persuaded by my identification of a portrait of the young Catherine, which shows her as blue-eyed and blonde (or at least auburn) in contrast with the sultry, doe-eyed Spanish beauty of the traditional image. The latter is clearly wrong, for there is no way that the features or coloration connect to the known portraits of her maturity. But the 'new' image is supported, as yet, only by probability.

As far as Henry's second Queen, Anne Boleyn, is concerned, there was neither the need nor the opportunity for such fundamental recon-siderations of character. This was because it has been Anne's fate to be vilified rather than idealized (and enemies, I feel, tend to be rather more honest than friends). It was also because she has been the subject of two scholarly biographers – Paul Friedmann in the nineteenth century and Eric Ives in the twentieth – who between them have settled most points of dispute.

But the revisions here are substantial nonetheless. They relate to the chronology of the early years of Anne's affair with Henry, c.1525–27. This is at once the most important and the worst documented period of her adulthood and such fragments of evidence as exist must be sifted with care. It is therefore extraordinary that historians should have persistently antedated the marriage of Lord Henry Percy, Anne's erstwhile admirer, to Mary Talbot. The negotiations for the match had begun, as is well known, as long ago as 1516 and its conclusion was confidently forecast for Spring 1524. On the assumption that it went ahead in 1524 as planned, historians have dismissed out of hand the story, given by George Cavendish in his *Life of Wolsey*, of Henry's ordering Wolsey to break off Percy's betrothal to Anne; there was no need for this, they argue, since, with Percy now a married man, any relationship with Anne must have long been over. But, as I show, Percy's marriage to Mary Talbot did *not* take place in 1524. Indeed it was not concluded for at least another year, till August 1525 or August 1526. This means that Cavendish's story remains plausible; indeed, bearing in mind his status as a reliable eye-witness to the events he describes, it is extraordinary that it should ever have been doubted.

And, just as important, it also means that we should believe Cavendish when he says that the incident led to Anne's nourishing a bitter grudge against Wolsey, which shaped the whole ensuing relationship of mistress and minister.

The other key evidence for this period is Henry's love letters to Anne. The letters are undated and often undateable. But I have been able to date letter V, in which Henry affirms his 'unchangeable intention' towards Anne (that is, his intention to marry her), to January 1527. This alters, at a stroke, the whole chronology of the Divorce: Henry first decides to marry Anne; only then does he launch the first secret trial of his marriage before a genuinely surprised Wolsey. And this in turn transforms our reading of the motivations and behaviour of the principal actors. Wolsey never really recovers his poise. Instead, as I show in my subsequent reworked narrative of the Divorce, his handling of the King's Great Matter was often inept and occasionally malign. Henry, too, emerges badly. It is now clear that he began the Divorce in thoroughly bad faith and that his supposed conscientious scruples were, as Catherine always insisted, a mere fig-leaf to hide his lust for Anne.

Only the two women cover themselves in something like glory: Catherine for her indomitable courage and resourcefulness, and Anne for her driving will and ambition. They, at least, were fairly matched.

Catherine and Anne were the two most important of Henry's wives, in terms both of the duration of their relationships with Henry and of their significance. This is why I devote the whole of Part I to the former, and most of Part II to the latter. But the Later Queens, who make up Part III, have their interest too. Here I have used the model of the short story for Jane Seymour, Anne of Cleves and Catherine Howard.

Jane emerges more firmly drawn than usual. For, despite her protestations of humility, she set herself up as the equal and opposite of her rival, Anne Boleyn. Jane was white to her black, a good conservative Catholic as opposed to Anne's religious radicalism. Particularly important is Jane's role in the great northern revolt known as the Pilgrimage of Grace. She endorsed, as far as she dared, the rebels' demands for a restoration of the monasteries, and, by a cruel twist of fate, her known sympathy with the aims of the revolt played an important part in tricking its leaders into submission.

This last point is new. In contrast, my treatment of Anne of Cleves is traditional. The essential material, in the form of the depositions about the King's invincible personal dislike for Anne, has been in print since the publication in the early eighteenth century of the *Ecclesiastical Memorials* by the great antiquary, John Strype. The depositions reproduce, verbatim and often in direct speech, the words of the participants and I have refashioned them into a narrative which tells the story of Anne's wooing, marriage and divorce largely in dialogue-form.

The reader may find it difficult to believe that the result is not fiction. But it is not. Instead, it is a word-for-word transcription of documents, which, thanks to this simple device, speak directly and without mediation to us.

That formal device apart, my only twist of novelty in the chapter is to show that Anne, far from retreating thankfully into the status of a well-endowed divorcée, never gave up hope of remarrying Henry and viewed each of his succeeding marriages with despair and renewed chagrin.

I have also depended on depositions and the dialogue-form for my life of Catherine Howard. But the result is new and fresh. As a child of the 'Sixties, I can describe Catherine's promiscuity without disapproval. I am also able, for the first time, to reproduce in full some of the more sensational material from the depositions, which includes the 'rudest word' in the language. Finally, in what again I suspect may be a first, I have read and transcribed the whole of the abstract of the interrogation of Thomas Culpepper, who was said to have conducted an affair with Catherine after her marriage to the King. The document is very long and very illegible. But deciphering it was well worth the effort. For, in place of the enthusiastic animal couplings of Catherine's premarital relationships, Culpepper's interrogation paints an altogether more ethereal picture. The couple never had sex: instead there were intense nocturnal conversations, anatomizations of their past love affairs and oblique humorous exchanges which might have come from the banter of lovers in a Shakespearean comedy.

It is all rather touching; while Catherine herself emerges as a sympathetic figure, who, alone among Henry's wives, was neither the tool nor the leader of a politico-religious faction.

Catherine also emerges more clearly in a literal sense as, for the first time, I establish the existence of a reliable likeness. The miniature by Holbein, now in the Royal Collection, was originally identified as a portrait of Catherine Howard by Horace Walpole. But the identification has never carried full conviction among scholars. Here, using the inventory of jewels given to Catherine on her wedding day, I have been able to prove that the picture is of her. It can even be dated as a wedding portrait.

*

With Catherine Parr, the book ends on a weightier note. I begin by discussing her origins in a rich, upwardly mobile family that remained – despite her father's premature death – at the centre of affairs at Court. This has been underplayed – especially by Strickland, who, because of her own surname, fancied that she too descended from a Westmorland gentry family – in a countervailing desire to dramatize Catherine's northern origins. Far more distorting, however, have been recent revisionist critiques of traditional claims about the quality of Catherine's early education and her early conversion to Reformed religion. I myself subscribed to these revisionist arguments in *Elizabeth*. But, as I show here with compelling new evidence, the traditional views of Catherine's education and religious affiliation are correct: she was well educated and she was a religious radical too, *even before her marriage to Henry.*

The consequences appear in the following three chapters. The first deals with the swift and dramatic impact of Catherine's marriage on the balance of religious faction at Court; while the second examines how her religious faith coloured her view of both her husband and his policies, and covered them both with an improbable glow of holiness.

But it is the last chapter which is, I think, the most original in the book. Here I show that Catherine was not only, in the hackneyed phrase first used by Strickland, 'England's first Protestant Queen'; she was also the first Queen of the Age of Print. She was a published, best-selling author; and she encouraged other people, including Henry's own daughters, to read and write books as well. The consequences led directly to the near fatal clash with her husband which is described so vividly in Foxe's *Book of Martyrs*. Doubt has been cast on Foxe's story; indeed, it has been dismissed as a pious fiction. But I am able to use the evidence of the appointment of royal doctors, who play a crucial role in the story, to demonstrate that it must be substantially true.

The result is to paint Catherine Parr, dismissed by Martin Hume as 'the last, and least politically important of Henry's six wives', as in fact one of the most substantial. She is also, thanks to her wonderful letters to Henry, which fuse religion and business and love into an intoxicating whole, the most immediately human. This means that it would have been agreeable to stay with her after Henry's death, through the eighteen months of her widowhood and remarriage. But the temptation had to be resisted. For this is a book about Henry's wives; and I have already told the end of Catherine's story in my *Elizabeth*.

So the book ends with Henry's death. It also begins with a Prologue which describes Henry's experience of marriage and his motives for entering into it. These, primarily, were love and an insistent, child-like desire to be happy. It was most unusual for a King to approach marriage in such a fashion. It is why he married so often and it sets the stage for the unfolding tragi-comedy of the book.

But it is also the last time that the King appears centre-stage. For the book is not about Henry but about the Six Wives who married him – for better and more usually for worse.

I have lived with this book for exactly two years. I owe much to my agent, Peter Robinson, and to my editor, Penelope Hoare, who have borne with the fits and starts of my writing and watched stoically as the book got longer and its completion more remote. I am grateful to Alasdair Hawkyard, who has helped in the compilation of the endnotes and family trees; to Rory Mcentegart, who has translated German documents for me; and to Dr Mark Falcoff, who has translated from the Spanish. But my greatest debt is to James Brown, who has read and criticized each chapter as it has been written. Indeed, without his encouragement and forbearance, nothing would have been written at all.

I am writing this on my fifty-eighth birthday. In one way, finishing the book is the best birthday present I could have had. In another, I am a little sad to let it go. But I shall be back. For there remains the even bigger task of the biography of Henry himself.

There, he takes the stage at last!

DAVID STARKEY
Highbury, London
3 January 2003

Henry's Weddings

Royal weddings in the early sixteenth century, like royal weddings now, were an opportunity for lavish public ceremony. And none was more magnificent than the first of the century: the marriage, on 14 November 1501, of the Prince and Princess of Wales in St Paul's Cathedral.

The preparations had been going on for weeks. A great elevated walkway had been erected from the west doors to the steps of the chancel, nearly six hundred feet away. The walkway was built of wood covered in red cloth and trimmed with gilt nails and it stood at head height. In the middle of the nave the walkway broadened out into a stage, several steps high. The wedding itself took place on the upper part of the stage, with the rest of the officiating clergy standing on the lower steps, so as not to obscure the view. After the wedding the young royal couple, both dressed in white, walked hand in hand (the gesture had been arranged beforehand) along the remaining section of the walkway towards the high altar for the nuptial mass. The musicians, placed high up in the vaults for maximum effect, struck up again and the cheers resounded. They became even louder, when, just before entering the gates of the sanctuary, the couple turned to face the crowds, 'that the present multitude of people might see and behold their persons'. Was there a royal wave? Did they actually kiss?[1]

This was the sort of occasion that was tailor-made for Henry. He was handsome, tall for his age and already with an indefinable star quality (two years earlier Erasmus, on first meeting him, had noticed 'a certain royal demeanour' in his bearing). It was a show for stealing, and steal it Henry duly did. All eyes were on him when he escorted the bride along the walkway. All eyes were on him again when at the wedding ball he cast his cloth of gold gown – and his dignity – to the winds and 'danced in his jacket'. His father and mother applauded indulgently.[2]

This was Henry's first experience of a wedding. But it was not his own. It was the wedding of his elder brother, Prince Arthur. Eight years later, it was his own turn. His brother, Prince Arthur, his mother, Queen Elizabeth, and his father, King Henry VII, were all dead, and he, aged only seventeen years and ten months, was King Henry VIII. His first independent act was to decide to get married. And his bride was the Princess he had escorted along that interminable walkway in St Paul's: Catherine of Aragon, his dead brother's widow.

But there all resemblances to the earlier ceremony end. There was no great cathedral. Not even the Chapel Royal was used. Instead, the wedding took place 'in the Queen's Closet at Greenwich' on 11 June 1509.[3]

Actually there were two Queen's Closets or oratories at Greenwich, just as there were in Henry's other principal palaces. They were known respectively as the Privy Closet and the Holyday Closet. The Privy Closet formed part of the Queen's suite of apartments, and was situated off the narrow corridor between her Presence Chamber (or throne room) and her Privy Chamber (a sort of private sitting room). The Privy Closet was divided by a screen. First thing each weekday morning the Queen knelt on one side of the screen and heard her chaplain say mass on the other. (Henry's Queens, whatever their religious proclivities, were expected to be pious, and probably they paid attention; Henry himself took a more masculine attitude and spent his time at the mass, as we might at breakfast, going through the morning mail.)[4]

The Holyday Closet, on the other hand, was, as its name indicates, used for high days and festivals. It was an enclosed balcony, rather like a dress circle, at the west end of the Chapel Royal. The balcony was divided in half by an internal partition, with one half forming the King's Holyday Closet and the other half the Queen's. Ordinary folk gained access to the Chapel at ground level; members of the royal family entered by a private, first-floor gallery, which connected directly with their own apartments, also on the first floor. Once inside, the Closets allowed them to hear the service, which went on for hours, in comfort and privacy: a fireplace protected them from the cold and a grille from prying eyes. At key moments of the ceremony, however, their presence was needed at the altar. So there were spiral staircases on either side of the Closets by which the King and Queen processed to the altar, knelt and made offerings, and then returned to the Closets.[5]

We do not know which Closet was used in 1509. Most probably it was the Holyday Closet, which Henry's father had built for his mother, Queen Elizabeth, though she had not lived to use it. But it does not really matter. For the important thing is that the Holyday Closet, though designed for days of estate or ceremony, was just as private as the everyday Privy Closet. And this is the point: when Catherine married Arthur, she did so publicly and splendidly in the heart of the capital; when she married Henry, it was in a private, almost furtive ceremony, in the bowels of a palace five miles from London.[6]

We know the names of only two witnesses: George Talbot, Earl of Shrewsbury and Lord Steward, and William Thomas. Shrewsbury, as Lord Steward, was departmental head of the King's Household; while Thomas, as a Groom of the Privy Chamber, belonged to the select group of personal body servants who alone had regular access to the private areas of the palace including the royal Closets. We also have the texts of the special oaths which Henry and Catherine swore in addition to their marriage vows. These were required because of the peculiar difficulties, diplomatic and legal, created by the fact that the King was marrying his own sister-in-law. But, apart from these isolated details, there is a veil of obscurity over the event. We do not even know the name of the officiating priest or bishop.

And that we know anything at all is due only to the breakdown of the marriage twenty years later and the depositions produced by Shrewsbury and Thomas in the carefully documented divorce proceedings.[7]

'All happy families resemble one another; each unhappy family is unhappy in its own way.' Nowhere is this better illustrated than in the marriages of Henry VIII, who, towards the end, complained bitterly of 'the sundry troubles of mind which had happened to him by marriages'. But, in one respect at least, each of his subsequent marriages followed in the footsteps of the first. They too, all five of them, were private and followed in detail the precedent of 1509.[8]

With the sole exception of the service at Dover where Henry first went through some sort of marriage with Anne Boleyn, the location was the same. Anne Boleyn was married (for the second time) 'in the upper chamber over the Holbein Gate at Whitehall, before dawn'; Jane Seymour in Whitehall, too, 'in the Queen's Closet'; Anne of Cleves in the same Queen's Closet at Greenwich where, thirty years before, Henry had married Catherine of Aragon; and Catherine Parr 'in the Queen's Privy Closet at Hampton Court'. The company was the same, with ladies and gentlemen of the King's and Queen's-to-be Privy Chambers predominating. The clergy, where they are known, were similarly confidential: Roland Lee, later Bishop of Coventry and Lichfield, is supposed to have married Anne Boleyn; Thomas Cranmer, Archbishop of Canterbury, married Anne of Cleves; and Stephen Gardiner, Bishop of Winchester, married Catherine Parr. All were intimate royal advisers.[9]

So there were no crowds, no trumpeters and no choirs. The only wedding music, in fact, for this most musical of kings, was the sonorous Latin of the service. But even the Old Church, whose liturgy Henry kept to the end of his reign, put the marriage vows into English. Each of the couples, when asked if they wished to marry, said 'Yea'. Then, in turn, they made their vows. The King swore first:

> 'I, Henry, take thee to my wedded wife, to have and to hold from this day forward, for better for worse, for richer for poorer, in sickness and in health, till death us do part, and thereto I plight thee my troth.'

Then each of the Queens replied. 'I take thee, Henry, to my wedded husband,' they swore, before making the same oath as the King with the additional, womanly promise to be 'bonny and buxom in bed and at board'.

Finally the King put on the Queen's wedding-ring.

Anne of Cleves's ring was engraved: 'GOD SEND ME WELL TO KEEP.' Few prayers can have been more brutally or more quickly rejected. Seven months later she was divorced and, after a consolatory dinner, returned the ring to the King, 'desiring that it might be broken in pieces as a thing which she knew of no force or value'.[10]

The question is now insistent: did Henry view marriage itself as being like that ring, 'a thing of no force or value'? Certainly, his attitude to it was peculiar. Just how peculiar has been obscured by the claim of most modern historians that royal marriages made in private, like Henry's, were the rule. They were so only because he made them the rule. The earlier practice, which he inherited, was variable. It is set out in the official handbook of English protocol known as *The Royal Book*. This was drawn up under the Lancastrians; then it was handed over, like a relay baton of legitimacy, to the succeeding dynasties: first to the Yorkists and then to the Tudors.

The ceremonies in *The Royal Book* fell into two main types. There were those which conferred divine sanction on the Monarchy, of which the most important was the coronation. And there were those which ensured the continuance of the royal line. This is why incidents in the Queen's reproductive cycle figured so heavily: the conception, her confinement, her delivery, the baptism of her child, and her churching, when, some forty days after giving birth, she was freed from the pollution of childbed. And the beginning of all these, naturally, was her marriage.[11]

Here *The Royal Book* offered a choice. 'Also it must be understood whether the King will be married privily or openly.' But, in offering this choice, it took for granted that the Queen (assumed to be a foreign princess) would have had a grand reception when she set foot on English soil, and that her marriage would be followed almost immediately by her coronation. How this worked out in practice is best seen in the sequence of ceremonies for Margaret of Anjou when she came to England in 1443 to be Queen of Henry VI. She was formally received at Southampton on 10 April; married quietly at nearby Titchfield Abbey on 22 April; and then, a month later, was crowned at Westminster on 30 May. And the coronation was of the most magnificent: it was preceded by a triumphal procession from the Tower to Westminster, with verses for the pageants written by the Lancastrian laureate, John Lydgate, and it was followed by three days of jousts.[12]

So for Margaret, a quiet wedding was a private interlude in the otherwise highly public complex of ceremonies which acknowledged her as Queen. Such, clearly, was the intention of the author of *The Royal Book*. Henry VIII followed it only in the case of his first two Queens, Catherine of Aragon and Anne Boleyn, who were indeed publicly and gloriously crowned soon after their rather hole-in-the-corner weddings. But Henry's other Queens were never crowned – though there was an intention to crown Jane Seymour which was put off, it was claimed, because of plague. There were acknowledgement ceremonies of sorts. But they were improvised and consisted in showing the Queen off to the Court (which could be controlled) rather than to the people (who were unpredictable).[13]

The lack of publicity of Henry's marriages does therefore make a point. Henry's marriages had more public, political consequences than those of any other sovereign. England threw off her ancient religion and destroyed old values and old, beloved ways of life, all for the sake of women – Henry's women. But, despite this, Henry refused to see his marriages as other than private acts. They were entered into for his personal satisfaction. And, if they failed to satisfy him, he broke them.

But this does not mean that Henry took marriage frivolously. Rather, he took it too seriously. In this one respect, at least, his attitude was curiously modern. Like us, he expected marriage to make him happy, rather than merely content, which is the most that sensible people hope for. Therefore, like us, when marriage made him unhappy, he wanted out. The result nowadays is a soaring divorce rate and a crisis of marriage. The result then was that Henry suffered from these same problems on a personal basis.

And he did suffer. So did his kingdom, his Church and his children. But those who suffered most of all were the Six Wives who became the Queens of Henry VIII.

PART ONE

Queen Catherine of Aragon

1. Parents: a power couple

Catherine of Aragon, the first wife of Henry VIII, was born on 16 December 1485. Her mother, the warrior-queen Isabella of Castile, had spent most of her pregnancy on campaign against the Moors (as the still-independent Islamic inhabitants of the southern part of Spain were known), rather than in ladylike retirement. Only after her capture of Ronda did she withdraw from the front, first to Cordoba and then to Alacala de Henares to the north-east of Madrid, where the child was born. The baby was named after Catherine, her mother's English grandmother, who was the daughter of John of Gaunt, Duke of Lancaster. She took after the English royal house as well, with reddish golden hair, a fair skin and bright blue eyes.[1]

The Englishness of her name and appearance proved prophetic. After a happy, secure childhood, Catherine's life was to become a series of struggles: to get married, to have a child and, above all, to protect her marriage and her child against her husband's determination to annul the one and bastardize the other. And the scene of these struggles was England.

Catherine's parents, Ferdinand and Isabella, were the most remarkable royal couple of the age. They were both sovereigns in their own right: Isabella of Castile, Ferdinand of Aragon.

Castile formed the larger, western part of what we now call Spain, stretching from the Bay of Biscay in the north to the marches of the Islamic kingdom of Granada to the south. It was a country of torrid, sunburned mountains and castles and high plains roamed by vast flocks of sheep. The territories of Aragon lay to the east. They were smaller, but richer and greener, encompassing the foothills of the Pyrenees, the fertile valleys of the Mediterranean coast and the great trading city of Barcelona. The traditions of the two kingdoms were as distinct as their landscapes. Castile was insular, aristocratic and obsessed with the crusade against the Moors in which lay its origin and continuing *raison d'être*. Aragon, in contrast, was an open, mercantile society: it looked north, across the Pyrenees towards France, and east, across the Mediterranean towards Italy.

To a striking extent, the two sovereigns embodied the different characteristics of their realms. Isabella was intense, single-minded and ardently Catholic, while Ferdinand was a devious and subtle schemer. But he was much more: a fine soldier, who won more battles, both in person and by his generals, than any other contemporary ruler; a strategist, with a vision that was European in scale and grandeur; and a realist, who had the wit not to let his numerous successes go to his head. Understandably, Machiavelli worshipped him as the most successful contemporary practitioner of the sort of power politics he himself recommended: 'From being a weak king he has become the most famous and glorious king in Christendom. And if his achievements are examined, they will all be found to be very remarkable, and some of them quite extraordinary.'[2]

Catherine manifestly took after her mother. But, I shall also argue, there was more in her of her father's qualities, both for good and bad, than has been commonly realized.

Neither Castile nor Aragon had belonged to the front rank of medieval powers. And their standing was diminished further by a particularly bad case of the disputed successions and civil wars which afflicted most European monarchies in the fifteenth century. In both countries, undermighty kings had bred overmighty subjects and the two royal houses had fissured into a tragi-comedy of divisions: brother was pitted against brother and father against son. Only the royal women seemed strong, leading armies and dominating their feeble husbands. It was a

Darwinian world, and none but the fittest, like Ferdinand and Isabella, survived.

They married in 1469, he aged seventeen, she a year or so older. Immediately Isabella was disinherited by her brother, Henry IV of Castile, in favour of his doubtfully legitimate daughter, Joanna. After the death of Henry IV in 1474, a civil war broke out between niece and aunt. This resulted in Isabella's victory and proclamation as Queen of Castile, and Joanna's retreat into a nunnery. Five years later, Ferdinand succeeded his father in Aragon. Ferdinand was the son of John II by his second marriage, and only after two deaths, both rumoured to be by poison, was he delivered the throne. Having fought everybody else to a standstill, Ferdinand and Isabella then threatened to come to blows themselves. He was determined to be King indeed in Castile; she was equally resolute to preserve her rights as Queen Regnant.

Finally their quarrel was submitted to formal arbitration. This established the principle of co-sovereignty between the two. Justice was executed jointly when they were together and independently if they were apart. Both their heads appeared on the coinage and both their signatures on royal charters, while the seals included the arms of both Castile and Aragon. And these were quartered, as a gesture of equality, rather than Ferdinand's arms of Aragon 'impaling' Isabella's arms of Castile, as was usual between husband and wife. Such power-couple equality was unusual enough in a medieval royal marriage. But, in fact, Isabella was the first among equals since, with the exception of the agreed areas of joint sovereignty, the administration of Castile was reserved to her in her own right.

Not surprisingly, Ferdinand jibbed. But he soon submitted and, united, the pair carried all before them. For, despite Ferdinand's four bastards by as many different mothers, he and his wife were genuinely, even passionately, in love. But even in this there was rivalry. 'My Lady,' one of Ferdinand's letters to the Queen begins, 'now it is clear which of us two loves best.' But they were in love with their growing power even more than with each other. Granada, the last stronghold of the Moors in Spain, surrendered in 1492 and the following year Columbus returned from his first voyage to America, having taken possession of several of the West Indies in the name of the 'Catholic Kings', as Ferdinand and Isabella were to be entitled by a grateful Pope in 1496. Catherine was at her parents' side to witness both these momentous events.[3]

And there is no doubt which had the most effect. Years later, when she was sent a present of a ceremonial Indian chair and robe, she ignored them. But the memory of Granada was forever green.

This is shown by Catherine's choice of badge. In both Spain and England it had become the practice for important people to have a badge as well as a coat of arms. A coat of arms was a given, as it was inherited. But a badge was a matter of personal selection. Some badges, it is true, ran in families – including many of the most famous ones, including the Red Rose of Lancaster or the White Rose of York. But even these were regularly modified, added to or discarded by individual family members to suit their own purposes or circumstances. Badges were also more freely used. They appeared on personal possessions, in interior decoration and on servants' clothing. At one level, therefore, they were a mere form of labelling – like nametapes; at another, they were a personal symbol, even a form of self-expression in an age where such opportunities were limited.

Catherine's choice fell on the pomegranate. This was a tribute to her parents' decision to add the pomegranate to the Spanish coat of arms in a punning reference to the conquest of Granada. (The word-play does not really work in English. But it is clear in a Romance language like French, where the name of the fruit and the city is the same: *grenade*.) But there were other layers of meaning as well. In Classical mythology the pomegranate is the symbol of Proserpina, the queen of the underworld, whose return to earth each spring heralds the reawakening of life after the death of winter. Christianity borrowed this idea, like so much else, and turned the pomegranate into a symbol of the Resurrection. Finally it represented the two, opposed aspects of female sexuality. These derived from the fruit's appearance. The outside is covered in a hard, smooth skin. But the inside (always revealed in Catherine's version of the badge by a cut in the surface of the fruit) teems with a multitude of seeds, each surrounded with succulent, blood-red jelly. The hard exterior suggested chastity; the teeming interior fertility.

This range of meanings was to play itself out, usually ironically, against the events of Catherine's life. But for her, I suspect, the fruit which she had seen growing in the gardens of the Alhambra came, more than anything else, simply to represent home.

2. Education for power

Catherine belonged to a large family as her parents had five children who survived infancy. The eldest, named Isabella after her mother, was born within a year of the marriage. Then there was a lengthy gap, occasioned in part by miscarriages possibly triggered by the Queen's active service in the wars against the Moors. At last, a son, Juan, was born in 1478, followed in quick succession by three younger children, all girls: Juana, Maria and finally Catherine, the baby of the family.

Juan, as heir, was the apple of his parents' eye. But Catherine, as the youngest, was something of a favourite too. Ferdinand proclaimed that he loved her 'entirely': 'for ever', he explained, 'she hath loved me better than any of my other children'. For the Queen, actions spoke louder than words, and in 1489, when Catherine was only three, Isabella held her up in public to watch a ceremonial bull-fight.[1]

Nor was this an isolated gesture, since Isabella was as hands-on as a parent as she was at everything else. She kept her daughters with her even on campaign and in 1491, for instance, at the siege of Granada, Catherine, her mother and sisters had to flee in the night when the Queen's tent caught fire. More importantly, Isabella also supervised the girls' education herself. She has been much praised – especially in this feminist age – for giving them almost as academically serious an education as their brother. But, as we shall see, there were some curious gaps in their training which in time were to cost Catherine dear.

Isabella's own education had been entirely conventional. She had been taught the rudiments of the Faith, housewifely skills and how to read and write Spanish. All these, especially the first, she passed on to her daughters. But, as an adult sovereign, she had also learned some Latin. There were practical reasons for this, since Latin was the prime language of law, government and, above all, of the diplomacy which she and Ferdinand were weaving across the courts of Europe like a spider's web. But Isabella, like Ferdinand, also had a larger vision and it seems certain that she saw the New Learning (as the reformed Classical curriculum came to be known) in the same light as the New World, as a territory to be conquered for her family and her Faith. And her daughters were to share in this inheritance as much as her son.

Isabella was greatly aided in her efforts by the close relations between Spain and Italy, which were the fountain head of the New Learning. Leading Italian Humanists, as exponents of the new studies were known, flocked to Spain and some of the best were retained in Isabella's service to educate her children. The most important was Pietro Martire d'Anghierra, known in English as Peter Martyr. His specific brief lay in the re-education of the nobility and the royal children above all. 'I was the literary foster-father of almost all the princes, and of all the princesses of Spain,' he boasted. Catherine's personal tutors, however, were two brothers: Antonio Geraldini and, after his death, his younger sibling, Alessandro.

Under their supervision, Catherine embarked on a formidable course of Latin literature. But it was not by the Pagan authors familiar to us. This is because they were considered risqué or, in the case of the poets, downright corrupting. So Catherine's direct acquaintance with works of the Golden Age of the Roman Republic and Empire was limited: to the moralists, including Seneca, and to the historians, who were also studied as a source of moral example. Otherwise, her reading was drawn largely from the first centuries of the Christian world: the Christian Latin poets, Prudentius and Juventus, and the Latin Fathers of the Church, Ambrose, Augustine, Gregory and Jerome.

This was Classical Lite, a mélange of authors who, with the exception of Augustine, are now largely forgotten, at least as literature. But then they were highly valued – as was Catherine's achievement in mastering them. She 'loves good literature, which she has studied with success since childhood', wrote the great Dutch scholar Erasmus, who later got to know her well. But what excited his admiration most was the fact that she had done all this as a woman. She 'is astonishingly well read', he wrote on another occasion, 'far beyond what would be surprising in a woman'.

What are also surprising, however, are the gaps in Catherine's education. She, like her siblings, was taught to dance and she performed confidently in public. Otherwise, there are no signs of musical skills or training, either instrumental or vocal. She was familiar with one of the great cycles of chivalric romance – if the presence in her mother's library of three well-thumbed volumes, in Spanish, of the tales of King Arthur and the Round Table is anything to go by. But it seems unlikely that she had read anything of the poetry of Courtly Love, and it is practically certain that she had never joined in its fancifully erotic games. Now, for a Christian Humanist, like Erasmus, the omission of such trivialities from Catherine's education was a positive virtue. But then Erasmus never had to make his way in royal Courts. Catherine and her sisters did: they were destined to have to woo husbands, to win friends and to influence people. In all of these, the Courtly arts, music, poetry and the game of love were the favoured instruments – especially for a lady. Isabella's daughters were sent out utterly untrained in them. Was it because Isabella herself was too mannish, or at least too successful a woman in a man's world, to care about such things? Was it because Isabella's entourage, perpetually on the move and almost always at war, was too much of a camp and too little of a Court for a Court culture to develop? Or was it, finally, because Spain was too isolated from the European mainstream?

If it were the last, the puzzle of Catherine's education deepens. For it was, precisely, the mission of Catherine and her sisters to end Spanish isolation. They were to marry foreign princes and, deploying the superior education which they had been given for the purpose, to bend their husbands and their husbands' lands to the service of Spanish interests. That at least was the theory. The practice was less impressive. For not only were these girls entirely lacking in Courtly skills, they were also sent out, as consorts to foreign rulers, with no training in foreign languages. They could speak Spanish, which scarcely anyone spoke abroad, and Latin, which only the clergy and diplomats did. But their education did not equip them to converse in the languages of their husbands. It was not an education for effective pillow-talk.[2]

3. Power weddings

18 April 1490 must have been a day of high excitement for Catherine, Maria and Juana. Isabella, their eldest sister, was being betrothed to Prince Alfonso of Portugal in Seville and the little girls formed part of the royal party. Catherine was aged five when she received this first lesson in the reality of royal marriages. Other lessons were soon to follow.[1]

For the Catholic Kings, Ferdinand and Isabella, took the customary view that a royal marriage existed, not for the personal satisfaction of the participants, but as a means to a political end. Historians call this use of family connexions to achieve political goals 'dynasticism'. And Ferdinand and Isabella carried it, as they did all forms of policy, to a high level of strategic sophistication. Like their foreign policy, from which it was indeed barely distinguishable, their dynastic policy had two principal aims. Within the Iberian peninsula, they wanted to consolidate their power by bringing Portugal, the only remaining independent crown, within the Spanish sphere of influence. And further abroad, they were determined to contain and challenge France. France was the greatest European power of the day; it also blocked Ferdinand's plans to recover his family's former territories in southern Italy and on either side of the Pyrenees. The marriage of his daughter, Isabella, would deliver Portugal to Ferdinand; his other children were available to bind France in a chain of golden wedding-rings that would, he hoped, turn into a ring of steel.

His plans received an immediate setback when Isabella's husband died at the age of twenty, and Isabella returned to Spain a youthful widow. Undeterred, the Catholic Kings pressed on. The year 1496–7 was the climacteric. On 22 August 1496 their daughter Juana sailed from Laredo in a great fleet captained by the Admiral of Castile. Its destination was the Netherlands, where Juana would marry the Archduke Philip.

Philip was another product of a successful dynastic marriage. His mother Mary was heiress of Burgundy (which included modern Belgium, the Netherlands and much of north-eastern France), while his father, Maximilian von Habsburg, was Archduke of Austria and Holy Roman (that is, German) Emperor. There was a long-standing hostility between Burgundy and France, which Ferdinand cleverly exploited. To make absolutely sure of the Burgundian alliance, he also secured a second marriage, and, on its return journey to Spain after delivering Juana, his fleet carried the Archduke Philip's sister Margaret, previously jilted by the king of France, as bride-to-be of Ferdinand's son and heir, Juan.[2]

On the way, the fleet was hit by tremendous storms and Margaret, in fear of her life, wrote a wry epitaph:

> CI GIST MARGOT LA GENTILLE DEMOISELLE
> MARIEE DEAUX FOIS, ET SI MOURUT PUCELLE
> Here lies Margot, the willing bride
> Twice married – but a virgin when she died!

This sums up one of the hazards of the royal marriage game. A bride could be sent 'on approval', only to be turned down on some technicality which the Church was usually happy to endorse, if a better bargain came along. Margaret need not have worried. Ferdinand and Isabella were enthusiastic for the wedding, and her husband, young Don Juan, Prince of the Asturias, proved an enthusiast after it too. Her virginity vanished in a trice and she conceived quickly.[3]

The bride and groom were then left in Valladolid, while the King and Queen, together with their unmarried daughters, Catherine and Maria, went on Progress down the valley of the Douro to the town of Valencia de Alcantara on the Portuguese frontier, there to deliver Isabella to her new husband. For death was not to interfere with the Catholic Kings' determination to secure the Portuguese alliance. Manoel had succeeded his brother Alfonso as heir apparent to the Portuguese throne, so it was decided that he should succeed his brother in his marriage bed also. Isabella was reluctant but resigned. In the middle of the celebrations, however, came terrible news. The Infante Juan was seriously ill. Ferdinand rode furiously back to Valladolid. But Juan died. His parents had been warned of the risks of over-enthusiastic consummation of the marriage for the eighteen-year-old groom but Isabella had brushed aside the warnings. 'Whom God hath joined together, let no man put asunder,' she had quoted.[4]

There was still hope for the future of the dynasty in Margaret's swollen belly. But, after a terrible labour, the baby was born dead. Then in 1498 Isabella, the young Queen of Portugal, died in childbirth. But at least she left behind a healthy boy. Two years later this child died, too.

This string of deaths of her children and grandchildren came near to breaking Isabella, as nothing else could have done. Her health declined and her religious fervour increased. But nothing, not her health and happiness, nor her children's, was to get in the way of the fulfilment of dynastic ambition. So Maria was sent off to Portugal to marry Manoel, though the Prince of Portugal had already been her brother-in-law twice over. It was a case of third-time lucky and the couple had a multitude of fine, healthy children. Finally, there came good news from the Netherlands too: in 1500 Juana was delivered of a boy. He was christened Charles, after his Burgundian great-grandfather. If he lived, he would be heir to a greater dominion than any ruler since an earlier namesake: the Emperor Charlemagne (that is, 'Charles the Great').

Maria's departure had left only Catherine in the nest. Her mother Isabella hesitated and prevaricated before letting her go. But finally Catherine, too, was sent forth from Spain, magnificently arrayed and accompanied like a sacrificial animal, to meet her marital destiny, far away in England.

4. England

That day in the spring of 1489 at Medina del Campo. Was it, perhaps, Catherine's earliest memory? She was wearing lovely new clothes and had been given fourteen young ladies, also prettily dressed, to wait on her. There were roaring crowds and a bull-fight. Her mother, rough with jewels and stiff with cloth of gold, held her up to see the spectacle. Then peculiarly dressed men, speaking a language which she did not understand, saluted her with low bows and a strange, unfamiliar title: 'our princess of England, Donna Catherine'. It was the Embassy come from England to negotiate a treaty of alliance between England and Spain, which was to be sealed with Catherine's marriage to Arthur, Prince of Wales.[1]

The intended bridegroom was two years old; Catherine, the bride, just over three.

About a hundred years previously, Catherine's English great-great-grandfather, John of Gaunt, Duke of Lancaster, had sent one of his daughters to marry in Spain and another in Portugal (she too had become one of Catherine's ancestors). England then had been the greatest military power in Europe. John of Gaunt's father, King Edward III, had conquered much of France, and Gaunt, for his part, was trying to acquire a Spanish kingdom for himself in the right of his second wife, Constance of Castile.

But subsequently, both England and Gaunt's House of Lancaster had a roller-coaster ride. The issue, as usual, was dynastic division. Gaunt's grandson, Henry V, had come within a whisker of uniting England and France in a Dual Monarchy. But Henry V died prematurely and, under his son Henry VI, who succeeded at the age of six months, his inheritance fell apart. First France was lost; then the English turned on themselves in civil war.

The civil war, later known as the Wars of the Roses, pitted the House of Lancaster (with its badge of the Red Rose) against the House of York (with its badge of the White Rose). Eventually the House of York won. In 1471 Edward IV made his claim secure by killing Henry VI and his son Prince Edward: the main Lancastrian descent was now extinguished.

But John of Gaunt, like most of his rank, had had a complex marital history. His marriage to his first wife, the heiress Blanche of Lancaster, was an affair of state. But, according to Chaucer's poem, *The Book of the Duchess*, it blossomed into a love-affair as well. Gaunt's second marriage, however, to Constance of Castile, continued as it had begun, as a marriage of convenience. Gaunt consoled himself with Catherine Swinford, the wife of one of his senior household officers. He had several children by her, whom he had legitimated by the surname of Beaufort, and he married her after Constance's death.

The descendants of the Beauforts, who were given the Dukedom of Somerset, had a claim to the throne, though it was rendered doubtful both by their original bastardy and by the terms of their legitimation.

Another satellite family of the Lancastrian dynasty was the Tudors. They descended from an extraordinary marriage between the Queen-Dowager Catherine, Henry V's widow, and a young, attractive Welsh yeoman of her household, Owen Tudor. His sons, Edmund and Jasper, were recognized as Henry VI's half-brothers and given the earldoms of Richmond and Pembroke respectively. Edmund, the elder, was then married to the heiress of the Duke of Somerset, Lady Margaret Beaufort. Margaret was only twelve but the marriage was consummated regardless. Shortly afterwards Richmond died and Margaret, after a terrible pregnancy and delivery which left her unable to have any more children, gave birth to a son, Henry Tudor, Earl of Richmond.

With the extinction of the main Lancastrian line in 1471, Henry Tudor became the Lancastrian claimant. It seemed of little importance at the time as he was a penniless exile in Brittany while in England Edward IV sat securely on the throne. But in 1483 Edward IV too died prematurely, of gluttony and lechery, and his young sons, Edward and Richard, were usurped by their uncle, Richard, Duke of Gloucester. He proclaimed himself Richard III and imprisoned the Princes in the Tower, where, almost certainly, he had them murdered.

Richard's usurpation split the Yorkist party down the middle and transformed Henry Tudor's position. Swearing to marry Edward IV's eldest daughter, Elizabeth, Henry set sail for England in the summer of 1485. The expedition was funded by the French and most of the troops were French mercenaries. The fleet landed in Milford Haven at the south-western tip of Wales (Henry always made much of his Welsh ancestry) and Henry marched to meet Richard III at Bosworth, near Leicester. Richard was defeated and killed, and Henry Tudor, crowned with the coronet which had fallen from Richard's helmet, was proclaimed Henry VII on the battlefield.[2]

Five months later, after his coronation at Westminster and his acknowledgement by Parliament, he fulfilled his promise and married Elizabeth of York in January 1486. The new House, which united the rival claims of York and Lancaster, was given a new badge, the Tudor Rose, which, white within and red without, combined the Lancastrian and Yorkist badges. Elizabeth conceived immediately and was delivered of a son in September. He was born in Winchester, the old capital of Wessex which was increasingly identified with the still older, mythical capital of Britain, Camelot. And he was christened Arthur, after Camelot's king.[3]

5. Negotiations

Henry VII's accession had presented Ferdinand with another opportunity for dynastic diplomacy. Here was another 'New Prince', who had reunited his country after a long civil war. Henry Tudor had inherited England's traditional enmity to France. And he had a son. What England had to offer and Ferdinand to give fitted like a plug and socket. Ferdinand made the first move and sent Spanish commissioners to England in 1488. The following year an English Embassy went to Spain to conclude matters. They agreed a treaty of alliance and an engagement to marry Henry's son Arthur to Ferdinand's youngest daughter Catherine. As was usual at the time, the marriage agreement provided for a set of reciprocal financial arrangements: Catherine's parents were to pay Henry VII a marriage portion of 200,000 crowns (about £40,000) in two instalments while, in return, Henry was to settle one third of the lands of the Prince of Wales on Catherine to generate a 'dower' or income for her in the event of Arthur's death. The treaty was signed in March 1489 at Medina del Campo and it was there, as we have seen, that the English envoys had caught their first glimpse of the little Princess who was to be their Queen.[1]

The English pressed for Catherine to be sent immediately. But over a decade was to elapse before she set foot on English soil and, many times during that period, it seemed likely that the marriage would be abandoned. For neither King had got what he wanted from the treaty. A joint intervention in Brittany had failed. Then, after many hesitations (after all, the French had effectively placed him on the throne) Henry VII had invaded France in 1492. But he invaded alone. After only a few weeks campaigning, he made the separate Peace of Étaples with France and called off his invasion in return for a pension (as the French called it) or tribute (as the English preferred to name it). Ferdinand riposted by making his own settlement with France, which recognized his gains in the Pyrenees.

Still worse, Henry's grasp on the throne soon looked shaky. A young

Fleming called Perkin Warbeck managed to pass himself off as Richard, Duke of York, the younger of the Princes in the Tower, and won widespread support, both within England and abroad. To try to counter his claims, Henry had his second son Henry, born in 1491, made Duke of York. The boy, though only three, was already able to ride a great horse to the ceremony. The King invested him with the coronet, the sword and the rod of a duke, then, in an uncharacteristically impulsive gesture of fatherly pride, picked him up in his arms and stood him on the table where everybody could see him.[2]

Perkin Warbeck, meanwhile, had been taken up by the young, ambitious King of Scots, James IV. James married Perkin to his relative, Lady Catherine Gordon, and, hostile as usual to his southern neighbour, swore to help him recover the English throne. In return, Perkin promised to cede Berwick and other disputed Border lands to Scotland.

Things now looked bad both for the Anglo-Spanish treaty and for Henry VII himself. But circumstances suddenly changed. Ferdinand, about to begin a life-and-death struggle with the French in Italy, discovered a new interest in the English alliance in the hope that Henry might be persuaded, once more, to distract the French in the north while he attacked them in the south. And Ferdinand's ambassador to England, Dr De Puebla, decided to help in the solution of Henry's domestic problems.

De Puebla had been one of the original ambassadors who had come to England to negotiate the alliance in 1488, and he was sent back there as resident ambassador in 1495. This time he stayed. He liked England and he respected the English King even more. Indeed, he had – so his many enemies in the Spanish diplomatic service whispered – become more English than Spanish. The truth probably is that De Puebla had come to think that English and Spanish interests were so closely interwoven that by serving the one he automatically advanced the cause of the other.[3]

In October 1496 the Anglo-Spanish treaties were renewed. Emboldened by this diplomatic backing, Henry VII decided to punish James IV for his support of Perkin by invading Scotland the following spring. The armies were marshalled but, just as they were marching north, the Cornish rose in a great revolt to protest against the taxation which had been imposed to finance the Scottish war. With the King's armies already on the way to Scotland, there was nothing between the rebels and London. Henry shadowed them to the north while Queen Elizabeth hastened to London and took refuge in the Tower with her second son, Henry Duke of York. The rebels marched round the city to the south and met the King, who by this time had gathered his forces, at Blackheath on 17 May. The King was victorious. But it had been a close-run thing.[4]

Meanwhile, De Puebla, working in concert with the Spanish ambassador in Scotland, had got James IV to wash his hands of Perkin. The Pretender was despatched with his wife and a few ships and made first for Ireland, which for once failed to rise, and then for Cornwall, in the hope of taking advantage of the aftermath of revolt. By the time he landed in September, however, it was too late and, after a forlorn attempt to besiege Exeter, he surrendered on 5 October. 'This day came Perkin Werbek,' Henry's account-book noted exultantly. Henry wrote personally to De Puebla with the glad tidings. His letter is addressed 'To our most beloved ... De Puebla' and, in his gratitude, he sought permission (which was not given) from Ferdinand and Isabella to reward their ambassador with an English bishopric.[5]

From this moment, Catherine's possible English destiny turned into a certainty.

6. *Arthur*

Catherine, of course, had never seen Arthur. But news of his appearance at different stages of his boyhood was sent back to Spain and, when she was old enough, was, no doubt, eagerly devoured by Catherine.

At first, the auguries were not favourable. Arthur had been born prematurely and had spent his first months fighting for his life. Almost all historians have assumed that this meant he grew up a weak and feeble child. And they have, as we shall see, built great superstructures of argument on the assumption. In fact, however, there is clear and repeated eye-witness evidence to the contrary – starting with the report of the first Spanish Embassy of 1488. The ambassadors were invited to inspect the infant prince first naked and then asleep. And they waxed lyrical at what they saw: 'He appeared to us so admirable that, whatever praise, commendation, or flattery any one might be capable of speaking or writing would only be truth in this case'.[1]

Arthur's development continued on these impressive lines. His tutors gave him an even more thorough grounding in Latin than Catherine herself. He was also introduced to a wider range of heavy-weight Classical authors. And his physical progress fully matched his educational achievement.[2]

His betrothal to Catherine took place in the summer of 1497 as his father, triumphant over the Cornish rebels, was waiting for the trap set by De Puebla to close round Perkin. On 18 July, Henry VII ratified the new treaties with Spain. The following month, at Woodstock Palace to the north of Oxford, in the presence of his father and mother and the whole Court, Arthur pledged his troth to Catherine, and Catherine, imper-sonated by De Puebla, gave hers to him.[3]

A few days later, Arthur was present when his father gave audience to the Milanese ambassador; he even spoke to the Embassy himself. The ambassador was as impressed as the Spanish had been ten years earlier. 'The Prince of Wales', he reported home, is 'about eleven years of age, but taller than his years would warrant, of remarkable beauty and grace and very ready at speaking Latin'.[4]

As such reports were read to her, did Catherine think of how much Arthur seemed to resemble her own brilliant brother, Juan, who had just died? Maybe she thought, too, of his namesake – that other Arthur, the mythical king of Britain about whose exploits she had probably read in the three old Spanish volumes of *The History of King Arthur and the Knights of the Round Table* in her mother's library.

7. *Preparations*

Then, as now, the finer points of wedding preparations tended to belong to the female sphere. So, soon after Catherine's formal betrothal, her future mother-in-law, Elizabeth of York, started a flow of more-or-less helpful advice from England. And behind Queen Elizabeth was the formidable figure of *her* mother-in-law, Lady Margaret Beaufort.

Lady Margaret, who enjoyed quasi-Queen-Mother status as 'my lady the King's Mother', was a termagant. She was an unlovely mixture of *dévôte* and snob, equally committed to precise religious observance, on the one hand, and to the finest nuances of social *punctilio*, on the other. She also fancied herself as an expert in household management. She was, in short, the mother-in-law from hell.

Catherine was to be much more fortunate in *her* mother-in-law. For Elizabeth, everybody agreed, was a real lady: 'the most distinguished and the most noble lady in the whole of England', as the Spanish ambassador (who belonged to a culture which had high standards in such matters) observed. She was beautiful, gracious, intelligent and, above all, a reconciler and healer in a royal family otherwise characterized by assertive and aggressive personalities. In short, hers was advice worth taking.[1]

Elizabeth began with a 'get to know you' letter to Queen Isabella in December 1497. She begged Isabella to write 'very often', both about herself and Catherine. And she promised to keep up a similar flow of information to Spain about her beloved Arthur. The letter was written in Latin. But that does not mean that it was an impersonal communication drafted by a Humanist scribe. For when letters came back from Isabella and Catherine, Elizabeth took personal charge of the replies. 'The Latin Secretary [said] afterwards that he was obliged to write the said letters three or four times, because the Queen had always found some defects in them.' Was the effort worth it? 'They are not things of great importance in themselves,' De Puebla commented in forwarding them to Spain, 'but they show great and cordial love.' Clearly, Elizabeth had struck the right note.[2]

Communications established, Elizabeth then turned to more serious matters. First to be addressed was the problem caused by Catherine's ignorance of modern languages. Ladies in England did not speak Latin, much less Spanish, the Queen and Lady Margaret explained to De Puebla. But they did speak French. They therefore suggested that Catherine should take advantage of the presence in Spain of her French-speaking sister-in-law, Margaret of Burgundy. They 'wish that [Catherine] should always speak French with the Princess Margaret . . . in order to learn the language and to be able to converse in it when she comes to England', De Puebla reported. Margaret was to remain in Spain for another two years, till 1499. And during this time she and Catherine became close. Though Margaret was five years the senior, they even shared Alessandro Geraldini's services as tutor for some five months. Thanks to this intimacy, Catherine's French came on rapidly. But English was still, as it was long to remain, foreign territory to 'our English Infanta'.[3]

Then there was the question of the bevy of ladies who would accompany Catherine to England. They should be of high birth ('the English', the Spanish ambassador explained, 'attach great importance to good connexions'). They should also, King Henry and Queen Elizabeth hinted in more informal conversations, be 'beautiful, or at least that none of them be ugly'. And, though Elizabeth did not fully spell it out, it is clear that, if push came to shove, looks were to be preferred to lineage. The English Queen's position was hardly feminist. But it was practical. For ladies-in-waiting were the chorus-line of queenly spectacle: they were there to sing, dance and, above all, to look nice.[4]

While these discussions for the real wedding were going on, a couple of extraordinary charades were enacted. These were the two proxy weddings between Arthur and Catherine on which the Catholic Kings insisted before they would trust their last-remaining daughter to the fickle English. We have already encountered De Puebla's role as proxy for Catherine at the betrothal; he played the same part, with increasing zest, at the proxy weddings. The first took place on 19 May 1499 at Bewdley, the pleasant country retreat which Henry VII had built for his son in the Welsh Marches. Arthur played himself; his Chamberlain, Sir Richard Pole, played the priest; and De Puebla played Catherine. Arthur and De Puebla joined their right hands and Pole held their hands between his. Then Arthur declared that he accepted De Puebla in Catherine's place as his lawful wife, and De Puebla, speaking for Catherine again, declared that she accepted Arthur as her lawful husband. This ceremony was known in contemporary Canon or Church Law as a 'contract *per verba de praesenti*' – 'that is to say that it was to be henceforth indissoluble'. To make doubly sure, the knot was tied a second time in December 1500. Here the play-acting extended to the point of treating De Puebla as the bride at the ensuing feast. He was 'placed at table above the Prince of Wales, and at his right hand'; he was also served first. The little ambassador was delirious with joy at such treatment. 'In general,' he boasted, 'more respect was paid to him than he had ever before received in his life.'[5]

Finally, between the two proxy weddings, there took place the remaining preparations for the marriage. These were different: real, strictly masculine and absolutely off-stage. They were the solution to the dynastic threat presented, by Perkin Warbeck and the Earl of Warwick to the Tudors and, by extension, to the marriage between Catherine and Arthur.

Warbeck was a Pretender; but Warwick was the real claimant to the throne, since he was the son of Edward IV's brother George, Duke of Clarence. If the Yorkist line were the true line, as most people thought, and if the succession belonged to males, as was again the common assumption, then Warwick was rightful King. He had been feared accordingly by both Richard III and Henry VII: Richard had held him at Sheriff Hutton Castle, his northern fastness; and, on his accession, Henry had immediately removed him to the Tower where, in the fullness of time, Warbeck was also imprisoned. Thence, in November 1499, it was alleged, the real and pretend Yorkist claimants had plotted their escape.

Both were condemned: Perkin was hanged, Warwick beheaded.

Henry VII wept crocodile tears, while De Puebla, who had been openly encouraging the executions, rejoiced. 'England has never before been so tranquil and obedient as at present,' he wrote in his New Year despatch to Ferdinand and Isabella in January 1500. 'There have always been Pretenders to the crown of England; but now that Perkin and the son of the Duke of Clarence have been executed, there does not remain a drop of doubtful royal blood.'

Catherine, of course, knew little of this. But eventually she, too, was to discover that her marriage to Arthur had been made in blood – Warwick's royal blood.[6]

8. Delays

With the executions of Perkin Warbeck and the Earl of Warwick, the English had done all that they could – and more than they should – to hasten Catherine's arrival in England. But still she delayed in Spain.

The treaty had specified that Catherine should marry Arthur at 'the end of his fourteenth year': that is, in September 1500. But this was the *latest* date provided for, and Ferdinand and Isabella had fed expectations that she would arrive sooner. En route to his posting in the Netherlands, Don Juan Manuel, the Spanish diplomat and brother of Dona Elvira, Catherine's duenna, had borne news that the Princess would be sent in spring 1500. But March came and went and still there was no firm word. 'The sums spent in preparation for the Princess are enormous,' De Puebla reported. The English, he continued, were on tenterhooks and Henry VII was getting impatient. For the English King did not like spending money 'on spec'.[1]

None of this, of course, was Catherine's fault. Instead, she was – as so often – the victim of her relatives and of circumstances.

The first problem lay in the relationship between her father, Ferdinand, and her future father-in-law, Henry VII. Both were too clever by half. They both, as it happens, wanted the marriage. But, since deceit was their second nature, neither could quite believe in the other's good intentions. The result was that Catherine's marriage – a prize for the grasping – nearly dropped through the slippery fingers of the two royal intriguers. For Ferdinand first to raise and then to dash hopes of Catherine's departure was an obvious negotiating tactic. But it was an increasingly dangerous one. The more nearly-adult Arthur got, the more valuable a prize he became – and there were other eager royal fathers with eligible daughters. The risk was real that Ferdinand, in his desire to strike a hard bargain, might find himself an underbidder – which would leave Catherine, still in Spain indeed, but also on the shelf.

The motives of Catherine's mother, Queen Isabella, in helping to delay her daughter's departure were more honourable. The deaths, first of her heir and only son, Don Juan, in 1496 and then in 1500 of her grandson by her daughter Isabella, Dom Miguel (who was her next heir), plunged her into a physical and emotional decline. Her energies, once inexhaustible, waned, and her religiosity deepened and became more morbid. She spent longer and longer at her devotions and under her robes of state – once so rich and gaudy – she wore the coarse habit of a Franciscan nun. This drove a wedge between her and her husband and, after the departure of her third daughter, Maria, to marry Manoel of Portugal, all that was left to her was Catherine, her youngest and dearest child. The bond between mother and daughter, always close, got stronger. So when the Catholic Kings protested that they would send Catherine as soon as 'the state of health of the Queen [Isabella] would permit it', they are for once to be taken at their word.[2]

But finally circumstances, stronger even than Ferdinand's deceit or Isabella's depression, took control. Already, in March 1500, a rumour had reached England via Genoese merchants. Her parents, it was said, had other 'very great and pressing occupations': the Moors of the Alpujarras had rebelled. The Alpujarras, a region of wild and craggy mountains and rich valleys to the south-east of Granada, had been given as a little fiefdom to Boabdil, the last Moorish king of Granada. Now its people rose in a savage and at first successful Revolt. The Christian general sent against them was killed and his troops massacred. Ferdinand and Isabella had to fight one more campaign together, which was to be their last, to preserve the Reconquest. Isabella raised troops and Ferdinand led them into action himself.

In April the English were formally told of the Revolt and its consequences for Catherine's departure: the Spanish royal family had been at Burgos, in the north of Spain, to speed Catherine on her way. But the news of the Revolt forced them to turn south and to abandon plans for the Princess's journey.[3]

The Revolt exposed the hollowness of the settlement with the Moors; it also casts a searching light on the nature of Catherine's own religious beliefs.

9. *Dogma*

At first sight, the terms agreed for the surrender of Granada back in 1492, while Catherine as a child was staying with her parents in the stone-built camp-cum-city of Santa Fé from which the siege was directed, were fair, even generous. The Moorish inhabitants were granted freedom of worship, language and dress. They were to retain their property, including most mosques, and, after a three-years' exemption from imposts, they were to be taxed as they had been under their own rulers.

All this amounted effectively to a guarantee of autonomy. It is certain that Ferdinand and Isabella never intended to keep the bargain. For their goal was not simply to restore the territorial integrity of Spain; they were determined also to unify it ethnically and religiously: to make it purely Spanish and purely Catholic.

The obstacles were overwhelming. Seven hundred years of Moorish occupation and five hundred years of creeping Reconquest had left Spain the most culturally rich and diverse of European societies. There were four main groups: the Catholic Spaniards; the Islamic Moors; the large Jewish minority, which had flourished under the tolerant rule of the Caliphs; and lastly, and most controversially, there were the New Christians or *Conversos*. These were former Moors or Jews, who had converted, more or less sincerely and more or less completely, to the now dominant Christian religion. To fuse so diverse a mass into a unity required a formidable force. Ferdinand and Isabella acquired it in the Spanish Inquisition.

The Inquisition was not a Spanish invention, any more than twentieth-century concentration camps were a German one. But the Spanish, like the Germans, perfected what they had borrowed.

Heresy – that is sustained, large-scale dissent from the teachings of the Church – had first appeared in western Europe, in southern France and northern Italy, in the thirteenth century. Heresy was seen as a menace to Church, State and society and to combat it special tribunals were established to enforce uniformity of Christian belief and practice. They were called Inquisitions (from the Latin verb *inquiro*, 'inquire into') because they were able to take the initiative in investigating and prosecuting, without waiting for complaints. The judges, known as inquisitors, were appointed directly by the Pope and were answerable only to him. They were usually drawn from either the Dominican or the Franciscan Order of Friars, who were often fanatical in their fervour and intolerance. The inquisitors were authorized to use torture in their investigations, and they could impose a formidable range of penalties, ranging from the confiscation of property, through life imprisonment, to death by burning. In theory, the last, ultimate penalty was not inflicted by the Church, which was forbidden to shed blood; instead the condemned were 'handed over to the secular arm' (that is, the State) to be burned alive.

In the mid-thirteenth century the Inquisition was introduced into Aragon, which had strong trading and political links with southern France and shared something of the problem of heresy. But the Aragonese Inquisition suffered from the weakness common to most forms of authority in that chaotic kingdom: one inquisitor was poisoned and the heretics even managed to strike back and revenge themselves by martyring a prominent Catholic, Bernardo Travasser.

Ferdinand and Isabella resolved on a fresh start and in 1478 they got papal authority to establish the Inquisition in Castile. Under their direct patronage, it started work in Seville. Its proceedings were so harsh and extra-legal that the Pope threatened to revoke its powers and imprison the inquisitors. Ferdinand and Isabella managed to save it. But they made one concession by agreeing to replace the discredited inquisitors. In their place the Pope appointed another royal nominee, the Dominican Tomás de Torquemada, who in 1483 was made Grand Inquisitor of both Castile and Aragon.

Torquemada's appointment was decisive. Not only was he a man of passionate Faith (not without reason is such conviction described as 'burning'), he was also an organizational genius. He created a network of provincial tribunals, all answerable to himself and his other creation, the High Council, which acted as a Court of Appeal. He issued statutes, to guide investigations and refine procedure. And he supplied energy and leadership. There were, in short, three monarchs in Spain: Ferdinand and Isabella and Torquemada. And there is no doubt whose powers were the more absolute. The Catholic Kings exercised their authority through a patchwork of different kingdoms and principalities. The powers of Torquemada's Inquisition, on the other hand, stretched without interruption from the Bay of Biscay to the Straits of Gibraltar, and from the Atlantic to the Mediterranean. It was the one national Spanish institution and it created a nation in its own image.

Torquemada's influence reached a peak in 1492 with the expulsion of the Jews. Torquemada and others of his ilk had long found the presence in Spain of a large Jewish population an offence against God and man. Had not Jews cried 'Crucify Him', when Pilate offered them a choice of the life of Jesus Christ or the life of the robber Barabas? Many Jews in Spain in the fifteenth century were also sufficiently rich and well placed to protect their *Conversos* brethren from Torquemada's officers. So, like those other persecutors, the Nazis, Torquemada persuaded himself of a Jewish conspiracy to Hebraize Spain; and he managed to persuade Isabella, who was only too willing to be convinced, that her victory over Granada required a thank-offering to God. The chosen sacrifice was the Jews, who were offered a choice between conversion and exile. Most opted for the latter, to the inestimable benefit of Spain's neighbours and rivals, from Venice to Ottoman Turkey. The comparative few who remained became easy pickings for the Spanish Inquisition.

By the time of Torquemada's death in 1498, the Inquisition had burned some two thousand men and women. Nowadays, the Spanish talent for turning sadism into spectacle finds its expression in the bull-fight. Then, its manifestation was the *auto da fé* (act of faith). This was the name given to the grand public ceremonies in which the victims of the Inquisition were condemned and executed. They were held at more or less frequent intervals in every city and substantial town of Spain, and each was a theatrical triumph of the Church Militant. Choirs and clergy processed, carrying the banners and relics of saints and wearing their finest vestments. The heretics were specially clothed, too, in a bizarre, humiliating parody of clerical dress. Sermons were preached and sentence pronounced. Then, before ecstatic crowds, the condemned were stripped, chained to stakes and incinerated.[2]

It was to avoid this awful fate that the Moors rose in rebellion in 1500 – thus, incidentally, delaying Catherine's departure for England. We have no idea of Catherine's thoughts on the events which led to the Revolt. But she is most unlikely to have disapproved. She was a conventional, fervently pious Catholic – in this, as in so much else, her mother's daughter. She had been with her parents in Granada when they had promulgated the expulsion of the Jews in 1492. She was at her mother's side when Isabella boasted that, in her eagerness to root out Unbelief: 'I have caused great calamities, and depopulated towns, lands, provinces and kingdoms.' Finally, it is clear that Ferdinand and Isabella hoped that the English alliance, of which Catherine was the pledge, would lead to England adopting the policies of the Inquisition. Prodded by the Spanish ambassador's denunciation of refugees in England, 'who have fled from the Inquisition [and] who speak ill of Spain and wish to excite hatred against her', Henry VII had made extravagant protestations. 'By the faith of his heart' he swore that the enemies of Spain were his enemies and that 'he would punish soundly any Jew or heretic to be found in his realm'.[3]

In the event, nothing much was done. But Catherine would have been an effective ambassadress for a policy of aggressive persecution, for she undoubtedly embraced the dogmatic attitude to Truth which underpinned it. Like all good Catholics, she understood 'religious belief as something objective, as the gift of God and therefore outside the realm of free private judgement'. She also understood that Holy Church was the exclusive custodian and repository of this objective and divine Truth – and also its appointed protector and defender.

> The Church established by Christ, as a perfect society, is empowered to make laws and inflict penalties. Heresy not only violates her law but strikes at her very life, unity of belief.

The penalties must therefore be appropriate: a life for a life. So Catherine believed. And so the best of her contemporaries, including Sir Thomas More, believed also.

But life was to play a cruel trick on Catherine (and indeed on More). For England, where her destiny lay, came to reject the fundamental principles of Catholic dogma. The conscience of her husband and King was to be put above the consensus of the Church. The English nation, not the Universal Church, was to be made the vehicle of God's purpose on earth. The new dogma was as aggressive and intolerant as the old. It also created a new nation. But Catherine was to stick to the old ways of her native Spain. The result was that the daughter of the unimpeachably orthodox Isabella became a dissenter in her adoptive country, and the persecutrix (at least by complicity) found herself a victim.

10. The journey

By 1500 the Moors of Las Alpujarras were crushed. Another rebellion broke out around the city of Ronda, perched defensively on its great ravine. But Ferdinand bought the new rebels off. He had more important business in hand: to bid farewell to his last child remaining in Spain, Catherine, the daughter whom he claimed to be his favourite. For Ferdinand and Isabella had, at last, given Henry VII a definite promise that Catherine would leave Spain for England on the Feast of St John the Baptist, 24 June 1501.[1]

But the sea voyage would be only the last leg of her journey, since Catherine was with her parents in the rebellious Moorish province of Andalusia in the extreme south of Spain. This meant she had to traverse over five hundred miles of mountain passes, river valleys and the vast central plateau known as the *meseta* – dusty, dry and featureless under the summer sun – before she even reached her port of embarkation on the northern coast.

On 15 May Ferdinand returned from the front to join his wife and daughter in Granada. But Catherine herself was too unwell to leave immediately. Her illness was described as 'an ague' or fever. It might equally have been the pain of departure, since she knew that she would, almost certainly, never see her parents or her country again.[2]

On the 21st she was fit to begin her journey. She travelled without Ferdinand and Isabella, since it was hoped that her comparatively small suite could journey more quickly unencumbered by the vast, slow-moving entourage of her parents' Court. And – also for speed – it was planned that she would lodge modestly, 'at inns and small villages' en route. But haste and the Spanish climate do not agree. 'The heat', Ferdinand and Isabella reported to England, 'is so great that she cannot make long [daily] journeys.' The pace indeed was snail-like: by 5 July she had only reached Guadalupe, the monastery and pilgrimage-site to the south-west of Toledo. After six weeks she was still less than half way to the coast. And she did not arrive in the maritime province of Galicia till early August. The fleet to escort her to England had been assembled in the port of Coruna for months. But she had one last duty to perform in her native land: a pilgrimage to the shrine of Santiago de Compostela to benefit from the indulgence which had been granted for the Jubilee year of 1501, when the Feast of St James (25 July) fell on a Sunday. The final ceremonies were performed and last farewells said and on 17 August she set sail.[3]

Within three weeks, she was in Spain once more, driven back by appalling Biscayan storms. The fleet had come near to foundering and had barely made land at Laredo, near Bilbao. The leading nobles escorting her, the Archbishop of Santiago and the Count of Cabra, managed to get word to England. But Henry VII had already heard of their plight and had despatched one of his best captains, Stephen Brett, 'to be on the look for the Princess, and to convey her in the best way to England'.

On Monday, 27 September at 5 o'clock in the afternoon Catherine and her fleet set sail again. The weather was reasonable until they rounded Cape Ushant, which juts into the Atlantic at the western tip of Brittany. Then, as they swung into the Channel, they were struck by gusting southern winds, huge seas and 'thunderstorms every four or five hours'. 'It was impossible not to be frightened,' one of Catherine's suite wrote to her mother.[4]

The intention had been that Catherine should land at Southampton, since, Isabella had heard, it was 'the safest harbour in England'. But needs must and at 3 p.m. on Saturday, 2 October, the fleet gratefully put in at the first possible English port, Plymouth, far to the west.

Catherine's first act was to go in procession to the church, to offer up thanks for her safe arrival. There, as one of the Spaniards piously observed, 'it is to be hoped that God gave her possession of all these realms for . . . long enough to enable her to enjoy life and to leave heirs to the throne'. They were fine hopes. But they were cruelly to be disappointed. Were the storms, as Catherine is later supposed to have seen them, an evil omen?[5]

11. *Arrival*

There were no signs of such gloomy thoughts when the townsfolk of Plymouth welcomed ashore their future Princess of Wales and Queen. 'She could not have been received with greater rejoicings if she had been the Saviour of the World,' Isabella was told in a phrase that must have swelled her mother's heart with blasphemous pride. The English took early to Catherine, and her hold on popular affection always remained secure.[1]

What makes it the more impressive is that Plymouth's welcome was entirely spontaneous. The English of course had made elaborate preparations for Catherine's reception. But everything had been based on the assumption that she would land at Southampton. So when she came ashore instead at Plymouth, the townsmen and local gentry were left to their own devices to offer their own, impromptu welcome. The town had already begun to enjoy the prosperity which, in the course of the next century, made it home to Francis Drake and the Pilgrim Fathers – those two contrasting products of the Reformation and English Imperialism that were to be the nemesis of Catherine, her House and her country. For now, however, Catherine benefited from the profits of Plymouth's trade and fishing, staying in 'the goodly house towards the haven' built by 'one Painter, a rich merchant'.[2]

She remained there over a week, as the arrangements for her official welcome were hastily revised. Plymouth is one hundred and fifty miles from Southampton, where the official welcoming party under Lord Willoughby de Broke was assembled. So it was decided that Catherine should be met part-way, at Exeter. First the slowest moving element of the cavalcade – a relatively plain horse-litter, for Catherine, and twelve palfreys (or riding horses) for her ladies – was despatched to Honiton. Then Broke himself followed in post, with a new, hastily drafted schedule that itself bore traces of further alterations as Henry VII's administrators adjusted to events on the ground. Having picked up the advance horses and litter, Broke was to arrive at Exeter on 17 October 'at the furthest'. By this time, Catherine had already left Plymouth with an escort of local gentry and nobles. The escorts had also been organized by Broke, who, fortuitously, was the most powerful landowner round Plymouth, and they had been instructed to cover the forty-four miles from Plymouth to Exeter to get Catherine there on the 19th for her formal reception.[3]

Broke was an obvious choice for the honour of receiving Catherine and conducting her to London. As one of the handful who had shared Henry Tudor's exile in Brittany before he became King, he was a member of the inner circle of Tudor government. He was also, as Lord Steward, the senior officer and administrator of the King's Household. And he was most carefully briefed. The rendezvous went according to plan – as did the rest of the new itinerary, which was stuck to with impressive precision. Catherine would have been struck immediately. Her parents were mighty monarchs, more powerful by far than the English King. But their domestic life and etiquette were relatively informal. Now she was in a different world. Instead of her summer ramble across Spain, there was the military precision of her English journey: she was being inducted into one of the most pompous and ceremonialized courts of Europe.[4]

Catherine's route to London followed roughly the line of the present A30. Every dozen miles or so there was a halt. The first stop was Honiton, 'a fair long thoroughfare and market-town', with, then as now, handsome houses strung along the highway which also doubled as the main street. Honiton was open, welcoming and snugly prosperous: it would be hard to imagine a greater contrast to the compact, fortified towns and villages of south and central Spain: red- or white-built, with thickly clustered houses and dense warrens of lanes.[5]

Two or three miles before the next staging post at Crewkerne, Catherine crossed the county boundary. The notables of Devon and Cornwall, who had accompanied her from Plymouth, bade her farewell and handed her over to the dignitaries of Somerset. They included Sir Amyas Paulet and Sir John Speke, who were figures in central as well as local politics. Their country houses lay to the north, that is to the left of the road, where the ground rose quickly: the Paulets at Hinton St George, where Sir Amyas had built 'a right goodly manor place of free stone, with two goodly high towers embattled (that is, with battlements) in the inner court', and the Spekes at White Lackington. Perhaps they pointed out the general direction to Catherine, focusing her eye on another novelty: the English landscape. It was hilly: 'but plentiful of corn, grass and elmwood, wherewith most part of all Somersetshire is enclosed'. No *meseta*, then, but a patchwork of fields, trim hedgerows and, above all, intense, variable greens now shading into the brighter colours of autumn and the greys and browns of early winter.[6]

Catherine's journey continued, first through Dorset, with halts at Sherborne and Shaftesbury, where she spent the great feast of All Saints Day (1 November) in the Abbey, and then across Cranborne Chase to Amesbury Abbey on the borders of Wiltshire and Hampshire. At Amesbury, where she arrived on the 2nd, there was another formal reception in which she was introduced to one of the greatest English families: the Howards.[7]

The Howards had narrowly escaped disaster when they fought on the wrong side at Bosworth. The head of the House, John, Duke of Norfolk, was killed, and his son and heir Thomas, Earl of Surrey, was captured and attainted (that is, declared legally dead) by the triumphant Henry VII. But he was brought back to political life through his willingness to transfer his loyalty to the new King. He was restored first to his earldom, then to his estates and finally, in 1501, was made Lord Treasurer. His eldest son, another Thomas, was even allowed to marry the Lady Anne, the sister of the Queen, Elizabeth of York.[8]

The Earl of Surrey was the nearest thing Catherine had yet encountered to one of the great Spanish nobles or *grandees* of her parents' court. He was a man of honour, proud of his lineage, mistrustful of novelty and, above all, a fighter. Fighting came as naturally to him as it did to the *conquistadors* of Spain: their foe was the Infidel; Surrey's enemy was the French and their sidekicks, the Scots. Accompanying Surrey at Amesbury was his aged relative, the Duchess Elizabeth, the widow of the last Mowbray Duke of Norfolk. The Duchess Elizabeth would have made her own impact on Catherine: she was a formidable personality, whose stained-glass portrait at Long Melford Church in Suffolk served as the model for Tenniel's drawing of the fiery Red Queen in Lewis Carroll's *Alice in Wonderland.* 'Off with her head!' the Red Queen cried. The Howards and their extended family experienced more than their fair share of beheadings in the course of the following decades: sometimes as Catherine's allies, more often as her bitterest enemies.[9]

The Duchess Elizabeth of course spoke no Spanish. So, to assist her in greeting Catherine, she was assigned the services of William Hollybrand, who gave a speech of welcome in the Duchess's name 'in the Spanish tongue'. The speech, like everything else, had been the subject of minute preparation and Hollybrand spoke according to a written text. How Catherine and her Spanish suite had hitherto overcome the language barrier is anyone's guess. As Plymouth traded with Spain, there would have been Spanish speakers among the merchant community. There were probably some resident Spaniards too – though they were regarded as a disorderly lot and were treated with disdain by metropolitan Spaniards. English and Spanish churchmen no doubt conversed in Latin, in which language Catherine herself was also able to communicate. Finally, her newly acquired French would have been put to the test by her more sophisticated hosts, including Lord Broke who had spent two years' exile in Brittany.[10]

Hollybrand himself probably combined the roles of merchant and minor royal bureaucrat as collector of the customs on wine in the port of London. He, too, was to become a part of Catherine's life, as Treasurer of her household as Princess of Wales.[11]

Beyond Amesbury the quality of the roads improved and Catherine was supplied with a 'chair' or chariot as an occasional substitute for her litter. The intention was now that she would make rapid progress towards London. But at Dogmersfield near Fleet in Hampshire, where Catherine was due to spend the nights of 5 and 6 November in a manor-house belonging to the Bishop of Bath and Wells, her iron schedule was suddenly broken. For Henry VII could contain his impatience no longer. The King would see his future daughter-in-law and introduce her to his son. And nothing would stop him.[12]

12. Meeting

Henry VII's decision to snatch a semi-licit glimpse of Catherine before her arrival in London was a last-minute one (the meeting does not appear in her itinerary); nevertheless, its effect was carefully considered. The King was accompanied by a reporter (probably a herald), who wrote up the event and turned it into the prologue to the official account of Catherine's reception and marriage. The herald's prose was purple, like most modern royal reporters'. He was also determined, like his royal master, to milk his story for all it was worth.[1]

Once again, the modern parallel is striking. For the early Tudors, like the Windsors, played the card of Family Monarchy, and turned the rites of passage of family life – the births, marriages and deaths – into public pageants. There was already a strong medieval tradition to this effect. But Henry VII, seated shakily on his throne, carried it to fresh heights in an attempt to curry popularity. And Catherine, like another young Princess of Wales, seemed type-cast to play a starring role in this royal charade.

Henry VII was staying at Richmond. He had just rebuilt the palace, with its fantasticated cluster of onion domes, and renamed it after the earldom he had held before he became King. Now, on 4 November, as though reluctant to leave his new creation, he did not set out till the afternoon. The short November day was soon spent, and the King and his party had to put up unexpectedly at Chertsey Abbey, with only a few miles of their journey accomplished. The next day he made better time and the morning mists had barely cleared when he left. The day turned out fine and sunny and the route was a pleasant one, through the southern part of the forest of Windsor. Soon the royal party was at a full gallop, until it reached Easthampstead, on the western border of the forest, near Wokingham. Here took place the first piece of family theatre, in the form of a public meeting between the King and his eldest son Arthur, Prince of Wales.[2]

Arthur was riding from his principality of Wales to his wedding in London. He was already well used to public events. When he had been received by his future subjects, as on his entry into London in 1499, he had been gravely courteous; when he had greeted his father, he had been elaborately deferential. So it was on this occasion. The inhabitants of Easthampstead were also used to frequent royal visitors to the King's hunting lodge on the edge of the village. So they cannot have been too surprised to find themselves pressed as extras into a Tudor photo-opportunity. 'The true and loving English people', as a few dozen villagers became in the reporter's grandiloquent phrasing, 'pleasantly perceive[d] the pure and proper Prince Arthur . . . solemnly to salute his sage father . . . which was great gladness to all trusty hearts'.[3]

Father and son, whose relationship under the hype was real and close, then spent the night together in the hunting lodge. The following morning they rode out together to 'the plains' – that is, to the flat heathland round Farnborough and Aldershot. Somewhere in the middle of the scrubby wilderness, the King and Prince met with the advance party of Catherine's suite.

Henry had sent word to Catherine at Dogmersfield that he was coming to see her. Catherine responded by sending the senior ambassador accompanying her to say that that was impossible; the orders of her father, the King of Spain, were clear: she was not 'to have any meeting, nor use any manner of communication [with her husband's family] ... unto the inception of the very day of solemnization of marriage'.

Henry's response was categorical. He summoned his councillors and they held a meeting there and then, on horseback and in the open air. Their decision was unanimous. Ferdinand might be King in Spain but Henry was King in England. And Catherine and her suite were now 'so far entered into [Henry's] Empire and realm' that they were subject to the English King and to English customs. It was a case of: when in Rome, do as the Romans do. Catherine and her advisers acquiesced graciously. They had, after all, no choice.[4]

Leaving his son behind, the King rode forward, as the advance guard, to lay siege to the Infanta in her castle. Catherine tried a final ruse. She would proclaim herself the Sleeping Beauty and send word to Henry that she was 'in her rest' after her journey. Henry refused to be put off. 'If she were in her bed he would see and commune with her, for that was the mind and the intent of his coming,' he said. He gave her a few moments to get herself ready; then, booted and spurred, strode into her 'third' (that is, her most private) chamber. Each spoke 'the most goodly words' in their own language.

The ice-maiden had melted. The King withdrew to change out of his riding dress and the Prince of Wales arrived at the manor-house at Dogmersfield. A second meeting now took place, between the young couple themselves. They had been betrothed and married repeatedly by proxy. Now they renewed their vows in person, with the bishops of both sides interpreting English and Spanish into their common language of Latin.

There followed supper and an impromptu ball. Catherine

summoned her minstrels and danced with her ladies. Arthur then danced 'right pleasant and honourably' with Joan, Lady Guildford.[5]

Joan was the wife of one of the King's leading ministers; she was also daughter of Queen Margaret of Anjou's most faithful lady-in-waiting. Through her mother, who was a native of Piedmont, she had acquired a skill in languages that was unusal in the Tudor court: as well as her fluent French she spoke good enough Latin for Erasmus to be impressed by her conversation, and she probably had Spanish too. These skills gave her an important role in the marriages of the early Tudors – though her fanatical devotion to the royal children meant that it was not always a happy one.[6]

But Joan was a mature woman, who was, moreover, married to someone else. Why did not Arthur dance with his own bride-to-be? It can hardly have been repulsion. For Catherine did not have the dark eyes and hair and sallow, creamy complexion of most of her ladies-in-waiting. Instead, with the looks inherited from her English ancestry, she corresponded closely to contemporary ideals of beauty.

Happily, we can see what Arthur saw thanks to a recently re-identified portrait of Catherine in her early teens. She is simply dressed, in a sort of smock, with her hair parted, pulled back and braided into a short, netted plait, and she holds a red rose, the badge of the Lancastrian ancestry she shared with Arthur. She is a country-girl, fresh and charming.

Was Arthur's failure to seize her in his arms then the result – as many writers have darkly hinted – of a lack of manhood? Hardly. Instead it was a straightforward question of etiquette. After all, there had been enough to-do about Arthur's merely seeing Catherine. For him to have embraced her and danced with her would have been – even in more relaxed England – a step too far, even an insult.

13. Hubris

After Dogmersfield, Catherine and Henry VII and Arthur went their separate ways. The King returned to Windsor and Richmond; Catherine continued her journey towards the capital. En route, there was another meeting, this time with the Duke of Buckingham. Buckingham was the richest noble in England, with a pedigree that made the Howards and even the Tudors look upstarts. Neither he nor the Tudors ever forgot the fact. His pride was to be his undoing. But for Catherine, used to the *grandees* of Spain, it seems to have been a bond of affinity. And they came to have enemies in common.

Finally, she was brought to Lambeth, to await her entry into London. There she would be shown to the English people and married to Arthur. For Catherine, it would be the fulfilment of her destiny; for her father-in-law, Henry VII, it was the achievement of his fondest ambition. Nothing was too good or too costly for the celebrations: he would make the streets of London run with wine, and gold would pour out of his carefully managed coffers.[1]

News of the scale of the preparations reached Spain and, just before Catherine's departure, Isabella wrote to Henry. 'I am told', she said, 'that the King . . . has ordered great preparations to be made, and that much money will be spent upon her reception and her wedding.' She was, of course, flattered and pleased at the attention shown to her daughter. Nevertheless, she continued, it would be more in accordance with her feelings if the expenses were moderate. She did not wish that her daughter should be the cause of any loss to England, either in money or in any other respect. 'On the contrary, we desire that she should be the source of all kinds of happiness.' Let Henry, therefore, be more niggardly with his money but lavish with his affection. 'The substantial part of the festival', she enthused, 'should be his love.'

This was Isabella at her gushing, sentimental worst. Subsequent events, however, were to make her words seem prophetic – as though the

Queen of Spain, Cassandra-like, had uttered a warning of the nemesis that follows hubris. But at the time, Cassandra-like again, she was ignored.[2]

Preparations for Catherine's wedding had begun at least two years previously, in 1499, when it was thought that she would soon be arriving in England. Henry VII appointed a group of commissioners, consisting of councillors and officers of the royal household, to plan and organize the event. But he was a hands-on King and he was certainly consulted on all of the commissioners' big decisions and many of their smaller ones as well. The commissioners' starting point was *The Royal Book*, with its collection of precedents for everything from christenings to funerals. But the rules it prescribed for weddings were of the vaguest. This was a challenge; it was also a chance to create something new in both scale and content. The commissioners (and Henry) seized the opportunity with both hands.

The key decision would be location. By the late fifteenth century, most important royal events consisted of four elements: an *entrée* or procession, the actual ceremony, the creation of Knights of the Bath, and a tournament. The various elements stretched over several days and took place in different venues. The first, the *entrée* or procession, followed a more-or-less fixed route, traversing the City of London at its widest, from the Tower in the east to Temple Bar in the west. This showed off the King or other member of the royal family to as many of the inhabitants of England's commercial capital and by far its largest city as cared to watch. For the support of the Londoners was worth having. They numbered some 50,000 and regarded themselves as a sort of proxy for the English: they *were* The People. In the fullness of time Londoners (and especially their wives) were to become Catherine's most vociferous partisans.

The remaining elements of royal ceremonies, however, were normally held outside the City boundaries in the suburbs. Westminster lay two miles to the west of the City and was connected to it by the Strand and King Street (the modern Whitehall) and by the more important highway of the Thames. Here the King had his main residence (and the only one formally entitled a palace): the Palace of Westminster. Here too, and forming part of the palace precinct, was Westminster Abbey. This was a specifically royal church. It contained the shrine of Edward the Confessor, England's royal saint, and it was the burial place of most of his successors, including King Edward III, from whom both Catherine and Arthur descended. Above all, the Abbey was where English Kings and Queens were crowned, with (in the King's case) the regalia taken from Edward the Confessor's own tomb. The coronation took place in front of the high altar in a specially designed area of the church known as the *theatre*. This combination of facilities, in the Palace and the Abbey, made Westminster the natural ceremonial capital, just as the City of London was the popular, commercial one.

But, whatever Westminster's attractions, Henry VII's commissioners ignored them. Instead, they decided that Catherine's wedding would take place in the Old St Paul's Cathedral in the City. This is because they had their sights on a single goal: audience. Large audiences were elusive in the sixteenth century. There were no modern media to take the event to the people; instead the people had to be able to take themselves to the event. Old St Paul's was in the middle of the largest potential audience in the country and it was an easy walk for most of them. It was also big enough to take all who were likely to come, with a standing capacity of ten thousand or more. It remained only to make sure that, in the absence of a *theatre* like Westminster Abbey, the vast crowds could see.

Here again the commissioners were highly innovative. It was already the practice at royal christenings that the baptism itself took place on a round, tiered stage with several steps. The massive silver font stood in the centre of the summit, which was reinforced to take its weight. The officiating priest and the godparents stood at this level too, with the assisting clergy on the lower steps – 'that the people may see the christening and press not too nigh'. The commissioners decided that Catherine would be married on a similar, if presumably larger stage. And the stage was to be placed in the middle of the nave. At a stroke, the ceremony would be visible, as a piece of theatre-in-the-round, to the whole of the congregation.

It remained only to get the wedding party from the west doors to the stage for exchange of vows and from the stage to the choir for the nuptial mass. At royal christenings the processions went at floor level, protected only by guards and footmen. But none ever took place in such a vast, uncontrollable space. The solution adopted had no precedent in English royal ceremony. It was decided to build an elevated walkway or bridge, with hand-rails and at head-height. The total length was well over five hundred feet. The walkway addressed the need both for visibility and for security; it was also a brilliant *coup de théâtre*, which gave the facility for spectacular processional movements, up and down the length of the nave, and all in full public view.

Among the commissioners, in short, there was one with the imagination of a great theatrical impresario. He had the eyes and ears, as well. For no detail was too small. Where should the trumpeters be placed for the best effect? When should they play? How should the fanfares be co-ordinated with the ceremony? Where should the gorgeously vested extras (for the assisting clergy were frankly treated as such) be placed so as not to get in the way? What should the young couple do to milk the scene? All these questions were thought of and answered.

The commissioners also dealt with the behind-the-scenes matters of logistics and accommodation. The King had only a single suitable City residence: Baynard's Castle (the other, the Tower, was too far away). But Baynard's Castle could lodge only the King and Queen and their immediate suites. Prince Arthur, the Spanish ambassadors and Catherine herself had all to be accommodated elsewhere, in buildings requisitioned and refurbished for the purpose. Then there were the horses, the servants, the uniforms and the thousand and one other little jobs that no one notices unless they are not done. These tasks, too, were remembered and assigned to specific, named individuals. Two commissioners were then assigned to progress-chase: 'not only to advertize every man that hath any charge to him to be ready to do their offices, but also to call upon them for the execution of the same'.[3]

In only one area did the commissioners delegate. *Entrées* were traditionally the responsibility of the City authorities and the custom was followed again in 1501. But an unusually close eye was kept. The commissioners chose the route (a new one) and picked the six exact locations for the pageants; while the City committee in immediate charge was directed to be in touch 'from time to time with the King's commissioners touching preparation to be made for receiving of the Princess that by God's grace shall come out of Spain'. The pressure worked and the City set itself to organize the most coherent and stylish *entrée* in the history so far of English pageantry.[4]

The King's servants had done their task well. As the moment for the ceremonies approached, Henry could be confident that neither Catherine nor his subjects had ever seen anything like it. It would be splendid and polished. But would there be room for the love which Isabella had craved for her daughter?

14. *London*

There was one thing, however, that not even Henry VII and his commissioners could control: the English weather. The original intention was that Catherine should make her *entrée* into London on Thursday, 11 November, 'if it be a fair day', or else on Friday the 12th. Predictably, bearing in mind the time of year, she had to wait the extra day.[1]

Catherine set out from Lambeth by 10 o'clock, in fine array. The commissioner's plans had already encountered one national obstacle, in the form of the English weather; now they confronted another: Spanish pride. It had been taken for granted that Catherine would make her entry, English-fashion, in a litter. Instead she chose to emphasize her

Spanishness by riding side-saddle on a great mule. She wore Spanish dress; her mule was saddled, harnessed and trapped Spanish-fashion; she even rode on the opposite side to the English practice, sitting on the animal's right.

The cavalcade proceeded east along the south bank of the Thames, riding a little inland. There were few or no buildings. Instead, the way lay through open countryside, interspersed with orchards and gardens. At St George's Fields (by the present Imperial War Museum) she was met by her English escort. It included the flower of the social and political élite, led by the King's second son, Henry, Duke of York.[2]

This was the first meeting of the pair whose lives were to remake English history. Henry was ten. Like Arthur, he was of above average height. Otherwise the brothers were very different in both appearance and character. Arthur took after his father and his father's Beaufort ancestry. He had a long face, a beaked nose and hooded eyes. Henry, however, resembled his mother, and still more his Yorkist grandfather, Edward IV. He had Edward's broad, flattish face, with auburn hair and a pale skin offset with small blue eyes, set rather close together, and a small rose-bud mouth. He also inherited his grandfather's charm (especially to women), his animal vigour and high spirits. Arthur, on the other hand, was his father's son in character too: he was serious, dedicated and watchful. The contrast between the brothers had been heightened by their very different upbringings. Arthur, from infancy, was reared away from his parents in his own separate Household. There his tutors had dinned into him his destiny as King. Henry, however, was brought up with his mother and sisters and spoiled as only a boy in a predominantly female household can be. Arthur was 'safe'; Henry was a young rogue, clever and attractive if perhaps a little dangerous. Did Catherine wish at that moment that Henry rather than Arthur was her chosen husband? Probably not. Henry was too young. In any case, her destiny (in which she had been trained as ruthlessly as Arthur in his) was to marry the heir of England. Henry was only the spare.

The much enlarged party rode on, with Henry at Catherine's right hand.

Soon they came to Southwark, the only built-up area south of the river. They turned north, into the high street. A few hundred yards brought them to the river bank. Then Catherine saw one of the great sights of Europe: the City of London.

Directly in front of her was London Bridge, with its two gate-houses, the Chapel of St Thomas of Canterbury, and a myriad houses and shops: tall, tight-packed and bursting over the structure of the bridge as every inch of valuable real estate was put to good use. On the opposite bank rose the City. Its buildings made an arc, as they followed one of the huge meanders of the Thames. The river was filled with shipping. Houses, warehouses and wharves were crowded together along the waterfront. The spires and towers of dozens of churches rose above the sharply-pitched roofs. To the right stood the Tower, looking much as it does today. In the distance were the hills of Islington and Highgate. And looming over everything was Old St Paul's. The cathedral was vast – in bulk, in length and, above all, in the height of its 489-foot spire. This was Catherine's destination. Here she would be married.[3]

But first there was the City and its welcome. Catherine was greeted by the City dignitaries: the Lord Mayor with his sword-bearer, the Recorder, the two Sheriffs and the twenty-four Aldermen, all in their robes. The officials then turned their horses round and preceded her on to London Bridge. There, in the middle of the Bridge, she encountered the first pageant of the series which the City had laid on for her entertainment and edification. The pageants were temporary, tower-like structures, built of wood and canvas and gaily painted and gilded with the King's arms, badges and beasts. On the upper floors were 'rooms' or stages with elaborately dressed figures and other devices. The figures addressed Catherine – resolutely – in English verse, of which of course she understood scarcely a word. To assist her and her party, there were painted captions in Latin. But these were very brief. Perhaps Henry told Catherine something of what was going on in his excellent French. He may even have tried out his Latin, which was also good, though naturally not yet as fluent as hers.

The first pageant contained the figures of two saints. First St

Catherine, complete with her wheel, explained to her namesake that the pageant series would show her how Virtue led to Honour. Then it was the turn of St Ursula, who told her that in this quest Arthur would be her helpmeet and companion. But thereafter things became complicated. For Arthur, according to Ursula, not only represented his namesake and ancestor, King Arthur, but also the star Arcturus and the constellation of Ursa Major. Arcturus is the brightest star in the northern hemisphere and Ursa Major the most recognizable constellation. They are allegorized in the *Book of Job* and the allegory in turn is elaborated into one of the set-pieces of Christian cosmology by Gregory the Great. All this would be woven into Catherine's pageant-journey across London. Partly, it was a mere excuse to display some of the astrological imagery of which Henry VII was known to be fond. More importantly, it disguised the fact that Arthur of Camelot, the obvious pageant-theme for Catherine's future husband, was an unsuitable subject for an *epithalamium* or celebration of marriage. For Arthur was incestuous and childless, while his wife, Guinevere, was an adulteress, who cuckolded her husband with his favourite knight, Lancelot. Arcturus and his constellation threw a pleasing cloud of star-dust over such unpleasantness.[4]

Catherine's procession continued over the bridge and entered Gracechurch Street. The street, like the rest of Catherine's route, was lined with rails. The leading citizens, the liverymen of the City Companies or Guilds, stood inside the rails in their hoods and gowns, while the ordinary folk crowded behind the rails. They also hung out of windows and perched on roof-tops and gutters. It was, the herald remarked, a sign of God's blessing on the marriage that no one fell or was crushed. Half way up Gracechurch Street, at its widest point, was the next pageant, which introduced Virtue herself. At the top of Gracechurch Street, by the corner of Leadenhall Market, Catherine turned left into Cornhill which in turn led to Cheapside.

Cheapside was the principal thoroughfare of the City and its main shopping street. Even Venetian observers were impressed at the goods on sale in the goldsmiths' shops. Catherine, however, had to be content with the increasingly precious words of the pageant-figures. For the next three pageants developed the cosmological theme of the series. The first, in Cornhill, was the Pageant of the Moon. It featured the moving circuit of the Moon (a treadmill, turned by three panting boys in armour) and a performer impersonating Catherine's ancestor, the astronomer-king Alfonso of Aragon, who prognosticated Catherine's future bliss with Arthur. Next, at the beginning of Cheapside, was the Pageant of the Sun. Here, inside his orbit (another revolving treadmill), sat a figure representing Arcturus/Arthur in his embodiment of the Sun. He gravely welcomed Catherine as his bride. This section of the series culminated in the next pageant at the Standard, the elaborate conduit-structure in the widest part of Cheapside. This was the Pageant of the Temple of God. Here sat the God-head himself, surrounded by burning candles and singing angels. He addressed Catherine. 'Love me, and my Church, your spiritual mother,' he enjoined. 'For ye despising that one despise the other.'

There stepped forward a second performer, dressed as a bishop. When he spoke to Catherine he had half an eye to another auditor, who watched and listened at the window of an adjacent merchant's house. It was the King. Henry VII had come 'somewhat privy and secretly', though his *incognito* was rather blown by the guards, who occupied every vantage point on the roof, and the crowd of hangers-on, who crammed both sides of the street below. The bishop's speech removed any remaining shreds of anonymity. He began by recalling the parable in St Matthew's Gospel, in which the Kingdom of Heaven is compared 'unto a certain king, which made a marriage for his son'. Just as, he continued, Henry VII was doing for Arthur. Then, bishop-like indeed, he warmed unctuously to his theme. Could not 'Our Sovereign Lord the King . . . be resembled to the King celestial/As well as any Prince earthly now living?' he asked. Was he not 'Most Christian King, and most steadfast in the Faith'? By this point, even Catherine must have become aware that the actor playing God the Father was made up to look like the father-in-law whom she had first seen when he burst into her chamber at Dogmersfield.[5]

The recording herald was with the royal party or its hangers-on, since it is at this point in his narrative that he describes Catherine's procession – one by one and group by group, just as they came into his view. Like all good reporters, he was most struck by the odd and the peculiar. He noted how the Spanish and English ladies in Catherine's suite (because they sat on opposite sides of their steeds) rode back-to-back. And he was particularly interested by Catherine's exotic dress and her 'little hat, fashioned like a cardinal's hat' with a 'lace of gold' to keep it on. The only personal feature he noticed was her hair, 'hanging down about her shoulders, which is fair auburn'. It was, we can safely assume, her best asset – in English eyes at least.

At the end of Cheapside, by the Little Conduit, Catherine came to the final pageant. She had succeeded in reaching the goal of Honour, and Honour himself pointed out two empty thrones on either side of him: one for Arthur, the other for Catherine. The Mayor and Aldermen, having given Catherine many fair words, now made her more substantial gifts of plate and money. Turning south by the church of St Michael le Querne (or 'at Corn'), whose east end abutted the Little Conduit, she made a half circuit of St Paul's Churchyard, by Paternoster Row and Ave Maria Lane, and re-entered it from Ludgate Hill. This brought her to the open space before the west front, where the Archbishop of Canterbury, in cope and mitre, was waiting to greet her. She offered up gifts and prayers at the Shrine of St Erconwald, the seventh-century Bishop of London and builder of one of the first cathedrals on the site. Then she withdrew to the Bishop's Palace, which lay to the north-west of the churchyard. Here she would stay for her wedding and honeymoon.[6]

15. Wedding and bedding

C atherine's wedding was scheduled for Sunday, 14 November (a Sunday or other Holy Day had always been the commissioners' preferred date for the celebration of the marriage, to take advantage of the extra elaboration of the religious ritual on such occasions). This left the intervening Saturday as a day of rest for Catherine. She had only one engagement, but it was an important one: her first meeting with her future mother-in-law, the Queen, Elizabeth of York.

Henry VII had already briefed his wife about his own encounter with Catherine at Dogmersfield; now the Queen would see for herself. The meeting as planned by the commissioners was a short and formal courtesy call.

Elizabeth had taken up residence with her husband a few days previously at Baynard's Castle. The house lay on the river, directly to the south of St Paul's. The way, down Paul's Chain, was short but steep and orders were given to sand the street to prevent Catherine's horses from losing their footing. According to her programme, Catherine would set out in the afternoon; be greeted at the foot of the stairs leading to the Queen's apartments by the Queen's Lord Chamberlain, who would conduct her to the presence; and then, having 'made a certain pause', she would return.

In fact, it turned into a much more sociable occasion. Elizabeth, as we have seen, was predisposed to like Catherine, and Catherine responded in kind. She did not arrive till 3 or 4 o'clock. Then, after a short formal audience, musicians were called for 'and with pleasure and goodly communication, dancing and disports, they passed the season full conveniently'. Time flew by and it was 'evening late' before Catherine left 'with torches lit to a great number'.[1]

Next morning, it was her wedding day. The great church was filled: people stood in the rood-lofts and vaults; they perched on window sills and packed the pavement. There were also two stands or boxes for the privileged. On the south side, the mayor and aldermen of London had an open stand; to the north, the royal family had a more elaborate box, modelled on the Closets in the Chapel Royal. It was enclosed and with glazed casements, which allowed the King and Queen to see without being seen. It also, again like the Holyday Closets, had private access. Henry VII and Elizabeth took their places. Then Arthur entered, inconspicuously like most grooms, through the south door and went to the wedding stage. Now it was time for the bride.[2]

Catherine left the Bishop's Palace, escorted as always by Henry, Duke of York. She entered in procession through the west doors, climbed up to the walkway and joined Arthur and the assembled clergy on the wedding stage. Trumpets, placed high in the vault as they are today to take advantage of the acoustic, rang out. But the real feast was for the eyes. Catherine's dress was white. Her skirt was stretched out over her hips by a great hoop or farthingale and on her head she wore a mantilla or veil of white silk, reaching to her waist and with a jewelled border an inch and a half wide. Was she the first bride in England to wear a veil? Certainly the herald had seen nothing like it.[3]

Now it was the lawyers' turn. First, the Papal dispensations authorizing the marriage were read out. Then, the terms of the marriage settlements were recited. As part of the theatre of the wedding, Henry VII and Arthur publicly sealed the deeds of the dowry; while for their part the Spaniards, equally theatrically, handed over the first instalment of the marriage portion. £20,000 in gold was a bulky item – and one shilling was paid 'for the carriage of the payment of Spain from [St] Paul's to the water' – that is, to the river Thames.[4]

Next came the actual wedding. This lasted some three hours, after which the party processed along the western end of the walkway towards the high altar. Arthur and Catherine went hand in hand, as specified in the commissioners' brief, and the trumpets sounded again. But, just before passing through the gates of the choir, the bride and groom paused and turned to the vast congregation – now to the north, now to the south, so that everybody could see them. It seems to have been a spontaneous gesture and it sent the crowds wild: 'Some crying King Henry!'; 'some in likewise crying Prince Arthur!' But no one, apparently, cried 'Princess Catherine!'[5]

There followed another interminable ceremony as the Mass of the Trinity was sung. Fortunately, the commissioners had not forgotten the needs of nature. Within the sanctuary, Arthur and Catherine each had a traverse or curtained enclosure, 'to serve when need shall be' for either to relieve themselves. The traverses also had fabric roofs to protect the Prince and Princess from the prying eyes of spectators in the vaults. At the end of the mass, refreshments of wine and spices were served.

Arthur left quickly and informally, to be ready 'to receive the Princess at her chamber door', when she returned to the Bishop's Palace, 'as the custom of England is'. But Catherine once more, like a mannequin on a catwalk, processed the length of the church, with Henry, Duke of York, at her side.

She was the focus of attention also at the wedding feast, where the guests ate rare meats and drank fine wines, were served by lords and knights, and remained at table until 5 p.m. At that hour, the Earl of Oxford, holder of the hereditary office of Lord Great Chamberlain, summoned a select party to prepare the wedding bed. It included the Lady Mistresses of both Catherine and Arthur.[6]

The Lady Mistress was what we might call the governess. She had oversight of the royal infant and supervised the staff of the nursery. It was a position of considerable seniority. Arthur's Lady Mistress was Lady Elizabeth Darcy, Catherine's was Dona Elvira Manuel.

When Catherine left for England, Dona Elvira accompanied her, with the augmented title of First Lady of Honour and First Lady of the Bedchamber. As was usual in royal Households, Dona Elvira's husband, Pedro, held equivalent offices on the male side of Catherine's establishment, serving as her Major Domo and First Chamberlain. But there is no doubt that Dona Elvira was the heavier hitter. At Catherine's entry into London, she had ridden second in her train, dressed all in black and cutting a formidable figure with her sombre veil or mantilla, also of black, 'like unto the fashion of a religious woman (that is, a nun), after the manner of Spain'. Building on the ascendancy established in Catherine's childhood years, Dona Elvira exercised a powerful and, it would seem, malign influence over her charge until the two of them split after a violent quarrel.[7]

In response to Oxford's summons, the Lady Mistresses and the other ladies left to supervise the preparation of the bedchamber and the marriage-bed in its proper form. The making of royal beds was an elaborate process, which is described at length in *The Royal Book*. The bed consisted of several layers and required a large team to assemble it. Its base was a bed or litter of straw. One of the yeomen of the guard jumped into the litter and 'rolled him up and down', both to make the straw lie smoothly and to check it for any concealed weapons or other devices intended to injure the occupant. Next a protective canvas was placed over the straw, followed by a feather bed, a fustian or blanket, a lower and upper sheet, another blanket, and two or three fur rugs, including one of ermine. The upper sheet was turned down, and the pillows put in position and covered with a head sheet. The feather bed and pillows were vigorously beaten and plumped; and the sheets and blankets stretched, made wrinkle-free and tucked in. Finally, the comfort of religion was added, as a few drops of holy water were scattered to banish bad dreams.[8]

Some two or three hours later, all was ready. First Catherine was undressed by her ladies and 'reverently laid and disposed' in the bed. Arthur's preparations were more rumbustious. The herald bowdlerizes them as 'goodly disports, dancings, with pleasure, mirth and solace'. Actually, custom dictated a sort of stag-night, with dirty songs and suggestive horse-play. The 'divinity that doth hedge a prince' imposed some restraint, but there was still plenty of scope for lewdness. The games over, a large group of nobles, gentlemen and clergy, led as always by Oxford, conducted Arthur to the bedchamber, where he lay down beside Catherine.

Solemnity returned as the bishops uttered the usual blessing over the marriage bed: 'Benedic, Domine Deus, thalamum hunc et omnes habitantes in eo . . .' 'Bless O Lord this marriage bed and those in it . . . that they live in your love and multiply [that is, have children] and grow old together in length of days.' Send, they implored God, angels to defend and protect the couple. The prayers concluded, they scattered holy water and swung censers. Finally, with the blessings of the Church and the good wishes of their friends ringing in their ears, Arthur and Catherine were left alone.[9]

What happened then, only God knows.

The herald, a strictly contemporary witness, assumed that nature had taken its course: 'And thus these worthy persons concluded and consummate the effect and complement of matrimony'. Many of those present, when questioned thirty years later, asserted the same. George Talbot, the Earl of Shrewsbury, remembered accompanying Arthur to the wedding chamber and leaving him there. The Earl said he had consummated his own marriage at fifteen; Arthur was a similar age, and he took for granted that Arthur had done so too. The Marquess of Dorset recollected Arthur getting into the bed where the Lady Catherine lay under the coverlet 'as the manner is of Queens in that behalf'. He, likewise, assumed that the marriage was consummated since Arthur was 'of good and sanguine complexion' – that is, fit and healthy.[10]

But Catherine was to tell a very different story.

16. The morning after

There had been hot competition to be part of Arthur's wedding-night party. One of those who struck lucky was Sir Anthony Willoughby, a body servant of Arthur's. He was sneaked in by his father, Lord Broke, the Lord Steward of the Household and Catherine's escort on her journey from the west country. The morning after, Willoughby claimed, Arthur had boasted of his exploits. 'Willoughby,' he had ordered, 'bring me a cup of ale, for I have been this night in the midst of Spain.' There were, Willoughby asserted, several witnesses to this remark. Later, the Prince had said openly: 'Masters, it is good pastime to have a wife.' The words stuck in men's memories, as well they might, and at least one other witness confirmed the story.[1]

Memories? False memories? Or downright lies?

Whatever had or had not happened on the wedding night, Catherine and Arthur had plenty of time to recover from their exertions. Catherine spent the day following, Monday, 15 November, in strict solitude, receiving no one, save Oxford who brought a warmly paternal message from her father-in-law. On the Tuesday, the King, the Prince and the Duke of York processed solemnly back to St Paul's to give thanks to God 'that so prosperously His Goodness had suffered everything of this laudable [marriage] to be brought to its most laudable conclusion'. For this ceremony, roles were reversed and it was Catherine's turn to watch from the privacy of the Closet on the north side of the nave. Afterwards, she received Henry VII in her lodgings and father- and daughter-in-law exchanged 'right pleasant and favourable words, salutes and communications'. That day, too, at dinner she was served for the first time as an English Princess, not as a Spanish Infanta.[2]

Would all this have been done if the marriage had not been consummated? Would Catherine herself have behaved as she did?

The scene then shifts to Westminster, whither the whole royal family went in a great river procession. First, there was a mass creation of seventy-six Knights and Knights of the Bath, 'whereof so great a number and multitude have not been seen heretofore in England at one season made'. Next, there followed four days of jousts, interspersed with masques, banquets and dances and the occasional day of rest. Once again, young Henry Duke of York contrived to steal much of the thunder. At the first evening's entertainment, he was the last of the royal family to dance. He and his partner, his elder sister Margaret, began by performing two 'base' dances. These were dignified and slow – too dignified for the boisterous Henry. Finding that his heavy cloth of gold clothes got in the way of his fun, he 'suddenly cast off his gown and danced in his jacket'. It was an outrageous breach of contemporary etiquette (stripping to the waist would be the modern equivalent). But, as he would do so often in the future when he broke the rules, Henry managed to carry it off: dancing 'in so goodly and pleasant manner that it was to the King and Queen right great and singular pleasure'.[3]

What of Catherine's reaction to this endless round of celebrations? Did she enjoy herself? Or did she have to rely on 'her agreeable and dignified manners' to conceal her boredom? We simply do not know.

On Friday, 26 November the great caravanserai that was the Court packed up and moved, again by water, to Richmond. Over the weekend, the King delighted in showing off to his guests the amenities of his new palace (which even included running water). The star-turn among the many entertainments was a performance by a Spanish acrobat on a tight-rope. But this was the finale and on Monday, 29 November, the Spanish ambassadors who had escorted Catherine took their leave. They carried with them a sort of souvenir wedding album, consisting of 'many goodly books, pictures and examples of this most excellent . . . marriage', as well as letters from the King, the Prince and the Queen. Arthur's letter assured his Spanish parents-in-law that Catherine was everything he could desire:

> He had never felt such joy in his life as when he beheld the sweet face of his bride. No woman in the world could be more agreeable to him. [He] promises to be a good husband.

Henry VII's letter similarly extolled Catherine's beauty and her good manners, in words that would have delighted Isabella. But he was unrepentant about the scale of Catherine's reception: her entry into London, he boasted, had been acclaimed by 'such masses of people as never before had been seen in England'; she was conducted to St Paul's 'with great splendour'; there had been 'great and cordial rejoicings', in which 'the whole people' took part.[4]

Everybody, it seemed, had got what they wanted.

Then the difficulties began.

The first problem was that Catherine suffered a bad attack of homesickness. It came on immediately after the departure of the high-ranking Spaniards. Catherine's mask of good manners slipped and she became 'annoyed and pensive'. Her reaction, as the herald sensibly noted, was entirely predictable: it was 'as nature, kind and manner will'. More surprising is Henry VII's response. For one of the many contra-dictory elements compounded into the King's complex and hard-to-read character was charm combined with an almost feminine sensitivity. These were turned to their full effect on the disconsolate Catherine. Guessing, probably correctly, that she was bored after the masculine war-games of the jousts (as well as homesick), he devised a gentler entertainment and invited Catherine and a mixed party of Spanish and English ladies to inspect his library at Richmond. Henry had serious scholarly interests (especially, according to Erasmus, in history). He was also a notable connoisseur of fine and costly workmanship. The pride of his collection was on display and he took a personal pleasure in showing Catherine 'many goodly pleasant books of works' (that is, illuminated manuscripts). The herald seems to have caught a glimpse, too, and found them 'full delightful, sage, merry and also right cunning, both in Latin and English'.[5]

But the King also knew that, while books are good for reading, diamonds are a girl's best friend – especially when she is down. So he had a jeweller on hand, 'with many rings, and huge diamonds, and jewels of most goodly fashion', and gave Catherine first pick, followed by her ladies. Such kind attentions 'somewhat a-slaked her heaviness'. They even, according to the herald, began to reconcile her to 'the manner, guise and usages of England' and to her place in the English royal family.[6]

But just what would that place be? For the assimilation of a foreign-born princess presented almost as many difficulties to the host-country as to the young exile herself. What, for instance, to do with Catherine's servants? She had been accompanied by a complete Spanish Household. Numbering some sixty strong, they had ridden with her across Spain and weathered the storms of Biscay. They were in no mood to go home and Catherine was equally reluctant to lose these last personal ties to Spain. Yet go home most of them must: they had no clear status in England, and they hindered Catherine's own necessary transformation into an English princess.

Francophone courts tended to be brutal and pack the lot off as quickly as possible. This had been the experience of Catherine's sister Juana when she was sent to Flanders as the bride of the Archduke Philip. It was also to be the fate of Catherine's English sister-in-law, Mary, when she became Queen of France. Mary had to say good-bye even to her Lady Mistress, Lady Guildford. For, despite her linguistic skills, Lady Guildford proved a particular obstacle to good marital relations between Mary and her much older husband, Louis XII. The moment she arrived in France, she set herself 'not only to rule the Queen' but everybody else as well. Louis was blunt: he declared he loved his pretty young wife, but if he could only have her with Lady Guildford 'he had lever [rather] be without her'.[7]

Dona Elvira was cast of the same brazen metal as Lady Guildford. But she was not Henry VII's prime target. Instead, the difficulties were 'especially with respect to the male servants' in Catherine's Household. The English 'even refused to hear mention of a Lord High Steward, of a Lord High Gentleman in Waiting, of a Lord Treasurer'. These were usual posts in the household of a Spanish Infanta so Fuensalida, one of the occasional ambassadors in England, was unable to understand the English objection to them. But the resident ambassador, De Puebla, who had lived in England for a decade and knew English ways, immediately grasped the difficulty. 'Lord High Steward (*Mayor Domo Mayor*)', he repeated, tut-tutting the while. The English, he explained to Fuensalida, 'especially abhorred a Lord High Steward'.[8]

The root of the problem lay in the differences between the English

and Spanish royal Households. Royal Courts, like the ancient universities of Oxford and Cambridge, look much the same to outsiders. But
seen from within it is the differences which count. English Queens (and
in this respect, as most others, the Princess of Wales was treated as
Queen-in-Waiting) had a Chamber or Household-above-stairs. It was
headed by a man, the Queen's Lord Chamberlain (the then holder of the
post was the elderly and distinguished Anglo-Irish peer, the Earl of
Ormond, who had conducted Catherine to Queen Elizabeth's presence
at Baynard's Castle). And there was a handful of other male officers under
the Queen's Lord Chamberlain, including the Gentlemen Ushers. But,
since the most important responsibility of the Chamber was the Queen's
body service, the great bulk of its servants were perforce women. The
organization of the Spanish Chamber (*camera*) was similar. But in Spain
the Queen or Infanta also had a Hall or Household-below-stairs. In
England, she did not. There was only one Hall, the King's, and there was
only one Lord Steward, who was the King's also. For its below-stairs
needs, the Queen's Household simply drew on the King's. In their
ignorance of English practice, the Spanish were giving Catherine as
Princess of Wales a Household more ambitious than her mother-in-law,
Elizabeth, as Queen of England. Naturally the English objected.[9]

And naturally too, Catherine's pompous establishment of male
servants soon found their grand foreign titles and functions clipped and
replaced with modest, familiar English ones. Her Master of the Hall
(*Maestra Sala*), Alonso de Esquivel, was told that 'he should not serve in
that quality'; instead, he was given the lesser position of Gentleman
Usher. Juan de Cuero, who, according to Spanish custom, had charge of
Catherine's state rooms, experienced a similar demotion. But the
principal target, naturally, was Catherine's *Mayor Domo Mayor*. As early
as January 1502, Ferdinand and Isabella had heard that Henry VII 'does
not wish Don Pedro Manrique to retain the office he has hitherto held'.
The Spanish responded by defending his position with equal tenacity (in
part, no doubt, because he was Dona Elvira's husband) and De Puebla
was instructed to make strong representations against such an 'affront'.[10]

Not for the first time, De Puebla must have despaired at the obtuseness of his own government. For not only did no English Queen or Princess have a Lord Steward, no one *at all* in England held the post of Lord *High* Steward. This is because the High Stewardship, as one of the hereditary great offices, had developed dangerously high pretensions, with its holders claiming to act as viceroys or even as anti-kings. The office had therefore been abolished as a permanent position and instead was only conferred from time to time, usually for no more than a day, for special ceremonial or judicial occasions. All this De Puebla had explained to Fuensalida in 1500. But he had neither understood nor properly reported the matter back home. Now De Puebla would have to try all over again.[11]

The finer points of the status, function and precedence of noble Household officers are infinitely remote from the concerns of the twenty-first century. But they were central to Catherine's world and to Catherine herself. Isabella was a notorious stickler for proper form and Catherine was her mother's daughter. Indeed, in the fullness of time, Catherine was prepared to stake everything – perhaps even life itself – on defending her own status as Queen, together with the titles, forms of address and style of service that went with it. She lost then, just as she lost in 1501.

But the final area of difficulty between Catherine and her in-laws was a universal one. It is important and comprehensible at all times and in all places, though the rules governing it differ. It was sex. Catherine and Arthur had slept together in the same bed on their wedding night, though just what happened remains a matter of unresolvable dispute. But should they continue to live together as man and wife? Or should they be separated?

When Catherine's arrival had first been seriously mooted, in 1500, there was no doubt which course would be followed. She was due to arrive in time to marry Arthur on his fourteenth birthday, 19 September 1500. Arthur would then be old enough to enter into a canonically binding marriage; but he was not quite old enough, his father felt, for him to live as a married man. Instead, as Henry VII told De Puebla more than once in the summer of 1500, it was 'his intention to keep the Prince and Princess of Wales, during the first year of their marriage, about his person and at his court'. But of course Catherine's arrival was delayed for more than a year. The result was that, when they were finally married in November 1501, she was sixteen and Arthur fifteen. They had, that is to say, reached exactly the age that Henry VII, speaking in 1500, had deemed old enough to allow them to begin to live together.[12]

Nevertheless, it seems to have remained his intention to keep them apart. Indeed, according to De Ayala, Henry VII had now lengthened the period he proposed to retain Catherine 'near his person' from one to two years. He was not of course protecting Catherine's youthful bloom (as modern sentimentalists assume), for no one then doubted Catherine's capacity at the age of sixteen to begin full sexual relations. The issue, rather, was 'the tender age of the Prince', who was nine months younger than his wife.[13]

But in the middle of December the question was suddenly reopened. Arthur, it was decided, should return to his government of Wales. But what of his wife? Should she remain at Court as planned? Or would it be better if she accompanied her husband? The King claimed that there was difference of opinion between his councillors and those of his son. And he tried to get Catherine to express a preference. In vain. With perfect propriety, she replied that 'neither in this nor in any other respect had she any other will than his'. Stonewalled by this submission, the King then set his son to work on Catherine, 'to persuade her to say that she preferred rather to go than to stay'. But she remained sweetly and immovably indifferent, or so she said.[14]

What was going on? At bottom, probably, was a division within both the Spanish Embassy and Catherine's Spanish entourage. De Ayala was disarmingly honest about the conflicts. At the moment, he wrote in December 1501, 'everyone reads, and asks and speaks what he likes'; surely it would be better, he implored the Catholic Kings, if they ordered 'that all we who are here, men as well as women, act in unison'. Some hope! Moreover, De Ayala was not an impartial witness. Instead, he was the leader of one faction, with Dona Elvira as his able second within

Catherine's Household. The leader of the other party was De Puebla. De Puebla correctly saw the Anglo-Spanish match as, in large part, his own personal achievement and he wished to do everything he could to further its development. The best way to that, he seems to have decided, was to bring Arthur and Catherine together as husband and wife, in fact as well as in name, so that Catherine would quickly bear a child as the literal fruit of the alliance.

De Puebla too had a powerful adjutant within Catherine's Household, in the person of Fra Alessandro Geraldini. Alessandro had been Catherine's tutor; now he was promoted to her confessor. As her tutor, he could claim an ascendancy over her mind; as her confessor, over her soul. Bearing in mind Catherine's piety and knowing his own authority, Alessandro set himself up as a rival to Dona Elvira for influence over the Princess. With Dona Elvira in cahoots with De Ayala, his own alliance with De Puebla was an obvious tactic.

Alessandro struck quickly and hard. He sought an interview with Henry VII and asked him, 'in the name of [the Catholic Kings and] as a man who knows your intentions', not to force Catherine and Arthur to live apart. 'On no condition in the world', he said, 'should [Henry VII] separate them, but send her with her husband.' Otherwise, Ferdinand and Isabella would be dissatisfied and Catherine 'he knows, would be in despair'. Meanwhile, De Ayala and Dona Elvira, claiming equally to know the minds of the Catholic Kings, were taking the opposite tack and insisting that Ferdinand and Isabella 'would rather be pleased than dissatisfied if they for some time did not live together'. It becomes, indeed, almost possible to feel sympathy for Henry VII in his dilemma.[15]

Both Elvira and Alessandro had, of course, their own private motives. From Alessandro's point of view, to bring Catherine's husband into Catherine's life was (as we have seen in the parallel case of Lady Guildford) the best way to ensure that there was no place for Dona Elvira. For Dona Elvira, on the other hand, the longer Catherine remained a child rather than a woman, the longer her own influence would endure.

Finally, there was a subplot. It had always been the intention that the jewels and valuable household goods brought by Catherine should count towards the dowry of 200,000 crowns payable by her parents. But the exact status of her possessions had changed between the original treaty, which formed part of the settlement reached at Medina del Campo in Catherine's girlhood, and the final treaty of 1497. In the former, the goods were to form part of the first instalment; they were to be accepted at face value, and they were to be retained by Catherine. All that, like the remainder of the settlement at Medina del Campo, was very much in Spain's favour. By 1496, things had changed. The goods were now to form part of the second instalment, with the first now consisting entirely of cash; they were to be appraised by London goldsmiths and accepted only at the London valuation; finally, their eventual destination became unclear, 'for [in the second treaty] it is said that Henry is to receive the ornaments'. These changes, as Ferdinand and Isabella complained in an aggrieved letter to De Puebla, were greatly to their disadvantage and, in 1500, at the eleventh hour, he was instructed to renegotiate them. In the event, the Catholic Kings accepted his protestation that such second thoughts would imperil the whole project and nothing was done.[16]

Nevertheless, the second treaty did leave Catherine's 'ornaments' in a curiously anomalous position. As soon as she arrived, they were valued and a receipt was demanded for them from the English. But, like the remainder of the second instalment, they were not due to be handed over for another twelve months. Meantime, they were jealously guarded by Juan de Cuero, who also fulfilled the function of Keeper of Catherine's Wardrobe. De Puebla, it seems, then came up with a scheme to liberate the 'ornaments' from their limbo to the heavenly benefit of Henry VII's coffers. If Catherine could be persuaded to use the goods, he told the King, they would lose part of their agreed value. Henry VII would therefore be justified in refusing to accept them and in demanding cash *in lieu*. Catherine's parents would have to pay, but they would also be reluctant to take the goods back from their daughter since she and her Household had already used them. Thus, at the end of the day, the English would have both the money *and* the property. Catherine herself, De Puebla assured Henry VII, had given her agreement: 'I have already spoken with the Princess, and won her over to my side.' It may be so. Unfortunately for De Puebla, however, De Cuero, who had charge of the property, was *not* on side. Instead he was an ally of De Puebla's enemies, De Ayala and Dona Elvira. He stuck rigidly by his brief and Henry VII experienced the humiliation of asking for something and being refused.

The Spaniards, including Catherine herself, were lucky that Henry VII had been taught in the school of hard knocks to keep his temper – unlike his second son, for example. Even so, De Ayala, bursting with indignation, persuaded himself that the scheme to send Catherine to Wales was part of the plot. Once she was there, he fumed, she would be under immense pressure to use the disputed goods. Firm instructions must be issued to the contrary, he wrote to her parents.

De Ayala's reading of the King's motives has been widely accepted. Yet it seems a calumny. For at this stage of Henry VII's reign there are few signs of miserliness. On the other hand, there is abundant evidence of his anxious concern for the well-being of his son and heir. Would he really have been prepared to risk compromising Arthur's welfare for a mere 30,000 crowns? I think not. De Ayala's charge also ignores other arguments in favour of allowing the couple to live together. Arthur had apparently enjoyed his wedding night. So when he pleaded with Catherine to agree to come with him to Wales, he spoke for himself at least as much as for his father. As for Catherine's own reaction, I believe Alessandro. She was uxoriousness itself and marriage was her destiny. At last, after so many delays, she had fulfilled it, only to be told that she was to live separately from her husband. No wonder she was 'in despair'. And no wonder she resisted the separation – just as she would fight, much more openly and vehemently, against her separation from her second husband.

So the English King changed his mind. And the most powerful motive was the one shared by Henry VII and De Puebla: the latter wanted Arthur and Catherine to have a child to cement the Anglo-Spanish alliance; the former wanted a grandson to guarantee the future of his dynasty. For both, the way to the future lay through Wales, so to Wales Catherine went.

'That we might observe the ancient customs of our realm', Henry VII wrote to Ferdinand and Isabella in a long-overlooked letter, 'we recently despatched into Wales the most illustrious Arthur and Catherine, our common children.' 'For though the opinion of many were adverse to this course by reason of the tender age of our son,' Henry continued, 'yet were we unwilling to allow the Prince and Princess to be separated at any distance from each other.'

Moreover, he added, Ferdinand and Isabella had no need to be concerned about Catherine's welfare, since '[she] has with her a venerable man, Alessandro Geraldini, her principal Chaplain, for whom we have the greatest regard, partly by reason of his virtues shown unto us in many ways, [and] partly because he has been [Catherine's] preceptor'. Geraldini would, no doubt, Henry ends, keep the Catholic Kings fully informed about both Catherine's welfare and the state of England.[17]

Arthur and Catherine left Court on 21 December, to begin their independent married life by keeping the great feast of Christmas together 'forty miles from here'. It was a journey which began with high hopes but ended in disaster.[18]

17. Nemesis

Arthur was a well-known figure in the Welsh Marches, where he had spent most of his short life. He was also a well-liked and respected one. Now he returned, with his new wife, Catherine. She was high-born, pretty and gracious. He was the hero of the hour. They were a golden couple, ready, it seemed, to usher in the new Arthurian age of which the Welsh poets had sung ever since the Prince's birth.

Arthur's principal seat, Ludlow Castle in Shropshire, was a not-unworthy Camelot. It stands on a rocky outcrop commanding a meander of the River Teme. At its core is a Norman keep. But in the thirteenth and fourteenth centuries the Mortimers, Earls of March, had transformed the castle into a magnificent palace-fortress, worthy of a family who were the mightiest Marcher lords and able to make and unmake kings. On the northern side of the inner bailey they built a symmetrical lodging, lit by large, traceried windows. In the centre is the great hall. It is elevated on a basement and entered by a broad stone stair that is as much ceremonial as functional. On either side are chambers in projecting wings. Catherine and Arthur occupied the block to the east, which was entered by a staircase from the dais of the hall. To the north, a massive square tower projects out beyond the curtain wall. It contains adjacent closets, with deep, embrasured windows overlooking the flood-plain. These were the couple's most private rooms.

But the most handsome building in the castle was one of the oldest. This is the chapel, which, like the keep, is Norman. It is circular. Outside, the doorway and windows are placed with absolute symmetry; inside, there is an arcade of pilasters supporting interlaced arches. In its severer, northern European fashion, the chapel is as pure and elegant an exercise of architectural geometry as any that Catherine had seen in the Alhambra.[1]

Nor did the Princely Household have to fear comparisons either. The President of the Prince's Council was William Smith. Bishop successively of Coventry and Lichfield and Lincoln, he was a scholar-administrator of the old school. He became Chancellor of Oxford University in 1500 and in September 1501 escorted Arthur on a visit to the university. Arthur stayed in Magdalen College, where the Bursar, a certain ambitious young don called Thomas Wolsey, was hurrying to complete the great tower and, allegedly, cooking the college books to raise the necessary funds. Arthur had paid his visit to Oxford on his way to his wedding with Catherine. On the way back, the couple probably passed through Oxford as well. They may indeed have spent Christmas at Woodstock, five miles to the north. And Oxford was always to remain

Catherine's favourite university – unlike the rest of the royal family whose patronage went to Cambridge. Another Oxford connexion was Arthur's tutor, Thomas Linacre. Physician, grammarian and pioneer scholar of Greek, Linacre was probably the most learned man in Europe north of the Alps. He was also an impossible perfectionist, who found writing a torment. He must have been a demanding teacher. But his efforts meant that Arthur could confront Catherine on more than equal terms of scholarship.[2]

But the most important members of Arthur's entourage from Catherine's point of view were Sir Richard Pole, Arthur's Chamberlain, and his wife, Margaret Plantagenet. Both had royal connexions. Pole was a member of Lady Margaret Beaufort's family of the half-blood, which issued from her mother's second marriage. Margaret Plantagenet was royal herself. She was daughter of George, Duke of Clarence and sister of the Earl of Warwick who had been executed in 1499 to make England safe for Catherine. Now Catherine learned the truth about the circumstances of her marriage – and from the woman who had been most injured by it. It could have been the beginnings of a vendetta: instead Catherine and Margaret became fast friends.[3]

We know about the incident through Margaret's third son, Reginald Pole. He was born in 1500 in Stourton, Staffordshire. This was a manor in the King's hands, where, no doubt, Arthur was staying at the time. In youth Pole was a friend and passionate admirer of Henry VIII; subsequently he became a partisan of Catherine and her daughter Mary. He knew all the secrets of the royal family as well as his own. So his story is to be believed. But we must not attach too much importance to it at this stage. There was a cloud over Catherine's marriage. But it was no bigger than a man's hand.[4]

Meanwhile, the outward splendour of Arthur's Household reached its height in the early months of 1502 and is described by the herald in his customary purple prose. At its core was Arthur's Council. This served a double purpose. It was to impose order and administer justice in the Welsh Marches, which were still an area of entrenched feuding and unlawfulness. It was also to provide Arthur with a practical training in the business of government. So we should envisage Arthur as listening to the deliberations of the Council and increasingly participating in them. Latterly he may even have delivered its verdicts in his own princely person. This I take is what the herald means when he says that Arthur 'governed [Wales] most discreetly, and after most righteous order and wisdom . . . upholding and defending the poor and rightful quarrels; repressing malice and unlawful disposition; amplifying and increasing the laws and the services of Almighty God'. All of which was 'to the great comfort and gladness of the Commons'.[5]

Arthur's own more personal needs were also satisfied during these months of his married life, if we believe the subsequent testimony of one of his most intimate body servants, William Thomas. Thomas had been Groom of his Privy Chamber for three years and attended him to Ludlow. There one of his tasks had been to prepare the Prince for the conjugal bed. Thomas 'made [him] ready to bed and . . . conducted him clad in his night gown unto the Princess's bedchamber door often and sundry times . . . and that at the morning he received him at the said doors . . . and waited upon him to his own privy chamber'. Arthur, it would seem, was an assiduous husband. Too much so, some later gossip suggested.[6]

But suddenly the idyll soured. On Easter Day, 27 March 1502, Arthur fell seriously ill. The herald's description of the malady is long on adjectives but short on precision. It was 'the most pitiful disease and sickness, that with so sore and great violence had battled and driven, in the singular parts of him inward, [so] that cruel and fervent enemy of nature, the deadly corruption, did utterly vanquish and overcome the pure and friendly blood'. Extracting a modern diagnosis from this is not easy. Most authorities have suggested a bronchial or pulmonary condition, such as pneumonia, tuberculosis, or the 'sweating sickness' which seems to have been a virulent form of influenza. But the phrase: 'the singular parts of him inward' has also been understood to point to testicular cancer. Some support for this theory may come from the testimony of an unknown witness, who remembered another of Arthur's servants as dating the Prince's decline from Shrovetide (8 February). Then 'he had lain with the Lady Catherine, and was never so lusty in body and courage until his death, which [he]said was because he lay with the Lady Catherine'. Testicular cancer, which is known to move rapidly in the young, would also explain the terrifying speed of the end. From Easter Day, when his illness became serious, to his death, took less than a week. On Saturday, 2 April, the Prince's 'lively spirits . . . finally mortified' and he yielded, 'with most fervent devotion, his spirit and soul to the pleasure and hands of Almighty God'.[7]

Sir Richard Pole immediately sent letters to the court at Greenwich. The messengers arrived late on the Monday. The task of breaking the terrible news was entrusted to the King's confessor. He entered the King's chamber early on the Tuesday morning, ordered everyone else out and then intoned in Latin from the *Book of Job*: 'What? shall we receive good at the hand of God and shall we not receive evil.' After these words of harsh comfort, he told the King of the death of his son.

Henry's reaction shows the reality of parental feeling behind the brutalities of dynastic politics. As a dynast, he moved his children like chess-pieces across the board of Europe's politics, to mate for the greater glory of the House of Tudor. But now he grieved for the loss of his son like any stricken father. His first thought was to summon Queen Elizabeth. She comforted her distraught husband and then returned to her own apartments to cry her mother's tears. Then she collapsed and King Henry came in turn to comfort her.

It is a touching scene. But even at this supreme moment of personal agony, the dynastic imperative could not be forgotten. 'Remember', Queen Elizabeth begged her husband, that they still had other children – 'a fair goodly Prince [and] two fair Princesses' – to carry on the family line. And remember, above all, she cried, 'we [are] both young enough' to have more children.[8]

It was a scene which Catherine's parents had played many times as death had cut down their heirs – first their eldest son, then their eldest daughter, then their first grandson. And it was a scene with which

Catherine herself would become all too familiar. Similar words, 'and we still young enough', would echo in her own birthing chamber, though this time spoken by the husband rather than the wife.

Etiquette forbade members of the royal family to see death, so neither Arthur's father nor his mother nor his widow accompanied him on his last journey. Instead, it was left to the stalwart Thomas Howard, Earl of Surrey, himself the father by two wives of twelve children who survived to adulthood, to supervise Arthur's funeral and to enact the rituals of grief as chief mourner. These took time to organize so, as usual, the body was embalmed: first it was eviscerated, then cauterized and finally stuffed with spices. The process was crude but on this occasion it was so effective that there was no need for the additional preservative of a lead coffin. Instead, chested only in wood, the Prince lay in state in his chamber for three weeks. On St George's Day, the funeral rites began, with requiem masses at Ludlow Parish Church and then at Bewdley where only three years previously Arthur had 'married' De Puebla as a proxy for Catherine. Spring that year in the Welsh Marches was unusually wet and windy, and between Ludlow and Bewdley the funeral car had to be pulled by oxen. The body was taken to Worcester Cathedral and buried on the south side of the choir.[9]

Henry VIII had a splendid chantry chapel built over the tomb, in which the heraldry and badges of Arthur and Catherine were combined. For Arthur, there were red roses of Lancaster and white roses of York, Beaufort portcullises and Yorkist falcons and fetterlocks and the Prince of Wales feathers; for Catherine, there were the yokes and arrows of her father and mother and her own pomegranate.[10]

Like Catherine's entry into London and her marriage ceremonies, this posthumous heraldic display tells of so many hopes invested and so much promise unfulfilled. It also suggests the overwhelming imperative to preserve the Anglo-Spanish dynastic alliance.

How this should be done became the great question of the moment.

18. A new marriage?

Catherine was now ill herself. Perhaps Arthur had died of something infectious and she had caught the same disease. Perhaps she had collapsed with the shock of his premature death. At all events, her parents were soon pressing for her to be removed from 'that unhealthy place'. Their concerns were superfluous. Long before their letters reached England, Catherine had been brought back from Ludlow to London. She was carried in one of the Queen's litters, which was covered in black cloth and trimmed with black ribbon and fringe as a sign of mourning. She travelled slowly and by easy stages, partly because of her state of health and partly because the English suspected that she might be pregnant. If the child lived and if it were a boy, it would be heir of England. Catherine would have fulfilled her dynastic role and her honoured place as mother of the future King would be assured. She reached Croydon by 4 May. It was soon apparent that she was not carrying Arthur's child.[1]

This fact changed everything. The heir was now the King's second son Henry, Duke of York, who on 22 June was granted an office as 'Prince of Wales' (though he would have to wait for eighteenth months before his formal creation). As for Catherine, what was she? She was a royal widow certainly. And, at the age of sixteen, might yet be a royal wife again. But whose?[2]

Answering these questions took seven long years as her parents and her father-in-law manoeuvred and bargained. Catherine was the person most concerned with the outcome. But no one thought to consult her. Nor apparently did she expect them to. Instead, to begin with, she was passive – as passive as the grain between the upper and the nether millstones.

In the negotiations between England and Spain, Henry VII held the trump card: he had control of Catherine's person. He played this advantage shrewdly and with increasing ruthlessness.

At first, he was all proper concern. As soon as her health was sufficiently recovered, Catherine was set up at Durham House in the Strand. Durham House, the London palace of the Prince-Bishops of Durham, was one of the finest residences in the City and was fully worthy of a daughter of Spain. Catherine was also attended exactly as her parents had provided. Her Spanish Household, which had accompanied her to Ludlow, had somehow struggled back from the Marches, complete with Juan de Cuero and his jealously guarded hoard. At Ludlow, Henry VII had been persistent in trying to reduce the status of Catherine's male servants to English norms. At Durham House, the pressures vanished and they were free to take up their old positions. Indeed the King concerned himself with only a single question: who would pay for Catherine's establishment and how much?[3]

The question should scarcely have arisen, since, in theory, the provisions for Catherine's dower, painstakingly threshed out at Medina del Campo and flamboyantly ratified at her wedding, made her one of the richest women in England. But the dower, as we have seen, was a reciprocal arrangement, made in return for the marriage portion. The first half of the portion had been paid on the nail at the wedding; the second half was due a year later. However, Arthur's death had supervened after only five months. The premature death of young princes was hardly unusual in the sixteenth century (Don Juan, Catherine's only brother, had also died shortly after *his* wedding). But, by some extraordinary oversight, the Anglo-Spanish treaties made no provision for what was to happen in such circumstances. Subsequently, the Spanish claimed that law and convention required the payment of Catherine's dower. Henry VII, on the other hand, took the view that, since only half the marriage portion had been handed over, he was under no obligation to fulfil his side of the bargain by paying the dower in full, or even in part. Henry VII, Ferdinand and Isabella were warned in the immediate aftermath of Arthur's death, 'would never fulfil his obligations to Catherine'. They were incredulous. But the warning proved all too accurate.[4]

Not that Catherine was left destitute – at least to begin with. Instead, Henry's first tactic was to pay her a monthly allowance in lieu. The sum

– £83 6s 8d a month, amounting to £1,000 a year – was a considerable one, since £1,000 p.a. was the income of a substantial baron. It was also exactly what the £20,000 capital value of the first instalment of the marriage portion would have yielded had it been invested in the contemporary land-market. I do not think that this is mere coincidence. The payments were made to William Hollybrand. Catherine had first encountered him when he had acted as spokesman and interpreter at her meeting with the Duchess of Norfolk. Now he seems to have joined her service as Treasurer of her Household. He was one of the few Englishmen in an almost wholly Spanish establishment and it cannot have been an easy position.

The King also augmented the regular payments to Hollybrand with substantial occasional gifts. Catherine was given £40 for her expenses in the weeks immediately following Arthur's death. In April 1503, she was given £100 on top of her allowance and double this sum in the September following. Henry VII accompanied the £200 with a fulsome letter in which he protested that 'he loves her so much that he cannot bear the idea of her being in poverty'. But the King found the fact that Catherine made large, irregular demands on his coffers hard to stomach. In September, Hollybrand was ordered 'to send directly an account of how the money is spent'. This was Henry VII presuming to control Catherine's expenditure by audit. In April, his act of generosity had been accompanied by a more ominous threat: '*for this time only*' was noted against the payment of £100 in the Treasurer of the Chamber's account book. The marginal note seems to be written in the King's own hand. If Catherine did not moderate her expenditure, Henry VII would cut her income off at source.[5]

For Catherine, it would seem, was extravagant or, in De Puebla's more tactful phrase, 'liberal'. But it would be a mistake, I think, to see this as a settled character-trait. Rather, Catherine was displaying a sort of childish self-indulgence, on a par with the generally slow pace of her development. For, at the age of seventeen or eighteen, she remained, to all intents and purposes, a child, with Dona Elvira as a domineering and demanding step-parent. Moreover, the mould of dependency was a strong one: it would take a succession of crises to force Catherine to break free.[6]

Meanwhile, Ferdinand and Isabella tried to regain the initiative in their dealings with Henry VII. Their representatives in England were ordered to put two proposals to the King. The first was to demand that Henry VII return the first instalment of the marriage portion and send Catherine safely back to Spain. The second was to offer Catherine to him once more as a bride for the new heir to the throne, Prince Henry. The proposals were of course contradictory. And, though the Spanish envoys were instructed to pursue the first with vigour, it was intended only as a cover for the second. Henry VII was well briefed about the real intentions of Spanish policy and played his cards accordingly.

The Catholic Kings were also aware that the Spanish position in England had been fatally weakened by the divisions in Catherine's entourage and they did their best to put a stop to them. They sent a new ambassador, Ferdinando Duque, to supplement and perhaps to supplant De Puebla. And they moved decisively against De Puebla's ally in Catherine's Household, her confessor, Alessandro Geraldini. Somehow, they had got wind of Geraldini's understanding with De Puebla; they had even got hold of one of his letters to the ambassador. There was, they wrote stiffly to Duque, 'no reason why such a man as Alessandro should remain in England'. Instead, he was to be lured back to Spain.[7]

The fear of the Catholic Kings was that Alessandro and his ally De Puebla would do damage to the negotiations for the new English marriage. This suggests strongly that Ferdinand and Isabella had got hold of the wrong end of the stick, since Geraldini and De Puebla had in fact been enthusiasts for Catherine's English destiny; it also points to their enemy, Dona Elvira, as the source of the deliberate misinformation. At all events, Geraldini's sudden recall left the duenna in unchallenged dominance over both Catherine and her Household. It also left her free to offer her own version of events.

This became a matter of moment when Ferdinand and Isabella demanded the truth from Duque about Catherine's condition: had

Arthur successfully consummated the union or was Catherine still a virgin? The Catholic Kings needed to know this fundamental fact about their daughter's first marriage to help in their negotiations for her second. And 'nobody', they complained, 'has told us'. As it happens, their letter crossed with one from Dona Elvira informing them 'for a certainty' that Catherine 'remains as she was here': that is, a virgin.[8]

Catherine's parents accepted Elvira's assurance. So have most succeeding generations. However, there are good reasons for doubting Dona Elvira's statement or at least for scrutinizing it more critically. As we have seen, there is circumstantial evidence, some of it contemporary, including the herald's account, for taking the consummation as a likelihood if not as a fact. Dona Elvira's own self-interested motives for insisting on her charge's virginity (and hence Catherine's continuing dependent status) are also very clear. Moreover, the only man who could have testified decisively to the contrary, Catherine's confessor Alessandro, had been got out of the country, probably at Elvira's own instigation, and, despite his fondness for mildly salacious gossip about the great, had doubtless been terrified into silence on this question at least.

But what of Catherine herself? Surely her steadfast affirmation of Dona Elvira's claim is decisive? But Catherine's insistence on her virginity is put on record only long, long after the event, in 1529. And the value we attach to it depends on our subsequent reading of Catherine's character and actions. Traditionally, Catherine has been regarded as a plaster-of-Paris saint, who could not tell a lie. Actually, she was both more complex and much more human.

We should also consider Catherine's position in the immediate aftermath of her marriage to Arthur. Did she know enough about sex to realize what had happened? On the contrary, everything suggests that she was and long remained both ignorant and, worse, misinformed. And was she in a condition to tell the truth even if she had known it? Here it is important to remember that the decision for Catherine to accompany Arthur to Wales had only been reached after long and acrimonious discussion. On one side, arguing for departure and living together, had been Alessandro and De Puebla; on the other, in resolute opposition, was Dona Elvira. If only by her acquiescence, Catherine had sided with her confessor against her duenna. We can imagine Catherine's girlish guilt when things turned out as they did. We can also imagine how that guilt was exacerbated by Margaret Pole's revelations about her brother Warwick's execution. Her marriage to Arthur, Catherine must have felt, had been made in blood and bitterness. It, her first marriage, and even he, her first husband, were things accursed, and Catherine wished to blot both out of her memory. How better than by claiming that the marriage had never been consummated? In other words, that it had never been a marriage at all and that Arthur had never been her husband?

All this is, of necessity, speculation. But it is striking that Dona Elvira's claim commanded by no means universal assent at the time. The English flatly denied it. The Spanish asserted it, but covertly. And Rome, judiciously, sat on the fence.

The Pope had been involved in the negotiations for Catherine's second marriage from an early stage. This is because the marriage was highly contentious. Catherine would be marrying her own brother-in-law and such a union raised profound questions of natural and canon law. Only the Pope could settle them with the absolute power of binding and loosing he claimed as heir of St Peter. At the time, the English were among the most fervent defenders of the Papal powers; later, and thanks to Catherine's own marriage, it was a different story. The Papal agreement to the marriage would be couched in the form of a document known as a 'dispensation' because it 'dispensed', or set aside, the moral and legal obstacles against the marriage.

The negotiations themselves had made rapid progress. The English asked, and the Spanish, by and large, granted. On Ferdinand and Isabella's own instructions, legitimate questions about Catherine's dower rights and the marriage portion were swept under the carpet. Nothing, neither Catherine's rights nor her welfare, must get in the way of the new English marriage. The treaties for the marriage were signed on 23 June 1503 at Richmond. Two days later, on the 25th, the young couple were betrothed 'at the Bishop of Salisbury's place in Fleet Street'. And three days later still, on the 28th, Henry celebrated his twelfth birthday.[9]

But then matters stalled in Rome. The first clause of the marriage treaty provided that both parties would petition Rome for a dispensation. The dispensation, it continued, was required because Catherine had previously contracted a marriage to Arthur:

> whereby she became related to Henry, Prince of Wales, in the first degree of affinity and because her marriage with Prince Arthur was solemnized according to the rites of the Catholic Church *and afterwards consummated.*

As agreed, both the English and the Spanish approached Rome for the necessary permission. Henry VII's overtures were straightforward. But Ferdinand muddied the waters by putting his own gloss on the case as outlined in the treaty. The treaty, he told his ambassador in Rome, asserted that the marriage had been consummated. The truth, Ferdinand wrote, was the opposite. He even claimed that 'it is well known in England that the Princess is still a virgin'. But, to satisfy the English, who are 'much disposed to cavil', 'it has seemed to be more prudent to provide for the case as though the marriage had been consummated'.[10]

Ferdinand's argument is a *non sequitur.* If it was 'well known in England that the Princess is still a virgin', why should it have satisfied English doubts to declare that she was not? No wonder that Rome seems to have been confused about the facts of the case and hesitated accordingly.

Henry VII knew nothing about Ferdinand's manoeuvres and was therefore in the dark about the reason for the consequent delays. Soon he was fearing the worst. Did Rome, like some of his leading councillors and bishops, such as Archbishop Warham of Canterbury and Bishop Fox of Winchester, oppose the marriage as a matter of principle? Pope Julius II tried to reassure him. He admitted that he had 'somewhat delayed to dispense with the obstacles to the marriage'. But he insisted that he had acted from the best of motives, taking his time 'only from the wish to consider the case more maturely'. The letter was intended to still the

English King's doubts. But it had the contrary effect of heightening them. The Pope had told Henry VII that he would hear from him by Robert Sherbourne, Dean of the Chapel Royal, who had been on Embassy in Rome. But Sherbourne began his journey home without the dispensation. The English King despaired.[11]

He need not have worried – or at least, worried too much. Julius had agreed the dispensation. But, as was frequent Papal practice with difficult decisions, he had not released the document. He would probably have continued to sit on it but for the circumstances of Isabella's poor health. Finally, as a compassionate gesture, he sent her the Brief in the autumn of 1504. Ferdinand wrote to Henry VII on 24 November to announce its arrival.[12]

It was a document which had been much pondered and on which much hung. Yet it contained an extraordinary error of dating. Following the normal practice of the Papal chancery, it was dated in two ways: by the year of grace and by the year of the pontiff's reign. But the two contradicted each other: the year of grace dating was 'the 7th of the calends of January of the year of our Lord's Incarnation 1503' that is, in the Roman calendar, 26 December 1502; whereas 'the first year of our pontificate' of the recently elected Pope Julius II only began on 1 November 1503. It was the sort of error which had invalidated many a lesser document.[13]

The Brief also contained one clause that outraged Isabella. For it stated, as a matter of fact, that Catherine's first marriage to Arthur had been consummated. But Dona Elvira had sworn the contrary! In response, no doubt, to Isabella's protests, the final, authoritative version of the dispensation, which took the form of a Bull, or papal letters patent sealed with lead, took a very different line. Like all the best redrafting, it achieved the desired result with extraordinary economy – indeed, by the insertion of only a single word.

The Pope, the Bull began, had been informed that Catherine had 'contracted a marriage with Arthur, Prince of Wales and that this marriage had, *perhaps*, been consummated'. The word translated as 'perhaps' is *forsan*. Its root is *fors* ('chance' or 'luck') and its usual meaning is indeed 'perhaps' or 'perchance'. In this usage, *forsan* expresses a strong doubt about the marriage having been consummated. But *forsan* is sometimes used to state a fact, just as in English we say 'something chanced or fortuned', when we mean 'something happened'. In which case the meaning becomes the opposite: 'this marriage happens to have been consummated'.

Was the ambiguity accidental, like the error of dating in the Brief? Or was it deliberate? In any case, it contrived to square the circle. By means of the single weasel word *forsan* the dispensation managed to contain both the English *and* the Spanish version of what had happened (or not) between Catherine and Arthur. Resolving the ambiguity, Julius might have decided, was a matter for another day and, or so perhaps he hoped, for another Pope. So it proved.

Such subtleties were by then beyond Isabella, who was on her death-bed by the time the Brief arrived. Two days later she was dead. Her death, as Ferdinand wrote to Henry VII, was 'the deepest grief that could happen to us in this world'. He had lost 'the best and most excellent wife'. Catherine had lost her mother. A new world of uncertainty had opened.[14]

19. Hard times

Her mother's death was a bitter personal blow for Catherine. Coincidentally, on the very day Isabella died, Catherine had written to her, anxiously enquiring about her health. 'She had', she said, 'no other hope or comfort than that which comes from knowing that her father and mother are well.'[1]

But, by a cruel irony, Isabella's death also devalued Catherine's worth in the royal marriage market. This is because the union of Castile and Aragon, on which the power of Spain depended, was a purely personal one: it was created by Isabella's marriage to Ferdinand and (at least in theory) it was dissolved by her death. Catherine, the daughter of the Catholic Kings, was one of the great catches of Europe; Catherine, the daughter of the widowed Ferdinand, King once more only of the insignificant realm of Aragon, was a paltry prize. Was Ferdinand an ally worth bothering with? Was Catherine a daughter-in-law worth having? These were the questions Henry VII now pondered. Catherine reaped the bitter harvest. She quarrelled with Dona Elvira, and she grew up. She plumbed depths for which her pampered upbringing had done nothing to prepare her. And finally, and with reason, she despaired.

Before news of Isabella's death reached England, Catherine marked the Christmas festivities with an extended visit to Court. This experience of the English Court *en fête* seems, for the first time, to have awakened feelings of independence. She became aware of the contrast between the relative freedom given to an English Princess, like her sister-in-law, Mary, and the purdah-like seclusion imposed on her as a Spanish Infanta. And with the awareness came resentment. But it was quickly curbed. Invoking Henry VII's authority as well as Ferdinand's, De Puebla moved decisively to shore up Dona Elvira's control over both Catherine and her forever-quarrelling servants. De Puebla was playing his usual double game. The more strictly Dona Elvira's discipline was enforced, the more intolerable it would become and the more likely Catherine was to throw it over. But, equally clearly, De Puebla, like Henry VII, took the view that Catherine, for the time being, was not yet fit to manage her own affairs.[2]

As it happened, Catherine's final rebellion against Dona Elvira was not long delayed. And this time, De Puebla played the part of her liberator. For all of them – the Princess, the duenna and the ambassador – were caught up in the great sea-change that followed Isabella's death.

As usual, family connexions and loyalties were the key to events and behaviour. Dona Elvira's brother was Don Juan Manuel, the Spanish ambassador in the Netherlands. He was a Castilian and, while Isabella lived, was one of the outstanding diplomatists of the new Spain. But, like many other Castilians, he saw Isabella's death as an opportunity to free his native land from the rule of the Aragonese Ferdinand. For Don Juan and his ilk, Ferdinand was doubly offensive, since he was both oppressive and a foreigner. He was now also vulnerable. For Isabella's heir was not Ferdinand, but the Catholic Kings' eldest surviving daughter, Juana, wife of Philip, surnamed the Fair. Philip was already Archduke of Austria through his father and Duke of Burgundy through his mother. Now he claimed to be King of Castile, Leon and Granada through his wife. If Philip could make good his claims, Spain would be fragmented and Ferdinand marginalized. Don Juan deployed all his considerable talents as an intriguer to achieve this aim.[3]

Juana was besotted with her husband and was dough in his hands. Don Juan's hope was that Catherine would prove equally malleable to Dona Elvira's will. France already supported Philip's immediate claim to the Castilian succession; Don Juan's aim was to get Henry VII's backing as well. With England on side, the encirclement of Ferdinand would be complete. Henry VII was sympathetic and in April 1505 he lent Philip £108,000 'for his next voyage unto Spain'. This was an immense sum (over five times the first instalment of Catherine's marriage portion, for example). All that remained to finalize Henry VII's investment, Don Juan felt, was to engineer a meeting between the English King and the King-Archduke, as Philip now styled himself.[4]

Here Catherine came in. Through Dona Elvira, Don Juan knew that Catherine, wretched after her mother's death, was desperately anxious to see her sister, Juana, who was so tantalizingly near in the Netherlands. Why not get Catherine to write to Henry VII to suggest a meeting? At such a meeting, Catherine and Juana could exchange sweet family nothings, while Henry VII and Philip plotted the downfall of the sisters' father, Ferdinand of Aragon. Formal proposals were put to Catherine to suggest a meeting and, under the promptings of both Dona Elvira and her own heart, she eagerly agreed and on the spot wrote a letter to Henry VII 'in the most affectionate and loving terms'.[5]

By pure coincidence, De Puebla was at Durham House as the plot unfolded. He, in contrast to Dona Elvira and her brother, had remained loyal to Ferdinand – and was determined to foil the scheme, which, as it happened, was developing under his nose. His first thought was to get Dona Elvira to promise to deliver the letter only through him as the accredited ambassador. Once in his hands, of course, Catherine's letter would have disappeared. Dona Elvira understood this very well and immediately despatched the letter by De Esquivel, the Master of the Hall.

De Puebla was informed. He abandoned his dinner uneaten and rushed back to see Catherine. Relations between them were poor and, despite all De Puebla's efforts on her behalf, Catherine regarded him with suspicion, even contempt. She, despite her surname 'of Aragon', was Castilian to the core and was imbued with the Castilian values of militant Catholicism. Central to these was a mistrust of converted Jews like De Puebla. De Puebla's sister had been seized by the Inquisition, and Catherine dealt with De Puebla with distaste.

Desperation gave him 'courage'. More importantly, it inspired him to hit on the single value that they shared: loyalty to Ferdinand. First swearing Catherine to secrecy (especially against Dona Elvira), he told her the whole position as he saw it. 'The interview was the work of Don Juan Manuel and Dona Elvira'. They 'intended to do injury to her royal father and to the Queen her sister [Juana] by means of it'. Nothing else would have made Catherine listen to him. And nothing else would have made her take De Puebla's side against Dona Elvira. But, with his appeal to her family loyalty, Catherine was his. She 'has an excellent heart', he reported to Ferdinand, 'and loves her father more than herself'. She immediately did what De Puebla recommended and wrote Henry VII a letter disowning her first communication as having been procured under false pretences.[6]

Catherine, however, was less successful in obeying De Puebla's other injunction to keep the matter secret. Concealing her true feelings was never her strong point (though some indeed would think it a virtue). Dona Elvira had betrayed her trust and still worse (did she not 'love her father more than herself'?) had betrayed her father as well. In the face of such double treachery, she could not remain silent. There was a furious quarrel and Dona Elvira took refuge with her brother in the Netherlands under pretext of seeking treatment for her failing sight. Years later,

De Esquivel remembered the 'horrible hour' when the duenna left. De Esquivel, too, as Elvira's instrument in carrying the first letter to Court, had shared in Catherine's displeasure and had been suffered to see her only three times in twenty-four months.[7]

Catherine's involvement in the affairs of the King-Archduke had yet to reach its miserable climax. In September 1505 Henry VII made Philip another substantial loan (of £30,000) and in January 1506 Philip and Juana set sail to claim their Spanish kingdoms. The armada made a triumphal progress up the Channel, with guns shooting and minstrels playing. But then it was struck with terrible storms. Each of the royal couple behaved characteristically in the face of drowning. Philip showed a cool physical courage. Juana sat with her arms entwined round Philip's legs, determined not to be separated from him even in death. Refusal to let go of a husband was a trait that Catherine was to share with her sister.

But the couple did not drown. Instead, separated from the rest of the fleet, they were driven ashore at Melcombe Regis in the lee of the Isle of Portland. The Aragonese party in Philip's entourage urged him immediately to set sail again for Spain. But Philip knew that he was effectively Henry VII's prisoner and, putting a brave face on things as he had done during the storm, he sent his secretary to the English King to suggest a meeting. The interview that De Puebla and Catherine had done so much to prevent was to take place nevertheless.[8]

Philip reached Windsor on 31 January. Catherine arrived shortly after. The King-Archduke and the English King were lodged in inter-communicating suites and competed in elaborate courtesies. Then sessions of hard negotiation alternated with entertainment. The entertainments ranged from the savagery of horse-baiting to the almost Victorian domesticity of the Sunday afternoon *soirée* presented by Catherine and her sister-in-law, Princess Mary. First Catherine and one of her ladies, both in Spanish dress, danced, and then Mary and one of her English attendants. The atmosphere turned suddenly sour when Catherine asked Philip, who was engrossed in conversation with Henry VII, to dance. At first he refused, courteously enough. But, when

Catherine persisted, he replied brusquely that he was a mariner, 'and yet you would cause me to dance'.[9]

This curious exchange has never been properly explained. It all goes back, of course, to Don Juan Manuel's plot and its debacle. Philip knew from Dona Elvira of Catherine's uncompromising support for Ferdinand, her father and his rival. Since De Puebla's revelations, all Catherine's wits had been devoted to preventing both Philip's voyage to Spain and his meeting with the King of England. Now Philip's rudeness, and the words in which he chose to express it, told her that he neither forgave nor forgot. 'I am a mariner,' he said, reminding her that she had tried to stop his voyage. 'And yet you would cause me to dance,' he continued, rubbing salt in the wound. Catherine had tried to prevent his meeting with Henry VII: why should he interrupt his confidential conversation with the King to dance with her, of all people? Mary offered Catherine sisterly comfort by going to sit with her on the edge of the carpet under the canopy of the cloth of estate.

Juana had travelled separately and more slowly and did not reach Windsor till Tuesday, 10 February. Juana is known to history as 'The Mad'. At this stage, as her behaviour during the storm shows, it would be fairer to call her neurotic. Fearful perhaps of embarrassments, the English royal family received her privately: not at the public entrance to the King's apartments, but at the privy or backstairs which gave on to the park. There she was greeted by Henry VII, her sister-in-law Princess Mary and her sister Catherine. The three ladies seem to have spent the day together. The following day Catherine and Mary went to Richmond. There they were joined by the King, who was anxious to show off his new palace to his royal visitors, just as he had done to Catherine in the aftermath of her wedding to Arthur. But Juana never saw the marvels of Richmond. Instead, Philip packed her off to the coast, while he enjoyed the continued hospitality of his royal host.[10]

In a later letter to Juana, Catherine recalled her joy at meeting the sister she had last seen ten years previously – and 'the distress which filled my heart, a few hours afterwards, on account of your hasty and sudden departure'. An older generation of historians blamed Henry VII for the cruelty of the separation. Instead, it is clear that the responsibility rests with Philip. He had snubbed Catherine a few days previously. Now he showed that he feared the influence she might have over her pliable sister. What if she recalled Juana to her filial duty to Ferdinand, as De Puebla had done so successfully with Catherine herself? What then of Philip's castles in Spain? Much safer to keep the sisters apart. Philip succeeded, and Catherine never saw Juana again.[11]

All this was bad enough. But the malign consequences of Isabella's death now threatened Catherine with a worse separation still – from Prince Henry, the second husband to whom she was espoused and yet not married.

20. Harder times

On 27 June 1505, the eve of Prince Henry's fourteenth birthday, a small party assembled in a certain lower chamber on the western side of the Palace of Richmond. But the mood was hardly festive. Prince Henry had come to renounce his marriage to Catherine.

Before Richard Fox, Bishop of Winchester and Lord Privy Seal, the Prince explained that he had entered into an agreement to marry Catherine. But the agreement was conditional since it had been made while he was a minor and could only be carried into effect when he came of age. Now, as he was 'attaining the years of puberty', he solemnly announced his intention not to proceed with the marriage. Instead 'contra eundem reclamo et eidem dissentio', he said. 'I protest vehemently against it and am [utterly] opposed to it.' Henry's protestation was witnessed by the Royal Secretary, the King's Chamberlain and Vice-chamberlain, by Prince Henry's own Chamberlain, Henry Marney, and by Dr Nicholas West, Archdeacon of Derby.[1]

West was a royal councillor and an expert in matrimonial law. When Henry, twenty-five years later, renounced his marriage to Catherine for the second time, West was to be a stalwart defender of both Catherine and the validity of the marriage. But in 1505 neither he nor anyone else told Catherine what Henry had done. She was left completely in the dark.[2]

In renouncing his marriage to Catherine, Prince Henry affirmed that he had acted 'neither by force, fraud or entreaty . . . but willingly and freely, in no way compelled'. The truth, however, was that he had spoken as the mere mouth-piece of his father.[3]

As events unrolled after Isabella's death, Henry VII became increasingly doubtful about the benefits of the Spanish marriage. He was also determined that, should it ever take place, it would be only when the marriage portion – every last escudo and crown of it – had been paid.

The attitude of Catherine's own father, Ferdinand, was more-or-less a mirror-image. In principle, he was unshakably committed to the marriage. Catherine must, he told his daughter more than once, 'speak of your marriage always as of a thing of which you have no doubt and no suspicion, and which God alone can undo'.

In practice, however, raising and sending the money for the second instalment of the marriage portion was another matter. There were other, infinitely more pressing, demands on Ferdinand's time and resources as he struggled to hold together the multitudinous kingdoms the possession of which was his lifetime's work. Excuses, to Catherine and to Henry VII, were always easier to find than cash.

Catherine thus found herself pig-in-the-middle as her father and her father-in-law entered into a sort of competition as to who could display the greater callousness about her plight. For mistreating Catherine, Henry VII quickly realized, was his best hope of putting pressure on Ferdinand to pay up. He was breathtakingly frank about this, telling De Puebla that, in behaving harshly towards her he acted out of Catherine's best interests, 'hoping to induce the King her father by that means sooner to send her marriage portion'.[4]

Ironically, the event which precipitated the sudden decline in

Catherine's fortunes was the final departure of her rejected duenna, Dona Elvira. Relations between them had been difficult for months. But her presence had guaranteed a sort of continuity. When Dona Elvira at last left for the Netherlands at the beginning of December 1505, the ground slipped from beneath Catherine's feet. Innocently, Catherine wrote to Henry VII, to ask either for the appointment of 'an old English lady' to act as chaperone in place of Dona Elvira, or that her father-in-law would offer her his direct protection 'and take me [in]to his Court'.

With his usual opportunism, Henry VII pounced. He gave Catherine what she wanted and took her to Court. But not in the fashion she expected. Instead, he used the move to strip her of her expensive and (to English eyes) useless male Household; he also separated her from her hoard of textiles, plate and jewellery, which he deposited in a place of safekeeping.[5]

Catherine's patience (or was it her sense of decorum?) snapped. 'Hitherto', she wrote to her father, 'I have not wished to let Your Highness know the affairs here, that I might not give you annoyance.' Now she poured out her troubles: 'for two months I have had severe tertian fevers, and this will be the cause that I shall soon die!'[6]

Things only got worse. The following April, Henry VII made explicit the link between Catherine's short commons and her father's failure to hand over the marriage portion. Catherine's reply – that 'I believed that in time to come your highness would discharge it' – only confirmed the English king's worst fears about Ferdinand's financial reliability.[7]

For Catherine, the pains of exile were now exacerbated by those of poverty. 'I have', she wrote to her father, 'nothing for chemises; wherefore, by Your Highness's life, I have sold some bracelets to get a dress of black velvet, for I was all but naked: for since I departed from Spain I have [had] nothing except two new dresses, for till now those I have brought from thence have lasted me; although I have now nothing but the dresses of brocade.' Poverty in black velvet and brocade is only comparative, but for Catherine, who had never wanted for anything, it was real enough.[8]

Worst of all, however, was the sense of being a stranger in a strange land. The previous year, Ferdinand, as part of his policy of setting Catherine's position in England in stone, had asked the English ambassadors about her progress in language. 'I am greatly desirous', he had said, 'that she shall be an English woman and to learn for to speak English.' The ambassadors had reassured him. 'Her Grace could speak some and that she understood much more', they had replied. As ever, diplomats spoke diplomatically. What was probably the real position was set out by Catherine in her letter to her father of April 1506. She had been without a confessor ever since Alessandro's enforced departure in 1503. Now she begged her father to send her a Spanish friar of the Order of Observant Franciscans. The issue was not so much his orthodoxy or nationality as his language, 'because', she admitted, 'I do not understand the English language nor know how to speak it'. So far, her years in England had been locust years: they had devoured her youth and given her nothing in return.[9]

Catherine reached the nadir, she thought, on the Feast of St John the Baptist, 24 June 1506. This was the final day provided for the delivery of the second instalment of her marriage portion. The day came and went and nothing arrived. Even the excuses of the Spanish were late and it was not until 15 March 1507, when Ferdinand was in Naples, that he wrote to Henry VII and Catherine. Each was given a different reason for the delay. To Henry VII, Ferdinand explained that the money was already collected and in the safekeeping of Isabella's trustees and awaited only his personal authority for payment on his return to Spain. Catherine likewise was assured that the money was ready. But, to her, Ferdinand blamed her brother-in-law, the King-Archduke Philip, who was 'always . . . hostile to him and to all his daughters', for preventing the payment. The inconsistencies are obvious, and, for the record, neither version was true.[10]

At least Ferdinand's letters made good speed to England, reaching Catherine and De Puebla in only a fortnight. Ambassador De Puebla had the coolest reception when he delivered the letter to Henry VII to the King's hands. Henry VII scarcely bothered to pretend to believe Ferdinand's reasons and, through his own ambassador, he lectured his brother monarch on the importance of honouring debts. 'Punctual payments', he later wrote to Ferdinand directly, 'is so sacred a duty and the sum of money is so moderate for so great a King as the King of Spain that he had not expected to be again requested to consent to a new postponement of the payment'. Nevertheless, after much persuasion, Henry VII agreed to a deferment until Michaelmas, 29 September 1507.[11]

Catherine's letters in reply to her father were equally frank. Please do not default again, she begged. 'For the contempt shown to her when the money of her portion did not arrive was great. Does not wish again to undergo such a humiliation. Though submissive, cannot forget that she is the daughter of the King of Spain.' But worse still than the poverty and the contempt was the fact that she was 'so seldom [allowed] to see the Prince of Wales, although he lived in the same house with her'.[12]

There is, in fact, a curious parallelism in the lives of Henry VIII and Catherine of Aragon in these years. Henry's mother died in February 1503. He was only eleven years old. Henry had been as close to Elizabeth of York as Catherine was to Isabella of Castile, and the loss affected him deeply. The news of his mother's death, he later wrote to Erasmus, had been 'hateful intelligence'. But the consequences were more than psychological. Elizabeth's death, following hard on the heels of the death of his brother Arthur, brought about a change in Henry's life – just as Isabella's death had done in Catherine's.[13]

Hitherto, as Duke of York, Henry had been brought up away from Court, under the general supervision of his mother. He had his own Household, which attended on him and his sisters as they moved between the smaller home-counties palaces including Eltham and Hatfield. Now everything changed. At the beginning of 1504 Parliament stripped him of his lands and title as Duke of York. On 23 February 1504 he formally stepped into Arthur's shoes with his creation as Prince of Wales. On 28 June he celebrated his fourteenth birthday and immediately afterwards, at the beginning of July, he joined his father at Richmond and accompanied him on the summer Progress. Like Catherine, Henry had been summoned to his father's Court.[14]

The summons came at a crucial moment. Henry was growing up fast.

Soon, the Spanish ambassador would note, 'he is already taller than his father and his limbs are of gigantic size'. But the King was reluctant to recognize his son's near-adulthood. It seems clear that he blamed himself for having given Arthur his head too soon. He could not afford to make the same mistake with Henry. So access to the young Prince was carefully controlled and his sports and pastimes were strictly supervised. In particular, he was forbidden to joust. Jousting was the sixteenth-century football. Star jousters made their fortunes and they were idols even to royal Princes. Henry's physique was ideally suited to the tilt-yard. But all his father would do was let him take part in the training bouts known as riding at the ring. 'The object of this sport', according to a modern authority, 'was to catch a suspended ring on the point of one's lance. It was far safer than jousting ... [and it was] a way of practising for jousting.' It was also, for a young man like Henry, sissy. He sat chafing at the bit as his seniors slugged it out with lances in the joust and hacked at each other with swords in the tourney.[15]

To compare this ban on jousting with the real deprivations inflicted on Catherine may seem far-fetched. But teenagers, like Henry, have little sense of proportion. He felt hard done by, just as Catherine was hard done by indeed. And the two had the same oppressor in Henry VII. Whether he knew it or not, the King was forging a common bond between his son and his son's wife-perhaps-to-be.

In the spring of 1507, however, Catherine was aware only that Prince Henry was so near and yet so far. Still worse, she suddenly realized that he might slip through her fingers entirely. She had always believed, as her father had taught her, that her marriage was a thing 'which God alone can undo'. Now her father-in-law made it brutally clear that more earthly considerations could intervene. The English King, Catherine reported to Ferdinand, 'has told her very positively that he no longer regards himself and the Prince of Wales as bound by the marriage treaty, because the marriage portion has not been paid'. Incredulous, Catherine asked De Puebla if Henry VII was indeed 'entitled by law to renounce her marriage' in the event of non-payment. De Puebla confirmed that he was. Still disbelieving, Catherine appealed to her confessor. If the marriage was conditional, he replied, 'and the conditions [were] not fulfilled by one party, the other should renounce the whole treaty'. The final authority had spoken and the verdict was damning.[16]

In her panic, Catherine wrote the second letter of the day to her father, warning him that her 'marriage will come to nothing if the marriage portion be not punctually paid on the day fixed'. She also sought for a scapegoat. The real culprits, equally if differently guilty, were her father and her father-in-law. But the sixteenth-century proprieties required unjudgemental submission from a child to a parent. Catherine was nothing if not conventional. Unable, therefore, consciously to think ill of Henry VII and Ferdinand, she turned instead on the nearest object, De Puebla, and poured out the vials of her wrath on him.[17]

He was spineless, dishonest and far too close to Henry VII, she told her father. He was also of the wrong rank and (though the words were unspoken) of the wrong race. Let her father send a real man and real Spaniard as ambassador, 'who will dare to speak an honest word at the right time', and all would be well. Her preference was for De Ayala, who had been in England at the time of her marriage and had tried to prevent her fatal journey to Ludlow. And if not De Ayala, then Gutier Gomez de Fuensalida, Knight Commander of Membrilla, would be the next-best thing.[18]

Catherine, did she but know it, was nominating her own nemesis.

21. Hope and despair

The twenty-two-year-old Catherine was indeed growing up almost as fast as Henry. He was becoming a man in the tiltyard; she was learning to be a woman in the no-less brutal school of hard knocks of Anglo-Spanish relations. There is a new worldliness in her letters. She even ventures confidently into unfemale spheres, like diplomacy itself. 'It cannot be doubted', she writes to her father *à propos* of the unspeakable De Puebla, 'that nothing contributes more towards the prosperity or adverse fortune of kingdoms than the sufficiency or incompetence of ambassadors.' Her interest was practical as well as theoretical. She had, she wrote to Ferdinand's all-powerful Secretary, Almazan, 'deciphered the last despatches without any assistance'. Now she 'wishes she were able to write in cipher' herself. Could she have the keys?[1]

Ferdinand had heard this easy authority once before from a woman. It was from his wife, Isabella. He responded in the same way. Picking up a hint from Henry VII, who had told him that he 'liked to hear [his news] from her [Catherine] better than from any other person', he decided that, in the interim before a new ambassador could be sent to England from Spain, Catherine herself should act as his envoy. She was sent credentials in form to present to Henry VII while De Puebla was instructed to share all communications with her. It would be difficult to imagine more uneasy bedfellows.[2]

Catherine, starved of purposeful activity as well as affection, threw herself into the new task. She presented her credentials to Henry VII. She started to write in cipher (braving, as she said, the laughter of Almazan and her father). And, above all, she learned the black arts of diplomatic deceit and double-cross.[3]

There was ample scope for these in her principal mission. This was to negotiate another dynastic marriage between England and Spain. The groom was to be her father-in-law, Henry VII, and the bride Catherine's own sister, Juana. The English King had been a widower since the death of Elizabeth of York in 1503, while Juana had been widowed three years later in 1506, when the King-Archduke Philip had died shortly after arriving in Spain to take possession of his wife's kingdoms. Juana was the beauty of the family and Henry VII, always susceptible to feminine charms, had been much smitten by her when he had briefly seen her at Windsor en route to Spain. That she was mad, or at least mentally unstable, counted for little. That she was young enough to be Henry VII's daughter counted for less. Nor was Catherine herself squeamish or scrupulous. Instead, she saw such a marriage simply as a device which could redress the balance of diplomatic forces between England and Spain. At the moment, these were wholly in Henry VII's favour. Ferdinand was eager for Catherine's marriage to Prince Henry; Henry VII was indifferent if not hostile. If, however, Henry VII wanted, or could be made to want, to marry Juana, then an obvious *quid pro quo* suggested itself.[4]

Catherine, forced for so long to play a merely passive role, rejoiced in this opportunity to turn the tables. 'I bait [Henry VII] with this [the marriage with Dona Juana],' she proudly told her father. Miraculously, her own treatment improved, which she pretended to take at face value. She even pretended to be happy with De Puebla's conduct of affairs:

> I dissimulate with him [her letter to Ferdinand continued] and praise all that he does. I even tell him that I am very well treated by the King, and that I am very well contented; and I say everything that I think may be useful for me with the King, because, in fact, De Puebla is the adviser of the King and I would not dare to say anything to him, except what I should wish the King to know.

Now there is nothing very reprehensible in this: 'dissimulation' is the practice of diplomats and politicians throughout the ages. But equally there is nothing very virtuous, either. To protect her own marriage, it seems, Catherine would lie with the worst. Not for nothing was she Ferdinand's daughter.[5]

Michaelmas 1507 came round and Ferdinand postponed the payment of Catherine's marriage portion for yet another six months. But by this time Ferdinand was back in the saddle. Fully in control in Spain, he could once more devote thought and resources to his daughter in England. The result was that on 22 February 1508 there arrived in London bills of exchange for the payment of the second instalment of Catherine's marriage portion. Ferdinand had also heeded his daughter's other suggestions. As she had begged, the bills were brought by a new ambassador. Ferdinand had even appointed one of Catherine's recommendations for the post, Fuensalida, the Knight Commander of Membrilla.

Fuensalida ran into immediate difficulties with that old bone of contention, the exact status of Catherine's trousseau. The Spanish insisted that it count towards the second instalment; the English refused. Despite his protests at Henry VII's covetousness and bad faith, Ferdinand conceded this point and in September drafts for the remaining 35,000 crowns were despatched. All should now have been plain sailing. But two other issues now threatened to shipwreck Catherine's marriage once and for all.[6]

The first was yet another dynastic alliance. With the death of the King-Archduke Philip and the incapacity of his widow, Juana the Mad, the heir of Castile was Charles, the eldest son of Philip and Juana and the grandson and eventual heir of Ferdinand and Isabella. Charles had been left behind in the Netherlands at the time of his parents' ill-fated voyage to Spain, and his aunt (and Catherine's sometime sister-in-law), the Archduchess Margaret acted as Regent on his behalf. But the real power in young Charles's life was his other grandfather, the brilliant but erratic Emperor Maximilian.

Henry VII and Maximilian now made common cause. Henry wanted another glorious marriage alliance for the House of Tudor; Maximilian, who was always strapped for cash despite his array of gaudy titles, wanted (as he bluntly wrote to the Archduchess Margaret) 'to get a good sum out of the King of England'. And both wanted to get at Ferdinand. The result was an agreement to marry Charles, aged eight, to Henry VII's second daughter, Mary, aged twelve. Ferdinand, whose kingdoms would supply the better half of young Charles's inheritance, was naturally put out. He ordered Fuensalida neither to agree to the marriage nor to do anything to countenance it. But nor, on the other hand, was he to veto it outright.[7]

All this put Catherine in a quandary. Mary's proxy wedding to

Charles was fixed for December 1508. As usual, a magnificent ceremony was planned, in which Catherine was expected to play a leading role. For, despite the slights and insults, she remained, as Prince Henry's as-yet-publicly-unrepudiated wife, the second-ranking woman of the English Court after Lady Margaret Beaufort, the King's mother. She was also on terms of close personal friendship with Mary herself. Nevertheless, Fuensalida, interpreting Ferdinand's instructions with his accustomed over-zealousness, forbade Catherine to take part. Catherine was torn. Normally she was all obedience to her father. But following his supposed orders in this instance would imperil her rank at the English Court, which she had fought so hard to maintain. It would put at risk one of her few friendships in England. It would even, Catherine could tell herself, contradict her father's over-riding wish that she should 'be an English woman'. As was proper in such a dilemma, conscientious Catherine consulted her confessor. His advice was clear-cut: she should take part. It was of course the advice Catherine wished to hear and she promptly followed it. She was Mary's principal attendant at the wedding ceremony in the cloth of gold-hung Presence Chamber at Richmond Palace; she dined with her in state afterwards and sat with her at the celebratory jousts. For the first time in her life, Catherine's adoptive nationality had triumphed over her native Spanishness.[8]

Fuensalida, who was Spanish to his backbone, was not best pleased. What made Catherine's treachery (as he saw it) worse was the fact that she had chosen to convey her decision to him via her confessor. This was to add insult to injury. For her confessor was a typical turbulent priest: he was young, footloose, attractive to women and fancy-free. His name was Fray Diego Fernandez. He was a Spanish Franciscan Observant, such as Catherine had asked her father to provide two years previously. But he was far from an official appointment. He seems to have made his own way to England (perhaps hearing of Catherine's call for members of his Order to come hither to wake up the Faith from its native torpor). He taught himself the language. And by spring 1507 he had become Catherine's confessor. Soon he had established a hold over her that exceeded even Dona Elvira's authority at its zenith. It was also a more

ambiguous power. Dona Elvira had exercised the quasi-maternal control
of a forceful woman over an immature girl. Fray Diego, on the other
hand, was a man who had an attractive young woman kneeling adoringly
at his feet. That she knelt to him as a priest was, Fuensalida felt, beside
the point. Moreover, he had heard dark rumours that their relationship
went beyond the merely confessional.[9]

Fray Diego was, in short, a bad influence on Catherine who must be
removed. Fuensalida found ready allies in Catherine's Household.
Catherine's Household had always been divided. But now the division
lay between Catherine and the rest. Her male servants had, of course,
long abandoned any hope of an English future. Some had managed to
return to Spain and the remainder were anxious to do so. Similar doubts
now infected the rump of five ladies-in-waiting who still attended on
Catherine at Court. They had served her loyally. But they had also seen
their looks begin to fade, their fine dresses wear out and the English
suitors, who at first had eagerly sought their hands, withdraw as
Catherine's star set. Now, they decided, they had had enough. Only one
person sustained Catherine's sense of her English destiny: Fray Diego.

Leader of the opposition among Catherine's women was Francesca
de Carceres. She visited Fuensalida in his lodgings in the house of
Grimaldi, the Genoese banker who was handling the bills of exchange
for Catherine's marriage portion. She told Fuensalida all the gossip about
Fray Diego. And she caught the eye of Grimaldi himself. Catherine
learned of her disloyalty and denounced her furiously. Francesca took
refuge in Grimaldi's house and, deciding that a bird in the hand was
worth two in the bush, accepted his offer of marriage.[10]

Fuensalida's disastrous intervention in Catherine's domestic affairs
was enough in itself to lead to a breach between them. Still worse was his
mishandling of the final stages of the negotiations for her marriage.
Catherine herself had called for an ambassador who would call a spade a
spade. Fuensalida prided himself on his ability to name it a bloody
shovel, though he would not have used so crude a phrase. While he was
ambassador in the Netherlands he had written 'these people are only
docile when they're treated roughly'. Now he proceeded to apply the

same maxim in England. At first, Catherine applauded the slap of firmness. But soon she understood its malign consequences. Fuensalida's relations broke down, first with the Council, and then with the King who flatly refused to see him. Not even the offer to pay the marriage portion in full assuaged English feelings. Instead, the difficulties about the trousseau were multiplied and molehills ingeniously transformed into mountains. Soon, Fuensalida persuaded himself, the mountains would fall and bury him and Catherine alike. He decided that the English, emboldened by Mary's proposed Burgundian marriage, had resolved to make war on Spain. His only thought was to get the marriage portion and Catherine herself out of the country before the storm broke.[11]

For Catherine, this was the final treachery. It was also the last straw. So far, she had held firm in the face of adversity. But this was too much. She had demanded the payment of her marriage portion. It had been paid. She had asked for a new, plain-speaking ambassador. He had been sent. And then everything had gone wrong. Even De Puebla's handling of her affairs acquired a retrospective, roseate glow. 'De Puebla', she wrote to her father, 'is accustomed to behave with the greatest gentleness towards Henry [VII], while the ambassador [Fuensalida] bears himself very audaciously towards him and his Council.' At last, she understood the logic of De Puebla's position: 'as she is constrained to submit to [the English authorities], no one can be of use who does not behave with moderation'.[12]

But the insight came too late. Soft means had been tried and failed. Hard means had been attempted, with even worse results. She had done everything she could, to no avail. She was at a dead end. The enterprise of the English marriage was over. She admitted her failure to her father and, what was more difficult still, to herself. 'Do not let me perish', she begged Ferdinand, 'otherwise . . . I am afraid I might do something which neither the King of England nor your Highness, who has much more weight, will be able to prevent.' Above all, 'send for me [to Spain], that I may conclude my few remaining days in serving God. That would be the greatest good I could have in this world.' Catherine's will, the will of the daughter of Isabella, had been finally broken.[13]

*

Catherine wrote this despairing letter on 9 March 1509. Six weeks later Henry VII was dead and Catherine's world was turned upside down.

22. Queen

It was indeed a new world that was ushered in when, on 21 April 1509, in great agony of body and mind, King Henry VII died. At fifty-two, he was not an old man, even by the standards of the sixteenth century. But the deaths, in quick succession, of his eldest son and his wife, had aged and soured him. His health broke down and he became increasingly oppressive: to members of his wife's family, to anyone with money, and, above all, to Catherine herself.

For Catherine, then, Henry VII's death could hardly make things worse. But would it make them any better?

On the whole, Catherine thought that it would. Back in September 1508 she had ventured to express 'the hope that the Prince would be better than his father'. Fuensalida, looking on the black side as usual, had replied: 'Please to God that the hope prove true, but he saw no likelihood of it.' For once, Catherine proved the better prophet.[1]

How had Catherine arrived at her optimistic reading of Prince Henry's character and inclinations? After all, the two had been allowed to spend very little time together and none in private. But Catherine was friendly with Mary, Henry's favourite sister. Perhaps, too, the courtship of her lady-in-waiting, Ines de Venegas, with William Blunt, Lord Mountjoy, which blossomed into marriage a few months into the new reign, had already begun. If so, this would have told Catherine all that she needed to know. For Mountjoy, though some thirteen years older than

Henry, was his 'socius studiorum' or 'companion in studies'. And it was Prince Henry's education, above all, that made him so different from his father.[2]

Henry, like Catherine herself, had been largely schooled in the Classics. Unlike Catherine, however, his education was influenced directly by the great Erasmus himself. Once again, the conduit was Mountjoy. Mountjoy had been Erasmus's favourite pupil in Paris and, when Mountjoy returned to England and took his place in Prince Henry's household, he kept up an enthusiastic correspondence with his former teacher. He also made sure that Henry was thoroughly inculcated both in Erasmus's characteristic style and in his moralizing approach to the Classics. He even brought Erasmus to England and introduced him to the eight-year-old Henry in 1499.[3]

But Mountjoy was a gentleman as well as a scholar. He came from a great military family, while his stepfather, the aged Earl of Ormond, was the source of the stories about Henry's namesake, the all-conquering Henry V, that formed another important aspect of the Prince's upbringing. Here history merged into legend. For when, late in the fifteenth century, Sir Thomas Malory came to write *Le Morte D'Arthur*, the definitive version of the Arthurian cycle, he remodelled the deeds of the mythical Arthur on the achievements of the real Henry V. For the young Henry, devouring *Le Morte D'Arthur* in Caxton's printed edition of 1485 and listening spell-bound to Ormond's reminiscences, the real and mythical hero-kings became one. He would be another Henry V, another Arthur: brave in war and peace, generous, bold and gallant.[4]

For Henry, aged seventeen years and ten months when his father died, was young – young enough to believe what he read and young enough to think that it could be put into practice. Erasmus's influence, also exercised primarily through books, supplied spice and intellectual ambition. From this source came Henry's sense of justice and virtue as the proper business of kings, as well as a fierce hunger for fame and for the acquisition of that most elusive of accolades for a ruler: to be known to contemporaries and to posterity as 'the Great'.

This was the young man whom Catherine, it seems, had glimpsed and in whom she put her hope. She probably knew, too, of more personal motives for his reaction against his father. From Margaret Pole, she had learned, perhaps, of Prince Henry's resentment at Henry VII's mistreatment of his mother's Yorkist relatives. And Catherine's own eyes would have told her that he hated being cooped up at his father's Court. That he wanted to joust and that only his father stopped him. That he had sat in the royal seat during one of Henry VII's bouts of illness; and that, like Prince Hal after he had tried on his dying father's crown, he had never wanted to give it up.

Now was his chance; now was Catherine's.

The old King died at 11 o'clock at night on the 21st. But his death was kept secret for two days. Councillors came to and from the royal apartments as though the King were still alive. And his son continued to appear publicly as Prince Henry and to be addressed as such. Not till the evening of 23 April was the truth made known and not till the 24th was the new King proclaimed in London. The concealment was to facilitate a political *coup*. Behind the smooth, uninterrupted façade of Court ceremony there took place a vicious faction struggle. This resulted in the downfall of two of the old King's leading councillors, Edmund Dudley and Sir Richard Empson, and the disavowal and reversal of the oppressive policies with which they were identified. The real author of these policies had, of course, been Henry VII himself. But he could not be blamed, openly at least.

The most dramatic reversal of policy was the decision that Prince Henry, now King Henry VIII, should marry Catherine after all. This decision, too, was probably taken behind closed doors in the first forty-eight hours of the reign. Certainly by 8 May it was a *fait accompli*. Fuensalida was bewildered and even Ferdinand, normally so quick on his feet in an emergency, struggled, against the disadvantages of distance, to keep up with events.

Nevertheless, there was no heedless rush to the altar. Instead, the English continued to extract the last drop of advantage from the situation. They made sure that the remainder of Catherine's marriage portion was paid in full and in cash. Catherine and her family also renounced any claim to the return of the money in the event of the premature death of either spouse. And not until the necessary deeds were signed and sealed were Henry and Catherine married on 11 June. The hard bargaining continued even into the couple's exchange of vows. 'Most illustrious Prince,' Henry was asked, 'is it your will to fulfil the treaty of marriage concluded by your father . . . and the parents of the Princess of Wales, the King and Queen of Spain; and, as the Pope has dispensed with this marriage, to take the Princess who is here present for your lawful wife?' 'I will,' Henry replied. Catherine was asked the equivalent question. 'I will,' she replied.[5]

Thus the vows were made; it remained to be seen how they would be kept. It also remained to be seen who would benefit from the marriage. So far, all the advantage had been on the English side. But Ferdinand rarely gave something for nothing. He had paid 200,000 crowns for the English marriage. He would expect a commensurate return on his investment.

Catherine's second marriage, in contrast with her first wedding to Arthur, was a private, almost furtive affair. There were probably lingering doubts about the propriety of the marriage, which, despite the Papal dispensation, never disappeared. Also, the wedding was over-shadowed and overtaken by preparations for a much greater ceremony. The Feast of St John the Baptist, 24 June, and, by their reckoning, Midsummer Day, had previously been a day of ill-omen for Catherine. This was the day when her father had been due to pay the second instalment of her marriage portion; he had twice defaulted and twice exposed her to intolerable humiliation. Ever since 1505, she had dreaded the day. Now she could look forward to it with joy. For Henry had decided that it should be his coronation day – and hers, as well, since she would be crowned alongside him.

The day before, she processed through London, as she had done on the eve of her wedding to Arthur. Then, she had been dressed as a Spanish Infanta, and had ridden Spanish-fashion, side-saddle on a mule.

Now, she appeared every inch the English Queen. She was carried, English-style, in a litter. And everything about her was vestal white: the horses, the covering of the litter, Catherine's own dress. She wore her hair like a bride: long and loose and covered only with a 'coronal set with many rich orient stones [that is, pearls]'. It became her: even a hostile witness conceded that her hair was 'beautiful and goodly to behold'.

But it is important to understand the meaning of the display. It was not, as many writers have assumed, a proclamation of the fact that she was a virgin when she married Henry. Instead, Catherine was only following precedent: every detail of her equipage, from the colour of the horses, the litter and the dress, to the 'dishevelled' state of her hair and 'the rich circlet' on her head, was specified by *The Royal Book* in its provisions for the coronation of a queen.

But, just as the Queen's procession reached the Cardinal's Hat tavern in Cornhill, the blue sky darkened and the heavens opened. The rain was so violent that it overwhelmed the silken canopy borne over Catherine and, in all her finery, she had to take shelter 'under the hovel of the drapers' stalls'. The shower was as short as it was sharp and Thomas More made light of it, in a little poem he appended to the collection of coronation verses he presented to the King. Others saw it as a darker augury. Had Catherine really escaped the curse of Midsummer's Day?

After Catherine followed her ladies-in-waiting and the gentlemen of her Household. Most were now English. They were headed by Lady Elizabeth Stafford, the sister of the Duke of Buckingham, who himself made a magnificent showing during the ceremonies as acting High Steward of England. Also in attendance on the Queen were Margaret Plantagenet and Elizabeth Boleyn. The latter was sister of the Earl of Surrey, wife of Sir Thomas Boleyn and mother of three young children, Anne, Mary and George, who was the baby of the family. Catherine's Spanish servants were not forgotten: Ines de Venegas, Maria de Gravara and Maria de Salinas all figured honourably among her ladies. Room was found even for Alonso de Esquivel and Juan de Cuero, despite the fact that both had fallen foul of their mistress. But the face Catherine was possibly most pleased to see was that of Fray Diego, who took his place in the procession with the rank of 'the Queen's Chancellor and Confessor'.

On the 24th itself the coronation took place. Two thrones were placed on a platform in front of the high altar in Westminster Abbey: the higher for Henry, the lower for Catherine. First came the coronation of the King. Then it was Catherine's turn. The ceremonial for a queen consort was somewhat simpler than for a king. No oath was administered to her, nor, as a woman, was she invested with the sword or spurs. But she was anointed on the head and the breasts; the coronation ring was put on the fourth finger of her right hand, the crown on her head, the sceptre in her right hand and the ivory rod surmounted with the dove in her left. Catherine was now Queen, as sacredly and inalienably as Henry was King. As she returned to her throne, she bowed to Henry 'honouring, as is right, his majesty'.

Catherine, of course, was both learned and devout, so for her the words of the elaborate Latin prayers uttered over her would have meant as much as the symbols and ritual. One by one, the names and stories of the great women of the Bible were recalled and applied to her. Grant, God was beseeched, that Catherine may be a vehicle of victory, even as '[Thou] didst sometimes cause Thy people to triumph over a most cruel enemy, by the hand of Judith, a woman'. Might her marriage endure: just as God, 'for the good of Thy people the Jews . . . didst deliver Queen Hester from captivity and bring her to the bed of Ahasuerus and to the society of his kingdom', so, for the good of England, might He keep Catherine with Henry that 'she, continuing always in the chastity of princely wedlock, may obtain the crown that is next unto virginity'. But, above all, God was begged, let her have children: like Sarah, Rebecca, Rachel and the Virgin Mary herself, may she 'multiply and rejoice in the fruit of her womb'; might she have a Son, a Christ for England.[6]

Thus Catherine was dedicated to a service greater than herself, greater even than Henry.

On 27 June, three days after their joint coronation, Henry wrote to the Archduchess Margaret, the Regent of the Netherlands, to explain why he had married Catherine. It was, he claimed, in fulfilment of his father's dying wish: 'he, being then on his death bed ... gave us express command that he should take in marriage the Lady Catherine ... which we would not, neither in this nor a thousand other things whatsoever they be, disobey or infringe'.[7]

Henry's words cannot be faulted as an expression of filial piety. But I do not think they should be taken seriously as an explanation of his behaviour. For, far from respecting his dying father's every wish, Henry had, while the breath was scarce out of the body of the old King, endorsed a comprehensive overthrow of the key policies and personnel of his reign. In any case, had Henry VII really come round to the Spanish marriage? If so, he had done a good job of concealing his kingly intentions from Catherine.

The truth seems to be that Henry VIII married Catherine because he wanted to. He wanted her father, Ferdinand of Spain, as an ally in the war which he intended to wage against France. He wanted to be married to show that, despite his youth, he was fully adult and able to wield sovereignty without limitation. And finally, despite the fact that Catherine was twenty-four-and-a-half years old to his eighteen, and that she was four feet something to his six feet two inches, she was still young enough and attractive enough to be wanted for herself. 'Even if we were still free,' Henry assured Catherine's father on 26 July, 'it is she, nevertheless, that we would choose for our wife before all other.' This time Henry is to be believed.[8]

Catherine's own motives for the marriage were also a mixture of the personal and the dynastic. It was her duty and destiny to be Queen of England. With a King like the young Henry VIII, who was the most handsome and brilliant prince in Christendom, it was a pleasure too. But Catherine had not been taught to set much store by pleasure. Instead, it is duty, to her father and to her House, which shines through the letter she wrote to Ferdinand in July 1509. 'I have no other good except that of being your daughter,' she assured him. She was 'so well married' indeed. But the marriage was the work of Ferdinand's hands. As for Henry, her principal reason for loving him was not that he was her husband, but that he was 'so true a son of your highness'. 'I have performed the office of ambassador' to England, she reminded Ferdinand. And she would continue to perform it with the additional power that came from presenting her credentials in the marriage bed.

Ferdinand knew his daughter well. He would now begin to receive the return on his investment in her marriage.

But, even in this letter, Catherine shed a little of her Spanishness. Juan de Cuero and his wife Janina had stepped into the shoes of the Manriques after their flight into exile. Janina de Cuero had replaced Dona Elvira as Catherine's Lady Mistress, while Juan had become her Chamberlain. Now Catherine, more independent in spirit, got rid of them both. She told Ferdinand that the De Cueros 'with my other servants, set off from hence to their homes'. She paid the members of her Household their eight years' arrears of wages (save for the ever-unforgiven de Esquivel, who got only six). But this payment, Catherine made clear, was to discharge a debt of honour, not to reward good service. Instead, she wrote, her followers deserved censure for their misbehaviour but forgiveness for her sake, 'by reason that they can call themselves mine'.[9]

The stick-and-carrot treatment Catherine suggested for her former Household servants was scant reward for their years of purgatorial exile in England. But, though ungenerous, it was an accurate assessment of the damage which their foolish quarrels had done her. Would the handful left behind, in particular her confessor, Fray Diego, serve her better?

23. Honeymoon

Catherine's honeymoon with Henry lasted for far longer than the customary 'first month after marriage, when there is nothing but tenderness and pleasure'. Instead, many months went by and still the King, the Queen and the Court devoted themselves to a round of entertainment. 'Our time is ever passed in continual feasts,' Catherine informed her father. Henry, also writing to Ferdinand, catalogued their pleasures in great detail: 'diverts himself with jousts, birding, hunting and other innocent and honest pastimes, also in visiting different parts of his kingdom'. This last is a reference to the Progress. The Progress this year lasted all August and September, as the Court wandered in leisurely stages from palace to palace and park to park in the home counties.

Amidst all the pleasure, there was time for tenderness too and at some time, probably during the Progress, Catherine became pregnant. By 1 November, the fact was made public. 'Your daughter, her Serene Highness the Queen, our dearest consort,' Henry informed Ferdinand, 'has conceived in her womb a living child and is right heavy therewith.' Henry was overjoyed and the realm exulted. A fruitful marriage was a good marriage: the decision to wed Catherine was about to be vindicated.[1]

Christmas was spent at Richmond. On 12 January, Henry made his boldest gesture yet and took part in a tournament. He had long been itching to do so. But hitherto he had felt it wise to defer to the continuing anxieties about the succession and had refrained from risking his life in public combat. It was these fears which had led his father to ban him from the tilt-yard in the first place. But now, confident in his impending fatherhood, he cast them aside and rode out to take his chance with the rest. He had his reward: he shivered lance after lance and scored repeatedly. The cheers of the crowd rang out; he was a sporting hero at last.

Henry, however, had only half come out of the closet, since he and his aide, William Compton, rode incognito, 'unknown to all persons and unlooked for'. But the King's cover was blown when Compton was badly injured in a bout. 'God save the King!' cried out someone in on the secret, terrified lest the injured knight was Henry himself. Amid the general consternation Henry had his helmet taken off and made himself known 'to the great comfort of all the people'.[2]

The Court then removed to Westminster where the boisterous fun and games continued. On the 18th, a group of twelve men, dressed like outlaws in short coats of Kendal Green, burst into the Queen's Chamber. It was Henry and his companions, disguised as Robin Hood and his Merry Men (complete 'with a woman like Maid Marion'). The entertainment was mounted 'for a gladness to the Queen's Grace'. But a contemporary account suggests a different, less happy reaction. According to the chronicler Hall, 'the Queen, the ladies, and all other [in the Queen's Chamber] were abashed, as well for the strange sight, as also for their sudden coming'.[3]

Was Catherine worrying at the risks her husband took? Were his adolescent antics becoming a strain?

At all events, on the morning of 31 January the Queen suddenly miscarried of a daughter. There had been almost no warning, 'except', her confessor, Fray Diego reported, 'that one knee pained her the night before'. The miscarriage was kept so secret, Fray Diego continued, 'that no one knew about it . . . except the King . . . two Spanish women, a physician and I'. But, instead of Catherine's belly diminishing with the delivery, the swelling continued and increased enormously. Probably this was the result of infection. But, disastrously, her physician persuaded himself that 'the Queen remained pregnant of another child and it was believed'. More extraordinarily still, the belief was persisted in, even when the Queen's menstrual cycle recommenced.[4]

Shrove Tuesday, the eve of Lent, was a day of celebration at Court. In 1510 it was also the last major occasion in the Court calendar before the Queen's expected confinement. So Henry decided to mark it in style. On 13 February, the King led in the Queen, to all appearances still heavily pregnant, and placed her in the royal throne, to preside over the banquet and the merry-making. He himself 'would not sit, but walked from place to place, making cheer to the Queen' and his guests. It was a remarkable public display of affection for Catherine, and of pride in her state.[5]

Towards the end of the month, the preparations for Catherine's confinement began. On the 24th the Court removed to Greenwich, where Henry himself had been born and where he hoped his own first-born would see the light of day. And on the 26th a warrant was issued for the refurbishment of the royal nursery, 'God willing', and the Queen's Chamber. The 'cradle of estate', or baby-throne, in which Henry himself had been laid, was re-covered in crimson cloth of gold, while the pommels at each corner were re-painted to include Catherine's arms alongside Henry's. Bedding was got ready for the wet-nurse, who would suckle the child, and for the two rockers, who would take it in turns to rock the cradle. And Mrs Elizabeth Denton, who had presided over Henry's own nursery as Lady Mistress, was brought out of retirement.

Meanwhile, Catherine's own apartment was got ready. *The Royal Book* laid down elaborate rules for the Queen's confinement. The bed, bed-hangings and wall covering were all to be of 'a suite', that is, of a single design. Figurative tapestries were avoided, lest they provoke fantastic dreams in the Queen and thus affect the child's mental state. The ceiling, floor and windows were covered in fabrics too, fitted close and nailed down. The tapestry was left loose only at one window, so that the Queen could have light 'when it pleased her'. There was a cupboard, stacked with gold and silver plate as a mark of her status, and an altar, covered with images and relics, where she could pray. At the foot of her bed stood a canopied day-bed on which, almost certainly, labour was intended to take place.

Some time in March Catherine entered this specially prepared apartment in the ceremony known as 'taking to her Chamber'. She took wine and spices with the Court in her Presence Chamber or Throne Room. Then her Lord Chamberlain, the Earl of Ormond, who had been Chamberlain to Henry's mother, Queen Elizabeth, called on the company to pray that 'God would give her the good hour' – that is, a safe delivery. A procession formed and accompanied the Queen to the door of her Chamber. There the gentlemen of the Court bade her farewell, while the Queen and her ladies entered. Catherine would now dwell in an exclusively female world until her delivery and her churching, when, some four weeks after the birth, she would be purified of the pollution of labour.

Inside, in the close, darkened room that was almost womb-like in its seclusion, Catherine had nothing to do but wait. Outside the King and Court waited too. But Henry diverted himself on 18 March by organizing a running at the ring. The new Spanish ambassador, Luiz Caroz, who had come to replace the disgraced Fuensalida, was mightily impressed to see Henry in armour for the first time.

Caroz was less happy with Catherine's condition. He had not heard about the miscarriage. But he had got to know about Catherine's resumed periods and, with a knowledge of gynaecology which seems to have been sounder than Catherine's, doubted whether her pregnancy could be real. His fears proved all too well founded.

Catherine continued to wait; Henry continued to wait. And still nothing happened. Finally, according to Fray Diego, 'it has pleased our Lord to be her physician in such a way that the swelling decreased'. She was not pregnant; there was no child. The preparations, the ceremonies had all been in vain. Catherine was left only with the humiliation – as public as the shame which had been visited on her when her marriage portion had not arrived, and far more serious.

Wise after the event, Caroz railed at the folly of those who would 'affirm that a menstruating woman was pregnant and . . . make her withdraw publicly for her delivery'. He also worried about the immediate consequences. He pressed the Council to consider carefully the official explanation of events which they would have to offer. He reported gloomily the fears of many concillors that, 'since the Queen was not pregnant, she was incapable of conceiving'. And he made helpful suggestions for improving Catherine's diet and hence the regularity of her menstruation. For 'the fact that she did not menstruate well', he had been told, was the reason for her failure to conceive.[6]

The honeymoon was over. The false pregnancy had got the marriage off to the worst possible start. And Henry and Catherine had their first quarrel.

The Duke of Buckingham had two sisters. The elder was Elizabeth, who had married Viscount Fitzwalter. She was Catherine's principal lady-in-waiting and quickly became a favourite of the Queen's. The younger sister was Anne. She married Lord Hastings and, more importantly perhaps, caught the King's eye. Catherine's extended lying-in provided an opportunity and an incentive for the affair to develop. Henry used Compton, who had recovered from his jousting injury, as go-between.

The task was more-or-less part of Compton's job-description as Groom of the Stool. The Groom's original and continuing function was to attend the King when he relieved himself on the close-stool or commode. But round this had developed a whole range of other responsibilities, which, by 1509, made Compton, as Groom, head of the King's private service. He controlled access to the King, looked after his personal money and papers, and handled his confidential relations – with men and women alike.

It was also his business to cover the King's tracks. Which is how the rumour got about that Compton was pursuing Anne on his own account. Elizabeth became concerned for her sister's virtue and warned their brother, Buckingham. Buckingham confronted Compton and the two had a furious quarrel. Henry then intervened to protect his confidential servant and bawled out Buckingham, who withdrew from Court in a huff. Hastings likewise removed Anne from Court and temptation, and deposited her in a convent to cool her heels. Once more Henry retaliated. He blamed Elizabeth and her intervention, and dismissed her from Court. It was now Catherine's turn to be outraged and the King and Queen had a very public falling-out.[7]

But the most interesting aspect of the whole business is Catherine's own reaction to her miserable experience. In the modern phrase, she coped by 'going into denial'. She also hid within the protective walls of her

Chamber. She was still there at the end of May, when the concern about her behaviour had become serious. The English, Caroz reported, 'wish she should go out and be no longer withdrawn; it is however not known when she will go out'. She also did her best to keep most of what had happened from the person she most valued: Ferdinand.

Her father could not of course be left entirely in the dark and on 27 May she wrote him a letter. 'Some days before' she had miscarried of a daughter. 'That her child was still born is considered to be a misfortune in England.' Hence the delay in her letter and hence the fact that she would allow no one else to write.

Clearly this version of events was severely edited. Catherine post-dates her miscarriage by almost four months. And she makes no mention of her subsequent false pregnancy nor of the fact that she had taken to her Chamber. Yet there can be no doubt that these events had happened. For, behind her back and to cover theirs, both Fray Diego and Caroz sent full accounts to Spain. Their motives were different: Fray Diego wrote to exonerate Catherine; Caroz to undermine Fray Diego. Nevertheless their accounts are mutually complementary. They are also confirmed by the English records of the preparations for Catherine's lying-in.

So Catherine had lied to her father. And earlier, she had deceived her husband about her phantom pregnancy, or at least had acquiesced in the deceit and muddle. In both cases, she acted out of fear and desperation. She was desperate to fulfil the pressure on her to have children. And she was fearful of the consequences when she failed. Do not 'be angry with her', she begged her father, 'for it has been the will of God'.[8]

But Catherine had more to fear than her father's wrath. There was her position in England to consider. Her marriage was contentious. Her first pregnancy had been a debacle. Her husband had quarrelled with her and he had an eye for another woman.

Fortunately, at this moment, Catherine's luck turned. When she was in labour on 31 January, Catherine had vowed to present one of her richest headdresses to the Spanish shrine of St Peter the Martyr of the Order of Franciscan Friars. One prayer at least was answered. For, even as she wrote her muddled, half-truthful excuses to her father, she was again pregnant. Henry must have slept with her up to the last moment before she had taken to her Chamber.[9]

This time surely she would carry the baby to term. This time surely it would be a boy.

24. *A son*

Despite its extraordinary beginnings, Catherine's second pregnancy was smoother than her first. The King went on a summer Progress to the south of England. But wisely Catherine opted out of part of it and spent July with her ladies at Eltham. By the end of October the couple were back at Richmond, where they were to remain. In November, the formal preparations for the lying-in and birth began and the Prior of Canterbury, who kept the great silver font which was used for royal christenings, was warned that it would shortly be needed again. Catherine took to her Chamber before the Christmas festivities and, on New Year's Eve, went into labour. The Gentlemen of the Chapel Royal sang prayers for her safe delivery and, at 1.30 in the morning of New Year's Day, her child was born. It was a boy.[1]

The King and England went mad with joy. Two hundred and seven pounds of gunpowder was spent firing salute after salute in the Tower. Bonfires burned; fountains ran with wine and processions of thanksgiving wound through the streets of London. For greater ceremony, the christening was 'deferred' until Sunday the 5th. It took place in the church of the Observant Friars (Catherine's favourite Order) at Richmond Palace. Rails and posts were erected from the Great Hall to the church to make a processional way, twenty-four feet wide. This was gravelled and hung with tapestry. Inside the church, the great silver font stood on a high, stepped platform. The boy's godfather was King Louis XII of France and his godmother the Archduchess Margaret. And he was christened Henry. The heralds cried his name and titles – 'Prince Henry, first son of our sovereign lord King Henry VIII' – and the proud father rewarded them with the extravagantly large sum of £20.[2]

As protocol dictated, neither Catherine nor Henry was present at the christening. Instead, Catherine remained within her Chamber. After the christening, her son was brought back to her in procession, preceded by his baptismal gifts. These were carried in the order of the rank of the giver and were headed by the magnificent presents from his godfather, Louis XII: a great salt, weighing fifty-one ounces, and a cup, weighing forty-eight ounces, both of fine gold. The gifts and the child were presented to the Queen by her ladies.

But the reunion between mother and son was brief. Immediately, as protocol again dictated, the child was borne to the nursery and handed over to the Lady Mistress, Elizabeth Denton, and the wet-nurse, Elizabeth Poyntz. The latter was clearly Catherine's own choice. The husband of the wet-nurse was John Poyntz, the second son of Sir Robert Poyntz of Iron Acton in Gloucestershire. Sir Robert was Catherine's Vice-chamberlain and John had followed him into the Queen's service. The French ambassador, D'Arizolles, who was in charge of distributing Louis XII's largesse at the christening, was clearly surprised at Elizabeth's social standing. He had been told, he reported, 'that it would be well to present a chain of 200 crowns [£40] to the Prince's nurse, and tell her that the King prays her to nurse well his godson. She is a gentlewoman of good house.'[3]

Meanwhile, Henry also left Catherine, to go on a pilgrimage of thanksgiving to the Shrine of Our Lady at Walsingham. Walsingham, on the north Norfolk coast, is a round trip of over two hundred miles from London. Henry set out from the Tower on the 12th and took about ten days to reach his goal. At Walsingham he said his prayers, kissed the relic of the Virgin's milk and made offerings of £1 13s and 4d. On the way back, he sent a messenger to Catherine, with a present of two does, which he had probably killed en route. He arrived back at the

Tower on the 31st and rejoined his wife at Richmond at the beginning of February.[4]

Henry's absence on pilgrimage had, happily, coincided with the boring aftermath of Catherine's pregnancy. This was now out of the way. Catherine was churched and out of her confinement and back in his bed. And it was almost time for the celebratory jousts. Henry had proclaimed these on the day of the christening itself. The King, with three aides, challenged all comers to meet him at Westminster on 12 and 13 February. The tournament was the most splendid of Henry's reign and it is recorded, uniquely, by a sixty-foot-long illuminated vellum roll. Here the various scenes of the pageant are represented in vivid colour and burnished gold-leaf.[5]

The roll begins with the mounted procession to the lists on the second day of the tournament. First comes the Master of the Armoury, with his staff on foot carrying the lances; then follow the trumpeters and the gallants of the Court. The trumpeters puff out their cheeks and the gallants preen. More sober are the heralds, who are in charge of both the ceremony and the sport. They directly precede the King's three aides, each of whom rides under a canopied pavilion. Their pavilions are magnificent. But they pale before the splendour of the King's, which is made of broad strips of cloth of gold alternating with blue velvet. The blue velvet is thickly strewn with golden letters of 'K' for Catherine.

The central portion of the roll shows Henry jousting before Catherine. Catherine is housed in a grandstand, which is elaborately painted and gilded with royal badges and livery colours. She sits under a canopy of cloth of gold, with Henry's sister Mary next to her. The Queen's face is notably plumper and her figure full and maternal. She applauds enthusiastically as Henry breaks his lance on his opponent's helmet, jerking the head sharply backwards and upwards. The trapper of Henry's horse is also made of blue velvet, sprinkled with more golden 'K's. As well, there are large golden hearts and, along the lower border, other golden letters spell out 'Loyall'. This is Henry's chivalric name for the tournament: he is Catherine's 'Coeur Loyal', 'Sir Loyal Heart'.

Never, I believe, had Henry been so in love with Catherine as at that moment; never would he be so fully again.

For, ten days later, on the 22nd, Prince Henry was dead. The baby was brought from Richmond and buried in state at Westminster Abbey on the 27th. Catherine was heartbroken: 'like a natural woman, [she] made much lamentation'. According to the chronicler, Henry took it like a man, concealing his feelings the better to comfort his wife. But D'Arizolles tells a different story. He had been advised by the Council, he reports, not to present Louis XII's letters of condolence on the death of the Prince, 'or say a word about it at present, as it would only revive the King's grief'.[6]

25. War

S o far, Catherine had failed at making love – or, rather, at making babies. Would she be any more successful at making war? For war was the reason that Ferdinand had emptied his coffers to pay the last instalment of her marriage portion. Two decades previously, he had signed the Treaty of Medina del Campo with Henry VII King of England, in order to complete the encirclement of his enemy, France. Now, with his daughter's marriage to the younger Henry safely accomplished at last, he had brought the scheme to fruition. Catherine was its symbol: she was also expected to play an active part in unleashing war.[1]

Ferdinand was quite open about this. Caroz, the Spanish ambassador in England, was instructed to do everything he could to get Henry VIII to declare war on France. If he failed, he was to invoke Catherine 'and ask her to persuade her husband'. And if Catherine were sufficiently unfilial to prefer peace to war, then Caroz was to use Fray Diego to persuade Catherine to persuade Henry. Ferdinand even wrote directly to Fray Diego, to promise him favour and preferment in the Church.[2]

Ferdinand's willingness to resort to the black arts against even his own child is characteristic. But it proved unnecessary. Catherine was Isabella's daughter: she had practically been born in camp and she felt at home there. War was her element and showed her at her best. Nor did Henry take any persuading to fight the French. Instead, he began his reign with a calculated gesture of bellicosity. The French ambassador, the corpulent Abbot of Fécamp, arrived to thank Henry VIII for his letter proposing the continuation of Henry VII's policy of peace and friendship between the two countries. The new young King was outraged. 'Who wrote this letter?' he demanded fiercely. '*I* ask peace of the King of France, who dare not look me in the face let alone make war on me!' And yet the letter proposing the renewal of peace *had* been written. And, despite Henry's protestations, the peace *was* renewed. For though the King wanted war, the members of an important party on his Council were determined to maintain peace.[3]

It was Catherine's first responsibility – and one which was congenial to her – to stiffen Henry's determination to over-ride the peace party. Thereafter, she had a choice. She could remain the tool of Ferdinand's schemes, as her father hoped and intended. Or she could work with her husband to the glory and benefit of England. Catherine never hesitated: had not her father told her that she must become English?

Ferdinand's first use of Catherine was indirect. Her letters home had told her father, excitedly, how much she was enjoying the endless round of entertainment laid on for her by Henry. In one of his first despatches, Caroz went into greater detail. He was especially struck by the twice-weekly foot combats with javelin and sword that were known as fighting at the barriers. They had been instituted, he solemnly informed Ferdinand, 'in imitation of Amadis and Lancelot, and other knights of olden time, of whom so much is written in books'. Many young men of the Court excelled in this sport. 'But the most conspicuous ... the most assiduous and the most interested [combatant] ... is the King himself'.

There was much froth and nonsense about such Court tournaments – as when, on one memorably absurd occasion, Henry made his entrance sitting, fully armed, in the middle of a fountain fashioned out of precious fabric that spouted real water through eight gargoyles. But there was high chivalric purpose and seriousness as well.[4]

Ferdinand decided to exploit this latent idealism for his own ends. In February 1511 he sent letters asking the English to help him launch a crusade against the Moors in North Africa. The bait was obvious. You all take part, Ferdinand told the young men of England, in mock combats fought on fictional grounds. Now fight, he challenged them, a real war for a real reason: 'against the Infidels, enemies of Christ's law'. Thomas, Lord Darcy, immediately volunteered to lead the expedition, and chose as his provost-marshal 'a lusty young man and well beloved of the King', Henry Guildford, whose father, Sir Richard, had died, within sight of Jerusalem, on pilgrimage to the Holy Land.

Darcy's troops sailed to Cadiz, only to be told on arrival that Ferdinand had been forced to abandon the crusade against the Moors because of the threat from nearer home of the King of France. Darcy returned to England not best pleased.[5]

But Guildford, determined to extract some adventure from the affair, rode to Ferdinand's Court at Burgos. There the Spanish King knighted him in the names of Saint James and Saint George, the patron saints of Spain and England. He also gave him an augmentation or addition to his coat of arms of 'a canton of Granada': that is, of a pomegranate on a silver square at the 'dexter chief' or top left of his shield. The pomegranate was Catherine's badge, and Guildford was to remain loyal through good times and bad to the daughter of the King who had knighted him.[6]

Ferdinand's efforts to involve England in war were also helped, unwittingly, by the intended target, the King of France. Pope Julius II and Louis XII had been allies. But they had quarrelled over the division of the spoils of their successful war on the Republic of Venice, and Julius had attacked the French armies in Italy. Stung, Louis decided to turn the tables. If the Pope could use secular weapons, he, the Most Christian King of France, would riposte with spiritual ones. He summoned a

Council of the Church to Pisa, and threatened to depose Julius. But the manoeuvre backfired since it enabled the opponents of France – in particular Ferdinand and the Pope – to present Louis as the common enemy of Christendom, who would reopen the wounds of the Great Schism which had torn the Church apart in the fifteenth century. This line found an especially ready hearing in England, where Henry and Catherine outdid each other in conspicuous piety.

But Ferdinand's best allies in England were the English nobility. Fighting came as naturally to them as it did to the *hidalgos* and *grandees* of Spain. The leaders of the pack were the Howards. Thomas Howard, Earl of Surrey, had three fine sons by his first wife, Elizabeth Tilney: Thomas, the heir, Edward and Edmund. Now, each was spoiling for a fight: on land or at sea, in the tilt-yard or on the battlefield. All were expert jousters. But they preferred the real thing since the risks and the rewards of war were greater. The problem was that England remained officially at peace. Then, in June 1511, two Scottish ships captained by Andrew Barton entered English waters. The Scots claimed that Barton, a favourite of King James IV, was a privateer: in other words, that he had been licensed by his sovereign to carry out specific reprisals to redress wrongs done. The English called him a pirate. Sir Edward Howard (who was acting as deputy to the ageing Lord Admiral, the Earl of Oxford) and his brother Lord Thomas, fought a naval battle with Barton off the Downs. Barton was killed, his two ships captured and his men brought back in triumph to London in September 1511.[7]

The swaggering return of the Howard brothers with their prisoners and their spoils brought the divisions in the King's Council to a head. James IV was Henry VIII's brother-in-law and, thanks to the renewal of the Anglo-Scottish treaty in June 1509, his ally also. On both grounds, the King of Scotland was outraged by the treatment the Howards had meted out to Barton. He wrote to remonstrate with Henry accordingly. But Edward Howard was shameless in his aggression ('wanton' is how a contemporary describes his attitude) and 'marvellously incendith [fires] the King against the Scots'. The result was a letter from Henry that added insult to James's injury. It was no business of a prince, Henry loftily told his brother monarch, to equate 'doing justice on a pirate or a thief' with a breach of amity and alliance.[8]

The feverish atmosphere at Court was further heightened when Darcy returned to Windsor, nursing his grievances. The King and Caroz co-operated to repair his damaged ego and his injured purse. Caroz paid him an over-the-odds daily rate for his men; Henry turned his loan of £1,000 for the expedition into an outright gift. 'Thus the King's money goeth away in every corner', one of the peace party complained.[9]

Meanwhile, Henry's envoy, Dr John Young, had been sent to France to demand that Louis XII make proper submission to the pre-eminence of the Pope. Louis had returned a dusty answer and Young complained that 'never man had worse cheer than he in France'.[10]

Events, in short, were on a knife-edge and the set-piece debate in the Council on the choice of war or peace was a close-run thing. At first, the peace party carried the day. But the return of Young, with Louis's dismissive message, provided Henry with the ammunition he needed to reverse the verdict. Responding to the King's cry of 'the Church in danger', the Council decided on war.

In November 1511 England joined the 'Holy League' of Ferdinand of Aragon, the Emperor Maximilian and Pope Julius. Thus, ironically, Henry, the future Supreme Head of the Church of England, fought his first battles in defence of the most extravagant temporal claims of the Papal monarchy. For, in return for his attack on the 'schismatic' Louis XII, Pope Julius had promised to transfer the kingdom of France to Henry – providing he defeated the French first.[11]

While the debate about war or peace still raged, Catherine had wisely kept in the background. Whatever her influence behind the scenes, the decision was Henry's and had to be seen as Henry's. But, once war was decided upon, Catherine began to emerge as an important force in her own right. Her first role was to help hold together the Anglo-Spanish alliance, which proved shaky from the start. This was inevitably difficult, since it cast her yet again as pig-in-the-middle between her husband and her father. Her actions were ambiguous then and they remain a little hard to interpret even today.

The plan of campaign was for England and Spain to launch a joint attack on France by 1 April 1512. Ferdinand suggested that the attack take place in the area of Guienne. Situated in the extreme south-west of France, just across from the Spanish frontier, it formed part of the Duchy of Aquitaine to which the King of England had a historic claim. An impressive expeditionary force set sail under the Marquess of Dorset and landed at the frontier town of Fuenterrabia. But then Ferdinand indeed made April fools of his allies by repeating his tricks of the previous year. Instead of his army under the Duke of Alba joining the English in laying siege to Bayonne, it overran the defenceless little Pyrenean kingdom of Navarre.

Meanwhile, the English, without the victuals and transport which Ferdinand had promised, were stuck in Fuenterrabia, where, very conveniently from Ferdinand's point of view, they blocked the path of any French force sent to rescue Navarre. Dorset's soldiers behaved as English youths do in Spain. They ate too much garlicky food, drank too much wine, caught the sun and got diarrhoea. They chatted up Spanish girls and got into fights with Spanish men. Finally, when Henry, giving in at last to Ferdinand's cajolery, instructed them to join the Spanish army in Navarre and over-winter abroad, they refused. Dorset, faced effectively with mutiny, had to agree to return to England.

The debacle was almost entirely Ferdinand's responsibility. But he resolved to brazen it out and sent envoys to England to throw the blame on Dorset's mismanagement and the English lack of experience in warfare.[12]

The Spanish envoys had separate letters of credence to Catherine and naturally sent first to her. She, however, replied that it would be improper for her to receive them before they had audience with her husband. Instead she gave them good advice. Don't rush things, she advised: 'the King was already informed how shamefully the English had behaved, and that he was very angry with them'. The ambassadors were then invited to a show 'trial', in which the English captains all accepted

Ferdinand's version of events and likewise threw the blame on Dorset, who, handily, was absent and seriously ill. Finally the ambassadors had a private audience with the Queen. She informed them that 'she had told the King and some of his councillors that they ought to give money to [King Ferdinand] with which to carry on the war in Guienne, if they wished to win that duchy'.[13]

What was Catherine doing? If we accept the Spanish despatches at face value there is no doubt: Henry's wife had sided with her father. She was using her superior age and worldly wisdom to lead her inexperienced husband by the nose to the benefit of Spain and the detriment of England. It is not a pretty portrait of a marriage. Henry appears weak to the point of simplicity and Catherine deceitful, even treacherous. But the picture depends on assuming, with the Spanish envoys, that Henry really had swallowed Ferdinand's bluster. In fact, we have Catherine's own word for it that Henry had been aware of Ferdinand's duplicity for months. As early as September, he had been speculating on the possibility of having to carry on the war effort alone in the event of Ferdinand and the Pope backing out – though in public he protested that he 'firmly believed that neither ... would ever desert him'. Likewise Henry's ministers wrote of Ferdinand's 'slackness' and dismissed his envoy as a 'man full of words'. But equally Henry, his advisers and, above all, his Queen were aware that Ferdinand was England's only serious ally in the war against France. If Henry wanted to keep Ferdinand on side for the campaign of 1513, he had to pretend to accept Ferdinand's version of the Guienne campaign of 1512. And he had to make the pretence convincing.

This is where Catherine came in. *She* told the Spanish envoys that Henry accepted their master's version of events. Then the King and his ministers laid on the show trial to give substance to Catherine's words. There are signs that the Spanish themselves suspected that they might be being taken for a ride. Most of the proceedings of the 'trial' were conducted in English, and they had to rely on Henry's Latin translation of what the accused captains said in their excuse. Clearly suspicious about the unanimity of the replies, as translated by Henry, the envoys afterwards asked some councillors in Latin and five others in French for their version of the answers. Exactly the same formulae were repeated. The element of collusion and rehearsal is obvious. The participants even found it hard even to keep a straight face. Half way through, apparently, the accused asked and were granted permission to rise from their knees to await the verdict. Such consideration was a rare luxury in a Tudor court of law. Moreover, the 'trial' was extra-judicial. Despite the confessions of the accused, no one was punished, and no one, not even Dorset himself, seriously lost favour. Instead Dorset went on to play a leading part in the French campaign of the following year. But the ritual humiliation of the English commanders (most of whom deserved it anyway for their spinelessness in the face of their badly behaved men) had done enough. Honour was satisfied all round and Ferdinand's ambassadors could proceed to renew the treaties for another year of campaigning against France. Catherine's final comment in her private audience with the Spaniards held out the additional bait of an English subsidy for a new invasion of Guienne: sign on the dotted line for cash, Ferdinand was told.[14]

But is this really a more attractive picture of Catherine's behaviour? Does it not simply reverse her role and show her deceiving her father on behalf of her husband? Actually, as Catherine well knew, you had to be up very early in the morning to deceive Ferdinand. Rather, she was telling him what he wanted to hear. And she was doing so to preserve his great creation: the Anglo-Spanish alliance.

Since her marriage, as Catherine was also aware, the alliance had worked to Ferdinand's benefit. Now she threw herself into making sure that England reaped at least equal reward.

The decision to continue the war in 1513 offered the opportunity. Wisely, Henry and his advisers had decided to learn from their mistakes in 1512 and do better. Catherine was in the thick of the attempt, working alongside her husband and using her unique position and her own expertise to complement his efforts.

She played an important role in the diplomacy. One of the key advantages of England as a member of the Holy League was that, with the Pope as an ally and fighting in his name, it could call on the censures of the Church to demoralize its enemies and keep waverers and neutrals on side. But these spiritual weapons had to be handled carefully. If they were deployed in too obviously partisan a way they lost their edge: as James IV of Scotland sneeringly told the English ambassador, Henry VIII 'was fortunate that ye had such a Pope so favourable to your Highness, and that was entered the League'. Catherine was especially useful in heading off such criticism. As Henry's confidante as well as his consort, she was known to speak for him. And yet, as Queen Consort, she had no constitutional role. Instead, she was a sort of 'official spokesman', authoritative yet disavowable.

And it was in this capacity that she intervened decisively in Anglo-Scottish relations.

England's drift to war with France had placed the little kingdom of Scotland in an awkward dilemma. Its historic traditions tied it to France in the 'Auld Alliance'; more recently, Ferdinand had brokered the settlement with England as part of his policy of encircling France. Would Scotland return to its old alignment or stick with the new? No one, including James IV himself, quite knew. And neither he nor his brother-in-law Henry handled things well. Henry was heavy-handed, using the stick when the carrot would have been more effective. Meanwhile, the mercurial James played with fire, assuring England of peace on the one hand while, on the other, renewing the 'Auld Alliance' with France and making threatening manoeuvres against the great Border fortress of Berwick-on-Tweed.

Amid all this male posturing, Catherine played a cool feminine hand and on 18 September 1512 she wrote to Richard Bainbridge, Cardinal-Archbishop of York, who was in Rome. There Bainbridge had an important double role: he was the English ambassador to the Pope; he was also, as a resident cardinal, a leading member of the Papal Court and a personal favourite of Pope Julius II himself. In both capacities, he was frankly partisan: a true John Bull in a cassock. The French ambassador in Rome, wrote Bainbridge, was 'as partial a Frenchman as I am an

Englishman' – 'I pray God give him an evil trist!' he added uncharitably. Catherine's letter to Bainbridge was ostensibly purely personal, a 'familiar letter'. And it contained only news, beginning with a highly coloured account of James IV's manoeuvres against Berwick and going on to describe how the English had countered by sending the Earl of Surrey to the Borders to shake up the military organization of the north. There was no hint of what Bainbridge might do with this information, much less instructions as to what he should do – instructions which Catherine of course was not empowered to give.

Yet Bainbridge did not hesitate. Catherine's letter reached him in early November. The moment he read it he hurried to Pope Julius and, by 24 November, had obtained a Papal Brief or letter threatening James with excommunication for attacking Henry while Henry was engaged in Holy War against the French, the enemies of the Church.

The following spring, the Brief and a Bull giving effect to the threat were delivered to James by Dr Nicholas West, the English ambassador to Scotland. James blamed the excommunication on Bainbridge's meddling, 'albeit', he said, 'it was by information given from England'. This West denied. 'It was the Pope's own motion, helped on by the Cardinal,' he asserted smoothly. Thanks to the fact that Bainbridge's 'information' had come from Catherine rather than from Henry, West stood – just – on the right side of the truth.[15]

Catherine also played a direct part in the preparations for the next season's campaigning, which began the moment the treaties with Spain were renewed in November. She showed a particular interest in naval warfare. Here, in contrast to the debacle in Guienne, England had won victories and acquired heroes. The key engagement had been fought with the French fleet off Brest in August 1512. One of the two big French vessels had fled, the other, the *Cordelière*, had been boarded by Sir Thomas Knyvet from the *Regent*. But suddenly the magazine of the *Cordelière* blew up, setting fire to both ships and killing most on board, including Knyvet. His death had something of the impact of Nelson's in 1805. Especially affected was Knyvet's companion-in-arms and commander, Sir Edward

Howard, who vowed 'that he will never see the King in the face till he hath revenged the death of the noble and valiant knight, Sir Thomas Knyvet'. Meanwhile, the French Channel fleet was reinforced by Prégent de Bidoux with a squadron of heavily armed galleys. Prégent, or 'Prior John' as he was usually known by the English, was an outstanding contemporary exponent of galley warfare and the English were rightly alarmed. Galleys (ships powered by oars), could operate in shallow waters, where deeper keeled sailing ships fouled the bottom. They could also go into action when sailing vessels were becalmed.

Catherine wanted the English to be able to reply in kind and in conversation with the Venetian ambassador in November she discussed the possibility of hiring galleys from the Republic's ample arsenal. She asked for four galleasses (that is, ships powered by both oars and sail) and two 'bastard galleys' to match the ones which she had heard the French were building. What was 'the monthly cost of a galley completely found'? she enquired – 10,000 ducats (£2,000), the ambassador replied. This figure is so enormous (more than the cost per month of the entire English fleet of twenty ships) that the guess has to be that an extra zero had somehow crept in. But even at £200 a month each (assuming that that is the real amount) the galleys were still very expensive and the plan was not pursued. Catherine lived to regret this.[16]

Why Catherine should have interested herself so closely in naval matters is unclear. Perhaps it was in conscious rivalry with her opposite number, Queen Anne of France. Anne was also Duchess of Brittany in her own right and, as such, had her own fleet which, since Brittany was the scene of the action, bore much of the brunt against the English. Or perhaps it was simply a matter of personalities. For the navy, rather like the Royal Air Force in the Second World War, seems to have attracted the most flamboyant and risk-taking individuals. In peace and at Court, they were the stars of the joust; in war, they were naval heroes. And in both capacities they performed for Catherine.

For jousts were invariably held to honour Catherine or to delight her. She presided and she awarded the prizes – as in October 1510, when she watched with her ladies from a special standing in the park at

Greenwich as Sir Edward Howard felled 'one Gyot, a gentleman of Almain [Germany], a tall man and a good man of arms' in the fight with battle axes. And it was this incident, or one like it, which Howard recalled 'in the *Mary Rose*, the 5th day of April [1513]' when about to go into action against the French at the start of the new campaigning season. 'I pray you', he wrote, 'recommend me also to the Queen's noble Grace (and I know well I need not to pray her to pray for our good speed) and to all good ladies and gentlewomen.'

Howard, that is to say, identified with Catherine as his lady, whether in the lists or in the fleet. There seems every reason to suppose that she, in turn, identified with him as her knight and captain. So she worried about his ships. She worried about his armament. Unfortunately, she did not concern herself about his provisions.[17]

For it was the arrangements for victualling the fleet which led to the downfall of Edward Howard. This time, the French, comfortably protected by the guns of Brest, refused to stir. A blockade would have been the obvious response. But, because of the failure of provisioning, Howard could not sustain it. He had therefore a choice. He could retreat in ignominy, with nothing done, like the English army in Guienne. Or he could attempt the impossible. He had done the impossible once before, in Catherine's presence when he had overcome the mighty German man-at-arms. Now, inspired by her memory (as well as by a brutal challenge from Henry), he would do the same with the French captain, Prégent.

Prégent's galleys lay inshore, protected by the rocks and shallows against Howard's big ships and heavy guns. All Howard could pit against them were a few unarmed row barges. To throw these against the galleys was a suicide mission. Howard was told as much. He persisted. His own craft came up alongside Prégent's flagship and he managed to board it with a score of others. But his men lost heart and cast off. 'Come aboard again! Come aboard again,' he cried. But he was ignored. Realizing it was over, he tore off the golden whistle that was his badge of office and threw it into the sea. Then the French thrust him with pikes against the rails of the galley and threw his body overboard.[18]

After the battle was over, two English prisoners told Prégent that one of his victims had been their admiral. Delighted with this information, Prégent ordered his men to fish among the dead. The corpse was discovered and brought to him. Prégent had the body of Howard opened, eviscerated and then salted, as a temporary preservative measure. An apothecary, who would complete the embalming in a more conventional way, was due to arrive the following day. Meanwhile, Prégent sent Howard's gold chain and 'whistle of command' (as opposed to the 'whistle of office' which he had flung in the sea) to the French Queen, and his clothes or 'spoil' to the King's daughter, Madame Claude, who was married to the heir to the throne, the Duke of Angoulême. The heart Prégent was anxious to keep for himself. He humbly begged the King and Queen this favour; it would be to their advantage, he promised.[19]

Thus ended the man I have guessed to be Catherine's favourite: stripped, gutted and salted like a fish, his clothing and effects distributed for the delectation of the ladies of the French royal house and his heart bid for as a souvenir by his killer.

Edward Howard had promised to avenge the death of his companion-in-arms, Thomas Knyvet. Catherine, I think, did not forget what had happened to Howard. And soon she would have vengeance in kind.

26. Regent

Catherine's involvement in the war preparations became common knowledge. Indeed, to one observer she seemed the real driving force. 'The King [is] bent on war,' noted the merchant Lorenzo Pasquaglio of the Venetian 'factory' or depot in London, 'the Council [is] averse to it; the Queen wills it.' But if the campaign of 1513 was indeed Catherine's war, it had got off to a bad start – especially in the areas where she was most concerned. But Henry and Catherine were not deflected. Nor was their mutual trust weakened. War, instead, proved the best aphrodisiac, and the campaign of 1513 was to leave their marriage stronger and Catherine's position more impregnable than ever.[1]

But in the spring of 1513 such an outcome seemed unlikely. For April had indeed proved the cruellest month. On the 25th, Sir Edward Howard had met his spectacular death, and the naval campaign never recovered. He was immediately replaced as Lord Admiral by his elder brother Lord Thomas Howard. But Thomas, though a brave man and a fine soldier, was solid and steady. He was lead to his brother's mercury, and the kamikaze daring went out of English seamanship, not to return tillthe Elizabethans. Meanwhile, Catherine's father Ferdinand betrayed England for the third time. On 18 April, ambassador Caroz signed a new treaty with England that provided for a joint attack on France in two months. But the left hand of Spanish policy in London did not know what the right hand in Spain had been doing. For less than three weeks earlier Ferdinand had agreed a truce with France. This truce, signed on 1 April, made a fool of his ambassador in England, and it made a dupe or worse of his daughter. For the truce, Ferdinand claimed, had been brokered en route by the Aragonese Franciscan whom he was sending as Catherine's confessor.[2]

But Henry and Catherine brushed these disappointments aside. They would fight on land; without allies and, if need be, on two fronts.

The first front would be opened in north-eastern France. The army would be led by Henry himself and it would be launched from the English bridgehead of Calais. The undertaking was on the largest scale and, sensibly, the troops were mustered gradually. At the beginning of May the foreward under the Earl of Shrewsbury left for Calais. The rearward under Charles Somerset, Lord Herbert, followed later in the month. Both commanders were well known to Catherine through their posts at Court, where Shrewsbury was Lord Steward and Herbert Lord Chamberlain. The advance parties of troops then moved into camp, leaving Calais clear for the King and his retinue which made up the middleward of the army.

Catherine accompanied Henry on the English leg of his journey. They left Greenwich on 15 June, and 'with small journeys' rode through

Kent. It was a brilliant cavalcade. The guard had been raised to a wartime strength of six hundred and bought new liveries of green and white, trimmed, at vast expense, with embroidery and spangles of silver and silver-gilt. The retinues of the nobles were scarcely less splendid or large. By 20 June, the King and Queen reached Canterbury, where they prayed and offered 'at the martyrdom of St Thomas [Becket]' for the success of the eighth Henry who, unlike the second Henry, fought on behalf of the Church and its authority. On the 28th the royal party arrived at Dover. The harbour was a sea of ships, 'such as Neptune never saw before'. They were painted, trimmed and gilded, with banners and pennants flying. The Pope's arms mingled with Henry VIII's. The King and Queen stayed the night at Dover Castle, then, the following day, Henry set sail.

One of his last acts before leaving English soil was to constitute Catherine as 'Regent and Governess of England, Wales and Ireland', during his absence 'in his expedition against France, for the preservation of the Catholic religion and the recovery of his rights'. She was given sweeping powers to raise troops, to make ecclesiastical appointments (apart from bishoprics), to pick sheriffs, to issue warrants for the payment of money and generally to use her sign manual or signature to set the machinery of government in motion. Henceforward, until the King's return, her signature, 'Katherina the Qwene', would have as much force as 'Henry R'. Mere Queen Consort no more, she was now, like her mother, Co-sovereign of the lion's share of her husband's dominions.[3]

Catherine did not weep at the parting. But a strong man nearly did. For Thomas Howard, Earl of Surrey, found himself left behind. Before stepping aboard, Henry had taken him by the hand and said, 'My Lord, I trust not the Scots, therefore I pray you be not negligent.' The Earl had replied, 'I shall so do my duty, that Your Grace shall find me diligent, and to fulfil your will shall be my gladness.' Surrey 'could scantly speak when he took his leave'. The King and 'the flower of all the nobility' were about to win glory on the fields of France; for him, there was only the slog of border warfare. Once he had recovered his composure, he swore a vengeance on the man who had deprived him of his birthright of accompanying his King 'in such an honourable journey'. 'Sorry may I see him or I die, that is the cause of my abiding behind, and if ever he and I meet, I shall do that in me lieth to make him as sorry if I can.' The intended object of his vengeance was James IV of Scotland. For James's recent behaviour had made it clear that England would indeed have to face war on two fronts: in the north of England as well as the north of France.[4]

Surrey's appointment as Lieutenant of the Northern Marches made it safe for Henry to leave England: the Earl would supply the iron inside the velvet of Catherine's regal mantle. His support began immediately. Once Henry was gone, Catherine let her feelings show. And, as the two rode north from Dover, Surrey 'attended on the Queen to London, comforting her as best he might'. But he was not to be at her side for long.

Catherine's formal support came instead from the small Council that was appointed to assist her. Most of the Council had accompanied Henry to France. But it would be wrong to think of the handful left in England as the dregs. Instead, Catherine's two leading advisers, William Warham, Archbishop of Canterbury and Lord Chancellor, and Sir Thomas Lovell, the Treasurer of the Household, were among the weightiest members of the whole body.

Lovell had been a leading member of Henry VII's government. He was soldier, lawyer and administrator, and showed himself ruthless in all three roles. This aspect of his character is captured by his bronze portrait medallion by Torrigiano. It shows him in profile, and firmness is its essence. His cap is pulled down firmly on his head; his chin is firm; and his mouth is firmly clenched and turned down at the corners in an image of formidable authority. He was now ageing. But he was a tower of strength to Catherine. He acted as her Lord High Everything Else, deputizing as Lord Steward for Shrewsbury, who was in France, and as Earl Marshal for Surrey, who was on the borders. He also served as a sort of honorary consort to Catherine, fulfilling the military duties which, as a woman, she was felt to be unable to discharge herself.[5]

Warham, in contrast, was probably expected to run the civil government. He was a councillor of long-standing and vast experience.

He was also, as Archbishop of Canterbury, the King's first subject, and, as Lord Chancellor, his senior minister. But he was out of place in a war government. He had been a last-ditch supporter of peace; he was also engaged in a long-running dispute about ecclesiastical jurisdiction with his fellow bishop and councillor, Fox of Winchester. The dispute came to a head during the campaign, to Catherine's embarrassment and Warham's fury. He became at best a semi-detached member of Catherine's regency Council.

Under the Queen and Council there was a skeleton administration. Warham's Chancery acted as a general secretariat, while the Chamber, under its Treasurer, John Heron, dealt with finance. Catherine as Regent was specifically authorized to issue instructions to both these bodies.

For Catherine, the first three weeks after Henry's departure were a period of phoney war. Her husband was still in Calais and Surrey was still in the south, busy raising his following from his own estates. Meanwhile she took up residence at Richmond and her Council busied itself organizing Lord Admiral Thomas Howard's naval expedition. Its mission was to take the heavy guns of the royal artillery directly to Newcastle by sea, whence they would be deployed by land against the expected Scottish invasion. The warrants for payment were signed by Catherine; they were paid on 16 July and the force was to set sail on the 21st. The pace of events now quickened. Surrey had finished raising his men. They were a crack force of 500 'able men', part gentlemen, part tenant farmers. On 21 July, they paraded in London before Sir Thomas Lovell and, the following day, the Earl rode north to Doncaster to take up his command. On the 21st also, Henry left Calais to join the other divisions of his army under Shrewsbury and Herbert, who were already laying siege to the strongly fortified French town of Thérouanne.

So three English expeditions — two by land and one by sea — left within twenty-four hours of one another. It was a remarkable example of combined operations and bade fair for the outcome. The English, helped by Catherine, had indeed learned from the previous year's disasters. Europe would have to sit up and take notice.

But, despite this good start, Catherine now experienced the worries of every woman whose husband goes to the front. Letters became her lifeline and she set up a chain of messengers. As she explained on 26 July to Thomas Wolsey, the King's Almoner and the rising star in the Council, she had sent her servant to France with the present letter. He was 'to tarry there till another cometh and this way I shall hear every week from thence'. Understandably, Catherine's principal concern was for her husband's health and safety: 'for with his life and health there is no thing in the world that shall come to him amiss by the grace of God, and without that I can see no manner good thing shall fall'.[6]

Catherine, as a war-wife, is hardly unique in having such thoughts. But her concerns have been misrepresented. In several accounts, Catherine is portrayed as showing herself to be more Henry's nanny than his wife, while the King himself appears as an overgrown schoolboy who had to be reminded to change his socks, wash behind his ears and avoid catching cold. Actually, there is nothing in Catherine's letters on such trivial topics. Instead, she was concerned lest Henry needlessly exposed himself to the enemy. These fears came to a head when he arrived at Thérouanne and joined the siege. Henry VIII had already played Henry V once, when he had stayed up all night, touring the camp to put his troops in good heart. Now he seems to have thought that he was at Harfleur, though the walls of Thérouanne were as yet unbreached. His Council in France warned him against such posturings. But the warning was quickly forgotten, and, during a later siege, Henry walked close to the walls, 'occasionally, for three hours and a half at a time'. Other royal women had similarly rash menfolk, and the Archduchess Margaret, Catherine's sometime sister-in-law, wrote to her father, the Emperor Maximilian, in a similar vein, after he had joined Henry on the campaign. 'As such things are not conducted without great danger,' she wrote following one engagement, 'she begs him to be careful.' But in the case of Catherine and Henry there was a special, unspoken fear. Henry had no heir. If he fell, his dynasty fell. And the reason for this state of affairs was Catherine's own failure to have children. On 1 August, Catherine took matters into her own hands and wrote directly to the

Archduchess Margaret, to ask her to send Henry a physician.[7]

But Catherine's letters were not only about wifely concerns and womanish fears. She wrote also as her husband's Regent and coadjutor in policy. She commented on morale on the home front: 'everybody here is in good health, thanked be God, and the Council very diligent in all things concerning the expedition of the King's service'. She showed a shrewd managerial touch. It would be a good idea, she suggested, if the King wrote to the Council about her good reports of their conduct, 'that he is very well content therewith and give them thanks for it, bidding them so to continue'. She reported news, like the message which had just come from Lord Admiral Howard. And she did her best, even at a distance, to encourage Henry to stick to the 'England alone' policy which they had agreed after her father's third betrayal. 'I trust to God that the King shall come home shortly with as great a victory as any prince in the world; and this I pray God send him', she continued, '*without need of any other prince.*'

Catherine's next weekly letter is missing. But it would have told Henry of the continuing preparations to resist the impending Scottish invasion. She had already sent out letters to local notables in the southern shires and boroughs, requiring them to report on the numbers of men and quantities of harness or armour they could supply. The town of Gloucester failed to respond and was sent a sharp reminder on 4 August. 'Writings and news from the Borders show that the King of Scots means war,' she told them. They must send the required information within fifteen days. They did.

On 9 August, Catherine transacted a more awkward piece of business. Responding to Henry's direct orders, she summoned Warham to appear before her and justify his conduct with Fox. It was an extraordinary occasion. Catherine, assisted by Lovell and another councillor, sat quasi-judicially. And Warham, Chancellor and Primate of All England, found himself demoted from judge to accused. The Queen demanded an answer. Warham took evasive action, promising to set out his case by letter. Both the Queen and the Archbishop found the meeting an uncomfortable one and Catherine, wisely, tried to avoid involvement as much as possible. For once, she emphasized that she was a mere agent, acting in her husband's name and according to his letters, 'for the matter was so new to me I would go no further in it'.[8]

By the time of Catherine's next letter, on 13 August, the long-threatened war with Scotland had materialized. On the 11th, Lyon King had delivered James IV's declaration of war to Henry in person in France. High words had been uttered on both sides. But the exchange had ended with Henry dismissing the herald with a munificent reward. Back in England, Catherine had the wit to turn her labours into a joke: 'Ye be not so busy with the war, as we be here encumbered with it,' she told Wolsey. Morale remained good, she continued. Everyone was pleased that the phoney war was over 'and all [Henry's] subjects be very glad, I thank God, to be busy with the Scots, for they take it for a pastime'. For herself, 'my heart is very good to it, and I am horribly busy with making standards, banners and badges'. It is a prettily feminine picture: Catherine, sitting with her ladies, embroidering (perhaps a little more hastily than usual) lions, pomegranates and crosses of St George. Or it would be prettily feminine, were not the standards and banners to fly over Catherine's own army, to be led by the Queen in person.

Three days later, on 16 August, Henry had the victory that Catherine had prayed for. A large French cavalry force, made up of the crack *gendarmerie*, tried to force its way through the English besiegers in order to re-provision Thérouanne (by throwing sides of bacon over the walls!). But they were caught off guard by the English archers and guns, and they turned tail and fled. In their haste to escape, the knights slashed the heavy bards and trappers off their horses and flung away their weapons and horse-armour. It was a *sauve qui peut*, in which only one weapon was used effectively: the spurs which gave the battle its name. Even so, they did not ride fast enough and many distinguished prisoners were taken, headed by the Duke of Longueville, who was of the blood royal, and the seigneur de Bayard, the *chevalier sans peur et sans reproche*, who had been the hero of the Italian wars.

Henry did not fight himself. But he made up for it by his chivalrous magnanimity after the victory. He had Longueville clad in a gown of cloth of gold and summoned him to sup with him. The Duke said, 'Sire, I will not.' The King replied, 'You are my prisoner and must do so.' While Henry and his prisoner ate elegantly, the inhabitants of Thérouanne, deprived of their bacon, faced starvation. They had no hope now of relief and, a week later, they surrendered the city.[9]

English historians, characteristically deprecating English achievement, are dismissive of the Battle of the Spurs. The French were not so foolish. They had done more than lose a battle and a city; they had lost their reputation. Henceforward, until they were redeemed by another victory under another king, the *gendarmerie*, once the flower of French chivalry, were known derisively as 'hares in armour'. And the reputation lost by the French now belonged to Henry.[10]

Catherine knew this and her response was ecstatic: 'The victory hath been so great that I think none such hath been seen before. All England hath cause to thank God of it, and I specially.' But as important as the victory, Catherine thought, was the way that it had been won. For the Emperor Maximilian, the titular ruler of Christendom, had joined with Henry, not as an ally but as a paid soldier, wearing 'a cross of St George with a rose' and taking the King's shilling (in fact, rather more, since 70,000 crowns worth £14,000 were transported to Gravelines 'for use of the Emperor'). The two rulers met on 11 August. On the one side, the Emperor Maximilian and his suite wore black cloth as mourning for the late Empress; on the other, King Henry and his attendants shimmered in cloth of gold. Even the King's horse was harnessed with gold and trimmed with gold bells. The Emperor played the poor relation in behaviour as well as appearance: 'declaring publicly that he came to be of use to the King of England, and calling the King at one time his son, at another his King and at another his brother'. Catherine lapped up the contrast. 'I was very glad to hear the meeting of them', she wrote to Wolsey, 'which hath been to my seeming the greatest honour to the King that ever came to Prince.'[11]

But, though she basked in her husband's glory, she never forgot that she was engaged in mighty enterprise of her own. 'Ye shall see', she told

Wolsey, 'how Almighty God helpeth here our part as well as there.' The good news to which Catherine referred was the defeat of an advance Scottish raiding party under Lord Hume. Their losses were so heavy that it became known as the 'Ill Raid'.

On 22 August, nevertheless, James IV and the main Scottish army crossed the border. At first, he carried all before him. He took Norham Castle (to the anguish of its proud owner, Thomas Ruthall, the Prince-Bishop of Durham) and three smaller castles; then, about 4 September, he established himself in a strongly fortified camp on Flodden Edge. It was protected from the south (the likely direction of English attack) by a steep slope and it commanded the road north from Wooler through the valley of the Till. The English response, agreed in advance but co-ordinated on the ground by Catherine and her Council, was designed to provide cover in depth. Three armies were available. The first was the northern army commanded by Surrey. He had been in the north since the beginning of August, cajoling, organizing and winning hearts and minds. His plans now rolled smoothly into operation. The whole strength of the north was summoned to muster with him at Newcastle on 1 September. His son Thomas, the Lord Admiral, was already in the port with the fleet and the artillery. The guns were put ashore and Thomas, together with 1,000 men from the fleet, joined his father. The result was a formidably armed and disciplined force of 20,000 men which took the field at Bolton in Glendale.

It was hard to think that even the flower of Scotland could defeat it and certainly the Howards, father and son, harboured no such doubts. But the English government *had* dared to think the unthinkable – and to provide for it. For if James won and if he broke the northern army he still had to face and overcome two more armies. The first was commanded by Catherine's right-hand-man, Sir Thomas Lovell. Between 3 and 7 September, Lovell was empowered to raise the Midland counties, to punish all who resisted and to use martial law. All the commissions were signed by Catherine, and the fact that Lovell was 'subject to the com-mands of Queen Catherine, Regent' was made explicit. By 9 September, he was at Nottingham, with 15,000 men and marching north.

Finally, if James had also broken through Lovell and the Midlanders, he would have had to deal with Catherine herself, who had taken the field with all the might of the south of England.[12]

Like Surrey in the north, Catherine had spent August mustering and preparing her forces. On 2 September, 'the Scots being so busy as they now be', she was 'looking for my departing every hour'. On 8 September, she ordered the royal standards and banners to be issued from the Great Wardrobe. And shortly thereafter, Catherine marched out, from Richmond, with two 'standards of the lion crowned imperial', and with banners bearing the arms of England and Spain and images of the Trinity, the Virgin and St George. She had a herald, a pursuivant and six trumpets. Her artillery alone cost £100 to transport. She had 100 carriages, each with a pennant. She may even have worn armour, since in September Robert Amadas, the royal goldsmith, was paid for 'garnishing a headpiece with crown gold'. By 10 September she was at Buckingham, sixty miles north of London, with an army variously described as 'a numerous force' or 'a great power' and estimated (with probably spurious precision) at 40,000.

Catherine's martial behaviour was widely commented on. Writing from the Venetian 'factory' in London, Lorenzo Pasquaglio turned English in his enthusiasm: bursting with pride he informed his brother that not only had 'our magnanimous King' won great victories, but 'our Queen' had also taken the field. But the man who was perhaps proudest and most understanding of Catherine's behaviour was her sometime director of studies, Peter Martyr. He kept a sharp eye on English affairs from his post at Valladolid and on 23 September reported that Catherine, 'in imitation of her mother Isabella', had made a splendid speech to the English captains. She told them 'to be ready to defend their territory, that the Lord smiled upon those who stood in defence of their own, and that they should remember that English courage excelled that of all other nations'. If we take Martyr's report literally, this speech must have been delivered on 21 July, when Surrey had mustered his men in London. But it seems unlikely that Catherine would not have made a similarly rousing oration to her own troops. She had indeed learned English, become

English and made herself mistress of both the language and the people's hearts.[13]

Just before she left Richmond, Catherine had briefly to turn away from English affairs and deal with the aftermath of her husband's victories in France. Wolsey had informed her that Henry's prize trophy, the Duke of Longueville, was being sent to England, where he was to be lodged in her household. Catherine protested that the proposed arrangement was impossible. She was about to depart for the front, while her Chamberlain, Lord Mountjoy, who was the only person of status to 'attend upon him', was also about to leave to take over as Captain of Calais. In the circumstances she suggested that Longueville should be kept in the Tower. Her advice was acted on and Catherine herself authorized the payment of £13 6s 8d 'for lodging and boarding Duke Langevile and six persons with him in the Tower'. But her mind was on other, more important things: pray God, she begged Wolsey, 'to send us as good luck against the Scots as the King hath there'.[14]

She had her prayer. Surrey tried first to lure James IV from the protection of his camp on Flodden Edge by a knightly challenge to battle. James replied that it was not for an Earl to dictate terms to a King. Chivalry having failed, Surrey resorted to stratagem. He marched off to the north, apparently with the intention of launching a counter-invasion of Scotland. But he halted overnight, and, very early on the morning of 9 September, swung to attack the Scots from the north, where the slope of the ground was gentle and offered little protection. At first the Scots did well. They scattered the extreme right of the English under Surrey's youngest surviving son, Sir Edmund, and Lord Thomas, who commanded the vanguard and the artillery, in despair tore the *Agnus Dei* from his neck and sent it to his father in a plea for reinforcements. But the day turned. The English guns and archers needled the Scots into mass charges which came to grief on English pikes. James and his Household charged with the rest and the King of the Scots fell only a spear's length from Surrey's banner.

The day now became a rout. For once figures tell the true story: with the King died an archbishop, a bishop, two abbots, twelve earls, fourteen lords and at least 10,000 ordinary folk. The English, in contrast, lost no more than 1,500. In the confusion and among the piles of bodies, most of which were quickly stripped and reduced to the anonymity of nakedness, James's corpse was not at first identified. It was learned from Scottish prisoners that he had either been captured or killed but his actual fate still remained unknown when Surrey sent the first news of victory to Catherine.[15]

The messenger probably reached Catherine within a little over twenty-four hours – say, late on the 10th or early on the 11th. She wrote immediately to her husband in Lille, where Henry was staying as the honoured guest of Maximilian and Margaret. Her letter has not survived. But a report of its contents went round the city like wildfire on the 13th.

> The Queen of England has written to the King in reply to his letter about the encounter with the French and about the Duke of Longueville, whom he sent as a present. She says she thanks his Majesty for the good news and for the present of the Duke. . . . She says she has shown no less prowess than he in fighting the Scots . . . With regard to the gift of the Duke, which is truly a great gift, she hopes to surpass the King in this also, and instead of a Duke she hopes to send him a King.

The writer is the Milanese ambassador. No doubt his tale lost nothing in the telling. But he is usually well-informed and the tone of Catherine's actual letter of the 16th is only a little less triumphalist. Its contents are of a piece as well. It compares, favourably, her own achievements with Henry's, and it also refers to an earlier promise to send him James as a prisoner (in return, no doubt, for Longueville). The Milanese report, in short, is to be believed.[16]

By the time of this further letter, Catherine was fully informed about the outcome of Flodden. James's body had been found on the 10th by one who 'knew him well by his privy tokens'. When the body was stripped, it was discovered that he had died of two serious wounds, one inflicted by an arrow and the other by a pike. Surrey sent part of James's coat-armour (that is, his surcoat of the royal arms of Scotland) to Catherine, along with letters, to her and to Henry, fully describing the battle. Then he had the Scottish King's corpse disembowelled, cauterized and embalmed to await a decision about burial. For James had died under the threat of excommunication, and excommunicates were denied Christian burial.[17]

As soon as Catherine learned the full extent of the Scottish defeat, she halted her march north, disbanded her troops and began to travel east on a very different mission. And it was from her stopover at Woburn Abbey on the 16th that she wrote her only letter of this momentous year that is addressed directly to Henry himself, rather than mediately to Wolsey.

Catherine begins her letter formally enough: 'Sir'. But she quickly becomes more intimate: 'my husband', even 'my Henry'. And her tone is frankly exultant. 'To my thinking, this battle hath been to your Grace and all your realm the greatest honour that could be, and more than ye should win all the crown of France.' She is also competitive. She had not been able to send the piece of James's coat-armour by the previous messenger; it comes with this, she told Henry. 'In this your Grace shall see how I can keep my promise, sending you for your banners a King's coat.' 'I thought,' she continues referring to her earlier promise 'to send himself unto you [as a prisoner], but our Englishmen's hearts would not suffer it'. James's fate is a cue for a reflection on the due deserts he has had for his perfidy: 'It should have been better for him to have been in peace than have this reward.' 'All that God sendith is for the best,' she concludes piously. She ends the letter with a formal submissiveness that its contents rather belie, 'Your humble wife and true servant'. And she signs simply 'Katherine'.

Catherine's piety was undoubtedly real. But it was also a touch complacent. This is understandable enough, since the last few months had granted her everything she could wish. The war, her war as well as Henry's, had been a triumphant success. Together, they had proved the doubters wrong: England could fight and win. The doubters had been headed by Catherine's own father. Now he would have to eat his words. Catherine was also avenged: the eventual fate of James IV's body parallels the wretched humiliations of Sir Edward Howard's abused corpse. Catherine even found time to settle accounts with her former rebellious servant, Francesca de Carceres, whose elderly husband had died, leaving her unprovided for. Ferdinand suggested putting her in the service of his daughter Maria; Wolsey in that of the Archduchess Margaret. Catherine would have none of it. 'She is so perilous a woman that it shall be dangerous to put her in a strange house,' she insisted. She must be sent back to Spain and to a nunnery. The French, the Scots, and her own servant had all found that it was dangerous to cross Catherine.

But God's goodness to her was not over. On the 16th she told Henry 'now [I] go to our Lady at Walsingham that I promised so long ago to see'. She was at the shrine on 23 September and, among other prayers, offered up thanks for the fact that she was with child.[18]

27. The breach with Spain

Catherine's war regency was the climacteric of her life. It had promised much. But the promises turned to dust. Her pregnancy ended mysteriously – presumably in a miscarriage. War, in which she had thrived, turned to peace, in which there was no political role for her. And her husband broke decisively with her father. The Anglo-Spanish alliance had been the *raison d'être* of her marriage. Without it, and without children, what was her marriage worth? Within six months of the 'loving meeting' between the King and Queen after Henry's return from France in October 1513, Catherine started to find out.[1]

In the autumn of 1513, Henry of England, the Emperor Maximilian and Ferdinand of Aragon had signed a treaty committing them to a three-pronged invasion of France in June of the following year. All three parties had also renewed their commitment to the marriage of

Henry's sister, Princess Mary of England, with Prince Charles of the Netherlands.

But Ferdinand immediately had second thoughts. He calculated that France, conveniently weakened by Henry's successful assault, would be so anxious to make peace with Spain that it would be willing to pay for it. And he persuaded the flighty Maximilian that he, too, could benefit more from such a settlement. The Franco-Spanish truce was renewed in March 1514 and was joined by Maximilian shortly thereafter. And the wedding of Mary and Charles, due to take place by 14 May, was hastily postponed.[2]

Now, there was nothing new about Ferdinand betraying England. As we have seen, Ferdinand's perfidy had become a fixed event in the political calendar. What was new this time was Henry's reaction. Instead of turning a blind eye as before, he reacted with fury. And he decided to turn the tables.

Henry's triumphs of the previous year had given him a fresh confidence. He had proved he could fight a war; now he would show that he could win a peace. Moreover, he had spent so much on the war (£500,000 in the single month of June 1513), that peace was a tempting prospect on financial grounds alone. Finally, he had a new minister: Thomas Wolsey.

Wolsey, after a series of false starts, had joined the royal service at the end of Henry VII's reign. And his rise continued under Henry VIII, when he was made royal Almoner. Nominally, the Almoner was a middle-ranking clerical official of the Court, who was responsible for the King's charitable doles of food. But Wolsey's real job was to act as Court agent for Richard Fox, Bishop of Winchester. Henry never really trusted Fox: 'Here in England they think he is a fox', he told Caroz, 'and such is his name.' But Fox was the weightiest councillor and leader of the peace party. So long as the peace party was in the ascendant, Wolsey served Fox with his inimitable enthusiasm and efficiency. But after the defeat of the peace party at the crucial Council meeting in October 1511, Wolsey changed tack. He read, correctly, Henry's commitment to war, and adapted himself to it. And in promoting Henry's war aims, he was as successful as he had been in serving his former master, Fox. The will driving the war might have been Catherine's, as Pasquaglio suggested, but the organizing and strategic genius behind the triumphs of 1513 was Wolsey's.[3]

And it was Wolsey, not Catherine, who benefited. In his modest Almoner's robes, he had been the *éminence grise* of the French campaign, always at Henry's side and acting, significantly, as intermediary even between Henry and his wife. But thereafter the modest garb and demeanour were cast off, and Wolsey became in quick succession Bishop of Tournai (Henry's grandest acquisition of the French campaign), Bishop of Lincoln and (after the mysterious death of Bainbridge in Rome) Archbishop of York. Finally, in 1515, he pushed Warham aside and became Chancellor as well. With each promotion, his plumage became more magnificent, his wealth greater and his hold over Henry more complete. The King, one of Wolsey's creatures informed him, spoke of him as 'though ye were his own father'. Where would that leave Henry's wife?[4]

Under Wolsey's guidance the diplomatic revolution of 1514 moved apace. Early in the new year, secret negotiations were opened with France. They were greatly facilitated by the enforced presence in London of Longueville, who found himself transformed from honoured prisoner into a trusted go-between. The logic of the negotiations was simple. England had been France's most dangerous enemy in 1513, therefore France would pay even more to make peace with England. Louis XII indeed was prepared to concede almost anything: Tournai, a massively increased pension (as it was called by the French) or tribute (as the English preferred to describe it), even himself. And what Louis offered, Henry and Wolsey were happy to accept. On 10 August, peace between England and France was proclaimed, and, three days later, it was re-affirmed by a proxy marriage.[5]

And this, it turned out, was the most astonishing *volte-face* of all. For instead of Mary marrying the youthful Prince Charles of the Netherlands, her groom was to be the ageing Louis of France. According to the Venetian ambassador, who was present at the betrothal, Mary was 'so pleased to be Queen of France' that she was prepared to overlook the fact that her new husband was, at fifty-two, nearly three times her own age and sickly. Mary herself later said that she had protested at the marriage; indeed she claimed she had only agreed to it after making Henry promise that, next time, she could marry whom she wished. Perhaps. But being Queen of France, as the Venetian said, was a fine thing. And the betrothal gave her a foretaste of the glories of her future position.[6]

The ceremony took place at Greenwich. Archbishop Warham officiated and preached the sermon. Longueville impersonated Louis. Mary, in so far as she was allowed to be, was herself. Longueville took her right hand and recited the oath. Mary took his right hand and made her promises. Then each signed the written agreement, the Princess writing her name as 'Marye'. Finally, Longueville gave her a ring which she placed on the fourth finger of her right hand. She was now Queen of France. As for Longueville, he was now a rich man, as Henry gave him his cloth of gold gown and a reward of 10,000 crowns. It was worth it, Henry VIII probably felt, for the pleasure of dishing Ferdinand.[7]

Ferdinand's daughter, Catherine, was present at the ceremony. She was dressed almost identically to the bride, who was now her equal in status. We do not know her thoughts. But probably she felt pity for the childish excitement of her sister-in-law and womanly sympathy for what she suspected Mary might face in the marriage bed. But her worst fears would have been reserved for herself. For Mary's French marriage undid everything that Catherine had done since she came to England from Spain. It might even undo her own marriage.

Certainly, this was the conclusion in both France and Rome, where news of the marriage of Mary and Louis was linked to a rumour that 'the King of England meant to repudiate his present wife, the daughter of the King of Spain and his brother's widow, because he is unable to have children by her'. Instead it was claimed, Henry intended to marry, like his sister, in France, by taking a daughter of the Duke of Bourbon as his bride. It used to be thought that the rumour was lent substance by an entry in the index to the secret archives of the Vatican which, under the same year (1514), notes the 'original of a letter written by the Pope to Henry, King of England, about the supposed nullity of his marriage'. But the entry now appears to be an error. So the story is no more than a rumour after all – albeit an extraordinary anticipation of later events.[8]

Moreover, Catherine, supposedly incapable of bearing children, had a not-so-secret weapon: at Mary's wedding she was pregnant and visibly so. Her condition had been apparent five weeks earlier to an envoy from the Archduchess Margaret. 'The Queen', he reported, 'is believed to be with child, and is so, as far as the writer can judge.' A fortnight later, Henry himself confirmed the news in a letter to Margaret.[9]

By October, preparations for the lying-in had begun. Blue say was ordered to hang the Queen's bed, while a cradle covered in scarlet 'without a frame' and a couch were to be supplied 'for the use of our nursery, God willing'. The political preparations had started too. Louis XII, Henry's new brother-in-law, discussed the forthcoming birth with the English ambassador. 'If God should send [Henry] a son', the King of France said, he was as eager to stand as godfather, as he had been last time for the late Prince Henry. Louis promised to send 'a good and honourable personage to be there against the Queen's deliverance to represent his person, and to do the act in his name'. Wolsey transmitted the good news to Henry 'who', he reported, 'is marvellously rejoiced'. Wolsey claimed, implausibly, that Catherine was equally pleased at the prospective godfather. But she had no choice.[10]

Catherine was due to take to her Chamber shortly after 15 November. This time, she probably looked forward to the enforced solitude and sequestration. For the atmosphere at Court had become intolerable. Henry was not satisfied that he had double-crossed Ferdinand, he wanted vengeance as well. And he opened negotiations to turn the Anglo-French peace into an offensive alliance against Spain. One immediate victim of Henry's vendetta against Ferdinand was Caroz. The English, Caroz complained in early December, had ceased to use him as the Spanish ambassador. Instead, they treated him 'as a bull, at whom everyone throws darts'. Henry was particularly rude, and 'behaves in the most offensive and discourteous manner'. In the circumstances, Caroz begged for his recall.

The other target of Henry's indignation was Catherine. She had no such easy escape as Caroz. She had to put a brave face on things, and did so with such success that Caroz complained that she had become English, and forgotten her duty to her father. He fingered the usual suspect, her confessor, Fray Diego, with whom he had waged guerrilla warfare since the earliest days of his Embassy. But the remaining members of her Household were almost as bad. 'The few Spaniards who are still in her household', Caroz explained, 'prefer to be friends of the English and neglect their duties as subjects of the King of Spain.' Worst of all was Dona Maria de Salinas, 'whom [the Queen] loves more than any other mortal'. Not only was Maria anglicized, like the rest; she was also the cat's paw of Ferdinand's inveterate enemies, the Castilian exiles at the court of Prince Charles.

The result was that Ferdinand's ambassador reaped no advantage from the fact that Ferdinand's daughter sat on the English throne. He could 'make no use of the influence which the Queen has in England, nor can he obtain through her the smallest advantage in any other respect'.

Caroz saw what Catherine wanted him to see. The breakdown in relations between England and Spain had forced her to choose between her father and her husband. Apparently, she had not hesitated. She had put her husband before her father and her acquired Englishness before her native Spanishness. But she could not escape her origins so easily. For Henry would not let her. Instead he was visiting the sins of his father-in-law on his wife's head. 'He had reproached her with her father's ill faith, *et conquestus suos in eam expectorabat* [and he got his loud complaints to her off his chest]'. As Henry had a rugby-player's chest (forty-two inches and expanding) the complaints were loud indeed.[11]

They resounded in Catherine's ears even in her Chamber, where, according to Peter Martyr, they led to disaster. 'The Queen of England', he reported, 'has given birth to a premature child – through grief, as it is said, for the misunderstanding between her father and her husband.'[12]

28. The quest for an heir

B ut Catherine's cup of sorrow was not yet full. For the last nine years, her confessor, Fray Diego, had been a central figure in her life. For her sake, he had endured the 'thirst, hunger, nakedness and poverty' visited on her servants under Henry VII. After her marriage to Henry VIII, he had helped acclimatize her to England and to the realities of wedded life. He seems even to have told her most of what she knew about sex. Catherine repaid him with uncritical devotion. Others formed a very different view of the opinionated friar and the list of his enemies grew long and powerful. It included Bishop Fox of Winchester who had done him 'many wrongs' under Henry VII, Lord Treasurer Surrey and his Countess who had her own bone to pick with the Queen, as well, of course, as the Spanish ambassador Caroz.

Eventually, Fray Diego's way with the ladies, which was the basis of his hold on Catherine, proved his undoing. He was convicted of fornication before the Council. Winchester and Surrey, as his personal enemies, took pleasure in announcing the sentence. He was to be deprived of his offices, expelled from the kingdom and sent back to Spain. The last filled him with particular terror. He knew that Caroz had painted him as the source of most of his problems in dealing with the English and he feared Ferdinand's revenge. He would return to the King of Aragon, he said, only 'with fifteen regiments of cavalry' – though whether the troops were required to protect him or to drag him there is not clear.

In his despair he wrote directly to Henry to beg him reconsider the case. The letter is written in an extraordinary Latin: ungrammatical, unclassical and heavily hispanized. Yet, in its way, it is fluent, even eloquent. And, in both form and content, it takes us very close, I suspect, to the persuasive mutterings to which Fray Diego had subjected Catherine, both within the confessional and without.

He began by singing his own praises: ancient princes, he said, were agreed in giving the highest rewards to the servants of their wives, especially when they had forsaken their native land to serve their mistresses. Then, drawing deep on his reserves of innuendo and gossip, he counter-charged his two accusers in Catherine's Household, Diego de Badillo, one of Catherine's yeomen, and Master Pedro Morales, one of her chaplains. Diego, he could prove, had carnally known a woman in the Queen's Household at Windsor. Geoffrey, one of the Queen's footmen, was a witness to the fact, since he had seen them with his own eyes. As for the chaplain, the servant he kept, who was called by his own name, was really his natural son. And so on. Finally, there was a threat. He was surprised, he said smoothly, that Henry's councillors had no fears in expelling from England someone who knew as much as he did. For he knew all the secrets of Henry's Household and kingdom. In particular he was familiar with all his dealings with Spain. He had seen all Henry and Catherine's replies to Ferdinand, and he had personally encrypted them in the Queen's own cipher. Think what someone who was less devoted to Henry's service than he might do with such information! But the secrets of which Fray Diego knew most were those of Henry's marriage-bed: 'I pray you may have sons,' he ended.[1]

It is unlikely that Henry saw the letter. But if he did, he was indifferent to both the blandishments and the blackmail, and Fray Diego was put on the next boat back to Spain.

Catherine, on the other hand, remained staunchly loyal. She wrote on Fray Diego's behalf to her father, praising him as a good servant to her and to Spain. If only he had been suffered to remain in England, she claimed confidently, relations between England and Spain would not have sunk so low.

Fray Diego was replaced by another Spaniard, Jorge de Athequa, who became Bishop of Llandaff. Athequa was 'a good, simple, timid soul' – in other words, everything that Fray Diego was not. Fray Diego was certainly a scamp and perhaps a bit of a scoundrel. But, in his way, he had been good for Catherine and, when he left, some of the life left Catherine with him.[2]

His departure was a depressing conclusion to a bad year for Catherine. But, just as the promises of 1513 had proved illusory, so the threats of

1514 failed to materialize – at least immediately. The peace with France collapsed; Henry and Ferdinand kissed and made up and Catherine and Henry, kissing more intimately, returned to the business of getting an heir.

Louis XII, despite his age and diseases, had been looking forward to his marriage with Mary. But it proved too much for him and he died only a few weeks afterwards on 31 December – of his exertions, it was said. Since he had only daughters, he was succeeded, according to French dynastic custom, by his nearest male relative, Francis, Duke of Angoulême. Francis I was even younger than Henry VIII, and as vainglorious. In particular, he was eager to rescue France's military reputation from the debacle of 1513. He promptly invaded Italy and, fighting at the head of his own troops, won the great set-piece battle of Marignano against the Swiss. Henry's glory was eclipsed and the English King was bitterly envious.[3]

There was nothing for it but for Henry to swallow his resentment of Ferdinand. Ferdinand had the sense to sugar the pill by making Henry a present of magnificent jewellery and in October 1515 new Anglo-Spanish treaties were signed.[4]

Catherine was delighted that the storm clouds of 1514 had blown over so quickly. But there is a new note in her letter to her father. She writes, not as she had done before, as more English than the English and as Henry's better and more devoted half. Instead, she sets herself to explain, with detachment, even with cynicism, the behaviour of both her adoptive country and her husband.

> There is no people in the world more influenced by the good
> or bad fortune of their enemies than the English. A small
> success of their enemies prostrates them, and a little adversity
> of their antagonists makes them overbearing. Such being the
> case, he may judge for himself how much the English love him,
> and how much they are persuaded that his friendship is
> necessary to them.

And by 'the English', of course, Catherine meant the King of England in particular. It is a sharp but scarcely flattering analysis of her husband's psychology.

In her letter Catherine referred, almost in passing, to the fact that she had had another miscarriage in the spring. But she did not tell her father that she was already pregnant again. Had repeated failure taught her that it was safer not to boast? This time, however, she carried the baby to term.

But not even Ferdinand could cheat death forever. It had been a miracle, Peter Martyr felt, that he had survived the last few winters as his asthma had turned to dropsy and worse. Finally, in January 1516 he died. Catherine had already taken to her Chamber when the news arrived in England. According to the Venetian ambassador, Sebastiano Giustiniani, the fact was 'kept secret during some days on account of the expected delivery of the Queen'. The precaution worked. Catherine was success-fully delivered. And the child lived. But it was a girl.[5]

The sense of deflation was palpable. Writing two days after the birth, Giustiniani assured the Republic that he would offer their congratu-lations; 'had an heir male been born', he added, '[he] would have done so already'. He eventually got to Court on the 24th and congratulated Henry 'on the birth of his daughter and the well-being of the Queen'. 'The State would have been yet more pleased', he continued, 'had the child been a son.'

Henry's reply to Giustiniani was both chivalrous and loyal: 'We are both young,' he said. 'If it was a daughter this time, by the grace of God the sons will follow.'[6]

But Catherine was already thirty-one. This was relatively old for child-bearing by sixteenth-century standards, and it was two years before she conceived again. In April 1518 Lord Mountjoy, Catherine's Chamberlain, gave the news in confidence to Wolsey's Court agent, the royal Secretary, Richard Pace. Pace added his own fervent hopes: 'Prays to God heartily it may be a Prince, to the surety and universal comfort of the realm'. He also suggested that Wolsey write 'a kind letter to the Queen'. By early June, the word had spread, and Giustiniani was 'assured of it by a trustworthy person, who heard it from the King's own mouth'. The ambassador added the same rider as Pace: 'It was an event most earnestly desired by the whole kingdom.'[7]

And no one, of course, desired it more earnestly than Henry. About this time, or perhaps a little earlier, he wrote a letter in his own hand to Wolsey. Since the King hated writing, this was a method of communication that he used only for the most important and secret business. His news was both. 'I trust', he told Wolsey, 'that the Queen my wife be with child.' This was why, he continued, he was reluctant to return to London from Woodstock, the Oxfordshire palace where they were staying. 'Because about this time is partly of her dangerous times and because of that I would remove her as little as I may now.' In other words, Henry is saying, Catherine had reached that stage in her pregnancy where she had previously proved to be most vulnerable to a miscarriage. It was a lesson learned from bitter experience. Bitter experience had also taught Henry not to count his chickens. 'I write this unto [you],' he continued, 'not as a ensured thing, but as a thing wherein I have great hope and likelihood ... [but] *nisi quod Deus velit inceptum opus bene finiri* [only if God will the beginning does the work end well].' It was a prayer which Catherine, no doubt, uttered as fervently as Henry.[8]

At the beginning of July Henry paid a flying visit to Wolsey at Greenwich, leaving the Queen and most of the Court at Woodstock. He returned on the 5th at 8 o'clock at night to the best homecoming present of all. 'And the Queen did meet with his Grace at his chamber door, and showed unto him, for his welcome home, her belly something great, declaring openly she was quick with child.' Catherine's 'dangerous time' had passed. Henry immediately ordered a *Te Deum* to be sung at St Paul's and another at Woodstock.[9]

It was decided that the lying-in should take place at Greenwich, and, in the second half of July, the Court moved there by slow stages. In August, the Pope asked whether Catherine were with child, and expressed himself delighted when he was told she was. 'Hopes it will be a Prince who will be the prop of the universal peace of Christendom,' the Cardinal Protector of England added for himself. In October, Giustiniani expressed the same hope more baldly: 'God grant she may give birth to a son, so that, having a heir male, the King may not be hindered from embarking, if necessary, in any great undertaking.' The delivery, he reported, was expected 'within a month or rather more'. The Prior of Canterbury was warned to be ready to send the font for the christening. The anticipation was now overwhelming.[10]

On 10 November Catherine went into labour and, during the night, was delivered of a child. It was another girl, 'to the vexation of everybody', Giustiniani reported, for 'never had the kingdom so anxiously desired anything as it did a Prince'. As though aware of her irrelevance to the great scheme of things, the baby died shortly thereafter.[11]

The great font was returned to Canterbury. It would not be needed again while Catherine was Queen.

29. On the shelf

Catherine was now on the shelf – in the sense that she was stuck in that limbo reserved for wives whose husbands do not much care about them one way or another. She became uglier and duller and more devoted to learning and religion. Meanwhile, Henry took mistresses, spent time with the boys and even, occasionally, immersed himself in the serious business of government. There was no public scandal and the structure of the Court, with its separate apartments for the King and Queen, staffed by separate Households, easily accommodated their increasingly separate and different lives.

The decline in Catherine's appearance in her thirties was very marked. The last wholly favourable comment about her was made in 1514, when she was in her thirtieth year and at the beginning of her fourth pregnancy. 'The Queen', the Netherlands ambassador reported, 'is of a lively and gracious disposition; quite the opposite of the Queen her sister [Juana the Mad] in complexion and manner.' But the breach with Spain and two miscarriages in quick succession took their toll. By spring 1515, the new Venetian ambassador Giustiniani and his suite thought that Catherine cut a poor figure. Overdressed and unattractive, she was out-shone, not only by her magnificent husband, but by her ladies as well. 'She is rather ugly than otherwise', the ambassador wrote 'but the damsels of her Court are handsome, and make a sumptuous appearance'. Four years later, in 1519, Giustiniani was reduced to scraping the barrel of compliment. 'She was not handsome, though she had a very beautiful complexion.' Francis I, speaking at the same time, was blunter. 'He [King Henry] has an old deformed wife,' he said, 'while he himself is young and handsome.'[1]

'Deformed' is, of course, a characteristic Gallic sexual hyperbole. Francis meant only that Catherine had become very fat. Unfortunately for Catherine, early sixteenth-century fashion favoured slimness in women. So did Henry's own preferences. Nor, alas, did Catherine have the build to carry it off. For she seems to have been very short. When she was young and pretty and svelte, the effect was charming. But with con-tinuous childbearing (she was pregnant at least seven times in the nine years from 1509 to 1518) and repeated stress and disappointment, her once trim figure broadened and layers of fat swelled her face and body. By the time she reached the menopause, which seems to have come to her very early at about thirty-five, she was (like the middle-aged Queen Victoria) nearly as wide as she was tall.

What made it worse, of course, was that she had married a husband who was younger and better-looking than she, and who had kept his youth and looks longer. Hence the contrast brutally noted by Francis. Catherine was probably aware of it too. Once, she had gloried in appearing at Henry's side. Now, she seemed to avoid all but essential Court ceremony and Giustiniani, who witnessed everything worth noticing at the Tudor Court between 1515 and 1519, reported on his departure that he 'had seen her but seldom'.[2]

Alienated, or perhaps self-exiled from English life, Catherine re-identified with her native Spain. Ambassadors were quick to note the change and to exploit it. So when the new Venetian Embassy visited her in 1515, Pasquaglio, 'knowing it would please her, addressed her in Spanish ... The Queen answered also in Spanish, and then entered into a long familiar conversation about the affairs of Spain'. It was more than a matter of language and when, in 1519, Prince Charles, her sister Juana's son, was elected Holy Roman Emperor, 'the Queen of England, *being a Spaniard*, evinced satisfaction at the success of her nephew'.[3]

In her altered circumstances, the Other World became as attractive as Iberia. Catherine had always been religious – more seriously so even than Henry, who prided himself on his piety. The difference is clear in Catherine's correspondence as regent, in which she is as anxious about her husband's spiritual health as his physical. 'Thanked be God of it,' she wrote to Henry after Flodden. 'And I am sure your Grace forgetteth not to do this, which shall be cause to send you many more such great victories, as I trust He shall do.' She rammed the point home in her letter to Wolsey, written the same day. 'This matter [the victory of Flodden] is so marvellous that it seemeth to be of God's doing alone. I trust the King shall remember to thank him for it.' But all of this was private, between the royal couple alone, even when mediated through Wolsey. By 1519, Catherine's piety had taken on a public dimension. 'The Queen', Giustiniani concluded his thumb-nail sketch, '[is] religious and as virtuous as words could express'.[4]

Nowadays, I suppose, we would talk of a change of image. In the first six years of her marriage to Henry, Catherine was 'lively and gracious'. She was young and pretty and sometimes flighty. She presided over jousts and the Court of Love. She was a powerful political influence on the King, and, for a few months, she ruled England as regent. She showed herself able, at least as able as Henry, and under her regency Tudor England won its greatest military victory before the Armada. She was religious. But the God she worshipped was the God of Battles.

In her thirties, Catherine lost most of this. She lost her looks, her political power and her husband's love. She had also failed to give him a son. But she found something that replaced them all: the love of God. She also retained the love of the people. For, like her, most Tudor women lost their looks and their figures in child-bearing. And many took to religion as a consolation. The difference, of course, was that Catherine performed on a wider stage.

So far, in her life in England, Catherine had trod many stages: the great walkway in St Paul's at her first wedding; the *theatre* in Westminster Abbey at her coronation; the painted grandstand in Palace Yard at the jousts for the birth of Prince Henry. But the largest and most important was in Westminster Hall after the 'Evil Mayday' riots in 1517.

These riots were a series of ugly, xenophobic attacks on foreigners in the City of London. Like such attacks nowadays, the actual violence was perpetrated by young, footloose men – the City apprentices. But the youthful rioters received tacit support from their elders and betters. The resulting disorders nearly got out of hand, and the King and Court, who were far more sympathetic to foreigners than the common folk, took a terrible revenge. The Duke of Norfolk (as Thomas Howard, Earl of Surrey, had been made in reward for Flodden) put the City under military occupation and decided to inflict exemplary punishment. Thirteen of the rioters, some of whom were little more than children, were convicted of high treason (since their foreign victims enjoyed the King's protection) and put to execution.

As usual, the Howards operated as a family firm. The executions were supervised by Norfolk's youngest son, now known as Lord Edmund Howard after his father's promotion, as Knight Marshall. The punishment for treason – hanging, drawing and quartering – was always horrible, but the actual pain inflicted varied greatly, depending on how the execution was carried out. Edmund Howard spared nothing: he 'showed no mercy but extreme cruelty to the poor younglings in their execution'. Some Londoners, no doubt, remembered his actions when, twenty-five years later, Lord Edmund's daughter, Catherine Howard, stepped on to the scaffold in her turn.

The stand-off between Court and capital had now become

dangerous. Four hundred other rioters were in gaol, equally at risk of execution. At this point Catherine intervened. According to the Papal Nuncio, 'our most serene and compassionate Queen, with tears in her eyes and on bended knees, obtained their pardon'.

The formal granting of the pardons was turned into a grand public display. The King came into Westminster Hall and sat in the seat of judgement. Fifteen thousand Londoners crowded into the body of the Hall, and the prisoners, stripped to their shirts and with nooses round their necks, were brought in. They fell on their knees and cried: 'Mercy!' Wolsey and the lords interceded for their pardon, which the King granted. The cheers rang out. But the person they were really cheering was Catherine.[5] Later, when Catherine came, in turn, to suffer, Londoners and their wives never forgot their loyalty to her.

30. Mary

But, even as they grew apart, Catherine and Henry kept one thing in common. This was the welfare of their only surviving child, the daughter born in February 1516. She was named Mary, after Henry's favourite sister, and she turned into a fine child. Catherine doted on her and Henry, when the mood took him, was also a proud and indulgent father, who delighted in showing off his pretty little daughter.

One such occasion took place on 23 February 1518, when the Venetian ambassador, Giustiniani, had an audience at Windsor. The King ordered the Princess, who had just celebrated her second birthday, to be brought in. Solemnly, Wolsey, ambassador Giustiniani and the attendant lords kissed the child's hand. Then Mary caught sight of Friar Dionysius Memo, the great Venetian organist, who was then resident keyboard virtuoso at Henry's Court. 'Priest! priest!' she 'commenced calling out in English' and would not stop until Memo agreed to play for her. Henry was delighted at the display, which showed that Mary was in truth her father's daughter: musical, precocious and imperious far beyond her years. Taking her 'in his arms', he came over to Giustiniani and started singing Memo's praises in Latin: '*Per Deum! iste est honestissimus vir . . .*' (God's Name! That man is a most worthy gentleman and one who is very dear to us . . .)

'Greater honour,' Giustiniani concluded, 'was paid to the Princess than to the Queen.' Catherine would not have minded: it showed that her daughter, despite her gender, was England's heir.[1]

And raising Mary as a worthy heir to the throne became the major objective of Catherine's fourth decade. She drew on her own experience; she consulted leading scholars and commissioned educational treatises. Above all, she herself mothered her child, in a way that was highly unusual in a royal parent. Years later, when Mary had a serious teenage illness, Catherine, surely recollecting these childhood days, announced she would take personal charge of her daughter. 'There is no need', Catherine insisted, 'of any other person but myself to nurse her . . . I will put her in my own bed where I sleep, and will sit up with her when needful.' Rare even is the modern royal child who has such loving attention.[2]

Henry, too, was an unusually hands-on royal father. In the sixteenth century royal daughters – and even second sons, like Henry himself – were brought up by their mothers with little or no interference from their fathers. Instead kings concentrated largely on their eldest son and heir. They did not raise them themselves. But they did take care over the choice of those who did. They nominated their governors (the male equivalent of the Lady Mistress) and Households, and drew up elaborate regulations for their education and upbringing. The most important set of these regulations was issued by Edward IV, Mary's great-grandfather, 'as well for the virtuous guiding of the person' of his eldest son, Edward, Prince of Wales, 'as for the politic, sad [wise] and good rule of his Household'. These Ordinances served in turn as a model for the upbringing of Catherine's first husband, Arthur, and, in the fullness of time, for that of her daughter, Mary, as well.[3]

For Mary, of course, was not only Catherine's daughter; at this time she was Henry's only child and therefore his heir. And, long before she was sent off to Ludlow in the footsteps of Arthur and the Yorkist Prince Edward, her father treated her as Prince[ess] of Wales. Just as though she had been a boy, he hand-picked her governess, vetted the organization of her Household and watched anxiously over her health.[4]

The result was that Mary had a hybrid upbringing. Sometimes she was reared like a royal daughter; sometimes like a Prince of Wales. And sometimes her mother took the lead and sometimes her father. But Catherine's, it seems safe to say, was the constant guiding hand. Catherine had her reward. For, when Mary had to choose, it was to her mother, not to her father, that she gave her unshakable loyalty.

Mary was christened in the Church of the Observant Friars at Greenwich on 20 February 1516 in a magnificent ceremonial which, inevitably, had been prepared for the expected prince. The canopy over her was borne by four knights. They included Sir Thomas Parr, father of Catherine, and Sir Thomas Boleyn, father of Anne. The godparents were the King's minister, Thomas Wolsey, who had been made Cardinal in 1515, Mary's great-aunt, Catherine Plantagenet, daughter of King Edward IV and widow of the Earl of Devon, and the Duchess of Norfolk. At her confirmation, which, according to the usual royal practice, followed immediately after the christening, Margaret Pole acted as her godmother.[5]

Catherine clearly had a hand in all this. Both Parr and Boleyn had wives who were ladies-in-waiting to Catherine, while Margaret Pole was Catherine's friend from the old days at Ludlow, during her first marriage to Prince Arthur. In 1513 Henry, probably prompted by Catherine as much as by his own conscience, had restored Margaret in blood and status by creating her Countess of Salisbury. But the restoration was incomplete: she was given the lands of the earldom of Salisbury but not the far greater inheritance of the earldom of Warwick, to which she was also heiress.

After the christening and confirmation, Mary, preceded by her godparents' gifts, was carried back in triumph to the Queen's Chamber and presented to Catherine. Then the baby was handed over to the staff of the nursery. Once again, its leading members seem to have been hand-picked by Catherine. The wet-nurse, who was critical to the child's immediate survival, was Catherine Pole. Her husband, Leonard, was another member of Lady Salisbury's family. The Lady Mistress, Lady Bryan, had also been one of Catherine's ladies. Under Margaret Bryan was the usual nursery staff of four rockers, who took it in turns to rock the royal cradle, and a laundress, who was needed to wash the large amounts of linen which even the best-behaved royal babies soil. The little establishment was completed by a gentlewoman and a chaplain.

But Lady Bryan's appointment also shows that Henry took a strong interest in the arrangements for his daughter. 'When the Lady Mary was born,' Lady Bryan recollected, 'it pleased the King's Grace to appoint me Lady Mistress; and [he also] made me a Baroness.' Lady Bryan was writing many years later. But her memory is confirmed by the fact that Wolsey, Henry's *alter ego*, personally signed the letters patent which authorized the payment of her wages.[6]

For the first few years of Mary's life, Catherine kept her daughter close to her at Court. Mary's name appears in all the household lists of the period and her expenses and the wages of her servants were paid on an *ad hoc* basis by the Treasurer of the Chamber, who was the principal paymaster of the Court. In the larger palaces, she had her own 'Chamber', or set of rooms, which formed part of the Queen's much larger suite. The Princess herself had two rooms: an inner one, where she slept in her everyday cradle, and an outer one, where she received visitors in infant state in her great 'cradle of estate', with its canopy, royal arms and quilt of ermine. Lady Bryan had a room, and the laundress another where she both worked and slept. Finally, there was probably a dormitory chamber for the lesser female servants, and slightly better accommodation for Mary's chaplain.[7]

Finding room for so many was impossible in all but the largest palaces. And the problem got worse as male servants, in considerable numbers, were added to the original female nursery staff. The Princess had twenty-two menservants by 1519 and thirty-one a year later. So Mary and her Household had to move out, to an adjacent manor-house. This is what happened during the Christmas season of 1517–18. Catherine and Henry were spending the holidays at Windsor, while Mary was lodged at nearby Ditton Park. Ditton Park is only a couple of miles from Windsor. But it lies on the north bank of the Thames while Windsor Castle is on the south. Fortunately, there was a convenient river-crossing at Datchet ferry, and Mary and her servants were ferried over on two separate occasions.[8]

One such journey from Ditton to the Castle almost certainly took place on 1 January 1518. For then Mary, aged one year and eleven months, participated in her first recorded ceremony and received the customary New Year's gifts. Her godfather, Cardinal Wolsey, sent her a gold cup by one of his servants; her godmother, the Countess of Devonshire, sent a gold spoon and the Duchess of Norfolk, her other godmother, a primer, from which no doubt Mary was soon expected to learn to read. The servants who delivered the presents each got a reward or tip, strictly graduated according to the rank of their master or mistress. Tips to Henry's and Catherine's servants are not recorded, however, which must mean that Mary's father and mother gave their gifts to their baby in person – probably in the Queen's Presence Chamber in the Castle.[9]

The problems of accommodation were particularly acute during the summer. This was the time of the Progress, when the King and Queen wandered from house to house, hunting in the parks as they went. Often, the houses they stayed in were little better than hunting lodges, and Henry and Catherine could scarcely accommodate their own, much reduced, travelling Household, let alone that of Mary. The summer was also the time of the plague, when disease struck apparently at random. Henry, rightly, was terrified of infection and maintained a policy of strict quarantine. On Sunday, 18 July 1518, Pace reported to Wolsey from The More (now Moor Park near Rickmansworth, Hertfordshire) that Henry had just learned that one of the Princess's servants had fallen 'sick of a hot ague'. He had recovered but Henry decided to take precautions and Wolsey was ordered to prepare 'such gists [list of stopping places] as shall be most for the King's surety and my Lady's'.[10]

The effect was that Mary spent the rest of July following in her parents' footsteps. She was brought forthwith to Bisham Abbey, Berkshire, which the King and Queen had left on the Saturday, and she stayed there till the following Tuesday. That Tuesday was also Henry and Catherine's removing day from The More, which they vacated for Enfield. This left a few hours to clean and tidy The More, before Mary's arrival there, which was planned for the Wednesday. The arrangement, which required considerable logistical skills to organize, nicely squared the circle. It kept Mary close to the Court. It avoided the mingling of the two Households, with the risk of cross-infection. And it gave Catherine ample opportunity to see Mary whenever she chose. The Queen and Princess were never more than fifteen miles apart and often less. And Catherine was still a good horsewoman. 'The Queen', Pace reported on the 18th, 'intendeth to hunt tomorrow four miles hence in a little park of Sir John Peachy's.' Sometimes, no doubt, her quarry included her daughter.

At the end of the following year, 1519, Wolsey, acting in Henry's name, carried out a general reform of the royal government and Household. Mary's little establishment received attention as well. It was assigned a fixed income of £1,100 a year from the Treasurer of the Chamber (the same amount, incidentally, on which Catherine herself had so conspicuously failed to make-do as Princess-Dowager a decade and a half previously). And responsible head-officers were appointed. It had now become the fully-fledged, independent household appropriate to Mary's status as Princess-Inheritrix of England.[11]

More importantly, from Mary's point of view, there was also a change of Lady Mistress at about the same time. Lady Bryan was a highly competent manager of the nursery (and went on to perform this role for all Henry's other children). But, good though she was with babies, it seems to have been felt that she lacked the status and perhaps the talents to supervise the education of the rapidly developing little Princess. Her replacement was Lady Salisbury. It seems an ideal appointment. The Countess was Catherine's *confidante* and she was royal, religious and virtuous.

She was also seriously interested in learning. One of Margaret Salisbury's own sons, Reginald Pole, the future Cardinal, was the most scholarly and most pious English aristocrat of his generation. And, while she was Mary's governess, the Countess commissioned a translation of Erasmus's 'sermon', *De immensa dei misericordia* (*On the Boundless Mercy of God*). The translation, published in 1526, was dedicated to the Countess as one who bore 'great mind and deep affection toward all manner of learning, and especially toward that which either exciteth or teacheth virtue and goodness and concerneth the way of our salvation'. She was certainly in post with Mary by early 1520. But the actual date of her appointment may go back much earlier, to the beginning of 1518 when a royal messenger was sent to Birling to 'my Lady Mistress'. Birling in Kent was the house of Lord Abergavenny, who was a close friend and family connexion of Lady Salisbury's. It would have been a natural place for her to have spent Christmas before taking up her duties at Court.[12]

Lady Salisbury proved a great success. Lady Bryan's memory was effaced and Mary became devoted to her new governess, regarding her 'as her second mother'. Henry, on the other hand, was more doubtful of her influence on his daughter. Was it because Margaret Salisbury was too close to Catherine?

The results of the Countess's care were clear in 1520 when Mary carried off her first State visit. A party of French gentlemen had come to England to see the sights. These now included the King's talented daughter, who was then in residence at Richmond. The gentlemen were rowed there on the afternoon of 30 June, with the benefit of a following tide. They were received in the Presence Chamber by Mary, who was attended by her governess, Lady Salisbury, her godmother, the Duchess of Norfolk, and a galaxy of other noble ladies. Mary was on her best behaviour. She welcomed her visitors 'with most goodly countenance, proper communication, and pleasant pastime in playing at the virginals, that they greatly marvelled and rejoiced at the same, her young and tender age considered'. Her parents were delighted: her father with her musicality, her mother with her deportment and linguistic skill.[13]

But the new arrangements for Mary's Household had little immediate impact on her movements. In part, this may have been because Lady Salisbury fell under a cloud. Her daughter Ursula had married Henry, Lord Stafford, the son and heir of the mighty Duke of Buckingham. Buckingham had sought and received the King's blessing for the match. Even so, it represented a potential danger. Both the Staffords and the Poles had a royal descent and a possible claim to the throne. Now the two claims were fused. Buckingham made matters worse by his ostentatious dislike of Wolsey, his quarrels with Compton, the King's favourite, and, above all, his loose talk about the succession.[14]

Henry was nervous about this, as well he might be with only Mary as his heir. In the spring of 1521, the King and Wolsey decided to nip matters in the bud.

Catherine and Henry had spent Christmas at Greenwich. They celebrated Candlemas, as the Feast of the Purification of the Blessed Virgin was known, there as well on 2 February. Mary was with them and her offering at the altar in the Chapel Royal was made by Mountjoy, Catherine's Chamberlain. Then, in the middle of the month the King and Queen journeyed north. They travelled together to Enfield, after which they separated. Catherine, who had not quite abandoned hope of another child, continued on pilgrimage to Walsingham 'to fulfil a vow'. But Henry turned east to his recently rebuilt palace of Beaulieu or New Hall near Chelmsford. Here he spent the next month alone and worrying: about epidemic disease, about his own state of health, and about Buckingham.[15]

By the time Catherine rejoined him at Beaulieu in mid-March, the die was cast. She had many ties of friendship with the women of Buckingham's family and she had always got on well with the Duke personally. But, even if she had wished to intervene, it was too late.

Buckingham was summoned to London at the beginning of April and shadowed en route by the royal guards. On 16 April he arrived and was sent to the Tower. That same day, Henry was at Greenwich, personally interrogating the witnesses against Buckingham. He quickly decided that their evidence was sufficient and that the Duke would be found guilty. Buckingham was tried on 13 May, condemned and executed four days later; his son-in-law Abergavenny was stripped of his offices and subject to penal fines and the Poles were expelled from the Court.

The treatment of the Countess of Salisbury herself was 'under discussion', as Pace cryptically noted in Latin, 'because of her nobility and goodness'. But one thing was certain: in the circumstances, she could not remain in charge of the heir to the throne.

The quest for a replacement occupied much of the rest of the year. Henry's first thought was to turn to the Dowager Countess of Oxford. But, as expected, she refused on grounds of ill-health. Henry's second choice was the husband-and-wife appointment of Sir Philip and Lady Calthorpe: Lady Calthorpe to be Lady Mistress and her husband Mary's Chamberlain. This was first mooted in late July. But it took until October to sort out their fee (£40 a year) and the formalities of appointment.[16]

Henry had originally emphasized the urgency of the need to find a solution to Mary's care: he 'intendeth within brief time to depart hence [from Windsor] to Easthampstead, and to pass his time near hereabouts, in such places as he shall have no convenient lodging for my Lady Princess'. In fact, he remained at Windsor, with only shortish visits to Woking and Guildford, until mid-November. And Mary remained with him, staying either in the Castle itself or at Ditton Park. 'The King, Queen and Princess continue at Windsor,' Lord Darcy's Court agent informed him on 12 October. And when Henry and Catherine moved on 21 November, the Princess followed them and 'was [still] with the King at Richmond'. Not till 2 December 1521 did Mary and her parents go their separate ways. The King and Queen left to spend Christmas at Greenwich; Mary was taken from Richmond to her old abode at Ditton Park, giving alms on the way. And there she had her first Christmas in her own house, complete with a decorated boar's head and a lord of misrule. This year, too, for the first time, her father's New Year's gift, of a silver cup filled with money, was sent by a servant. But Catherine, paying a flying visit, gave hers in person.

In the course of the first six months of 1522, Mary rejoined her parents for long stays at Greenwich and Richmond. But this year, the summer Progress, which traversed East Anglia from Ipswich in the east to Walsingham in the north, was unusually extended. So, in early July, Mary bade farewell to her parents at Windsor and, escorted by Catherine's footmen, rode the short distance to Chertsey which served as the first of her summer residences. She was apart from her family for the whole of August and September. By October, the Progress was over and the separation was felt to have gone on long enough. The King and Queen had remained in East Anglia, alternating between Hertford Castle and Hatfield Palace, while Mary had moved to Richmond. She was now brought to Bedwell, a manor-house in Hertfordshire three miles east of Hatfield.[17]

The location of the house was obviously a crucial consideration. But so too was its ownership. For Bedwell was one of the principal seats of the wealthy knight, Sir William Say, father-in-law of Lord Mountjoy, Catherine's Chamberlain. It was lavishly furnished and its estates were well-stocked, especially with pigeons from its dovecotes, to which Mountjoy was partial. Once again, the Queen's footmen provided an escort for Mary's journey, which took two full days on the 17th and 18th. Mary thereafter remained at Bedwell, within easy reach of her parents, for the next two months. During this time Catherine also communicated more formally with Mary's Council by letter. And when mother and daughter went their separate ways for Christmas, Catherine provided for Mary's transport in fine style, with both a palfrey on which she could ride when she wished and a litter in which she could rest when she was tired.[18]

Mary was now approaching her seventh birthday. The sixth or seventh year was an important threshold in Tudor childhood. Before that age, boys were brought up with their sisters 'among the women', from whom they received elementary instruction in reading and writing; afterwards, they were given over to male schoolmasters and began their formal education. Girls, on the other hand, remained with their mothers to be inculcated in domestic tasks. Which direction would Mary take? Would she continue to be educated informally by her mother, who was, after all, by virtue of her own superior education, unusually well qualified as teacher? Or would she follow the masculine road of a formalized education with male teachers and a more intellectually demanding curriculum?

Catherine, as usual, considered the matter carefully. She also had one notable example to hand. Sir Thomas More had four children, three daughters and one son, who were born about a decade before Mary. In his *Utopia*, More had thought the unthinkable. In the upbringing of his children, he decided to do the unthinkable as well and give his daughters, who turned out to be brilliant, and his son, who did not, exactly the same rigorous education. All four children studied at home and had the best masters, who taught them Latin, Greek, mathematics and astronomy. Catherine knew about this experiment. It had been made famous by Erasmus's praise of More's household academy and More himself was a familiar figure at Court where he was a resident Councillor from 1518. But Catherine turned elsewhere.[19]

Predictably, her chosen adviser was a Spaniard. Juan Luis Vives was born in 1492 in Valencia. After a thoroughly traditional education in scholasticism and logic at the academy in his native city, he proceeded to further study in Paris and the Netherlands. In his late teens he underwent a sort of conversion. He passionately rejected his youthful studies as arid and destructive and embraced instead the new literary programme of Erasmus with its emphasis on clarity and personal integrity and its appeal to the heart rather than the head. He also built up a reputation as a brilliant teacher. By 1522, however, his career was in crisis. The actual business of teaching had become 'in the highest degree repulsive' and his former pupil and patron, William de Croy, Cardinal-Archbishop of Toledo, had died. Vives needed a new patron and a new job.[20]

At this point, Catherine of Aragon offered her patronage. Vives leapt at the opportunity. He would spend part of the year in England. And he would exchange the drudgery of the classroom for the well-paid role of educational consultant. It did not quite work out like that. Vives was snapped up as Wolsey's Reader in Rhetoric at Oxford. But this appointment left him with plenty of time for attendance at Court. He complained that his lodgings were mean and in the City which was a long way from the usual seat of the Court at Greenwich. But, despite his protests, he enjoyed the excitement of being at the heart of things. He also came to hold Catherine herself in respect and affection.[21]

But what did Catherine see in Vives, apart from his Spanishness? There were the things in him that everybody found attractive, such as his youth, his brilliance, his engaging personality, his freedom from the usual scholarly bile and malice. For Vives was a most unscholarly scholar. Most scholars were not gentlemen. Instead, they were low born, in priestly orders and, rather often, like Erasmus himself, 'not the marrying sort'. Vives was a world apart. He was of gentle birth, with a good pedigree, a coat-of-arms and a motto, *Siempre vivas*. He was a layman. And in 1524 he was to marry. All this appealed powerfully to Catherine: she liked gentlemen, she was conventional and she was passionately devoted to marriage.

Vives therefore was 'one of us' – unlike Erasmus. He was also, unlike More, 'a safe pair of hands'. Catherine could ask him for his advice on a programme for Mary's future education and be confident that the result would not frighten the horses – or, more importantly, her husband.

Vives did not disappoint. Catherine must have made her request early in 1523. Vives worked with his usual speed (he had written twelve books by the time he was twenty-eight) and the dedicatory letter to *De institutione feminae christianae* (*The Institution of a Christian Woman*) is dated 5 April 1523 at Bruges. 'I have been moved [to write]', Vives told Catherine, 'partly by the holiness and goodness of your living, partly by the favour and love that your Grace beareth toward holy study and learning.' But Catherine, he continues, was to be more than the inspiration of the treatise, she was herself to be the model of the educated Christian woman, whose example Mary was to follow in all things. 'Your dearest daughter Mary shall read these instructions of mine, and follow in living. Which she must needs do, if she order herself after the example she hath at home with her, of your virtue and wisdom.'

This sets the tone immediately. But another woman is an even more powerful presence: Blancha Maria, Vives's mother. Blancha also came from a good family, which had literary tastes and had produced several poets. Her love for her son was deep but undemonstrative. And his feelings for her only strengthened with the passage of time. 'Therefore,' he recalls in *De institutione*, 'there was nobody that I did more flee, or was more loath to come nigh, than my mother, when I was a child. But after I came to a man's estate, there was nobody whom I delighted more to have in sight.'

But it is Blancha's relations with her husband, Luis, not with her son, which are principally at issue. Vives remembered, 'I could never see her strive with my father'. Instead, she had two habitual sayings. 'When she would say she believed anything well, then she used to say, "It is even as though Luis Vives had spoken it." When she would say she would [wished for] anything, she used to say, "It is even as though Luis Vives would it".' The result, Vives said proudly, was that 'the concord of Vives and Blancha was taken up and used in a manner for a proverb'.

All this, Vives claims artfully, is an aside. 'It is not much to be talked in a book, made for another purpose, of my most holy mother.' But the disclaimer is itself an artifice. For the invocation of his patron Catherine, in the dedicatory epistle, and of his mother, Blancha, in the text, serve to announce the principal theme of his book: that the new education is entirely compatible with the old woman and with the old, subordinate place of women. Fathers, according to Vives, have nothing to fear from educated daughters, nor husbands from learned wives. As for women themselves, they too have everything to gain from education, as it will fit them better for their proper role, as handmaidens to man and God.

But when Vives turns from principles to practice, *De institutione* disappointingly runs out of steam. Instead of an educational programme, there are two lists, one of 'good' books and one of 'bad'. The 'bad' books are vernacular romances. Vives lists many examples in Spanish, French and Flemish but not in English since he was familiar with neither the language nor the literature. Romances were the Mills and Boon of the day and their content was recognizably the same. It consisted of bold knights, handsome heroes, wicked villains, distressed damsels, unrequited love and nights of passion – sometimes occurring outside marriage, sometimes before it, but rarely, alas, after the knot was tied. Such works, according to Vives, were '*libri pestiferi*' (noxious books): they inculcated false values and incited women's imaginations, which in any case were more fevered than men's, to lust. He wanted them banned, for Mary and for all other women.

Vives's list of 'good' books, which he would substitute for the bad, is much less sensational. It fell into three groups. The first consisted of much of the Good Book itself, including part of the Old Testament, together with the Gospels, the Acts of the Apostles, and the Epistles. Then there were the three Fathers of the Church, Saints Cyprian, Jerome and Augustine. Finally, Mary was to read something of the best moral philosophers of the Classical World, such as Boethius, Plato, Cicero and Seneca, as her teacher would select.

Vives also disapproved of cards and dice and fine clothes, which Mary came to enjoy, and dancing, at which she already excelled.

Catherine was enthusiastic about the general arguments of *De institutione*. But she wanted more and more detail. Her opportunity came six months later, after Vives had taken up his post at Oxford. From 22 September 1523 Catherine and Henry were at Woodstock Palace, five miles from Oxford. They had bade farewell to Mary at Richmond on 13 August and then travelled west by easy stages. The main purpose of their visit to Woodstock was to hunt the magnificent park. But they interrupted their sport to hear Vives deliver one of his lectures. Probably Catherine repeated her request in person. With his usual efficiency, Vives dashed off a more detailed programme of study for her daughter, *De ratione studii puerilis*, which he prefaced with a letter, dated at Oxford on 7 October, dedicating the work to Mary herself.

So the *De ratione* was a practical work, intended for actual classroom use. It shows. Vives gave rules for the pronunciation of Latin and Greek (for Mary, like other Tudor children, was expected to have a spoken as well as a written knowledge of the ancient tongues). He advised that something should be learned by heart (*memoriter*) every day, and read over two or three times before bedtime to impress it permanently in the memory. He recommended a Latin and English dictionary and discussed the latest available grammars (the one, for instance, prepared for Mary by the late Thomas Linacre was sophisticated in intent but rather slapdash in execution with misprints and errors in the examples). He refined his earlier list of recommended reading and leavened the diet with some poetry. Since Mary would be Queen, he added some political science, including Plato and Thomas More's *Utopia*. And, since she would be Defender of the Faith, she was to read the New Testament night and morning. She was also to learn by heart the main examples of ancient proverbial wisdom, which had been conveniently collected together by Erasmus in a single little volume.

Finally, Vives remembered that all work and no play makes a dull girl. 'Let her be given pleasure in stories which teach the art of life. Let these be such as she can tell to others.' There follows a list of improving stories – of Joseph in the Bible, of Lucretia in Livy, or (a rare concession) of patient Griselda in popular fiction. In thus prescribing Mary's leisure-reading as well as her schoolwork, Vives had the same intention as the authors of politically-correct fairy-stories today: to harness a child's perennial interest in story-telling to the fabrication of a new culture. But Vives, like Erasmus, quickly realized that the number of suitable ready-made stories was inadequate. So he turned his own considerable gifts as a narrator to the telling of new ones. The result was a compendium, *Satellitium vel Symbola*, of stories designed to amuse and edify Mary. It was published in 1527, and it included an account of a conversation that Vives had with her mother in the Queen's barge.

There was clearly a good deal of direct contact between Vives and Catherine and between Vives and Mary too. But Vives was never Mary's teacher: he gave only advice to the mother, not lessons to the daughter. Catherine had appointed a teacher, whom Vives knew and respected. And he is careful to explain their relative input. 'Since thou', he tells Catherine, 'hast chosen as her teacher a man above all learned and honest, as was fit, I was contented to point out details, as with a finger. He will explain the rest of the matters.' Unfortunately Vives never mentions the teacher's name. Nor does any other source. Equally, it is clear that the teacher, whoever he was, enjoyed only delegated authority. For Catherine remained in control. She might have consulted the leading authorities, commissioned reports and appointed expert staff. But it made no real difference: in infancy, she had nursed Mary through her childish ailments; now she corrected her Latin exercises, kept her up to scratch with her handwriting and assessed her progress. 'Time will admonish her as to more exact details,' Vives advised Catherine, 'and thy singular wisdom will discover for her what they should be.' This sort of parental interest places a child under immense pressure. Fortunately, Mary had the talent to respond. Aged twelve, she was able to make a translation of a prayer by St Thomas Aquinas, that, like all the best prayers, is both stately and euphonious; in her twenties, and responding to the encouragement of another Queen Catherine, she was author of a published translation of one of Erasmus's Biblical paraphrases. The achievement is considerable; the credit is largely Catherine of Aragon's.[22]

31. Marrying Mary

On 5 October 1518 Catherine had stood next to her husband in her Great Chamber at Greenwich. This was the first and largest room of her suite and it had been 'very sumptuous[ly]' decorated for the occasion. In front of Catherine was her daughter Mary, 'dressed in cloth of gold, with a cap of black velvet on her head, adorned with many jewels'. Mary was two and a half years old and it was her wedding day.

First, Cuthbert Tunstall, the most brilliant English scholar of his day and Master of the Rolls, gave an oration *de laudibus matrimonii* (in praise of marriage). The address lasted some time and Mary (probably tired and bored by all the talk) was 'taken in arms' by her Lady Mistress. Then the representative of the bridegroom, who was a year younger than Mary, stepped forward. Hands were held and oaths exchanged. Finally, Cardinal Wolsey, Mary's godfather, put the ring on the fourth finger of her right hand, and the proxy-groom passed it over the second joint. Mary was now a married woman. She was, however, probably more interested in the ring, which, though made small to fit her tiny finger, was set with a large diamond 'supposed to have been a present from the Cardinal'. Wolsey always had an eye for the perfect gift.

The ages of the bride and groom, which seem so outlandish to us, presented no difficulty to Catherine. She was a dynast herself and had been pledged at the age of three to Arthur when he was aged two. Instead, her sticking-point was the nationality of the bridegroom. For he was the Dauphin Francis, the heir to the French throne. Mary's marriage was the seal on a new Anglo-French alliance. This revolted Catherine's deepest instincts. She was Spanish herself and consistent in her desire for England to stick to the old certainties and remain the friend of Spain and the enemy of France. Now she was required to welcome a French prince as her son-in-law. Unfortunately, neither her husband's minister, Wolsey, nor, increasingly, her husband himself, any longer shared her commitment to old certainties.[1]

For times had changed yet again. In particular, the coming of age of Catherine's nephew, Charles, the son of her sister, Juana, who is known to history as the Emperor Charles V, reignited the struggle for dominance in Europe between France and Spain.

At first Charles seemed the underdog. Only eighteen and inexperienced, he was lantern-jawed, slow of speech and, so many thought, slow of wit as well. He was of course heir to vast territories: Burgundy and the Netherlands from his father, the Archduke Philip, Spain from his grandfather, Ferdinand, and, from his other grandfather, Maximilian, who was to die in 1519, huge swathes of Germany. But he had yet to make good his claim to many of these lands. Characteristically opportunist, his rival, the brilliant and mercurial Francis I of France, decided to strike first, before Charles had consolidated his hold on his inheritance. Francis scored some easy victories. But Charles quickly gave the lie to those who had underestimated him.

Henry and Wolsey also saw their opportunity. In terms of size, population and wealth, England came a poor third after France and the territories of Charles V. But, not for the last time, England was able to punch above its weight. For Francis and Charles were evenly-balanced opponents. The support of England, Wolsey and Henry reckoned, could make all the difference to the outcome of their struggle. *Cui adhereo praeest* (Whom I back wins) became their motto and they resolved to sell England's support to the highest bidder. The visible prize in the auction would be the hand of Catherine's daughter, Mary.

Francis, eager for England's support against Charles, or at least its neutrality, made the first bid. Henry and Wolsey were receptive and agreement was quickly reached. It consisted of three elements: the marriage of Mary and the Dauphin; a settlement of outstanding Anglo-French differences, which was wrapped up in a grandiose Treaty of Universal Peace (a sort of pan-European security pact); and a still-more grandiose summit conference, to be held as soon as possible, to 'nurture love' between Henry and Francis.

It was another woman, Louise of Savoy, the mother of Francis I, who best understood Catherine's feelings about the settlement and her consequent conflict of loyalties. Not that she sympathized. Instead, Louise's awareness was a product of anxiety. She knew that the Anglo-French alliance was a recent plant of sickly growth and she feared that Catherine would use her influence to uproot it entirely.

Catherine was not short of opportunities. The first hitch arose over the proposed summit conference between Henry and Francis. This was postponed several times – so often, in fact, that the French started to doubt whether it would happen at all. To try to clear the air, the two kings swore an oath, promising, as was then fashionable, not to shave until they met.

On 9 November 1519, the French ambassador to England arrived in France with terrible news: King Henry of England had cut off his beard!

Louise summoned the English ambassador, Sir Thomas Boleyn. Boleyn immediately pointed the finger at Catherine, saying, 'as I supposed, it hath been by the Queen's desire'. But Catherine's motives, Boleyn insisted, were entirely innocent: she simply hated beards. 'I have here aforetime,' he told Louise, 'known when the King's Grace hath worn long his beard, that the Queen hath daily made great instance, and desired him to put it off for her sake.' Louise remained suspicious, asking 'if [the] Queen's Grace was not aunt to the King of Spain (Charles V)'. Boleyn replied that Charles was indeed her sister Juana's son. But, he assured Louise, it was Henry's feelings that mattered, and he 'had greater affection for [Francis] than any King living'. Mollified, Louise ended the exchange by exclaiming that 'Their love is not in the beards but in the hearts!'[2]

But the delays continued and Louise's doubts revived. She put them point-blank to Boleyn's successor as ambassador, Sir Richard Wingfield. 'She demanded me of the Queen's Grace, and whether I thought her to have any great devotion to this assembly.' Wingfield prefaced his reply by describing Catherine's attitude to the proper submission of women in marriage:

> There could not be a more virtuous or wise princess anywhere than the Queen my mistress was, having none other joy or comfort in this world but to do and follow all that she may think to stand with the King's pleasure; and considered by her as well it pleased him to be entirely affectionate to the said assembly, as also the alliance and marriage to be passed and concluded between the Princess and the Dauphin, he thought none could be more desirous [for the meeting] than she.

In other words, for Catherine of Aragon read Blancha Maria: 'It is even as though Luis Vives would it.'[3]

*

However, the Imperial ambassadors in London, writing only three days later than Wingfield, picked up a different story: Catherine 'had made such representations, and shown such reasons against the voyage [to meet Francis], as one would not have supposed she would have dared to, or even to imagine', they reported. Henry rarely responded well to confrontation. But on this occasion he took it in good part. 'She is held', the ambassadors concluded, 'in greater esteem by the King and his Council than ever she was.'[4]

Actually, the various reports are not as contradictory as they seem. For Henry and Wolsey had already decided to hedge their bets by reopening negotiations with Charles V.

Suddenly, Catherine's family connexions ceased to be unmentionable and became an asset once more. And suddenly, Catherine stepped back into the inner circle of power from which she had been excluded since Wolsey's rise. Or, at least, she appeared to. When, on Sunday, 18 March, the Imperial ambassadors arrived at the Court at Greenwich they found Henry, Catherine and Wolsey deep in conversation. Henry broke off to inform them that he had decided to meet Charles V before his encounter with Francis I. He was therefore writing to the French King to ask him to postpone their meeting for a few days – though of course without telling him the real reason. Catherine uttered a heartfelt plea. 'Raising her eyes to heaven, with clasped hands [she] gave praise to God for the grace she hoped he would do her that she might see Charles.' To see her nephew 'was her greatest desire in the world'. Then she thanked Henry, and curtsied to him deeply. Henry, ever the gentleman, doffed his hat to his wife. It was just like old times.[5]

Catherine had her wish and met her nephew, when she and Henry were en route to France. Charles landed at Dover where Wolsey and Henry met him. They overnighted and then, early on the morning of Whitsunday, 27 May, rode to Canterbury. There, on the landing of the grand staircase in the archbishop's palace, was Catherine, magnificent in cloth of gold and pearls. 'She embraced her nephew tenderly, not without tears,' and Henry, Catherine and Charles proceeded to a family breakfast. On Whitmonday, there was a splendid banquet. In compliment to Charles as King of Spain, all the entertainment was in the Spanish fashion – in dress, music and dancing. Catherine was in her element. The following day, Henry and Charles first slept off their hang-overs and then devoted themselves to business. Charles took his leave late that night and, with long wax torches to light the way, was escorted to Sandwich. Thence, on Wednesday the 30th, he sailed to Flanders.[6]

Meanwhile, Henry and Catherine continued to Dover and then Calais for the much postponed meeting with Francis I. It took place in a sort of no-man's-land between Calais and the French town of Ardres. This is a flat and dusty part of France. But in 1520 an army of English and French craftsmen, working in competition with each other and against the clock, transformed it into fairyland. Even the tents were made of cloth of gold. But it was an outdoor summer event in northern Europe and no one could control the weather. There were violent winds, which blew down the tents and whipped up blinding storms of dust, and torrential rains, which turned the dust into a sea of mud. Bishop Fisher, who was there in Catherine's train, saw the bad weather as a sign of God's anger at the pointless pomp and circumstance. But the event survived the setbacks and caught the imagination. It still does. It was The Field of Cloth of Gold.

Thanks to the earlier meeting with Charles V at Canterbury, Catherine had gone to The Field of Cloth of Gold in better spirits than she had dared hope. She played her part, wore magnificent clothes and hung a fortune in jewels on her person. She was even agreeable to Francis I, though he had called her old and deformed. She could afford to be polite because she knew that it was all a sham – from the blood-brotherhood of the two Kings in the tournament to the concluding ceremony on 23 June when they took communion together at Wolsey's hands and renewed their oaths of eternal friendship.[7]

A fortnight later, Catherine and Henry met Charles once more, first as his guests at Gravelines, and then as his hosts at Calais. For Catherine at least it was a much more agreeable four days.[8]

What had happened, of course, was that Charles had made a counter-bid for English support. And it was a much higher one, since Charles V needed England in a way that Francis I did not.

For the succession to Charles's vast inheritance had reached a moment of crisis. All had gone smoothly in the Netherlands, where he had been born and brought up. He had also, having outbribed his rival, Francis I, been elected King of the Romans (Holy Roman Emperor-elect) in succession to his paternal grandfather Maximilian. But Spain, Catherine's native land and the jewel in the crown of her nephew's inheritance, looked as though it might slip through his fingers.

On 20 May 1520 he had set sail from Corunna for his meeting with Catherine and Henry in England. Even as his Court was embarking, widespread disorders had already broken out. They turned into a great revolt, known as the *Comuneros*. The rebels were protesting at Charles, his foreign advisers and his demands for heavy taxation to pay off the debts he had incurred in winning the Imperial election. The *Comuneros* won sweeping victories and set up a *junta* (a revolutionary government). The unpopular foreign Regent, Cardinal Adrian of Utrecht, who was Charles's former tutor, was driven out of Valladolid and royal authority, painstakingly established by Catherine's parents, looked as though it might collapse entirely.

For the moment there was nothing Charles could do about Spain since he was needed elsewhere in his dominions. He had to be crowned King of the Romans at Aachen and to settle accounts with Francis I. But then he would have to return to Spain – or lose it. The expedition would need money and ships. He had neither. But England had both ships and money. And Charles knew he would have to pay – or promise – dearly for them.

But Henry and Wolsey were in no hurry to close the deal. After all, Francis I, smarting from his defeat in the Imperial election, might yet bid higher still. The result was an extraordinary diplomatic dance between England, France and the Empire. England, in the person of Cardinal Wolsey, played the part of a coy maiden, turning now to Francis as her partner and now to Charles. The farce reached its conclusion at the conference at Calais in 1521. In theory, Wolsey sat as mediator, to adjudicate the differences of Francis and Charles. In reality, Henry had already decided to throw over France and ally with Charles.

To secure the English alliance Charles was prepared to promise anything. He promised to marry Mary with a dowry heavily discounted by the repayment of his and his grandfather Maximilian's debts to England. He half promised to procure Wolsey's election as Pope. He promised to help make Henry king of the rump of France, after he had settled his own claims against French territories. He even promised to make good the pensions that Henry and Wolsey would forgo by declaring war on France. If the English had asked for the moon, Charles would have promised that as well. And he would have found it scarcely more difficult to deliver than the rest.[9]

But such realities were for the future. For the present, Catherine was delighted at the new direction of policy. She now had the prospective son-in-law of her dreams. And things were different for Mary as well. At her proxy marriage to the Dauphin in 1518, she had been an infant, oblivious to the real meaning of the event. Now she was six years old, precocious and perhaps a little spoilt, and in love with the idea of being in love. Encouraged by Catherine, she had chosen Charles as her Valentine and wore a golden jewel at her breast, with the name 'CHARLES' picked out in jewels. She also had another, even larger, brooch with letters spelling out the title of her husband: 'THE EMPEROUR'. She wore the brooch when she sat for a portrait miniature, which, almost certainly, was intended as a lover's gift to Charles. If Mary, who had never seen Charles, was in this state already, what would it be like when they met face to face?[10]

A meeting in fact was due in the following spring. As part of the Calais settlement, it had been agreed that Charles would come to England on his way back to Spain, to pick up ships and reinforcements. Charles was all for making it a severely practical event and spending the money thus saved on the war. 'We prefer', he protested, 'to visit Henry like a son coming to his father's house . . . and hope that too great pomp and ceremony will not impede the friendly familiarity which we hope will continue, not only throughout our life, but throughout that of our successors.' There is an echo here of his grandmother Isabella, expressing her anxieties about the lavish reception planned for Catherine on her arrival in England, twenty years previously, in 1502. But Charles protested in vain. Henry and Wolsey, like Henry VII before them, wanted a triumph: it was not every day that they had an emperor to parade through London.[11]

Catherine also pressed her more sincere hospitality on her nephew. 'Her greatest desire', she told the Emperor's ambassador, 'was to see you here and to receive you with the greatest honour and best cheer possible.' But Catherine had not finished with the ambassador. Before he took leave, she said firmly, he must first see the Princess dance. Mary 'did not have to be asked twice' and performed without a trace of childish shyness or false modesty. First she danced a slow dance and a galliard 'and twirled so prettily that no woman in the world could do better'. Then she shifted to the keyboard and 'played two or three songs on the spinet'. The ambassador was impressed, as was the intention. 'Indeed, sire,' he reported to Charles, 'she showed unbelievable grace and skill and such self-command as a woman of twenty might envy. She is pretty, and very tall for her age . . . and a very fine young cousin indeed.'[12]

The ambassador's words were exactly what Catherine had wanted him to write. But did she stop to consider the risks for her daughter in encouraging these performances? Mary was wearing Charles's name, dancing for Charles, living and breathing Charles. Such romantic fantasies were hard enough to sustain even in aristocratic marriages. But Charles was royal. And, though he was Catherine's nephew, his projected marriage with her daughter was a dynastic one. It had been made for reasons of power politics; if the circumstances changed, it could equally be broken for dynastic reasons. Where would that leave Mary, now that Catherine had taught her love along with Latin?

Charles arrived at Dover as planned on 26 May. After inspecting the fleet, the two monarchs made their way to Greenwich. There Charles found Catherine and Mary waiting for him at the Hall door. Charles knelt and 'asked the Queen's blessing' and had 'great joy to see the Queen his Aunt and in especial his young cousin germain the Lady Mary'. Catherine and Mary in turn received him 'with much love'. Three days were spent in 'banquets ... pageants, jousts and tournaments'. Henry showed off his skills in the lists; and Mary, no doubt, performed in person for Charles on the dance floor and the spinet. Charles and Henry then made a joint *entrée* into London, each with a naked sword born upright before them.[13]

Then the two monarchs moved to Windsor, to perform the ceremonies of the Garter and get down to serious negotiation. Here Catherine joined them, and brought Mary too. The representative of Charles's brother, the Archduke Ferdinand, caught sight of her and, blinded by the charms of neither mother nor daughter, delivered a cool assessment. 'She promises to become a handsome lady,' he reported of Mary, 'although it is difficult to form an idea of her beauty as she is still so small.' And that of course was a problem: there was a sixteen-year age-gap between Charles and Mary. Was it feasible for him to wait so long? Was it even desirable?[14]

From Windsor, Charles went to Southampton, where he embarked for Spain. Henry accompanied him to the coast but Catherine and Mary took their leave of him at Windsor. Charles had become a familiar figure in Catherine's life. She had met him three times within the space of two years. She had also renewed her personal friendship with her former sister-in-law, the Archduchess Margaret. Margaret had continued to act as Regent of the Netherlands for the frequently-absent Charles, and had accompanied him to the post-Field of Cloth of Gold summit conference. It seemed, in short, that Catherine's family was reconstituting itself in her own generation. And, thanks to the forthcoming marriage between Mary and Charles, there was hope that it would continue into the next.

With Charles, her favourite nephew and prospective son-in-law, Catherine had been all smiles. But his brother Ferdinand's ambassador had to deal with a harder, less familiar Catherine. Charles had left Ferdinand as his Regent in Germany and Austria. There he had to confront the growing menace of the Turkish or Ottoman Empire, then at the height of its power. He had sent his ambassador to Windsor to remind Henry and Charles that Christian Europe's south-eastern frontier was about to collapse. He got short shrift, even from Catherine, and even after he had played the family card. The ambassador 'told her that [Ferdinand] regarded her as his true mother, and asked her not to forsake him, but to see that the King of England should send him succour against the Turks'. Catherine replied briskly that 'it will be impossible'. Could anything be done next year, he persisted. She would write her answer, she said. The ambassador then asked Charles to make an approach. And, on this topic, Charles 'had not found her at all gracious'. The ambassador tried again himself. Catherine said she was too much occupied to write.

Catherine was of course right. Her husband and her nephew had their hands full with France, and France, as Wolsey remarked with his characteristic verve, 'was the real Turk'. 'I know no other Turk,' he added.[15]

Over the next few years, Catherine had need for her cool political realism, as the new alliance with Spain under her nephew proved almost as problematic as the old, under her father, the slippery Ferdinand.

The English fleet, under Lord Admiral Surrey, escorted Charles part-way to Spain. But, as it cleared the Channel, it broke away and turned to launch a lightning amphibious attack on Brittany in which Morlaix was taken and sacked. Admiral Surrey, as ruthlessly effective on land as on sea, was then launched on France from the east. He left Calais in late August, with two companies of Burgundians among his troops. They marched south, burning and looting the lightly-defended towns and villages as they went. Not till they reached Hesdin, which lies mid-way between Agincourt and Crécy, did they encounter serious resistance. Surrey wanted to launch an assault on the castle; his Burgundian co-commanders demurred. The expedition turned back, acrimoniously.[16]

It was not the best of starts to Anglo-Spanish co-operation. And a much greater challenge lay ahead. This was the project, to which Henry and Charles had committed themselves, to conquer and dismember

France. Known as the 'Great Enterprise', it needed commensurate preparations. With his usual energy and efficiency, Wolsey took matters in hand and in 1522 he carried out the 'Great Proscription'. This was a new Doomsday survey of the nation's population and wealth and it enabled both troop-recruitment and taxation to be put on an up-to-date, accurate footing. But, however effectively England directed its resources, it could not conquer France alone. Nor, under the terms of the treaties, was it expected to. Where, Wolsey and Henry wanted to know, were Charles's troops? The answer, as under Ferdinand, was in the south. Once more, England seemed to be invading France only to provide cover for Spain's aggrandisement in the Pyrenees or in Italy. Once more, the divergent interests of Spain and England bred distrust between the allies. And once more, Catherine found herself caught in the middle.

But this time she was older, wiser and spoke more bluntly. 'She told us vehemently', Charles's ambassadors reported in January 1523, 'that the only way for you to retain the friendship of this King and of the English was to fulfil faithfully everything you have promised.' But that, Catherine knew, was easier said than done. Charles had promised the moon: how could he deliver? 'It was much better', she continued, 'to promise little and perform faithfully than to promise much and fail in part.' Catherine had put her finger on the essential problem in Anglo-Spanish relations. But not even she could suggest a solution.[17]

Finally, despite constant bickering, the threatened invasion of France was launched in autumn 1523. This was late in the season for so great an undertaking. But the decision to invade had been triggered by the revolt against Francis I of the Constable de Bourbon. He was the premier peer of France and had done what Buckingham had only dreamed of. The enemies of Francis I had great hopes of him. Bourbon himself was to advance through Provence in the south-east; Charles to attack from the south-west into Guyenne; while the English were to march on Paris from Calais.[18]

The English commander was Henry's brother-in-law, Charles Brandon, Duke of Suffolk, who had married Henry's sister Mary after the death of Louis XII. Suffolk's reputation (except on the jousting field and in bed) does not stand high. But in 1523 he faced the French alone. He got the English within eighty miles of Paris, then had to turn back. Part of the problem was the weather, which turned viciously cold. But he had also been hamstrung by the failure of Archduchess Margaret to supply the promised transport, victuals and reinforcements. Bourbon's attack had fizzled out in Provence; while in the south-east Charles had not even crossed the frontier. Instead, like Ferdinand a decade earlier, Charles saw his main interests as lying in the Pyrenees and contented himself with recapturing Fuenterrabia.[19]

After this debacle, relations between Henry and Charles threatened to break down entirely. Catherine was powerless to act: she could only inform, encourage and, above all, warn Charles. As early as January 1524, her warnings became insistent. Henry had been complaining loudly of Charles's failure to meet his financial, let alone his military, obligations. He had not received a penny of the promised indemnity for the French pension; nothing had been paid of the loan of £30,000 which he had made to Charles to speed his return to Spain. 'Matters have gone so far', Charles's ambassador reported, 'that the Queen sent her Confessor to me in secret to warn me of Henry's discontents.'

At the same time, Catherine renewed her lament that Charles had over-extended himself. 'She is very sorry', the report continued, 'that your Majesty ever promised so much in this treaty, and she fears it may one day be the cause of a weakening of the friendship between you two.' But, above all, the ambassador begged, 'keep this communication of the Queen's secret; it would be regrettable if it came to the ears of certain English'. By which he meant, I suspect, Cardinal Wolsey. By November, the tensions between Wolsey and Catherine were out in the open. The Archduchess Margaret's ambassador explained that he would have communicated more frequently with Catherine, 'but I have been warned by some of her friends that it would not be discreet'. And when he had spoken to her, 'I have often noticed that the Cardinal was very restless . . . and often interrupted our conversation.'[20]

*

Henry's disillusionment with Charles meant that no English army left for France in 1524. With no threats to detain him at home, Francis I led a great expedition to Italy in person and at first seemed to carry all before him. But Charles's troops, led by Bourbon, put up unexpectedly strong resistance. Sir Thomas More was with Henry at Hertford when the news was brought and he reported the King's reaction. Whatever Henry's doubts about Charles, he was delighted at Francis's discomfiture. Catherine rejoiced too, with a simple, partisan patriotism. '[She] said that she was glad that the Spaniards had done it somewhat in Italy in recompense of their departure out of Provence'. Wolsey presciently guessed that Francis might have bitten off more than he could chew with his Italian expedition and Henry concurred, 'think[ing] it will be very hard for him to get thence'. He laughed with pleasure at the thought. But he did not lift a finger to help Charles.

Wolsey's guess proved correct and on 24 February 1525 Charles's troops defeated and captured Francis at the battle of Pavia. Even the plumes of Francis's helmet were plucked off as he lay pinned to the ground under his horse. It was Charles's twenty-fifth birthday. He was now true Emperor of the West. And he no longer needed England.[21]

At first, Henry did not realize how the balance had changed. On 31 March he wrote a letter of congratulation to Charles, in his own hand and in French. He would have sent Wolsey in person, he said, if his health had been good enough to stand the journey. Instead he sent an Embassy. Its purpose was to propose the formal partition of France. Since God had punished Francis 'for his high orgule, pride and insatiable ambition' with his defeat and capture, it was Henry's and Charles's divinely ordained duty together to complete the task and strip him of his kingdom. And so forth.[22]

Catherine avoided such bombast in her letter. It was written on 30 March, the day before Henry's, and it told Charles of 'the great pleasure and content I have experienced at hearing of the very signal victory which God Almighty . . . has been pleased to grant to the Imperial arms in Italy'. In thanks, she told him, Henry had ordered prayers and solemn

CATHERINE OF ARAGON 193

processions; she was sure Charles was doing the same. It was the tone of her own letters about Flodden.[23]

But Catherine's letter also showed a sharper understanding of political realities than her husband's. She had heard nothing from Charles for a long time. Diplomatically, she attributed Charles's silence to the 'inconstancy and fickleness of the sea'. But she suspected that the real reason was his displeasure with her husband's performance as an ally. So in the rest of her letter Catherine mounted a loyal defence of his performance. Henry, she insisted, 'has never failed to be the constant and faithful ally of your Highness'. Therefore, she begged, 'I humbly beseech your Highness to persevere in the path of friendship and affection towards us'. On her own behalf Catherine pleaded the 'love and consanguinity' which should unite aunt and nephew.

Charles brushed it all aside. Henry had been captious and demanding. Now he would pay him in his own coin. He affected to take Henry at his word and proposed an immediate joint invasion of France. But there were conditions. Mary must be handed over immediately. Her dowry must be paid in full. And an additional loan, equivalent in size to the dowry, must also be granted. It was an ultimatum that was intended to be refused. And Henry and Wolsey duly rejected it. The Anglo-Spanish alliance was over. Henry's dreams of conquest in France were at an end. And Mary, infatuated Mary, would have to be found another husband.[24]

As for Catherine, her desolation was complete. Not only had her daughter lost her husband, she (she feared) had lost her nephew. Charles did not bother to reply to her letter of congratulations. Indeed, he did not write at all. By November, it was 'upwards of two years' since she had had letters from Spain. Finally, she had to admit the truth to herself. Charles was angry with her and had forgotten her. But she protested hotly at the injustice of his behaviour. 'And yet I am sure I deserve not this treatment, for such are my affection and readiness for your Highness's service that I deserved a better reward.' She protested in vain. It would take another, larger revolution in her affairs to make Charles notice her again.[25]

For Catherine was about to lose her husband.

PART TWO

Rival Queens

Divorcing Catherine
Anne Boleyn
Jane Seymour

Divorcing Catherine

32. The preliminaries

As long ago as 1514 there had been an unsubstantiated rumour doing the rounds in Rome that 'the King of England meant to repudiate his present wife ... because he is unable to have children by her'. The Duke of Buckingham, speaking about the same time, expressed similar doubts. 'God', he said, 'would not suffer the King's Grace's issue to prosper, as it appeareth by the death of his son, and that his daughters prosper not, and that the King's Grace has no issue male.' Buckingham, who had discussed the matter with his personal soothsayer, the Carthusian monk, Dan Nicholas Hopkins, was confident he knew the explanation. 'The Duke [was] discontented ... that the Earl of Warwick was put to death and said that God would punish it, and that he had punished it in that he would not suffer the King's Grace's issue to prosper.'[1]

Catherine, who, we know, was deeply troubled by the execution of Warwick to clear the way for her own marriage to Arthur, may even have shared such doubts herself for a time. But Mary's birth, and Catherine's joy in her child, put an end to them. 'She was', she said under the seal of the confessional, '*and had been for many years* ... unconscious of guilt in connexion with her marriage.'[2]

But if Catherine had moved from doubt to certainty about her marriage, Henry followed the opposite path. In 1516, he had still been breezily confident that he would have a son; by about 1520, he knew that he would not; by 1525, he was pondering the consequences of his 'childlessness' (as, despite the birth of Mary, he persisted in seeing it); and by 1527, he had decided on the explanation. He had also, though

Catherine was one of the last to realize it, fallen in love with another woman.

Catherine was slow to grasp the changes in her husband's thinking. This was hardly surprising since they no longer confided much in each other and their lives had gone in different directions. She was absorbed in religion, in good works and increasingly in her daughter's upbringing; he busied himself fitfully with the business of government and whiled away endless hours of leisure. He also kept his anxieties to himself, brooding on them until his doubts hardened into conviction. He discussed them with his confessor, Bishop Longland of Lincoln; then, much later, with his minister, Cardinal Wolsey. But he never confided in his wife.

It therefore came as a brutal shock to Catherine when, in the summer of 1525, she heard that Henry's young bastard, Henry Fitzroy, was to be recognized as the King's son and showered with titles and honours. The boy was installed as Knight of the Garter, created Earl of Nottingham and Duke of Richmond and Somerset (all of them royal titles), and appointed Lord Admiral and Warden-General of the Marches against Scotland. At the same time, his education was put on a formal footing; he was given a great Household, with head officers and a Council, and sent off to Sheriff Hutton Castle in Yorkshire to be nominal head of a regional government for the north. Such a concentration of peerages and great offices had never before been held by a subject, let alone a six-year-old. It could mean one thing only: Henry VIII had decided that gender was more important than legitimacy. Catherine feared that he would recognize Richmond as his heir, and would exclude Mary from her rightful inheritance.[3]

Henry, characteristically, never went quite so far.

But Catherine was not appeased. Contrary to her usual policy of wifely submission, she let her indignation become public knowledge. 'It seems', reported the Venetian envoy, Lorenzo Orio, in a private letter, 'that the Queen resents the earldom and dukedom conferred on the King's natural son and remains dissatisfied.' According to Orio, Catherine's displeasure had been 'instigated' by three of her Spanish ladies, whom Henry in turn 'had dismissed . . . [from] the Court'.[4]

Actually, it seems unlikely that Catherine's indignation would have needed 'instigating' by anybody. Rather, we should see her talking over her feelings with a sympathetic audience. For her Spanish ladies, like Catherine herself, were familiar with a world where female succession was taken for granted. Catherine's mother, Isabella, and her eldest surviving sister, Juana, had inherited the crown of Castile, in turn. And Catherine saw no reason why her daughter, Mary, should not one day inherit England.

But Henry saw things otherwise. He was familiar with English history, which (we have Erasmus's word for it) had formed a major part of his education. Here the position of women was very different. In England there was no formal exclusion of female succession, as in France; and, again unlike France, women could transmit a claim to the throne to a male descendant. But no woman had actually sat on the English throne. Back in the twelfth century, the Empress Matilda, daughter of Henry I, had tried. But her attempt to enforce her rights had led to civil war. And civil war was a sensitive topic for Henry VIII. In 1497, aged six, he had taken refuge in the Tower with his mother, Elizabeth of York, while the Cornish rebels fought with his father at Blackheath in the name of the Pretender, Perkin Warbeck. If the rebels had won, his father would have been slaughtered on the battlefield, like Richard III, and Henry himself would have shared the fate of the Princes in the Tower. He had never, I think, forgotten that moment and he was determined that it would never recur. That was why Buckingham had gone to the scaffold. And that was why Henry became so reluctant fully to accept Mary as his heir. If Matilda, married to the Emperor Henry V, had failed to make her claim good, why should Mary be any different – especially when the Emperor Charles V had just rejected her as his bride?[5]

But the succession of a bastard, like Richmond, was at least as problematical as the succession of a woman, like Mary. Moreover, Henry was just as proud of his daughter as was Catherine, and he was almost as demonstrative. He was not going to disinherit his child lightly.

Nor would Catherine let him, if she could help it. According to Orio, 'the Queen was obliged to submit and have patience' after Henry had slapped down her objections to Richmond's extravagant advancement and had dismissed her Spanish ladies. My guess is slightly different: I think she simply changed tactics. Instead of confronting Henry, which was rarely successful, she reverted to her usual methods and set herself to persuade him. It seems to have worked.[6]

The result was an explicit recognition of Mary's status as heiress to the throne.

On 26 July 1525, as Richmond began his journey north from Stoke Newington, Wolsey was putting the finishing touches to yet another reorganization of Mary's Household. This time it was turned into an entourage fit for a Princess. She was given a Steward and Chamberlain, both of whom were barons; a Lady Mistress, who was, once again, the Countess of Salisbury; and a Lord President of the Council, who was a bishop. Under them were about three hundred other officers and servants, including Mr Featherstone, her schoolmaster, two officers of arms, Chester Herald and Wallingford Pursuivant, and two gunners to man Mary's personal ordnance and artillery. The superior officers were attired in black velvet, while the rest wore Mary's livery of green and blue – in silk damask for the middle ranks and in cloth for the lower. The cost, in wages, food and other provisions, was a staggering £5,000 a year.[7]

It was a Court in miniature. And, as Mary also had a Council under the Lord President, it was a government in miniature too.

In August, Henry signed a set of orders transferring the day-to-day government of Wales and the Marches to his daughter and her advisers. The Princess was about to enter into her Principality. The long absence of a resident 'Prince', the preamble began, had led to disorder and maladministration of justice. Therefore the King had decided 'to send at this time our dearest, best beloved and only daughter, the Princess, accompanied and established with an honourable . . . Council, to reside and remain in the Marches of Wales'.

Catherine could hardly have asked for more. The head officers of Richmond's Household were knights and esquires, Mary's were peers.

The President of his Council was an archdeacon, Mary's was a bishop. Richmond's governorship of the north was an established career path for a cadet prince of the royal house. Richard, Duke of Gloucester, had administered the north for his elder brother, Edward IV, and Henry himself, as Duke of York, had almost certainly been intended to take a similar route. But Mary's government of Wales belonged to its titular Prince(ss), the heir. She was following in the footsteps of Prince Edward, the eldest son of Edward IV; of Prince Arthur; and, of course, of her mother when she had gone to join her husband at Ludlow. Whatever her memories of that time, Catherine rejoiced at the recognition of her daughter's position.[8]

There were only two drawbacks. The first was that Henry, maddeningly, held back from a formal recognition of his daughter's position. She was always known as Princess, and sometimes as Princess of Wales or Prince of Wales (as when Vives dedicated his *Satellitium* to Mary as *Princeps Cambriae*). But she was never invested with either the title or the lands. (Nor, for that matter, had Richmond been formally legitimated – an omission that Catherine was hardly likely to object to!) It was as though Henry could not choose.

Catherine's other regret, of course, was that Mary's move to the Marches meant that her daughter was further away and absent longer than ever before. Probably in August, Mary and her entourage began their journey west. Their first base was Thornbury, the great castle to the north-east of Bristol, which, like the rest of Buckingham's possessions, had been seized by the crown after his fall. Mary spent the autumn there while her officers supervised the repairs to Ludlow Castle, which had been neglected since Arthur's death and Catherine's departure, over twenty years before.

Catherine quickly missed her daughter. Mary, dutiful child that she was, had written to her to 'know how I would do'. Catherine, however, delayed her reply. The reason was not forgetfulness, she assured her daughter when she finally wrote in late October, but depression. 'I am in that case that the long absence of the King and you troubleth me.' She tried to console herself. She hoped that God 'doth it [make Mary absent] to the best', and that He would shortly 'turn [Henry's absence] ... to come to good effect' also. Meanwhile, she was glad to hear from Mary, to learn that her health was better, and to see that she had written in Latin. Even here there was a note of regret, since it was Catherine who had taught Mary the rudiments. But Catherine put a brave face on it. 'As for your writing in Latin,' she told her daughter, 'I am right glad that ye shall change from me to Mr Featherstone, for that shall do you much good, to learn by him to write right.' But she wished to remain involved and asked her daughter to send her some of her exercises after Featherstone had read them. 'For it shall be a great comfort to me to see you keep your Latin and fair writing and all.'

Catherine ended with her recommendations to Lady Salisbury and signed herself 'Your loving mother, Catherine the Queen'. It is the letter of every mother when her only child first leaves home.[9]

But the separation proved less absolute than Catherine feared. By September 1526 Mary was back at Court, where her new entourage made a great impression. 'Her Grace was not only well accompanied with a goodly number', Wolsey's then Court agent, Richard Sampson, reported, 'but also with divers persons of gravity, *venerandam habentibus canitiem* [having reverend grey hairs]. I saw not the Court, Sir, better furnished with sage personages many days than now.' But Sampson reserved his best superlatives, in two languages, for the Princess herself. In English, she was 'of her age, as goodly a child as ever I have seen'; in Latin, she so behaved herself '*ut splendidius nusquam, decentius, iocundius videri potest mortale nihil* [that no one, nowhere could seem more distinguished, proper, and joyful]'. Neither Featherstone nor Lady Salisbury had let Catherine down.[10]

This autumn visit was only a temporary one. But, by the following year, Henry and Wolsey were on the point of abandoning the regional Households for the rival heirs to the throne. The establishments were hugely expensive, and Henry had set his eyes on an even more exalted destiny for Richmond: he would make him King of Ireland. The scheme, according to the Spanish ambassador, was hugely unpopular, since 'it will be tantamount to having a second King of Scotland for this kingdom'. And the ever-watchful Catherine was ready to pounce: 'The Queen is very dissatisfied with these proceedings, though little of it is communicated to her.'[11]

But, within a few months, the advancement of Richmond seemed very small beer. The boy had threatened Mary's position only; now Catherine's own status was at risk. For Henry had decided on a radical solution to the succession. He would no longer tinker with the symptoms, and swing between his bastard and his daughter; instead he would go to the root of the matter and tackle his marriage and his wife.

Or rather, he would deal with the fact – for such he had persuaded himself it was – that his marriage was not a marriage and that Catherine was not his wife. Indeed (or so he convinced himself), in the sight of God, she never had been. So he was free to marry and have sons by another, younger, more fruitful woman. He had already chosen the girl and plighted his troth. And she, on New Year's Day 1527, had accepted him as her betrothed. It was now just a question of getting the rest of the world to see things as Henry did.

The King thought that it would be easy. For the facts of the case, as they presented themselves to him, were obvious. Like many others, including Buckingham and Catherine, he had pondered on why 'God would not suffer the King's Grace's issue to prosper'. Unlike the rest, he had come up with an answer from the Word of God. *If a man shall take his brother's wife*, it states in *Leviticus* 20.21, *it is an impurity: he hath uncovered his brother's nakedness; they shall be childless.* The words struck Henry like a revelation. He had married his brother's wife, and he had been childless or at least son-less, which amounted to the same thing. Clearly, his marriage had transgressed the divine prohibition and had been punished accordingly. It was an 'impurity', a thing accursed and it should be ended forthwith.

But what of the Papal dispensation which had been obtained for the marriage? Was not that sufficient? Evidently not, said Henry. Indeed, since the dispensation had been powerless to ward off the curse of childlessness, it was clear that the Pope himself had erred in granting it. Everyone agreed that the Pope was empowered to dispense human or ceremonial law. But not even the heir of St Peter could set aside the law of nature and of God. Julius II had sought to do just that when, in defiance of *Leviticus*, he had permitted the marriage of Henry and Catherine. Julius had been wrong. Henry had suffered for that wrong. Now Julius's successor, Clement VII, must right it.

That, in a nutshell, was Henry's case. Over the next seven years, it underwent innumerable shifts of emphasis. It was infinitely elaborated and refined. Sometimes it was diluted to try to make it possible for the current Pope to undo the error of his predecessor without damaging his own authority. But, from its essence, Henry himself never varied.

Catherine was just as immovable, matching her husband's commitment with an equal and opposite one of her own. She was as convinced of the rightness of their marriage as her husband was of its wrongness. And, to begin with, her defence was vastly more effective than his attack. For Catherine, though she liked to present herself as a lone woman, had powerful allies. They included public opinion, the great weight of conventional legal and theological authority, and, above all, the political and military muscle of her nephew, the Emperor Charles V. Henry, in contrast, had only his own conscience and his own power as King of England. And he was trying to deploy them in areas where the individual conscience (even that of a king) and the power of the State had not hitherto dared to trespass.

So it was a not unequal struggle: Henry liked to call himself a lion but Catherine fought like a lioness, in defence of herself and of her child.

33. Trial in secret

O n 18 May 1527, Don Inigo de Mendoza, the new Spanish ambassador in London, made a sensational report to the Emperor. Henry had 'secretly assembled certain bishops and lawyers that they may sign a declaration to the effect that his marriage with the Queen is null and void on account of her having been his brother's wife'. The King was 'bent on this divorce' and Wolsey was 'scheming to bring [it] about'.

The Queen had been told nothing and feared the worst. 'She is so full of apprehension', Mendoza's report continued, 'that she has not ventured to speak with him [directly].' Instead, she 'communicated by a third person, who pretended not to come from her, though Mendoza suspected that he came with her consent'.[1]

The Divorce had begun. And, simultaneously, Catherine and her friends had taken their first step to frustrating Henry's wishes. Everything, from Henry's point of view, depended on secrecy and speed. Catherine, with her messenger to the Spanish ambassador, had threatened to make both impossible.

The day before, on 17 May, Wolsey had opened the court to try the King's marriage. The court met privately, in Wolsey's town palace of York Place. Wolsey sat as judge by virtue of his special ('legatine') powers from the Pope. His fellow-archbishop, Warham of Canterbury, was assessor. The defendant was Henry. And the charge was one of unlawful cohabitation with the wife of his deceased brother, Arthur.

Henry, of course, was not in the dock; indeed he sat on Wolsey's right hand. And the proceedings began with Wolsey asking Henry's permission to cite him to answer the charge. Henry graciously agreed. Wolsey then put the facts of his marriage to him. Henry concurred. Then the King appointed his proctor, or counsel, and withdrew. Here we enter a looking-glass world. Since the proceedings were inquisitorial, it was the task of Henry's counsel to argue the *opposite* of what his master wanted, and to defend the marriage. The case against was presented by the promoter or, as we might say, the counsel for the enquiry.[2]

He was Dr Richard Wolman and he had done his job thoroughly. Over a month previously he had interrogated Bishop Fox of Winchester at his episcopal palace at Winchester. Fox was the sole surviving member of the government who had been intimately involved with the negotiations for both of Catherine's marriages. He was now old and blind. But his memory was sharp and, prodded by Wolman's questions, his answers built up a full picture of the circumstances. One exchange in particular stands out. Had the marriage between Arthur and Catherine been consummated? Fox testified that the couple had lived together in both London and Ludlow and that he believed consummation had followed this cohabitation. Using Henry's arguments and Fox's evidence, Wolman built up an impressive case against Pope Julius II's dispensation, which he presented on 31 May. Wolman then requested Wolsey to weigh his arguments, test his evidence and arrive at judgement.[3]

So far, things were running strongly in Henry's direction. Catherine had received neither official notification of the trial, nor a summons to it, nor had she any opportunity to put her side. All was set for a snap decision, which could only be for Henry.

But, at the eleventh hour, something happened. Instead of proceeding to judgement on the 31st, as Wolman demanded, Wolsey pronounced the case to be so difficult that he was referring it to a panel of learned theologians and lawyers for elucidation. With that, the court rose, never to reconvene. Catherine could breathe again.

What had gone wrong (from Henry's point of view) or right (from Catherine's)? We shall never know for certain. But, most probably, Wolsey, for once, was telling the plain truth when he had pronounced the case too difficult for summary judgement.

For there was more than one Biblical text dealing with the question. And if *Leviticus* forbade marriage with a brother's widow, then the other text, in *Deuteronomy*, appeared, in certain circumstances, to require it:

When brethren dwell together, it declared, *and one of them dieth without children, the wife of the deceased shall not marry to another; but his brother shall take her, and raise up seed for his brother.* There were two ways to resolve the contradiction. The first, preferred by Henry, dismissed *Deuteronomy* out of hand. It belonged, it was argued, to the ceremonial law, which applied only to Jews, not Christians. And even the Jews themselves had ceased to conform to it. The other solution effected a partial reconciliation of the texts. It followed *Leviticus* in acknowledging the general principle that marriage with a brother's widow was prohibited. But it made a single exception for the circumstances envisaged by *Deuteronomy:* that is to say, when the dead brother was childless. A respectable body of opinion, especially the Early Fathers of the Church, had agreed with Henry in dismissing *Deuteronomy* and applying the prohibition in *Leviticus* strictly as a matter of divine law. But the development of later medieval canon law had been towards the 'compromise' position, which generally forbade marriage with a brother's widow, *except when the deceased was childless.*

And, unfortunately for Henry, the facts of his case fitted the exception perfectly.

Wolsey probably knew all this already. In any case, he was forcibly reminded of it when, in the last days of the trial, he consulted Bishop Fisher of Rochester, who was one of the proposed panel of experts. The consultation was an informal one, and Wolsey carefully omitted the names of the parties. But the signs are that Fisher guessed the truth. Worse, from Henry's point of view, he came out strongly for the 'compromise' position and hence for the right of the Pope to adjudicate the case. 'Otherwise', Fisher noted, 'it is in vain that Christ has said [to St Peter]: "whatsoever thou shalt loose on earth shall be loosed in heaven".'[4]

Wolsey forwarded Fisher's opinion to the King on 2 June, with a covering letter of his own in which he did his best to soften the blow for Henry. He hinted that Fisher's judgement had been warped by his partiality for Catherine: 'that, having some conjecture or smelling of the matter, his said opinion proceedeth rather of affection, than of sincerity of his learning or Scripture'. He also suggested that Fisher had 'extorted' or twisted Christ's words to Peter beyond the limits of reason. But, whatever palliatives Wolsey might apply, Henry now knew the worst: the weight of expert opinion was against him and for Catherine.[5]

But that was not the only bad news contained in Wolsey's letter. The Cardinal enclosed other reports, from France and Italy, 'confirming the piteous and lamentable spoils, pillages, with most cruel murders, committed by the Imperials in the City of Rome'. An Imperial army, led by the Duke of Bourbon, had mutinied for lack of pay and seized and sacked Rome. Bourbon had been killed and Pope Clement had taken refuge in the Castel di Sant'Angelo, where he was effectively a prisoner. The Emperor Charles V piously disavowed the actions of his troops but was happy to exploit the consequences, which were so advantageous to him.

For Henry, on the other hand, the consequences of the Sack of Rome, as it became known, were little short of disastrous. The aborting of Wolsey's tribunal meant that Henry's Divorce could not be settled unilaterally in England; instead it would have to be referred to Rome. But the news in Wolsey's package told Henry that both the city of Rome and its Pope were now in the hands of Charles V. And Charles, Henry needed no reminding, was Catherine's nephew.

In three days, between 31 May, when Wolman had presented his carefully crafted case against the dispensation, and 2 June, when Wolsey wrote his letter, the world had been turned upside-down. Henry had had certain victory snatched from his hands; Catherine had been rescued from the jaws of defeat.

It took Henry another three weeks to summon up courage to broach matters directly with his wife. He found her in no mood to compromise. There were tears, then tantrums and finally an ultimatum.

The confrontation took place on 22 June. There are two versions of what happened. The first comes from Catherine herself, via the Spanish ambassador. Henry had told her

> that they had been in mortal sin during all the years they had lived together, and that this being the opinion of many canonists and theologians whom he had consulted on the subject, he had come

to the resolution, as his conscience was much troubled thereby, to
separate himself from her *a mensa et thoro* [from board and bed] and
wished her to choose the place to which she would retire.

Catherine had then, according to this account, resorted to a woman's
prerogative, 'bursting into tears and being too agitated to reply'. The
effect (and no doubt the intended one) was to unman Henry. Instead of
forcing a separation as he intended, he made a clumsy attempt to comfort
her. 'All should be done for the best,' he mumbled. Then he 'begged her
to keep secrecy upon what he had told her' and fled. It was a less than
convincing display of patriarchal power.[6]

But the evidence from Henry's side suggests that there had been steel
behind Catherine's tears. 'The Queen', Wolsey wrote to Henry, relaying
what he had heard from his Court agent Sampson, 'was very stiff and
obstinate, affirming that your brother did never know her carnally, and
that she desired counsel [that is, legal advice] as well of your subjects as
of strangers.'[7]

Wolsey had immediately smelled a rat. Catherine must have been (as
we know she was) forewarned and forearmed. 'This device could never
come of her head, but of some that were learned [legally expert].' Indeed,
to his anguish, Wolsey realized that Catherine had put her finger on the
weakness in Henry's case. 'These were the worst points that could be
imagined for the impeaching [preventing] of this matter ... that she
would resort to the counsel of strangers [foreigners] ... and ... intended
to make all the counsel of the world, France except, as a party against it.'
Henry had envisaged the case as England *versus* Catherine. Thanks to
Catherine's intrepidity, Wolsey feared, it was turning into the World
versus England and England's King.

It was Round One to Catherine. Hence Wolsey's urgent advice to Henry
to avoid alienating her further. Instead, he recommended, 'your Grace
should handle her both gently and doucely [sweetly or softly]'. Henry,
after a moment of doubt when he thought that Wolsey himself was going
soft on the case, agreed.

The new treatment seemed to work, as Sampson reported on 25 July. The royal family – Henry, Catherine and Mary – were all at Court and Sampson, as he told Wolsey, had carefully observed their mutual demeanour. It was most satisfactory:

> The Great Matter [the code name for the Divorce] is in very good train; good countenance, much better than was in mine opinion; less suspicion or little, the merry visage is returned not less than was wont. The other party [Catherine], as your Grace knoweth, lacketh no wit, and so sheweth highly in this matter.

The Court had moved from Hunsdon to Beaulieu on the 23rd. The King had been ready early. 'Yet he tarried for the Queen. And so they rode forth together.' They were once more the very image of a happy couple.[8]

But Catherine could dissemble too. As Wolsey suspected, she had immediately seen that if Henry needed secrecy, she could only gain from broadcasting her plight. Rumour and the force of public opinion would do part of her work for her. Indeed their operations had already started and, according to the Spanish ambassador, 'the affair is as notorious as if it had been proclaimed by the public crier'. But Catherine had a more specific target, her nephew Charles V. For the last few years he had neglected her. But now, in her hours of need, she was confident that he would not let her down. She was right.[9]

But first, she had to get in touch with him directly. The Spanish ambassador, though he reported her plight sympathetically, was reluctant to be involved too openly, lest he wreck the already shaky relations between the two countries. So she would have to find her own messenger. She had the ideal candidate: her Spanish servant, Francisco Felipez. Felipez, who was one of the Queen's sewers (waiters at table), had been in her service since her days as Princess of Wales. He was utterly loyal to her, 'and hath been always privy unto the Queen's affairs and secrets'. She decided to send him to Charles in Spain 'with a letter explaining the position in which she is now placed'. But how to get him past the English authorities?[10]

There now ensued an elaborate game of bluff and double bluff. Felipez approached the King directly to ask for permission to go to Spain, using the excuse (which was, even then, an old one) of 'visit[ing] his mother, who is very sore sick'. To divert suspicion, Catherine ostentatiously refused her consent and asked Henry to do the same. Henry immediately saw through the scheme. But instead of keeping Felipez at home, he decided to outwit both his wife and her servant. Publicly, he gave Felipez permission. But, privately, he ordered Wolsey to have Felipez picked up in France. Wolsey, though he praised Henry's cunning to his face, immediately realized that the King might have been too clever by half: what if Felipez by-passed France and sailed directly for Spain? Which of course he did.[11]

Felipez arrived at Valladolid by late July and Charles's response was immediate. He was shocked 'to hear of a case so scandalous'. And he was galvanized into action. He wrote to Henry, to ask him to think again. He wrote to Catherine, to offer his full support. He wrote to Pope Clement, alerting him to 'this ugly affair' and suggesting that, in view of Wolsey's partisanship, he revoke his legacy (special powers). Finally, he sent to Rome a special envoy, Quinones, the General of the Order of St Francis, who was 'fully ... qualified for this sort of business', and who indeed became an ardent and effective partisan of Catherine's. [12]

Catherine had appealed to Caesar. And the Emperor, as she hoped, had informed the world. He was also, as Catherine likewise hoped and Wolsey feared, beginning to get the world on side – on Catherine's side against Henry.

With the single bold gesture of the Felipez mission, Catherine had turned 'the Great Matter' from an English question into an international one. In so doing, she had turned the tables: Henry might win in England; she would be victorious abroad.

34. Between trials

Catherine's coup in 1527 with the Felipez mission had internationalized the Divorce; it would take Henry and Wolsey almost eighteen months of frantic effort to repatriate it. She had also torn the veil of secrecy off the Great Matter and it could never be put back. Things were out in the open, and when the case next came to trial it would be in open court. The tribunal would be a stage, towards which the eyes of all Europe would turn. And Catherine would give the performance of her life.

But, meanwhile, she had to wait and to see. What would King Henry do? How would Pope Clement respond? Who would take her side and who her husband's? She was not passive, of course. But, as Henry was the aggressor, the initiative belonged to him. The strain, the insecurity began to tell. Above all, she suffered bitter pangs at her husband's personal rejection of her. That autumn, she found a confidant in Juan Luis Vives.

Vives had left England in May 1527 to spend the summer in the Netherlands. He returned, as agreed, in late September, 'to teach the most illustrious lady Princess the Latin language, and such precepts of wisdom as would arm her against any adverse fortune'. Instead, he found another more in need of his services as a comforter: Mary's mother, Catherine herself.[1]

Catherine took the first step. 'Troubled and afflicted with this controversy that had arisen about her marriage, [she] began to unfold . . . this her calamity' to Vives 'as her compatriot and [one who] used the same language'. It was probably the first time she had been able to talk freely about the matter in her native tongue to an intelligent and sympathetic listener. The emotional release proved too much. She broke down and cried like any other woman.

She wept over her destiny, that she should find him, whom she loved far more than herself, so alienated from her that he thought of marrying another; and this affected her with a grief the more intense as her love for him was the more ardent.

Vives offered her Job's comfort: God chastised those whom He loved. 'Who can blame me', Vives demanded, 'that I listened to a miserable and afflicted woman? that I soothed her by discourse and conversation?'

But the talk soon turned from these pious generalities to the more dangerous topic of the Great Matter itself. 'As we went on, we spoke more warmly, and proceeded to the discussion and examination of the cause.' Catherine told Vives that she was unable to find out what Henry had decided to do next, 'for it was concealed from all excepting very few'. But the 'report and common opinion was . . . that the cause was remitted to Rome'. She was desperately anxious that her case should not go unheard in Rome, as it had threatened to do in Wolsey's court at York Place. So, once again, she turned to the Emperor. Her agent lay to hand: she would use Vives as her go-between. He was commanded 'to go to the Emperor's ambassador, and to ask him, on her behalf, to write to request the Emperor that he would deal with the Pope that she might . . . be heard before his Holiness decided on her cause'. Ambassador Mendoza promised Vives that he would write as Catherine wished.[2]

Mendoza was as good as his word. On 26 October he wrote in unusually blunt terms to his master. 'The divorce is more talked of than ever,' he reported. 'If therefore the Emperor really has the Queen's honour and peace of mind at heart, orders should be sent to Rome for a trusty messenger to bring us the Pope's decision.' Catherine had also sent the ambassador, probably by Vives as well, an appeal in her own name to her nephew. Mendoza explained that he was sending Catherine's letter separately, 'that it may be safe in case of [this] being intercepted'.[3]

The precaution worked and Catherine's letter reached its destination. It also shows that her claims of ignorance need to be taken with a pinch of salt. Her particular fears, she explained to Charles, arose from a meeting summoned for 15 November, when 'all the lawyers of the kingdom shall meet together and discuss whether I am or am not his lawful wife'. Their opinions, she continued, were to be collected together and forwarded to Pope Clement to serve as the basis for his decision.

Catherine, indeed, was extraordinarily well informed. The 15 November meeting, which followed up an earlier discussion at Hampton Court in October, was to take soundings on the 'King's Book'. This was an elaborately referenced position-paper, setting out Henry's case. It had been assembled that summer by a team of theologians and canon lawyers working with Henry's active participation and under his personal direction. The work had proceeded in strict secrecy; likewise the discussion-seminars. The Queen can only have heard about the November meeting from one of those summoned.[4]

This pattern would repeat itself. For the Divorce was a parting of the ways for the political establishment of Tudor England. Some remained true to Henry through thick and thin. But others found that they were drawn, inexorably and against their better interest, to Catherine. For some it was a matter of high, conscientious principle; for others, there were mundane reasons, such as family ties to the Queen's Household or the ancient, semi-feudal loyalty of servant to mistress. Those who sided with the Queen included many whom Henry regarded as his closest friends and advisers. Only the bravest of them dared act openly for her. But many betrayed Henry in secret by a whispered word or a carefully discarded paper: his ambassador in France; the Clerk of the Privy Council; one of his key agents in Rome. The result was that the King could do nothing in his Great Matter without Catherine knowing, and without Catherine broadcasting it to the world. The walls of his private apartments seemed to have ears. Was he safe in the Council Chamber? Or the confessional? Could he trust even Wolsey?

A cancer of suspicion and paranoia had planted itself in the King's mind. It would grow until it destroyed the whole political world of his youth – that carefree world of jousts and revels which he and Catherine had built together.

One of the first victims was Richard Pace, scholar, gossip and the sharpest pen in early Tudor England. The strain of serving two masters – Wolsey and Henry – had already driven him to a sort of nervous breakdown. He gave up politics and went back to the world of scholarship in which he had begun. The rest-cure worked and he recovered. But he could not escape his past, for the Divorce had now politicized scholarship itself. In the earliest days of the controversy, Pace was a strong supporter of Henry and recruited, for the King, Robert Wakefield, the greatest Hebrew scholar in England. But in the summer of 1527 Pace underwent a conversion and, swinging from one extreme to the other, became a violent partisan of Catherine.[5]

As usual with him, it was all or nothing. He spoke 'to the King touching this matter of the Queen and the government of the Cardinal' (Wolsey was widely blamed in the Queen's circle for instigating the Divorce). And he went beyond words to action. The result was pure cloak and dagger. Pace got in touch with Mendoza via a friendly English merchant. The message was: 'if he only would send one of his servants to speak with him [the Emperor's] interests might be served'. Mendoza duly sent one of his staff, who spoke English. Mendoza must meet with him at once, Pace insisted, 'and named the Church of St Paul's as the place of meeting least likely to arouse suspicion'. Wisely, ambassador Mendoza did not keep the rendezvous. But his member of staff had been tailed to Pace's house. On 25 October Pace was arrested and sent to the Tower. He knew too much.[6]

The following February, Wolsey was able to make a wider trawl through the ranks of the Queen's supporters. At the end of January, England joined France in declaring war on Charles V. High words were exchanged but no gunfire, since neither side actually wanted conflict. But the phoney war gave the opportunity to break diplomatic immunity. In Spain, Charles V carried out a mass detention of ambassadors; in England, Wolsey ordered the lightning arrest of Mendoza. It was done under cover of a summons to Court. But, instead of being taken to the palace, the ambassador was led to 'a house which he did not know' and told that, unless he handed over the key to the strong-box containing his papers, it would be broken open. Mendoza managed to slip the key to his Secretary, who got back to the Embassy before the guards and removed and secreted safely 'all the letters and ciphers relating to the Emperor's affairs'.[7]

Others were less lucky. A week later, Sir John Russell informed the King, as instructed, that Wolsey had 'examined Francisco Felipez and Vives in the gentlest manner he could without force, thinking that this was more to the King's honour'. Felipez, whom Henry had personally dismissed from his post in the Queen's Household after his return from Spain the previous autumn, can hardly have been surprised. But Vives took a tone of high moral indignation in the written statement which was wrung out of him. He had heard, he began, 'great complaints of the Emperor, that he had violated the law of nations [*jus gentium*] by taking the ambassadors of many nations'. But his own treatment at the hands of Wolsey was equally, Vives insisted, an offence against the laws of decency and friendship. 'This is not less an outrage to compel anyone to divulge what was secretly entrusted to him, especially a servant trusted by a mistress whose fidelity to her husband is undoubted.' Not that he or Catherine had done anything to be ashamed of. 'But the example is a bad one, for a great part of the intercourse of life rests on the faith of secrecy, which, if destroyed, everyone will be on guard against a companion as against an enemy.'[8]

Vives, alas, was right, in both his analysis and his prophecy. The sanctity of private conversations, even the security of one's own thoughts, were also to be among the victims of the Great Matter. And the government soon became less nice about the means it used to extract information about them.

Meanwhile, Wolsey had at last made some headway in Rome on the Great Matter. Ever since he had aborted his own court at York Place, he and the King had been trying to get the Pope's agreement for the case to be heard again in England on a more regular footing. But on what terms? There were two methods by which a Pope could authorize such delegated jurisdiction. The first was known as a 'general commission'. This simply instructed named judges to investigate a case, deliver a verdict and carry out whatever consequential action was necessary – for example, to separate the spouses of a marriage which had been found to be invalid. The disadvantage of such a commission from Henry's point of view was that it left the outcome of the trial dangerously open; that the verdict was subject to appeal to Rome; and that the case could be 'revoked' or recalled even before a verdict had been reached. So a general commission would offer Henry neither the certainty he needed nor any guarantee of the 'right' verdict. This led his advisers to propose instead the use of the other form of Papal authorization known as a 'decretal commission'. This was an altogether more restrictive document. It set out the law on the question, leaving the judges only to discover the facts and deliver their verdict accordingly. The advantages from Henry's point of view were obvious. Provided the statement of law was framed appropriately, the verdict could be guaranteed. It would be like ticking the boxes on a form.

The decision rested with Giulio de' Medici, who had reigned as Pope Clement VII since 1523. He was a wily Florentine, who turned prevarication into an art form. He would talk, at inordinate length, without ever reaching a conclusion. And he knew every word, in mellifluous Italian or fluent Latin, apart from 'yes' and 'no'. His other dominant characteristic was a certain timorousness. But then he had plenty to be afraid of. The Lutheran heresy, which abusively rejected his power as Pope, was making great strides in Germany and threatened to take most of the country into schism. The troops of the Emperor Charles V had not only sacked his capital but threatened his hold over the Papacy's territories in central Italy. His family, the Medici, had been driven out of their hereditary city state of Florence, which they had ruled as dukes. Now Wolsey was threatening him as well and telling him that, if Henry were not enabled to get rid of Catherine, England would go the way of Germany.

Clement was aware of the risk and anxious to do what he could for Henry. Indeed, bearing in mind that England was far away and Charles V's troops near at hand, he was not ungenerous. He was also hoping that something would either turn up (like a French victory in Italy) or go away (like Henry's infatuation with his new woman) to let him off the hook. So Clement was playing for time. He would offer Henry *almost* everything he wanted in the pre-trial commissions, but not quite. And he would stretch out the negotiations as long as he could.

The result was a policy which led to Clement being vilified by both sides in turn: first by Catherine and her supporters, since he seemed to be offering Henry too much, and later by Henry, since he took back what he had given. Clement shrugged. He had to keep afloat both those leaky ships of State, the Papacy and the Medici dukedom. And if that meant he lost England, so be it. 'I do', he said to one of the English agents in a rare moment of frankness, 'consider the ruin that hangs over me; I repent what I have done. [But] if heresies arise, is it my fault? My conscience acquits me.'[9]

It would be hard to think of a man more alien to Catherine, with her hard-edged Spanish certainties. The Papacy, Catherine proclaimed, 'should stand firmly on the Rock which is Christ'. It should be a fortress, proud and immovable. But Pope Clement, unlike Queen Catherine, had seen what happened to proud buildings in warfare. All over Rome and the Papal states were shattered palaces and castles and monasteries, roofless, windowless and gutted, their treasures pillaged and their inhabitants murdered or raped or held hostage. Better by far, Clement thought, to lie low, to show the wisdom of the serpent and the meekness of the dove and to survive.[10]

But Catherine would never understand such supineness, as she saw it, and she would never understand why the Pope seemed so anxious to please her husband. For Clement willingly granted a general commission for the trial of Henry's marriage. He was also happy to follow Wolsey's suggestion and appoint Lorenzo Campeggio as the English Cardinal's fellow-judge and legate. Campeggio was Cardinal-Protector of England at Rome and absentee Bishop of Salisbury. His appointment led to an obvious charge of bias, in that both judges were English bishops and took the King of England's shilling. Catherine and her supporters pressed the charge vigorously. Clement ignored them, since he knew that Campeggio's true loyalties lay to the Papal service, in which most of his extended family had made their careers and fortunes.

But even Clement baulked at the decretal commission. Its blatant bias to Henry was certain to offend Charles V mortally. It also offended Clement's own sense of justice. But finally Clement was brought to grant this too, though only on strict conditions: the decretal commission was never to leave Campeggio's hands; it was to be shown only to Wolsey and Henry; and if possible, it was never to be used. Even so, he regretted his action immediately. He would have given one of his fingers not to have signed it, he said.[11]

By now it was August 1528. After endless delays, real and diplomatic, Campeggio had begun his journey to England. The first leg, from the port of Tarquinia, fifty miles north-west of Rome, to Provence, was by sea. But thereafter he had to cross France by land. Here his progress was slow – and agonizingly so, because of his gout. Riding even his slow-paced mule was intolerable; instead he had to be carried in a horse litter. And he could stand this for no more than a few hours a day. By 14 September he had only reached Paris and he did not reach Calais till the end of the month. The journey had taken nine weeks. But he was about to arrive in England at last.[12]

And at last the curious, eighteen-month-long armistice in the Great Matter would be broken. Since the abrupt ending of the York Place tribunal, direct hostilities had been suspended. Instead, each side had used the time to develop their own arguments and to probe the weaknesses of their opponents'. Not surprisingly, since they were talking only to themselves, each had come to the conclusion that they had got the better of the other. Now their confidence would be put to the test.

We know the state of mind of the two parties on the eve of battle thanks to a conversation between Wolsey and Catherine's Almoner, Dr Robert Shorton. After beginning with other matters, Wolsey had quickly steered the talk to the Great Matter. 'What tidings had he heard of late in the Court?' Wolsey asked. 'None', Shorton replied, 'but that it was much bruited that a Legate should come hither into England.' And what, Wolsey continued, did 'the Queen [think] of his coming?' 'She was fully persuaded and believed that his coming was only for the decision of the cause of matrimony depending between her and the King's Highness,' Shorton answered.

This gave Wolsey his opening. Swearing Shorton to secrecy by everything he held sacred – 'his fidelity, his oath and *sub sigillo confessionis* [under the seal of confession]' – he pumped him on the Queen's intentions. Shorton made no bones about replying, probably because Catherine had spoken plainly enough herself and had not greatly cared who heard her. 'He heard the Queen oft say, that if in this cause she might attain and enjoy her natural defence and justice, she distrusted nothing but that [she should win].' She had four reasons. First, because 'it was in the eyes of God most plain and evident that she was never [carnally] known of Prince Arthur'. Second, because neither of the judges was competent to try the case, since both were the King's subjects and appointed at his instance. Third, because she had no access to 'indifferent counsel [impartial legal advice]' in England. And fourth, because 'she had in Spain two Bulls, the one be[ar]ing later date than the other, but both of such efficacy and strength, as should soon remove all objections and cavillations [nit-picking objections] to the infringing of this matrimony'.

Shorton's testimony is important. Often, Catherine is presented as taking a simple, untutored stand on right and conscience alone. She *would* make such a stand, and very effective it was too. But, as we can see from Shorton's report, there was nothing spontaneous or untutored about it. Instead, it was part of a carefully considered legal strategy. Catherine, like Henry, had been doing her homework. She was as intimately involved in the niceties of argument about the case as he, and just as much in command of the details. And she had rather better ammunition.

This was clear from Wolsey's response. First, he blustered about Catherine herself. Her statement, he protested, was so full of 'undiscreet, ungodly purposes and sayings' that Wolsey doubted whether she was of 'such perfection [or] virtue' as he had once thought. Then he began a point-by-point refutation of her arguments – on her virginity, on the partiality of the judges, and on her lack of access to 'indifferent', that is, in effect, overseas counsel. He went on at inordinate length, especially on the issue of the consummation of her first marriage with Arthur. The

Spanish ambassadors, he claimed, 'did send the sheets they lay in, spotted with blood, into Spain, in full testimony and proof thereof'. But on the fourth head of Catherine's case, the two Spanish Bulls, this matador of debate said nothing. Was it because he had nothing to say?[13]

Campeggio arrived in London on 9 October and, more dead than alive, was lodged at Bath House. Bath House, then the town house of the bishops of Bath and later the residence of the earls of Arundel, lay just beyond the Temple, with pleasant gardens reaching down to the Thames. Thence, it was a short journey downstream by boat to Henry's city palace of Bridewell. On the 21st, Henry and Catherine took up residence in Bridewell. On the 22nd, Campeggio, accompanied by Wolsey, was formally received at Court, and the King 'came out to the very foot of the staircase to meet them'. First there was a grand public ceremony, in which Charles V was denounced as a tyrant and the common enemy of the Pope and Christendom. Then the King and the two Cardinals, Campeggio and Wolsey, retired to the King's Privy Chamber, where they were closeted 'a long time together'. The pre-trial negotiations had begun.[14]

Catherine was about to experience the politics of the Papal Court at first hand. And, it turned out, they rested, not on a rock, but in quicksand.

35. The legate

For Campeggio, the priesthood was only a second career. Until he was in his mid-thirties, he had been a teacher of law at Bologna university and a married man. Then in 1509 the death of his wife opened the way to a new life in the Papal service. His rise was rapid: priest in 1510, cardinal in 1517, Protector of England in 1524. But none of this made much difference to the man. He became neither a *dévôt* nor a Renaissance Prince of the Church. Instead, he remained the north-Italian bourgeois he had always been. He was devoted to the advancement of his numerous family of three sons and four brothers and countless remoter relations. He had a sincere love of money. And he was an excellent diplomat and deal-maker, with a negotiator's characteristic indifference to principle. As far as he was concerned, differences were for splitting, chasms for bridging, while walls were always to be probed for their weakest spot. And the weakest spot in England, Campeggio decided, was likely to be Catherine herself.[1]

Despite his state of health, Campeggio got to work quickly, with a series of private, face-to-face meetings with the principals to assess the situation for himself. He began with Henry, who came to Bath House the day after the formal reception at Court on 22 October. The two were closeted together for four hours and had a frank exchange of views. By the end, Campeggio was in no doubt that Henry was immovable. The King had decided, Campeggio wrote to a friend in the Papal Court, that his marriage was invalid 'and I believe that an Angel descending from heaven would be unable to persuade him otherwise'.

Campeggio then pulled his white rabbit from the hat: why not persuade Catherine to enter a nunnery? This would square the circle. It would leave her status and that of her daughter intact. And it would also, by a little stretching of the law, free Henry to remarry. Henry was delighted with the idea. Moreover, Campeggio reflected to his correspondent, there was much to recommend it from Catherine's point of view. She would gain much and lose nothing – not even her marital rights, since Henry had already given up sleeping with his wife two years previously, 'and will not return however things turn out'. Henry agreed that Campeggio should put the proposal to the Queen the following day, the 24th.

This time Campeggio was accompanied by Wolsey. Campeggio began with deliberate obliqueness. Pope Clement would of course offer

Catherine justice, he said. Nevertheless, to avoid scandal, it was much better that the matter should not come to open trial. Instead, Catherine, 'should, of her prudence, take some other course which would give general satisfaction and greatly benefit herself and others'. 'I did not further explain the means to her,' Campeggio told his correspondent, 'in order to discover what she would demand.'

This was a proper opening gambit, polished in a thousand difficult negotiations. But Catherine, refusing to play the game by Campeggio's rules, immediately named names. 'She had heard', she said, 'that we were [come] to persuade her to enter some religion.' Campeggio was taken aback at such bluntness but quickly shifted ground. 'I did not deny it,' he reported. Then he proceeded to try to sell her the idea. To take the veil, he informed Catherine, would 'satisfy God, her own conscience, [and] the glory and fame of her name'; and it would preserve 'her honours and temporal goods and the succession of her daughter'. There was also, he concluded, 'the example of [Jeanne de Valois], the Queen of France that was, who did a similar thing, and who still lives in the greatest honour and reputation with God and all that kingdom'.[2]

Wolsey echoed Campeggio's arguments, at greater length and more urgently.

The Cardinals, Wolsey and Campeggio, two of Europe's most experienced and wily men of business, had been jumped into declaring their hands. Catherine, however, refused to show hers. Instead, protesting pathetically that she was 'a woman, a foreigner and friendless', she said she would once more demand 'indifferent' counsel from the King. 'Then she would give us audience.'

The pathos of Catherine's situation is real. But it should not disguise the fact that she had just issued an ultimatum. Until she got the advisers she wanted from Henry, she would not give her reply to Campeggio's proposal and the best hope for a quick solution to the Great Matter would remain in suspense.

She saw Henry on the 25th to reiterate her demand for 'indifferent' counsel. It was something which Henry had hitherto resisted absolutely.

The Great Matter touched the English succession too closely, he claimed, for any foreigner to be allowed to deal in it. Catherine put her case once more, and this time Henry yielded. She was assigned seven English counsel, two Flemings, and 'a Spaniard, Luis Vives, whom she herself nominates'. Her ultimatum had worked.

Having got her way on the issue of foreign counsel, Catherine became submissive once more and asked Henry permission to confess to Campeggio. His heart must have leapt. Was she about to accept the bait and become a nun? Why else would she wish to see the Cardinal in private? For a moment, I guess, Henry thought that his troubles were over. He gave her leave with alacrity.

Catherine came to see Campeggio at 9 o'clock the following morning, the 26th. The visit lasted a long time, because she had so much to say, beginning with 'her first arrival in this kingdom' and continuing to 'the present'. But the principal matter was her virginity.

> She affirmed, on her conscience, that from 14 November, when she was married to the late Prince Arthur, to 2 April following when he died, she did not sleep with him more than seven nights, and that she remained intact and uncorrupted by him, as she came from her mother's womb.

In making this solemn affirmation, Catherine was addressing the Pope through his legate and the world through the Pope. So she not only gave Campeggio permission to break the seal of the confessional and inform Clement VII of what she had said, she positively encouraged him. But England was a different matter. Here she had to be more cautious. She said 'she would declare her intentions in proper place and time' and, meanwhile, asked that Campeggio swear his secretaries to silence.

But what, Campeggio wanted to know, of his suggestion that she should take the veil? Would she consider that? Her answer was crushing.

> She assured me she would never do so; that she intended to live and die in the estate of matrimony, into which God had called

her, and that she would always be of that opinion and never change it.

'She repeated this so many times and so determinately and deliberately', Campeggio reported, 'that I am convinced she will act accordingly.'

For once, this man of so many fluent words was at a loss for a single one. 'Nothing more occurred to me [to say]', he wrote, 'and she left me.' He was impressed and exasperated at the same time. 'I have always judged her to be a prudent lady, and now more so.' Nevertheless, he lamented 'her obstinacy in not accepting this sound counsel'. It 'does not much please me', he ended querulously.[3]

But Catherine was no longer in the business of pleasing him or any other man. The weakest spot in the wall had turned out to be stronger than Campeggio had thought.

36. The Brief

Catherine's fear was that Henry would force the Great Matter to a quick, summary judgement. With Campeggio's arrival, the threat of this now seemed very real. Campeggio had shown the decretal commission to Henry on the 24th. The following day, the King boasted to Catherine about its effects. 'The Pope had condemned her at Rome', he told her triumphantly, 'and the Legate Campeggio had come for the sole purpose of having the sentence executed.' She knew Henry well enough not to believe everything he said. But in this case she could take no chances. Even her own actions had contributed to the emergency. By rejecting so decisively Campeggio's suggestion that she should take the veil, she had destroyed the possibility of a compromise solution and had brought the moment of trial nearer. Indeed, she had welcomed it: 'she insists', Campeggio reported, 'that everything shall be decided by [judicial] sentence.' 'Neither the whole kingdom on the one hand, nor any great punishment on the other, although she might be torn limb from limb, should compel her to alter this opinion', she had told him. She would be a martyr to marriage and the trial would be her scaffold.[1]

But she knew that under no circumstances must she be tried by the decretal commission. It was time to use her secret weapon and, probably in the second week of November, she showed Campeggio her 'Spanish Bulls'. The effect was cataclysmic.

The decretal commission was based on the Bull of dispensation, which had justified the dispensation for the marriage of Henry and Catherine by the need to preserve the peace between England and Spain. For this Bull to stand in law, the reason had to be sufficient. Henry and Wolsey were advised that it was not, and the decretal commission rested on this advice. The commission recited the contents of the Bull; noted its likely defects; and required the legates to proceed to judgement on the basis of three questions, all derived from the supposed inadequacies in the Bull. Would the peace between England and Spain have continued without the marriage? Was it true that Henry did not desire the marriage in order to conserve the peace? Had the rulers, or one of them, among whom the peace was to be kept, died before the marriage took place? If all or any of these objections were found to be valid, the Bull would be void and the marriage null.

One of the documents Catherine now produced was also a Bull (so-called because of the lead seal or *bulla* which authenticated it). This turned out to correspond word-for-word with the Bull of dispensation cited in the decretal commission. Catherine's other document was not a Bull, but the Brief or letter, sealed with wax, which Pope Julius II had sent to comfort Isabella on her deathbed.

The Brief in the main followed the text of the Bull. But it varied from it at the crucial points which Henry's advisers had identified as the weak spots of the Bull. The Bull stated that the marriage was necessary to maintain the peace between England and Spain. The Brief made the same point but less absolutely. Existing peaceful relations, it claimed, 'would probably not last so firmly' if the marriage did not take place. The Brief also broadened the reasons for the dispensation. It was granted, it stated, not only for the sake of maintaining peace, but for *et certis aliis causis* (for certain other reasons).

These 'other reasons' were unspecified but they were enough to make good the errors in the Bull. If the Brief stood, the decretal commission and its captious objections fell. And there were doubts, even about the general commission. Henry and Wolsey, it seemed, would have to start all over again.

In one elegant move Catherine had undone eighteen months of frantic, expensive English diplomacy in Rome. She had also made her husband look a fool. It was not a bad morning's work.[2]

The response was swift. The same day Catherine's counsel asked permission to wait on her. They had serious matters which had been submitted by the 'other side'. The King, they said, had been informed that there was a conspiracy to assassinate both him and Wolsey. It was undertaken on her behalf by the Emperor's agents. The King, they continued, would like to give the Queen the benefit of the doubt and assume she was not involved. But her behaviour in other matters gave him pause. 'Your Grace does not show such love to [Henry], neither in nor yet out of bed . . . as a woman ought to do to her husband.' 'What was done in bed between both your Graces we pass over,' they said. But her public demeanour left much to be desired. The King was 'in great pensiveness by reason of this matter'; Catherine, on the other hand, showed every appearance of happiness. She exhorted 'other ladies and gentlemen of the Court to dance and pastime' and she dressed and behaved cheerfully herself.

But, worst of all, she was courting the people. There had been demonstrations against the Divorce and in favour of Catherine. It was her duty to help repress them, she was told; instead she had encouraged them by making her public behaviour more expressive than previously. 'By beckoning with your head and smiling otherwise than in times past your Grace was wont to do, your Grace has rather comforted them in so doing than rebuked or refrained them.' Catherine, in short, it was alleged, had been playing the Diana-card, and turning the People against the Prince.

Catherine dismissed the charges with contempt. But they were a mere warm-up to the subject of the Brief. There should be no secrets between husband and wife, she was told. Yet she had kept the Brief 'close', which showed she had not been 'so loving as your Grace ought to be'.

At this point the tone shifted suddenly, from lofty exhortation and reproof to something more brutal. She was warned that it was foolish to 'strive' with the King. She was reminded of her 'ill-success' in childbed. Then she was subjected to a barrage of questions on the Brief. How long had she had the Brief? Whom did she send for the Brief? What letters did she write for it and to whom? Who brought her the Brief? And did she have any similar letters?[2]

In her replies Catherine was economical with the truth. She had received the Brief, she claimed, six months previously from Mendoza, the Spanish ambassador. And she denied receiving any letters from the Emperor at the same time.

In fact, Mendoza was still pressing his home government for the document as late as September.

A copy of the Papal Brief of dispensation for the Queen's marriage to the King is much wanted here [he wrote on the 18th]. It ought to come forthwith, but so fully and legally attested that it may be presented in court. The one [he] has is a mere transcript.

Catherine sent a messenger to warn Mendoza that he too was likely to be interrogated on the subject. 'If so', he assured the Emperor, 'I shall so shape my answer that it may not disagree with the Queen's declaration, nor make it appear as if she had stated an untruth'.[3]

This was only the beginning of Henry's fight back. The Brief had arrived too conveniently. And it answered the objections to the Bull too fully. Surely it was a forgery? But how could he tell? Catherine had produced only a transcript. He must get his hands on the original. All the efforts of the King and Wolsey were now bent to this end – and all Catherine's to frustrating them.

By 23 November Catherine was sufficiently alarmed at Henry's activities (of which, as usual, she was well informed) to summon the Spanish ambassador to see her at Greenwich. But it was hardly a regular audience. Instead, she ordered him 'to go thither in disguise, and with the greatest possible secrecy'.

They had a long conversation, in the course of which she told him that the King was planning to send one of his most trusted friends and advisers, Sir William Fitzwilliam, the Treasurer of the Household, to Spain to demand the original of the Brief. Catherine wanted Mendoza to warn Charles V of Fitzwilliam's mission, and to advise the Emperor that in no circumstances was the Brief to be handed over. She had heard that Fitzwilliam had secret orders 'to get that document into his hands and, if successful, place it where it cannot be found again'. Charles must take no chances. She had been advised that such Briefs were not registered in Rome, so the original in Spain was unique. And 'all the strength of her case now lies in [it]'.[4]

But Henry changed his mind about sending Fitzwilliam (as Mendoza thought he would). Instead, he would try a subtler approach and get Catherine herself to write to demand the original of the Brief.

We can only guess at the means that were used, but they were successful. Having sworn Henry a 'solemn oath' to get the Brief 'by all possible means', Catherine wrote the necessary letter to Charles. The letter was sent by the overland route via France with two messengers: one the King's servant; the other the Queen's, Francisco Felipez.

Felipez was already a marked man. Before he left, he was told that on no account was he to carry any other letter from the Queen. He swore accordingly. And watches and searches were available to make sure he kept his word.

Mendoza, however, got round the precaution simply enough and 'made the messenger learn by heart all that was required'. He was to tell Charles to ignore Catherine's letter, as it was not 'a free act of her will'. But Felipez's journey was no sooner begun than it was over. 'He fell at Abbeville and broke an arm' and had to come back to London.

Everything had to be done again. Catherine's letter was rewritten and given this time to her Chaplain, Thomas Abel. Abel was to prove one of Catherine's bravest and most devoted defenders. But he was English, and Henry's subject and servant before he was hers. That alone in 1529 was enough for Catherine. 'Unwilling to deliver the [oral] message to the King's servant [Abel], in whom she placed no trust', she paired him with Montoya, another Spaniard, 'who might also retain by heart the ... message'.[5]

Abel and Montoya made the journey to the Franco-Spanish frontier in company with another royal courier, Curzon, who was carrying letters informing the English ambassadors in Spain of the mission to get hold of the Brief. They reached Fuenterrabia together on 2 February. But there Curzon was stopped, though Abel and Montoya were let through. Abel had seemed particularly keen to press ahead. The result was that Abel was in Valladolid ten days before the English ambassadors knew anything about his arrival.[6]

He put his time to good use. He got audience of the Emperor to whom he gave the letter extorted from Catherine. He also gave him a covering note. The gist was the message which Montoya and, before him, Felipez, had learned by heart. But Abel elaborated the simple message into a six-point memorandum. Charles was to remonstrate with the Pope, for his apparent favour to Henry. He was to send a good canonist (canon lawyer) as his ambassador to England, to take charge of the case. And he was to match Henry's research effort and 'order good canonists and legists to examine the matter, and write to the Queen thereon something that she can make use of'.[7]

What was going on? Was Abel indeed acting on Catherine's orders, as he claimed? Or had he taken over Montoya's mission on his own initiative? And what of Catherine's role? Was her earlier distrust of Abel real? Or was it a subterfuge, in which she deceived even the Spanish ambassador, to keep Abel 'clean'? We shall never know for certain, since, as in all the best spy stories, the controller (Catherine) and the agent (Abel) had covered their tracks so well.

One thing is clear, however. Despite the incident at the frontier, the English ambassadors in Spain had no inkling that Abel might be a double agent. Instead, they consulted him and confided in him as a colleague. Especially on the matter of the Brief. For the Emperor denied them only one thing. He refused, courteously but absolutely, to hand over the original of the Brief. (The English ambassadors could not understand why!) Otherwise Charles V was generous in allowing them access to it. The Brief was read to them; they were given a notarially attested copy; they were even allowed, under supervision, to transcribe it and examine it.[8]

One of the ambassadors was Edward Lee, who was Henry's main legal expert on the Great Matter. He found Abel, who was a fellow Court cleric, particularly helpful in his analysis of the Brief. The Brief stated that it was obtained at the request of Henry and Catherine. But Catherine, Abel confirmed, had never heard of it till she received the transcript from Spain in 1528. The Brief also stated as a matter of certainty that Arthur had carnally 'known' Catherine. Abel confirmed that the Queen denied this on oath. Finally, when Lee came to draw up his list of points which suggested that the Brief was a forgery, he arranged them under twelve heads, as was 'partly suggested by his conversation with Master Abel'.[9]

These conversations have a surreal quality. On one side, there is Henry's chief legal expert; on the other, the man who was to emerge as one of Catherine's most effective propagandists. And they are engaged in an animated exchange of ideas. But only Abel knew who was on whose side. And only he and Catherine were able to benefit from the knowledge.

*

The Abel mission was Catherine's third hammer-blow against Henry. Once again (as with the production of the Brief and the Felipez mission), she had proved that she had better intelligence, better and more daring agents and finally, I think, a better tactical sense.

There is a curious footnote to the affair of the Brief. The Imperial Chancellor Gattinara told Lee that 'he thought that the Holy Ghost, foreseeing what might follow, had preserved it'. For the Brief was found, he admitted, not in any official archive, but 'the hands of . . . a cousin of the person who had the handling of both marriages of the Queen'. Lee asked if his name perhaps was De Puebla. Gattinara acknowledged that it was.[10]

So De Puebla had done one last service for Catherine's marriage – even from beyond the grave.

37. *Trial in open court*

Old habits die hard, as do old marriages. Catherine and Henry had been married for almost twenty years. Recently they had grown apart emotionally. But a whole network of connexions and assumptions remained. There was their shared love for their daughter Mary. And there were the little routines of half a lifetime of shared living. Catherine made Henry's shirts (and, to his dying day, he never lost his taste for the black-thread embroidery round the collar and cuffs that was known as Spanish work). When they were apart, they exchanged messages every few days, as they had done since their first separation in the French war of 1513. To authenticate the messages, they used secret tokens, known only to each other. Breaking these ties would take years of mounting pain and bitterness – bitterness on Henry's part and pain largely on Catherine's.[1]

Even Court ritual drove them together. The Court calendar revolved round the 'Days of Estate'. These were the main feast days of the Church which were also marked by high ceremony at Court. The King and Queen wore matching robes, whose colour depended on the occasion (purple or scarlet for celebration, blue for mourning). They processed to the Chapel Royal. They heard mass in their adjacent Closets or Pews and they participated in special ceremonies at the altar. Then they dined publicly and in state. On certain days, such as Twelfth Night or Shrove Tuesday, they watched a play in the Great Hall in the evening or took part in a banquet. And they did all this together.

The greatest concentration of 'Days of Estate' lay in the extended Christmas celebrations, which lasted from Christmas Day, 25 December, when the King and Queen wore the purple, to Epiphany, 6 January, when they appeared in their crowns and most of the coronation regalia. So, as Christmas 1528 approached, all eyes were on the Court. Would the time-honoured rituals be observed, or would Henry carry out his repeated threats to separate from Catherine?[2]

In the event, habit and perhaps a sense of decency more or less prevailed. The King and Queen had moved to Greenwich on 17 November 1528. Catherine remained there, though Henry broke off to pay several short visits to Bridewell. Ostensibly, these visits were to enable him to consult more freely with the legates about the Great Matter. But they had a covert purpose as well. Henry 'had lodged [his mistress] in a very fine lodging, which he has prepared for her close by his own'. There, 'greater court is ... paid to her everyday than has been to the Queen for a long time'.[3]

Did Catherine know about her rival's nights of pleasure and days of pomp in London? If so, she chose to ignore them. Instead, she took advantage of her husband's absence in town to summon Mendoza, the Spanish ambassador, to see her incognito in her apartments at Greenwich. She confirmed that Henry had reiterated his determination to separate from her, on the grounds of his personal safety. It was not Catherine herself that he mistrusted, he assured his wife, but 'he is not quite so sure of her servants, both English and Spanish, and especially of the latter'. But Henry had not, Catherine said with relief, carried out the threat. Instead, whenever he came to Greenwich, 'he very seldom fails to visit her, and they dine and sleep together'. Catherine, understandably, did not go into details. So we will never know if Henry had resumed the sexual relations, which, according to Campeggio, he had broken off at the time of the first trial of the marriage in 1527. But it seems unlikely.

Mendoza then speculated on Henry's motives. The King had received legal advice, he guessed, that he must not appear too flagrantly to deprive Catherine of her conjugal rights while the Great Matter was still *sub judice*. This is probably true. But Henry was not only acting legalistically. He preferred, of course, to spend his time with his other woman. But, when he was under the same roof as Catherine, he ate with her and accompanied her out of habit and because he always had. And he kept Christmas in the old fashion too.

Henry joined Catherine at Greenwich on the 18th. On Christmas Day, he heard two masses and tipped the boys of the Chapel Royal two pounds for their singing of *Gloria in excelsis*. The same day, the French ambassador reported that 'the whole Court has retired to Greenwich, where open house is kept both by the King and Queen, as it used to be in former years'. But things were not quite as usual. For the King's mistress was at Greenwich too, 'having her establishment apart, as . . . she does not like to meet with the Queen'. Did she fear Catherine's tongue or Catherine's tears?

But Catherine had more important things to worry about than her husband's mistress. Ever since Campeggio's arrival in England, her strategy had been clear. It was to persuade Pope Clement to revoke the commission to his two legates, Cardinal Wolsey and Cardinal Campeggio, and take the trial of her marriage back into his own hands in Rome.

Charles V's envoys in Rome were bringing heavy pressures to bear to the same effect. The pressures culminated on 27 April 1529 when a formal written protest was presented to the Pope in person, requiring Clement 'to have the case adjudicated in his Court, since, were it to be tried in England, Queen Catherine would never obtain justice'.[4]

Catherine's hope was that her nephew's request would have the force of a command. But it fell on unwilling ears. Clement, caught as he was between the upper and nether millstones of Charles V's power and Henry VIII's wrath, had little sympathy for Catherine's plight. 'Would to God', his Secretary, Sanga, wrote to Campeggio, 'that [Wolsey] had allowed the matter to take its course [in 1527], because if the King had come to a decision without the Pope's authority, whether wrongly or rightly, it would have been without blame or prejudice to his Holiness.' And would to God also that Catherine would agree to take the veil. 'The course would be portentous and unusual', Sanga readily admitted, but it would involve the injury of only one person: Catherine. And that Clement could 'readily entertain'.[5]

Only one thing would force the Pope to act: a direct, personal appeal from Catherine herself.

Now it was Catherine's turn to hesitate. So far, she had moved purposefully and decisively. But, faced with this decision, she postponed, prevaricated, grasped at every straw. It was not that she did not understand what was required. Rather, she understood its consequences all too well. A sixteenth-century wife, especially a royal wife, was expected to have no will apart from her husband's. Or, at least, she was never to display such a will publicly. In all her previous actions in the Great Matter, Catherine had stayed – just – on the right side of this principle. Everything she had done had been secret and, in so far as it was known to her husband, disavowable. But an appeal to Rome would be open, and an open challenge. It might enable her to keep Henry as her husband. But she would forfeit his trust for ever. For Catherine to appeal was to choose the weapon of a suicide. The first result would be, as she herself wrote, '*suum manifestum excidium* [her own certain ruin]'. The appeal was to be used only in the last extremity.

For several months, Henry's own hesitations spared Catherine the need to make this terrible choice. Ever since Catherine had detonated the bombshell of the Brief, Henry and his agents in Rome had been trying to make the basis of the Legatine Trial in England more watertight. But Pope Clement, even-handed in his dissimulation, had blocked them at every turn. Without additional assurance from Rome, Henry was reluctant to risk an open trial of his marriage. These delays were Catherine's salvation, as the Imperial ambassador, Mendoza, pointed out. To Mendoza's profound relief, he had left London for the Netherlands in late May. At the time of his departure, he reported, 'the Queen's case was at a standstill, and there were no symptoms of its being proceeded with. There was, therefore, no occasion or need for a protest, nor for making an appeal to the judges.'[6]

But, within a few days, the world had been turned upside-down. Henry lost patience and decided, whatever the defects in the Legates' authority, to force matters to a conclusion. Perhaps he hoped that bullying and bribery would win the day (the vast wealthy Bishopric of Durham had already been dangled in front of Campeggio's nose). Perhaps he believed in the force of his cause.

On 30 May, Henry authorized Wolsey and Campeggio to proceed with the trial. The next day, the two Cardinals met in the Parliament Chamber, otherwise the Upper Refectory (or Upper Frater), at Blackfriars. The Pope's general commission was read and they formally accepted it. Their first act was to appoint two bishops to summon the King and Queen to appear before them on 18 June. The summons was served on Catherine the next day in her Privy Chamber at Windsor. Her decision on the appeal could be postponed no longer.[7]

Even so, she hung on till the eleventh hour and beyond. On 14 June, the King and Queen left Hampton Court to take up residence at Greenwich 'in order to be present [at Blackfriars] at the day fixed'. Henry travelled by water; Catherine by land. En route, she 'crossed the water', and went to call on Campeggio. He was laid up, as he reported, with 'my gout, which is accompanied by a slight feverishness'. But Catherine, 'very anxious and perplexed about her affairs', threw etiquette to the winds and was ushered 'even to my bedside'. Her first anxiety was the fact that her advocates had not arrived from Flanders. She did not fully trust her English counsel, she said. What should she do? Hope for the best, Campeggio replied. But all this, I suspect, was so much beating about the bush for Catherine's real concern: how could the case go ahead in England when the Emperor had asked for it to be revoked to Rome? Had the revocation in fact taken place? Campeggio had to admit that it had not. Once more, he pressed the matter of taking the veil. She brushed him aside. Her mind was made up. 'On the Queen's departure from me she went to her lodgings here in London, and there met her counsellors.'[8]

The 'Queen's lodgings' in London were situated in Baynard's Castle, where Henry VII and Elizabeth of York had stayed during the celebrations for Catherine's first marriage with Prince Arthur. This time, they witnessed a very different ceremony. Catherine remained with her advisers all that day and into the next. Then, on the 16th, in their presence and in 'a certain upper chamber', she made her formal appeal from the Legates to Rome. She did so in the presence of two notaries, who recorded the fact in proper form in 'a public instrument'. The die was cast.

Catherine knew she had to act. But she was wife and woman enough to regret what she had to do. 'She is very sad and disconsolate', Mendoza reported on the basis of direct information, 'because, though when sick in her very heart, she swallowed the potion prescribed for her, she yet sees no relief at hand in her misfortune.' The reason for her sorrow, he explained, was that 'she apprehends that instead of calming her husband's irritation against her, she has rather increased it by her act'. She was right. But her conscience, and her sense of affronted right, drove her to yet more open defiance of Henry.[9]

The place chosen for the public trial of Catherine's marriage was the Parliament Chamber of the Dominican Friary of London. Invariably known as Blackfriars, because of the colour of the friars' robes, the Friary occupied an enormous site at the western corner of the City walls. To the north it was bounded by Ludgate Hill, to the west by the Fleet river and to the south by the Thames. Internally, the precinct was divided by Water Lane, which ran north-south from the Great Gate off Ludgate Hill to the Water Gate on the Thames. The western half of the precinct was largely empty, save for orchards and gardens. The eastern side of Water Lane, however, was thickly developed with the Friary buildings.

The buildings lay on a north-south axis. The Church was to the north, with two cloisters, the Great Cloister and the Inner Cloister, one after the other, to the south. On the first floor of the west side of the Great Cloister was the Friary Guest House, and, directly to the south, the Parliament Chamber, which, likewise, formed the first floor of the west side of the Inner Cloister. The two buildings were linked by a staircase tower. The Refectory occupied the whole of the range and was an enormous room, a hundred and ten feet long and fifty-two feet wide. The rooms of the Guest House were narrower, since the west side of this range was taken up with a gallery, ten feet wide and a hundred and ten feet long. At its northern end, the gallery was joined by another two-storey gallery, which crossed the Friary gardens and orchards diagonally, from south-east to north-west. At the north-western end, a covered bridge across the Fleet river connected this gallery directly to the private apartments of Bridewell Palace, which lay on the opposite bank of the Fleet River.[10]

The bridge and galleries were the final stage of the construction of Bridewell Palace. Henry had started building the palace in 1515, to replace the accommodation he had lost when the private lodgings at Westminster burned out in 1512. The works took seven years and cost the enormous sum of £20,000. But, when they were finished, Henry had a palace-monastery complex that more than substituted for Westminster. Bridewell itself offered residential accommodation which was modern, compact and fashionable, in contrast with the sprawling, half-ruinous medieval splendours of Westminster, while Blackfriars had facilities, sacred and secular, which rivalled those of Westminster Abbey. The site, on the boundaries of the City, rather than in a suburb (as was Westminster), was also well suited to a king who was popular and knew it. Now, with the hugely ambitious network of galleries linking the palace and monastery, Bridewell-Blackfriars was set to displace Westminster and become the royal capital of Tudor England.

The newly-completed buildings were first used in 1522, for the visit of Catherine's nephew, Charles V. The following year, Parliament was summoned there. The King stayed in Bridewell; heard the customary mass of the Holy Ghost in the Friary Church; and opened the Parliament in the Parliament Chamber or Upper Refectory.[11]

The decision to use the Parliament Chamber for the Legatine Trial was thus a natural one. No one could have guessed that the outcome of the Trial would be a triumph for Catherine. Nor that it would alienate Henry from the palace and the City and destroy the prospects for Bridewell as a royal habitation forever.

In early May, Thomas Garton, Page of the Wardrobe of the Beds, was ordered to prepare the Chamber for the trial. A 'dormant' or fixed table and two chairs, covered in cloth of gold with cloth of gold cushions, were placed for the judges on the dais at the southern end of the room. The dais was railed and 'all covered in carpets and tapestry . . . like a solemn Court'. On the right hand side of the Chamber was a throne, with a cloth of gold canopy, for the King, and on the left, another throne, also canopied but lower, for the Queen. In the body of the court were bars at either end for the advocates, benches for the assembled bishops, and more benches and tables for the clerks.

Some of the weightier items, including the benches, bars and dais, may have been still in situ from the last Parliament. The rest – the chairs, carpets, cushions and precious textiles – would have come from the storehouse of the Great Wardrobe. This lay directly to the east of Blackfriars, at the junction of Carter Lane and St Andrew's Hill, and was connected to the monastery by another gallery. The proximity of the Wardrobe and the re-use of existing materials kept Garton's costs for 'making ready the Parliament Chamber' to a modest six shillings.[12]

The second session of the court took place, as arranged, on Friday, 18 June. This again was intended to be a formal occasion, in which the two parties would answer their citation or summons by proxy.

Henry duly sent his proxies. But Catherine created a sensation by appearing in person. This took everyone by surprise: according to

Campeggio, her arrival was 'unexpected and unknown till the last moment'. She entered in solemn state, accompanied by four bishops, the rest of her counsel, and 'a great company' of ladies and gentlewomen. Then, 'sadly and with great gravity', she read the written protestation against the jurisdiction of the Cardinals which she had made on the 16th, and required it to be registered and returned to her. The judges agreed and informed Catherine that they would answer her protestation on the following Monday, 21 June.[13]

Between 9 and 10 o'clock on the Monday morning, the full court duly assembled. Catherine entered first, then the two Cardinals, Wolsey and Campeggio, and finally Henry VIII himself, who was the first to be seated. 'It was', according to George Cavendish (who, as Wolsey's Gentleman Usher, was an eye-witness), 'the strangest and newest sight' that a King and Queen should 'appear in . . . court [as common persons] . . . to abide the judgement of their own subjects'. The court crier cried: 'Silence!' Then the judges' commission was read and the parties summoned into court. 'King Harry of England, come into court!' called the crier. 'Here, my lords!' answered the King, as he rose from his throne.

Then, standing but still under the canopy, the King addressed the court. He 'said a few words in English', asking for a swift decision 'to determine the validity or nullity of his marriage, about which he had from the beginning felt a perpetual scruple'. Wolsey spoke next and also set out his *bona fide*. He acknowledged the infinite benefits he had received from the King; nevertheless, he protested, both he and Campeggio would judge the case only according to the facts and their conscience. Wolsey's speech was designed to answer the substance of Catherine's objections. It remained only for Campeggio formally to reject her protestation and to reassert the competence of the judges.

That done, Catherine was cited to appear. 'Catherine, Queen of England, come into the court!' called the crier. Catherine was now on a stage, and the eyes of all the world were on her. She did not falter. First, she addressed the judges. Once more she rejected their competence and appealed directly to Rome. Then she turned to her husband. He had spoken of his scruples. But now, she bitterly replied, 'it was not the time to say this after so long silence'.

Stung, Henry defended himself. He had remained silent, he insisted, only because of 'the great love he had and has for her [and] he desired, more than anything else, that the marriage should be declared valid'. Then he, too, went on to the attack and denounced her appeal to Rome. It was unreasonable, he argued, 'considering the Emperor's power there'. And was not England, the country of which she was Queen, 'perfectly secure for her'? Did she not have 'the choice of prelates and lawyers' as her counsel?[14]

For the King publicly to bandy words with his Queen was undignified. It was also a blunder. As Anne Boleyn later pointed out, whenever Henry got into an argument with Catherine, he lost. He did so spectacularly this time.[15]

Suddenly the Queen left her dais, which was placed opposite her husband's. But it was separated from it by the body of the court with its bars and throng of lawyers, clerk and bishops. These obstacles made it impossible for the Queen to cross the room directly; instead 'she took pain to go about unto the King [and knelt] down at his feet'. Twice Henry tried to raise her up, according to Campeggio, but still she knelt. Then, 'in the sight of all the court and assembly', she spoke 'in broken English':

> [She begged] him to consider her honour, her daughter's and his;
> that he should not be displeased at her defending it, and should
> consider the reputation of her nation and relatives, who will be
> seriously offended; in accordance with what he had said about his
> good will, she had throughout appealed to Rome, where it was
> reasonable that the affair should be determined, as the present
> place was open to suspicion and because the cause is already
> [begun] at Rome.

Catherine, for all her 'broken English', made the speech of her life. But its effect was not so much rhetorical as forensic. By appearing to take her husband's protestations of continuing love at face value, she had twisted his words to devastating effect. If Henry was so keen for the marriage to be found valid, she had said, how could he possibly object to her appeal to Rome? Surely it was the most natural thing in the world?

Still worse from Henry's point of view was his own response. The heat of the moment, his instinctive gallantry, the overwhelming sympathy of the audience for his wife – all drove him to give some sort of agreement to Catherine's request.

It is unclear just how far he went. Campeggio understood the exchange to mean that Henry had *actually* 'granted [Catherine] full liberty to write and send messengers to Rome and to his Holiness [with her appeal]'. Catherine understood the same. But Henry, appalled at what he had done under pressure, later tried to introduce qualifications. It proved impossible. He had given his wife the word of a King, spoken in public, that she could appeal to Rome. *He* could never retract. *She* could act with a clear conscience.

It was Catherine's final and most effective coup against the Great Matter. She had knelt. But she had fought and won.[16]

There was nothing more for her to do in the court. 'She rose up, making a low courtesy to the King, and departed from thence.' It was supposed that she would have returned to her former seat; instead 'she took her direct way out of the house, leaning, as she was wont always to do, upon the arm of her General Receiver called Mr Griffith [Richards]'. Seeing his prey escape, Henry ordered the crier to call her back. 'Catherine, Queen of England, come into the court!' he cried. Richards said to her: 'Madam, ye be called again.' 'On, on,' she replied. 'It makes no matter, for this is no indifferent court for me; therefore I will not tarry. Go on your ways.' Twice more the crier repeated his summons. But Catherine ignored him. She never returned.[17]

In this extraordinary exchange, both Henry and Catherine were playing to the gallery. The court was open, and the common folk, male and female, of London packed the lower end of the Parliament Chamber, overflowed into the anteroom and stood on the stairs. And there was no doubt who got the applause. 'If the matter was to be decided by the women', the French ambassador, the shrewd, worldly Bishop Jean du Bellay, noted, '[the King] would lose the battle; for they did not fail to encourage the Queen at her entrance and departure by their cries, telling her to care for nothing, and other such words; while she recommended herself to their good prayers, and used other Spanish tricks (*castellanneries*).'[18] There had been earlier demonstrations too. When Henry and Catherine 'were passing from their royal residence [Bridewell] to the Dominicans through a gallery communicating with that convent, the Queen was ... warmly greeted by immense crowds of people, who publicly wished her victory over her enemies'. Enraged, Henry ordered his guards that 'nobody should be again admitted to the place'.

It was easier said than done: the banks of the Fleet were a public highway and not even Henry VIII could divert a road at his pleasure. Some of his councillors, according to the Spanish ambassador, drew the obvious conclusion: if the King could not remove the Londoners, it might be better if he removed himself. 'It is far better for him', they advised, 'not to live in London, because he will be less open to slander.'

Henry took their advice, but his absence lasted only a few days. For if he wished to drive through his Divorce, he had to be on the spot. And Bridewell was his only central residence. Until he had another, he had to inure himself to the people's cheers for Catherine and their muttered jeers and curses for himself.[19]

After Catherine's walk-out from the Court at Blackfriars, the Great Matter became a double race. In London, the King and his lawyers were moving heaven and earth to rush the trial to its conclusion and obtain (they took for granted) a favourable verdict. In Rome, on the other hand, Catherine's family and friends were exerting themselves just as manfully to persuade Pope Clement to accept Catherine's appeal, 'advoke' the case to Rome and abort the Legatine Trial in England. It was anybody's guess who would win.

At first, the shrewd money would have been on Henry's team.

Catherine's withdrawal of course made their task easier. Her lawyers, especially Fisher, performed miracles and earned Henry's undying hatred for their pains. But, without the Queen, there was a limit to the resistance they could offer. And the pressure on Campeggio, in particular, was immense:

> If your Lordship [he wrote to his friend and colleague, Cardinal Salviati] saw me in bed with a cruel attack of gout in seven places, accompanied with fever, although only incidental, brought on by the pain, and surrounded by fifteen doctors with two piles of books to show me all they conclude is according to law, and nothing else can or ought to be done, I am sure you would have compassion on me, especially as I am obliged to have myself carried to the place where the trial is held, God knows with what discomfort to me and danger in moving, in ascending and descending staircases, and in embarking and landing from the vessel.

Campeggio's wry humour, and the constant stream of letters he wrote to his friends in the Curia (as the Papal Court was known), saved his sanity. But they would offer no protection should the trial come to a natural conclusion. His secret instructions from Clement VII, which were repeated with every letter from Rome, were to drag things out as much as possible. But the English had grown wise to this tactic and, Campeggio ruefully observed, 'it is no longer possible to entertain them [string them along]' as previously. What then should he do, he asked Salviati, 'if the process be finished before any provision [that is, an order from Rome to abandon the trial] comes?' 'I beg your lordship to think how I can in such a heat avoid giving sentence – I mean if judgement be for the King.' He could say that he was unable or unwilling to give judgement. But, in that case, the commission authorized Wolsey to deliver a verdict alone. And there was not much doubt what that would be. 'God help me,' Campeggio concluded.[20]

But, as Campeggio winced and fretted, Henry (despite the vast issues at stake) was enjoying the whole thing. The King was an amateur theologian and lawyer, with a shrewd eye for quiddities, distinctions and super-subtleties. The trial was a feast of such, and Henry glutted himself. He turned up in person to swear his depositions; he debated in private with Campeggio; he had endless discussions with his lawyers.

Meanwhile, as Campeggio feared, the trial was drawing towards its end. There was a final adjournment. Then Friday, 23 July was fixed as the day that judgement would be given. Henry, casting his kingly dignity to the winds, decided to eavesdrop. According to Cavendish, he came 'and sat within a gallery' next to the door of the Parliament Chamber. The door gave a view of 'the judges where they sat, whom he might see and hear speak, to hear what judgement they would give in his suit'. The Court assembled at its usual time, between 9 and 10 o'clock in the morning. The counsel for the enquiry exhibited the written record of the trial and pressed the judges to give sentence. Henry's moment of liberation, he thought, was at hand.[21]

Catherine's behaviour throughout this frenetic period could not have been more different from Henry's. After her dramatic walk-out from the court, she left Bridewell and went to Greenwich, where she remained, despite repeated written summons to reappear before the legates.

For she had done her work; she could only hope and pray that it would take effect in time.

Others, however, had laboured frantically on her behalf. The moment she had formally executed them, three documents had been rushed over to Brussels: her protestation against the legates, her appeal to Rome, and her power of attorney for the Spanish ambassador to the Curia. Her messenger was an un-named gentleman of her Household. It would be satisfactory to think that it was Francisco Felipez, now recovered from his broken arm. In Brussels, Mendoza, the former Spanish ambassador in London, took charge of the papers and ensured that they were 'sent to Rome by an express messenger'. By 5 July, they were in the hands of Miçer Mai, Charles V's ambassador to Pope Clement.[22]

Mai was Catherine's ardent partisan. He dashed with the letters straight to Clement and upbraided him mercilessly for his failure to 'advoke' the case to Rome. Wearily, Clement agreed that Mai should set the machinery in motion. 'You have the Queen's powers to act for her,' he told Mai, 'let a petition be presented in her name and justice shall be done.' Five days later, on the 10th, Mai got firm information about the first stages of the Blackfriars Trial: that Catherine had appealed; that the legates had rejected her appeal; and that Catherine, in consequence of her failure to appear, had been declared 'contumacious' – that is, wilfully disobedient to the summons of the Court.[23]

Contumacy, Clement did not need telling, opened the way to more-or-less summary proceedings. There was now real urgency. The Pope summoned a meeting of the *signatura*, the advisory body which made recommendations on petitions of justice, for the 13th. Its unanimous advice was that Catherine's appeal should be allowed. But, to give the decision added weight (and probably to put off the inevitable for a few more days), Clement resolved that the 'advocation' should first be ratified by the Consistory: that is, by the Pope and cardinals meeting in solemn council. This was fixed for the 16th. But, the evening before, Clement collapsed with an illness that was either diplomatic or psychosomatic, and it was announced that the Consistory was postponed. Mai exploded with fury at one of the senior cardinals, threatening that the Emperor 'could and would find other means' to protect Catherine. Cowed and cornered at last, Clement allowed the advocation to be decreed as planned on the 16th in a Congregation: that is, a meeting of the cardinals without the Pope.[24]

The English representatives in Rome had fought Mai every step of the way. And even now they had a final ploy: let the advocation be sent only to Catherine, they requested. Mai saw through that immediately. Their intention, he guessed, was either to waylay the single messenger or to have the document suppressed when it reached England. Once again Mai went directly to the Pope, who, weary and sick at heart about the whole business, told him 'I might do what I liked' about publication.[25]

It was a task Mai relished. No fewer than six copies were drawn up. One was to be posted in Rome on the 23rd. Two more were to be sent to Flanders, to be posted in Bruges and Dunkirk. And no less than four were to be sent to Catherine via the Archduchess Margaret. That would teach the English.

In the event, one of Catherine's copies was sent by her faithful Gentleman of the Household.[26]

But Mai's haste, it transpired, was superfluous. On 23 July, the day that the advocation was posted in Rome, the Legate's Court assembled at Blackfriars. But, instead of delivering its verdict, Campeggio, 'taking his faith upon the word of a true prelate' announced that, since 'the reaping and harvest vacation' had begun in Rome, the case would stand 'prorogued and continued' until the beginning of the new term on 1 October. Campeggio (or was it his friend Salviati?) had come up with the solution to his dilemma: he had decreed neither for Henry nor against him but had simply adjourned the case.[27]

The leading members of the royal Court had come to hear the expected verdict. As soon as Campeggio announced the adjournment, the Duke of Suffolk, Henry's brother-in-law, stepped forward and struck the table in front of the two judges: 'By the mass,' he swore, 'now I see that the old . . . saw [proverb] is true, that there was never Legate nor Cardinal that did good in England.'[28]

Du Bellay, the French ambassador, had got wind the day before that something had gone wrong with the expected smooth delivery of the verdict for Henry. But, despite such premonitions, the adjournment was a terrible blow for the King.[29]

So far, Catherine had won every battle in the Great Matter. But Henry could not, would not, let her win the war. He would change his general. He would use new weapons. He would show who was master in England.

Then let his wife see how she would cope.

38. The aftermath

The advocation of the case by the Pope altered, as was intended, the balance of power sharply in Catherine's favour. It looked as though the Great Matter would eventually have to be tried in Rome, where Catherine was at least as strong as Henry. But first, if due process were followed, there was the 'citation' or summons. As soon as the necessary documentation arrived in England, Henry, as the respondent party, would be summoned to appear before the Papal tribunal like any other litigant and with the usual penalties for non-compliance. Now, it was one thing for Henry to respond to such a summons as part of a collusive action which he himself had initiated, as in May 1529; it was quite another for it to be served on him against his will and by his wife or her agents. This, Wolsey informed the English ambassadors in Rome, 'is no more tolerable than the whole amission [loss] of his . . . estate and dignity Royal'.[1]

Would Catherine dare to press home her advantage and use a weapon that was guaranteed to humiliate and alienate her husband beyond recall? Henry (in his own words) 'feared' that she would.[2]

He was right to be fearful. During the Blackfriars Trial, Catherine had shown her customary courage. But, in the weeks that followed, her mood turned sour. The trial had ended inconclusively, and still there was no firm news of what had happened to her appeal in Rome. Under the strain, she succumbed to resentment and mistrust. She resented what Henry and Wolsey had done to her, and she was mistrustful of what they might yet do. Her anxieties centred on the Legatine tribunal. This was adjourned rather than dissolved and so might still, she feared, be employed against her.

The man charged with rescuing Henry from the toils of his wife's ill-feeling was Wolsey himself.

By any standards, Wolsey was a man of extraordinary despatch in the conduct of business: he was able to write for twelve hours, from four in the morning till four in the afternoon, without rising 'once to piss', as Cavendish, his Gentleman Usher, reported. But even his fiercesome efficiency was at the mercy of the vagaries of contemporary transport. For communications in the sixteenth century could go no faster than a man could ride along pot-holed roads, through treacherous passes and in the teeth of brigands and customs- and frontier-officials who were scarcely less lawless. In the circumstances, the news of the advocation of the case and citation of Henry to Rome reached England promptly. But the documentation and official notification followed much more slowly. This protracted timetable set the framework for Wolsey's actions.[3]

The English ambassadors in Rome wrote to Wolsey on 16 July, to inform him that the advocation had been granted. But they warned him that they were 'obliged to send this letter by a private courier and by an unsafe route', since the regular posts had been closed as 'the Pope does not wish the King to know anything until the advocation is [officially] sent'. Clement himself wrote to Wolsey three days later, on the 19th. He informed him of the advocation, apologized for having to grant it and trusted that Wolsey would take it in good part.[4]

Despite the fears of the ambassadors, their letter of the 16th made good time to England and was in the King's hands by Monday, 2 August. In the interim, Henry had at last started to contemplate seriously the possibility of a trial of his marriage at Rome – and what Campeggio's role in it might be after his return to the Curia. For an unavoidable consequence of Campeggio's extended stay in England was that he knew where all the bodies were buried. Acting on Henry's orders, Wolsey tried to tie his fellow legate's hands by getting him to sign a written undertaking or 'pollitication'. Wolsey sent the pollitication to Henry by the hands of Brian Tuke, the Master of the Posts, who arrived at Greenwich on Friday, 30 July 'towards evening'. The pollitication, Tuke reported, was unexpectedly well received. The King was especially pleased with Campeggio's undertaking that, if Henry objected to the advocation, he (Campeggio) would use his best efforts with the Pope *ut nec a serenissma Regina permittat dictam causam prosequi aut tractari* (that he shall not permit her Serene Highness the Queen either to pursue or to conduct the case). He was even more satisfied with Campeggio's assurance that he had 'no intelligence [understanding] with the Queen'.[5]

Campeggio's apparently favourable attitude to Henry made him the King's first line of defence when, the following Monday morning, the letters from Rome with firm news of the advocation were put in his hands. Immediately, Henry invoked Campeggio's undertaking in the pollitication. Wolsey was to require Campeggio that, 'according to his promise', 'he will use all ways and means possible that it come into his hands (before) it comes into the Queen's sight'. 'For his Highness', the instructions continued, 'feareth lest she would not facilely [easily] agree the alteration, but use it as it maketh most to her benefit.'[6]

The 'alteration', to which Henry referred, was the scheme to draw the fangs of the citation by removing the elements most offensive to his royal dignity. Wolsey had earlier listed these as citation of the King to Rome, either in person or by proxy, 'with any clauses of interdiction, excommunication, incurring into contempt, *vel cum invocatione brachii secularis aut poenis pecuniariis* [either with the invocation of the secular arm or with financial penalties]'. If these were included, he said, 'the dignity and prerogative Royal of the King's crown, whereunto all the nobles and subjects of this realm will adhere and stick unto the death, will not tolerate nor suffer that [the citation] be obeyed'. Wolsey was instructed to reiterate these arguments to Campeggio and get him in turn to press them on Catherine: 'to be content to procure that no such thing be comprised in the said advocation as shall irritate the King's Highness and his nobles, and say that a King in his own realm may not be violently [compelled]'.[7]

It is unclear whether Campeggio agreed to undertake the task assigned to him. If so, he failed. There was now nothing for it but to open direct negotiations with the Queen's counsel in which he, the King, would appear in the unaccustomed role of suitor. Henry finally agreed to this disagreeable expedient during his short visit to Wolsey at his house of Tyttenhanger near St Alban's on 14–15 August. A few days later Wolsey reported on the progress he had made. He had summoned

Catherine's senior legal adviser, John Clerk, Bishop of Bath and Wells, to a meeting. Tracking him down had taken some time, since the bishop had left London for his summer retreat at Dogmersfield in Hampshire, where, twenty-eight years previously, Catherine had first met Henry VII and Prince Arthur.

Wolsey put the case to Clerk with his accustomed forcefulness. Thus far, he began, Henry 'had never showed himself as a party' to the suit, since the procedure had been *ex officio* or inquisitorial. In the circumstances, it was highly undesirable for 'the Queen [now] to show or make herself a party against the King' or to have a citation, with all the offending clauses, served on him 'at her suit'. This, Clerk was bluntly warned, would 'irritate and exasperate [the King] against her' – with consequences that Wolsey laid on with a trowel. 'Great danger . . . may arise to the Queen . . . if the King is cited.' Likewise, Catherine would be personally blamed if the citation led to a breach of the peace between Henry VIII and Charles V, and 'she would incur the indignation of all the nobles and people of the realm'. But the greatest risk, Wolsey pointed out with relish, was run, not by the Queen, but by the Queen's counsellors: if Catherine pushed things, as was feared, it was they who would bear the brunt of Henry's wrath and face 'extreme undoing'.

Since Clerk himself was Catherine's leading counsellor, the tactic was none too subtle. But it had its desired effect. Quickly, the bishop protested his agreement. Now that the legates' 'hands are closed by the . . . advocation of the cause', Clerk acknowledged, the Queen should go no further. Instead, he proposed a mutual suspension of legal hostilities: 'the Queen ought to be content to proceed no further in the process at Rome, like as the King will nothing attempt by way of law'. And he undertook to try to get the agreement of Catherine's other principal counsel and of the Queen herself.

Clerk returned to London and met his colleagues, including Cuthbert Tunstall, the Bishop of London, and Catherine's Almoner, Dr Shorton. They came up with a scheme by which the letters of advocation and citation would not be served on Henry but only 'secretly notified' to the two legates. This seemed to square the circle. It would spare Henry's pride but, at the same time, it would still be effective in extinguishing finally the authority of the Legatine Court, which was Catherine's minimum requirement. Clerk wrote to this effect to Wolsey who forwarded his letters to Court.[8]

Henry replied by his new Secretary, Stephen Gardiner. He thanked Wolsey for his 'pains, letters and study'. But he was by no means satisfied. For Clerk's letters had revealed new details about the citation. It now required Henry's response, it appeared, 'under pain of 10,000 ducats [£2,500]'. Henry was 'not the best content and marvelleth much *de adjectione poenae pecuniariae* [about the addition of a monetary penalty]'. This, Henry felt, was so 'prejudicial to his person and royal estate', that he could not consent to the citation being formally 'showed to his subject [Wolsey], within his own realm'. Instead, he suggested another device. Clement's Brief of 19 July, in which he informed Wolsey of the advocation of the case, had finally arrived. Would not the formal exhibition of the Brief to the legates suffice to extinguish the jurisdiction of their Court?[9]

Gardiner's letter reached Wolsey at 11 p.m. on 4 September. By this time, Wolsey's guests at The Moor included not only Clerk but Campeggio himself. The following morning, Campeggio eagerly endorsed Henry's suggestion 'that the execution of the brief to me (Wolsey) directed . . . shall be sufficient'. He also agreed to help persuade Clerk. Clerk finally conceded, 'albeit after good and long debating'. But the obstacle, he feared, would be Catherine herself. 'Considering her stiff heart, replenished with great mistrust . . . he doubted what she would do'. At any rate, it would take more than him to convince her.

Clerk's anxieties about Catherine's reaction were evidently shared by Wolsey. Aware that he would have one chance only, he decided to get Henry's direct endorsement first. He sent two distinguished canon lawyers to Court to explain in detail what was proposed 'without that any overture shall be made to the Queen thereof till I may be advertised how the King's Highness and ye of his counsel do like of the same'. Henry was happy to give his seal of approval. But he too feared the worst: 'In case *omnibus tentatis, hoc non successerit* [having tried everything, this should not succeed]', he was prepared to make a choice of evils (*de duobus malis*). 'Rather the [advocation and citation] should be privily execute upon [Wolsey] and the Cardinal Campeggio, than the same with rumour to be divulged in Flanders'.[10]

Armed now with Henry's agreement, Wolsey got to work on Catherine's full counsel. They were no push-over. 'They make much sticking as yet,' he reported, 'alleging that in the . . . brief there be none effectual and express words whereby the Queen might be sured of the effectual closing of the judges' hands; and that she, being full of mistrust, shall be with great difficulty induced thereto.'[11]

Somehow, Wolsey pulled off the trick. On 11 September the two Cardinals came to London for the formal renunciation of their powers. This too had been the subject of much debate 'both on the King's part and on the Queen's'. 'At length the form of intimation was agreed on,' Campeggio reported, 'and it was made to us by a proctor of the Queen's, who announced that we had no powers, and that neither of us could proceed any further.' Wolsey and Campeggio then signed a declaration to this effect, which was embodied in 'a public deed'.

The English trials of Catherine's marriage were over.[12]

Henry was delighted, and hoped to extract the maximum advantage from Catherine's reluctance to press home her advantage. Even if Catherine wanted to 'resile [withdraw] and go back', he trusted that Wolsey had so arranged matters that 'it should not be in her power so to do'. He also hoped that 'this act, done before [Wolsey] and the Cardinal Campeggio' would prejudice her future chances of legal action, 'by the letting and impeaching of further prosecution, and of any citation or process' whether 'here, at Rome or elsewhere'. It was a characteristically grasping and mean-spirited response.

But why had Catherine given in? Was it gratuitous generosity? Her early mood hardly points to that. Had her counsel been panicked by Wolsey's threats into pressurizing her? If so, it is difficult to understand why the negotiations were so long and so tough. Catherine herself offered a more straightforward explanation.

> The Queen [she was reported as saying] had at one time resolved to be herself the bearer of the inhibition, and, since there was no one to execute [it], to present the same to the King; but on the latter representing that it would be quite sufficient that the two Cardinals should resign, and exhorting her not to take such a step, she [the Queen] agreed to desist, *on condition of her counsel declaring that no harm or detriment should ensue to her interests*, and that the inhibition to the Cardinals should be considered sufficient.

Which indeed seems to be what happened.[13]

Once again, therefore, Catherine was one step ahead of Henry. *Before* she agreed to the form of Wolsey and Campeggio's renunciation, she had made sure that she would do no damage to her legal position. But even *after* the renunciation, Henry was still nursing the hope (which his wife already knew to be delusory) that her action would be 'prejudicial' to her. As so often, Henry had been too clever by half – and too devious. But it was Catherine who scored the solid points.

Why? Was it that Catherine's legal advice, for which indeed she paid dearly (£514 in 1527–8 and £704 in 1528–9), was better than Henry's? Rather the difference lay in the King and Queen themselves. Catherine was a good client, who was prepared to take advice. Henry was an impossible one, who always thought he knew better than his lawyers. He paid the price – until he could change the law to fit his notions.[14]

The agreement of the 'alteration' with Catherine and her counsel was Wolsey's last service for Henry. In the immediate aftermath of the Blackfriars Tribunal, Catherine herself had prophesied that its failure would mean Wolsey's ruin:

> The Queen [Mendoza reported] writes that such are the King's disappointment and passion at not being able to carry out his purpose that the Cardinal will inevitably be the victim of his rage.

The Queen spoke true. On 19 September, with the 'alteration' safely concluded, Henry relented and allowed Wolsey to come to Grafton where the King was enjoying the hunting. But the circumstances were designed to humiliate: the man who had ruled the roost so long was not even given a room of his own where he could change his riding clothes.[15]

A fortnight later the blow fell. On 9 October, as Wolsey presided in the Court of Chancery, he was himself indicted in the Common Law Court of King's Bench. The charge was one of *Praemunire*: that is, the illegal exercise of Papal authority in England in his capacity as legate. The penalty was the confiscation of all property and imprisonment at the King's pleasure. On the 22nd, Wolsey anticipated the inevitable verdict by acknowledging his offences and surrendering himself and his vast possessions into the King's hands. On the 30th, his person was placed outside the King's protection and his property declared forfeit. Meanwhile, he had been forced to surrender the Chancellorship.

Wolsey was the man Catherine blamed for putting the idea of the Divorce in the King's head. For fifteen years, he had come between Catherine and her husband. Now he was gone.

On 3 November, Henry opened the fifth Parliament of his reign, later known as the 'Reformation' Parliament. It was immediately 'prorogued' or adjourned to Westminster. For Henry now had a new palace to replace Bridewell of baleful memory.[16]

A few days previously, on 24 October, Henry had gone by boat from Greenwich to Wolsey's former town-palace of York Place in Westminster. The King was accompanied only by his mistress, her mother and Henry Norris, the Groom of the Stool and, as head of the Privy Chamber, the King's principal body servant. This select party inspected both the building and Wolsey's treasures, which had been laid out for them like the goods in a Harrods' sale. They were mightily impressed: 'it is added', the Imperial ambassador reported, 'that the King was much gratified and found [them] more valuable even than he expected'. On the evening of 2 November Henry left Greenwich to take up residence in the splendidly equipped palace.[17]

He and Anne Boleyn were setting up house together.

It was a new world. It was unclear what place, if any, there was in it for Catherine. Certainly there was none at York Place, which had no apartment for the Queen.

Anne Boleyn

39. Beginnings

Anne Boleyn had the gift of arousing strong feelings. People were never neutral: they either loved her or loathed her.

Even her family origins divided opinion. Her supporters lauded her ancestry while her opponents sneered at her as an upstart. In reality, she was the product of a characteristically English social mix.

On her father's side, Anne descended from a line of merchants made good. Her great-grandfather, Geoffrey Boleyn, was the founder of the family's fortunes. He was a London mercer, who served as Mayor in 1457–8 and received the customary knighthood. Since it was fashionable, then as now, to invest new City money in land and country living, he bought two family seats, Blickling in Norfolk and Hever in Kent. He died in 1463. Sir William, Anne's grandfather, was Geoffrey's second son and eventual heir. In contrast to his aspirant father, he was content with the life of a prosperous country gentleman. But William's eldest son, Thomas, Anne's father, acquired a taste for politics and joined the royal service, where he rose rapidly. He was helped by his family's wealth, by his education (he was fluent in French and, what was more unusual for a layman, in Latin) and, above all, by his family connexions.

For all the Boleyn menfolk had married well, into established noble families. And, with each succeeding generation, the rank of their wives rose: Geoffrey married a baron's daughter; William married the daughter and eventual co-heiress of Thomas Butler, Earl of Ormonde and Catherine of Aragon's Lord Chamberlain; and Thomas did best of all, since his wife Elizabeth was the daughter of the second Duke of Norfolk and sister of the third.

This galaxy of aristocratic female ancestors meant that, in the fullness of time, Anne was able to display a most impressive shield. It quartered the arms of Butler, Rochford, Warenne and Thomas of Brotherton, with augmentations for the English and French princedoms of Lancaster, Angoulême and Guyenne. That Anne descended from these families was incontestable; that she had the right, as a remote descendant in the female line, to display their arms was much more debatable.

Even in her heraldry, it seems, Anne tried too hard and asserted too much.[1]

Thomas and Elizabeth were married in about 1500 and had their three surviving children in quick succession. The eldest, Mary, was a placid and unremarkable girl. But she was very attractive to men, and found them irresistible too – or, at least, her resistance never seems to have lasted long. But the two younger children, Anne and her brother George, the baby of the family, were different. They were intelligent, ambitious and bound by a fierce mutual affection. Their father recognized their talent and did his best to nurture it.

George is supposed to have been 'educated among the Oxonians', though there is no trace of him in university or college records. But either at Oxford or elsewhere he received an excellent education. Having inherited the family talent in languages, he shone in Latin and French. He was also an accomplished poet and translator, and developed a taste for abstruse speculation in religion and political theory. All this marked him out from the run-of-the-mill English gentleman of the day, who was more at home with the sword than the pen. But equally it provided a link with his future brother-in-law Henry VIII, who likewise prided himself on his intellectual sophistication.[2]

Curiously, Anne's education is much better documented than her brother's. Her 'Oxford' was a succession of French-speaking continental royal households which, in everything but Latin, gave her a training at least as good as George's.

Her first placement was in the household of the Archduchess Margaret. Margaret, the daughter of the Emperor Maximilian, had become the favourite aunt of the much-intermarried royal families of Europe. In her youth she had been married three times in quick succession: to Charles VIII of France, who repudiated her; to Catherine of Aragon's brother Juan, who died prematurely; and to the Duke of Savoy, who likewise died young. Widowed for the third time at the age of twenty-four she returned to her native Netherlands, where two years later she became Regent for the future Charles V, who was her nephew through his father, Philip the Fair, and Catherine of Aragon's nephew through his mother, Juaña the Mad. She also supervised the education of Charles and his sisters Eleanor, Elizabeth and Mary.[3]

It was a task for which Margaret was well suited, both emotionally and intellectually. Despite her three marriages, she had no children of her own to distract her and she was multi-lingual, a competent poet in both Latin and French, an important patron of Flemish painting and the builder of an architecturally progressive palace at Mechelen. Much of the palace still stands, and, with its brightly patterned brick and long galleries supported on stone columns and arches in the classical style, it anticipates the buildings Henry and Anne were to throw up together at York Place. Finally, the Arch-duchess was an able politician and a formidable character, whose formal style of address was (not without reason) *Très Redoutée Dame* ('Most Dread Lady').

The result was that her household became an international finishing school, where the élite of three or four countries vied to put their sons and daughters. There, their parents could be confident that they would not only be well educated and trained but also brought up alongside Charles, who was the future ruler of half Europe, and his sisters, who were the Queens-to-be of Portugal, Denmark and Hungary. For, in the sixteenth century as in the twenty-first, who you knew was at least as important as what you knew.

Thomas Boleyn encountered Margaret's household for himself when he was sent as English ambassador to the Netherlands in 1512–13. He made a good impression and was impressed himself in turn. When he had audience with the Archduchess, he found her surrounded by ladies-in-waiting who included natives of France, Spain and England, as well as the Netherlands. Thomas Boleyn, ever with an eye for the main chance, decided that his clever second daughter should join their number.

Soon after his return to England in the spring of 1513, Thomas Boleyn sent Anne to Margaret with an escort and a letter to the Archduchess. Anne was most welcome, Margaret replied, and she hoped to treat her as her father would wish. 'At the least', she continued, 'I trust that, on your return [to the Netherlands], there will be no need for any other interpreter [*truchement*] between you and me than her.' About the girl herself, she was as flattering as any father could wish. 'I find her so well behaved and agreeable for her young age, that I am more obliged to you for sending her than you are to me [for receiving her].'[4]

Anne was given formal instruction in French by Symonnet, a tutor in the Archduchess's household. She began her lessons by writing out letters which he had composed for her to copy. Then, at the next stage, they moved on to dictation. One of these dictation exercises survives, in the form of a letter sent to her father. It was written at La Vure. La Vure, now known by its Flemish name of Terveuren, was the *château*, set in a seven-hundred-acre park on the outskirts of Brussels, that Margaret used as a summer retreat for herself and her young charges.

Anne begins by thanking her father for his letter in which he set out his hopes for his daughter. 'Sir, I understand from your letter that you desire me to be an entirely virtuous woman when I come to the [English] Court.' As an inducement, Boleyn had held out the prospect of conversation with Catherine of Aragon. 'You tell me,' Anne continued, 'that the Queen will take the trouble to converse with me and it gives me great joy to think of talking with such a wise and virtuous person.' The prospect, she assures him 'will make me all the keener to persevere in speaking French well'. It also reminded her of her present deficiencies. 'Sir, I beg you to excuse me if my letter is badly written.' Then she (or rather Symonnet composing in her name) offered the explanation, which contains a vignette of his teaching methods. 'I assure you the orthography is my own, while the others were only written by my hand. Symonnet dictates the letter to me and leaves me to write it myself.' Anne's spelling in the letter is indeed bad – so bad that at times the meaning is scarcely comprehensible.[5]

But – thanks to Symonnet's teaching and the Archduchess's encouragement – Anne made rapid progress. In May the following year the Archduchess announced her intention of spending the summer once more at La Vure. Then, in August, there came a bombshell.

It had been the assumption that King Henry VIII's sister, Mary, would marry the Archduchess Margaret's nephew, Charles, shortly after his fourteenth birthday in February 1514. Mary had been betrothed to him in 1508, and in the English Court she was always addressed as the Princess of Castile. Margaret was a supporter of the English alliance. She was still sore at her own humiliating rejection by Charles VIII of France. And she was well aware that the prosperity of the Netherlands was largely dependent on the English trade: London merchants exported English wool and cloth to the Netherlands and imported in return the luxury goods, including tapestries, illuminated manuscripts, sculptures and paintings, at which Flemish craftsmen excelled. But while Margaret enthused about England, her menfolk sent out mixed signals. Ferdinand of Aragon, Charles's maternal grandfather, double-crossed Henry VIII and scarcely bothered to conceal the fact; while Margaret's father, Maximilian, the boy's paternal grandfather, postponed the marriage-day yet again – waiting, Micawber-like, for something better to turn up (for, like Micawber, Maximilian was always short of cash).

The result, as we have seen, was that Henry VIII lost patience, threw over the Habsburg alliance and married Mary instead to Louis XII of France. The Anglo-French treaties were proclaimed on 10 August 1514. Four days later, Thomas Boleyn wrote to Margaret to inform her of the marriage and to tell her that Mary had specifically asked for his daughter, 'la petite Boulain', as one of her attendants. Would the Archduchess give Anne leave to return with the escort he had sent?

Boleyn begged 'Ma très redoutée Dame' to be pleased with the

news. She certainly was not. England was now allied to her old enemy
the French. And 'la petite Boulain', whom she had taught French, was
now going to put her skills to use by smoothing relations between the
French King and his wife who, despite the best efforts of her teachers,
did 'not have the language perfectly'. It was a poor return for her
efforts.[6]

As it happened, Anne was not back in England in time to travel to
France with Mary and her household. Instead, she seems to have made
the journey directly, by land. Did this mean that she also missed the
spectacular falling-out between the French King and his wife's Lady
Mistress, Lady Guildford, which resulted in Louis's packing off most of
Mary's attendants back to England? At all events, Anne survived the
purge.

Soon, however, she was caught up in the much greater upheaval of
Louis's death and Mary's widowhood, which was terminated abruptly by
Mary's clandestine marriage to her brother Henry's favourite, Charles
Brandon, Duke of Suffolk. Was Anne's role in these events the basis of
the life-long enmity between her and the Duke and Duchess of Suffolk?
It seems probable. At any rate, Anne did not return to England with Mary
at the beginning of 1515. Instead – how and through whose good offices
we do not know – she was placed in the Household of the new Queen of
France, Claude, daughter of Louis XII and wife of the new French King,
Francis I.[7]

Queen Claude, in contrast with the Archduchess Margaret, had little to
teach Anne. Claude was the same age as Anne. She had no influence over
her husband, Francis I, who was devoted to his mother, the domineering
Louise of Savoy. And she was plain to the point of deformity, pious and
more or less constantly pregnant. Henry VIII, as we have seen, was a
model of uxorious tenderness during Queen Catherine's 'dangerous
times'. Francis, on the other hand, displayed a callous indifference to his
wife's sufferings and dragged her and her belly from pillar to post in his
continual wanderings: 'I assure your Grace,' the English ambassador
wrote to Henry in 1520, 'you would have no little compassion if ye saw

the poor creature with the charge she beareth.' Anne, we may guess,
decided that no man would ever treat *her* like that.[8]

The other lessons Anne learned in France were more agreeable.
Francis's Court was the centre of an advanced, brilliant, Italianate
culture. And the French King himself was the perfect gentleman to every
woman except his wife. Anne thrived in this atmosphere of stylish
cultivation. Years later, her accomplishments were still remembered at
the French Court. She perfected her knowledge of French. She polished
her musical skills, learning 'to sing and dance . . . [and] to play the lute
and other instruments'. But the instrument on which she became most
adept was herself. 'She was beautiful, had an elegant figure and eyes that
were even more attractive.' For her eyes were large and black and she
deployed them with a practised skill: 'Sometimes keeping them in
repose; on other occasions, sending them forth as messengers, to carry
the secret witness of the heart.' 'Such was their power, that many men
were hers to command.'

In short, by her late teens she had become the perfect, quintes-
sentially French, *cocotte*. 'You would have never taken her for an English
woman in her manner and behaviour,' wrote Lancelot de Carles in his
poetic reminiscences about her, 'but a native-born French lady.' For a
Frenchman, this was the ultimate accolade.[9]

Once again, the vagaries of foreign policy intervened. Anglo-French
relations soured rapidly in the wake of the Field of Cloth of Gold and in
late 1521 Anne was recalled to England. She had made enough of an
impact for Francis I himself to complain at the removal of 'the daughter
of Mr Boullan', 'who was in the service of the French Queen'. Wolsey,
when the complaints were submitted to him, had his answer ready. 'He
himself was responsible for her recall', he explained, 'because he
intended, by her marriage, to pacify certain quarrels and litigation
between [Sir Thomas] Boleyn and other English nobles.'[10]

At the age of twenty, Anne Boleyn was launched both into the
English Court and the aristocratic marriage market.

40. Debut

At some point in the winter of 1521–2 Anne arrived back in England. Her birth, her father's office in the royal Household and her own lengthy training in France more or less entitled her to a position at Court and, by early in the New Year, she seems to have been in post as one of Queen Catherine's ladies-in-waiting. She must have made an immediate impact, since she was given a leading part in the festivities for Shrovetide.[1]

Shrovetide (the modern Pancake Tuesday) was a time of celebration and release before the rigours of Lent. It was often marked by the performance of a play in the King's Hall; in 1522, however, the festivities took a more complex form. There was a joust on 2 March and a revel on the night of Shrove Tuesday itself, 4 March. The two had a linking theme: the power of women and love, and the corresponding weakness of men. It was a subject on which Anne, thanks to her experience in France, was a past-mistress.

In the joust, the King led a band of eight knights, each of whom rode under the double device of letters of 'L' and a wounded heart embroidered on the trapper of his horse. 'L' stood for *Elle* or She, the personified powerful Woman; the heart was the Man's heart that She held in her thrall. Each of the jousters also had a personal motto, likewise embroidered on his horse-trapper. Henry's was *mon naverray*, which, with the letters of 'L' and the tormented heart, signified *Elle mon coeur a navré* (She has broken my heart). The opposing band of knights, led by the Duke of Suffolk, had trails of pansies embroidered on their trappers, which, no doubt, like Ophelia's, were 'for thoughts' (of love).

The joust took place in the tilt-yard at Greenwich and was watched by Queen Catherine, Princess Mary and their ladies-in-waiting. The six-year-old Mary wore her Valentine's brooch spelling out the name of her fiancé, none other than Charles V, in jewels; while Anne Boleyn, we can guess, turned her eyes of jet-black – now hot, now cold – on whichever

jouster had proclaimed himself her servant. She had plenty of opportunity, as the festivities continued.

The theme of women's power over men's hearts was continued in the
Shrove Tuesday revel. In this Henry and his companions, now dressed in
cloth of gold caps and blue satin cloaks, laid siege to the *Chateau Vert* (the
Green Castle). The Castle had three towers, with battlements clad in
green tin-foil and each flying a banner: the first of 'three rent [torn]
hearts', the second of 'a lady's hand gripping a man's heart' and the third
of 'a lady's hand turning a man's heart'. The Castle was defended by eight
noble ladies. Each lady impersonated one of the virtues of the ideal
wife/mistress and had the name of her virtue embroidered in gold on her
caul or hair-net of silk. Assisting these ladies in the defence of the Castle
were the eight female vices: Scorn, Disdain, Malebouche (Badmouthing)
and the rest. These vices were played with gusto by the boys of Wolsey's
Chapel.

First, Ardent Desire stepped forward to begin the action. This was a
speaking part probably played by William Cornish, the Master of the
Children of the Chapel Royal, and the likely deviser of the revel.
Dressed 'all in crimson satin with burning flames of gold', he called on the
ladies of the Castle to surrender. The vices, Scorn and Disdain, proudly
refused. Then, with a salvo of real guns (fired outside), the siege began.
The attackers hurled oranges and dates; the defenders replied with rose-
water and comfits (sweet cakes). In their enthusiasm, three of the boys
tore off their cauls and 'cast . . . them down out of the castle'. Eventually,
the boy-vices were driven out and Henry and his lords 'took the ladies of
honour as prisoners by the hands, and brought them down, and danced
together very pleasantly'.

The ladies of the Castle were the *crème de la crème* of the Tudor Court.
They were led by Henry's sister Mary, Queen Dowager of France and
Duchess of Suffolk. Then came Gertrude, daughter of Lord Mountjoy
and wife of Henry's cousin, the Earl of Devon. And in third place,
immediately after these two royal ladies, was 'Mrs Anne Boleyn'.[2]

There are some signs that the ladies were typecast for the parts they
played. Mary, who still had the looks which had driven her elderly first

husband, the French King Louis XII, to over-exert himself into an early grave, was Beauty. The Countess of Devon, wife of the first peer of the Blood Royal, was Honour. It would, therefore, be nice to know why Anne was chosen for the part of Perseverance. Why? Was it the set of her jaw? Or her confidence, polished like marble by her years in France? And would the characterization prove accurate?

Anne had arrived indeed. She had been back in England for only a few weeks. But she had taken, as of right, a position at the centre of Henry VIII's Court. She would never leave it.

Anne's debut in the marriage market, which had provided the pretext for her recall from France, was equally high-flying. Her proposed husband was a member of the nobility. The marriage was suggested by her uncle, Thomas Howard, who was soon to succeed his father as Duke of Norfolk. The King himself was interested in the outcome and the negotiations were handled on his behalf by the King's minister, Cardinal Wolsey.

It was not the last time that Wolsey and Norfolk were to find themselves involved in the quest to find Anne a husband.

The background to this first marriage scheme lay in Anne's own tangled family history. As we have seen, Anne's paternal grandmother, Margaret, was the second daughter and co-heiress of Thomas Butler, Earl of Ormond. When Ormond died in 1515, Anne's father, Thomas Boleyn, inherited the lion's share of Ormond's English estates, including the honour of Rochford in Kent. But there was no agreed succession to the earldom itself. Instead, it was disputed between Boleyn and Piers Butler, Ormond's cousin, heir male and unchallenged head of the Butler family in Ireland. As the Butlers were one of the two great 'Old English' families in Ireland, the dispute became a running sore in Irish politics. An obvious solution was to unite the rival claims by marrying Anne Boleyn to Piers Butler's son and heir, James, who was kept as a sort of hostage for his father's good behaviour in Wolsey's Household in England.

Thomas Howard first floated the idea in 1520 when he was governing Ireland (in so far as Ireland was ever governed) as a harassed and reluctant Lord Lieutenant. And he revived it in 1521 after he had fallen ill and was pressing urgently for his recall. His unspoken motive was that the marriage would smooth the way for Piers Butler to be recognized as Earl of Ormond and appointed Lord Lieutenant of Ireland in his place. Wolsey threw his weight behind the scheme, assuring the King that, on his return from the Calais peace conference, he would 'devise with your Grace how the marriage betwixt [James Butler] and Sir Thomas Boleyn's daughter may be brought to pass'.

But, despite Wolsey's assurances, the 'perfecting' of the marriage never happened. Had something gone wrong between the young couple? James, to judge by his later portrait drawing by Holbein, was a handsome, strapping fellow. But he was still a teenager. So perhaps he was too young – or Anne too old. The more likely explanation, however, is that the two fathers failed to reconcile their differences. Piers Butler was confident he could make good his claim to both the title and the estates in Ireland, by force if necessary; Thomas Boleyn was equally confident that the King's favour would grant him the victory. Without common ground between the two men, the scheme foundered and James was allowed to return to Ireland in 1526. By then Anne had found another prospective husband in Wolsey's Household – and lost him as well.[3]

The 1522 Shrovetide entertainment had taken place at Wolsey's palace of York Place. Perhaps it was then that Anne first saw Henry Percy. Percy, almost exactly of an age with Anne, was the son and heir of the Earl of Northumberland. Like James Butler, he was resident in Wolsey's household as a sort of hostage for the good behaviour of his father, who was the greatest of the northern lords and was never fully trusted by Henry VIII.

The acquaintance between Percy and Anne ripened quickly. Percy accompanied Wolsey on his visits to Court. And while Wolsey transacted business, young Percy 'would then resort for his pastime unto the Queen's Chamber'. Anne's eyes 'went forth as messengers, bearing the secret witness of her heart'. And Percy, starved of love by his proud and oppressive father, responded with passion.

The trouble was that prudence, in the form of his father, had already disposed of him otherwise. As long ago as 1516, the Earl of Northumberland had been in negotiation with George Talbot, Earl of Shrewsbury, for a marriage between Henry Percy and Shrewsbury's daughter, Mary. In terms of dynastic policy, the marriage made a lot of sense. The Percy and Talbot earldoms were among the oldest and richest in England; their estates were contiguous, and Mary Talbot came with the promise of a substantial dowry of 2,500 marks (£1,666 13s 4d). But the fathers moved slowly. In 1516 Northumberland protested that the deal was done, insisting that 'I have concluded with my lord of Shrewsbury'; almost eight years later, however, in December 1523 Shrewsbury was still corresponding with Northumberland about the exact terms of the marriage, which 'he trusts will take effect' the following spring. But this deadline too was missed.

Meanwhile, Percy and Anne had become secret but acknowledged lovers. They entered into a form of betrothal, being 'ensured together intending to marry'. Some have even thought – though it seems unlikely – that they anticipated the ceremony and slept together.[4]

But Percy was not Anne's only admirer. Thomas Wyatt, poet, diplomat and man of action, was to become one of the outstanding figures of the age. He was also handsome, sensual and a known lady-killer. Anne caught his eye. But she proved no easy prey.

Anne Boleyn and Thomas Wyatt had a great deal in common. Their fathers were both senior courtier-administrators: Sir Thomas Boleyn was now Treasurer of the Household, while Sir Henry Wyatt, Thomas's father, was, as Treasurer of the Chamber, the principal royal paymaster. They were neighbours in Kent, where Sir Henry had bought Allington Castle. And Thomas Wyatt, born in 1503, was of an age with Anne's beloved brother George. He had the same sort of education (though he went to the more fashionable Cambridge). And he shared the same sort of ambitions.

These ambitions could only be accommodated at Court, so to Court Wyatt went. He began by odd-jobbing for his father, and in 1523 acted as courier for several large sums sent from the King's treasure to York. Then, on 24 October 1524, Wyatt senior vacated one of his lesser posts, the Clerkship of the Jewels, in his son's favour. It would be hard to think of anybody less temperamentally suited to accountancy as a career than young Wyatt and he resigned the Clerkship six years later. But at least it was a start in the royal service.

Wyatt, however, differed from Anne in one important respect: he had gone through with an arranged marriage in his youth. In about 1520, when he was only seventeen, he had married Elizabeth, daughter of Thomas Brooke, Lord Cobham. Cobham was one of the largest landowners in Kent and a neighbour. In terms of family advantage, the marriage made excellent sense. But it proved a personal disaster. The couple had two children, a son called Thomas after his father and a daughter christened Elizabeth after her mother. Then they separated. Information picked up much later by the Imperial ambassador dated the separation to 1525 or 1526 and stated it was 'on grounds of [Elizabeth's] adultery'. But Wyatt's own comments to his son on the failure of the marriage suggest something more complex. 'The fault', he admitted 'is both in your mother and me, but chiefly in her.' The separation was not a judicial one but a personal, unilateral act on Wyatt's part. And it was evidently accompanied by great bitterness: for many years Wyatt would neither see his wife nor pay her maintenance.[5]

Now, with the notorious, very public failure of his marriage, Wyatt stood outside the rules of conventional contemporary morality. His response was to make his own rules. 'I grant', he wrote with characteristic pithiness, 'I do not profess chastity, but yet I use not abomination.'

Wyatt's involvement with Anne, in which he tried to tread this fine line, is difficult both to date and to document. It belongs, most probably, to the period around the final breakdown of his own marriage in 1525–6. And the key documentation for it consists of a handful of his poems. As so often in creative literature, his was emotion recollected in tranquillity. Long after, when Anne was dead and Wyatt himself was settled into a long-term liaison with his mistress, Elizabeth Darrell, he looked back on his relationship with Anne and pitied his younger self.

In the sonnet, 'If Waker Care', he compared the two women under fanciful, symbolic names. Anne was 'Brunette' because of her colouring, but also because there was something dark and smouldering about her. Elizabeth, on the other hand, was 'Phyllis' (meaning 'green bough') who was an innocent wood-nymph of Greek mythology. Both aroused intense, oscillating sensations of love in Wyatt: 'sudden pale colour', 'many sighs', 'now joy, now woe'. But they did so to very different effect. Anne – 'her that did set our country in a roar' – had been exciting, difficult and tantalizing; Phyllis, in contrast, offered 'unfeigned content'. Other poems elaborate this characterization of Anne. She was a 'fire that me brent'; a briar-bush which had ensnared and torn him; a deer, which had seemed 'tame' but was 'wild' and had led him on a fruitless chase.

According to Wyatt's grandson, George Wyatt, the poet's passionate approaches had confronted Anne with a dilemma. On the one hand, she found him attractive. She was also well aware that, in the intensely competitive world of the Court, to be pursued by a man of repute, like Wyatt, increased her own reputation. To that extent, therefore, she encouraged his attentions: 'which might the rather occasion others to turn their looks to that which a man of his worth was brought to gaze at in her'. But equally Wyatt, for all his charm and intelligence, could not give her what she wanted. Married already, he could only make her his mistress, not his wife. And that was not enough for Anne. Since she had already been sought on behalf of the heir to one earldom and was clandestinely betrothed to the heir of another, she had no practical reason to settle for the position of mistress. It also seems likely that she found it morally repugnant – as she did when it came to being mistress to a man of far higher status than Wyatt.

Anne's solution to her dilemma was, as Wyatt found to his cost, to blow hot and cold: hot enough to keep him in play, but cold enough to freeze him out whenever things threatened to go too far.

Wyatt's final complaint about Anne was that he had to share her attentions with so many others. In 'Who so list to hunt' he compares her to an elusive hind chased by a pack of hunters, each striving to outdo the other and get the honour of the kill for himself. And 'I', Wyatt, laments, 'am of them that furthest cometh behind'.

The image of Anne as the quarry and her throng of would-be lovers as the hunt-pack is, of course, a poetic metaphor. But the *situation* Wyatt describes appears to have been sober reality. Anne, with her dark looks and exotic stylishness, had cut a swathe through the English Court, and men of all ranks – lords, knights and mere gentlemen like Wyatt himself – were competing to win her. She may even, like an English Helen of Troy, have provoked a (mock) war for her possession.[6]

In the autumn of 1524, there was only one topic of conversation at Court. A group of fifteen young bloods had got the King's permission to mount a novel form of entertainment for the Christmas season. They would build a mock castle to their own specifications in the tilt-yard at Greenwich and defend it against all-comers. They also offered to meet any who would take up their challenge in other more conventional forms of combat: the joust, the tournament and the fight at the barriers.

The challenge was formally proclaimed in the Queen's Great Chamber at Greenwich on St Thomas's Day, 21 December. The herald explained that the King had given the keeping of the castle, romantically entitled the Castle of Loyalty or the *Chateau Blanc* (the White or Virgin Castle) to four 'Maidens' of the Court. Their names are not given. But one might have been Anne Boleyn. The four Maidens, the herald continued, had in turn deputed the protection of the castle to fifteen defenders.

Prominent among the defenders was Thomas Wyatt. Equally prominent among the attackers, it was intended, should be Henry Percy. On 19 November, Percy wrote a begging letter to his brother-in-law, Lord Clifford. He told him that 'the King hath appointed me to be one of them which shall assault the Castle of Loyalty'. His master, Cardinal Wolsey, had arranged the nomination 'for my advancement to honour'. But he would require money to rig himself out in appropriate style. His father, he knew only too well, 'will do nothing for me but would be glad to have me put to lack'. Could Clifford lend him the necessary £150 by the end of the month? The sum was enormous and shows that Percy was determined to put on the best display possible.

But most striking is the King's own involvement: Henry threw himself into the scheme. On 6 November he ordered the Revels Office to put its resources at the disposal of the defenders. He picked the challengers, as Percy's letter shows. He was present in person at the proclamation of the combat. And he took great interest in the technical problems of assaulting the castle. He 'devised engines [for the assault], but the carpenters were so dull, that they understood not his intent, and wrought all thing contrary'. To everyone's frustration, therefore, the siege had to be postponed till the New Year.

The first of the regular chivalric contests, however, went ahead as planned on 29 December. Six defenders of the castle rode out fully armed across the draw-bridge to the tilt-yard. But, before they could fulfil their promise to meet all-comers, there was a sudden interruption. Two 'ladies' (once again played by a couple of the ever-useful boys of the Chapel Royal in mock-antique drag and women's wigs hired from Mrs Pike of Cheapside) rode in, leading two 'ancient knights'. The knights had false hair and beards of silver and hats and robes of purple damask. When they came before Queen Catherine and her ladies-in-waiting, the two 'ladies' presented a petition on behalf of the two old knights:

> Although youth had left them [the petition explained] and age was come, and would let [prevent] them to do feats of arms; yet courage, desire and good will abode [remained] with them, and bade them to take upon them to break spears, which gladly they would do, if it pleased her to give them licence.

The Queen and her women, after reading the petition, praised the courage of the two ancient knights and graciously gave them leave to compete. 'Then the knights threw away their robes' to reveal themselves as the King and the Duke of Suffolk.

The unexpected appearance in the tilt-yard of Henry and his longest-standing friend was a piece of calculated drama – a play within a play that transformed the meaning of the whole event. What had begun as the debut of a new generation at Court was turned into a battle between Youth and Age. The defenders of the White Castle of Loyalty were mere striplings, ranging in age from their late teens to their early twenties. In contrast, Henry, aged thirty-three, and Suffolk, aged thirty-nine, were men in the prime of life. The theatre of their entry – their disguise of silver beards and wigs, their outlandish costume, their petition to Queen Catherine – heightened the contrast with the youthful defenders. It also made their eventual triumph all the sweeter.

For Henry proceeded to thrash his opponents. In the tilt, he amazed observers, 'for they saw his spears were broken with more force than the other spears were'. In the subsequent combat with swords (known as the tourney) it was Anthony Browne, aged twenty-four, who felt the full force of the King's attack. Henry launched such a furious assault on him that he 'had almost cut his pouldron [a piece of defensive armour for the neck]'.

But was extra force lent to Henry's strokes by the fact that this was also a battle for a woman? The King's opponent in the tourney, Anthony Browne, had been resident at the French Court during Anne Boleyn's later years there. There is no suggestion of intimacy between Anthony Browne and Anne Boleyn. But, with some of the other key participants, it was a different story. As we have seen, one of the defenders of the castle was Thomas Wyatt, now self-proclaimed as Anne's devoted follower; one of those nominated to attack the castle was Henry Percy, her secret betrothed; while Anne Boleyn herself, I have guessed, was one of the Maiden-keepers of the White Castle. Was King Henry also fighting in Anne's presence? And for her? To show that he alone was fit to match with Brunette, the new toast of the English Court?[7]

It is impossible to be sure. But the winter of 1524–5 *is* a likely starting point for Henry's interest in Anne. There is a single contemporary account. Its author is George Cavendish, Wolsey's Gentleman Usher, who, many years later, wrote the *Life* of his former master. Cavendish correctly identifies Henry's love for Anne as the beginning of Wolsey's fall, and so pays particular attention to it. His account is not without problems and there is an infuriating absence of dates (which are, in any case, the weakest point of his narrative).

Henry's infatuation, Cavendish remembered, started as a secret passion: 'not known to any person nor scantily to [Anne's] own person', the King began 'to kindle the brand of Amours' towards her.[8]

Henry's intention, almost certainly, was to install Anne as his 'official' mistress. So far, two women had occupied this position. The first was the young, talented and exquisitely beautiful Elizabeth Blount. She became Henry's mistress soon after her arrival at Court as one of the Queen's ladies in 1513, and in 1519 she gave him a son, Henry Fitzroy. Six years later, as we have seen, Henry, recognized the boy and created him Duke of Richmond. But the birth marked the beginning of the end of the love affair: babies, Henry seems to have felt, were for wives and not for mistresses, who should inhabit a more ethereal realm of chivalric fantasy.

In 1522 Elizabeth Blount, with Wolsey's help, was married off to Gilbert Tailboys, who was later created a baron. At the same time, Henry transferred his affections to a new mistress: Mary, elder sister of Anne Boleyn. Mary was already married to William Carey, one of the King's favourite Gentlemen of the Privy Chamber. The wedding had taken place on 4 February 1520 in the Chapel Royal at Greenwich and Henry himself had been present. How Mary's husband and father were squared we can only guess. But probably their acquiescence was bought by a stream of grants of office, land and title: Carey, whose income was assessed at £333 6s 8d for the Subsidy (income tax) of 1527, became a rich man; while Thomas Boleyn was made Viscount Rochford. These transactions might seem to turn Mary into the merest prostitute, with her husband and father as her pimps. But Mary, if her later behaviour is anything to go by, had been in love with Henry, and, being in love, had done what came naturally.

In 1525 Mary had a son, Henry Carey. Was her husband the boy's father or was it the King? In either case, childbed marked the end of her love affair with King Henry, just as it had done for her predecessor. Henry's old distaste for a mistresses after she had given birth had reasserted itself. He also had a new love: Mary's sister, Anne.[9]

*

Neither Elizabeth Blount nor Mary Boleyn had put up much resistance to the King. Henry probably expected the same easy acquiescence from Anne. But first there was the little matter of Henry Percy. Anne was in love with Percy, who, as far as she was concerned, was to be her husband. According to Cavendish, it was Henry's discovery of the pre-contract between Anne and Percy which first led him to take Wolsey into his confidence about his feelings for Anne. Wolsey would have been neither surprised nor shocked. He was himself the father of at least two bastards and he had been closely involved with Elizabeth Blount: she had been useful to him while she was royal mistress and he had helped to provide for her when she was honourably discharged. Naturally, therefore, the minister set about offering his services to the King's new liaison.[10]

Wolsey's first task was to eliminate Henry's young rival. This he was well placed to do, since Percy was a member of his own Household. Immediately on his return to York Place from the Court, Wolsey summoned Percy. Then he set about browbeating him into submission. All the arts of the accomplished bully were used. He interviewed the young man in the Gallery at York Place, which was a semi-public space, and in front of his Chamber servants (who of course included Cavendish). And he employed his customary violence of language. 'I marvel not a little', he began, 'of thy peevish folly that thou wouldst tangle and ensure thyself with a foolish girl yonder in the Court – I mean Anne Boleyn.' Wolsey brutally pointed out the difference in status between Percy – 'like to inherit and possess one of the most worthiest earldoms of this realm' – and his prospective bride. Percy's rank made his marriage a question of State, on which it was his duty to consult the King. By failing to follow proper form, he had offended both the King and his father.

Moreover, Wolsey concluded his tirade, Henry had already planned another marriage for Anne herself. Anne knew nothing of it. But, Wolsey was confident, 'she, upon the King's motion, will be . . . right glad and agreeable to the same'. Wolsey, no doubt, was thinking of the proposed match between Anne and Piers Butler. But (unknown to Wolsey) had

Henry already begun to toy with the prospect of another husband for Anne: himself?

In the circumstances, Percy's reply was not without courage. He wept (tears were as fashionable in the early sixteenth century as in certain circles today). But he stood his ground. He was an adult, he said, and thought himself fit to chose a wife 'where as my fancy served me best'. He defended Anne's descent and cited her Howard and Butler connexions. And he stood by his word to marry her: 'which I cannot deny nor forsake'. Wolsey, unused to such resistance, redoubled his attack and denounced him as 'a wilful boy'. Percy returned once more to the facts: 'I have gone so far before so many worthy witnesses that I know not how to avoid myself nor to discharge my conscience'.

Percy's steadiness is remarkable. He has the reputation, not altogether fairly, of a weakling and a wastrel who nearly destroyed his family. But somehow he found the strength to hold out against the King's all-powerful minister. The strength can have come from only one source: his love for Anne Boleyn.

Finally, Wolsey summoned Percy's father from the North. Northumberland, whose relations with his son were in any case bad, first administered another tongue-lashing to the boy and then did as Wolsey wished. The betrothal with Anne Boleyn was broken off and Percy's marriage to Mary Talbot was, at long last, concluded.[11]

It is a good story. But is it true? For over a hundred years now historians have had their doubts. These centre on the date of Percy's eventual marriage to Mary Talbot. There was indeed a renewed flurry of activity about the proposed match in late 1523 and the wedding itself was confidently expected in the following spring. If it had gone ahead then, as recent historians have assumed, Cavendish's narrative must be wrong: there is not the time for Henry to have fallen out of love with Mary Boleyn and into love with Anne Boleyn, which Cavendish's account of the King's motives requires.

But the match between Percy and Mary Talbot did not proceed in early 1524. Indeed, as late as March 1525, Percy was referring to his marriage as a future event. He was definitely married by September 1526, when one of Northumberland's servants sent his commendations to 'my young lord and my young mistress', as well as to 'my lord and lady'. And it was on 23 August that one of the Earl's officers had begun an annual account for the 'expenses of Lord [sic] Henry Percy and Mary his wife'. Why 23 August? It is not one of the quarter days, which provided the usual commencement dates for accounts. Instead, it must have been the date, on or shortly after their wedding day, when they had set up house together. Which in turn fixes the wedding itself to August 1526, if this is the first set of annual accounts, or to August 1525, if it is the second. The latter is the more likely. In either case, there was plenty of time for Henry's interest in Anne to have kindled.[12]

Establishing the proper range of dates for Percy's marriage to either August 1525 or August 1526 thus vindicates Cavendish's essential accuracy. It also suggests that he should be believed about the consequences. Anne, according to Cavendish, was furious with Wolsey for his role in breaking off her love-match with Percy and vowed her revenge. 'If it lay ever in her power', she said, 'she would work the Cardinal as much displeasure' as he had her. Her enmity, at first judiciously concealed, was to have profound consequences.[13]

But, even more importantly, the dating of Percy's marriage to Mary Talbot makes good Cavendish's principal defect: it supplies the foundation for a chronology of Henry's love for Anne.

It started, I have guessed, around Christmas 1524–5; and the King's exhibitionist behaviour in the chivalric contests of the White Castle was probably its first symptom. Early in 1525, Henry took Wolsey into his confidence and the Cardinal set himself to break up Anne and Percy. Probably in June 1525, when Percy's father, Northumberland, was in London for the creation of Henry Fitzroy as Duke of Richmond, the deed was done and the marriage followed in August. It was a predictable disaster. There was a single, still-born child and the couple separated within a couple of years.[14]

Henry, with Wolsey's cruelly effective help, had achieved his first goal. There are signs that Anne and Percy resisted to the end. According to Cavendish, Percy was forbidden to see Anne, and Anne herself was rusticated from Court to get the young man out of her system. When she returned, possibly for the autumn season of 1525, Henry must have imagined that he had a clear run. He was quickly undeceived: no minister could help him now; instead he had to work his own passage.[15]

For Anne made sure that, for the first time in the King's life, his gratification was delayed. But even she could not have guessed for how many weary years the delay would last.

41. Henry in love

Anne kept Henry in suspense for over a year. He cajoled and pleaded. He made promises and gave gifts. Above all, he wrote letters. Anne, whether out of sentiment or prudence, kept his letters. But she was betrayed: somehow, seventeen of the letters, belonging to two widely different periods, were purloined and sent to Rome, no doubt to serve as evidence against Henry's Divorce from Catherine. And there, in the Vatican Library, they remain. Henry almost certainly kept Anne's letters to him. But they have vanished – probably because he destroyed them years later, when his love for Anne had turned to hate and he tried to eradicate every memory of her. The result of this asymmetric survival of evidence is that our knowledge of their courtship is one-sided. Henry's letters document each fluctuation of his feelings. Anne's emotions, on the other hand, can only be glimpsed, refracted and perhaps distorted, in Henry's replies to her letters.

But though her presence is off-stage, as it were, it remains the dominant one: Henry might be King, but he could neither command this woman nor her love.

*

The first batch of Henry's letters are written in his own, heavy hand and composed in his best literary French. They are wonderfully polite, and labour under the weight of simile and circumlocution. Henry anatomizes his heart and compares his love to the sun which (according to contemporary astronomy) was hottest when it was furthest away. He addresses Anne as 'my mistress and friend' and he signs himself 'your loyal servant'.[1]

These letters, in other words, still belong to the fantastical world of the masques and revels where Henry had first glimpsed Anne. It is the realm of Courtly Love, with its conventions, its artifice and its elaborate games with words. Henry's previous extra-marital relationships, with Elizabeth Blount and with Mary Boleyn, had remained at this level. But, at some point, Anne wrought an alchemy. She turned Henry's stilted sighs into real passion. She made him, for the first and last time in his life, fall in love. Like his rival Wyatt, he experienced the vicissitudes of passion: 'now joy, now woe'. He burned for fulfilment – in vain. And, the least patient of men, he had to school himself to wait.

But, revealing in so many ways, Henry's letters have a crucial defect: they are undated. And, since they deal with the never-never land of Courtly Love, they are almost undatable by the usual scholarly techniques. The result is that historians have assigned them to a wide range of dates: from 1526 at one extreme to 1528 at the other. As I shall show, the earlier date is probably correct for the first batch of letters: whatever else it was, Henry's love for Anne was not a thing of quick growth and rapid accomplishment.

What is probably the first letter in the sequence was written after Anne had withdrawn from Court and returned to her parents' house at Hever. The likeliest date is the late summer of 1526. Henry had spent many months pressing his suit and thought that he had persuaded her. Anne was not so sure and had gone away to escape his importunity – and to think. To begin with, however, Henry was all confidence.

His pains at their separation would be, he writes, 'almost intolerable' were it not 'for my firm hope of your indissoluble affection'. Since he could not be with her himself, he sent the next best thing: 'my picture set in a bracelet with the device [motto] which you already know'. But, above all, he longed to be in the place of his gift and in her arms himself.[2]

The exchange of symbolic jewellery, like the bracelet which Henry sent Anne, formed another important part of the rituals of Courtly Love. The great Hans Holbein himself, for whom no commission seems to have been too small, designed several similar pieces for presentation to Anne. None matches the miniature in a jewelled setting, which Henry sent on this occasion. But almost all incorporate a 'device' or 'cipher' of inter-laced letters. These vary from straightforward initials, including the 'AB' pendant which hangs round Anne's neck in her standard portrait, to complex and esoteric sequences of letters, whose meaning, always intended to be private, can now only be guessed at. Sending such trinkets conveyed messages between lovers. But wearing them in a prominent place might speak of commitment and possession – as when little Princess Mary wore her 'Emperour' brooch at her breast and dreamed of her husband to be.[3]

By the time of the next letter, Henry's confidence in his possession of Anne had taken a severe knock. He had heard, though not from Anne herself, that she had 'wholly changed' her mind. She would not come back to Court. He told her frankly that he 'marvelled' at the report: he was sure he had never wronged her, and that it was a poor return for 'my great love' to be kept at a distance from the 'conversation and person of the woman whom I most respect in the world'. Did not she suffer from the separation, even a little? And was it really her will to prolong it? If so, he warned her, he would try to wean himself from his passion: 'I could do no other than complain of my ill-fortune, while abating little by little my great folly.'[4]

Anne ignored the implicit threat. It was, she probably guessed, beyond Henry's power to give her up. Her intuition was right. Soon Henry was writing again, begging for news of her. He sent her a buck, freshly killed with his own hand. When she ate it, he hoped, it would 'remind you of the hunter'. The present was nicely calculated: Anne seems to have acquired a gourmet's palate in France, and relished all kinds of rare meats. But the venison was also intended to remind Anne that Henry, like Wyatt, was hunting a different quarry: herself.[5]

In vain. Anne eluded Henry's clutches, just as she had Wyatt's. And what she gave with one hand, she took back with the other. She relented enough to agree to return to Court. But it would not be, she insisted, as Henry's mistress but as his wife's servant. The King protested at her decision as unbefitting and ungrateful. And he ended his short note with a riddle:

> v. n. A. 1. de A. o. na. v. e. r.

Historians have found it hard enough to transcribe the letters accurately, let alone to understand them. And full interpretation remains elusive. But the gist is fairly clear. It depends on a series of multi-lingual plays on 'Ann' (English), 'Anne' (French) and 'Anna' (Latin). 'Un an' is the French for 'a year'; 'anno' is the Latin for 'in the year', and is often abbreviated as 'Ao'. So Henry's riddle seems to commemorate the first anniversary of their involvement: a year of Anne, even the first year of Anne's reign over his heart.[6]

Probably mindful of the same anniversary, Anne at last replied in writing. But far from quelling Henry's anxiety, her letter put him to greater 'agony' still. He could not understand it, since it seemed so ambiguous. Did she want him or not? Did she love him or not? 'Having been for more than a year now struck with the dart of love', he demanded she put his mind at rest, one way or the other. For some time, he explained, he had stopped calling her his mistress.

> For if you only love me with an ordinary love the name is not appropriate to you, seeing that it denotes a uniqueness very remote from the ordinary. But if it please you to do the duty of a true, loyal mistress and friend, and to give yourself body and heart to me, who have been, and will be your very loyal servant –

Then he would make a corresponding vow. 'I promise', he continued,

> That not only the name will be due to you, but also to take you
> as my sole mistress, casting off all others than yourself out of
> mind and affection and to serve you and you alone.[7]

Henry wrote this letter just before Christmas. Anne probably brooded on
her response over the holidays. Then, at New Year, she gave him a
double response, in the form of a gift and a letter. It is the former that
dates the whole letter sequence. For in his reply Henry thanked her for
her 'estrene'. Historians usually translate the word as 'gift'. But *étrenne*, as
it is written in modern French, is a special sort of gift: one given on New
Year's Day. It has no other meaning. And only one New Year's Day is
possible as the occasion for this gift: 1527. That of 1526 is too early. It
would mean that Henry's solemn engagement to Anne was followed by
eighteen months of inaction – which, bearing in mind what we know of
Anne's character, is inconceivable. Equally, 1528 is too late. For what
would have been the point of the exchange of vows months after Henry
had begun formal Divorce proceedings in both London and Rome and
when, as a result, his affair with Anne had become notorious throughout
Europe?[8]

The date of 1 January 1527 for this letter acts thus as a sort of anchor
for Anne's story. First – bearing in mind Henry's earlier reference to the
period of 'more than a year' that he had been in love – it fixes the
beginning of the King's serious infatuation with her to the later part of
1525. Second, it makes sense of the subsequent course of their affair and,
in particular, of its sudden eruption into the public domain in the course
of 1527.

In short, it rewrites history.

Anne's New Year's gift to Henry was another symbolic jewel. It was set
with a fine diamond and took the form of a ship in which a lonely maiden
was storm-tossed. The gift was accompanied by a letter, which contained
'a beautiful interpretation' of the jewel. The 'interpretation', no doubt,
explained that the maiden was Anne herself and that Henry would,
henceforth, be her refuge from the storms of life. She had done what he

wanted. She had made 'a too humble submission' to his proffered love.

He would match her devotion; he would even outdo it, if it were possible. He was hers and wholly hers – mind, soul and body. Or rather, his heart was hers, and his body he hoped might be. 'Again assuring you', he wrote, 'that henceforward my heart shall be dedicated to you alone, with a strong desire that my body could also be thus dedicated.'

Evidently, Anne had not made an unconditional surrender. She had given Henry only half of what he wanted: her heart and her love. But, as for her body, he would have to wait. Only when – if – they were married would she give him that.

For a woman thus to bargain with the King was audacious. To put the bargain into writing, which Anne appears to have done, was unheard of. But there can scarcely be any other interpretation of Henry's reply. He spoke of his 'immovable resolution' (*immuable intention*). He swore *aut illic aut nullibi* – 'either there or nowhere'. He prayed, he said, 'once a day' for the circumstances which would enable him to consummate his love – 'which God could bring about if it please him'. The oath, the prayers, the resolution, can only be for one thing: for his marriage to Anne and therefore, of course, for his divorce from Catherine.

Henry signed his letter with a new device: in the centre is a heart enclosing the initials 'AB'; on either side are his own initials 'HR' and the motto *aultre ne cherse.* 'I seek no other'.[9]

The gesture is that of a love-sick schoolboy. But the resolution behind it was kingly. It needed to be, as the obstacles in the way of its fulfilment were so formidable. Ranged against Henry were his people, his Church, his nobility, his own past – and, above all, his wife, Queen Catherine. His minister, Wolsey, was ambivalent and even Anne's own father sometimes hesitated. Only a single voice spoke out unequivocally in favour of the great revolution Henry proposed: Anne herself.

Would it be enough?

42. Sole mistress

Even after their exchange of vows, Anne kept Henry waiting. Her father was to be her escort back to Court from Hever and problems – real or manufactured – rendered the timing of his departure uncertain. Now it was planned for this day; now that. Henry was on tenterhooks and was reduced to petitioning Thomas Boleyn, his own servant and councillor, like any humble suitor. Please come two days earlier, he begged. Or at least at the time originally agreed. 'For otherwise', Henry wrote lamely to Anne, 'I shall think he has no wish to serve the lovers' turn as he said he would.'[1]

But, whenever Anne returned, her reception was assured. Just as her absence, Henry told her, had given him 'greater heart-ache than the Angel [Gabriel?] or Scripture could express', so their reunion would be more than the joys of Heaven. He was her 'secretary'; he longed to be with her 'privately'; he was 'and ever will be, your loyal and most assured servant, HR, who seeks no other than AB'.

He was well and truly caught.

Now at last Anne could return to Court, confident that Henry would fulfil his vow and more: she would be his 'sole mistress' certainly, and, if he (and she) could manage it, his wife and Queen as well.

Four months later, Anne appeared with Henry in public for the first time. The occasion, one of the grandest and most lavish events of Henry's reign, was the reception given for the French ambassadors at Greenwich in May 1527. It took place in a specially constructed banqueting house and theatre: the decorations of the theatre were painted by Holbein, while the banqueting house was hung with Henry's most precious tapestries and stacked with his finest gold and silver plate. The festivities culminated in the evening entertainments of 5 May, when, by the King's command, De Turenne, the principal French ambassador, danced with the Princess Mary, 'and the King with Mistress Boleyn, who was brought up in France with the late Queen [Claude]'.[2]

What the two women thought of each other during this encounter we can only guess.

Mary, in fact, probably noticed nothing. After all, she was the star of the ball. She was publicly doted on by her father, who showed off her splendid auburn hair (so like his own before he had begun to go bald) to the ambassadors. So if she deigned to acknowledge Anne at all it would only have been as a courtesy to a nobody, who was enjoying a brief moment of glory with her father because she could communicate with the ambassadors in her excellent French. And the King's partner seems to have been similarly invisible to the rest of the English Court, no doubt for the same reason.

But Anne knew better. She knew, though Mary did not, that she and Mary would be inveterate enemies in a struggle that would last for both their lives. And she knew that the struggle would start soon.

43. Henry and Anne: 'Our Matter'

On 17 May 1527, only twelve days after the Court ball and only four months after Anne's New Year's exchange of pledges with Henry, Wolsey opened the Secret Trial of the King's marriage. 'Our Matter', as Henry called the Divorce in his love letters to Anne, had begun.

Henceforward, in the Divorce, Anne and Henry were one. They debated it and discussed it; they exchanged ideas and agents; they devised strategies and stratagems. And they did all this together. Even when they were apart (in absences that were themselves calculated to further the Divorce) they communicated almost daily by letter. They were, in short, Macbeth and Lady Macbeth – and Anne, like Lady Macbeth, frequently took the initiative. She was the bolder one of the pair, the more radical and, arguably, the more principled. The girl from Hever, the cocotte of the Court of Queen Claude of France, had metamorphosed into 'one of the makers of history'. It was an astonishing transformation.

But, in the crucial early months of 1527, Anne is almost invisible. No English source mentions her. And only the French, to whom she was already a familiar figure, noted her appearance at the Court ball on 5 May.[1]

The silence is curious. I suspect that Henry kept Anne out of the limelight *because* of her importance to him. Not only was she Henry's partner in the Divorce, she was, in fact, the *reason* he was seeking to annul his marriage in the first place. The chronology alone, established here for the first time, virtually proves the case: Henry had promised to marry Anne on or shortly after 1 January and he launched the first trial of his existing marriage to Catherine on 17 May. It was cause and effect. But, of course, Henry could never publicly admit to the connexion between the two events. To have done so would have been to acknowledge that he was dumping Catherine because he wanted to marry Anne. And that overnight would have destroyed the moral, if not the legal, case for the Divorce.

Instead, both Henry and Anne had to pretend and conceal. Their promise to marry had to be kept secret, as had the very existence of their relationship. Both found the game a strain. Henry was proud of Anne (and perhaps prouder still of his conquest of her) and wanted to show her off. Anne was as bold as brass and wanted to show off too. Hence the extraordinary risk of their appearance together at the Court ball. But they were good enough actors to get away with it.

Probably indeed only Anne's parents and her brother were fully in on the secret. The confidential servants of the Privy Chamber must have guessed that something was up, as must Wolsey. But it is unclear how much even Wolsey was told at this stage.

Fortunately for historians, one well-informed observer made it his business to cut through the deliberate obfuscation and secrecy. This was Reginald Pole. Pole, unusually, had a foot in both camps. He was Henry's cousin and protégé, while his mother, the Countess of Salisbury, was Catherine's closest English confidante. In 1529 Pole was to use his influence as a scholar of the royal blood to help get Henry a favourable verdict on the illegality of his marriage from the Sorbonne. But Pole's doubts about Henry's case were to harden during his subsequent period of extended study in Padua in 1530–5, and in 1536 he made them public in his *Pro ecclesiasticae unitatis defensione* (*In defence of Church unity*).

In the treatise, which took the form of an open letter addressed to Henry, Pole turned his spotlight on to the murkiest corner of the King's case: his relationship with Anne Boleyn. As we have seen, Henry's *bona fide* depended on concealing or at least marginalizing Anne's role in the Divorce. Pole, on the contrary, showed that it was central and that it was Henry's desire for Anne, and not his conscience, which first led him to challenge the legality of his marriage with Catherine. All this confirms the case that I have presented here. Indeed Pole may very well have based his conclusions on the same evidence, in particular Henry's love letters to Anne which had, almost certainly, already been spirited away to the Vatican. But Pole also goes further and claims that it was Anne, not Henry, who had come up with the arguments in favour of the Divorce.

> She herself sent her chaplains, grave theologians, as pledges how ready her will was, not only to declare to you [Henry] that it was lawful to put her [Catherine] away, but to say that you were sinning mortally to keep her as your wife even for a single moment, and to denounce it as a high crime against God unless you straightway repudiated her.

'This', Pole concludes, 'was the first origin of the whole lying affair.'[2]

Henry, who had been led by Pole's English friends to expect a defence of his own case, was to receive the shock of his life. But, as he read, the King's surprise was to turn to anger and to a settled determination to be revenged on Pole and his entire family. Henry's feelings are understandable. They are also the testimony to the truth of Pole revelations – and to the extent that they had hit home.

So Pole's account, written after the event in 1536, was to present a unique picture of Anne's activities in 1527. She was working with Henry on the Divorce, recruiting expert opinion, introducing him to the arguments based on the 'Divine Law' prohibitions in *Leviticus*, and stiffening his resolve. And she was astonishingly successful. By late March Henry was ready to act. The basic arguments against his marriage were worked out (and were to change little in the years that followed). He had chosen a lawyer and agreed a procedure. It remained only to set the machinery in motion.

From its earliest stages, therefore, Henry – that is to say, the collectivity of Henry and Anne – had assumed personal charge of 'Our Matter'. And they would never relinquish it. How could they? Its successful resolution was central to their happiness. Henry, in his letters to Anne, is open about this: 'which [thing], brought to pass ... you and I shall have our desired end, which should be more to my heart's ease and more quietness to my mind than any other thing in this world'. Getting the Divorce meant everything to Henry and Anne. It was their all in all. How could they fully trust anyone else to act on their behalf?

Henry's chosen lawyer was Dr Richard Wolman, Archdeacon of Sudbury and later Dean of Wells. Wolman – a 'doctor in both laws', that is, in both civil (or Roman) law and in canon law – was one of the small group of royal councillors who were required to give 'their continual attendance' at Court. The group assembled twice each day, at 10 a.m. and 2 p.m., in the Council Chamber or, if the King's residence were too small to have a special Council Chamber, in the King's Dining Chamber. There they were to be ready either to advise the King on matters of current policy or to administer justice to the poor. Organizing the latter was Wolman's special responsibility. The position, later known as Master of Requests, was the most junior in the Council. Yet it brought its holder into close daily contact with the King. He had to present 'poor men's suits' to the King and to recommend a solution. And, since the cases were trivial, he had to do so with a light touch.[3]

Wolman evidently got it right. The result was that Henry decided that he was the man to prepare and conduct the case against his marriage. Wolman's forensic skills were of course important in the decision. But so too was his proximity to the King. For Henry was determined to control the process at every stage.

The extent of the King's personal involvement became clear when, in April 1527, Wolman rode to Hampshire to interrogate Bishop Fox about Catherine's two marriages. He had Henry's own letters to present to Fox and an oral message from the King as well. And when the aged bishop at first refused to sign the transcript of his examination, on the grounds that he was blind and that none of his own counsel had been allowed to be present, Wolman was able to extort his signature 'out of deference to the King's command'.

Fox also understood that Wolman was acting as the King's direct agent. He was likewise well aware that his own behaviour as a half-reluctant witness was open to misconstruction. So, on 7 April, the day after the two-day interrogation was over, the seventy-nine-year-old bishop dictated a letter to the King which mingled dignity with pathos. He had answered, he insisted, according to his 'conscience'. But he also begged for Henry's 'gracious consideration of my great age, blindness and lack of good hearing'.[4]

The fact that Henry and Wolman had done the ground-work meant that, when Wolsey opened the Secret Trial of the King's marriage in his own house of York Place on 17 May 1527, he came to the case relatively fresh. As of course, as a judge, he should. Henry must have taken him into his confidence to some extent. But Wolsey's own voluminous papers show no trace of his involvement in the preparation of the Trial.

Why was the usually omni-present minister not involved? It may indeed have been due to a sense of judicial propriety (though that rarely bothered Wolsey whose whole career was a living defiance of the

Separation of Powers). Or he may have disqualified himself by opposing, in principle, the King's wish for an annulment. 'I have often kneeled before him in his Privy Chamber on my knees the space of an hour or two', Wolsey protested on his deathbed, 'to persuade him from his will and appetite, but I could never bring to pass to dissuade him therefrom.' Or it may have been that Wolsey, knowing Anne's animus against him, feared the ensuing marriage of Anne Boleyn and Henry VIII, and was reluctant to do anything to bring it about.[5]

But, whatever the reason for Wolsey's initial non-involvement, it could not last. His own decision to abort the Trial on 31 May saw to that. Anne had told Henry that his case against the marriage was water-tight and Henry had believed her. Henry had also worked closely with Wolman in the preparations for the Trial and had become confident of the outcome. But his own creature, Wolsey, in his capacity as Papal legate, had denied him his fondest wish! It would now be Wolsey's task, in his other capacity as Henry's minister, to get him the Divorce by some other means.

Or Wolsey's head would pay the price.

Wolsey's personal feelings about the Matter were unimportant. He was there to do, not what he wanted, but what his King wanted. That, in the sixteenth century, was the minister's job, and he excelled at it. Nothing was too big or too small or too dirty. For almost fifteen years now, Wolsey had made war and peace, organized executions and revels, poured out millions at one moment and retrenched fiercely the next – and all at the King's bidding. When Henry wanted a new husband for his daughter Mary, Wolsey had found him one, and then, at the King's behest, changed him for a new model; when Henry wanted to get rid of his mistress, Elizabeth Blount, Wolsey had organized that too. Henry had turned to him even to eliminate his rival for Anne, Henry Percy.

Naturally, the King and Cardinal had not always seen eye to eye. Nor was Wolsey ever a mere passive instrument. Rather, it was a sort of partnership in which Henry called Wolsey his 'friend'. The word had a stronger meaning then than now, and for the King to apply it to his own subject was a unique distinction. In this friendship Henry, of course, had the final say. But Wolsey often seemed the dominant character. He was older, more experienced and more worldly-wise. Henry, for his part, trusted him, with a trust that was almost without limit: he was prepared to give him latitude, a free rein, and a nearly infinite degree of discretion.[6]

But could it continue? For Henry now called Anne his 'friend' also. Could Henry have two friends: one his minister and the other his mistress?

Above all, could Wolsey, with the best will in the world, turn the mistress into the King's wife?

And was his heart in it anyway?

For Anne had a very different perspective on Wolsey from Henry. The Cardinal had already meddled twice in her private life, each time disastrously. He had failed to carry through her marriage with Piers Butler. And he had succeeded, much against her will, in calling off her wedding with Henry Percy. Would he serve her any better this time?

But, whatever doubts Anne might have nursed about the minister, Wolsey had none about himself. Instead, he announced his take-over of the Divorce with his usual brazen confidence. 'I have now in hand [the Divorce],' he wrote to Henry on 2 June, only two days after he had suspended the Secret Trial *sine die*, 'wherin such good and substantial order and process hath hitherto been made and used, as the like, I suppose, hath not been seen in any time heretofore.'[7]

Despite Wolsey's bustle, however, the fissures soon became clear. And they were provoked by the other main party: Catherine. For it was apparent to Wolsey, if not to Henry and Anne, that Catherine's devastating intervention in the aftermath of the Trial had changed everything. Her determination to involve foreign counsel blew apart the cosy circle of English canon lawyers, who, with a few notable exceptions, had been prepared to do what Henry wanted. Even more important was Catherine's assertion that Arthur had never had sex with her. For if she had indeed emerged a virgin from her first marriage then *Leviticus* and its curse did not apply. She had been Arthur's spouse in name only – which meant in turn that she was now Henry's wife fully and perhaps finally.

Wolsey, as he later explained to the King, had discussed these awkward consequences with Dr Richard Sampson, the Dean of the Chapel Royal and one of Henry's legal experts. The minister's arguments depended on a technical distinction in canon law between 'affinity' and 'public honesty'. 'Affinity' is the relationship between a man and his wife's relations which, after his wife's decease, puts marriage with her female kin out of bounds. 'Public honesty' has the same effect. But the former requires proof of consummation or full sexual relations between the sometime spouses; the latter does not. Instead, the mere fact of a valid, publicly celebrated marriage is sufficient. Wolsey entered into the distinction with an amateur's enthusiasm, for he was no lawyer by training.

'If your brother had never known her,' he told Henry he had said to Sampson, then 'there was no affinity contracted.' 'Yet,' he had continued, 'in that she was married in *faciae ecclesiae* [in the face of the Church] . . . there did arise *impedimentum publicae honestatis* [the impediment of public honesty].' And this he had explained, warming to his theme, 'is no less *impedimentum ad dirimendum matrimonium* [an impediment that invalidates matrimony] than affinity.' Moreover, he concluded triumphantly, the 'Bull maketh no express mention' of public honesty. Which in turn would render the marriage invalid. Q.E.D. – *quod erat demonstrandum* ('which is what was to be demonstrated'), as old-fashioned exercises in geometry used to conclude.[8]

Wolsey's argument, for which some historians including J. J. Scarisbrick have expressed enthusiasm, might just have won in Rome – on a good day and with a favourable political wind behind it. But it was excessively, nit-pickingly technical and lacked the aweful simplicity of *Leviticus*. Nevertheless, it *did* offer an escape from the impasse into which Catherine's insistence on the non-consummation of her first marriage had driven Henry's case. But Wolsey got no thanks from Henry – or from Anne.[9]

Instead, Henry's immediate reaction had been to smell treachery or at best backsliding in his minister. The King jumped to the conclusion (as Wolsey put it) 'that I should either doubt or should [word illegible] your secret matter'. And, to rub salt in the wound, Henry sent Wolman, his new confidant in the Divorce, to tell Wolsey of his displeasure.

Wolsey received Henry's message on the morning of 1 July. It left him 'not a little troubled [in] ... mind' and a few hours later he wrote to Henry to defend himself. 'Most humbly prostrate at your feet', he begged Henry to believe in his loyalty, 'whatsoever report shall be made [to the contrary]'. And he solemnly vowed him his unswerving devotion. 'In this matter', he swore, 'and in all other things that may touch your honour and surety [security], I shall be as constant as any living creature; not letting [failing] for any danger, obloquy, displeasure or persecution; ye, and if all did fail and swerve, your Highness shall find me fast and constant.' 'I shall stick', Wolsey ended his letter, 'with your Highness, *usque ad mortem* [unto the death].'[10]

Only one month into his management of the Divorce, Wolsey was reduced to volunteering to die in the last ditch. It was not a good beginning – especially since there were many who would be delighted to see him taken up on the offer.

What had gone wrong? As usual in such situations, both sides were to blame. Wolsey had badly misjudged the King's feelings. Not having been involved in the early stages of the Divorce, he had discussed it with Sampson as just another item of policy. One approach (affinity based on *Leviticus*) had failed, so another (public honesty based on the canon law of unconsummated marriages) should be tried. But Henry did not see the arguments in this cool way at all. *Leviticus* could not be dumped, as circumstances dictated. Instead, belief that his first marriage was forbidden by divine law had already become an article of faith with him. And to question it was already an act of treachery – even for his 'friend' and minister.

But why, for his part, did Henry, who was normally tolerant of differences of opinion with Wolsey, leap so quickly to impugn his motives? We shall never know for certain. But Wolsey's letter drops heavy hints, since he begs Henry, 'of your high virtue and most noble disposition' to protect him 'against all those who will speak or allege to the contrary [of his loyalty]'. Had Anne already started to poison Henry against Wolsey? And were others already jumping on the band-wagon?[11]

44. *Mistress and Minister*

The summer Progress of 1527 was a climacteric – both in Anne's life and in the history of England. When the year began, her relationship with the King of England was the most closely guarded of secrets. When it ended and the rhythms of political life resumed in the autumn, all was out in the open. She had become Henry VIII's acknowledged consort-in-waiting and was queening it over a Court where she already exerted more power than the unfortunate Catherine had ever done. Meanwhile, as Anne rose, Wolsey, the great minister, declined. He spent the summer away from England, on Embassy to France. And, during his absence, his grip on policy, in particular the policy of the Divorce, weakened alarmingly. Was this Anne's work? Had she engineered his convenient exile? Or did she only exploit it?

Cavendish, who accompanied his master, Wolsey, to France and gave a remarkable picture of his mounting discomfiture there, was in no doubt: Anne, determined to be revenged on Wolsey for having prevented her marriage to Henry Percy, was responsible for everything. In the early summer, according to Cavendish, she joined in a conspiracy with Wolsey's enemies on the Council. She set a trap for him by persuading him – with fair and flattering words – to go on the mission to France. She then worked on Henry during Wolsey's absence to undermine his reputation and destroy his favour. And she succeeded beyond her wildest dreams.

Cavendish's account has been dismissed by the fashionable band of 'revisionist' historians, who are blessed with the happy confidence that they understand the past better than those who were alive at the time. But, in outline, it seems to me to be correct. It errs, in fact, at only one point. Written with the benefit of hindsight, it is neat and pat, and it exaggerates the extent to which the outcome was planned from the beginning. There was, I would guess, no great conspiracy against Wolsey in the early summer: too few knew of Anne's relationship with Henry to supply the necessary breadth of support, nor had Anne either the occasion or the motive to act. Rather, Anne took advantage of events as they unrolled. She had the necessary political skill ('a very good wit', as Cavendish put it). She also had the strength of character to impose herself as the leader or 'chief mistress' (in Cavendish's phrase again) of Wolsey's opponents, who increased in number and confidence as his power waned. And, above all, she had the luck – which equally deserted Wolsey.[1]

The scheme to send Wolsey on a mission to France originated during the lengthy French Embassy to London in the spring of 1527. It was intended as the culmination of the policy of 'peace with honour', by which Wolsey had kept Henry at the centre of European affairs ever since the Treaty of London of 1518. Each successive negotiation was more ambitious in scope; the 'Universal' Peace of 1518 was trumped by the 'Eternal' Peace of 1527. And each was designed to show Henry and Wolsey in a yet more glorious light. The 1527 Embassy was the *ne plus ultra* for Wolsey. As Henry's 'lieutenant' or viceroy, he was accorded full royal honours during his journey to France (and enforced them to the last jot and tittle). He was also hailed in pageants by the French, who were not to be outdone in sycophancy, as the Holy Ghost who had brought peace to earth and goodwill to men (at least if they were not the subjects and soldiers of the hated Emperor Charles V).

It was a heady brew, and explains why Cavendish thought that Wolsey had been tricked into undertaking the Embassy by having his vanity tickled. But, behind the public pomp and circumstance, Wolsey's mission also had another, more secret purpose. His fertile brain had quickly spotted that the Sack of Rome, and the Pope's subsequent imprisonment at the hands of Charles V's troops, were as much an opportunity for Henry's schemes as a threat to them. Someone would have to serve as acting head of the Church if the Pope's captivity were prolonged. And who was better qualified than Wolsey? Once seated on St Peter's throne, if only temporarily, he could exercise the plenitude of Papal power and grant Henry his Divorce. The world – and Catherine – would be presented with a *fait accompli.*

Wolsey discussed this scheme fairly widely – though in the strictest confidence and in the highest political circles. He talked it over with Henry before he left London on 3 July on the first leg of his mission to France; indeed the two may have worked it out together. Then, the night after his departure from London, he raised the matter with William Warham, the Archbishop of Canterbury, when he reviewed the state of play on the Divorce with him at Dartford. Warham, no mean political player himself in his younger days, had immediately detected Wolsey's ulterior motive, remarking smoothly that 'the same shall much confer to [Henry's] Secret Matter'. Wolsey seems even to have mentioned it to some of the galaxy of international diplomats, who were gathering in northern France in anticipation of the summit conference with Francis I.[2]

But, despite all the talk, Wolsey *did* nothing. He did not even sketch out a programme of action till 29 July, and it was only two weeks later still, on 11 August, that he was finally goaded into action.[3]

The result was the worst of all possible worlds. Wolsey had said more than enough to alert Henry's enemies to his intentions (a version of the plan for a Papal vice-gerency was known, for instance, in the Imperial Court, then at Valladolid, by 14 July, to the horror of the English ambassador there). But he had done much too little to persuade Henry that he was working seriously to implement the scheme. And if the Great Matter was not top of his minister's agenda, Henry wanted to know why.[4]

Anne, with her own axe to grind, was now able to offer Henry an all-too-convincing explanation for the minister's inactivity. Wolsey was doing nothing because he had never wanted her to marry Henry anyway. He was incompetent. He was not to be trusted. And, in any case, she and her friends had a much better plan. But it must be kept from Wolsey, since he would do everything he could to frustrate it.

Would Henry, despite Wolsey's decade-and-a-half of service, fall for this rival scheme? And who would win the King's ear, his minister or his mistress?

In the circumstances of the summer of 1527, there was no contest. Wolsey was two hundred and fifty miles away in France. Anne was ever-present at Henry's elbow (if not yet in his bed). Wolsey had only a couple of friends at Court: Sir William Fitzwilliam, who had succeeded Anne's father as Treasurer of the Household on Boleyn's elevation to the peerage, and Dr William Knight, who had replaced the occasionally demented Richard Pace as royal Secretary. And Knight was to prove treacherous. In contrast, Anne's friends and relations surrounded the King during this most unusual of royal Progresses.

Normally, the Progress or royal summer holiday was a roving hunting party, which moved, at intervals of two or three days, from country house to country house. Accommodation was strictly limited, and the royal entourage was cut to a handful of intimates and a skeleton staff of domestics. This year, however, it was different. Instead of going on his travels, Henry spent a full month in a single house: Beaulieu or New Hall, two-and-a-half miles to the north-east of Chelmsford in Essex. The house had originally belonged to Anne's father, who had inherited it through his mother, Lady Margaret Butler, the daughter and eventual heiress of the seventh Earl of Ormond. Thomas Boleyn had sold the house to Henry in 1516, but he retained a substantial landed stake in Essex and took the title of his viscountcy from Rochford (also a former Butler possession) fifteen miles to the south-east.[5]

The royal party arrived at the ex-Boleyn mansion, which Henry had extended into a full-scale palace, on 23 July. There the King was joined by the Dukes of Norfolk and Suffolk, the Marquess of Exeter, the Earls of Oxford, Essex and Rutland, and Viscounts Fitzwalter and Rochford.

This was a conclave of Henry's most trusted friends and relations: Norfolk was the King's uncle by marriage; Suffolk was his brother-in-law and sporting partner; Exeter was his first cousin and closest male relation; while Essex, Rutland and Fitzwalter were rather more distant royal connexions through the Yorkist and Woodville lines. It was also – since Rochford was Anne's father and Norfolk her uncle – a gathering of Anne's relations as well.

On 31 July Fitzwilliam alerted Wolsey. 'The King is keeping a very great and expensive house', he wrote. He listed the King's house-guests and noted the even more select band of Norfolk, Suffolk, Exeter and Rochford who usually supped apart with the King in his Privy Chamber. Fitzwilliam complained of the havoc wrought on his plans to use the Progress to continue Wolsey's schemes for economical reform in the royal Household. But, with characteristic discretion, he left it to Wolsey to draw his own conclusions about the political threat posed by the gathering.[6]

For the house party at Beaulieu turned into an extended think-tank on the Great Matter. Indeed, that is probably why it was assembled in the first place. Like a modern company 'away-day' at a country-house hotel, it was designed to combine business with pleasure and to offer a relaxed atmosphere of country sports and pastimes which encouraged the participants to say the unsayable and think the unthinkable. To judge by the results, it succeeded. It also took its decisions, not only in Wolsey's absence, but deliberately behind his back. For the first time in his career, Wolsey found himself excluded from the centre of power – and by a woman. And for the first time in hers, Anne, the hunter/huntress of Wyatt's poem, used the hunt as a political device in the battle to control Henry. It was not a lesson she forgot.

On 6 August the whole party rode off to the Earl of Oxford's fine ancestral Norman fortress at Castle Hedingham to enjoy the sport there. By the time it returned, the die was cast and on 7 August Secretary Knight wrote to Wolsey to inform him that 'the King's pleasure is that your Grace do send hither immediately Mr Doctor Stephens; for his Highness desires to communicate and confer divers things with him which cannot so readily follow the pen as they should'.[7]

'Mr Doctor Stephens' was Stephen Gardiner, later Bishop of Winchester, Lord Chancellor and a hate-figure for English Protestants. Gardiner, born in about 1497, was the youngest son of a prosperous cloth-worker of Bury St Edmunds, Suffolk. His father, who died when he was a boy, left him a substantial legacy to pay for his education and Gardiner seized the opportunity. By 1522, he had obtained a double doctorate from Cambridge in civil law and canon law. Three years later, still aged only twenty-eight, he was elected Master of Trinity Hall. Moreover, most unusually for a sixteenth-century academic, he had a fluent knowledge of French. This he acquired during a sort of gap-year between school and university spent in Paris in the company of one of his guardians, Thomas or Richard Eden. A frequent visitor to Eden's house in the rue St Jean was the great scholar Erasmus. And Gardiner became used to preparing the scholar's favourite salad of lettuce 'dressed with [melted?] butter and vinegar'. He did it, as he did most things, exceptionally well.[8]

Cambridge left a permanent mark on Gardiner. But, even before his election as Master of Trinity Hall, he had taken a decisive step into the wider world when, in 1524, he was talent-spotted for Wolsey's Household. Wolsey made him his Secretary and, from the beginning, had used him as his own principal agent in the Secret Matter. On 8 June 1527, Gardiner, 'in the Legate's name', had collected the crucial documentation on the Divorce in the form of 'a box containing eleven pieces of evidence about the matrimony of Spain' from the archives of the Treasury. Thereafter he had been Wolsey's only 'help and instrument' in drafting and working up Wolsey's schemes to obtain the Divorce.[9]

Thus, to send Gardiner to Henry, as the King was now demanding, was tantamount to Wolsey's handing over the management of the Divorce to Henry. And that, as Wolsey knew, was his own passport to oblivion. So, writing on 11 August, Wolsey refused Henry's request for Gardiner; he also leapt into action.

But first came the excuses for his delay: he had not wished to weaken his bargaining hand against the French by mentioning the Secret Matter; he had been waiting for news from Rome; he had other 'importable [insupportable] business, both day and night'. But now, he concluded, circumstances had changed, since the Secret Matter was secret no longer. 'I have received out of Flanders', he informed Henry, 'letters from . . . your Grace's agent there, containing that it is come to the [Archduchess] Margaret's knowledge, by secret ways and means . . . that your Grace intendith to be separate and divorced from the Queen.'

No doubt. But nothing could conceal the fact that the real trigger to Wolsey's action was not the news from Flanders, but Henry's demand for Gardiner. Nevertheless, Wolsey's flurry of activity was impressive. And he made sure that Henry knew it. He had approached the Pope, he wrote to the King, for his consent to the scheme for Wolsey to take over the administration of the Church during the Pope's captivity. He was sending him three separate envoys, each with excellent contacts in the Roman Court, that 'if the one expedition fail, the other may take effect'. He would throw money at the problem. He would do anything, in short, he assured Henry, 'which may confer and be beneficial to your Grace's purpose'.[10]

Henry's reaction was, apparently, sweetness and light. On 17 August the trusty Treasurer Fitzwilliam (whom Knight punningly called Wolsey's 'treasure') informed Wolsey that 'the King is much pleased with Wolsey's letters and likes all that he has done'. But, he continued, he was sure that Wolsey had already been told of all this by Secretary Knight, 'whom [he] esteems a right honest man and a friend to Wolsey'.[11]

Knight's letter (written, in fact, two days later on the 19th) confirmed Fitzwilliam's sunny tone. 'The King', Knight told Wolsey, 'command[ed] me to give unto you his most hearty thanks.' Henry had made his councillors at Court, Norfolk, Suffolk, Rochford and Fitzwilliam, 'privy' only to Wolsey's other letter dealing with general business. But this reply to Wolsey's letter 'concerning the secrets' had been handled by the King alone. And Henry was delighted: since Wolsey's approaches to Rome were all that he wished for, the sending of Gardiner was superfluous. Knight's letter went on to reinforce the picture of his own loyalty to Cardinal Wolsey. He praised Fitzwilliam as another of

Wolsey's 'faithful and loving servants'. And he told Wolsey of the ugly rumours spreading at Court about the activities of Wolsey's agents in raising funds for his great educational foundations at Oxford and Ipswich by dissolving a swathe of smaller monasteries. 'I have heard the King and noblemen speak things incredible', Knight confided.[12]

The story about the 'things incredible' was true, and shows how far and how quickly the general atmosphere on the Progress had turned against Wolsey. Otherwise, Knight's letter was a tissue of lies. It was designed to lull Wolsey into a false sense of security; it was also intended to disguise Knight's own forthcoming role as Judas.

Wolsey was not altogether deceived and sent John Clerk, the Bishop of Bath and Wells, to explain more fully to Henry his actions concerning the Divorce. But nothing prepared Wolsey for what was to come.[13]

The house party at Beaulieu broke up as planned on 27 August. Most of Henry's guests left Court while the King, with a small entourage, made for Greenwich. Secretary Knight, however, took a different direction. He travelled to London to make arrangements for a lengthy journey: he was to be ambassador to Rome.

Knight's mission was the final decision of the Beaulieu think-tank: Knight would be Henry's envoy to the Pope, not Wolsey's. He would take his instructions directly from the King, not the minister. And he would do what Henry and Anne wanted – not what Wolsey, in his wisdom, thought they ought to want. For Henry and Anne were weary of Wolsey's delays and tergiversations. Instead, they had decided to try a frontal approach that was stunning in its directness. Knight would ask Clement VII for a dispensation that would free Henry from all impediments to his *immediate* remarriage: it would allow him to marry, even though he was *still* married to Catherine; it would also permit him to marry Anne, even though her sister Mary had been his mistress. And all this would be done without Wolsey's knowledge.

Some of the Beaulieu deliberations leaked and reached Mendoza, the Spanish ambassador in London, by mid-August. 'It is generally believed', he reported home on 16 August, 'that if the King can obtain a divorce he will end by marrying a daughter of Master Bolo [Boleyn] . . . who is now called Milord de Rochafort [Rochford].' But the secret of Knight's mission was well kept – even from Wolsey.[14]

The letter which Wolsey received from Knight thus came as a bombshell. King Henry, Knight wrote from London on 29 August, had decided to send him to Rome 'for the procuring and setting forth . . . of [the King's] secret matter'. He was about to depart and would see Wolsey shortly in France to receive the minister's own further orders 'concerning such other things as [Wolsey] should think necessary to be sped [in Rome]'. This last went a little way to protecting Wolsey's dignity. But, finally, it was a mere sop.[15]

Wolsey now stared into the abyss. If Knight's mission went ahead, Wolsey would be rendered redundant; if it succeeded, Anne would be made Queen. And what would happen to him then?

Knight's letter was delivered to Wolsey at Compiègne on 5 September. Cavendish, who was in attendance, became an eye-witness of Wolsey's efforts to salvage his career.

Wolsey 'rose early in the morning about 4 of the clock' to compose his reply to Henry. He then remained glued to his desk for twelve hours. 'All which season', Cavendish noted with amazement, 'my Lord never rose once to piss, nor yet to eat any meat but continually wrote his letters with his own hand, having all this time his night-cap and kerchief on his head.' Towards four in the afternoon he finished writing. But even then he took no refreshment until he had ordered the messenger, 'Christopher [the] Gunner, the King's servant, to prepare him without delay to ride in post in to England with his letters'.[16]

Wolsey's feat has often been cited by historians as an example of his typical industry and energy. But the context (which those historians have not recognized) was hardly typical: Cardinal Wolsey was writing for his political life.

Wolsey's messenger was, therefore, carefully chosen for his speed and intrepidity. Christopher Morris (to give him his proper name) had been sent as diplomatic courier to Spain in early 1527. Communications had been disrupted by severe floods. But Morris somehow fought through, to the admiration of the ambassador, Dr Edward Lee. 'He wondered', Lee wrote, 'how he escaped the waters, which have done much hurt here.' Perhaps in reward for his efforts, Morris was appointed Chief Gunner in the Tower of London.[17]

But not even Morris could make the round to England and back in less than five or six days. Wolsey therefore had to wait on tenterhooks, as Cavendish observed, 'expecting the return of Christopher [the] Gunner'. Instead, on the 10th, a much less welcome face appeared: Secretary Knight himself, en route for Rome as he had promised.

Wolsey was astonished. After all, he had written a letter, a long, brilliant letter to Henry. It was full of knowledge of the world, of Rome and, above all, of the King's own character. How could it have failed to scotch the wild-cat scheme for Knight's mission? It was scarcely possible. Instead, he ordered Knight to delay, confident, as Knight reported confidentially to Henry, that 'by the coming of Christopher Morris I should have been by your Grace countermanded'.

To pacify Wolsey, and 'for the avoiding of suspicion', Knight did as he was told. Morris duly arrived the next day. But, as Knight knew all along, Morris bore letters ordering Knight to proceed on his mission and Wolsey to assist him. Wolsey was beaten. He first despatched Knight and then made immediate preparations to return to England. Europe, even the Great Matter, could wait; it was his own position at home which now mattered most.[18]

But his humiliations were not yet over. The original intention, as Fitzwilliam had informed Wolsey back in July, was that Henry would remain 'near Greenwich till Wolsey comes home'. Henry would then have gone to meet Wolsey part way on his journey across Kent and there would have been a loving, public reunion between the King and his trusty minister followed by long conversations in private. This is what had happened on Wolsey's return from his previous mission to France in 1521. But Anne's advent and the events of the Progress of 1527 made sure that there was no repetition.

Instead, Henry deliberately moved west, to Richmond. He came to

Greenwich for the reception of the French ambassadors, who had arrived for the ratification of the treaties, on 22 September. But he stayed only for a single night before returning to Richmond.

And it was at Richmond that Wolsey arrived on the 30th. There he had a reception like no other. He immediately sent to Henry to know when he should 'repair to the King's Privy Chamber' for his usual private audience. But Anne was with Henry when the messenger arrived. She was now an acknowledged figure at Court and, according to the Spanish ambassador, presumed to reply to Wolsey's messenger on the King's behalf. 'Where else is the Cardinal to come?' she snapped. 'Tell him that he may come here, where the King is.' Henry confirmed Anne's commands and Wolsey came into the presence of Henry – and of Anne.[19]

At a stroke, she had established herself as consort in all but name.

But where did that leave Wolsey? Rumours were already circulating of a conspiracy against him by Norfolk and Rochford, Anne's uncle and father. Meanwhile, Wolsey was fighting back. The Beaulieu think-tank had thought the unthinkable. The Cardinal therefore decided to respond with his own gathering of the great and the good at Hampton Court. And, since those invited were lawyers and canonists, they could be relied on to take a more cautious approach.

Who would win? The radicals or the conservatives? Wolsey or Anne?

But perhaps Henry, despite his apparent decisiveness in the summer, was not yet ready to choose.

45. Anne's envoy

Late in the autumn of 1527 a priest, John Barlow, left the royal palace in haste. He had just had a private audience with the King (and probably with Anne too) and was carrying further, top-secret instructions for Secretary Knight on his Embassy to Rome.[1]

Barlow was a striking man. 'He is short, red-haired, very moderate in eating and drinking, and keeps himself to himself, unless he is spoken to', one observer reported. Not the easiest of company, he had few social skills and knew (as he admitted himself) 'neither music nor games of chance'. But he was utterly trustworthy. 'You may assuredly send me whatsoever you will [by him]', Henry told Knight in the letter which Barlow was carrying, 'for he will with diligence bring it me and wisely enough too.' Barlow's qualities, good and bad – his sobriety, his unsociability and his lack of small talk – all point to the single-mindedness of a man with a mission, even a fanatic. And there is no doubt about the object of his devotion: it was Anne Boleyn. Barlow, one of his many enemies later reported (for Anne's was not a popular cause), had 'always belonged to her, had his promotion by her, and had been ambassador for her in divers places beyond sea'.[2]

This was his first such mission. It was also the most important. For if he and Secretary Knight were successful, Henry would be free to marry Anne in a matter of months.

No one, least of all Knight, underestimated the difficulty of this mission. In particular, Knight was frankly sceptical ('whereof I doubt') that he could persuade the Pope to dispense Henry to marry Anne *before* his marriage with Catherine was formally dissolved. That, as we have seen, had been Henry and Anne's great hope. But, by the time Henry despatched Barlow with Knight's additional instructions, Henry too had come round to Knight's point of view.[3]

For, after his return to England, Wolsey had got his hands on the draft of 'the secret bull' that it had been Knight's mission to obtain. The King was aware of the source of the leak: 'by whose means I know well enough', he wrote darkly. And his irritation was only increased when Wolsey had pointed out the impossibility, even the absurdity, of what Henry was asking. But finally the King had to concede the truth of Wolsey's criticisms: the first draft Bull was indeed 'too much to be required and unreasonable to be granted' and Knight, Henry now ordered, was to pursue it no further.

Instead, Henry sent him a second draft Bull via Barlow, which would dispense him to marry Anne only *after* his marriage with Catherine was annulled. This second Bull, Henry was convinced, was Wolsey-proof: 'no man', he told Knight, 'doth know [of it] but they which I am sure will never disclose it to no man living for any craft the Cardinal or any other can find'. But, just to make the deception of Wolsey complete, Henry had agreed another, double set of instructions with Wolsey, which, he instructed Knight, he was to ignore.

This second Bull, Henry swore, was '[that] which I above all things do desire'. To secure it, Knight was to use 'the best counsel, so they be secret' and to employ the most persuasive arguments. In particular, he was to reassure Pope Clement that 'this bull is not desired except I be *legittime absolutus ab hoc matrimonio Katherinae* [legitimately absolved from this marriage with Catherine]'. Above all, the King enjoined, Knight was to do everything possible 'to get access to the Pope's person'. '[For] I fear me sore that if you find not some by ways beside them that my lord Cardinal did devise with you to have access to the proper persons, it will be long or [before] you attain the same.'[4]

Clearly, the breach which Anne had opened up between Henry VIII and Cardinal Wolsey in the summer had not healed. Indeed, if anything, Wolsey's subsequent attempts to rehabilitate himself had been counterproductive. In the summer, the King had distrusted the Cardinal enough to deceive him. Now, in this letter to Knight, there is a new note of resentment, almost of fear, of Wolsey's cleverness ('craft') as something quasi-diabolic. For the moment Wolsey's craft held Henry in thrall: he could evade it but he did not dare to confront it directly.

Only Anne, the original source of the disagreement, could steel Henry to a decisive break. But, evidently, she did not. Was she, too, despite her bravado, still a little in awe of Wolsey?

Barlow, riding fast, caught up with Knight at Foligno, an agreeable city in Umbria, eleven miles to the south-east of Assisi. Knight had chosen Foligno as his base for two reasons. It was partly (as he told Henry) because 'I have acquaintance [there]' – no doubt from the days, back in 1501, when he had been a law student at Ferrara. And Foligno was also convenient for the Papal stronghold of Orvieto, where the Pope was expected to take refuge when he regained his freedom.[5]

Knight's original intention had been to await Pope Clement's release before doing anything. But Barlow's arrival galvanized him into action. With astonishing courage, even foolhardiness, Knight ventured into a Rome that was still under Spanish occupation: there were even Spaniards staying in the house where he lodged. Nevertheless, under their noses and no doubt using his excellent Italian, he contrived to smuggle a message to Clement in the Castel Sant'Angelo. The Pope, more fearful than Knight, begged him to flee from Rome, where his presence had become known to the Spanish command. But he assured him that, as soon as he was at liberty, 'he would send unto me your Grace's requests in as ample a form as they be desired'. Knight withdrew once more to Foligno, whence he wrote to Henry on 4 December to inform him that the Pope's release was expected any day.[6]

It took place early in the morning of 6 December when the Holy Father, disguised as a gardener, according to some accounts, or as a merchant with armour under his clothes, or as one of his own servants, according to others, fled from the Castel Sant'Angelo and took refuge, as expected, at Orvieto.

Knight, with his usual vigour and efficiency, which belied his fifty-one years, was one of the earliest to make his way to Orvieto and offer Henry's congratulations to Clement on his escape. These, he reported, the Pope received most gratefully since 'I was the first that made like salutation in any great prince's name'. His success received a backhanded acknowledgement from the Spanish envoys in Rome, who worried about the effect of such a hostile presence at the Papal court-in-exile. Knight himself pressed home his advantage by immediately requiring Clement to honour the pledge he had made during his imprisonment and grant Henry his dispensation, as well as a commission to Wolsey to try the marriage.

But the liberated Pope at Orvieto proved less generous than the prisoner of the Castel Sant'Angelo. Excusing himself on the grounds that he was 'not expert in the making of commissions', he referred the documents to one who was, Lorenzo Pucci, Cardinal of the Church of the Four Crowned Saints and Papal Datary, for advice.

Pucci found fault with both documents (what else, after all, are experts for?). But, in the event, they were treated in different ways. The changes made to the dispensation were comparatively slight, even after Clement himself had put in his twopenny-worth. But the commission, drafted under Wolsey's direction, was another matter. As it stood, Pucci said warmly, it could not be sealed 'without perpetual dishonour unto the Pope, the King and your Grace [Wolsey]'. Pucci first put his criticisms into writing; then, at Knight's suggestion, he prepared an alternative text. Both parties eventually agreed to this and Bulls in the revised form were issued: for the dispensation on 17 December and for the commission a few days later.[7]

But had the changes vitiated the documents? It seems to be the consensus of historians that they had. However, Knight, who was himself an Italian-trained canonist, was confident that they retained their efficacy. They were not, he conceded to Henry 'in the form that was conceived in England'. But they were, he insisted nevertheless, couched 'after such manner as is sufficient for the cause and as I trust shall content your Highness'.

More to the point perhaps, Clement himself was also convinced that he was granting things that were usable – and things, moreover, that he very much feared Henry would leap to use, to his own deep detriment. The dispensation, by itself, the Pope speculated to Knight, 'might encourage your Grace [Henry] to cause my lord Legate [Wolsey] *auctoritate legationis* [by virtue of his office of Legate] to hear and discern [determine] in the cause' of the Aragon marriage. While the commission would, of course, explicitly authorize Wolsey to hear the case.[8]

The trouble was, as Clement explained to Knight, that he had already solemnly promised the Emperor 'not to grant unto any act that might be preparative, or otherwise, to divorce to be made between the King and Queen'. The promise had been made under the duress of his imprisonment and he felt no moral obligation to honour it. On the other hand, he very much feared what the Spanish might do to him if he were discovered to have broken his word – as, of course, his grants to Henry had just done.[9]

Knight, familiar with Italy in a way that few other of Henry's advisers were, sympathized with Clement's fears and endorsed them in his report to Henry:

> I cannot see, but in case [the dispensation and the commission] be put into execution at this time, the Pope is utterly undone, and so he saith himself. The Imperial [troops] doth daily spoil castles and towns about Rome; monsieur de Lautrec [the French commander] is yet at Bononye (Bologna) and small hope is of any great act he intendeth.

The solution to the dilemma, Clement and Knight agreed, was for Henry to keep the Bulls secret and, for the present, to refrain from acting on them. Subsequently, the King and the Pope were to co-ordinate their moves. Henry would give Clement good notice of the time to be fixed for the trial: 'that ye do certify the Pope that ye intend within 15, 20 or 30 days to move your cause before my lord Legate'. And Clement, thus alerted, would try to turn the ever-changeable Italian political climate to his and Henry's advantage by reissuing the commission 'with a date convenient'.

The most 'convenient' circumstances for such a manoeuvre, Clement explained, would be the arrival of the French army at Rome. If that happened, Knight reported:

> the Pope thinketh that he might by good colour say that he was required by your [Henry's] Ambassador here and by M. de Lautrec [to issue the commission], to whom, being here with great power . . . he could not say nay.

'This might be', Clement concluded hopefully, 'a sufficient excuse towards the Emperor.'[10]

310 THE QUEENS OF HENRY VIII

It was, of course, a long shot. Under sixteenth-century conditions of transport and communication, it was difficult to orchestrate events in London and Rome in the way the scheme demanded. And a major victory for French arms in southern Italy was – and remained – elusive. But politicians have to deal with the world as it is, with all its uncertainties, not as they would like it to be. Knight and Clement acknowledged that hard necessity and the way forward they suggested was probably Henry's best hope.

Knight wrote all this to the King on 'New Year's Day in the morning at Orvieto'. One year ago to the day, Anne had used a New Year's gift to convey her acceptance of Henry's vow to give her his hand. Now, it seemed, Henry and Anne had received an even better New Year's gift in the form of the Pope's agreement to their marriage.

Properly pleased with himself and the successful conclusion of his mission, Knight ended his letter by announcing his return home and sending Henry his wishes 'for a prosperous New Year, and many'. By 28 January 1528, his report of his success had reached England, and Wolsey, then sitting as judge in Star Chamber, broke off from the case to forward the package to Henry. 'There seems to be a good towardness in affairs there [in Italy]', his short note concluded.[11]

But, within a few days, the minister was singing a very different tune.

As instructed, Knight had scrupulously kept Wolsey in the dark about his real mission. 'I could do no less at this time than write unto my lord Legate that the commission and a dispensation for your Highness be sped,' he informed Henry. But he had not told him *which* dispensation. Nevertheless, the text was in Wolsey's hands by the beginning of February. Had Henry triumphantly shown him the results of his handiwork himself? Or had the Papal messenger, Nuncio Gambara, who first brought a copy to England, handed it to Wolsey, whether inadvertently or on purpose? We do not know. But Wolsey, once he had the documents in his hands, went to work with a will: he would show Henry what happened when the King tried to act without his advice and behind his back.

The result takes the form of a closely annotated copy of the dispensation. It is written in two columns: the dispensation to the right and the notes to the left. The latter are excoriating.

The dispensation began by reciting Henry's case against his present marriage. He had married Catherine, his brother's widow, without a valid dispensation, thus both falling into sin and incurring the penalties of excommunication. He did not wish to remain in this state a moment longer and so begged the Pope to lift the ban of excommunication and declare his marriage null. After his marriage had been annulled, he sought a dispensation to marry another woman, even within the first degree of affinity, and whether or not that affinity had arisen from licit or illicit intercourse. He further requested a declaration that the issue of this second marriage would be legitimate, to avoid in future the sorts of disputes about the succession which, as 'ancient chronicles' assert, had dogged England in the past. Providing once more his marriage with Catherine had been annulled, he also sought licence to marry a woman even though she had previously contracted, but not consummated, a marriage. All this, the enacting clause stated, the Pope was graciously pleased to grant, 'by our apostolic authority, of our certain knowledge, and out of the plenitude of our apostolic power'.

The annotator's greatest scorn was reserved for the initial 'narration,' which recited Henry's doubts about his present marriage. Its statements were, it was to be hoped, 'most false'. And, even if they were true, they were dishonourable, unworthy of such a King and indecent to be stated in public. *Expungatur itaque hoc totum* (therefore all this is to be struck out), it concluded.

The annotator likewise declared the principle of a conditional dispensation to be fundamentally flawed. It made uncertain and questionable what should be 'most certain and most valid', namely a change in the royal line of succession. The dispensation should therefore be made an absolute permission, that did not depend in any way on the validity or otherwise of the first marriage.

As well as these large questions of approach and principle, the annotator found important technical omissions. The type of marriage contract, from which Henry's future bride was dispensed, had not been specified. To clarify matters, the words *de presenti* should be added. Even the enacting clause was defective, as the words *de mero motu summi pontificis* (by the mere motion of the Supreme Pontiff) had been left out. They should be restored.[12]

We do not know the identity of the annotator, though there are clues in his unusually fine italic hand, his pungent Latin style and his absolute command of canon law. The great nineteenth-century scholar, James Gairdner, guessed that, whoever he was, he wrote at the dictation of Cardinal Wolsey. He certainly wrote for Wolsey's benefit. For, by the time that he had finished, Henry's confidence in the document, which was his work and Anne's, had shrivelled like a pricked balloon. King Henry VIII's rebellion was over. Cardinal Wolsey was back in charge of the Divorce.

Whether that was a good thing in the long run, either for the Divorce suit or for Wolsey, remains to be seen.

The first victim of the change was, of course, Secretary Knight. He had been the chosen instrument of Henry's rebellion and Wolsey made sure that he paid the price. The achievements of his Embassy were comprehensively trashed – 'in their present form', Wolsey now asserted, the dispensation and the commission 'are as good as none at all' – and Knight himself was left marooned in France, denied permission even to return home. On 21 April, he wrote pathetically to Henry. 'It pierceth my stomach deeply', Knight began, 'that any charge committed unto me by your commandment should not be likewise by me performed accordingly unto your pleasure.' However, he insisted that he had throughout acted 'as it became your true servant' – as 'if my good fortune had been to come unto your presence I should evidently have shown unto your Highness'.[13]

Whose verdict on Knight's Embassy was right: Knight's or Wolsey's? Most historians have been eager to endorse Wolsey's condemnation of Knight's efforts. There is, however, as I have already suggested, little reason to do so. Far from Knight's embassy being a disaster, Henry was never nearer to a papally recognized divorce and remarriage than on New Year's Day 1528. That he threw the chance away was his own fault, for listening to Wolsey. But the final blame must rest with Wolsey, who was happy to damage Henry's case in order to cling on to his own power.

Anne cannot have been over-pleased at Wolsey's restoration to something like his old favour and, as soon as he was out of the way, she was probably instrumental in making amends to Knight who, in December 1529, was appointed to the wealthy archdeaconry of Richmond.

Her protection was exercised much more effectively, however, over her own creature Barlow, who had couriered the offending documents. In August 1528 her father, Lord Rochford, asked Wolsey to appoint Barlow to the living of Sundridge in Kent. Wolsey obliged but his office confused the name of the living by writing 'Tonbridge' instead of 'Sundridge'. Anne wrote to him to request him to clear up the difficulty and make the grant to Barlow in proper form. It would, she assured him, 'be very well bestowed'. 'For all these that hath taken pain in the King's Matter,' she continued, 'it shall be my daily study to imagine all the ways that I can devise to do them service and pleasure'.[14]

She was as good as her word: Barlow got Sundridge.

46. *Wolsey reascendant*

By the time Nuncio Gambara arrived in England with the dispensation and the commission, Anne had already left the Court for her parents' house at Hever.[1]

This, probably, was to preserve the decencies. The fact that Henry had sought the dispensation showed of course that he was eager to marry again; while the particular provisions of the dispensation pointed directly to Anne as the woman in question: the 'affinity contracted whether by licit or illicit intercourse' arose from Henry's affair with Anne's sister Mary; 'the previous betrothal' referred to Anne's aborted marriage with Percy. Indeed, her actual name seems already to have become known in Rome, together with a not very favourable view of her virtue: she was 'not', it was considered, 'of so excellent qualities as she is here esteemed [in England]'. None of this was helpful to Henry's case. But it was not seriously damaging either. On the other hand, for the Papal Nuncio to have found Henry and Anne living together in apparently open sin at Greenwich would have entirely destroyed Henry's moral *bona fide*.

So Anne had to leave. At least it spared her having to witness Wolsey's triumph. But equally her temporary rustication probably smoothed Wolsey's path. *His* absence in France in the previous summer had led directly to Knight's secret mission to Rome; now *her* absence in turn helped Wolsey to regain control of the Divorce suit.

Cardinal Wolsey moved with his customary single-mindedness and expedition. In little more than a week, Gambara was debriefed; the dispensation was dissected and a new mission to Rome was agreed on. Gambara would return to Rome, this time effectively as Henry's ambassador to the Pope. And he would be accompanied by two new English envoys: Stephen Gardiner, Wolsey's brilliant young aide, and Edward Fox.[2]

Foxe came from the same stable as Gardiner. He went up to Cambridge in 1512, the year after Gardiner, and became Provost of King's College in 1528, three years after Gardiner became Master of Trinity Hall. The two men enjoyed, as they said themselves, 'old amity and fast friendship', with Foxe deferring to Gardiner as the elder and the more brilliant. In the Embassy, for instance, Foxe had been given the precedence, since he was already a royal councillor, though it had always been intended that Gardiner was to do the bulk of the talking. But, between the two of them, they agreed that Gardiner should be named first, as well as speaking first. They also had rather different functions:

Gardiner was the hard-hitting lawyer; Foxe, a Doctor of Divinity, was there to argue the theology of Henry's case. It was a quieter role. But, in the long-run, it proved to be the more subversive.

The two had a long private meeting with Wolsey 'in his chamber' at his town palace of York Place on the night of Friday, 7 February. They probably accompanied the minister to Greenwich on Sunday the 9th and had an audience with Henry. Then, on the Monday, as Wolsey returned to London, they rode off, post-haste, on the first leg of their two-thousand-mile round trip. They left in such a hurry that much of the documentation of the Embassy – still in preparation at the time of their departure – had to be sent on after them by the courier Thaddeus. He was a crack rider; even so, dreadful weather conditions meant that he did not catch up with them until they were in France.[3]

Meanwhile, Henry and Wolsey proclaimed their renewed agreement on policy with a typical fireworks-display of co-ordinated speeches and actions. On Tuesday, 11 February, Henry went to stay the night with Wolsey at York Place. Late that same evening, in retaliation for the arrest of the English ambassadors in Spain, Mendoza, the Imperial ambassador, was arrested at his house in St Swithin's Lane in the City and taken to Sir John Daunce's house in Mark Lane near the Tower. On the Wednesday, the King and Cardinal summoned the ambassadors of most other powers to York Place jointly to explain their actions. The Emperor, they claimed, had persistently rejected their overtures for peace; therefore they had no choice but to declare war to protect the freedom of Italy and all Christendom from Charles V's overweening power. That at least was what they said; their real motive, of course, was to free the Pope from Spanish control so that he could be brought to agree to Henry's Divorce.[4]

Finally, on Thursday the 13th, Wolsey alone tried to justify the declaration of war to an assembly of English notables in the Star Chamber. They were more sceptical about the prospect of war with England's major trading partner and her traditional ally. So, according to the chronicler Hall, the speech was received badly: members of the audience nudged each other ('some knocked other on the elbow') and whispered hostile comments. But that, for the moment, was the limit of the opposition.[5]

Publicly, therefore, Henry and Wolsey stood as one, shoulder-to-shoulder in support of a policy that carried high risks at home and abroad – and big opportunities too.

But all was not quite as it seemed. Just before he dismissed Foxe and Gardiner at the end of their audience on Sunday, Henry slipped Foxe a letter. It was for Anne, on whom the envoys were to call at Hever on their way to Dover.[6]

In contrast to Henry's earlier, florid epistles in French, this letter was in English. And it was short, even terse. 'This bearer and his fellow', Henry told Anne, 'be despatched with as many things to compass Our Matter and to bring it to pass as our will could imagine or devise.' Henry drove the point home: the mission *would* result in rapid action: everything possible *was* being done. 'Yet I will assure you,' he continued, 'there shall be no time lost that may be won, and further cannot be done; for *ultra posse non esse.*'

Henry doubtless intended that his excess of rhetorical devices – the repetition, the proverbial phrases, the rhyme, the translation into Latin for extra emphasis – would underscore his resolution and confidence. But they have the opposite effect. Was Henry doubtful about what he was doing? Or, more likely, did he fear that Anne was?

'Keep him not too long with you, but desire him for your sake to make the more speed,' Henry concluded, 'for the sooner we shall have word from him the sooner shall Our Matter come to pass.'[7]

For both Henry and Anne, however, there was immediate consolation. Nuncio Gambara had left London on the same day as Gardiner and Foxe. So the coast was clear and Anne could come back to Court. Henry trusted she would make a 'short repair [a quick return]'. But it could not be short enough for him 'which desireth as much to be yours as you do to have him'.[8]

Then a hitch occurred. Somehow, Henry's longing for Anne's return became public knowledge. It was 'better known at London than with any that is about me', Henry informed Anne in another short, urgent note. He 'much marvelled', suspecting 'lack of discrete handling [appropriate secrecy]'.[9]

He was right. For the cover of the one-time Secret Matter was long since blown. Instead, whether in public or (as they thought) in private, their love was played on an open stage. Henry reacted with irritation to the perpetual scrutiny, to the leaks and the rumours, whether true or false; Anne, in contrast, had the confidence of a natural celebrity and almost seemed to welcome the exposure.

Did she also see it as a sort of guarantee? As something which ensured that Henry was in too far to go back on his word?

47. Co-operation?

When Anne returned to the Court at Windsor in late February, she found a new face in the King's personal entourage: Thomas Heneage. Heneage had been the most important member of Wolsey's Privy Chamber, and, as such, Cavendish's boss. Now Wolsey, flushed with his success in regaining control of policy, had engineered Heneage's appointment to a similar position in Henry's Household. His task was to hold a watching brief on Henry – and on Anne.

Anne quickly found work for idle hands.

'As the King was going to dinner', Heneage noted in his first report to Wolsey on 3 March, 'Mistress Anne spake to me, and said she was afeared your Grace had forgotten her.' The reason for her anxiety was that Wolsey had sent a messenger to Henry and, in his haste, had omitted to instruct him to pay his compliments also to Anne. Heneage made excuses for his former master. But Anne was not satisfied. She would make sure that Wolsey never forgot her again. And she would use Heneage as the means.

That night at supper, Henry ordered Heneage to take a dish from his table 'down' to Anne, who was evidently lodged beneath the King's private apartments at the foot of the Privy Stairs. Heneage did so and found himself invited to supper with Anne. She immediately turned on the charm. But she also made demands. 'She wished', Heneage reported to Wolsey, 'that she had some of your good meat, as carps, shrimps and other.' Meanwhile, her mother, Lady Rochford, had already pressed Heneage for 'a morsel of [Wolsey's] tunny [tuna-fish]'. Heneage, finding the business fishy in both senses of the word, excused himself for getting involved in it. 'I beseech your Grace to pardon me', he wrote, 'that I am so bold to write unto your Grace hereof: it is the conceit and mind of a woman.'[1]

But Wolsey understood better. Anne required tribute, and he paid it, sending her a letter and, no doubt, her carps. Anne transmitted her elaborate gratitude, again via Heneage. 'Mistress Anne', he informed Wolsey on the 16th, 'thanketh your Grace for your kind and favourable writing unto her, and sayeth she is much bounden unto your Grace.'[2]

This charade of mutual compliment, beautifully played and patently insincere, testified to the fact that, after the political ebbs and flows of the winter of 1527–8, Wolsey and Anne were now in need of each other. Wolsey had recovered power on the premise that he had found the key to Henry's Divorce and remarriage. So he needed to keep Anne on side by convincing her that he was serving her cause effectively and with enthusiasm. Anne, in turn, had been told by Henry that Wolsey was her best, perhaps her sole, hope of marrying the King. So it was in her interest to sweet-talk Wolsey and encourage him in his efforts (as she did all others who laboured on the Divorce).

A moment's reflexion, however, shows that the need was not reciprocal. Wolsey needed Anne more than she needed him. Anne – and her marriage – was, after all, the end; Wolsey was only the means. If he failed, he would be discarded, as had nearly happened in late 1527.

But this time, it is clear, Wolsey intended to put up a fight.

*

Wolsey's weakness in 1527 had been his lack of reliable intelligence about the King. Treasurer Fitzwilliam had been loyal but did not form part of Henry's inner circle. And Secretary Knight, who did, had betrayed Wolsey.

Heneage's appointment to Henry's Privy Chamber went some way to remedying this deficiency. Even more important was Wolsey's placement there of Sir John Russell, the ancestor of the Dukes of Bedford. Russell was one of Wolsey's oldest and most loyal clients: 'I have', he later protested to Wolsey, 'borne my heart and service unto your Grace above all men living, saving only the King.' Russell's appointment to the Privy Chamber took place in January 1526 at the latest. But he spent most of the subsequent two years as a sort of military attaché with the Imperial armies in Italy. It had been intended to send him to Italy again in late 1527, this time as Henry's representative with the French armies of Marshal Lautrec. But the mission was aborted. Wolsey had a more important campaign for him at home: the minister's own political survival.[3]

But Wolsey was not the only one who was manoeuvring for advantage around the King. Back in January 1526, with the major Household reforms known as the Eltham Ordinances, Wolsey had at last seemed to get full control of the Privy Chamber. He secured the expulsion of some persistent troublemakers, including the brothers-in-law Sir Nicholas Carew and Sir Francis Bryan. He bought out others. And he even managed to get rid (for a consideration) of Anne's own brother, George Boleyn, who had been one of the King's pages.[4]

In the winter of 1527–8, however, with the temporary eclipse of Wolsey's power, those whom he had driven out came knocking on the door of the citadel once more. In December, Sir John Wallop, the intimate friend of Sir Thomas Cheyney, one of the few long-serving Gentlemen of the Privy Chamber to have survived all Wolsey's purges, was appointed to the department. Wallop's appointment was noted by the French ambassador, who added, with evident surprise, that 'Bryan is not yet reappointed.' Instead, Bryan's brother-in-law Carew beat him to it when Carew was reinstated in the Privy Chamber in January 1528.[5]

There is no evidence that many of these men had close links with Anne. Indeed some, including Carew, were to be among her most dangerous enemies. But all were profiting from the weakening of Wolsey's power which she had brought about. And one or two decided to capitalize on her position more fully.

Most important was Sir Thomas Cheyney, who, as it happens, had much in common with Anne. Like her, he came from an important Kentish family and was 'well couched in the French tongue'. But he was not related to her, as some have supposed (it was the Cheyneys of Northamptonshire, a different family, who were connected with the Boleyns). Cheyney had no reason to love Wolsey, who had treated him outrageously while he was ambassador to France in 1522. But, with the political skill which enabled him to thrive as 'a favourite and Privy Councillor to four successive Kings and Queens, in the greatest turn of times England ever beheld', he had kept his feelings well hidden.

But in March 1528 he seems to have fallen into Wolsey's deep displeasure. The occasion is unknown, though probably it was connected with his subsequent, long-running quarrel with Wolsey's client, Sir John Russell, over his determination to secure the wardship of Russell's wealthy step-daughter, Anne Broughton, whom he later married. Faced with Wolsey's wrath, Cheyney turned to the only person able to defend him against Wolsey and sought Anne's protection.

Anne's reaction is instructive. She did not approach Henry directly on Cheyney's behalf, which would only have exacerbated matters. Instead, she acted as a peace-maker and used Heneage to try to sort things out directly with Wolsey.

'As your most bounden bead[prayer]-woman', Heneage reported, Anne had 'commanded me to write unto your Grace, humbly desiring the same to be good and gracious lord unto Sir Thomas Cheyney'. 'She is', he continued, 'marvellous sorry that [Cheyney] should be in your Grace's displeasure.' As for Cheyney himself, Anne claimed, perhaps implausibly, he was as repentant as could be: 'Also she sayeth that the same Sir Thomas Cheyney is very sorry in his heart that he hath so displeased your Grace, more sorry than if he had lost all the good he hath.'[6]

This was to lay it on with a trowel. Nevertheless, Anne's good intentions towards Wolsey were manifest. And they would remain so, as long – but only as long – as his approach to the Great Matter seemed to bear fruit.

In fact, Wolsey's strategy received an immediate set-back. With the declaration of war on Charles V, in which France joined, Wolsey was aiming to weaken Charles's grip on his Italian territories in the south by attacking him in the north of his vast empire. But the scheme quickly came adrift since English public opinion was resolutely opposed to the war. There were riots in several counties, including Kent, where Anne's father was one of those delegated to contain the disturbances. 'I believe', the French ambassador himself admitted, '[Wolsey] is the only Englishman who wishes a war with Flanders.' 'You may be sure', he added, 'he is playing a terrible game.'[7]

The terrible game was quickly up. On 16 March, Henry informed Wolsey privately that he was 'loath' to prosecute the war. By early April it was agreed that trade between England and the Low Countries should continue. And, with effect from 15 June, a formal truce was proclaimed with Flanders, though England remained in a state of hostilities with the Emperor's other territories. The failure of the war was a blow to Wolsey's prestige. But he quickly recovered since the Flemish campaign had only ever been a side-show to the real theatre of war in Italy.[8]

Back in December 1527, Gregorio Casale, the permanent English representative at the Papal Court, had spelled out the geo-political realities of the Divorce campaign. 'If Lautrec [the French commander in Italy] advances,' he reported on the 22nd, 'the Pope will do all [Wolsey] wants. But, if not, he will do nothing.'[9]

Fortunately for Wolsey, Lautrec's successes continued. In the summer of 1527 he had conquered all Lombardy, apart from its capital, Milan. In the autumn, on Francis I's direct orders, he left behind the still-undefeated Imperial garrison in Milan and marched south. In the New Year, he overran the Romagna and on 9 February he invaded the Kingdom of Naples. His advance turned into a promenade and by the end of April he had reached the suburbs of Naples itself. In the Bay, a Genoese fleet, commanded by a nephew of Andrea Doria, France's principal Italian ally, blockaded the city and cut off supplies. On 28 April, the Spanish fleet tried to break out but the admiral was killed and his ships destroyed. The fall of Naples was imminent.

Lautrec *had* advanced, and Clement was prepared to do all, or almost all, that Wolsey wanted.[10]

It was the best possible background to the mission of Foxe and Gardiner. Contrary winds kept them at Dover for four days, and they spent another two in Calais, recovering from the crossing and waiting for the courier Thaddeus to catch up with them with the remainder of their instructions. Diplomatic business then consumed another three days in Paris and they allowed themselves a day off at Lyon to mark the half way stage of their journey. Thereafter, taking full advantage of their youth, they had ridden hard, 'travelling evermore from before the day till it was within the night' and, after Lyons, 'never lying two nights in one place'. They were off the road for about ten days and on it for about thirty. Which gave an average of some thirty-three miles a day.[11]

It was fast. But was it fast enough for Henry and Anne? Foxe and Gardiner had their doubts. So, anxiously they begged the King to take account of the bad luck and unavoidable delays they had suffered. Then, they trusted, he would see that 'we have made as diligent passage by post hither, as any courier could, not riding the night'.

They finally arrived at Clement VII's refuge of Orvieto on 21 March. They were filthy, soaked to the skin and without a change of clothes since, for speed, they had left their baggage behind in Paris. This led to another two days' delay while clothes were made for them. The alternative, they explained, was to appear in borrowed garments. But that would have been doubly difficult. Most people in this refugee Court seemed to have only one set of clothes and they were cut, moreover, in the Spanish fashion. It would have been curious indeed if the English envoys had appeared before the Pope in the black 'Spanish cloaks' that were worn by their bitterest opponents.[12]

Foxe and Gardiner had their first audience with Clement on the 23rd. They were not impressed. Orvieto, in ancient times an Etruscan stronghold, was known in Latin as *Urbs Vetus* (the Old City). And the name, they joked bitterly, was only too appropriate, for the city was indeed old 'in all languages'. So too was everything in it. The Papal palace was old and ruinous, with bare rooms and fallen ceilings. The furnishings were threadbare and worth only a few pounds. The attendants consisted of 'thirty person, riff-raff and other, standing in the chambers for a garnishment'. The Pope was ineffectual and worn-out. And – above all – the Papacy itself was at its nadir. 'It is a fall from the top of the hill to the lowliest part of the mountain', they wrote with a sort of poetry of contempt, and the power which had once ruled the world was now plundered and exploited by every petty Italian principality.[13]

Clearly, they – and especially the forceful Gardiner – expected Clement to be a push-over. They were quickly undeceived.

For all the fallen state of the Papacy and for all the apparent weakness of the man, there was something plastic, even resilient about Giulio de' Medici, now Pope Clement VII. He seemed to yield quickly, but he just as quickly bounced back. To seek to force a decision from him was thus, as Foxe and Gardiner eventually realized, to try to squeeze rubber into shape or to write in water.

Nevertheless, despite the impossibility of their task, they went to it with a will. Their mission was to get Clement's agreement to two documents: a new dispensation for Henry to marry Anne, and a new commission to Wolsey to settle the Great Matter once and for all. The former Clement agreed to without difficulty. But the latter he absolutely refused, at least in the form of the decretal commission which Wolsey so desperately wanted.

In session after session, Gardiner tried to get him to change his mind. They met in the Pope's little Privy Chamber or in his study which also doubled as his bedroom. Clement placed himself with his back to the wall, while the English envoys and two or three cardinal-councillors sat on stools in a semi-circle around him. Law books were brought in and experts were consulted. Occasionally Clement, who was well-informed about England as its former Cardinal-Protector, diverted to discuss entertaining tit-bits of English news and gossip. Otherwise, they ground on remorselessly, traversing and retraversing the same territory until far into the night and then resuming, bleareyed, the following morning.

On 31 March Foxe and Gardiner reported the stalemate in letters sent home by the trusty Barlow, who was standing by. Then they returned to the attack. This time Gardiner's language became more violent and his threats more open. To no avail. Sometimes Clement parried with tears; sometimes with a flash of humour. God, he wryly observed, had put all the laws in his bosom but had, unaccountably, forgotten to give him the key!

Easter was approaching and the English were desperate to get something. Finally, a compromise was brokered. The Pope would grant only a general commission. But the English would add some key clauses taken from the decretal commission. There would be provision, in case of necessity, for one judge to act without his fellow. Appeals would be excluded after a fashion. And Rome would give its *imprimatur* to the proceedings by sending Cardinal Campeggio to England as papal legate and Wolsey's fellow judge. Earlier drafts were produced and fought over line by line. Agreement was reached just before Easter. On Easter Monday, 13 April, both the dispensation and the commission were sealed by the Papal Chancery and, the same day, bearing these precious trophies, Foxe set out on the return journey.

He also carried a letter from Gardiner to Wolsey, in which Gardiner frankly admitted that, 'by reason of crying, speaking, chafing and writing, [he was] ill distempered'. Clement had worn even Gardiner down.[14]

Foxe's speed home disgraced their earlier efforts. He was in Paris by the 26th and at Calais by the 28th. There he had to wait four days for a favourable wind, before setting sail on 2 May. The crossing was uneventful and he arrived at Sandwich that night. He had taken only fifteen days on the road from Rome and had ridden on average over sixty miles a day. It was twice as fast as on the outward journey.

The following day was Sunday, when Wolsey paid his regular weekly visit to Court in term time. Once again, Foxe rode flat out for Greenwich, hoping to arrive before Wolsey left. But an excess of hospitality from town dignitaries en route held him up and he did not arrive till 5 p.m. It was too late: Wolsey's barge had left two hours previously to take him back to town.

Instead, the King ordered Foxe to go to Anne's chamber and debrief himself directly to her.[15]

48. Wolsey's triumph

Normally, it seems, Anne was still lodged with the Queen's women on Catherine's side of the palace. But disease had struck and 'my lady Princess [Mary] and divers other the Queen's maidens were sick of the small-pox'. So Anne had moved to a lodging in Tilt-yard Gallery, to the south of the main palace complex. This was remote enough to offer her some protection from infection. It also enabled her to maintain an independent, semi-royal state that would have been quite impossible in the Queen's lodgings.

And it was in the lodgings in the Tilt-yard Gallery that Foxe found Anne. First, he was 'admitted unto her presence'; then he gave her a quick summary of the achievements of the Embassy. He told her that the Pope had granted the key documents and agreed to the despatch of a legate. And he gave the credit to Gardiner's 'singular fidelity, diligence, and dexterity'. Anne was ecstatic. The only problem was that she found it difficult to distinguish one young, eager, travel-stained cleric from another – 'oftentimes in communication', Foxe reported to Gardiner, 'calling me Mr

Stephens' (the name, as we have seen, by which Gardiner was usually known). Finally, she made Gardiner 'promise of large recompense'.

At this moment, Henry entered unannounced (evidently, ease of access for the King was another advantage of Anne's present lodgings). Anne withdrew and Henry ordered Foxe to tell him, *quam posse brevissime* ('just as briefly as I could'), 'what was done in his cause'.

Foxe began with the dispensation. As we have seen, this was the document over which Wolsey had launched his bid to regain control of the Great Matter. He had shredded the first version obtained by the now-disgraced Knight. And he had drawn up a new version, incorporating all his criticisms. Gardiner, Foxe reported to Henry, had presented this new dispensation to Clement with a characteristic, hyperbolical flourish – claiming it to be such that, for the peace of Europe, the Pope should 'grant unto all princes christened the like thereof'. But Clement's response to a document over which the mountains had laboured had been deflationary. For he had treated it, if not quite as the ridiculous mouse of the proverb, then certainly as something utterly uncontentious, which he could accept on the nod, 'very promptly and facilely'.

Foxe, in his report to the King, put as good a gloss on this as possible. It was, he said, a mark of Clement's special favour to Henry that he 'had passed the same without alteration of any sentence or word and sent the same by me'.

Here Foxe, for all his rhetoric, spoke the literal truth. For Wolsey's draft of the second dispensation survives in the Vatican archives. This shows that it was used by the Papal Chancery as warrant for the Bull of dispensation, which was copied from it pretty much word for word (Foxe apologized for the bad writing of this transcript, since there were no calligraphically qualified scribes in the skeleton Curia-in-exile). The draft is endorsed: *Minuta dispensationis missae per Thadeum cursorem* ('Draft of a Dispensation sent by the courier Thaddeus'), showing that it formed part of the supplementary packet of instructions which, as we have seen, was sent on to Foxe and Gardiner after their departure from London. And the draft is docketed by the Papal secretary, Motta, as having been registered in the Apostolic Chamber.

After describing their (rather too easy) success with the dispensation, Foxe moved to the more delicate matter of their failure to secure the decretal commission. But he put this in a good light too. The general commission, which they had got, contained, he claimed, all but two of the essential points of the decretal commission. The omissions – the Pope's definition of the law on the case and his promise not to revoke the commission – were, Foxe conceded, important. But Clement, he assured Henry, had faithfully promised to make them good by his subsequent letters.

Henry was persuaded. He 'made marvellous demonstrations of joy and gladness' and summoned Anne to join in.

After he had been joined by Anne, the King peppered Foxe with questions about the Pope's attitude to his case. In his answers Foxe, as he reported to Gardiner, 'took occasion' to puff Wolsey's role. 'Without [Wolsey's] letters', he told Henry and Anne, 'we should have obtained nothing there'. It was also thanks to Wolsey that Clement had changed his opinion of Anne. The Pope had previously been informed that, in his love for Anne, Henry was driven by *privatum aliquem effectum* ('a certain private lust'); that Anne herself 'was with child, and of no such qualities as should be worthy that majesty'. But, Foxe asserted, thanks – and thanks only – to Wolsey's testimony to the contrary, Clement had been persuaded of the truth.

At this point, Foxe must have turned to Anne, who had of course been present throughout this extraordinary recital. Was she properly grateful to Wolsey? Or outraged at the impertinence of his agent, Foxe?

Finally, Henry asked Foxe about the issue of 'recusation and appellation' – that is, refusal of jurisdiction by one of the parties and appeal. This matter loomed large because it was already clear that Catherine intended to resort to these devices to abort any trial in England – as indeed she was to do. Once again Foxe had his answer ready. These cases were covered by the new commission, he claimed, 'so far as the law would suffer and might be expressed by words'. He then quoted the relevant clause of the commission. But, faced by this technicality, Henry remitted the matter to Wolsey. 'He said he would my lord Grace's judgement' and ordered Foxe to go immediately to Wolsey that night.

For the moment, Wolsey's own town-palace of York Place was uninhabitable, since he was rebuilding the Hall and other chambers 'most sumptuously and gorgeously'. Instead, he was staying at Durham House on the Strand. By the time Foxe arrived there it was past 10 o'clock at night and Wolsey had gone to bed. Foxe was admitted nonetheless and explained what had happened. Wolsey's first reaction was unfavourable. He was 'marvellously perplexed, thinking this Commission to be of no better value than that was sent by Gambara' and obtained by the despised Knight. But he decided to sleep on the matter.

By the following afternoon, he had changed his mind. He summoned a high-powered delegation, consisting of Foxe, Dr Bell (Henry's first and most trusted adviser on the Divorce), and Anne's father, Lord Rochford, and told them that he was fully satisfied with the commission. Other experts concurred and sang Gardiner's praises: *O! non aestimandum thesaurum, Margaritumque regni nostri* ('O inestimable treasure and pearl of our realm'). Which was, Foxe reported to the subject of these extravagances, 'to the great comfort and rejoice of us your poor friends here'.

But, despite these outpourings, Wolsey wavered again. Finally, he decided he must have a decretal commission. It would settle his conscience and defend him against his detractors. It would deal with the possibility that Clement might die before a verdict was reached – or that he might change his mind. Above all, it would protect Wolsey's own political position.

Here Wolsey got carried away. He spoke with extraordinary bluntness and gave Foxe a complete rhetorical question-and-answer script for Gardiner to use with Clement. What, Gardiner was to ask, would most conduce to the recovery of Papal authority? Surely, he was to answer his own question, it would be to render Wolsey impregnably secure in Henry's favour? So 'that what his Grace [Wolsey] should advise . . . his Highness [Henry] should . . . facilely condescend . . . unto'. 'And by what means', Gardiner was to continue, 'may that be so perfectly attained?' By

Clement's granting a decretal commission, he was to reply, '*only at the contemplation (petition) of my lord's Grace*'.[1]

It was A. F. Pollard who, almost a hundred years ago, observed that for Wolsey 'the Divorce was . . . a means not an end'. The point has been played down by Wolsey's apologists. But it seems to me to be no more than the truth. For, from the moment he found out about Knight's secret mission, Wolsey had a single aim. It was not to get the Divorce for Henry. Instead, it was to recover control of the Great Matter for himself. He pursued this objective with single-mindedness and – it would seem from his words to Foxe – self-awareness also.[2]

But were Wolsey's objectives in the Great Matter compatible with Henry's and Anne's? In other words, were Wolsey's policies as effective in procuring the Divorce as they were, for the time being, in bolstering Wolsey's own position? Only time, once again, would tell.

Barlow rode off, yet again, to Orvieto with Foxe's letter and Wolsey's instructions. And Gardiner, once more, had to lay siege to Pope Clement. At first he failed and his golden reputation risked crumbling to dust. The only thing that would recover it, Foxe reported to his friend, would be for him to secure Legate Campeggio's despatch with the decretal commission. 'And in case he never come, ye never to return.' It was the fate of exile, which Wolsey had visited on the wretched Knight.[3]

Gardiner fought tooth and nail to avoid it. Finally, he was successful. On 11 June he wrote to Henry in triumph: Campeggio was en route for England with the decretal commission. On 28 June, Wolsey received the news. Gardiner's triumph was his triumph. He had got what Henry wanted; now, surely, he was impregnable.[4]

Less than a week before, Anne had been at death's door.

49. The sweat

T he sweating sickness, or the sweat for short, seems to have been a kind of acute influenza, perhaps combined with pneumonia. The principal symptom was profuse sweating (hence the name). The disease moved with extraordinary speed: within twenty-four hours the patient was generally past the worst – or dead. The epidemic made its first recorded appearance in England at the end of the fifteenth century. Thereafter, it struck again, invariably in the summer and with undiminished ferocity, every few years. The outbreak of 1528 was one of the worst.

Certainly, it had the most momentous consequences.

On Tuesday, 16 June, one of Anne's ladies-in-waiting fell sick of the disease.

It was in any case a day of upheaval at Court as it was the beginning of the Progress. The whole Courtly apparatus of 'portable magnificence' – the tapestries and cushions, jewels and plate, household utensils and the King's own clothes, bedding, travelling library, medicine chest and personal petty-cash – had been packed into their special bags, boxes and chests and loaded on to carts. The carts had been covered with bear-hides to protect them against the elements and the great caravanserai of the Court stood ready to depart from Greenwich to the first port of call of the Progress: Waltham Abbey in Essex.

But, with the news of the disease, these orderly arrangements were abandoned. Henry immediately rode off to Waltham while Anne was sent to stay with her father at Hever.[1]

Such a flight to safety was Henry's invariable reaction to plague and other epidemic diseases. No one would have expected him to behave differently – with the exception, it appears, of Anne herself. She seems to have protested at the abrupt separation from her royal admirer. At any rate, Henry was soon writing to her, to comfort her and remove her 'unreasonable thoughts'. He trusted that the disease had spared her as it seemed to have done him. He heard that she had had, as yet, no symptoms. And, in any case, he asserted, 'few if any women' had been affected.

But the real purpose of the letter was to assure Anne that, despite his flight and their separation, his love for her remained the same. 'Wherever I may be I am yours,' he protested, reverting both to the Courtly French and the extravagant phraseology of his earliest letters to her. And, once more, there was a fanciful signature: his royal cipher between the syllables of the French word *immuable* – the whole meaning 'King Henry the Constant' or 'King Henry the Immovable.' The fact that the 'Constant' and 'Immovable' Henry was actually in a state of perpetual motion, fleeing from house to house to escape the sweat, may have escaped Henry. But Anne is unlikely to have missed the irony.[2]

A day or so later Henry's hardy optimism was dashed: Anne had fallen ill, along with her father. The news was brought to Henry at night. Immediately, he wrote to her again. It was the worst possible thing that could have happened. He loved her more than the whole world. He desired her health as much as his own. He would gladly suffer half her illness to have her cured.

With the letter Henry sent Anne a physician. His favourite doctor (probably Dr Chamber) was unfortunately absent, just at the moment when he was most needed. But, in his place, Henry was despatching his second medical adviser. He prayed to God that this physician would be able to make her well. Anne, for her part, 'was to be governed by his advice regarding your sickness'. That way, Henry wrote, 'I hope soon to see you again, which will be a better restorative to me than all the precious stones of the world' – and here the King, who was himself a keen amateur of medicine, referred to the supposed curative properties of certain jewels.[3]

The physician's name was Dr William Butts. He had gone up to Cambridge about ten years before Foxe and Gardiner. But, since he was a slower developer than that brilliant pair of friends, he was an elder contemporary of theirs. He commenced his MD in 1518 and in 1524 he became the Principal of St Mary's Hostel, which lay a few yards from both Gardiner's Trinity Hall and Foxe's King's College. His practice began in the mid-1520s and he quickly made his name with his treatment, first of the always sickly Princess Mary and then, as recently as May 1528, of the usually robust Duke of Norfolk. Norfolk sang his praises, as one 'without whose aid he thinks he should not have recovered'. But Anne was his test-case.[4]

At first, it was touch and go. 'By returning in of the sweat before the time', Anne was in grave 'jeopardy'. Though no one knew it at the time, the whole future of England, England's Church and England's State, hung in the balance. But 'the endeavour of Mr Butts' (or, more likely, the vigorous Boleyn constitution) carried her through. She survived.[5]

Butts's career was now made. 'If he can put you in health again,' Henry had vowed in his letter to Anne, 'I shall love him better than ever.' He kept his promise. By Christmas, Butts had been appointed Royal Physician with the then enormous salary of £100 a year. With Anne herself, Butts's relationship became, if anything, even more intimate. For he helped take charge, not only of Anne's physical health but of her spiritual welfare and religious patronage as well.[6]

Anne recovered rapidly. However, Henry's invariable practice was to impose a lengthy period of quarantine on members of his entourage who had been sick or otherwise exposed to infection. He made no exception – not even for Anne – and she remained in Kent for several weeks. But they communicated frequently by letter. And her absence not only made Henry grow fonder (as the French ambassador noted with apparent surprise) but also more generous to her 'suits' or petitions on behalf of her relatives and clients.

The ability to get jobs and procure favours was, then as now, a mark of political power. As soon as Henry's passion for Anne was clear, Cavendish notes, 'it was . . . judged . . . throughout all the Court of every man that she being in such favour with the King might work mysteries with the King and obtain any suit of him for her friend'. Anne, for her part, grasped the opportunity eagerly. Unlike Catherine, a foreigner and with no ties binding her to Court parties or factions, Anne had wheeling-and-dealing in her blood. She was the daughter of a man whose ambition was to serve the King 'in the Court all the days of my life'; her uncle was the politically supple Duke of Norfolk; her brother-in-law, William Carey, was a gentleman of the Privy Chamber; and her cousin, Sir Francis Bryan, known as 'the Vicar of Hell', was one of the most colourful characters of the Court. For Anne to press suits on the King, and turn her power over his heart into power over his patronage, was as natural as breathing.[7]

Anne showed a particular interest in the appointment of the next Abbess of Wilton in Wiltshire. The house was a rich one and many of the nuns were the unmarriageable daughters of important families. They had little by way of religious vocation and lived the life of ladies of leisure – gadding about the countryside, feuding with each other and occasionally conducting not very well concealed love affairs with local clergy. The last Abbess had died in April and two candidates quickly emerged to replace her: Dame Isobel Jordan and Dame Eleanor Carey. Eleanor was sister of William Carey, who pressed hard for her appointment. But William Carey was one of the first victims of the sweating sickness. Anne then took over the suit, as a kindness to her sister Mary's stricken family, and got Henry to promise faithfully that Eleanor should have the post.

But here other forces came into play. Dame Isobel had powerful backers, too, including, it soon became clear, Wolsey himself. Both sides in the struggle played dirty and the easy-going life of the Abbey provided plenty of scandalous material. Dame Eleanor admitted that she had 'had two children by two sundry priests and further since hath been kept by a servant of the Lord Broke that was, and not long ago'. There were nasty rumours, too, about Dame Isobel – though, it was conceded, she 'is so old that of many years she could not be as she was named'.

The upshot was a stalemate that was submitted to Henry himself for resolution. He reported his decision to Anne in a letter written at the beginning of July. Her sister-in-law, Eleanor Carey, was barred out of hand. 'I would not', Henry wrote to Anne, 'for all the gold in the world cloak your conscience or mine to make her ruler of a house which is of so ungodly demeanour.' That might seem to open the way to Dame Isobel. But Henry arrived at a Judgement of Solomon. 'Yet notwithstanding', he assured Anne, 'to do you pleasure, I have done that neither of them shall have it; but that some [other] good and well disposed woman shall have it.' This was an ingenious solution, calculated to save face all round.[8]

But Wolsey rejected it. The minister's mind at this time is unusually hard to read; probably, indeed, he was unsure of it himself as he was buffeted by contrary experiences. There were long delays in the suit for the decretal commission, on which he had hung his whole future. These filled him with fears and forebodings, which he confided to the French ambassador. And the sweat was carrying off so many in his own household that it seemed impossible that he should escape infection himself. At this moment, suddenly, the clouds parted and Gardiner's letter arrived with news that Clement had, at last, conceded the decretal commission. Swinging now wildly between depression and a sense of mission, between talk of retirement and a determination to do the right thing at all costs, Wolsey's mood became dangerously unpredictable. At the beginning of July, he even managed to pick a quarrel with the faithful Russell. This was rather like fighting with himself. Even more dangerously, however, he resolved to take on the King.[9]

Henry's decision in the Wilton affair had been communicated to him in a letter written by the Court cleric, Dr Bell. Wolsey decided on his response probably on 5 July. Contrary to his usual practice, he did not inform Henry immediately. Instead, he sent him a strange letter. If these were 'the last words' he wrote to him, he assured the King, 'I dare boldly say and affirm, your grace hath had of me, a most loving, true and faithful servant; and that for favour, meed, gift or promise of gift, at any time, I never did or consented to [any]thing that might, in the least point, redound unto your dishonour or disprofit.' It was a magnificent valedictory, written in fear of imminent death. Unfortunately, perhaps, Wolsey lived – and had to live with the consequences of his actions.[10]

Two days later, on the 7th, Bell was still pressing Wolsey for a reply to his letter. What had he done about Wilton? Henry, under pressure no doubt from Anne, was keen to know.[11]

Wolsey delayed another few days still, before writing, and his letter did not reach Bell till the 10th. Bell trembled as he reported Henry's reaction. The King was 'somewhat moved'; Bell, for his part, protested that 'I would rather than part of my small substance' that Wolsey had acted otherwise. The next day Heneage confirmed Henry's displeasure: 'he was not best content'.[12]

For Wolsey, it transpired, had appointed Dame Isobel Jordan Abbess of Wilton. In so doing, he had defied Henry's direct command. Still worse, perhaps, he had humiliated the King in front of Anne.

50. Turning point

Henry wrote his letter of reproof to Wolsey on the morning of 14 July. After he had finished it, he summoned Wolsey's two leading Court followers, Russell and Heneage, and read the letter aloud to them.[1]

Clearly, he was proud of his efforts and of the effect he knew his rebuke would produce.

And with reason. It was almost a year since Henry had first quarrelled with Wolsey over the management of the Divorce. Then, the King's own behaviour had been duplicitous, even furtive. His letter to Knight, his instrument in deceiving Wolsey, 'reads', a great nineteenth-century historian wrote, 'more like the composition of a schoolboy found out by the master against whom he plots, than . . . the letter of an absolute King, who might have dismissed and ruined Wolsey at a moment's notice'.[2]

This time, however, there was no diffidence in either Henry's mind or his pen. To defy, the King wrote to his minister, his direct order in the matter of Wilton was bad enough. But worse than his defiance, was his attempt at deceit by claiming 'ignorance of my pleasure'. Henry refuted the claim by quoting word for word from previous letters to Wolsey. He then issued the blunt warning: 'wherefore, good my Lord, use no more that way with me for there is no man living that more hateth it'.[3]

It was Wolsey's turn to tremble like a schoolboy at this verbal lashing and to receive what comfort he could from his creatures Heneage and Russell.

Henry, the playboy king, had grown up at last. He had had to. His determination to marry Anne had forced him to stand alone; it was Henry against the world.

But, as usual, behind a newly strong man was a stronger woman: Anne herself. Henry was not only fighting for her, to keep and to marry her; *she* was helping to direct the blows and to plan the strategy.

And nowhere does this show more clearly than in the couple's handling of Wolsey during that long, disease-ridden summer.

'As many as I love, I rebuke and chasten', Henry had begun his letter to Wolsey – assimilating himself (not for the last time) to the Deity with this reference, from the *Book of Revelation*, to God's cruel-to-be-kind treatment of the faithful.[4]

And, for the moment, Henry meant it: everything which stood in the way of the full resumption of the 'loving' relationship between the King and his minister was swept aside. Abruptly, the King declared the question of Wilton closed. 'It is no great matter', Henry wrote to Wolsey a few days later, 'and though the case were much more heinous, I can be content for to remit it.' He also affected a conscious even-handedness as the tension between Russell and Cheyney over the wardship of Anne Broughton turned into open feuding. Indeed, he went one better and inclined rather against Anne's client Cheyney, whom he cast as the aggressor towards Wolsey's follower Russell. Cheyney 'was proud and full of opprobrious words', Henry said publicly. And only if he would admit his fault and be friends with Russell would he be readmitted to the Privy Chamber.[5]

The clue to Henry's behaviour, of course, was Gardiner's coup in securing the despatch of the Legate Campeggio with the decretal commission. This vindicated (it seemed) Wolsey's approach to the Divorce and rendered him indispensable – to Anne at least as much as Henry.

The result was that Anne sought to turn the renewed love-in between Wolsey and Henry into a strange sort of threesome. 'I am', she wrote to Wolsey, 'most bound of all creatures, next the King's Grace, to love and serve your Grace.' She would, she swore, never 'vary from this thought as long as any breath is in my body'. And she thanked the Lord 'that them that I desired and prayed for are scaped [the sweat], and that is the King and you'.[6]

Anne wrote this letter while she was still convalescing from the sweat. After her return to the Court in late July she wrote another, in terms of equally extravagant affection. 'I do know', she assured Wolsey, 'the great pains and troubles, that you have taken for me both day and night, [are] never like to be recompensed on my part, but alonely in loving you next unto the King's grace above all creatures living'. But her love, of course, was cupboard-love. 'I do long', she continued, 'to hear from you news of the Legate.'

She finished writing and turned to Henry who was by her side and wheedled him into adding a postscript. 'The writer of this letter', Henry began his note, 'would not cease till she had caused me likewise to set my hand.' 'I ensure you', he continued, 'there is neither of us but that greatly desireth to see you.' Then there followed the same sting-in-the-tail as in Anne's own letter. 'The not hearing of the Legate's arrival in France causeth us somewhat to muse', Henry ended, 'notwithstanding, we trust by your diligence and vigilancy (with the assistance of Almighty God) shortly to be eased out of that trouble'. There followed the double signature:

By your loving sovereign and friend, Henry R
Your humble servant, Anne Boleyn[7]

And still their trust in Wolsey seemed to be rewarded. After all their anxieties, Legate Campeggio arrived in France. Once more, for

338 THE QUEENS OF HENRY VIII

decency's sake, Anne was packed off to stay with her mother in the country. And there she received the news she had hoped for, in a scribbled note from Henry himself. 'The Legate which we most desired', he informed her, 'arrived at Paris on Sunday or Monday last past [13 or 14 September] ... and then I trust within a while after to enjoy that which I have so long longed for to God's pleasure and our both comfort.'

Henry's hopes, of course, far outpaced not only Campeggio's gouty limbs but events themselves. It took the Legate till the end of September to reach Calais and another week before he finally arrived in London. Then began his interminable round of meetings: with Henry, with Wolsey, with Catherine – with everybody in short apart from Anne herself. Away from her royal admirer and the Court, and flagrantly excluded from events, Anne's patience (never her strong point) snapped. Henry administered a slap of firm comfort in a letter which has disappeared. Then he welcomed her restoration to a better frame of mind. 'What joy', he exclaimed, 'it is to me to understand of your conformableness to reason, and of the suppression of your inutile [useless] and vain thoughts and fantasies with the bridle of reason!'

Never was she to think such black thoughts again, he wrote. The preparations for the wedding were in train: 'I have ... dress[ed] up gear for you, which I trust ere long to see you occupy' – 'and then', he added meaningfully, 'I trust to occupy yours.' As for Campeggio, only 'the unfeigned sickness of this well willing Legate doth somewhat retard his access to your presence'. When his health recovered, Campeggio would, Henry assured Anne, despatch their business quickly. And it was a calumny that he was favourable to Charles V: 'for I know well where he hath said', Henry confided, 'that it should be well known in this matter that he is not Imperial'.

But, as it turned out, it was Anne's 'inutile and vain thoughts and fantasies', not Henry's masculine reason, which proved correct. For in Italy events suddenly turned against Henry's French allies. In June 1528 Doria broke with the French and on 4 July his nephew withdrew his blockading fleet from the Bay of Naples. The Spanish could now revictual and reinforce the city. Still worse, on 17 August Lautrec died of the plague – which had already carried off two-thirds of his army. The stricken French forces, depleted and effectively leaderless, first retreated and then surrendered. On 9 September, as Campeggio was approaching Paris, Charles V's commander informed him that he was once more master of the south of Italy. Other disasters for the French followed in the north, as Genoa rebelled and regained its independence. Finally, on 21 October, just as Campeggio's negotiations were fully underway in London, the last French garrison on the Ligurian coast surrendered as well.[8]

'If Lautrec advances', Casale had presciently written the previous December, 'the Pope will do all [Wolsey] wants.' But Lautrec was now dead and the French conquests in Italy had collapsed like a house of cards. Wolsey's hopes collapsed with them.[9]

For the moment, however, Henry's mind was on matters nearer home. He was missing Anne horribly – so much so that current language was inadequate and he had to reach back into the already antique vocabulary of English Romance to find the word to describe his condition.

51. Disillusionment

'These', Henry wrote to Anne, 'shall be to advertize you of the great *elengenesse* that I find here since your departing'. '*Elengenesse*' means loneliness, dreariness or misery. Henry had encountered the word, almost certainly, in the continuation of the *Romaunt of the Rose* by a follower of Chaucer:

> She had a . . . scrippe (bag) of faint distresse
> That full was of elengenesse.

Anne, familiar probably with the poem in its original French as well as in the English translation, would have got the reference immediately. For the 'she', whose attributes include *elengenesse*, is the personification Abstinence, who cruelly parts lovers from the object of their desires – just as she and Henry were parted.

As usual, therefore, Henry, the most literary of Kings, had chosen his words carefully: *elengenesse* is a word for lovers, to describe the pangs that only lovers – separated by distance, or necessity, or a false parade of virtue – know.[1]

And the knowledge, it seems, had taken Henry unawares, as he was surprised by the strength of his own feelings. A day or two since Anne had gone seemed longer, he wrote, than 'a whole fortnight' while they were together. His pains were worst in the evening. He wished 'you were in my arms or I in yours'. He fantasized about embracing her. Above all, he longed to kiss her 'pretty duckies [breasts]'.

Only two things, he told Anne, lifted his depression. One was the 'book' he was composing to argue the case for his Divorce. The 'book' was based on the materials produced by his team of theologians. As we have seen, according to Pole, this group had first been assembled by Anne herself; latterly it was almost certainly headed by the bright young theologian, Dr Edward Foxe. That day Henry had 'spent above four hours' in writing and he was delighted to find that the result 'maketh substantially for my matter'.

His other consolation was more material: 'now that I was coming towards you', Henry wrote, 'methinketh my pains half relieved'.[2]

For Henry had decided that, if Anne could not come to London, then he would come to her. Or at least he would come almost half way and meet her in the vicinity of Beddington. This was the country seat of his friend and Anne's cousin, Sir Nicholas Carew. Beddington is near Croydon in Surrey: it is some ten miles from London and about sixteen miles from Anne's parents' house at Hever. There Carew had turned his old family home into 'a fair house (or palace rather) . . . which by advantage of the water is a paradise of pleasure'. Even in November, it was a fitting retreat for the would-be lovers.[3]

*

According to the Spanish ambassador, of course, Henry's departure from London had scarcely been voluntary: instead, he had been driven out by demonstrations in support of Catherine. Perhaps. But it seems more likely that the attraction of Anne was at least as powerful as the repulsion of popular feeling. Moreover, Henry intended to do more than canoodle with Anne: he needed to consult her on the sudden worsening of their position on the Great Matter.[4]

Only five weeks previously Legate Campeggio had arrived in England, bringing, Henry had convinced himself, and had almost convinced Anne, the solution to all their problems. But Henry's hopes had been quickly dashed – to his embarrassment and Anne's irritation. Campeggio, instead of pressing forward with the trial, was trying every device to put it off: from the non-starter (from Henry's point of view) of reconciliation, to the equally unacceptable notion (from Catherine's perspective) of persuading the Queen to withdraw to a nunnery. Still worse, Catherine had struck back by revealing the Spanish Brief, which, if it were genuine, nullified all Henry's gains in Rome and rendered the decretal commission worthless.

Finally, and underlying everything else, were the larger realities of the French collapse in Italy and the triumph there of Catherine's nephew, the Emperor Charles V.

Henry, in short, desperately needed to regain control of events. Already, in such circumstances, he had formed the habit of turning to Anne for inspiration. Now he did so again, and, as usual, she obliged. When he returned to London on 14 November, after four intense days of business and pleasure at Beddington, a further initiative had been decided on. Henry would send a new Embassy to Rome; he would try new approaches; above all, he would employ new men.

The chief of the new Embassy was Sir Francis Bryan, Henry's favourite and, since their mothers were half-sisters, Anne's 'cousin'. The sixteenth century took ties of kindred and marriage much more seriously than we tend to. But, even by those standards, the relationship was not an especially close one. Nevertheless, Bryan had identified himself wholly with Anne. On 25 June, he had been finally reappointed to the Privy Chamber to replace her brother-in-law, William Carey, who had died of the sweat two nights previously. Now he was being sent to Rome as her eyes and ears as well as Henry's.

And he could be relied on to report frankly what he saw and heard. For one of the principal features of Bryan's strange, contradictory character was an addiction to plain speech. He called a spade a spade, and often, as one would expect from 'the Vicar of Hell', a bloody shovel as well. As with other famously plain-speakers, a mixture of motives was involved. Bryan had a genuine commitment to the truth; he also enjoyed making mischief. The mission to Rome would offer him plenty of scope for both.[5]

Assisting Bryan was the expert Latinist and native Italian speaker, Peter Vannes, who served as Latin Secretary to both Wolsey and Henry. Vannes was intended to hold a watching brief for Wolsey, with whom he maintained a separate Latin correspondence. But equally he was a pliable careerist, bending to every prevailing wind. And the likely direction of the wind was indicated by the fact that it was also planned to include in the Embassy Dr William Knight, Wolsey's *bête noire*, after he had co-ordinated approaches to Rome with Henry's ally, Francis I of France.

Clearly, if the rather skewed composition of the Embassy was anything to go by, Henry and Anne were deciding to find their own way to Rome – without Wolsey and perhaps against him.

Bryan and Vannes left at the end of November. After a terrible Channel crossing, during which one of them (they would not specify which) suffered from 'dreadful nausea and vomiting of blood', they arrived in Calais on 6 December. Travel by land then proved almost as problematic as by sea, as the 'shortness of the days and the bad state of the roads' kept them to a snail's pace.

It was not a good beginning, as their defensive letters home showed.[6]

Meanwhile, Henry had lost patience with his enforced separation from Anne. To bring her back to Court would defy public opinion; it also risked alienating Campeggio. But Henry was beyond caring. As for Anne, she was always less sensitive than Henry to outward appearances. She also seems to have calculated that, with the sudden darkening of the political skies, she could do more good at Henry's side than languishing in the country.

So back to Court she came. Wolsey, as usual, was left to sort out the logistics, which he did with his accustomed efficiency. 'As touching a lodging for you, we have gotten one by my lord Cardinal's means', Henry informed Anne in a brisk, business-like letter in English, 'the like whereof could not have been found hereabout for all causes.' Work in preparing the new establishment, he continued, was proceeding rapidly, and her father had been instructed 'to make his provisions with speed'. Soon her accommodation would be ready and they would be together.

As for 'our other affairs', Henry assured Anne, 'there can be no more done; nor more diligence used, nor all manner of dangers better both foreseen and provided for'. All, he vowed, would turn out well, as 'shall be hereafter to both our comfort'.

The endless iteration suggests a doubt in the mind of the writer; there was certainly one in the reader's.[7]

The 'hereabout' in Henry's letter was, almost certainly, Bridewell, Henry's London palace, which he was using as his base to conduct negotiations with the barely mobile Campeggio. There have been several guesses as to the exact building allocated to Anne. They include Durham House in the Strand, Suffolk Place in Borough High Street or even an apartment in Bridewell itself. None seems very plausible. More likely was a site on the South Bank, where Anne's father had his London house. Thence it was only a short boat-ride to Bridewell and Henry's arms.

Wherever it was, Anne was installed by early December. 'The King', the French ambassador reported, 'has lodged her in a very fine lodging, which he has prepared for her close by his own.'

Any pretence about Anne's position was now abandoned: she was close to Henry physically, and she was close also, ceremony soon made clear, to the throne itself. 'Greater court is . . . paid to her every day', the French ambassador continued, 'than has been to the Queen for a long time.' The ambassador, the shrewd and worldly prelate, Jean du Bellay, assumed that Anne's sudden public prominence was a deliberate tactic: 'I see', he informed Montmorency, Francis I's favourite and minister, 'they mean to accustom the people by degrees to endure her, so that when the great blow comes it may not be thought strange'.[8]

Du Bellay had a vested interest in the dethroning of the Spanish Queen Catherine. But even he doubted the efficacy of Anne's move to London. 'The people', he reported, 'remain quite hardened' in their hostility to both the Divorce and Anne as its intended beneficiary. 'And I think', he continued, 'they would do more if they had more power.' But the government was alert to the risk of public disorder, and took elaborate precautions.

Anne scarcely left Henry's side again, with the result that Henry's letters to her, which cast such a powerful if one-sided light on their love affair, cease.

But, of course, Anne's public visibility continued to fluctuate with the exigencies of the Great Matter. The Christmas holidays of 1528–9 were such a moment. The King joined the Queen at Greenwich on 18 December, and Anne moved to Greenwich as well, but had a separate establishment. Perhaps, as du Bellay guessed, the reason was that Catherine's lofty disapproval unsettled Anne. But it seems unlikely that someone who was ordinarily so brazen was intimidated thus easily. A much more likely explanation for Anne keeping a low profile was the presence at Greenwich for much of the festivities of Cardinal Wolsey and Cardinal Campeggio. Henry poured his charm on Campeggio; knighted his son, who had been born in wedlock before he became a priest; and dangled, Du Bellay heard, the vastly rich bishopric of Durham under his nose. Anne would have been out of place while these games were being played.[9]

She would come into her own soon enough.

Within a few days of the ending of the festivities, extraordinary news arrived at the English Court. Secretary Knight, after the usual dreadful winter Channel crossing, had reached Paris at the beginning of January. There he met Vincento Casale at the French Court, en route to Henry with letters from his brother Gregorio in Rome. The letters painted the blackest picture of the Pope's mood: 'he was never more afraid of the Imperialists than now'; he was surrounded by pro-Imperial advisers; 'he daily shows signs of repentance for having granted the [decretal commission], saying that he is undone if the decretal comes to the knowledge of the Emperor'. In short, Knight concluded, Clement was utterly 'untoward . . . in the King's Great Affair'.

Knight, who had been through a similar *renversement* before, wrung his hands at the ill-luck which seemed to dog Henry's efforts: surely, he wrote, there is 'some *cacade* [?cassation or annulment] that inturbeth [confuses] all godly devices'. But, bravely, he acted and advised according to his best judgement. It would, he informed Henry and Wolsey, be folly to continue with his mission to Rome, since its only effect would be to alert the now pro-Imperial Clement to Henry's most secret plans. He would therefore continue on his way with deliberate slowness (to put the French off the scent) and await the countermand which he was sure would come.[10]

Both his reasoning and his recommended course of action were excellent. But, as before, Knight got no thanks for them. And the reason was the same as before: he had, once again, got across Wolsey. What he said might be true. But it was not the truth that Wolsey wanted to hear – nor, still more importantly, that Wolsey wanted Henry to hear.

The Papal Chamberlain, Francisco Campana, who had been sent as an envoy from Clement himself, arrived in London on 11 January 1529, preceded by Casale who had reached the city a day or two earlier. Wolsey now worked furiously to undo Knight's advice. His argument was a model of revisionism – that is, of proving conclusively that black is white and that the best scientific evidence demonstrates the moon to be made of green cheese. So what, Wolsey blustered, if the Pope was frightened of the Emperor? Were not the instructions of the English ambassadors designed to obviate that very fear by offering him an Anglo-French garrison or 'presidy' in Rome? This would enable him to defy Charles V and his Spanish army of occupation. Let the presidy be pressed on the Pope and all would be well.

Moreover Campana, Wolsey informed Knight, had sung an entirely different tune about the Pope's attitude. Far from being Imperial, Campana had assured Henry, Clement was his fast friend. So the Pope would not only do all he could for Henry according to 'law, justice and equity', he would go further and act on his behalf *ex plenitudine potestatis*. The latter, as we have seen, means 'from the fullness of his power'. In one sense it is a mere technical phrase, which was included in all formal Papal acts. But it might mean more. For, in theory, the plenitude of Papal power was absolute. Understood in this sense, therefore, Campana's words were an unequivocal assurance that the Pope would settle the Great Matter in Henry's interest.[11]

Dispute was later to rage about Campana's words and their exact meaning. But there is no doubt that Wolsey persuaded Henry at the time that the second, 'strong' interpretation was the right one. And there is no doubt that this saved the day for Wolsey. Knight was seen off once more and was loftily upbraided by Wolsey for his panic and cowardice.

But equally, as previously in 1527, there is no doubt that Knight's reading of events was right and that Wolsey's was wrong. For, despite all the Papal Chamberlain's smooth, equivocal assurances to Henry, his real mission spelled the end of Henry's hopes of the Pope. Acting in strictest secrecy and on Pope Clement's direct command, Campana ordered Campeggio to continue his policy of delaying the Legantine Trial; he also instructed him to destroy the decretal commission. Campeggio obeyed and the rest of his legacy in England was to be a mere postscript to this action.

Wolsey's performance was magnificently audacious. But, like all high-wire acts, it left him dangerously exposed. Du Bellay, the French ambassador, realized this immediately. 'Monsieur the Legate', he reported on 25 January, 'is in grave difficulty, for the affair has gone so far that, if it do not take effect, the King his master will blame him for it, and terminally.' But, Du Bellay was convinced, Wolsey would make a fight of it. Henry, he predicted, 'would have to deal with a tough nut', and one that even the King would find it hard to crack.

Anne, too, was quick to realize Wolsey's vulnerability, and, in the same despatch Du Bellay described her dramatic move against him at Court. The long-running quarrel between Russell and Cheyney had flared up again. 'Cheyney', Du Bellay reported, 'had given offence to the Legate within the last few days, and, for that reason, had been expelled the Court.' But, instead of trying to pour oil on troubled waters, as she had done before, Anne had gone on the offensive against Wolsey too. 'The young lady', Du Bellay continued, 'has put [Cheyney] in again, whether [Wolsey] would or no, and not without sending him a message couched in disrespectful words'.[12]

Historians, if they have noticed this incident at all, have rather played it down. In fact, it was a watershed. Hitherto, whatever Anne may have thought about Wolsey in private, her public dealings with him had been correct, even warm. Now she had broken with him with deliberate, public ostentation. It can only have been because she had decided that his initiatives in Rome were doomed to failure.

In taking this line, Anne was opposing her judgement to Henry's. For the King, formally at least, was giving his full backing to his minister. Who would be proved right: the mistress or the minister? And where would that leave Henry?

Wolsey, of course, also understood the risks of his game. And, he quickly decided, a reluctant envoy like Knight was worse than useless. So Knight was countermanded and, in his place, it was decided to send the young Turk, Stephen Gardiner. The decision was extraordinarily sudden, so much so that Gardiner had not time even to say farewell to his closest friend in Wolsey's household, Thomas Arundel. Instead, he sent him a touching letter. 'Though I depart from you in body', Gardiner wrote, 'I depart not in mind and soul, which ... shall be ever where you be during my life, wheresoever this body shall fortune to wander.'[13]

It was a rare flash of sentiment in a man who would show none in his public life.

This aggression was one reason for Wolsey's choice of Gardiner; the other was – Wolsey thought – Gardiner's proven loyalty to himself. But

Gardiner showed himself free of sentiment in this area too. Wolsey, he decided, had launched his career, but only Anne could take it to the summit. So, shortly after his arrival in Italy, he wrote to Anne, protesting his 'willing and faithful mind' to do her 'pleasure'. Anne replied promptly, thanking him for his offer and accepting it enthusiastically: 'not doubting, but as much as possible for man's wit to imagine, you will do'. But then she added a note of caution. 'I do trust in God', she wrote, 'that the end of this journey shall be more pleasant to me than your first. For that was but a rejoicing hope, which causing the like of it, doth put me to more pain.' 'Therefore I do trust', she concluded, 'that this hard beginning shall make a better ending'.[14]

It was done tactfully. But equally there is no doubt that, from Anne's point of view, Gardiner was on probation. His last mission to the Pope had failed; this one had better succeed.

Gardiner joined Bryan and Vannes at Rome in early February. They found a Papal Court in turmoil. Clement was dangerously ill and there were even rumours that he was dead. The rumours turned out to be exaggerated. But his convalescence was long and slow. It was also a perfect excuse to put off even seeing the English envoys, much less addressing their business.

But, as they were fobbed off from day to day, they came at the truth by other means: as Knight had reported two months earlier, the political climate in Rome had turned decisively against the English. There was now, they became sure, no chance that Henry would get what he wanted.

The position was clear to them by mid-February. Gardiner wrote to Henry in guarded terms; Bryan in much blunter ones. For some reason, these particular letters were delayed and did not reach Wolsey till 19 March. Early the following morning Wolsey sent Brian Tuke, the Master of the Posts, to Greenwich to deliver the letters in person and report on Henry's reactions.

As it happened, the moment was ill-chosen. Henry had sprained his foot the day before and it was 11 o'clock before it was dressed and he had breakfasted. Tuke was ushered in as soon as he had finished and presented the letters. Their contents were not calculated to improve the King's mood. Gardiner's letter to Henry, Tuke reported, was written 'with as much or more desperation, than that was to your Grace'. Still worse was Bryan's letter, which was 'totally of desperation'. The King shared only the odd paragraph with Tuke, but these gave the flavour of the whole. Bryan 'could not believe that the Pope would do anything for his Grace', adding the characteristic Bryan-ism that: 'It might well be in his Pater Noster (Our Father), but it was nothing in his Creed'. Worst of all for Wolsey, Tuke spotted that there was another letter enclosed with the one to Henry. It was 'directed I wot [know] not to whom, but I suppose to Mistress Anne'.[15]

The minister's monopoly of information was broken and the ambassadors had opened up separate channels of communication – not only to the King but to the King's mistress.

Henry gathered up his miserable morning's mail and kept it for consideration. It was now Palm Sunday Eve and the beginning of Holy Week. The King and Cardinal spent Easter separately, Henry at Greenwich and Wolsey at Richmond. And they did not meet till the following Saturday, 3 April, when Wolsey visited the Court with his colleague Campeggio.

During their audience, Henry and Campeggio had a conversation about the most recent sensation: the circulation of a Lutheran pamphlet at Court during Holy Week itself. Henry teased Campeggio by repeating the pamphlet's arguments for the confiscation of Church property and Campeggio did his best to reply. Finally the King called a halt to their argument and assured him that he 'always would remain a good Christian'.[16]

It is impossible to be sure of what was going on. But it looks like a struggle for the King's mind. Anne, for it must be she, had despaired of a solution at Rome and was pressing for more extreme measures, including probably those outlined in the Lutheran pamphlet. Wolsey, on the other hand, was doggedly sticking to his existing policy. Let Henry's ambassadors only push hard once more and Clement would – must – concede what he wanted.

Wolsey, for the moment, won.

His victory was embodied in the separate letters which Henry and Wolsey sent to the English ambassadors in Rome on 6 April. Both had the same message: the ambassadors were not to despair but to act! But the tone of the letters was different. Wolsey's had the icy calm of barely suppressed hysteria. Nothing, he insisted, must stand in their way and they must press the Great Matter on the Pope *etiam in ipso articulo mortis* – 'even in his very death throes'. Henry's, however, breathed the confidence of superior and particular knowledge. No credence, the King stated flatly, was to be given to 'common report'. Such were mere vulgar rumours, like the stories about Campeggio's Imperialism. Here Henry went out on a limb. 'We find and certainly know Campeggio to be of a far other sort in his love and inclination towards us than was spoken, not having such affection towards the Emperor, as in him was suspected.' Then he became confidential, tipping his ambassadors the wink. 'And to be plain with you,' he continued, 'if ever he had been of other mind, we have said somewhat to him as might soon change that intention.' Had Henry applied the stick of a threatened schism from Rome? Or the carrot of the promise of the bishopric of Durham? Or both? In any case, his confidence in his kingly cunning was supreme. He was riding high, and, as it turned out, for a fall.[17]

The letters were given to the courier Alexander, who made excellent time, arriving in Rome only a fortnight later on 21 April.

As it happened, Bryan had settled down to write another personal report to Henry that day. 'Sir', he had begun, 'your Grace hath sent me hither to the intent I should instruct you, from time to time, of all your affairs here, as I could know, see or hear.' For those who knew Bryan, as Henry did, it was an ominous beginning.

And it got worse.

They had seen the Pope several times, Bryan told Henry, and they had reported the entirely negative results in their joint letters to Wolsey, 'whereby ye [Henry] may perceive that plainly [the Pope] will do nothing for your Grace'. 'There is no man living', Bryan added, 'more sorrier to write this news to you, than I am. But if I should not write this,

I should not do my duty. I would to God my former letters might have been lies, but I feared ever this end.'

As Bryan was concluding the despatch, the courier arrived with the letters from England. Bryan broke off to read them and added a postscript:

> The courier Alexander arrived here bringing certain letters from your Grace and my lord Cardinal, wherein your Grace and my said Lord marvelled that we should write so extremely that the Pope would do nothing for your Grace ... seeing as then we had not spoken with him. Sir, we wrote as we saw and know by substantial and credible men. And now your Grace may perceive by [the Pope's] answer the sequel of the same.

It was as near as even Bryan dared to get to saying 'I told you so' to Henry.

But there was someone else, Bryan knew, who would have no such inhibitions. 'Sir', he had written in the body of the letter, 'I write a letter to my cousin Anne. But I dare not write to her the truth of this because I do not know whether your Grace will be contented that she should know so shortly or no.' Instead, Bryan threw the responsibility of breaking the news on Henry himself: 'I have', he added innocently, 'said to her in my letter that I am sure your Grace will make her privy to all the news'.[18]

How willingly Henry undertook the task and how Anne responded we can only guess.

Bryan despatched the courier Thaddeus with his letters that same afternoon. Thaddeus also made good time and presented Bryan's letters at Court on 6 May. Still Wolsey tried to put his own gloss on things, telling Campeggio that the English 'ambassadors did not despair of obtaining something from the Pope'. This was, of course, a flat lie. On the other hand, Henry, fresh perhaps from a bruising conversation with Anne, recognized that the game was up. On Sunday

9 May he informed Campeggio that he was sending Thaddeus to Italy
with letters recalling Bryan and Gardiner from Rome. The courier left
on the 13th, bearing letters from Wolsey which announced a complete
change of policy.[19]

In view of 'this ingratitude in the Pope's holiness', Wolsey informed
the English ambassadors, Henry had decided to abandon the attempt to
get cast-iron guarantees from Rome. Instead, 'taking as much as may be
had and attained here to the benefit of his cause', he would proceed 'in
the decision of the same here, by virtue of the Commission already
granted unto me and my lord Legate Campeggio'. Gardiner and Bryan
were to return in post to England, since Gardiner's expertise, in
particular, was wanted in the forthcoming trial.

This option, to go it alone in England, had been open to Henry as
long ago as December 1527, when Knight had obtained the first
Commission. In the subsequent eighteen months, Henry, advised solely
by Wolsey, had laboured mightily at Rome. He had squandered money
and diplomatic credit. And he had nothing to show for it. Indeed, his
position was actually worse. Had he decided to go ahead in early 1528 on
the basis of Knight's Commission, he would have had a favourable
military and diplomatic wind behind him. By 1529, however, Catherine's
nephew, Charles V was master of Italy. The Pope was about to proclaim
himself Imperial, and, Henry's ambassadors informed him from Spain,
was on the point of revoking the case to Rome.

All this, the King could bitterly reflect, was the reward for listening
to his minister rather than his mistress.

But Henry and Wolsey had not yet plumbed the depths. On
5 May, Bryan wrote to Henry to inform him of their final audience
with the Pope. The meeting had been an acrimonious one and high
words had been uttered on both sides. One of the issues had been
Campeggio's supposed promises to Henry. The English had thrown
his assurances at the Pope. The Pope had countered with Campeggio's
own letters, in which 'he hath written . . . that he, neither Francisco
Campana, never promised nothing to your Grace particularly but in
general words'.

Bryan, of course, was fully aware of the effect of his revelations. 'If my writing', he told Henry, 'sound anything against the Cardinal ... [or] other, who feels himself grieved, let him kick; for I do it not of no malice, but according to my duty, to inform your Grace.'[20]

But, whatever Bryan's motives, the effect was the same. Henry had been revealed as gullible – to his own servant Bryan, and, still worse, to Anne, whose fears about Campeggio's being Imperial he had so loftily dismissed the previous autumn.

Events were now running hard against Wolsey. On 14 May the Wolsey loyalist, Sir John Russell, had been countermanded as ambassador to France at the last moment. His horses had already been embarked at Sandwich and he himself was on the point of boarding when the new orders arrived. In Russell's place, Henry sent Charles Brandon, Duke of Suffolk. Brandon was even closer to him than Bryan and the consequences were to be even more electric.[21]

The day before, Du Bellay, freshly back from France, whence he had ridden with most unclerical speed and bravado, had had an audience with Wolsey in which he invited him to the forthcoming peace conference at Cambrai between Francis I's mother, Louise of Savoy, and Charles V's aunt, the Archduchess Margaret. Wolsey, recognizing immediately the risk to England of a merely bi-lateral agreement between France and Spain, was desperate to attend. But Henry, whom Du Bellay saw twenty-four hours later on the 14th, refused to give him permission to go. Du Bellay, as he explained to Montmorency, could not write Henry's reasons 'at present, having no cipher'. But, almost certainly, Henry felt that he needed Wolsey at home, to handle the Divorce. Indeed, his minister's willingness to rush off abroad at such a moment must have seemed like desertion, even betrayal. Such, at any rate, was Du Bellay's retrospective reading of events. 'What has most served to put him in discredit with the King', he wrote later to Montmorency, 'was that, at my coming, he declared too openly his wish to go to Cambrai.'[22]

It is true that Wolsey's attitude to the peace conference did not help. But Wolsey's ruin was from a different quarter. On the night of 17 May the courier Alexander reached Windsor with Bryan's letters from Rome. The following morning Wolsey, who had been peremptorily summoned to Court by Henry, commanded Campana and Campeggio's Secretary to Windsor. They arrived at sunset and found Wolsey at table. He had been with Henry all day and was exhausted. So they were put off till 9 the following morning. They turned up at the appointed hour and greeted Wolsey as he emerged from his chamber. Wolsey, normally so voluble, said nothing but took the visitors to the King, introduced them and then left it to Henry to interrogate them.

'Do you not remember', the King asked Campana, 'that the first time you spoke to me you told me that his Holiness would do for me all he could *etiam de plenitudine potestatis?*' Campana said he recalled the occasion perfectly but denied 'the form of words specified'. Wolsey tried to refresh his memory. But Campana stuck to his guns. Then the letters from Rome were thrust under his nose and they 'wished to read the very words which the ambassadors had read in [Campeggio's] letter'.

Henry blustered furiously. But, as the envoys took leave, he besought their help. 'Be good friends to me', he begged, 'and have pity on me.'[23]

It was to this that Wolsey's advice had brought him.

Also on the night of the 17th, Suffolk, who, Du Bellay heard, had been substituted for Russell as a result of Anne's direct intervention, had his final audience with Henry VIII before leaving for France. His 'secret charge' was to pump Francis I on Wolsey's reliability on the Divorce. In his reply Francis damned Wolsey with faint praise and subtle innuendo. Wolsey wanted the Divorce, 'for he loveth not the Queen'. But Henry should 'not put too much trust in no man, whereby he may be deceived'. Instead, he should 'look substantially upon his matters himself'. And, above all, he should remember that Wolsey 'had a marvellous intelligence with the Pope, and in Rome, and also with the Cardinal Campeggio'. Which, Francis added mischievously, made it all the stranger that neither Clement nor Campeggio were doing what Henry wanted.[24]

From this moment, probably, Wolsey was finished. Or he would be, if Anne had her way.

52. Wolsey's fall

B ut Anne could not destroy Wolsey just yet – if, indeed, Henry
would let her destroy him at all.

First, the Legatine Trial at Blackfriars had to be gone through.
Then, after the abrupt adjournment on 23 July, the proceedings had to be
brought to a seemly conclusion. This was easier said than done, and it
took two months to find a formula that satisfied both Catherine's quest for
certainty and Henry's determination to preserve his kingly dignity.

While this dragged on, Wolsey enjoyed the twilight of power. He received
and wrote letters. He kept the machinery of government ticking over. And
he proffered advice, which was received more or less graciously. But the
real foundation of his authority – Henry's favour – had gone.

The minister had last seen his King on 14–16 August 1529 at
Tyttenhanger, when Henry's terms for agreeing to the winding up of the
Legatine Court dominated the conversation. Thereafter, though he
pressed his hospitality on the King and was often only a few miles distant,
he was forbidden the Court. The fact soon became notorious, and fed, as
it was intended to, rumours of his impending fall. The Cardinal, the new
Imperial ambassador reported on 21 September, 'was under sentence of
exile from the Court, and ordered to reside three miles away from it, and
not to appear unless summoned'. Probably there was nothing so formal
as a 'sentence of exile'. But the consequences were the same and when on
about 10 September Wolsey had begged a personal audience as he had
something to say that was better in speech than on paper, he was sharply
told not to trouble the King with false mysteries and to write the matter
briefly and under clear heads.

This stylistic requirement, apparently innocent in itself, was possibly
the cruellest blow of all. Once, Wolsey's orotund and prolix style, for
which he was notorious, had charmed the King; now, he was told, it
merely bored him.[1]

Meanwhile at Court, that magic citadel into which Wolsey would never again freely enter, a new government was forming. Its work-horse was to be Stephen Gardiner, Wolsey's former Secretary, who had expiated his past by the fervour with which he worshipped Anne's rising sun. As soon as the Blackfriars Trial was over, he was appointed royal Secretary in place of the more-or-less permanently absentee Knight. And on 28 July, as he proudly wrote to his friend Peter Vannes, he went off to Court at Greenwich to take up his appointment.[2]

Wolsey's initial expectation, clearly, was that the new Secretary would, like his predecessors, act primarily as intermediary between himself and the King as equipollent powers. Henry had other ideas: this time his Secretary would be his alone. So on 28 July, when he assigned Gardiner his lodgings at Court and his fees, he gave him special orders not to absent himself. He then drove home his command with a tag taken from the parable of the wise and foolish virgins. Be vigilant, he warned him, for 'you know neither the day or the hour'.[3]

Gardiner, of course, had no intention of proving a foolish virgin and he resisted all Wolsey's blandishments to lure him into visiting him. He 'would gladly come to Wolsey', he informed him in one letter, 'but dares not'. 'I should have come myself', he wrote in another, 'but the King's Highness specially commanded me to tarry.'[4]

Slowly and unwillingly, the truth dawned on Wolsey: he was being boycotted by the King's new ministers on the King's own orders.

Gardiner, as Du Bellay recognized, had the talent to turn, in time, into another Wolsey. But in 1529 he was barely out of his apprenticeship. The real locus of power is shown, instead, in the first item of business Gardiner transacted for Henry. This was to act as intermediary in the negotiations about the future of the wealthy and powerful prince-bishopric of Durham.

Durham had been vacant since Wolsey had formally exchanged it on 8 February 1529 for the even more valuable see of Winchester. The vacancy presented a double opportunity for the Crown. While the see remained empty, its 'temporalities' (as its landed income was known) reverted to the King. The sums involved were vast: Durham's gross receipts totalled £3,200, while about £2,400 was actually paid net into the bishop's coffers. When, on the other hand, in the fullness of time the bishopric was filled, it would be a plum piece of patronage, to be bestowed carefully and in expectation of some commensurate gain for the government. In the circumstances of 1529, this meant only one thing: Durham would be used to further the Great Matter.[5]

The King first, as we have already seen, dangled it as bait in front of Campeggio. But Campeggio, despite his Bolognese bourgeois values, managed to resist. Henry then swung, as he increasingly would, from one extreme to another. Campeggio burned his English boats when he adjourned the Legantine Trial on 23 July. A few days later, Henry gave the temporalities to Thomas Boleyn, now Lord Rochford.

The gesture was perfectly calculated, both practically and sym-bolically. At a stroke, it gave Anne Boleyn's father, who, as Lord Rochford, was still only a junior member of the peerage, the magnate income and status that was necessary for him both as the King's future father-in-law and (if both Anne and her father had their way) as his new first minister as well. It also supplied him with a suitably grand London residence in the form of Durham House. This had been Catherine's home during the first years of her widowhood after Arthur's death; more recently, it had served as Wolsey's temporary London house during the rebuilding of York Place. Henceforward, it would be the headquarters of Boleyn power in the capital.[6]

But the symbolic effect was at least as important. Back at Easter, Henry had teased Campeggio about confiscating the goods of the Church. Now he showed that he was in earnest. And the first victim, appropriately enough, was Wolsey.

The details were set out in Gardiner's letter to his former master of (probably) Sunday, 1 August. Wolsey had already been informed of the King's decision about Durham. Once (as with the choice of an Abbess for Wilton) he would have fought tooth and nail. But the fight had gone out of Wolsey and he fell over himself to be co-operative. He had always, he told Henry, regarded the last half-year's rental income for Durham as due to the King, not to himself. So far, he continued, he had received nothing. But, he informed Thomas Boleyn separately, he would now write to his former officials in Durham ordering them to hand over direct the rents payable on Lady Day (22 March) 1529.[7]

This eagerness to please gave Thomas Boleyn pause. He thanked Wolsey for his offer but declined it through Gardiner. 'He does not wish it to be known', Gardiner explained, 'that he had laboured for that half year's rent.' Instead, 'he would be content to receive it from Wolsey, without making business with his officers for the receipt'. At first sight, this looks like a piece of scrupulosity on Thomas Boleyn's part. He already had an ugly reputation for greed and was, it appears, unwilling to add to it. But Gardiner glossed the proposal very differently and made clear that it was in fact an ultimatum. Thomas Boleyn was not prepared to wait for the rents to trickle in and be shipped from the north. Instead, he wanted cash. Now. Or at least tomorrow – when, Gardiner advised Wolsey, 'he had better make some arrangement' for payment. Thomas Boleyn had also calculated the amount to the last hundred pounds. 'Rochford', Gardiner reported, 'reckons it at MCC [£1200].' This, as we have seen, is exactly half of the expected net receipts of the bishopric. Anne's father can have arrived at the figure only by checking the records.

Alongside Lord Rochford, the other key members of the new Council were the two Dukes, Norfolk and Suffolk. They, perhaps, belonged more to the dignified than the efficient part of the administration. But their rank gave them an automatic weight. Norfolk also drew strength from his role as Anne's uncle and his assiduity at business. Suffolk, in contrast, though idle, was even closer to Henry. But his relations with Anne were awkward. And his wife, Mary, the King's sister, frankly hated her. Caught between his friendship with Henry and his increasing enmity with Anne, Suffolk acts as a litmus test of power during these months.[8]

The new political world that emerged in the summer of 1529 also had a new observer. This was Eustace Chapuys, who replaced Inigo de Mendoza as the Imperial ambassador to Henry VIII.

The contrast could scarcely have been greater. Mendoza was a Spanish bishop, fervent in his Catholicism and equally fierce in his national pride. Chapuys, in contrast, was that altogether cooler figure, a Savoyard lawyer. Savoy was one of the debatable lands of Europe: linguistically, it was suspended between French and Italian; while politically it was disputed between the kingdom of France to the west and the Italian territories of Charles V to the east. Polyglot and polyvalent in his identities, Chapuys was the perfect servant for the multi-national, multi-lingual empire of Charles V, who himself (it was said) spoke French to his councillors and his wife, Spanish to his God, and German to his dogs. Faced with this choice, Chapuys sensibly opted to write his despatches to the Emperor in French. He also preferred to speak in French 'being the language most in use' to Henry 'which the King understands and speaks best'.[9]

In terms of his personal history, therefore, Chapuys seems the very embodiment of the Renaissance revolution in diplomacy which has been described by historians such as Garrett Mattingly. He was also equipped with conciliatory instructions and was warned by Catherine herself that too open zeal on her behalf could only make her predicament worse.

Nevertheless, once settled in England, Chapuys threw Catherine's advice to the winds. Soon, his heart was ruling his head, and he became the Queen's partisan as whole-heartedly and intemperately as Mendoza had been. And he was correspondingly savage about Anne Boleyn. No word was too coarse for her; no motive too low; no action too immoral. She was *la putaine* (the whore); a vengeful harpy, who harried her opponents from the Court; a murderess, in thought if not in deed, who would not stop at poison to rid herself of her rival Catherine; and, above all, a heretic, who was at once the bitterest and the most dangerous enemy of the Faith in England.

But if Chapuys hated Anne, he was also fascinated by her. He reported her every word and action and collected every tit-bit and scrap of gossip about her. Mostly it was scurrilous. But occasionally, despite his better judgement, he found himself impressed by her courage and strength of will. And he had the honesty to report this too. The result is paradoxical: the despatches of one of her greatest opponents provide the most vivid picture of Anne's character and her role in events. The picture, too, is surprisingly nuanced. There is light and shade. There is even humour. And, above all, there is colour.

So Chapuys's portrait is plausible. It is even seductive. But is it to be believed?

Understandably, Chapuys's open, violent prejudice against Anne has led some historians to dismiss his evidence almost in its entirety. This, however, is a mistake. There is in principle no reason why a person's enemies should be less likely to tell the truth about him than his friends. The former exhibit one set of prejudices; the latter another. And both kinds of testimony should be handled accordingly. There is also a more particular point. For Chapuys, despite his evident bias, was careful about his sources. He usually gives the names of his informants and, on inspection, they turn out to be an impressive bunch. They include leading councillors and courtiers, as well as intimate hangers-on about the great, such as doctors and priests. All were in a position to see and hear the incidents they reported, and frequently they corroborate each other. Where this happens, Chapuys is to be believed. Elsewhere, in view of his demonstrable reliability, I have given him the benefit of the doubt. And, on the occasions where I have not, I try to indicate my reasons.

Chapuys arrived in England in late August. It was the dog-days of summer, when normal politics slept during the Progress. But the times were not normal; instead, there was the sea-change as Wolsey's ministry tottered to its fall. Chapuys grasped the position immediately. In his first despatch, written on 1 September, he reported on the visible signs of Wolsey's decline: not only was Wolsey forbidden the Court; foreign ambassadors were now forbidden to visit him. Chapuys had also glimpsed the sort of regime that was replacing him. But, before going into details, he wanted to check his facts: 'the people who have thus sworn the Cardinal's ruin', he informed the Emperor, 'I shall name in my next despatch, when I have obtained more credible information on the point'.[10]

It took Chapuys a day or two to complete his investigations and, on the 4th, he wrote up the results. 'The Dukes of Suffolk and Norfolk and Lord Rochford, the father of the Lady Anne Boleyn, are the King's most favoured courtiers and the nearest to his person', he reported. They also 'transact all state business'. But Chapuys then distinguishes between this 'transaction of business' and real power. This, Chapuys had discovered, lay elsewhere:

> If the Lady Anne chooses [he informed Charles] the Cardinal will be dismissed, and his affair settled; for she happens to be the person in all this kingdom who hates him most and has spoken and acted the most openly against him.

Chapuys had not yet met Anne. But already he had arrived at a judgement. 'The King's affection for La Boleyn', he continued, 'increases daily. It is so great now that it can hardly be greater; such is the intimacy and familiarity in which they live at present.'[11]

Ten days later he secured his first audience with the King at Grafton in Northamptonshire. He found a Court where Queen Catherine enjoyed only the shadow of a consort's place while the substance belonged to Anne. Even diplomatic business waited on Anne's whim. Chapuys had outlined his instructions to Henry before 'dinner' (about 11 a. m.) and was expecting a reply when the King had finished eating. But he found himself denied an answer as Henry had a more pressing appointment, the nature of which he scarcely bothered to disguise. 'The King', Chapuys reported, 'was in a great hurry to repair to the meeting place of the morning, where the Lady [Anne] was ready to open the chase'.[12]

This is the Anne of Wyatt's poem, at once the hart and the hound, the hunted and the huntress:

> *Noli me tangere*, for Caesar's I am
> And hard for to hold, though I seem tame.

And Anne had her own quarry, too: Wolsey.[13]

The hunting season, and with it the Progress, normally ended at Crouchmas, that is, the Day of the Elevation of the Holy Cross. This falls on 14 September. Coincidentally (or perhaps not), Chapuys's first audience with Henry had been on this day. And its significance was quickly brought home to him by the King's eagerness to conclude their conversation. 'He was', as Chapuys explained in a separate despatch to the Archduchess Margaret, 'in a hurry to go to dinner, in order to repair afterwards to the hunting field and take leave of the chase, as he is in the habit of doing at this time of year.' The fact, as Chapuys discovered later, that Anne herself was mistress of the hunt only lent a further edge to Henry's impatience.[14]

But despite the cavalier treatment of the new Imperial ambassador, neither the Progress nor the hunt were to end at Crouchmas. Instead, both were prolonged for almost a fortnight after their usual time. And it was not till 29 September that Henry reached Windsor, which was to be his autumn residence that year.[15]

There were probably straightforward reasons for the extension of the holiday season. It was Henry and Anne's first uninterrupted summer together and naturally they revelled in the experience. Anne also had her own reasons for not wanting the summer to stop. She was an expert sportswoman and could show off to advantage her intrepidity in the chase, in contrast with Catherine's much staider enjoyment. Finally, the sport in Northamptonshire must have been unusually good that season.

But there were also deeper motives at work. The King's extended absence from the vicinity of the capital made it easier to prolong Wolsey's political purdah. And when that purdah ended, and Wolsey was allowed to visit the Court, the restricted accommodation offered by a house such as Grafton would also make it easier to manage the meeting. For Wolsey might be down but, as Anne and her friends were well aware, he was not yet out. And a meeting between Henry and his not-yet-quite-fallen minister could not be postponed much longer.

By the beginning of September, the negotiations about the winding-up of the Legatine Trial had reached a reasonably satisfactory conclusion and on the 11th Cardinals Wolsey and Campeggio formally renounced their powers. The latter was now eager to be off from a country where he had outstayed his welcome. He was granted an audience at Grafton on 19 September; he was also given permission to bring Wolsey with him.

Cavendish, who accompanied his master, gives a set-piece description of the scene. Bets were laid that Henry would not speak to Wolsey. And the odds must have shortened considerably when it became clear that no Chamber had been allocated to him in the little palace. Instead, and highlighting the King's ambiguous role, Henry Norris, the Groom of the Stool and the royal *alter ego*, offered Cardinal Wolsey his own room in which to change from his riding clothes.

The two Legates, Cardinals Wolsey and Campeggio, were then summoned to the Presence Chamber, where the Council stood in a row in order of rank. Wolsey doffed his cap to each, and each similarly uncovered himself to Wolsey. The rest of the Chamber was crowded with courtiers. They were there for one thing: to see how Henry would greet his former favourite. Would it be with smiles? Or frowns?

They did not have to wait long. Henry entered and stood under the Cloth of Estate. Wolsey eased down his great bulk and knelt to him. Henry first gave him his hand and then 'took my Lord up by both arms'. All bets were off. The Cardinal seemed safe.

The King and his minister then stood in earnest conversation, which Cavendish was able to overhear in part. 'I heard the King say, "How can that be? Is not this your own hand?" and plucked out from his bosom a letter.' Wolsey's answer apparently satisfied the King and they went off to dine separately: Wolsey with his fellow councillors and Henry with Anne. Neither had an easy time.

For Anne was 'much offended with the King' that he seemed to be letting Wolsey off so lightly. Cavendish was not of course there. But he got a report of the conversation from 'them that waited upon the King at dinner'. Anne launched furious accusations, which Henry batted away. Wolsey had brought the King into debt with his own subjects by the forced loan, she said; he had dishonoured and slandered him; if any nobleman had done half so much, he would have lost his head. 'I perceive', Henry observed coolly, 'ye are not the Cardinal's friend.'

After dinner, Henry saw Wolsey again: first in the Presence Chamber and then in the Privy Chamber, where they were closeted alone till nightfall. And Wolsey was told to return early the following morning.

The situation now seemed black for Wolsey's enemies. The minister had had only a few hours with the King but already he appeared to have recovered his former influence. What would be their fate if he was restored to power? Doubtless, the betting was running on that too.

It was time to invoke Anne.

The two Cardinals spent the night in a nearby house at Easton Neston. Early the following morning, according to the King's command, Wolsey returned to the Court. But there were to be no more private conversations. Instead Henry was booted and spurred. He ordered Wolsey to meet with the Council, took his farewell and rode off to the chase. Anne had done her work well.

Cavendish is clear about what had happened. 'The King's sudden departing in the morning', he asserts, 'was by the special labour of Mrs Anne, who rode with him to lead him about because he should not return until the Cardinals were gone.' Just to make sure, she had arranged a picnic dinner at the site of a new park which they were to inspect. The park, Cavendish concludes, 'is called at this day Hartwell Park'.[16]

Anne had got her kill.

It is a brilliant narrative: the detail is circumstantial and the psychology plausible. But, alas, the story is flawed. The only question is by how much.

For another of Wolsey's Chamber servants, Thomas Alvard, also accompanied him to Grafton and described his reception in a letter written only three days after the event. As far as the Sunday is concerned, Alvard's account agrees closely with Cavendish's. But for the Monday he tells a very different tale. According to Alvard, Wolsey *did* see Henry again in the morning. The two had another long private conversation in the Privy Chamber; then they sat together with the Council. In the afternoon, Wolsey escorted Campeggio to the King and they took their leave 'in as good fashion and manner . . . as ever I saw before'.[17]

Only then did the King go hunting. And there is no mention of whether it was with Anne.

Does this mean we must discard the whole of Cavendish's story? Anne's best academic biographer thinks so. My guess rather is that Cavendish, who rarely makes fundamental mistakes about events to which he was an eye-witness, simply telescoped things. At thirty years' distance, he remembered only the King's hasty departure for the field. Alvard's account fixes this to the early afternoon; Cavendish placed it instead for dramatic effect first thing in the morning. But, whenever it happened, the *effect* on Wolsey was the same: a conversation begun was unfinished; a deal half-brokered remained unclinched.[18]

Just the same thing, after all, had happened to Chapuys a few days previously, when Henry's post-prandial departure for the hunt, also instigated by Anne, had broken off his business with the King. The ambassador was sanguine: he would soon have another audience at which he could pick up the threads.

Wolsey, on the other hand, would have no second chance.

After Grafton, Henry VIII and Cardinal Wolsey went their separate ways: Henry moved by slow stages to Windsor; while Wolsey rode first to his nearby house at The More and thence to London for the start of the legal term on 9 October. On that day, with magnificent courage or supreme blindness or some mixture of the two, he processed as usual to Westminster Hall. There he sat in judgement as Chancellor. But he could not preside over Star Chamber because 'all the lords and other the King's council were gone to Windsor to the King'. A shift in the centre of political gravity had occurred – from Wolsey's entourage to the Court and from Wolsey himself to Anne.

That same day in King's Bench the Attorney General, Christopher Hales, launched the legal proceedings that would complete Wolsey's fall.

On 17 October, when the Great Seal was finally prised from Wolsey's grasp, Du Bellay reflected on the former minister's fate. He was 'the greatest example of fortune that one could see'. But 'the worst of his evil is that Mlle de Boleyn has made her friend promise that he will never give him a hearing, for she thinks he could not help having pity on him'.

This, of course, is an ambassador's gossip. But Wolsey himself took the same view of his plight in a letter written a few days later. The letter is damaged. But the drift is clear enough. 'If the displeasure of my Lady Anne be somewhat assuaged', Wolsey wrote, 'as I pray God the same may be, then it should be devised that by some convenient mean she be further laboured.' 'For this', he continued, 'is the only help and remedy. All possible means must be used for attaining of her favour.'[19]

And all means were used. Her favourite, her brother George, was bribed with the offer of great pensions from Wolsey's ecclesiastical preferments. And eventually Wolsey screwed up courage to write directly to Anne. To no avail. 'She gave kind words', Wolsey was informed, 'but will not promise to speak to the King for you'.[20]

He was naked to his enemies. And she, it seemed clear, was the worst of them.

Meanwhile, the ascent of the Boleyns continued and on 8 December 1529, in one of the first royal ceremonies to be held in Wolsey's confiscated palace of York Place, Anne's father Thomas Boleyn, Lord Rochford, was created Earl of Wiltshire in the English peerage and Earl of Ormond in the Irish. The following day there was a celebratory banquet. The greatest ladies of England were present, including the King's sister Mary, the Queen Dowager of France and Duchess of Suffolk, and the two Duchesses of Norfolk, the Dowager and the wife of the present Duke. But Anne took precedence of them all. She was 'made', Chapuys noted with outrage, 'to sit by the King's side, occupying the very place allotted to a crowned Queen'. 'After dinner', he continued, 'there was dancing and carousing, so that it seemed as if nothing were wanting but the priest to give away the nuptial ring and pronounce the blessing.'[21]

Thomas Boleyn now had both wealth and status. It remained only to give him appropriate great office. This was done, once more, at the expense of a churchman. Cuthbert Tunstall, the distinguished humanist and friend of More and Erasmus, was Bishop of London and Lord Privy Seal. In the New Year, he was promoted to the still-vacant bishopric of Durham. But at a price. He was required to resign the Privy Seal, the third ranking office in the kingdom, so that it could be conferred on Boleyn. He also had to confirm the transfer of Durham House to Boleyn and agree to make it permanent. Finally, he had to wait till 25 March, when the half-year rents were due, for a grant of the temporalities of his see. By this transparent device, Boleyn had managed to get his hands on another £1,200.[22]

It is a story of pillage that anticipates the vast secularization of the 1530s. In this, as in so much else, the Boleyns were pioneers.

Thomas Boleyn had attained the summit of ambition for a subject. Neither Anne nor her family could go any further till that 'nuptial ring', which Chapuys had seemed to see proffered to her at the December banquet, were hers indeed.

But, for that, new measures and new men were needed. Anne set about to provide them.

53. Injurious remedies

Back in November 1528, when the English negotiations in Rome were about to enter their last, desperate phase, Wolsey had instructed Henry's ambassador to remind the Pope of the terrible consequences that would follow if the Divorce failed. Pope Clement VII was to be told that Henry VIII would be driven 'to adopt those remedies which are injurious to the Pope, and are frequently instilled into the King's mind'. 'I cannot bear up against the storm,' Wolsey had continued. The Devil himself was at work. And 'the sparks of that opposition here, which have been extinguished with such care and vigilance, will blaze forth to the utmost danger of all'.[1]

Wolsey, even more obscure and orotund in Latin than in English, had failed to name names. But his words were all too easy to gloss. The 'injurious remedies' or 'the spark of opposition' were the Lutheran heresy. And the person 'frequently instilling [them] into the King's mind' was the individual best placed to do so: Anne Boleyn.

Anne Boleyn's religious preferences, like most other aspects of her character, seem to have been formed by her years in France. France, in common with the rest of western Europe, was undergoing religious ferment in these first decades of the sixteenth century. There were three key figures: the scholar and humanist, Jacques Lefevre d'Étaples; Guillaume Briçonnet, Bishop of Meaux; and Marguerite of Angoulême, Francis I's beloved sister.

Lefevre was the creative spark. Like Luther, he became convinced that true Christianity could reach the people only if they could read and hear the Word of God in their own language. Accordingly, in 1523 he published a translation of the *New Testament* into French. Like Luther again, he attached particular importance to the *Epistles* of St Paul, from which he also derived the doctrine that faith, not works, saves mankind. Unlike Luther, however, he trusted to reform from within, and never formally broke with the Catholic Church. Briçonnet, for his part, put Lefevre's theory into practice in his own diocese of Meaux, while Marguerite supplied the high-level political patronage that was needed to protect the reformers against the highly conservative Faculty of Theology in Paris, known as the Sorbonne, and its allies in the powerful and quasi-independent law court, the *parlement* of Paris.

But the main events in all this had happened late in Anne's stay in France or after her departure. It was only in 1518 that Briçonnet invited Lefevre to Meaux and only in 1521 (the year of Anne's return to England) that the bishop began to correspond with Marguerite. Nevertheless, Anne seems to have got a real sense of what was underway. And certainly she kept up with developments, from England, and came to regard Marguerite, whom she had met, as a role model.[2]

The evidence comes from the early stages of her relationship with Henry. In January 1530 Louis de Brun, a French teacher resident in England, gave her a French treatise on letter writing as a New Year's gift. Addressing her as Madame de Rochford (the title she had acquired, rather irregularly, by her father's elevation to his earldoms the previous month), De Brun commended her reading habits.

> One never finds you [he noted] without some French book in your hand ... such as Translations of the Holy Scriptures ... And principally, last Lent and the one before last ... I always saw you reading the salutary Epistles of St Paul that contain the complete teaching and rule of good living according to the best moral principles.

Paul's *Epistles* were, as we have seen, the prime source for Lefevre's religious revolution. And, no doubt, Anne paid particular attention to the passages the great Frenchman highlighted. 'Therefore being justified by faith', Anne would have read in the *Epistle* to the Romans, 'we have peace with God through our Lord Jesus Christ.' But this faith, she would also have learned, was not dead or passive but a living, breathing thing: a 'faith', according to the *Epistle* to the Galatians, 'which worketh by love' and which, according to the *Epistle* to the Corinthians, revealed itself by 'charity'. Indeed, it was empty without it:

> Though I have all faith, so that I could remove mountains, and have not charity, I am nothing.
> ...
> And now abideth faith, hope and charity, these three; but the greatest of these is charity.

Now there is nothing accidental about this. Anne's Scriptural readings were noticed and were, of course, intended to be noticed. And she continued this practice of conspicuous piety throughout the days of her prosperity, reading improving works herself and encouraging her ladies to read them as well.[3]

There is every reason to think that these activities of Anne's were sincere. But she was also following the example set by Marguerite in France. And she had another role-model nearer home in England. For Anne's rival Queen Catherine was also notably devout. But Catherine's piety was very different. It was Catholic, orthodox and Spanish. Anne set herself up as a sort of equal and opposite force to Catherine, in this as so much else. In place of Catherine's unbending conformity she embraced Reform. She was not Protestant of course (even the word had yet to be invented). But her passionate attachment to the Scriptures shows her to have been an evangelical. And if Catherine's piety was Spanish, with Spanish devotional practices, Spanish books and a Spanish confessor, Anne's was proudly and consistently French.

'She was', her former Chaplain, William Latymer, recalled many years later, 'very expert in the French tongue, exercising herself continually in the reading of the French Bible and other French books of like effect and conceived great pleasure in the same.' 'Wherefore', he continued, she 'charged her chaplains to be furnished with all kinds of French books that reverently treated of the whole Scriptures.'

Latymer can hardly have seen De Brun's treatise, but his testimony is an almost word-for-word echo of the earlier tribute.

But of course the books that Latymer and De Brun had seen Anne reading were not only in French, they came from France. 'I remember', the daughter of William Lock, King Henry's silk merchant, recalled in her memoirs, 'that I have heard my father say that when he was a young merchant and used to go beyond sea ... Anne Boleyn ... caused him to get her the Gospels and Epistles written in parchment in French together with the Psalms.'

Some of these books, or their first cousins, survive. One is Anne's splendidly illuminated *Psalter*. It is decorated with Anne's arms, badges and mottoes, and gives the text of the *Psalms* in a new, radical French translation probably by Lefevre's disciple, Louis de Berquin, who was burned for heresy in 1529. Another is Anne's French Bible, in Lefevre's own translation. This is printed rather than written, but it still has its original binding, gold-tooled with Henry's and Anne's cipher, 'HA', and evangelical mottoes.[4]

This trade in foreign religious books was illegal. Lock, no doubt, was able to use his status as a royal merchant to conceal books among his bundles of precious silks. Even more impudent was Anne's brother George. He went on five diplomatic missions to France and seems to have used his diplomatic bag to smuggle back increasingly controversial works that were banned in France as well as England. They were small, cheaply produced volumes, and were designed for concealment, not display. But, taking advantage of the immunity conferred by status and family connexion, George had two turned into magnificent presentation manuscripts for his sister.

The original works on which the manuscripts were based were again by Lefevre. The first was his *Epistres et Evangiles des cinquante et deux sepmaines de l'an* (*The Epistles and Gospels for the Fifty-two Weeks of the Year*). This gives the Biblical reading for each day of the liturgical calendar, followed by a commentary. The second was also a Biblical text and commentary – the text in this case being the Old Testament *Book of Ecclesiastes* or The Preacher with its refrain of 'Vanity, vanity, all is vanity!' In both books, the texts and readings were in French, while the commentaries emphasize, in clear and vivid language, the need for a living Faith in Christ as opposed to the moribund practices of the orthodox Church. Finally, the books were the product of the same printer/publisher, Simon du Bois, who had fled from an increasingly hostile Paris and found refuge with Marguerite in Alençon, the capital of her husband's duchy.

When George Boleyn had Du Bois's modest volumes turned into magnificent manuscripts, he left the Scriptural texts in their original French, but he gave the commentaries in English, in his own translations. George also prefaced *The Epistles and Gospels for the Fifty-two Weeks of the Year* with a dedicatory letter to Anne, in which, as 'her most loving and friendly brother, [he] sendeth [her] greeting', and invoked as well 'the perpetual bond of blood' between them.[5]

And it was blood that was to be spilled, at least in part, because of their joint commitment to religious reform.

But it is time to return to De Brun's treatise and its date. 'Last Lent' was Lent 1529 (10 February–13 March), while 'the one before last', when De Brun had first seen Anne reading the Pauline *Epistles*, was Lent 1528 (26 February–4 April).

It was in January 1527 that Anne and Henry had exchanged their pledges of love. Now, a mere thirteen months later, Anne was advertising her piety conspicuously, and in ways which were heterodox at least.

And soon she moved from advertisement to action.

It was probably in the autumn of 1528 that Anne added a postscript to a letter to Wolsey. 'My lord,' she wrote, 'I beseech your Grace with all my heart to remember the Parson of Honey Lane for my sake shortly'.

The request seems innocence itself; in fact, as Anne well knew, it was acutely provocative. For the 'Parson of Honey Lane' was up to his eyes in a programme to import religious books that were more radical and more dangerous than anything Anne's agents handled: they were in Latin or English, not French, and their author was not the carefully moderate Lefevre, but the firebrand, Martin Luther himself, or some or other of his disciples.[6]

Thomas Forman was a Fellow of Queens' College, Cambridge, where Erasmus had studied. He took his Doctorate in Divinity in 1524, and in 1525 was given the rectory of Allhallows, Honey Lane in the City of London. The same year, he was also elected president of his college. He had fallen foul of Wolsey because of the activities of his curate, Thomas Gerard or Garrett.[7]

Garrett is a figure straight from R. H. Tawney's *Religion and the Rise of Capitalism*: he was part missionary and part entrepreneur. And it was in this double role that he arrived in Oxford on Christmas Eve 1527 as a sort of travelling salesman for radical reform. There he won souls for God, and also turned in a nice profit by selling his converts the key works of the New Learning. His catalogues, neatly arranged and marked up with the prices, included Luther's *De captivitate babylonica* (The Babylonian Captivity [of the Papacy]), William Tyndale's *New Testament* in English, and the key source book, *Unio dissidentium*. The *Unio* is an anthology of extracts from the Church Fathers, which covers the main topics of Reformation controversy, including Faith and works, the Eucharist, the veneration of saints, and the Antichrist.

Garrett had brought a full selection of such books with him in his luggage; he also seems to have replenished supplies by getting 'two fardells [parcels]' shipped from London to Oxford that were 'very heavy', as the servant who bore them to the carriers testified. To Wolsey's genuine distress, Garrett had particular success with the students of Wolsey's own great new foundation of Cardinal College – like bright young men everywhere, they were eager for the latest thing.

A two-pronged investigation was launched in both Oxford and London. In Oxford, Garrett was first arrested; then escaped in disguise after picking the lock of his prison; only to be recaptured, interrogated and forced to recant. In London, Forman, an altogether weightier figure, was also picked up. Interrogated by Cuthbert Tunstall, Bishop of London, he denied sending suspect books to Oxford, but freely admitted having several in his own possession. When Tunstall asked him why, he replied smoothly that it was 'to the intent that he might see what opinions were among the Lutherans and be the more ready to impugn them, for the defence of the Church'. Tunstall was unconvinced and advised Wolsey to take sureties of Forman for good behaviour. 'I think he might find a great sum to be forthcoming', he observed meaningfully.[8]

It was presumably at this stage, while Wolsey was pondering Forman's fate, that Anne intervened on his behalf.

Her intervention came at a crucial moment. Hitherto, England had been the vanguard of the resistance to Luther. Henry himself had written his *Assertio septem sacramentorum* against the heresiarch and had been rewarded with the title of *Fidei Defensor* by the grateful Pope Leo X in 1521.

And Wolsey had not been far behind. According to Henry himself he had 'moved and led' him to write the *Assertio* and therefore deserved to be the 'partner of all honour and glory he had obtained by that act'. More particularly, while the King strutted on the European stage, the Cardinal-minister concerned himself with enforcement in England. Correctly, the Church had identified imported heretical books as the prime source of 'infection' (as the inquisitors themselves called it) and Wolsey, as Legate, set himself to stamp them out. He presided, in the full panoply of his legatine rank, over the first public burning of heretical books in St Paul's churchyard on 12 May 1521. And another book-burning, in the same location, took place a few months after the first publication of Tyndale's *New Testament* in 1525.

Wolsey was equally active against individual dissenters and, at the opening of the first trial of the proto-martyr, Thomas Bilney, he made a formal declaration of his legatine jurisdiction over heresy. Tunstall, as Bishop of London, objected to this encroachment on his power as diocesan. But the matter was quickly smoothed over and the two co-operated effectively in matters such as the Garrett/Forman investigation.[9]

Of course, the persecutions were not as successful as the orthodox would have wished. For every book that was burned another dozen seemed to get past the searchers at the ports. And though some recanted, many evangelicals quietly and quickly reverted to their real beliefs.

Nevertheless, Wolsey could take a measure of pride in what had been achieved. Under his leadership, the English Church had, as he reminded Pope Clement VII, shown 'care and vigilance'. And if the 'sparks' of Lutheranism were not as fully 'extinguished' as he claimed, they had been thoroughly damped down.

But would they remain so? Or, as he warned Clement, would they 'blaze forth to the utmost danger of all'? And why, in the early winter of 1528, did Wolsey show such sudden alarm?

The answer, almost certainly, was Anne's intervention on behalf of Forman. Anne had an irritating and unbusinesslike habit of not dating her letters. Nevertheless her intervention must have taken place in the autumn of 1528, between her father's letter to Wolsey of 20 August (to which the body of Anne's letter was a sequel) and Forman's death (whether as a result of his harassment is not known) in about October 1528. A month later, Wolsey was unburdening himself of his fears to Clement.[10]

Wolsey was right to be alarmed. It was political support that had turned Lollardy under Richard II from mere academic deviance into a major, if temporary, force. And it could have the same effect on Lutheranism.

Anne had dared to reveal her hand, as a patroness of dissent. Whether it proved to hold trumps would depend, as both Wolsey and Anne well knew, on Henry.

It would also depend on the direction taken by the opponents of the Church. Hitherto, led by Luther abroad and Tyndale in exile, they had mounted a frontal challenge to the central dogmas of Catholic belief, including the nature of the sacraments and the nature of grace. At Easter 1529 there was an apparent change of strategy. It was reported, in anxious terms, by Campeggio in a letter to Clement VII's confidant Sanga:

> During these Holy Days certain Lutheran books, in English, of an evil sort, have been circulated in the King's Court. . . . I understand that by this book the Lutherans promise to abrogate all the heresies affecting the articles of the Faith and believe according to the Divine law, providing that this King . . . will undertake to reduce the ecclesiastical state to the condition of the primitive Church, taking from it all its temporalities.

'I told the King', Campeggio continued, 'that this was the Devil dressed in angels' clothing.' Henry (as we have already briefly seen) teased Campeggio, now blowing hot, now cold about the 'Lutheran' scheme.[11]

It is impossible to identify the 'book' for certain. But it seems very likely that it was Simon Fish's *A Supplication for the Beggars*. Fish was unusual among religious controversialists, in that he was a layman and married, rather than a priest. And, in the *Supplication*, he wrote an equally unusual and effective piece of propaganda.

Little is known of Fish's life. According to Foxe, who is our chief informant, he was a lawyer and member of Gray's Inn. While he was in the Inn, he had taken the key part in a satirical play directed against Wolsey; he was also a leading figure in the Garrett/Forman ring and traded in illicit books, especially the Tyndale *New Testament*, on a substantial scale. Naturally London soon became too hot for him and he fled to join Tyndale in the Low Countries. And there he composed his masterpiece.[12]

The first peculiarity of the *Supplication*, and the one from which all its other distinctive features sprang, was that it was written by a layman for laymen. This meant that, amid the welter of theological point and counterpoint that passed for Reformation argument, it struck a refreshing note of simplicity and brevity. It was only 5,000 words long and took up only fourteen small pages. It could be read at a sitting and was easy to conceal. It was also cheap enough to scatter free, as seems to have been done on a subsequent occasion. The language was straightforward too, addressing laymen's issues in laymen's words. Finally, and what lifted it quite out of the ordinary, it had a Big Idea, that caught the contemporary imagination and set the agenda for supporters and opponents alike.

A 'supplication' is a petition: in this case from the Beggars of England to the King. The Beggars complain that they are starving because Churchmen beg so much more effectively than they do. Churchmen have begged away the substance of England, stealing land from the King and the Lords, and wives from every husband, and daughters from every parent. They are corrupt, deceitful and parasitical. Only once they are justly deprived of their ill-gotten gains will England recover prosperity and religion its purity.[13]

This was music to the ears of a powerful strand of opinion that was instinctively anticlerical. Anticlericals (who were opposed to the power and wealth of the Church, rather than to its beliefs) were to be found among the lawyers and burgesses (or leading townsmen) who made up a significant part of Parliament. Some gentry families were also affected by anticlerical beliefs, as were a handful of the nobility. But what they lacked in numbers, anticlericals made up for in influence – especially if the King could be brought in on their side.

And it was to that end that Fish bent his propagandist's genius. For the *Supplication*'s address to the King was much more than a nominal device. Instead, Fish with a virtuoso's skill played on Henry's prejudices. Henry liked his policy papers short. The *Supplication* was a masterpiece of brevity. It also pandered to Henry's vanity, to his theological learning and to his fondness for playing the role of Solomon as king and judge. Fish similarly probed and irritated tender spots in Henry's memory, such as the humiliation inflicted on him by the tax-payers' strikes of 1525 and 1527, which had hamstrung his grandiose schemes for European military intervention. Both strikes still rankled and both were now attributed to widespread impoverishment as a result of clerical exactions. Fish even knew the right names to mention as exemplars of clerical excesses – including Wolsey's former 'audiencer and commissary', Dr Alen, whose name so stank in Henry's nostrils in 1527 that Secretary Knight begged Wolsey, absent on his ill-fated mission to France, on no account to use him as his messenger to Court.

But Fish's masterstroke was, according to Foxe, to send his pamphlet to Anne.

Anne, 'who lay then at a place not far from the Court', began to read it. Her brother George, always on the look-out for religious novelty, noticed the new pamphlet and read it too. He immediately recognized its potential and 'willed her earnestly' to show it to Henry, 'which thing she did'. Henry, as George foresaw, was impressed. He questioned Anne about the authorship of the anonymous pamphlet, summoned Fish's wife and recalled Fish himself from exile. He even had a personal interview with him.[14]

Some historians have questioned Foxe's story. But, it seems to me, for no good reason. Foxe's source was Fish's own wife, who played a significant role in events. Even more importantly, Foxe's critics have ignored the Forman incident. Fish, as we have seen, was part of the same ring of illicit book-dealers as Forman and Garrett. In the close-knit world of London proto-Protestantism, he would certainly have known of

Anne's intervention on behalf of Forman; conversely, Anne herself would have been aware of Fish's identity, commitment and energy. Each therefore was prepared to play the part Foxe allots them. He is to be believed.

But the most important testimony is that of the bitterest enemy of Fish, Anne and George Boleyn and everything they stood for: Thomas More.

Cuthbert Tunstall, the Bishop of London, was in the front-line of the fight against heresy. He was also one of the most intelligent and widely read of the bishops. So he quickly grasped that persecution alone was not enough; there must also be persuasion. And it must be persuasion in *English*, since that was the language that the heretics and their friends were using so effectively. But who was to produce the counterblast?

The greatest English theologian and controversialist was John Fisher, Bishop of Rochester. Fisher had joined battle against Luther early, writing three important Latin books, as well as delivering two set-piece sermons, in 1521 and 1526, that were printed in both Latin and English. These works have been described as a 'massive contribution' to the defence of orthodoxy. And so they were – up to a point.[15]

For Fisher was, inescapably, a cleric. And he wrote and thought like a cleric, even in English and even in his works that were intended primarily for a lay audience, such as his sermons. These are peppered with Latin quotations, admittedly translated. And their whole structure of argument depends on analogy, similitude and authority. They are a world away from Fish. For Fish, like Charles Dickens's Mr Gradgrind, had no interest in tropes and poetry and other such fine stuff. Instead, what Fish wanted and what he gave were facts and anecdotes – or whatever tendentious assertion he could pass off as fact, and whatever tall story he could dress up as true.

It is a style with which we are familiar and which strikes us (unlike Fisher's) as being somehow modern. This is because Fish and his like were journalists, though the word had yet to be invented.

All this was, in today's fashionable phrase, a paradigm shift, and adapting to it was beyond Fisher. But More was a better bet. For he was a Londoner, a layman and a lawyer. He came, in other words, from the same milieu as the most effective reformers. If knowing your enemies was the issue, More did. He could think like them and write like them. He too could be a journalist.

In March 1528, therefore, at the height of the campaign against Garrett and Forman, Tunstall decided to commission More to mount a counter-attack. The heretics, Tunstall explained in his florid Latin commission to More, were 'translating into our mother tongue some of the vilest of their booklets and printing them in great numbers'. By these means they were 'striving with all their might to stain and infect this country'. If good men did nothing, they would succeed.

Therefore heresy must be answered with orthodoxy and lies with truth. And it must be done in English, in print and in works intended for the man in the street (*simplicibus et ideotis hominibus*).

Here More came in. For he was able, Tunstall proclaimed, to 'play the Demosthenes in our native tongue just as well as in Latin'. He was also a doughty fighter, 'wont in every fight to be a most keen champion of Catholic truth'. Finally, he was following in the distinguished footsteps of another layman – those 'of our most illustrious Lord King Henry VIII, who stood forth to defend the Sacraments of the Church against Luther'.

But perhaps the most important point remained unspoken. Not only was More following in Henry's footsteps, he was also personally close to the King, who had consulted him in the preparation of the *Assertio* and had used him to polish and arrange the finished work. If anybody could persuade Henry's subjects, More could; with luck, he might even persuade the King himself.

Accordingly, Tunstall licensed More to possess and read heretical books, blessed him and sent him forth into battle 'to aid the Church of God by your championship'.[16]

Thus equipped, More produced a stream of controversial works in English. The second was a reply to Fish. It was called *A Supplication of Souls* and it was written in the summer months of 1529. How More found the time is a mystery, since he spent the whole of July and much of

380 The Queens of Henry VIII

August as a delegate (along with Tunstall) at the international peace
conference at Cambrai. Nevertheless, he somehow managed to turn out
a work that was more than ten times as long as Fish's – if probably less
than half as effective.

Why did More think it necessary to use so large a hammer to crack
so small a nut? The answer lies in More's analysis of Fish's strategy. So
far, More says towards the end of the first book of his *Supplication of Souls*,
the heretics had gone 'forth plainly against the Faith and Holy
Sacraments of Christ's Church'. But this frontal attack had rebounded.
Instead, they had decided to 'assay the Second Way': they would avoid
open impiety and 'make one book specially against the Church and see
how that would prove'. And Fish's was the book.

We have heard all this before, of course, as Campeggio had said as
much (and in much smaller compass) in his letter to Sanga in early April.
It is unlikely that Campeggio had come up with the idea himself. He
understood English only imperfectly and had not, he admitted, seen the
offending work. Instead, it is much more probable that Campeggio had
spoken to More, and had taken his analysis straight from him.

This realization is important: it means that More had understood
immediately Fish's line of attack. He had also realized that it was deadly
in its efficacy. The 'Second Way' worked.

And, above all, More feared, it would work on Henry. So he saved his
bitterest words for Fish's attempts to enlist Henry's sympathy. 'Rolling
his rhetoric from figure to figure', More sneered, '[Fish] falleth to a
vehement invocation to the King'. But nothing, he protested, could be
less plausible than his subsequent arguments. Fish misunderstood
English history, with his appeal to the reign of King John. He misunderstood parliamentary procedure (said More, who had been Speaker
of the Lower House and was about to preside over the Upper). Above all,
he misunderstood the King. For Henry, More insisted, had already
decided. He had written the *Assertio*. He was Defender of the Faith. He
would never be Enemy of the Church.[17]

They were bold words. But, even as they were written, they were
only half true.

*

The *Supplication of Souls* was published in the late summer of 1529, as the work of Sir Thomas More, knight, Chancellor of the Duchy of Lancaster. But, within a few weeks, Wolsey fell and More exchanged the Chancellorship of the Duchy for the Chancellorship of England. It was Wolsey's old office and More seemed marked out as the great minister's immediate successor. He delivered, as was then customary, the speech at the opening of the 1529 parliament and he used it to launch a savage attack on his predecessor as the 'great wether', who, diseased and deceitful, had led the flock astray.[18]

The reality of course was more complex. According to Chapuys, the Imperial ambassador, More got the office of Chancellor only as a compromise, after Norfolk vetoed Suffolk's appointment to such a powerful position. Indeed, it has been claimed, it was Suffolk who was in the driving seat in these months, with a parliamentary programme that drew directly on Fish's anticlerical masterpiece.[19]

The evidence comes from a paper prepared by Thomas, Lord Darcy. Darcy, a leading councillor to Henry VII, had commanded the English army sent to assist Ferdinand, Catherine's father, in Guienne in 1512. Subsequently, he became an ardent partisan of Catherine's cause in the matter of the Divorce. And in 1537 he was executed for his treasonable complicity in the great Catholic rising known as the Pilgrimage of Grace.[20]

His is not a biography that would seem to typecast its subject as a radical anticlerical. But that is how Darcy has been presented on the basis of an item in the 'Memorandum [on] Parliament Matters', which he drew up on 1 July 1529. 'Item', the eleventh of Darcy's eighteen points began, 'that it be tried whether the putting down of all the abbeys be lawful and good or no, for great things hang thereupon'. The words seem straightforward. In fact, they are ambiguous. What is their tense? Do they deal with the past or the future: with the abbeys that *have been* 'put down' by Wolsey to fund his colleges at Oxford and Ipswich; or with those that *would be* put down by the King on parliamentary authority? And what is the intentionality of the writer? Is Darcy *against* such 'putting down of all the abbeys'? Or is he *for* it?[21]

The current interpretation favoured by scholars plumps in both cases for the second of these alternatives: Darcy is assumed to be raising the legality of a future general dissolution. And he is presumed to be as heartily in favour of it as the notorious Simon Fish himself.

This double assertion, for it is no more, has been little debated. This is extraordinary. For, if it were correct, the whole history of the Divorce and Reformation would surely have been different. Instead of a long, slow process that dragged itself out over almost a decade, there would have been a Big Bang. For Darcy was an out and proud religious conservative, who looked back to a golden age of universal pious observance, when 'the Lents, Embers, vigils and other days accustomed of Commandments and Councils of Holy Church, [were] justly observed and kept, and the offenders, if any, were duly punished'. If such a man was signed up to the dissolution, why did it not happen in the first session of the 'Reformation' Parliament of 1529? And why did not Parliament, as Catherine feared it would, move immediately to authorize Henry's divorce and remarriage?[22]

Why, in short, did Henry and Anne have to wait so long? And why did Anne have to fight so hard? And why did More, Tunstall, Fisher and the rest even bother to go through the motions of fighting a battle that was – it would seem – already lost?

The answer of course is that Darcy has been comprehensively misunderstood. He was not looking forward (in both sense of the words) to a parliamentary dissolution. Instead he was looking back to Wolsey's 'putting down' of several monasteries – and he was looking back in anger. What Wolsey had done, Darcy insisted, was an 'abomination'. Wolsey's actions, and the 'seditious and erroneous violations used at the pulling down of the abbeys by his commissioners... may be weighed to the worst act or article of Martin Luther's, as will be proved if good trials and examinations be had thereof'. He should be punished accordingly.[23]

That and no other was the meaning of Darcy's eleventh article.

It contained no comfort, of course, for Wolsey. But equally it contained little either for Henry or for Anne. For Darcy was as traditional in his politics as in his religion. He objected to Wolsey for trespassing in the temporal sphere (as well as trampling on the rights of his fellow clergy). But he would react with equal horror to any intrusion by the temporal power on the rightful authority and liberties of the Church. And such an intrusion was what was needed if the deadlock over the Divorce were to be broken. Darcy would never countenance it.

Nor, it turned out, would his fellow members of Parliament – at least for the time being. Following the clear lead of More's opening speech (as well as the detailed suggestions of Darcy's 'Memorandum'), the parliamentary session that began on 4 November 1529 clipped some of the more luxurious growths of clerical power that had flourished under Wolsey.

Probate, that is the authorization of wills, was then a matter for the Church. Wolsey had introduced a steeply rising scale of fees for the granting of probate, so that large estates paid much more heavily than small. Nowadays this would be called social justice; then a Parliament of property-owners denounced it as an outrageous exaction and proposed a cap on the amount payable. There were also complaints in the Lower House that abbots were trading as tanners and wool-merchants, like laymen.[24]

This sort of thing was inconvenient to the Church. But it hardly merited Bishop Fisher's angry intervention in the Lords when he accused the Commons of acting 'for lack of Faith'. Norfolk replied sensibly that the greatest clerks were not always the wisest men. And Henry brokered an awkward compromise in which Fisher ungraciously explained away his words without retracting them.[25]

The compromise pleased neither the Commons nor the Lords Spiritual. But, when the session ended on 17 December, just in time for the Christmas festivities, the great edifice of the English Church still stood intact. Parliament had indeed limited a few clerical 'abuses'. But they all related to the Church's claims on lay property. And lay property, it was agreed by all but a few ultramontanist clerics such as Fisher, belonged absolutely to the temporal sphere. As such, it was subject to Common Law, which was properly made and unmade in Parliament. For all the skirmishes and alarms, both sides had finally respected these distinctions.

The result was a triumph for Darcy's programme (his real programme, that is) of restoring the proper relationship between the spirituality and temporality. This had been damaged by Wolsey's overweening and encroaching power. Now Parliament had restored the balance. But of course it had done nothing about Henry's marriage. For that belonged as firmly to the spiritual sphere as lay property did to the temporal.

Indeed, the Divorce had not even been mentioned – to Catherine's surprised relief and, no doubt, to Anne's corresponding irritation.

Other remedies, more or less injurious, would have to be tried.

54. Cranmer

A nne was not the only person searching for new ideas. In the wake of the collapse of Wolsey's whole strategy in the Great Matter, every member of the King's party was on the look-out for the key idea that would unlock the Divorce. And the nearer they were to the centre of affairs, the greater was the pressure to come up with something new.

Two of those who had benefited most from the Great Matter were the Cambridge friends, Stephen Gardiner and Edward Foxe. Gardiner was now royal Secretary, while Foxe – always more of a backroom figure than his ebullient friend – was the leading member of the King's Spiritual Council. On 2 August 1529, very shortly after the adjournment of the Blackfriars Court, Henry and Anne left Greenwich on the first stage of the summer Progress. Gardiner and Foxe formed part of the inner ring of courtiers and councillors who accompanied them. The first scheduled stop was Waltham Abbey.[1]

The Abbey was able to accommodate only the immediate royal party, and Gardiner and Foxe were lodged instead in the neighbouring township now known as Waltham Cross. The harbingers (the royal officials responsible for billeting courtiers) placed them in the house of a certain Mr Cressy. As they settled in, they recognized a familiar face from Cambridge. For Dr Thomas Cranmer of Jesus College was tutor to two of Cressy's sons and had taken refuge in his house, together with his pupils, when the plague had struck in the university.[2]

Cranmer belonged to a senior generation. He was born in 1489 and had gone up to Cambridge in 1503. But, in comparison with the brilliant Gardiner, he was a late developer. He only took his BA in 1511–12 and did not complete his doctorate of divinity until 1526, a full four years after the much younger Gardiner had secured his own double doctorate in canon and civil law.[3]

But what Cranmer lacked in brilliance, he made up for in steadiness: he was thorough, organized and a superb note-taker. In contrast with the instinctively partisan Gardiner, he was also blessed (and sometimes cursed) with an ability to see both sides of the question. This, combined with his essential fair-mindedness, meant that his opinions were in a state of slow but constant change. The individual steps were scarcely ever revolutionary. But his lifetime's journey – from orthodoxy to advanced reform – was. Finally, and unlike most of his contemporaries, he had acquired a style of written English which was clear, simple and, at its frequent best, of surpassing beauty.

Gardiner and Cranmer were, in short, the hare and the tortoise: radically different in temperament and abilities and destined to be rivals and eventually deadly opponents in Church and State. Even after five centuries, it is unclear who won.

But in 1529 they found themselves on the same side – that of Anne and the King.

At supper in Cressy's house, probably on the night of Gardiner's and Foxe's arrival, the three fell into conversation. All of them being Cambridge men, they talked about the university. Then the topic shifted to the burning issue of the day: the King's Great Matter. Cranmer's contribution was a characteristic mixture of diffidence and boldness. First, he excused himself by saying that, unlike his two acquaintances, he had made no particular study of the question. Nevertheless, he continued, he was sure that both they and, by implication, the King were pursuing the wrong strategy. 'I do think', he said, 'you go not the next way to work, as to bring the matter to a perfect conclusion and end, specially for the satisfaction of the troubled conscience of the King's Highness.'

This was because they were treating the case *legally*, by 'observing the common process and frustratory delays of these your courts'. At best, this approach would be slow; at worst, it would resolve nothing. But, Cranmer insisted, there was an alternative and superior strategy. For the issue, properly considered, was not legal but *moral*. And the moral laws, unlike canon law, were certain. 'There is', he asserted flatly, 'but one truth in it'. And this unique truth was visible, not to lawyers like Gardiner, but to theologians like himself. 'No man ought or better can discuss it than the divines', he claimed. It would be easy to canvass their opinion, 'with little industry and charge'. And, once done, Henry would have what he most craved: certainty. He would also be conscientiously entitled to settle matters on the basis of the theological ruling, whatever the state of the legal process and whatever the Pope might say or do.[4]

The view that truth, especially on moral questions, is one and indivisible, and that it is perceived as such by all men of goodwill, is a common one. It seems to be impervious to experience and invincible to argument and is still widely held even today. But it is especially characteristic of ages of faith and revolution – like the early sixteenth century. It also appeals particularly to academics with little experience of the outside world – like Cranmer.

Cranmer was on the threshold of this larger experience. When he stepped over it, the consequences would be huge – for himself, for Catherine, for Henry and, above all, for Anne.

Cranmer's recommended course of action was also a professional slight on Gardiner and his discipline of law. Was this the result of innocence?

Or was it a deliberate dig at a showy and, so far, much more successful colleague? As often with Cranmer, it is impossible to be sure.

But Gardiner's hurt feelings or envy, if there were such, had to be set aside. Cranmer, his naïve and donnish acquaintance, might have stumbled on the way forward for the Great Matter. At any rate, his idea was worth floating before the King. Gardiner and Foxe made haste to do so.

Choosing their moment, they recounted their conversation at Waltham to Henry and Henry, intrigued, decided to summon Cranmer to an interview.

Here an element of doubt enters. According to both versions of the story, Cranmer had his audience at Greenwich. But the Court did not return there for fully twelve weeks, until 24 October. By that time much water had flowed under the bridge. Wolsey had fallen and on the 25th, also at Greenwich, Henry gave his successor, Sir Thomas More, the Great Seal.[5]

Some historians feel that this gap before the interview is too long. In fact, it seems to me to make sense, since, in the interim, Henry's mind had been on other things. First there was the winding up of the Legatine Court. Then there was the engineering of Wolsey's fall. Finally there was the debate over his successor and the preparations for the forth-coming Parliament. Only in late October did the King have the leisure either to meet Cranmer or to respond to his audacious suggestion.

But, whenever the encounter took place, the meeting of minds was instantaneous. Cranmer was telling Henry what he wanted to hear. He was also repeating what, if we believe Reginald Pole, Anne had been telling Henry since 1527. 'That man hath the sow by the right ear, Henry is supposed to have said appreciatively about Cranmer.[6]

Cranmer's Cambridge days were over. On the spot, Henry 'retained him to write his mind in that his cause of divorcement'. Then, according to John Foxe's more coloured version of the story, the King summoned Thomas Boleyn, Anne's father. 'I pray you, my lord', he said, 'let Dr Cranmer have entertainment in your house at Durham Place for a time, to the intent he may be there quiet to accomplish my request, and let him lack neither books nor anything requisite for his study.'[7]

Cranmer's connexion with the Boleyns had begun.

This too was a meeting of minds – and interests. Thomas Boleyn, like his two bright children, Anne and George, was interested in the new religious ideas. This was enough for Chapuys to brand the whole family as 'Lutheran'. Cranmer was tending in the same direction, for reasons that were both personal and philosophical. He had interrupted his Cambridge career for what looks like a shot-gun marriage with the barmaid of the Dolphin Inn. The marriage ended quickly because of her early death. But Cranmer's interest in the opposite sex remained very much alive. During the lively conversation at Waltham, he had also argued that Papal power must yield to Scriptural truth. This too was a characteristically Lutheran position – as was the attitude he assumed, practically if not yet theoretically, to clerical marriage.

But of course it was the *political* implications of Cranmer's ideas which mattered and which made him so attractive to the Boleyns. For marriage and the extent of Papal power were the hot issues of the day. And Cranmer, it seemed, had something new to say on them. Or at least he said it better than anyone else. Soon he became Thomas Boleyn's chief theoretician and strategist on the Divorce. At the same time, and drawing largely on Cranmer's ideas, Lord Privy Seal Wiltshire, as Thomas Boleyn now was, turned himself into the minister for the Great Matter.

There was a sort of inevitability about this. Thomas Boleyn, as Anne's father, had the most obvious personal interest of all Henry's new councillors in bringing about the Divorce. He was also prepared to countenance measures that were, it soon became clear, too extreme for anyone else to stomach. And since the Divorce was the principal item of royal policy, the councillor in charge of it became, *ipso facto*, principal minister.

Historians have been slow to recognize Thomas Boleyn's position – as indeed were contemporaries. Instead, it was the showier power of the two Dukes, Norfolk and Suffolk, who attracted comment and adulation.

Understandably piqued, Thomas Boleyn decided to teach the French ambassador, Du Bellay, the new realities of power. The casus belli was an apparently trivial item of diplomatic business. Du Bellay thought that the matter had already been settled by Norfolk and Suffolk. Boleyn quickly showed him his mistake. 'He let everybody have their say', the aggrieved ambassador reported, 'then argued the opposite and defended it to the hilt.' His intention, Du Bellay added, was to display his displeasure that 'one had failed to worship the Young Lady [Anne]'. It was also to confirm the truth of what Boleyn had told him previously. 'That is to say that none of the other [councillors] have any credit at all [with Henry] unless it pleased the Young Lady to lend them some.'

Did Thomas Boleyn protest too much? I do not think so. Nor did Du Bellay. Thomas Boleyn's claim about the power wielded by his daughter, Anne, was, the ambassador concluded, 'as true as the Gospel'.[8]

All this meant, as far as Cranmer was concerned, that he reported not only to Thomas Boleyn but also to Anne, as the power behind her father and, evidently, the power behind the throne as well.

With this backing, Cranmer's rise as head of the Durham Place think-tank was rapid. Already, probably by November 1529, he formed one of a select group of four royal advisers who were nominated to try to persuade Thomas More, the newly appointed Chancellor, out of his unfortunate reluctance to support the Divorce. More lists the group as consisting of Cranmer; the Almoner, Edward Lee; Foxe; and Niccolo de Burgo ('the Italian friar'). And he describes them as 'such of his Grace's learned counsel, as most for his part had laboured and most have found in the matter'. Cranmer was indeed in exalted company and had come far, fast.[9]

But his main activity that autumn was to follow up Henry's instructions at his first audience and prepare a 'book' on the King's case for a Divorce. Foxe describes the result as follows: it contained, 'besides the authorities of Scriptures, of general councils and of ancient writers, also his own opinion, which was this: That the [Pope] had no such authority, as whereby he might dispense with the word of God and the Scripture'. The 'book' itself cannot now be securely identified and it is even unclear whether it survives. What is certain, however, is that it was sent to Cambridge. There it was circulated among the theology faculty with a view to softening up opinion on the Divorce. It was clearly effective – at least in persuading the already converted.[10]

It is, however, important to put Cranmer's contribution in context. There was, of course, nothing new about Henry consulting learned opinion. Such consultations had formed part of the King's armoury from the very beginning of the Great Matter. Moreover, in the dying days of his ministry, Wolsey had been eager for a canvass of French opinion and had tried on at least two occasions to persuade ambassador Du Bellay, who was sympathetic to Henry's position, to undertake it on the King's behalf. But what is characteristic of these schemes is their vagueness. 'Wolsey and the King', Du Bellay reported baldly, 'appeared to desire very much that I should go over to France to get the opinions of learned men there on the Divorce.'[11]

It was the same at the beginning of October when Henry decided to send his own envoys to France instead. Chapuys, it is true, reports that Catherine 'is very much afraid' that one of the envoys, Dr John Stokesley, the Dean of the Chapel Royal, was 'sent now to France for no other purpose than that of inducing the University of Paris to write in behalf of the King'. But Catherine, understandably, often anticipated movements against her long before they happened. So it was in this case. For the envoys' instructions replicate the vagueness of Wolsey's would-be commission to Du Bellay. Since Du Bellay had advised Henry that many French scholars were of 'semblable opinion and sentence', the King commanded Stokesley to consult with Du Bellay's brother, Guillaume, the seigneur de Langey, about whom he should approach. Then, 'having conference with such learned men ... he shall extend his wit and learning to conduce them, and attain their opinions and sentences conformable to the King's purpose'. There is no mention of the Sorbonne or any other university. Instead, the only body specifically named is 'the French Court' – though Stokesley was also authorized to extend his search 'elsewhere'.[12]

Chapuys is equally misleading on the status of the Embassy. He compared it dismissively to one sent at the same time to his own master, the Emperor, claiming that its personnel were men 'of less splendour in their equipage and condition': that is, of lower rank. He could not have been further from the truth, since the French Embassy was headed by Anne's own brother, George. Du Bellay, of course, knew differently. He had had some wry amusement at the choice of the Boleyns' 'little prince' as ambassador when he was still barely out of his teens. But he had no illusion about George's importance. Those who sent him, he advised, 'are most anxious for him to be given a good welcome and more honour than is ordinarily necessary'. The choice of Stokesley is equally significant since he too was a Boleyn client. 'Your good lordship', Stokesley wrote a few months later to Thomas Boleyn, 'hath fastly bound me to be your beadsman and servitor at your commandment during the little rest of my life.'[13]

In other words, even at this embryonic stage, the canvass of learned opinion was a Boleyn enterprise, to be overseen by members of the family and carried out by its clients. And so it would remain – and more so – after Cranmer's dramatic intervention transformed its nature.

For that, it is now clear, is what he did. In place of the earlier, vague proposals for consultation, Cranmer produced a fully thought-through scheme that had shape, strategy and a *modus operandi*.

The elements were already there in his remarks at Waltham. But they were refined and developed in his subsequent conversations with the King and Thomas Boleyn and, above all, in his Durham Place writings. We can also be sure that Anne made her own powerful contribution.

At Waltham, Cranmer had argued that the 'sentence [of the Divines] may be soon known and brought to pass'. This, in the fully developed scheme, translated into a systematic canvass of academic opinion. It was carried out university by university and it was designed to result in a series of formal, legally binding statements or 'determinations', agreed by the appropriate representative body of each university and delivered under its official seal. Cranmer, from the first, had also been clear that the matter was essentially one for 'the Divines'. This was to result in the targeting of faculties of theology. Faculties of canon law were also consulted. But, in general, fewer hopes were entertained of them and less importance was given to their verdicts. But most important was Cranmer's reduction of the complexities of the Great Matter to a straightforward, four-part formula or questionnaire. It was a talent for creative simplification that was to find its fullest and longest-lasting achievement in his later liturgical works. Here, however, he deployed it to devastating polemical effect.[14]

Was it, the universities were to be asked, permissible to marry the widow of your deceased brother, when the marriage had been childless but consummated? Or was it contrary to divine law? And contrary to natural law? And if it *were* contrary to both divine and natural law, could the Pope dispense from such a prohibition?

Henry's preferred answers to these questions were 'no', 'yes', 'yes' and 'no' respectively.

By late November 1529, Henry was fully up to speed on the new approach to the Great Matter and had persuaded himself that it would work. Indeed, he was confident enough to boast about it to Catherine.

The two, of course, were leading separate lives, albeit usually under the same roof. But they maintained the decencies. Whatever their increasingly acrimonious private disputes, they preserved a façade of public politeness, behaving, as the Milanese ambassador noted with some surprise, with 'so much reciprocal courtesy . . . that anyone acquainted with the controversy cannot but consider their conduct more than human'. They also kept up the ceremonial of the Court, processing together to the Chapel Royal on the great feast-days of the Church and dining together afterwards. And it was over these meals that their worst quarrels tended to occur.[15]

So it was on St Andrew's Day, 30 November 1529.

It was Catherine who commenced hostilities. According to Chapuys, she protested that she suffered the 'pains of Purgatory on earth' from

Henry's neglect of her. In particular, she complained of Henry's 'refusing to dine with her and visit her in her apartments'. Henry justified his neglect by pleading business: Wolsey had left things in such a mess that he was having 'to work day and night to put them to rights again'. Then he, in turn, went on the attack. As for 'visiting her in her apartments or partaking of her bed', that was impossible since he was not her husband. All respectable, authoritative opinion, he insisted, agreed on this point. He already had several such opinions, 'founded upon right and canonic law', and, when he had the rest, he would send them to the Pope. That should end the matter. But if the Pope did not 'in conformity with the above opinions . . . declare their marriage null and void, then in that case he would denounce the Pope as a heretic and marry whom he pleased'.

Catherine, who was as well informed on the case as both Henry and Anne, picked her husband's arguments to pieces. She ended by telling Henry triumphantly that 'for each doctor or lawyer who might decide in your favour and against me, I shall find a thousand to declare that the marriage is good and indissoluble'.

Did her crowing bring back Henry's memories of an earlier exchange, when, in the aftermath of Flodden, Catherine had told him that, in return for his captive French Duke, she was sending him the coat of the dead King of Scots?

Then, as now, his wife knew who was the greater victor.

Bested, Henry retreated to Anne. But he found cold comfort. 'Did I not tell you', Anne snapped, 'that whenever you disputed with the Queen she was sure to have the upper hand?' Some fine day, she continued, Henry would succumb to Catherine's arguments. Then what would happen to Anne? She would be cast off. 'I have been waiting long', she protested with increasing vehemence, 'and might in the meanwhile have contracted some advantageous marriage, out of which I might have had issue . . . But, alas!, farewell to my time and youth spent to no purpose at all'.[16]

One almost begins to feel sorry for Henry, caught as he was in the cross-fire between two such women.

In fact, whatever Henry had said to Catherine, it was not until New

Year 1530 that the campaign to secure favourable 'determinations' from
the universities really got under way, both at home and abroad.

At home, and even before the royal approaches were made, Cranmer's
own university of Cambridge was up in arms. The occasion was two
sermons delivered in Advent (the four weeks before Christmas) 1529 by
Hugh Latimer, Fellow of Clare Hall. As late as 1524, when he took his
degree of bachelor of divinity, Latimer had been a staunch traditionalist.
But shortly thereafter he was 'converted' by Thomas Bilney. Overnight
he became a powerful preacher and (like most brilliant lecturers) a thorn
in the flesh of the university authorities. Things came to a head in his
Advent sermons. They were outrageously populist, explaining Salvation
by analogy with the rules of a popular game of cards known as Triumph
or Trump. And their teaching was inflammatory too. Trumps, according
to Latimer were hearts: the heart prostrated and humbled in the Love of
God, like Mary Magdalen's. And in the love of your neighbour too. This
meant that traditional (Latimer called them 'voluntary') works of piety –
such as pilgrimages, offerings to saints and the setting up of candles in
church – were, at best, an irrelevance in the quest for Salvation. Instead,
saving, triumphing Love showed itself only by the necessary works of
mercy and charity, such as relieving the poor, visiting prisoners and
comforting the sick.[17]

Immediately, a battle of the pulpits broke out, with sermons and
counter-sermons. News reached the Court, where Cambridge men
including Foxe and Gardiner had the King's ear. On 24 January, Foxe
wrote to the vice-chancellor, Dr Thomas Buckmaster of Peterhouse,
warning him of Henry's impending intervention in the 'shameful
contentions' and urging him to put the university's own house in order
by enjoining silence on both parties. But Foxe's letter also reveals a new
dimension to the affair: the petty squabbles of Cambridge had been
caught up in the larger divisions over the Great Matter.

'It is reported to the King', Foxe wrote, 'that this malice is expressed
because Latimer favours his cause.' The suspicion was borne out, Foxe
continued, because Latimer's opponents had such strong connexions

with Bishop Fisher of Rochester, Catherine's great champion and the chancellor of the university. They were members of St John's, the Cambridge college which Fisher had encouraged Henry's grandmother, Lady Margaret Beaufort, to found. And they were egged on, it was reported, by Fisher's many friends in the university, including the master of St John's.[18]

Five days later, on the 29th, Buckmaster acted on Foxe's advice and, in a speech to the senate, ordered both parties to keep silence about matters of current controversy. It is unknown how effective this order was. But, in any case, feelings were still running high when, in early February, Foxe and Gardiner arrived at Cambridge as royal envoys to the university.[19]

Cambridge had been chosen for the honour of delivering the first verdict on Henry's marriage. And it was Foxe and Gardiner's task to make sure that the verdict was the right one.

Bearing in mind his multiplicity of connexions with the university, Henry was probably expecting a walkover. In the event, he met stiff opposition, as Gardiner and Foxe informed him in their initial report. They arrived in Cambridge on Saturday at noon and that night and the following Sunday morning they spent consulting and lobbying. But the other side were equally active: 'as we assembled, they assembled; as we made friends, they made friends'.

The result was that, when the university senate assembled on Sunday afternoon, Henry's opponents at first carried the day. The scene will be painfully familiar to anyone who has sat through such events. Vice-chancellor Buckmaster began, as was customary, by consulting the doctors of theology. There was no clear pattern to their replies *et res erat in multa confusione* ('and things were in great confusion'). *Tandem* ('at length'), as Gardiner feelingly puts it, it was agreed that the decision should be referred to a committee, known then as now as 'delegates'. There followed a concerted attempt by Henry's opponents to exclude from this committee anyone who was known to have 'allowed [accepted] Dr Cranmer's book' on the Divorce, which had already been circulated. This was fought off. But when the vice-chancellor's proposed terms of reference for the delegates were put to the vote, 'they would in no wise agree'. As it was already night, Buckmaster adjourned the meeting till the following afternoon.

Even then it was a cliff-hanger. The first ballot resulted in another negative. Then there was a tie. Finally, at the third attempt, 'by labour of friends to cause some to depart the house which were against it, it was obtained'. Gardiner and Foxe sent Henry a copy of this vote or 'grace' (as again it is still called), together with an annotated list of the delegates. 'All marked with "A"', they told Henry in their covering letter, 'be already of your Grace's opinion.' Six of the doctors were thus marked and seven of the masters, while three more names bore the note: *de isto bene speratur* ('of this one there is good hope'). It was, as Henry's agents concluded, just enough:

> Your Highness may perceive by the notes, that we be already sure of as many as be requisite, wanting only three; and we have good hope of four [sic]; of which four if we get two, and obtain of another to be absent, it is sufficient for our purpose.

Cranmer, it may be remembered, had thought that the canvass of academic opinion could be done 'with little industry and charge'. He had fallen at the first fence, even in his own university.[20]

Nevertheless, Cambridge finally delivered the desired verdict on 9 March. Immediately, a delegation headed by the vice-chancellor went to Court to inform the King in person. They arrived at Windsor on 13 March in the afternoon. It was the second Sunday in Lent, and the preacher appointed for this prestigious occasion was none other than Latimer. It was his first sermon at Court and he proved as much a sensation there as at Cambridge. Henry gave him an extra reward of £5 (the annual stipend for many clergy) from his Privy Purse, on top of the customary 20 shillings.[21]

There is no similarly direct evidence for Anne's reaction. But it is safe to assume that it was profound. She came to accept Latimer's distinction, which was then novel and controversial, between the two sorts of 'works'. 'Voluntary' works of traditional piety, he had proclaimed in his Cambridge sermons and probably repeated at Court, were useless; instead true works were the 'necessary' works of charity and mercy which flowed from Saving Grace and Love. Soon Anne's rapidly growing means would enable her to put her preferences into action. Foxe, the martyrologist, asserts that her charitable alms 'in three quarters of a year ... is summed to the number of fourteen or fifteen thousand pounds'. This is an impossibly vast amount, and it has been guessed that Foxe, who rarely makes such a straightforward mistake of fact, may have added a zero to his source. But everybody agreed that her benefactions were unusually generous. And she was to invoke them in her hour of need.[22]

A reluctant witness of Latimer's triumph was Vice-chancellor Buckmaster. Buckmaster had used the weight of his office to support the King's cause at Cambridge. But, like university authorities throughout the ages, he had little time for troublemakers – such as Latimer.

Buckmaster had arrived at Windsor in time to hear 'part of Mr Latimer's sermon', which was followed by evensong at about 5 o'clock. That done, Buckmaster presented the university's 'determination' to the King, 'in the Chamber of Presence, all the Court beholding'. Henry was delighted. It was the first 'determination' of a university and it was, he had been assured by Foxe and Gardiner, favourable. He glanced at the covering letter but did not bother to read the 'determination' itself. Instead he turned his charm on Buckmaster. 'His Highness', Buckmaster reported in a letter to his close friend Dr John Edmunds, master of Peterhouse and his successor as vice-chancellor, 'gave me great thanks ... [and] much lauded our wisdoms'. He then made clear that his thanks would be followed by a more substantial token of favour for Cambridge. 'He showed me also', Buckmaster continued, 'what he had in his hands for our University.'

Nevertheless, the King could not pass up the chance of having a dig at Buckmaster for his hostility to the new favourite royal preacher, Latimer. 'By and by [Henry] greatly praised Mr Latimer's sermon; and, in so praising, said in this wise: "This displeaseth greatly Mr Vice-chancellor yonder!"'

'And here is the first act,' Buckmaster interpolated, as the smooth high-table raconteur he was.

The second act took place next day. There were two scenes. In the first, the Cambridge delegation was presented with Henry's personal rewards: twenty nobles (£6 13s 4d) for Buckmaster and half as much (£3 6s 8d) for the junior proctor who accompanied him. The rewards were brought by Dr Butts, the favourite royal physician and master of St Mary's Hostel, Cambridge, who had clearly been carrying out some discreet lobbying for his university. Butts further informed Buckmaster that he should take the reward 'for a resolute answer, and that I might depart from the Court when I would'. Was Anne, to whom Butts was very close, intervening to get the delegation out of the way before Henry's mood changed?

If so, she was too late and Butts's orders were countermanded by Foxe. There then took place the second, and much less agreeable, scene of the act. It was set in a 'privy place' where Foxe brought Buckmaster to await the King's arrival. He entered at 1 o'clock. 'It was in a gallery', Buckmaster informed Edmunds, and 'there were only Mr Secretary [Gardiner], Mr Provost [Foxe], Mr Latimer and Mr Proctor and I and no more.' Henry kept them in intense debate for five hours. The reason was that he had discovered a crucial omission in what they had brought. 'He was scarce contented', Buckmaster reported, that the 'determination' contained no answer to the question: *An papa possit dispensare cum jure divino?* (could the Pope dispense with divine law?). Without an answer to this, the Cambridge declaration, won with such effort, was almost useless for Henry's purposes.

Foxe and Gardiner had already explained the reason: if the clause had been included 'it would never have been so obtained'. Buckmaster added his own excuses: 'I made the best, and confirmed the same that they had showed his Grace before'. Henry grudgingly accepted the explanation but demanded that the additional clause be adopted after Easter.

At 6 o'clock Henry departed, 'casting a little Holy Water of the

Court' (that is, fair words without meaning). And Foxe and Gardiner did not even ask Buckmaster to stay for a drink.

Buckmaster left the next day, 'thinking more than I said and being glad that I was out of the Court, where, as I both heard and perceived, many men did wonder on me'. 'And here shall be an end for this time of this fable,' he concluded with relief.[23]

Not for the last time, an academic had found himself out of his depth in the world of power politics.

There is no evidence that the additional clause, on the Papal dispensing power, was ever agreed. Nevertheless, despite Cambridge's failure fully to satisfy Henry, the university's 'determination' was a watershed. It was the moment when a generation chose. And at Cambridge, though not at Oxford, it had decided that it was on the side of Henry, of Reform – and of Anne. We do not know what the 'A' annotation stands for in Foxe's and Gardiner's list. Perhaps it was 'A' for *Amicus* or 'Friend'. It can hardly have been 'A' for 'Anne'. Yet it might just as well have been. For, of the seven Masters marked with an 'A', no less than four, Hugh Latimer, Nicholas Shaxton, John Skip and Thomas Goodrich, came to enjoy her enthusiastic patronage: Latimer became her chaplain, while Skip succeeded Shaxton as her Almoner.[24]

And just how vigorous and calculating Anne's patronage was emerges from the case of one of the doctors marked with an 'A', Edward Crome, DD. Crome also was to benefit from Anne's interest in his career. Indeed, she pushed him too far for his own liking. In 1534 she obtained for him the parsonage of the important City church of St Mary's, Aldermanbury. But Crome long hesitated about accepting the position. Finally, on 20 May 1534 Anne lost patience. 'By which refusal', she informed him bluntly, 'we think that you right little regard or esteem your weal or advancement.' He was also disregarding the larger questions that were so important to her. She had determined on his appointment, she informed him, as tending powerfully to 'the further-ance of virtue, truth and godly doctrine'. Therefore, she commanded, let him 'use no farther delays in this matter but take on you the cure and charge . . . as you tender our pleasure in any behalf'.[25]

Faced with this imperious command, Crome accepted.

One name, of course, is missing from the goings-on at Cambridge: Thomas Cranmer, the man who had started it all. This is because it had been decided that Cranmer would be better employed abroad.

In late January 1530, all the talk was of the despatch of an Embassy from Henry to the Emperor Charles V, who was about to meet Pope Clement VII at Bologna for his Imperial coronation. The Embassy was headed by Anne's father, Thomas Boleyn, Earl of Wiltshire, in his triple capacity as the King's first minister, future father-in-law and leading magnate (even Henry, according to Chapuys, insisted on referring to him as '*monseigneur*'). And it was an appropriately magnificent affair. On 20 January 1530, to confirm his status, Wiltshire was formally appointed Lord Privy Seal and given a valuable wardship. The same day, the eagle-eyed Chapuys noted that the advance luggage train of the Embassy, consisting of servants with eight mules, had left London. But this was only the beginning. 'It is thought', Chapuys reported, 'that the whole troop will consist of 60 or 80 horses, exclusive of the mules.' 'Early' the next day, Wiltshire himself set off. He was accompanied by two theologians, a canon lawyer, a herald and a clerk of the signet to act as secretary to the Embassy and to draw up documentation in the proper form. The initial costs, for wages and living expenses alone, amounted to the enormous sum of £1,743. This left such a large hole in the Chamber, the treasury which normally paid ambassadorial expenses, that Henry made good the amount out of his Privy Purse.

Apart from Wiltshire, Chapuys picked out only three members of the Embassy by name. One of the three, whom he identified as a royal chaplain and theologian, was Cranmer ('Croma').[26]

This, clearly, was no ordinary Embassy. Instead, it was an attempt at a comprehensive relaunch of the Great Matter. Cranmer's insights would be applied to diplomacy, in the form of a last-ditch attempt to win over Charles V, the key obstacle to the solution of the Divorce at Rome. His ideas would also be given practical effect, by a comprehensive canvass of academic opinion in France and Italy. In comparison with these ambitious goals, anything going on in England was small beer. Which is why Gardiner and Foxe were left to deal with Oxford and Cambridge, while Cranmer was sent off with Wiltshire. It is also why Wiltshire himself as chief minister was put in personal charge of the mission.

The last time anything like this had been tried was Wolsey's ill-fated mission to France in 1527. But then the diplomatic situation had turned against Wolsey; he was also fatally undercut at home. Wiltshire would have better luck. The fate, which had made Charles V absolute master of Europe, slowly began to turn. And Wiltshire could also relax on the home front: his daughter Anne would see to that.

Wiltshire's first port of call was Paris, the seat of the Sorbonne. This was the most prestigious faculty of theology in Christendom. A favourable verdict from the Sorbonne would go far to establish Henry's case; a negative one would destroy it. Henry had high hopes, since Francis I of France had thrown his weight behind the campaign for the Divorce. But Henry's approaches to the faculty, which had begun the previous November, had run into immediate difficulties. The first obstacle was the formidable Noel Béda, principal of the collège de Montaigu and the scourge of the proto-Protestant *Cercle de Meaux*. Béda was rigorously orthodox, too, on the question of Papal authority, which, he correctly perceived, was challenged by Henry VIII's claims. He was therefore implacable in his opposition. And, thanks to his authority, obstinacy and almost infinite deviousness, he waged a highly effective campaign. He was not short of allies either, whether in the *parlement* of Paris or in the substantial group of Spanish scholars in the Sorbonne. The latter were led by Dr Garay, who, with very little help from Charles V, conducted a freelance guerrilla war on Catherine's behalf.

It was like Cambridge, only worse.

Wiltshire was informed of the situation in a letter from his client Stokesley, one of the two English agents in Paris. The letter, dated 16 January, probably reached the Earl en route. It detailed the machinations of Béda and 'the unlearned Spanish Doctor Pedro Garay', and the steps which the English had taken to counter the 'authority' of the former and the 'fury' of the latter. But finally, Stokesley made plain, everything depended on direct intervention by the French King.

Anne's brother George, the other English agent, had ridden off in post to the Court at Dijon to try to procure it. But Stokesley was not optimistic. For Francis I's two sons, surrendered as hostages for the fulfilment of his treaty with his captor Charles V, were still in Spanish hands. Till they were released, the French would do nothing openly, 'for that they feared that thereby the Emperor might make a colour [pretext] to delay the deliverance of the . . . King's children.' Montmorency, the chief French minister, and De Langey, Du Bellay's brother, had been quite open about this, Stokesley reported: only let the Princes be in French hands 'and we should have of . . . them all aid and furtherance that we would desire'. But were they, he wondered, as sincere as they seemed? Would it not be wiser to continue to press ahead while the French were so dependent on the English for co-operation in the complex negotiations with the Emperor?[27]

Wiltshire seems to have endorsed Stokesley's advice. He then continued towards his own rendezvous with Francis.

The meeting had been fixed to take place at Moulins in the Auvergne on 18 February. The town had been chosen because it was convenient both for Wiltshire's journey south, towards the Italian frontier, and for the French King, who was still at Dijon. But Wiltshire, hastening towards Bologna, arrived three days early, on the 15th. Luckily Du Bellay was there to meet him. He immediately set himself to roll out the red carpet for Wiltshire, since, as he knew from his experiences in England, the feelings of the future father-in-law of the King of England ruffled easily. Wiltshire should be lodged in the *château*, he recommended. The French King should send Court officials to wait on him. Above all, Francis I should come to meet him himself. 'You know the man', Du Bellay advised Montmorency, 'he only wants to stay here till tomorrow!'[28]

In the event, the King of France *did* come to meet the Earl of Wiltshire – though since Francis only arrived in Moulins on the 19th, Wiltshire had only to stay three or four extra days.

Wiltshire then resumed his journey south. At Roanne, he heard that the Pope and Emperor were planning to leave Bologna soon after the forthcoming coronation on 24 February. Appalled at the risk of missing his goal, Wiltshire tried to ride post. But his constitution was not up to the strain, and at Lyon he was so 'broken' that he had to abandon the plan. But (as might be expected of Anne's father) what he lacked in strength he made up for in determination. 'If I know him', Du Bellay remarked, 'as soon as he's recovered, he'll make the best speed he can.' He did so and arrived in Bologna on 14 March, with a few days to spare before the Emperor's departure on the 22nd.[29]

Wiltshire had his first, formal audience with the Emperor on the 15th but the substantive discussions continued over the following few days. The courtesies were observed but high words were exchanged on both sides. As Wiltshire sought to recapitulate Henry's arguments on the Divorce, Charles cut him short and 'went very far with him'. 'He was not to be believed in this case', the Emperor said, 'as he was a party.' Despite this assault from the greatest ruler of Christendom, Wiltshire more than stood his ground. 'What he did', he replied, 'was not as a father but as a subject and servant of his master.' The English King, he continued, would have been delighted if the Emperor had been willing to understand and accept his conscientious objections to his marriage, 'nevertheless his pleasure would not hinder the execution of his intention'.

There was now a mutual stand-off.

At this point, as the attempt to broker a settlement had failed, Wiltshire was instructed to pull from the hat the rabbit of Cranmer's argument. The issue was one, he said, of the authority of Scripture versus the authority of the Pope. And there could be no contest between the two. Scripture was clear in it, so too were the canons and decretals (here Wiltshire cited the precise chapter). Finally, Wiltshire explained, Henry had received a sort of prophetic support:

The King [he said] is also encouraged by a wonderfully virtuous and wise man, who says that he is not to be considered pious but

404 THE QUEENS OF HENRY VIII

impious, who transgresses his Master's law for the sake of a
servant [this was a reference to the Pope's title of *servus servorum
Dei*, (Servant of the Servants of God)] and fears more to offend
man than God.

This 'wonderfully virtuous and wise man', whose judgement Henry so
much depended on, can only have been Cranmer.

Charles V listened to Wiltshire's exposition with a mixture of
impatience and incomprehension. He then announced his definitive
position. He intended that the affair would be determined by the ordinary
course of justice at Rome. 'If the marriage with his aunt be found to be
null, he will not maintain it, but if it is pronounced valid, he will.'[30]

And he refused to hear Wiltshire further.

Wiltshire had to endure another embarrassment. So far, Henry had
managed to avoid being served with the citation to appear in Rome for
the trial of his marriage. But, taking advantage of the presence of Spanish
troops in Bologna, Catherine's proxy served the summons on Wiltshire
as Henry's accredited representative. Wiltshire blustered. But, so long as
Charles was in Bologna, there was nothing he could do.

The moment the Emperor left, however, he complained vigorously
to the Pope of the indignity, and demanded a six-month delay, on
condition that Henry did not act unilaterally. The Pope refused to act
without consulting the Emperor. But when Charles V made no objection
the compromise was agreed.

The English were greatly helped in this damage-limitation exercise
by the French envoy to the Curia, the Bishop of Tarbes. Wiltshire was
properly grateful, as Tarbes informed Francis I: the events at Bologna,
Wiltshire said, 'will create a stronger affection towards you, in himself
and his master'. And Francis would have a more potent ally still. 'He told
me yesterday', Tarbes continued, 'he was sure, if his daughter came to be
Queen, she would be all her life your very humble servant, well knowing
that all their weal depends on you only.'[31]

The language is extravagant, but there was a sober reality behind it.

Anne's preferences were French, not only in culture, language and religion but, crucially, in foreign policy too. It was, after all, no more than a recognition of mutual interests.

In his despatches home, written on the 18th and 19th as events were still unfolding, Wiltshire made no attempt to gloss his failure with Charles. The Emperor, he wrote, was both resolute and immovable: 'stiffly . . . set in the contrary part of Your Grace's Great Matter and earnest . . . in it'. He was primed by Chancellor Gattinara. And Gattinara's influence was equally malign on Chapuys, 'the Emperor's ambassador being resident with your Grace in England', since he was, Wiltshire suspected, 'by many likelihoods . . . much led and guided by the Chancellor'. Finally, the Pope was and would remain in the Emperor's pocket: 'he is led by the Emperor, so that he neither will nor dare displease him.'

The enemy, in short, was now fully known and unmasked.

The courier made excellent time to England and the letters were in Henry's hands by the time of his audience with the French ambassador at the beginning of April. His worst fears were confirmed. 'The King', the ambassador reported, 'is so displeased with the Emperor's haughtiness that he has a great mind to recall his ambassador; which he adds, he is the more induced to do, as he believes it would lead the Emperor to withdraw his, for he is little satisfied with the Imperial ambassador here.' Henry also speculated openly on an English solution to the Divorce, 'by the advice of his Council and Parliament'. The Pope was 'simoniacal and ignorant', and other kingdoms, he was convinced, would follow his lead in refusing to recognize Rome.

All this suggests that historians have misunderstood the effects of the Bologna meeting. It was not a defeat for Wiltshire, as the Duke of Norfolk, already jealous of Boleyn power, was eager to insinuate to Chapuys. On the contrary, it demonstrated that the Boleyn strategy on the Great Matter had been correct. Anne and her father had long argued that, since Rome neither could nor would grant a Divorce, alternative means must be found. Now they stood vindicated by Charles's intransigence.[32]

Cranmer, it was clear, was right. The Boleyns as his patrons were

right. There was no alternative. And this in turn meant that the canvass
of university opinion became more important than ever.

The original intention had been for Wiltshire to remain in Italy till the
canvass was complete: he would then present the 'determinations' to the
Pope, who would stand confounded; the Pope might even yield . . .

Bologna challenged this cosy assumption. Now Wiltshire was
instructed to return to France, to hold a watching brief on the political
situation there. To replace him, Cranmer was given the day-to-day
charge of the Italian canvass. He proved exceptionally successful, and,
within a few months, favourable verdicts had been obtained from the four
leading universities: Padua, Pavia, Ferrara and Bologna. This is the more
remarkable since the English were operating in 'enemy' territory. It was
'serious', the Imperial ambassador to Venice reported, that the faculty in
the Pope's own city of Bologna should find for Henry, since 'they are
subjects of the Pope'. But find they did. The means used were not pretty
– on either side. English money was met with Imperial and Papal threats.
Academics intrigued, deceived and shamelessly changed their minds.
Inevitably, there were crises, in which Richard Croke, the most active and
excitable English agent, appealed beyond Cranmer and invoked the
Boleyns themselves. 'Advertise my Lord [of Wiltshire] or the King or else
all will be lost', he wrote in one letter. 'I pray you', he implored Cranmer
in another, 'to move my Lord of Wiltshire and my Lady Boleyn to move
the King to be good to me, and that I may have money and authority of an
ambassador.' Then his task would be easy.[33]

Other universities in France followed with declarations for Henry:
Orleans on 5 April, Angers on 7 May, Bourges on 10 June. But still the
great prize of the Sorbonne eluded him. For the haggling over the French
Princes was not yet concluded and, until they were safely released,
Francis and his agents were unwilling to defy the Emperor by applying
the necessary pressure to whip Béda and his followers into line. Finally,
and much against his better judgement, De Langey, who was acting as
Francis I's chief agent at the Sorbonne, was driven to act on 12 June: 'I

should have been glad if I could have dissembled further', he informed Francis, 'without creating more distrust in the King of England's men.' But he had put them off as long as he could. Indeed, he feared that Anne's cousin, Sir Francis Bryan, who had taken over from her brother George as the principal English agent in Paris, might have been withdrawn in disgust at French delays.[34]

But, reluctant and half-hearted as it was, De Langey's intervention was far from satisfying the English and three days later on the 15th they wrote to Wiltshire, who was being entertained royally at the French Court at Angoulême, to complain. De Langey was showing them one set of letters to Francis but actually sending other, milder ones, they grumbled. And they reported in horror the sort of language which Henry's opponents had used in the debates. Béda had exhorted his colleagues, they wrote, to remain fast, 'trusting that there were left many yet *qui non flexerunt genua Simulacro Baal* [who would not bend the knee to the Idol of Baal]'. 'Signifying', they continued, 'that the King our master and the French King were the idol of Baal, and all that followed their desires committed idolatry'.[35]

Finally, events broke the deadlock. On I July Francis's sons were handed over at the Spanish frontier. And on 2 July, certain that the release would take place, De Langey extorted the required verdict from the Faculty.[36]

The news reached the English Court only on the 11th. Henry rejoiced and Anne was triumphant. Who cares about the Emperor now, she crowed. 'She has been', Chapuys reported to Charles V, 'urging on the King and telling him that Your Majesty had it not in your power to do him any harm.' Why, she continued, 'her own family would provide for one year 10,000 men for his service at their own expense!'

More important, she offered herself. 'It is foretold in ancient prophecies', she said to Henry when he was remonstrating with her on the number of enemies he was making on her behalf, 'that at this time a Queen shall be burned; but even if I were to suffer a thousand deaths, my love for you would not abate one jot'.[37]

At last events were running her way.

55. The Royal Supremacy

Anne's father, the Earl of Wiltshire, arrived back from the Continent at the beginning of August 1530 – probably on the 4th. It was the Progress time and the Court was at Easthampstead, a hunting lodge in the depths of Windsor forest. For weeks, the King had done nothing but devote himself to the chase – and to Anne.[1]

Now, suddenly, he was galvanized into taking the most momentous step in the whole history of the Divorce: he decided that, as King of England, his marriage was not subject to the judgement of the Pope after all.

Chapuys was quick to notice the change in the pace of events. 'Immediately on the arrival of the Earl', he reported, 'the King despatched a messenger express to Rome.' Two or three days later Henry sent out summonses to leading members of the Council to meet in special session at Hampton Court.

The day appointed for the meeting was the 11th. Catherine (though not, one suspects, Anne) was left behind at Windsor and Henry took up residence at Hampton Court. The French ambassador was in attendance as well. The meeting turned into a mini-Parliament and continued for five days until the 16th. Chapuys naturally suspected that it had been convoked to discuss the Divorce. Equally naturally, he, as Imperial ambassador, received bland assurances to the contrary. But his suspicions were roused by the fact that on the 17th 'another courier was despatched to Rome', which must, he concluded, 'be in consequence of some resolution passed at that very meeting'.

Chapuys was right. The accounts of Sir Brian Tuke, the Treasurer of the Chamber and Master of the Posts, confirm that 'Francis Piedmont, courier, [was] sent to Rome', with letters dated the 16th. They also confirm that his 'letters [were] of great importance'.[2]

The letters have disappeared. But subsequent correspondence makes it possible to reconstruct their contents: Henry's ambassadors in Rome were instructed to inform the Pope that he had no jurisdiction in the case. On the contrary, 'the custom of England [is] that no one should be compelled to go to law out of the Kingdom.' 'This custom and privilege', they were also to assert, 'stand on firm and solid reasons and have true and just foundations.'[3]

This, the 'custom and privilege of England', was the germ, though no more, of the Royal Supremacy. The Supremacy asserted that the King, not the Pope, was rightful Head of the Church *in* England. It was key doctrine of the English Reformation, and provided the basis, not only for the Divorce, but also for the whole future constitution of the Church *of* England, as it became.

And, it is now clear, the doctrine was first conceived, or at least first put into words, at Hampton Court on 11–16 August 1530.

This answers one question but immediately raises another: where did the idea come from? One answer might be from Henry himself, who had said something similar during an earlier clash between 'Church' and 'State' in the Richard Hunne affair of 1514–15.

In December 1514 London was rocked by the discovery of the body of Richard Hunne, who was found hanged in the Bishop of London's gaol known as the Lollards' Tower. Hunne was a prosperous merchant-tailor of London, who had been charged with heresy on apparently flimsy grounds. Was his death suicide or murder? The ecclesiastical and secular authorities immediately took opposite sides in the affair. The Church courts gave a verdict of suicide and had his body burned as that of a heretic. The London coroner's jury, on the other hand, found a verdict of murder against both the bishop's gaoler and his chancellor. Finally, in a set-piece debate before the King himself, Henry intervened on the side of the lay authorities:

> By the ordinance and sufferance of God [he declared], we are King of England, and the Kings of England in times past have never had any superior but God only. Wherefore know you well that we will maintain the right of our Crown and of our temporal

jurisdiction, as well in this point as in all others, in as ample a wise as any of our progenitors have done before us.

The debate, curiously, took place at Blackfriars, almost certainly in the same Parliament Chamber where, in 1529, the Legatine Trial of Henry's marriage precipitated an even greater clash of jurisdictions.[4]

And the parallels go beyond location. For, at first sight, there does indeed seem to be a straight line from Henry's remarks in 1515 to the claim formulated at Hampton Court in 1530. But that cannot be. For if Henry was already convinced of his 'supremacy' in 1515, why, only six years later in 1521, did he argue so powerfully for the most far-reaching claims of the Papal monarchy in the *Assertio*? And why, eight years later still, did he sue so hard and so humiliatingly to the Pope for a Roman solution to the Great Matter?

There is no convincing answer to these points. Instead, it makes better sense to see Henry's words in 1515 as high-sounding but vague rhetoric, of a type to which he was prone on great public occasions. They could mean anything – or nothing. And in 1515, it became clear, they meant precious little: Wolsey saw to that.

The ideas of 1530 were therefore new, in substance, if not in formulation. And a much more convincing source for them is the Boleyns. The coincidence between the Earl of Wiltshire's return and the convening of the Hampton Court meeting itself speaks volumes. So does the nature of the mission which had kept him abroad for seven full months. During that period he had taken overall charge of the canvass of the universities in both France and Italy. He had been in close touch with the labourers at the intellectual coalface, such as Cranmer who had been sent to Italy, and Stokesley and latterly Foxe who had been sent to France. And it seems clear that he had immersed himself fully in the debate. It would be hard to think of a better forcing-house for the idea of the Supremacy.

For the key, I think, is to see the Supremacy, not as a radical departure in the strategy of the Great Matter, but rather as a logical outcome of the canvass of the universities.

Back in the immediate aftermath of his roasting by Charles V at Bologna, Wiltshire had given the French ambassador a remarkably cool analysis of England's immediate strategy. 'He said', the Bishop of Tarbes reported, 'the English would act for three or four months like those who look at dancers, and take courage according as they see them dancing ill or well. And as they should see Francis do, so would the King his master do.' 'You will understand what these words imply', the ambassador added portentously.[5]

During the next three or four months, Wiltshire, whether in Paris or at the French Court, had a front-row seat at the ballet of European politics. It was time enough for him to decide that Francis I could be trusted and that a joint plan of action should be agreed. The plan emerges most clearly from the correspondence of Du Bellay. By April Du Bellay was reporting his conviction that, 'if the King of England sees the Princes in France and that he has [the verdict of] the University of Paris . . . I think that he'll marry immediately'. He repeated the conviction at the beginning of May. By the end of June, his conversations with Wiltshire had crystallized into the outlines of an agreement. Henry, it was taken for granted, would act unilaterally; meanwhile Francis I *would* protect his back.[6]

The detailed negotiations, it was also agreed, would be undertaken by Du Bellay himself as special ambassador to England. As soon as the Sorbonne had delivered its verdict (which was to be extorted, of course, by his brother De Langes), Du Bellay would go post-haste to England to conclude a treaty for mutual defence. Francis, Du Bellay's subsequent instructions made clear, preferred the treaty to be in general terms. But, if Henry pressed, Du Bellay was authorized to include a 'special engagement about the matter of his marriage'. The engagement was formulated very broadly: if, in consequence of Henry's suit for the nullity of his marriage, England were attacked 'by any prince or potentate of what estate, quality or condition he be', Francis would come to his aid.[7]

It is hard to overestimate the importance of such a guarantee. The Emperor might threaten armies, or the Pope spiritual sanctions, but, shielded by his good brother of France, who was also the Most Christian King, Henry could regard them with something like indifference.

Anne, it now seemed, would be married in weeks rather than months.

Unfortunately, the plan unravelled almost immediately. Béda and his allies in the Sorbonne mounted a furious rear-guard action, in which they threatened to rescind the verdict, favourable for Henry, which the faculty had reached in July. De Langes, by invoking Francis's direct authority, managed to quell the revolt. But Du Bellay lost precious days in Paris, helping his brother to regain control of the Sorbonne and he did not arrive at Dover till 19 August. But by then it was too late. The Hampton Court meeting had already come and gone, with France represented only by the resident ambassador and no new treaty agreed. Moreover, at the meeting Henry had found some of his own councillors almost as recalcitrant as the die-hards of the Sorbonne. Warned by Chapuys, Archbishop Warham of Canterbury, who was the only possible English judge in the Great Matter, refused to act in defiance of Rome. Henry was blocked – both at home, and, temporarily, abroad. He had the verdict of the Sorbonne. But he could do nothing with it.[8]

Out of this frustration, I would guess, 'the custom and privilege of England' was born. The determination of the Sorbonne and the other universities provided Henry, it was now clear, with only *moral* authority. But what use was that, if neither Warham at home nor Clement in Rome would recognize it? 'The custom and privilege of England', when it developed into the Supremacy, would bridge the gap. For it would provide a *jurisdictional* authority that would compel recognition of the verdict of the determinations.

At least it would where Henry's writ ran.

For the moment, however, Henry contented himself with sending his vague but threatening letter to Rome. For there was still the summer – and Anne – to enjoy.

This was the second, uninterrupted summer that Anne had spent with Henry. But there was a new joyousness about it, as they had thrown all pretence and concealment to the winds. She would be seen as the King's companion and consort, outside the palace as well as within. She did not care who knew it. And she would go in appropriate state.

Henry's prodigal generosity saw to that.

Perhaps the clearest testimony to Anne's altered status had come on 27 May 1530 when Henry issued orders for her to be supplied with an astonishing range of luxurious velvet-covered and gilt horse-furniture, including saddles and harnesses for her own horses and trappings for the mules that carried her litter. Inevitably, bearing in mind her francophile tastes, most of the saddles were 'of the French fashion', while some of their trimmings were decorated in the latest Renaissance style and 'graven with antique works'. Also included in the warrant was 'a pillion of fine down, covered with black velvet, fringed with silk and gold, [and] lined with buckram'.[9]

It can only have been for her to ride behind Henry.

Indeed, she already had. The incident took place a few weeks previously, on 27 April, as the Court was removing from Windsor to its eventual destination at York Place. Normally the journey would have been done by water; instead, it was decided to travel by land in a sort of mini-Progress. The route lay via The More, Hunsdon and Enfield, all of which had fine, deer-filled parks which promised excellent sport. Henry was in holiday mood, and, to show it, on the first leg of the journey from Windsor to The More, he made Anne ride pillion behind him.

Kingship was forgotten. Anne had made him a young lover again.

But others noticed and, according to Chapuys, were shocked at the gross familiarity. 'The King shows greater favour to the Lady every day', Chapuys reported. 'Very recently', he continued, 'coming from Windsor, he made her ride behind him on a pillion, a most unusual proceeding, and one that has greatly called forth peoples' attention here.' Two men, he added, had been imprisoned for daring to gossip about it.[10]

Also in late May Anne had been fitted out with hunting gear, consisting of bows, arrows, shafts, broad heads, a bracer or wrist-guard and a shooting glove. These supplies were quickly exhausted and in June another four bows were supplied for her use.

For weeks she and Henry rode and hunted and did little else. 'For nearly a month', Chapuys reported in mid-August, 'the King has transacted no business . . . [Instead] he has given himself up entirely to hunting privately and moving from one place to another.' After the interruption of the Hampton Court meeting, the holiday resumed. In September it was marred by a disagreeable incident in which two packs of greyhounds, one belonging to Anne and the other to a Groom of the Privy Chamber, mauled a cow to death. But a royal tip of ten shillings smoothed matters over.[11]

At the beginning of September, however, Chapuys noticed a change. Anne's cousin, Sir Francis Bryan, returned from his Embassy in France at the end of August. Immediately, the ports were closed and Henry was 'continually engaged in Council'. Evidently, Bryan had returned with important news. But, despite his best efforts, Chapuys could not ferret it out. He did, however, reappraise his earlier judgement about Henry's idleness. 'This year', he decided on balance, '[the King] has attended more to business and less to sport than for a long time previously.' And Henry's new-found industry would continue into the autumn and through the winter. For at last he saw a way to the solution of the Great Matter – the Boleyn way which Henry would now make his own.[12]

The first to confront the 'new' Henry was the newly appointed Papal Nuncio, Antonio de Pulleo, Baron de Burgo. His choice as Nuncio is yet another testimony to Clement's tact and understanding. Sensitive to the rising tide of English anticlericalism, the Pope had chosen a layman as his representative, not a cleric. De Burgo was also as near to a neutral on the Great Matter as was possible in the increasingly polarized world of the 1530s. On the one hand, as a Sicilian nobleman, he was a subject of Charles V in his capacity as King of Naples. On the other, he was in the Papal service, was high in Clement's personal confidence and had the temperament of a natural diplomat, being 'well-mannered . . . and learned', as the Milanese ambassador described him appreciatively. Best of all from Henry's point of view, Miçer Mai, the fiercely partisan Imperial ambassador in Rome, viewed his despatch with grave misgivings. 'I have done all I could to prevent his nomination', he reported. And when, despite his best efforts, De Burgo was sent, Mai conceded defeat with the dry: 'We shall see'.[13]

Mai, it turned out, need not have worried. For, with all his patience and emollient charm, De Burgo found himself in an impossible situation. Acting on Clement's direct instructions, the Nuncio offered the compromise that Mai feared. But Henry rejected it. He had become as hardline as Mai himself.

All this was clear from the moment of De Burgo's first audience. He arrived in London on 9 September. The end of the hunting season, the Day of the Exaltation of the Holy Cross, was still five days away, and the time was normally sacred to the chase. But Henry interrupted his sport to receive the Nuncio at Waltham Abbey on the 12th. De Burgo explained that the six-month moratorium, agreed with Wiltshire, was coming to an end and the trial in Rome would have to begin. But Clement would, he continued, go to almost any lengths to compromise on the judges and even the place of trial.

Henry brushed these offers aside. Who cared what a modern Pope of these degenerate times would do? 'For . . . it had been enacted', he informed the startled Nuncio, 'by several ancient Popes [whose authority should, on account of their sanctity, be of more weight than that of recent ones], that no cause having its origin in this country should be advoked to another kingdom.' He had already informed the Pope of this privilege. If Clement refused to honour it, Henry declared, 'I can safely proceed to action.' And if, as a consequence, Charles V attacked him, he would see off the attack. But, in any case, his good friend and ally, Francis I of France, would come to his defence.[14]

Henry did not rely on words alone. Instead, on 12 September 1530, the very day of De Burgo's audience, he issued a proclamation. This forbade any suit 'to the Court of Rome', or any attempt to publish in England any Bull obtained in the last year, which contained 'matter prejudicial to the high authority, jurisdiction and prerogative royal' of England. The penalty was *Praemunire.* This was the device which had destroyed Wolsey. It was now threatened against Catherine and her supporters, if they tried to publish a hostile Papal verdict against Henry. It was even threatened against De Burgo, if he served any procedural writs on the King.[15]

On Sunday, 25 September, two days after the Progress ended, De Burgo went to Hampton Court to register a formal protest against the proclamation. He might have spared his breath. For the ministerial troika of Norfolk, Suffolk and Wiltshire maintained a united and vehemently anti-Papal front. 'They cared neither for Pope nor Popes in this kingdom', they bragged to De Burgo, 'not even if St Peter should come to life again; that the King was absolute both as Emperor and Pope in his own kingdom.' It was brave talk. It also suggests that the work of fleshing out and documenting the idea of the 'custom and privileges of England' was already well underway.[16]

Nevertheless, behind the united front, there were substantial disagreements between the three councillors. Suffolk (egged on by his wife, Henry's sister Mary) had always been opposed to the Boleyn marriage. Norfolk, as Anne's uncle, was willing to embrace it on grounds of self-advancement and personal dynastic advantage. But now he, too, was baulking at the means, if we believe his words at a private interview, arranged at his request, with the Nuncio. '[Do] not ... take any notice of the King's violent words,' he begged De Burgo in strict confidence, 'he would take good care that none of the King's threats should be carried into action.'[17]

In fact, only Wiltshire seems to have been fully on side. And his enthusiasm was limitless. While Norfolk went out of his way to signal moderation, Anne's father, on the contrary, flaunted his extremism and, to Chapuys's face, 'began slandering the Pope and Cardinals ... violently'. Indeed his language was so outrageous that Chapuys could stand no more of it. Instead, he reported, 'full of horror at what was being said, I took leave and left the room immediately.' 'Should the Earl [Wiltshire] and his daughter remain in power,' Chapuys concluded, 'they will entirely alienate this kingdom from its allegiance to the Pope.' His words were as shrewd as analysis as they proved accurate as prophecy.[18]

But the divisions within Henry's inner circle of advisers were nothing compared to those in the Council and the kingdom at large. Once again, in another meeting at Hampton Court at the beginning of October, Henry tried to get agreement to the proposition that the 'custom and privileges of the kingdom' allowed the Divorce to be settled in England. And once again he failed.[19]

His first reaction, as usual when he was thwarted, was rage. Then he turned to overcoming the opposition. There were two means. One was research, to make the case for the 'custom and privileges' more persuasive. Here Henry himself took the lead. The other was a stick-and-carrot approach to opponents. This, as we shall see, was Anne's province. And she would show an especial talent for wielding the stick.

Research, then as now, depends on books and a good library. So the first sign that Henry was turning himself into a researcher on the 'custom and privileges' came in October when Sir John Russell, Wolsey's former client who still held on to his position in the Privy Chamber, received a reward of twenty shillings 'for bringing of books'. A month later, in late November, Thomas Heneage, another former Wolsey client in the Privy Chamber, arranged for the transport of books by boat from York Place to Hampton Court, where Henry would spend most of the autumn. But the principal source of supply was the monastic libraries.[20]

Also in late November, the Abbot of Reading sent the King 'an inventory of books'. Two days later, the inventory was followed by a delivery of books from the same source. This would scarcely have given the King or his assistants time to read and mark up the list, as was done with another inventory of the libraries of Lincolnshire monasteries. But maybe Henry was working fast. At any rate, no fewer than seventeen books with a Reading provenance have been identified in the Old Royal Libraries, though it is unclear whether they were all sent in November 1530.[21]

418   THE QUEENS OF HENRY VIII

Why Reading? Proximity was probably one explanation: the House was quite near Hampton Court and Henry stayed there on at least twelve occasions in his reign. He also knew the Abbot, Hugh Faringdon. Faringdon was a monastic grandee of the old school, as much at home in the saddle as in the stall, and he kept in touch with Henry by sending him frequent presents of 'wood' or hunting knives.

Anne, almost certainly, had her connexions with the Abbey of Reading, too, and they make an instructive contrast with Henry's. In 1528, as Wolsey's henchmen were trying to purge Oxford from the consequence of Thomas Garrett's missionary book-selling, they discovered that the infection had spread further still. 'This Garrett', the Bishop of Lincoln reported to Wolsey, 'also hath, I fear, corrupted the Monastery of Reading, for he hath diverse times sent to the Prior there such corrupt books . . . to the number of three score or above, and received money of him for them.' 'How the said Prior hath used those books,' the bishop continued, 'and with whom, I know not.'[22]

The Prior (or deputy-Abbot) was John Shirburn. Evidently, Shirburn was thrown into gaol, like most of the suspects in the affair. We have already seen that, in late 1528, Anne intervened with Wolsey on behalf of another suspect, Thomas Forman, the rector of Honey Lane. Nine or ten months later, in the dying days of Wolsey's ministry, the King himself was brought to intercede for Shirburn.

The King's Highness [Gardiner informed Wolsey on 7 September 1529] willed me also to write unto your grace, that suit is made unto him in favour of the Prior of Reading, who, for Luther's opinion, is now in prison, and hath been a good season, at your Grace's commandment. Unless the matter be much notable, and very heinous, he desireth your Grace, at his request, to cause the said Prior to be restored to liberty and discharged of that imprisonment.

This letter has not had the attention it deserves. 1529 is extraordinarily early for Henry to be intervening on behalf of an acknowledged

Lutheran. His views on the subject were still harsh and it would have taken considerable courage to launch the suit on Shirburn's behalf. Who would have dared and who would have had the opportunity? It is difficult to think of anybody but Anne who, then and for the future, was to be the consistent protectoress of heterodox opinion.

If this guess is right, Anne knew Shirburn or at least his circle. She knew of the suspect books he had bought for the Abbey; she would also have had the opportunity of discovering the more orthodox riches of its collections.

Did she point Henry in the direction of Reading and its library when he was doing his research? It seems as likely as not.

In the following months, dozens more books were brought to Henry, from Ramsey (twice), Sempringham, Gloucester, Evesham, Spalding, and St Augustine's, Canterbury. And the more he read, the surer he became. He was indeed rightly 'absolute both as Emperor and Pope in his own kingdom'. Clement's powers, on the other hand, were a mere usurpation. In Henry's mind at least, the way was open to the Divorce – and to much else besides.[23]

As Henry's convictions hardened, Anne's confidence rose. Not that she ever quite trusted Henry's resolution. In November 1530, for instance, she placed herself at a window in the King's Chamber where she could 'overhear and overlook' Henry's audience with Chapuys in the adjacent gallery. And, as Chapuys's replies became tougher, Henry, he noticed, manoeuvred him out of Anne's earshot into the middle of the room![24]

But events were now moving beyond the power of Chapuys's repartee. Parliament, much prorogued since its first session in 1529, was due to reconvene in January 1531. Anne hoped and Catherine feared that it would take decisive action. In eager anticipation, Anne adopted a new livery for Christmas. Its motto was borrowed from the Burgundian Court, where, long ago, she had begun her career in the Archduchess Margaret's household at La Veure. 'Ainsi sera, groigne qui groigne, Et vive Bourgogne!' the full motto went. Anne dropped the last line 'And long live Burgundy'. This left her servants emblazoned with the boast: 'Thus it will be, Grumble who will'.[25]

And thus it was. But, contrary to expectation, the action took place in the Convocation (the 'parliament' of the clergy) which met alongside Parliament proper. Suddenly, the King called on the clergy to enact his own conviction that, 'as Emperor and Pope', he was indeed 'Supreme Head on Earth of the Church in England'. His spokesmen, headed by Stokesley, rehearsed the arguments. But Henry had a more powerful argument still. Once again, it was *Praemunire*. Once it had brought down Wolsey. Now it was turned against the entire clergy. All of them, Henry's lawyers argued, had recognized Wolsey's legacy. So all were guilty. The clergy fought and wriggled. But there was no escape. They had to acknowledge Henry's new title and pay a gigantic, collective fine of £100,000.

Only one thing was saved from the wreck: the sweeping claims of Henry's new title were modified by the addition of the phrase 'insofar as the Law of Christ allows'. It was Henry's turn to object to this, since, for the orthodox, the addition rendered his title meaningless. But finally he agreed. For of course *he* knew that Christ's Law, properly understood, indeed declared that he was 'Emperor and Pope'.[26]

Anne had no doubts either. When she heard the news, Chapuys discovered, '[she] made such demonstrations of joy as if she had actually gained Paradise'.[27]

In a sense, of course, she had. For Henry, she was sure, was in her grasp at last.

But first she had to remove the obstacles in her path.

56. *Wolsey's end*

Anne's first target was Wolsey. Once, she had vowed undying devotion to him. But it was always conditional and, after Wolsey had betrayed her cause (as she saw it) in the Blackfriars Trial, she had become his most dangerous enemy. She was also the best placed to give effect to her feelings. But not even she could move as quickly as she wished. For Henry himself stood in her way.

Henry *had* decided to get rid of Wolsey as his minister, and the old ascendancy of the Cardinal over his mind was gone forever. But he would not throw him to the wolves – yet. The King's 'love and friendship', which had been the real foundation of Wolsey's power, were still too strong for that. Nor had he forgotten Wolsey's vast talents, or the extent of his past services. There might even have been a sneaking sense that he might need them again.

It was this last which really alarmed Wolsey's enemies. But there was nothing they could do. Instead, they had to stand by while Henry (in the nice phrase of the Milanese ambassador) allowed his former minister to 'fall on a feather-bed'.[1]

No sooner, indeed, was his surrender to the majesty of the law complete on 30 October 1529 than Wolsey began (with Henry's covert encouragement) to hope for a restoration to favour and soon to more besides. Barely twenty-four hours later, on the night of 1–2 November, Henry sent Sir John Russell, Wolsey's old client, to him with a token and message. The latter was so encouraging that, in his letter of thanks to the King, Wolsey ventured to hope that 'as soon as it shall seem to your pitiful heart ... it may be openly known ... that your Highness hath forgiven me mine offence and trespass, and delivered me from the danger of your laws'. Less than three weeks later, on 18 November, Wolsey had his desire when he was formally readmitted to the King's protection which had been forfeited by his condemnation at law.[2]

But there was still the hurdle of Parliament to overcome. An important group in the Lords was determined to bring Wolsey to account and on 1 December a version of Lord Darcy's articles against him was passed by the House. The articles ended with a plea to Henry to inflict exemplary justice on the fallen minister and to make of him a 'terrible example' to all other like offenders. But, though the passage of the articles gave Wolsey another bad fright, Henry had no intention of unleashing Parliament against him. Instead, on 17 December, Parliament was prorogued till 26 April 1530. Wolsey could breathe again.[3]

Indeed, now that he was doubly secure, both against the ordinary processes of law and the extraordinary procedures of Parliament, he did more. Soon he was confident enough to begin to negotiate with the King and his new councillors to rescue as much from the wreck as possible. It was not so much *plea* bargaining as *fine* bargaining.

And it says rather a lot about Henry that Wolsey dared to undertake it all. For the Henry he appealed to was generous and merciful. He tempered justice with pity and moderated the rigour of his laws out of regard for Wolsey's long service, his grey hairs and (as Wolsey himself constantly predicted) the short span of life left to him.

This, in short, was a Henry that Anne had yet to toughen up.

In the negotiations, Wolsey of course used the language of profound abasement. But that was a front. Behind the verbal smoke-screen, there is no mistaking his sense of self-worth or his increasing outrage at the injustice (as he saw it) of his treatment. He had done nothing which deserved punishment, he insisted. Or at least nothing maliciously. He could not be expected to live on less than £4,000 a year (an enormous sum that was more than the income of a duke). This was not out of an appetite for filthy lucre – he calls it 'the muck of the world' – but only to look after his servants and kinsfolk and to live 'according to his poor degree'. The revenues of the archbishopric of York were 'sore decayed' and could not possibly produce this minimum sum. Let him therefore be given a pension of 1,000 marks (£666 13s 4d) out of the revenues of Winchester or the Abbey of St Albans (neither of which he had expected to surrender). Oh, and he needed ready cash. And Household stuff and provisions. Above all, the message was, he needed these things as a sign that Henry had not finally forgotten and rejected him.[4]

All the talents which had made Wolsey so formidable in the days of his power were now focused on the single task of his rehabilitation. And, as his horizons shrank, so his energies seemed to concentrate and become febrile in their intensity. He wrote letter after letter. He wheedled and pleaded. He appealed to his past services. He invoked pity by vivid descriptions of his present ill-health (which, since the symptoms included loss of appetite and insomnia, was probably the result of a nervous breakdown). And, crucially, he called in every favour.

Henry Norris, the Groom of the Stool, lived up to his usual epithet of 'gentle' and did his best to help. Russell, as always, was stalwartly loyal. Gardiner was outwardly helpful too. But, in the view of the shrewd, rising young man, Ralph Sadler, Gardiner could not be trusted. 'I think he will do little or nothing to [Wolsey's] avail', Sadler wrote after a frustrating visit to Court, 'more than he may not choose for very shame, considering the advancements and promotion he hath had at [Wolsey's] hands.'[5]

But most effective of all was the addressee of Sadler's letter: Thomas Cromwell.

Cromwell was a man of humble origins: as humble as Wolsey's. Wolsey was the son of an Ipswich butcher; Cromwell of a Putney blacksmith. But, unlike Wolsey, he was schooled in the university of life. Some stories make him a mercenary who, in his youth, fought his way even to Italy. Certainly he was well travelled, and, with a natural aptitude for languages, he seems to have picked up German, French and Italian on the way. He returned to England and became somebody in the City. There seems to have been a bit of trade and a bit of law, and he became reasonably adept at Latin too. Then, we do not know how, he was talent-spotted by Wolsey and became his key legal agent in a specialist and controversial area.[6]

Wolsey's two colleges at Oxford and his native Ipswich were his pride and joy. But their endowments were raised, not out of his own wealth, but by dissolving a host of lesser monasteries. Cromwell headed the team which handled the legal side of this first dissolution. And it made him a figure of universal hatred. Indeed, as early as 1527, Wolsey was warned on no account to use Cromwell as his messenger to Court, because Cromwell was so unpopular.[7]

As long as Wolsey remained in power, this opprobrium was water off a duck's back (and no back was broader or more impermeable than Cromwell's). But, when Wolsey fell, Cromwell stood utterly unprotected: 'You are', his friend Stephen Vaughan, the radical Antwerp merchant, wrote, 'more hated for your master's sake (in other words, for Wolsey's), than for anything which I think you have wrongfully done against any man.'[8]

This was a charitable view. But Cromwell's activities, as he himself well knew, left few disposed to charity, and his prospects were grim. The fact produced a rare display of open, unguarded emotion. It took place in Wolsey's Presence Chamber on the morning of 1 November (a few hours, that is, before Russell brought his comforting message from the King). There, Cavendish remembered Cromwell praying with tears in his eyes. Why was he so distressed, Cavendish asked. 'It is my unhappy adventure [fortune],' Cromwell replied, 'which am like to lose all that I have travailed for all the days of my life for doing of my Master's true and faithful service.' Cavendish tried to comfort him. Surely he had done nothing to be ashamed of, he said. But Cromwell was more realistic: what mattered was not *what* he had done but *how* it was perceived. 'An ill name once gotten will not lightly be put away,' he insisted.

Moping, however, did not come naturally to him. Action did. 'This afternoon', Cromwell announced at the end of the conversation, 'I do intend . . . to ride . . . to the Court, where I will either make or mar or I come home again.'[9]

He made it. Subsequently, he was to remake England, while, in the process, undoing hundreds of others, including, in the fullness of time, Anne herself.

Cromwell's immediate task was a difficult one. He had to square the circle of protecting the interests of his old master, Wolsey, on the one hand, and providing for his own future in the new world of a Boleyn ministry and Anne's likely marriage to the King, on the other. Unlike the too obviously self-interested Gardiner, he pulled the feat off brilliantly.

The trick, Cromwell realized, was to combine the appearance of loyalty with the reality of pragmatism. So no man was more conspicuously loyal to Wolsey; no man sued harder for him or was readier with comfort and good advice. All this won him golden opinions, since the theory of Tudor politics valued loyalty above all things, however treacherous the practice might be. But equally it was Cromwell who seems to have suggested that Wolsey give lavish bribes to those now in favour about the King: £100 a year to Norris (which was doubled by Wolsey); the reversion of an office with an augmented fee of £40 a year to Fitzwilliam; another £40 p.a. to Sir Henry Guildford; £20 p.a. to Russell, which once again Wolsey proposed increasing to £40 or even £50.[10]

The lion's share, however, of Wolsey's spoils went to Anne's brother, George, who extracted an annuity of £200 from Winchester and 200 marks (£133 6s 8d) from St Albans. Between them, these grants transformed George Boleyn's financial position. Before, he had been dependent on royal handouts; now he could plausibly maintain the dignity of his viscountcy. Even six years later, the two annuities amounted to seventy-five per cent of his total income.

The drafts of George Boleyn's grants survive. They are corrected by Cromwell, just as it was Cromwell who handled the delicate negotiations for the other handouts. Wolsey, of course, was the reservoir of gold. But it was Cromwell who opened the tap which gushed riches.

The result was a paradox. Wolsey had his wish and a phoenix rose from the ashes of his fortunes. But the phoenix was Cromwell, not Wolsey.[11]

Only Anne seems to have resisted Cromwell's blandishments and failed to join in the chorus of praise. For he was guaranteeing Wolsey's survival and even perhaps his ability to revive.

And that was not what she wanted at all.

But, for the moment, there was nothing she could do about it. On 11 February 1530 Wolsey agreed to the biggest bribe of all, when the title of York Place, which Henry and Anne had seized the previous autumn, was formally transferred to the King. The next day Wolsey was formally pardoned and restored to the archbishopric of York and on the 17th the deal was further ratified by the exchange of indentures between the King and the Cardinal. Winchester and St Albans were of course forfeit. But Wolsey got his pension of 1,000 marks; he also got £6,374 in cash, goods and livestock to enable him to resume living in something like the style to which he had become accustomed.[12]

It might have been much worse. And, save for Cromwell's efforts, it probably would have been.

On 5 April Wolsey set out from Richmond towards his archbishopric of York, which he had held for sixteen years but had not yet seen. This was not the only novelty. He who had been a by-word for luxury and soft living now wore a hair-shirt (at least occasionally). He devoted himself to his religious duties. He even washed the feet of the poor (all fifty-nine of them, one for each year of his life) on Maundy Thursday. There were other changes, too. He had always been lavish and generous in his hospitality. But now its purpose altered. Instead of entertaining kings and plenipotentiaries, he feasted his neighbours. And instead of riding roughshod over public opinion, he courted it – as only a professional courtier knew how. His tongue turned to honey and he became a peace-maker and reconciler.

But some things did not change. He started building again, as he tried to make his diocesan palaces (unlived in for decades) habitable. Above all, as he always had done, he longed for power. For twenty years it had been his element. He had lived it and breathed it. Like a drug it had energized him and like a drug he found he could not do without it.[13]

It was a fatal attraction.

Probably Wolsey's restoration had always been a forlorn hope. In theory, Henry could have done it at a stroke. In practice, even supposing he wanted it, he would have found it difficult to achieve. Anne and her family were against it; his Council was against it and an overwhelming majority in his Parliament was against it too. Indeed people who disagreed on everything else could at least agree on hating Wolsey. But it was the *means* that Wolsey chose to try to recover his position that finally undid him. For he changed tack on the Great Matter yet again.

The signal may well have come from Catherine herself. As early as December 1529, she had 'shown some pity for the Cardinal's fall'. This immediately led Chapuys to speculate on a grand *renversement d'alliances*. Wolsey would ally with Catherine. The former would regain power and the latter her husband. And the Boleyns would be dished, to the mutual advantage of Queen and Cardinal. At the time, Wolsey was too prostrate to have anything to do with the idea. But by the following summer he seems to have made the scheme his own.[14]

He began cautiously. As soon as he had arrived in his diocese at the end of April 1530, he put out feelers to Chapuys, vindicating his conduct and offering his services, such as they were, to Charles V. Chapuys's response had been non-committal but polite and designed to string Wolsey along. He did not have long to wait for the Cardinal to bite. In early June, Dr Agostino Agostini, Wolsey's Italian physician, who had carried the earlier messages, wrote to Chapuys again. The letters were obscure, deliberately so. But they seemed to hint that the Pope and Charles should co-ordinate their forces to intervene decisively in the Great Matter, the former with spiritual censures, the latter with an army. This would provoke a crisis which Henry had neither the power nor the will to resist. Anne would fall and Wolsey would be restored.

In his report home, Chapuys endorsed at least the broad outlines of the idea. 'It seems', he advised, 'as if your Majesty ought to have matters brought to a crisis at once.' A first step, he advised, would be for Rome to order Anne's removal from the Court.[15]

Charles agreed and instructed his ambassador in Rome to approach the Pope for the necessary Brief to Henry. Even in his remote exile, it seemed, Wolsey could reach far.

The fact, no doubt, was balm to his fractured ego. But it was also profoundly dangerous. It was not yet a crime, of course, to argue that Catherine's marriage was valid. It was equally permissible to advise her on the best means to protect her position. But Wolsey had gone far beyond this. He was advising foreign powers on the best tactics to use against his sovereign. He was trying to foment unrest in England. He was seeking to force his services on the King, with the threat and perhaps even the reality of violence. And, above all, he was aiming to coerce Henry into leaving Anne.

There was only one name for these acts: it was treason.

Wolsey of course was no fool. He was not a Buckingham, to blunder into treason. It is possible, on the other hand, that his burning sense of injustice destabilized him and blinded him to the reality of his actions. But it is much more likely that he acted with his eyes open. The key is his attack on Anne, which lay at the heart of all his schemes. For he had decided that she was *the* enemy. She was 'the night crow', who haunted Henry like an evil spirit, he told Cavendish. She 'called continually upon the King in his ear, with such a vehemency' that she was irresistible. And she called on him to destroy Wolsey.[16]

Wolsey had issued the challenge. Anne was not the woman to refuse to take it up.

It was a war to the death between them.

Nor had Wolsey limited himself to scheming with Chapuys. Complex as ever in his diplomacy, he also kept his channels open with the French. Indeed, before his departure for the north, he had been visited by the resident French ambassador, Giovanni Gioachino di Passano, sieur de Vaux, who was one of the many Italians in the service of Francis I. There were good reasons for De Vaux's visit. Wolsey had been the beneficiary of a generous pension from the French and had neglected to provide receipts for the last three payments. But to suspicious minds – and Wolsey seemed to be going out of his way to arouse suspicion – the question of the receipts could look like a cover for something more sinister.[17]

It was of course common knowledge that Wolsey was pulling every string at Court to return to favour. As early as May, indeed,

Cromwell passed on Henry's blunt warning that Wolsey should stop playing politics by trying to make bad blood between the King and the Duke of Norfolk. But these were domestic matters. Wolsey's foreign schemes, on the other hand, seem to have gone undetected till the late summer.[18]

The most likely spy-catcher is Anne's cousin, Sir Francis Bryan. He had played Wolsey's nemesis once already with his outspoken reports from Italy. Now he may have repeated the role by picking up rumours of the Cardinal's activities in France – hence the closure of the ports on his return to England at the beginning of September.[19]

Even then, Henry would not move precipitately against his former minister. Instead, a more careful watch was kept on his activities. The result confirmed his enemies' worst fears. 'Though I list to be blinded,' Norfolk told Wolsey's old servant, Sir Thomas Arundel, who was trying to press his master's suits at Court, 'I should blind no man here.' Arundel had claimed that Wolsey was quietly resigned to his fate. Nonsense, said the Duke, he was continuing to intrigue and call in favours. And to prove it he was even able to give the names of three men whom Wolsey had recently reminded of the benefits he had conferred on them and their families. 'All these messages are taken in the worst sense,' Arundel reported despairingly.[20]

That was in mid-October. At the end of the month more damning evidence still came to light. Letters were intercepted from Agostini addressed to De Vaux who was taking a sea-side holiday at Dover. When they were opened they were discovered to contain lines in cipher.[21]

Now surely Wolsey was finished.

But still Henry hesitated and the 'night crow' had to use all her 'vehemency'. Anne, Chapuys heard, 'has wept and wailed, regretting her lost time and honour, and threatening the King that she would go away and leave him'. Henry, terrified at this ultimatum (which, curiously, was the mirror image of Wolsey's own scheme to engineer Anne's judicial separation from the King), had pleaded with tears in his eyes. But Anne would not be pacified. 'Nothing would satisfy the Lady short of the Cardinal's arrest,' Chapuys reported.[22]

On 1 November, about noon, Walter Walsh, Groom of the Privy Chamber, left Court with a commission for himself and the Earl of Northumberland to arrest the Cardinal. At that moment, according to Cavendish, Wolsey was sitting down to dinner at Cawood Castle, seven miles outside York. He kept his accustomed state. His massive silver archiepiscopal cross was propped up in the corner against the wall hangings. Dining with him, but separated, according to etiquette, by the length of the table, were some of his senior servants, including Agostini. As Agostini rose at the end of the meal his 'boisterous' (that is, stiff-textured) gown of black velvet caught on the cross. It fell along the hangings. In its path, unfortunately, knelt one of Wolsey's chaplains. The cross struck him on the head and drew blood.

The company looked on, appalled. '*Malum omen* [an evil omen],' murmured Wolsey.[23]

Four days later, Walsh and the Earl of Northumberland entered Cawood. Northumberland, of course, was none other than Henry Percy, Wolsey's former ward and Anne's former suitor, who had inherited his father's title.

Northumberland, 'trembling' and speaking 'with a very faint and soft voice', said 'I arrest you of High Treason.' Wolsey, in return, humiliated him for one last time by denying his authority and surrendering instead to Walsh, as one of the King's Privy Chamber. 'For the worst person there', he said, 'is a sufficient warrant to arrest the greatest peer of this realm.' He should have known, because it was he who had sent Compton, the head of the Privy Chamber, to arrest Buckingham.[24]

Meanwhile, as the Cardinal and the Earl were having their altercation, Walsh, hooded and disguised like any modern secret police-man, had arrested Agostini. 'Go in, thou traitor', Cavendish heard him exclaim, 'or I shall make thee.' Hastily, Cavendish opened the door, and Walsh thrust Agostini violently into the room. His rough usage continued, as the next day he was sent off to London with an escort and his legs tied under his horse. This, on a journey of two hundred and fifty miles, cannot have been pleasant.[25]

They were in no such hurry with Wolsey. Instead, he was taken, by easy stages, to Sheffield Park, the Earl of Shrewsbury's house, where he remained under honourable house arrest for almost a fortnight.

This curious hiatus makes it clear that there were two stages to Wolsey's fall. The first, his arrest on 4 November, was a pre-emptive strike. Three days later, on the 7th, he had planned to enter York in state, to be installed as Archbishop and to meet his clergy of the Northern Province in Convocation. This was the ideal moment, it was feared, for Wolsey to rise up like another Becket against his King. He could have ordered Henry to submit himself to Rome and to separate himself from Anne. And he could have excommunicated him in the event of his refusal. In view of his known dealings abroad, the risk was too great. The installation had to be aborted.[26]

This was achieved by his arrest at Cawood. Meanwhile, Agostini's interrogation would reveal the extent of Wolsey's schemes. He seems to have arrived in London between the 10th and the 13th. Two hundred and fifty miles tied to the back of a horse had been duress enough and he confessed freely and without further torture. There was no need even to send him to the Tower.[27]

His confession has disappeared. But, to judge from reports of it, it seems to have been oddly skewed. Chapuys deduced that 'he had denied having any understanding or acquaintance with me'. On the other hand (Henry informed Bryan in France) Agostini *had* made much of a letter which Wolsey had instructed him to write to De Vaux. In it Wolsey is supposed to have suggested that the French should first provoke England into war with the Emperor and then turn on their ally. The scheme is fantastic and improbable. But, fantastic or not, Agostini said he was so appalled by it that he failed to deliver the letter. Conveniently, however, he remembered the incriminating paragraph word for word.[28]

Now why on earth should Agostini deny a set of contacts which had certainly happened, and 'confess' instead to a scheme which was an implausible fiction?

Actually, the mystery is easily solved. What we know is not what Agostini said but what the Council wanted it to be thought that he had said. He *had*, I strongly suspect, confessed to his contacts with Chapuys. It would have been mad to do otherwise. But equally, the last thing that the English wanted was a diplomatic incident with Charles V, in which an accusation against his ambassador might be the last straw in provoking the Emperor into war with England. Hence the concocted charge of trying to communicate with De Vaux. This established Wolsey's attempt to provoke foreign intervention, which was essential to a convincing charge of treason. But, as relations with France were good and as the attempt was supposed to have been abortive, it avoided any risk of diplomatic unpleasantness.

There is a sort of poetic justice here. In his time, Wolsey had fabricated more than his share of lies, white and black. It was only fair perhaps that he should be condemned by an untruth that was impudent even by his standards.

But, once again, Wolsey was to cheat his fate. Toward the end of his stay at Sheffield Park he was finishing his dinner with a dish of baked 'wardens' or pears. Suddenly, Cavendish noticed that he looked very ill. He changed colour and had a violent fit of colic. A prescription from his apothecary (carefully tested for poison) enabled him to 'break wind upward'. But the relief was only temporary. Diarrhoea set in and became more acute. By the time Sir William Kingston, the Lieutenant of the Tower, arrived on 22 November 1530 with a detachment of the Guard to conduct him to the Tower, Wolsey was already very weak. He managed to struggle as far as Leicester, where he died on the 29th.[29]

His last words did not mention Anne by name. But, since they warned Henry in apocalyptic terms against his Divorce and the threat of Lutheranism, she was their real target. Prudently, those who witnessed what he said conspired to suppress it – 'for in any wise', Kingston advised Cavendish, 'the [Council] would not hear of it'.[30]

'Such at length', the Milanese ambassador reported, 'was the end of the man who boasted that he ruled the whole world.'[31]

Anne, however, was never his willing subject and she was instrumental in destroying him at last. One great threat to her marriage had gone. But there still remained Queen Catherine. She would be next.

It is not clear which side broke the curious, three-year long truce between Anne and Catherine. But there can be no doubt as to the winner.

57. Attacking Catherine

Back in June 1530 Anne had set herself to cut one of the few, lingering threads of domesticity which still bound Henry to Catherine. Thanks to her mother's careful training, Catherine was (as we have seen) an excellent needlewoman. And, despite all that had happened, she and her ladies continued to make Henry's shirts. Henry – fond, like most men, of having his cake and eating it – saw nothing wrong with the arrangement. Anne did, and she intervened decisively to stop it.

As usual, Henry had sent some linen to the Queen with a request to have it made into shirts. Anne's response was to throw a very public scene and blame the messenger. According to Chapuys, she 'sent for the person who had taken the cloth – one of the Principal Gentlemen of the Privy Chamber – and . . . abused [him] in the King's very presence'.[1]

But Henry, of course, still needed his shirts. At first, it seems as though Anne intended to step into Catherine's shoes and wield the needle herself. That at least would be a plausible interpretation of the large delivery to Anne in September of linen cloth for which Henry paid 'the wife of the Dove' the sum of £10. But, predictably perhaps, sewing proved not to be Anne's forte. Maybe Henry was dissatisfied with the quality of her work. Maybe Anne simply gave up. At all events a professional solution was found and, by November, Mrs William Armerer, the wife of one of the King's footmen, and a practised seamstress, had stepped into the breach. Hitherto, she had made shirts for Henry's dependants, including the King's boy attendants, Mark Smeaton, his favourite musician, and his Fool. Now she started to make them (out of far finer fabric and at much greater cost) for the King himself.[2]

But Catherine also rebelled at the curious apartheid of her existence. She became convinced (on no very good grounds) that solely Anne stood between her and reunion with Henry. Only let Anne be forced from his side for a few months, even for a few weeks, and her husband would be hers again.

So, rather as Wolsey had done, she went on the offensive against Anne. And Anne, once more, took up the challenge – with relish and increasing confidence of victory.

The occasion for Catherine's broadside was Christmas Eve, 1530. Christmas, notoriously, is a time for family quarrels and the season began miserably enough with Catherine riding her moral high horse. Not only, she told Henry, was his conduct doing her a grave personal wrong, he was also setting a scandalous example by keeping Anne Boleyn in his company.

This was, as far as I can judge, the first time that Catherine had referred directly to Anne in her exchanges with Henry. And it immediately put her on the defensive. For Henry in turn was able to assume the moral high ground. She was altogether mistaken, he replied, in her insinuations about Anne. He was not living in sin with her and there was nothing wrong in their relations. True, he kept her company. But that was only to learn her character as he had made up his mind to marry her. And marry her he would, he added triumphantly, whatever Catherine or the Pope might say.[3]

Catherine, for once, was bested in a quarrel with Henry.

Anne followed up Henry's little victory, when, later in the holiday season, she said 'to one of the Queen's ladies-in-waiting that she wished all the Spaniards were at the bottom of the sea'. Scandalized, the lady-in-waiting replied that Anne 'should not for the sake of the Queen's honour express such sentiments'. But Anne was not to be abashed. 'She cared not', she replied, 'for the Queen or any of her family, and that she would rather see her hanged than have to confess that she was her Queen and mistress.'[4]

This was a declaration of open war.

Catherine responded in kind and her language about Anne took on the shrewish vehemence of the wronged wife throughout the ages. Anne was that 'woman [Henry] has under his roof'. And she was equally pointed about her husband. His conduct, she wrote to her nephew Charles V, was flagrant and displayed 'not the least particle of shame'.[5]

But, as so often in the Great Matter, it was events abroad that put the final spark to the tinder.

Here it is important to be clear about Henry's developing strategy. From the moment of the failure of the Blackfriars Trial, it had been taken for granted that an English verdict on the Divorce would somehow have to be sanctioned by Parliament. There was no mystery about this, as some modern historians like to claim. On the contrary, it was clear to supporters and opponents alike. This is why Catherine trembled as the date of each session of the Reformation Parliament approached, and why she breathed a sigh of relief as it was further prorogued. For Henry, these successive prorogations were infuriating but necessary as he did not dare to submit the Great Matter to Parliament unless he could be sure in advance that it would agree to it. He had been repulsed once by Rome. To court the same fate in his own kingdom would probably be fatal – certainly to his chance of remarriage; probably also to his hold on the throne.

So the King had to play a waiting game, as arguments were mustered, opponents discreetly muzzled, and neutrals massaged. But the great threat to this tactic was sudden action from the Pope. Papal excommunication of Henry, or an order to separate from Anne, could have brought down Henry's house of cards. Fear that Wolsey would invoke such ecclesiastical censures against Henry was the immediate occasion for Wolsey's arrest in November 1530. It also accounts for the sudden move against Catherine in the summer of 1531.

The issue was brought to a head by the failure of a French mission to get Pope Clement to agree to a formal suspension of the process in Rome. The Pope's letters instructing Nuncio De Burgo to inform Henry of his decision arrived in London on 30 May. Knowing the likely reaction from the King, De Burgo hesitated about asking for an audience. But Chapuys stiffened his resolution and, 'at my persuasion', the ambassador reported, the Nuncio went to the Court at Greenwich the following day.

Henry's reaction was curiously mixed. His own ambassadors had already told him of the substance of his message, he coolly informed De Burgo. Then he launched into his now accustomed abuse of Rome: 'Even if His Holiness should do his worst by excommunicating me . . . I shall not mind it', he boasted, 'for I care not a fig for all his excommunications. Let him follow his own at Rome, I will do here what I think best.' But then, mercurial as ever, he conceded Clement's essential goodwill. 'I take the Pope upon the whole to be a worthy man,' he said, 'but ever since the last wars he has been so awfully afraid of the Emperor that he dares not act against his wishes.'[6]

But if he spared the Nuncio, he made up for it by his subsequent treatment of Catherine. His wife, he now decided, was his opponents' weakest point. She was in his power and could be browbeaten or worse. This of course had always been true. But hitherto Henry had been restrained by caution or even the remains of his former tenderness. Time had diminished that. He had also been provoked by Catherine's increased stridency. For if her actions matched her words she was preparing to invoke the extreme measures against her husband which so far she had carefully avoided. And, last but not least, there was now Anne's open, passionate hostility towards the Queen and her supporters.

It was an explosive mixture.

As usual, Catherine's sympathizers in Henry's Council leaked his plans in advance, and the Queen was warned that she would be put under pressure to agree to a suspension of the case in Rome. She prepared herself by hearing several masses of the Holy Ghost, to inspire her and stiffen her resolve. Then, later that day, 'towards 8 or 9 o'clock at night, just as the Queen was going to bed', the promised delegation of the Council arrived and demanded audience.

The delegation was about thirty strong and was led by the senior members of the peerage. It was also reinforced by the leading legal experts on the Divorce. Clearly, it was designed to impress, even to overawe, by its size and weight. Predictably, it failed. Each councillor in turn went into bat with Catherine and each, if we believe Chapuys, was smartly bowled out. She was especially dismissive with the clergy. She told Lee that he spoke 'more for the sake of flattering the King than of adhering to the truth'. And she advised Sampson, Dean of the Chapel Royal, to spare his breath with her and go and argue the case in Rome, where it belonged!

Finally, having successfully taken on all-comers, Catherine rubbed salt in the wound by putting on a pretty display of feminine pathos. Why so powerful a delegation? she asked. 'What could have prevailed on them thus to assemble and come and surprise her, a poor woman without friends or counsel?'

The delegation retired, doubly defeated by Catherine's intelligence and her guile.[7]

But what was worse from Henry's point of view was the reaction of several members of his own Council. Instead of outrage, they seemed to enjoy the discomfiture of their colleagues at the hands of the Queen. And they scarcely bothered to conceal the fact.

Controller Guildford was most outspoken. 'It would be a very good thing', he said to no one in particular, 'if all the doctors who had been the inventors and abettors of the plan [for the Divorce] could be tied together in a cart and sent to Rome.' The Earl of Shrewsbury, who was Lord Steward of the Household and the holder of one of the oldest and richest earldoms, used politer language, but, for those who understood his words, actually threatened resistance. They, he reminded his colleagues, represented 'all the nobility of the Kingdom'. This was the dangerous doctrine of aristocratic collegiality which had scotched the ambitions of many medieval kings. Was it now to be invoked against Henry?

But probably most hurtful to Henry was the reaction of the Duke of Suffolk. Brandon was Henry's brother-in-law and his closest and oldest friend. But he, too, sided with Catherine. The Queen, Suffolk told Henry, 'was ready to obey him in all things, but that she owed obedience to two persons first'. And who were they, the King snapped, thinking that Suffolk meant that his wife put her allegiance to the Pope and the Emperor above her duty to him as her husband. His reaction laid him open and Suffolk delivered a magnificent rebuke. 'God was the first,' he said, 'the second was her soul and conscience.'

If Suffolk had turned against Henry, who would be for him?

Normally, Henry reacted to such open displays of defiance by losing his temper. This time, he kept it. It was a much more dangerous response. He had foreseen Catherine's intransigence, he said. 'It is now necessary', he added, 'to provide for the whole affair by other means.' Then, according to Chapuys's report, 'he remained for some time thoughtful'.

The 'other means', and the threat implicit in the words, were quick to materialize. And it was Anne who struck the first blow.

Her victim was Guildford. As soon as she heard of his remarks, she 'threatened him most furiously, saying that when she becomes Queen, she will have him punished and deprived of office'. Guildford replied that he would spare her the trouble 'for he himself will be the first to resign his post'. He then went straight to the King; told him what had happened; and surrendered his staff of office into Henry's hands on a transparently false plea of ill-health. Twice Henry refused his resignation and handed back the white staff, saying that 'he ought not to mind women's talk'. But Guildford was adamant and insisted on returning home to Kent.[8]

Like Suffolk, Guildford was one of Henry's oldest adherents, with a connexion going back to the royal nursery, where Guildford's mother,

Lady Joan, was one of the favourite attendants of the young Prince and his favourite sister, Mary.

Who else would Henry have to give up for Anne's sake? The answer, it quickly became apparent, was Catherine herself.

A few days after the extraordinary scenes at Greenwich, Henry and Anne, with the Queen still in tow, left for Hampton Court. They rested for a day at York Place and then continued to their destination upriver via Putney. On about 20 June, Chapuys sent a messenger to Hampton Court to ask for an audience. But the messenger returned empty-handed, with the report that Henry 'was already gone to Windsor and other places, to amuse himself and pass away the time, accompanied only by the Lady and the Master of the Horse [Carew] and two more'. It is, in fact, very difficult to establish Henry's precise movements at this time. Despite Chapuys's assertion, the King does seem to have been primarily based at Hampton Court. But he was in London for flying visits on the 23rd and the 29th; at Hanworth Park, four miles to the west of Hampton Court, on the 28th; and at Windsor on the 12th and 13th and again on 16th. The King's overnight visit to the Castle on the 12–13th was reported by no less an observer than Thomas Cranmer, who then formed part of the royal entourage at Hampton Court. 'The King and my Lady Anne', he informed Wiltshire on 13 June, 'rode yesterday to Windsor, and this night they be looked for again at Hampton Court'. 'God be their guide', he added piously. This pattern of restless movement was to continue for another six weeks. So was Henry's abandonment of Catherine.[9]

At first, Catherine seems to have noticed nothing very out of the ordinary about her errant husband's behaviour. But by 17 July she was thoroughly alarmed, and, as usual, informed Chapuys of her fears. The Queen, the ambassador reported, 'is very much distressed and in great tribulation'. Her reasons seemed compelling to him too. 'The King himself, the Lady and her adherents', he informed the Emperor, 'now speak out with much greater assurance than before.' Anne, he continued, 'declares that her marriage to the King will take place in three or four months at the latest'. She was also anticipating the fact by assuming more and more of her future royal state. 'During the last few days, [she has] appointed an Almoner, besides several other officers about her person.' But, worst of all, she had succeeded in excluding Catherine from her place at the King's side on formal occasions and even informal ones. 'She always accompanies the King at his hunting parties, without any female attendants of her own, whilst the Queen herself, who used formerly to follow him on such expeditions, has been ordered to remain at Windsor.'[10]

Obviously, something was going on. But what? The chronicler Edward Hall, writing at the end of Henry's reign, was in no doubt.

> The King after Whitsuntide [28 May] and the Queen removed
> to Windsor, and there continued till the 14th day of July, on
> which day the King removed to Woodstock and left her at
> Windsor. And after this day the King and she never saw together.

And where Hall led, modern historians have been happy to follow like sheep. But, also like sheep, they have gone astray. For Hall's account, with its picture of Henry, firm and resolute, taking a clear-cut decision to break with his wife, cannot be right.[11]

This was pointed out almost two centuries ago, by the great Regency antiquary, Sir Nicholas Harris Nicolas. But even Nicolas did not fully elucidate what happened. For events were more tangled and Henry's behaviour more messy and confused than even he suspected.[12]

The uneasy family party, in which, to quote another famously wronged royal wife, there were three in the marriage, in fact arrived at Windsor (after another brief visit to York Place) on 7 July. On the 14th, Henry indeed left Windsor. But instead of starting out boldly to distant Woodstock, he shifted only a short way to Chertsey Abbey, a mere seven miles to the east of Windsor. And there he and Anne remained for at least ten days, crossing and recrossing the river by the ferries at Hampton Court and Dachet, and hunting in the neighbouring parks which clustered round the great forest of Windsor: they were at Mote Park on the 17th, at Ditton Park near Windsor on the 19th and at Byfleet Park on the 22nd.

Only on the 26th did Henry make a more decisive move. But it was to the *south* – that is, in the opposite direction to Woodstock. He was at Guildford on the 29th, at Farnham on the 31st, and on 4 August reached The Vyne, near Basingstoke in Hampshire where he stayed for three days. There was good sport round about, and Henry and Anne hunted in Wolmer Forest on the 2nd, in Beaurepaire Park on the 5th and in Basing Park on the 6th. But they had other, human quarry as well.[13]

This had immediately been realized by Catherine, who saw events with the extra clarity of bitterness and disillusionment. 'She fancies', Chapuys reported, 'that his object in taking the Lady with him to such hunting parties is that he may accustom the lords and governors of the counties and districts he traverses on such occasions to see her with him, and that he may the better win them over to his party when Parliament meets again.'[14]

The targets of this charm-offensive are not far to seek. The Vyne was the seat of William, Lord Sandys, KG. He had been Lord Chamberlain of the Household since 1526 and he had recently added a noble long gallery to his house. It was decorated in the latest style with panelling carved with a rich assortment of arms and badges. The arms and badges included Henry's and Catherine's, as well as Sandys's own and those of his network of friends, colleagues and relations. There were Wolsey's cardinal's hat and his cipher, 'TW'; the peacock badge of Thomas Manners, Earl of Rutland; the shield of Cuthbert Tunstall, as Bishop of London; and the mitred coat-of-arms of William Warham, Archbishop of Canterbury.

These men were a broad cross-section of the political establishment of the 1520s – an establishment which, even as Henry visited The Vyne, was being rent apart by the Great Matter. Wolsey, so far, was its greatest victim, while in contrast Rutland had got his earldom at the same time as Anne's father, and was to be a reliable supporter. On the other hand, Tunstall's present bishopric of Durham had been fleeced for the Boleyns' benefit, while Warham's cautious obstinacy was emerging as a crucial obstacle to Henry's marriage to Anne.

Which side – bearing in mind the divergence among his friends and colleagues – would Sandys join? He was a sincere conservative in religion. Yet somehow he was kept on-side through all the traumas of Anne's rise. It is safe to assume that Henry's visit to The Vyne played its part in this. It might even have been the key.

Equally important was Sir William Paulet whose arms also appear in the panelling. He was Sandys's friend and neighbour at nearby Basing. And he was similarly conservative. Yet he too remained loyal and was even promoted when Guildford, who had finally agreed to remain in office, died the following May. Paulet now became Controller as well as retaining his existing office of Master of the Wards. Henry and Anne's visit to him at Basing on 6 August must once again have been intended to cement a relationship that otherwise threatened to become shaky.[15]

And evidently it worked.

It was while he and Anne were en route to The Vyne that Henry received a message from Catherine. It had always been the custom of Henry and Catherine, when they were apart, to communicate at least once every three days by means of a messenger and a 'countersign' or token. Invoking this old practice, Catherine sent to Henry 'to inquire about his health, and to signify the regret she had experienced at not having been able to see him before his departure for the country'. Even if she could not accompany him, would he not at least give her the consolation of bidding him farewell? She was brutally repulsed for her pains. 'He cared not for her adieux', Henry raged, 'he had no wish to offer her the consolation of which she spoke or any other.' She had humiliated him in front of the world. He only wanted rid of her.

Catherine replied with proper, wifely submission, though without conceding anything of her position. Henry did not deign to answer in person but sent a formal letter from the Council instead. This was the first time a letter had failed to address Catherine as Queen.

Neither Catherine nor Chapuys doubted for a moment who was responsible. 'If the Lady's authority and the good reasons [this was meant ironically, of course] . . . alleged [in the letter] be taken into consideration, [it] must have been decreed by her.'

Catherine was plunged into real despair. Chapuys tried to rouse her by a wildly optimistic reading of events. But her only effective consolation was the company of her daughter Mary. Banished by their husband and father, the two decided to make the best of things by having a holiday. 'They will pass their time', Chapuys reported, 'in sport and visiting the royal seats round Windsor.'[16]

But their pleasure was cut brutally short.

By the first week in August, after consolidating their hold on the conservative courtiers and gentry of north Hampshire, Henry and Anne were ready to return to Windsor. And the last person they wished to find there was Catherine, with Mary clinging to her like Niobe 'all tears'. For weeks Anne, like the goddess of the chase, had pursued her rival. She bullied Henry; she wheedled; she threatened; and, most devastatingly, she cried. Her arrows pierced his heart and hardened his judgement. It was how she had destroyed Wolsey. Now she would remove Catherine.

At last Henry had screwed himself up to deliver the final blow. 'The King', Chapuys reported, 'on the plea of wishing to hunt in the environs of Windsor, sent orders for his Queen to remove to The More, a manor close to the Abbey of St Albans, and for the Princess Mary to go to Richmond.' It was the final cruelty. Not only had Henry separated himself from Catherine, he was also separating Catherine from Mary. Mother and daughter never saw each other again.

How to interpret this brutality? The Court saw it as a portent. 'No doubt is entertained here', Chapuys reported, 'that the King is now resolutely intent upon obtaining his Divorce.' The ambassador, however, persisted in his own opinion that Henry's actions were a 'mere artifice' to bully Catherine into agreeing to a repatriation of the trial of the Great Matter once more to England. But to that, he predicted, she would never consent, however extreme the pressure that might be applied.[17]

Here at least he proved an accurate prophet.

By a curious coincidence, just as these fissures were taking place in the royal family, a Venetian tourist decided to pay a flying visit to England from Flanders. He was Mario Savorgano, the son of Girolamo, a Venetian commander and wealthy aristocrat. His itinerary is strikingly modern, with day-visits to Whitehall, Hampton Court and Windsor. But, unlike most modern tourists, he was well enough connected to have the entrée at Court. He caught up with Henry on 4 August, while the King was hunting in Odiham Park, mid-way between Farnham and The Vyne. 'I went to a park', he reported, 'some thirty miles from London where the King was, taking his pleasure in a small hunting lodge, built solely for the chase, in the midst of the forest . . . He embraced me joyously, and then went out to hunt with from 40 to 50 horsemen.'

Savorgano then expatiated on Henry's physical and mental qualities. He would be perfect indeed, he concluded, were he not wishing to divorce his wife. But this 'detracts greatly from his merits, as there is now living with him a young woman of noble birth, though many say of bad character, whose will is law to him, and he is expected to marry her'.

The day after this encounter with Henry and perhaps with Anne, Savorgano returned to Windsor and continued to The More, 'where the Queen resides'.

> In the morning [he reported] we saw her Majesty dine; she had some 30 maids of honour standing round the table, and about 50 persons who performed its service. Her Court consists of about 200 persons, but she is not so much visited as heretofore, on account of the King. Her Majesty is not of tall stature, rather small. If not handsome, she is not ugly; she is somewhat stout, and has always a smile on her face.

Still, in other words, Catherine enjoyed the dignity and state of Queen and still, as her constant smile shows, she was able to act the part, whatever she was feeling or whatever Henry or Anne could do.

Determined to complete the tally, late that same afternoon Savorgano presented himself at Richmond and 'asked the *maggiordomo* [probably the Gentleman Usher] for permission to see [Mary]'. 'He', Savorgano continued, 'spoke to the Chamberlain, and then to the Governess [Lady Salisbury] and they made us wait.' He filled in the interval by inspecting the palace. Then he was ushered into the Presence Chamber to await Mary's entrance. 'The Princess came forth, accompanied by a noble lady, advanced in years, who is her Governess, and by six maids of honour.' 'We kissed her hand', he reported excitedly, 'and she asked us how long we had been in England, and if we had seen their Majesties, her father and mother, and what we thought of the country.' Then she turned to her attendants and withdrew into her Chamber.

The audience was over and Savorgano was left only with the impression the Princess had made. It was very favourable. She was short but pretty and well proportioned 'with a very beautiful complexion'. She spoke several languages fluently and was very musical. In short, he concluded, 'she combines every accomplishment'.[18]

This is Mary just before the strains of her parents' divorce had damaged her character and spoiled her looks.

For Anne would give neither Mary nor her mother a moment of peace. It was not sheer vindictiveness, though there was an element of that. Instead Anne had convinced herself that Catherine's place was rightly hers. As for Mary, she was a bastard. And in any case, Mary would soon be brushed aside by the fine son who would crown Anne's own union with Henry.

That was a goal worth fighting for. Anne was good at fighting. And she had only just begun with Catherine and Mary.

58. Preliminaries to marriage

In the summer of 1531, the vicar of Kirk Holland, in Derbyshire, told his parishioners some extraordinary news: the King was about to marry another wife. And 'one Mr Cromwell penned certain matters in the Parliament House, which no man gainsaid'. One of his hearers, the vicar said, 'knew the gentlewoman, and that her father's name was Sir Thomas Boleyn'.[1]

This seems to be the first time that Thomas Cromwell and Anne Boleyn were linked in the public consciousness. Quite why Cromwell's activities in the brief and unremarkable parliamentary session of 1531 should attract such attention is unclear. Most likely, in fact, the vicar was confusing events in Parliament with those in Convocation. The confusion was easily made, since the place of meeting of Convocation had been shifted from the customary St Paul's to the Chapter House of Westminster Abbey. The Commons met in the nearby Refectory of the Abbey and the Lords in the Painted Chamber in the adjacent palace. It was only a few steps from the one assembly to the other, and the journey was frequently made as the intense negotiations over the Submission of the Clergy took place.[2]

In these negotiations, Cromwell, MP for Taunton and newly appointed King's Councillor, played a leading part. He came into the Chapter House on the morning of Friday, 10 February 1531 and had a secret conference with Archbishop Warham. The next day, Convocation acquiesced in silence to the King's new title of 'Supreme Head of the Church, in so far as the Law of Christ allows'.[3]

Anne, as we have seen, greeted the news with as much joy 'as if she had actually gained Paradise'. And was Cromwell the man whom she credited with unlocking the heavenly gates? And could he pull off the trick once more – this time to make her Henry's wife and Queen at last? It seemed as though he could.

But in spite of Cromwell's already acquired reputation as a Parliamentary Pickford, who carried everything, the next session, which opened on 15 January 1532, got off to a surprisingly shaky start. Almost a month was spent in acrimonious and inconclusive discussion about the King's feudal rights. Then, in the second week of February, Norfolk convened an informal meeting of the leading members of both Houses to consider an important new proposal. 'Many learned doctors', he reported, 'had concluded that all matrimonial causes belonged to the temporal, not to the ecclesiastical jurisdiction.' Were the parliamentary opinion-formers prepared to support the King's prerogative in this matter?[4]

The issue of the Church's jurisdiction in matrimony had already been aired in public by the distinguished lawyer, Christopher St German. In a series of books, the first of which was published in 1528, he argued for limiting canon law narrowly to matters of Faith and leaving questions of property (like wills and marriages) to the common law.[5]

Magpie-like as ever, Henry's councillors were seeing if Parliament would be prepared to accept St German's arguments – which would, in turn, open the way to a direct, parliamentary solution of the Great Matter.

In fact, though much has been made of St German by some modern historians, his ideas fell at the first fence. 'The first to answer [Norfolk]', Chapuys reported, 'was Lord Darcy, who said that his property and his person were entirely at the King's disposal, but that from what he had read and heard he believed that all matrimonial matters were spiritual and fell under ecclesiastical jurisdiction.' The majority of the meeting followed Darcy's lead, 'to the Duke's great disappointment and annoyance'.[6]

Another scheme, Chapuys heard, was floated by Anne's father, Thomas Boleyn, now the Earl of Wiltshire. Since Archbishop Warham was immovable on the subject of the Divorce, Wiltshire proposed the abolition of archiepiscopal authority over the Church and its transfer instead to the King. Anne, with her Lutheran sympathies, was supposed to have been enthusiastic about the idea. But it too disappeared without trace into that box marked 'too radical by half'.[7]

For Parliament, it became clear, was no more enamoured of Henry's new claims over the Church than any other reasonably representative group of his subjects. This proved true even in the contentious area of clerical taxation.

Annates or First Fruits was the fee, amounting to one year's income, which a new bishop was required to pay to Rome for the Bulls ratifying his appointment. The burden was considerable and appointees had to mortgage themselves to the hilt to pay it – with disastrous consequences to their families and friends if they died before they had been in post long enough to liquidate the debt. In view of this, it might be thought that the higher clergy would have rushed to welcome a government-sponsored Bill to abolish Annates. But the opposite was the case. The Council's motive, to put financial pressure on the Pope to agree to the Divorce, was too transparent, and the measure was fought bitterly at every stage. Indeed, the Act of Annates passed into law only through the King's heavy-handed personal intervention in both Houses. The government also made an important concession. The Act as passed was conditional, and it would only be put into practice, the Duke of Norfolk assured the English ambassadors in Rome, if the Pope continued to refuse Henry his Divorce.[8]

This was as far as Parliament would go by way of innovation. And for Anne it was nowhere near far enough.

It was time instead to return to the old, tried and tested tunes of anti-clericalism. These had proved a hit in the first session of the Reformation Parliament, even with convinced religious conservatives, like Lord Darcy or committed supporters of Catherine of Aragon, like Sir Henry Guildford. Now Anne and Cromwell, her new right hand man, co-operated to stage a revival.

From the beginning the mood in Parliament was favourable. According to the chronicler Hall, who as MP for Much Wenlock was an eye-witness of proceedings in the Lower House, 'the cruelty of the ordinaries [bishops]' ranked high among the Commons' initial grievances. Lay grumbles about ecclesiastical power were of course nothing new. But what gave them a special edge was the clamp-down on heresy which had followed Wolsey's fall. Spurred on by Lord Chancellor More, the bishops had gone on the offensive against heterodox opinion. And no one was spared. Anne's favourite preacher, Latimer, was arraigned on a heresy charge in the Convocation which met alongside Parliament. And the merchant William Tracy, the father of Cromwell's old friend and fellow MP Richard, was posthumously condemned as a heretic for making a will which was rude about clerical pretensions.[9]

All this meant that tensions between the clergy and the laity were already dangerously high when, a fortnight after the start of the session, they were deliberately inflamed by a gesture at Court. For Simon Fish's brilliantly subversive pamphlet, *The Supplication of Beggars*, which had opened the way to the first anticlerical wave of autumn 1529, was given a new lease of life. The fact has been obscured by the carelessness of many historians about detail. The text of *The Supplication* printed by Foxe begins with the note:

> A certain libel or book, entitled *The Supplication of Beggars*, thrown and scattered at the Procession in Westminster, on Candlemas day, before King Henry VIII, for him to read and peruse.

This, many have assumed, meant that Fish's pamphlet was distributed at Court on 2 February 1529, the Feast of the Purification of the Blessed Virgin Mary, which was known as Candlemas on account of the elaborately decorated candles which were offered up at the altar by the faithful, led by the King himself. But this date is impossible, since on 2 February 1529 Henry was not at Westminster but Greenwich. Nor did he have a palace in Westminster either. This lack was supplied, as we have seen, by his seizure of York Place from the fallen Wolsey in the autumn of 1529. Henry spent Candlemas at York Place in 1530, 1531 and 1532. Of these dates, 1532 is the most probable for the 'throwing and scattering' of the pamphlet in the procession before the King. And it is likely, too, that Anne, who had first brought Fish's work to Henry's attention, had a hand in its dramatic re-entry on to the public stage.[10]

Meanwhile, in Parliament, Cromwell was engineering his own, parallel reprise. Back in 1529, the Commons had begun to codify their anticlerical grievances into a series of petitions. The petitions seem not to have been submitted to the King before they were quietly allowed to lapse as part of Henry's scheme to call off the parliamentary attack on Wolsey. But Cromwell, always good with paper, seems to have kept copies – just in case they came in useful. And come in useful they did in 1532.[11]

The papers were reworked into a single, omnibus petition. It was retitled, in a deliberate, provocative echo of Fish's pamphlet, *The*

Supplication against the Ordinaries. And, in a series of carefully co-ordinated moves, it was rewritten and reused to force Convocation into a complete surrender of its legislative independence to Henry. All existing canons were to be submitted to him for approval; all future ones would require his consent. The surrender took place on 15 May 1532, when Convocation also acknowledged Henry as Supreme Head of the English Church, now without reservation. Parliament itself had been prorogued on the 14th and, on the 16th, Lord Chancellor More resigned. He had lost the behind-the-scenes battle for the King's mind.[12]

Henceforward, Henry's 'good servant' would be forced into an increasingly public struggle with the King himself. It could end in only one way.

The other great loser from the 1532 session was Gardiner. In the autumn of 1531 he had been given the choicest of Wolsey's benefices, the bishopric of Winchester, which was the richest see in England. And as late as January 1532, shortly before he was recalled from a brief Embassy to France, Henry (according to Cromwell) had complained of his absence as 'the lack of my right hand'.[13]

But the hand was to offend Henry, for, in the debates on *The Supplication*, Gardiner immediately took a high line in defence of the privileges and independence of the Church. The boy from Bury St Edmunds had not climbed to the top of the greasy pole to see it cut from beneath him. But, for once, he miscalculated.

The King, Chapuys reported on 13 May, 'is very angry, especially with the Chancellor [More] and the Bishop of Winchester'. Gardiner, however, had made a more dangerous enemy still. He had been one of Anne's earliest and most effective partisans in the Great Matter. But, as the Boleyns' anticlerical and even heretical policies became clear, his attitude changed. By the time of the Council's confrontation with Catherine in June 1531 he was showing, according to Chapuys, some sympathy with the Queen's position. In return, 'the Lady [now] strongly suspects and dislikes him'. Anne's suspicions were confirmed by his behaviour in Convocation and she became openly hostile.[14]

Henry, as usual, softened first. But Anne could be won over only by a valuable sacrifice. In 1530 Gardiner, then the King's newly fledged Secretary, had acquired the use of the royal manor of Hanworth. It was an up-to-date building, extensively remodelled by Henry VII; it had a fine park and gardens and it was very convenient for Hampton Court. It was, in short, good enough for Anne and certainly too good for one of Anne's enemies. So in June 1532 Gardiner, as a precondition for his forgiveness, was required to surrender his interest to the King. Henry promptly regranted Hanworth to Anne, and rebuilt it and refurbished it as her own country seat. That it had been prised from Gardiner only added, no doubt, to the delights of its strawberry beds and terracotta Classical medallions.[15]

But Parliamentary manoeuvres, however important, were not the be-all, still less the end-all of the Divorce – despite the fact that English historians, with their narrow national focus and their excessive concentration on 'the Constitution', often write as though they were. Instead, managing the Great Matter was a complex affair. It was like playing a game of chess or conducting an orchestra. Each piece had to be moved to its right place on the board; each section of the orchestra be brought in at the right time. One false entry and the harmony of the English political élite, which was already strained to breaking-point, might collapse entirely; one wrong move and the beleaguered Queen might yet escape.

Then where would be the climax, where the consummation of checkmate for Anne?

In this complex of factors, foreign policy was of paramount importance. The new understanding with France – the final achievement of Wolsey's foreign policy – had always been the precondition for Henry's freedom of manoeuvre over his first marriage to the Spanish princess, Catherine of Aragon. Only France was strong enough to make Catherine's nephew, the Emperor Charles, think twice about invading England or launching trade sanctions. And only France had enough influence at Rome to counter-balance the formidable pressure on the Pope of the Spanish cardinals and ambassadors.

But if Henry was at last to get rid of his Spanish-born Queen, England's understanding with France had first to be made water-tight.

Here Anne was in her element. Her skill in the French language, her understanding of French ways and her enthusiasm for her adoptive country, all conspired to make her the key instrument in the charm-offensive which Henry now launched against France.

It had got underway in late 1531, when, on Christmas Eve, the new French ambassador, Gilles de La Pommeraye, arrived to replace Giovanni Gioachino di Passano. Anne 'feasted' both the incoming and the outgoing ambassadors. And she mingled business with pleasure. 'With all their pastimes', Chapuys sourly reported, 'they were not idle, and have this day [29 December] sent [the Bishop of] Winchester to France.' In his turn, De La Pommeraye was frank with Chapuys about his own mission. 'Pommeraye is here', Chapuys informed the Emperor, 'for the process of the Divorce to be decided in this kingdom.' 'And', he continued, 'he tells me that it is impossible to conceive how much the King has the said affair at heart and that his master [Francis I] will refuse him nothing.'

Henry soon put Francis's good intentions to the test. His initial aim was to get the French King to agree the scheme for mutual aid against the Emperor which had first been discussed with Jean du Bellay, Bishop of Bayonne in the summer of 1530. This time, negotiations moved smoothly. On 5 May, De La Pommeraye re-embarked at Southampton for final consultations with Francis I, who was then in Brittany. De La Pommeraye returned to England on 10 June, with Francis's present of a brace of fine greyhounds for Henry. He also bore an even better gift in the form of Francis's agreement in principle to the treaty of mutual aid. There followed a fortnight of lavish entertainment mingled with intense negotiations at the end of which, on 23 June, the treaty was signed. The ambassador represented the French, and Anne's father and Dr Edward Foxe, her leading intellectual supporter, the English.[16]

The forces which either ally was to send to the aid of the other in the event of an attack by the Emperor were relatively small. Depending on the circumstances, each side was to supply a fleet manned by 1,500 soldiers, while the English were to send a force of 5,000 archers to France, if she were the party attacked, or the French a force of 500 spears to England, if the Imperial offensive were launched there. Archers or long-bowmen were (despite the increasing effectiveness of artillery) still regarded as the best English troops; while 'spears' or heavily armed cavalry, were likewise (despite their rout at the Battle of the Spurs) considered to be the crack French troops. The apparent disparity in numbers is accounted for by the fact that 'a spear' was not an individual but a small fighting formation, consisting of the mounted man-at-arms himself, supported by one or more mounted archers, light horsemen, and 'custrels' (that is, shields-bearers attending on the man-at-arms).[17]

But numbers, however calculated, were not really the issue. Instead the treaty was a statement of intent, as far as the signatories were concerned, and a warning, which the Emperor would have to heed. For it signalled that an attack on England was also an attack on France. And not even Charles V was strong enough to contemplate having to deal with both at once.

Chapuys, who had a scent for such matters, realized the meaning of the treaty even before it was formally announced or he had discovered its terms. For some days he had, he complained to its target, Charles, 'the bad odour of this new treaty in my nostrils'.[18]

Much would happen before he could free himself of the stench.

But the treaty was soon overtaken in importance for Henry by another, overtly symbolic scheme. He and Francis, he decided, would broadcast their union by a personal meeting of the two Kings and their Courts.

The model, of course, was the Field of Cloth of Gold in 1520. This was scarcely a happy precedent from the French point of view, since on that occasion the English, by a masterpiece of duplicity, had betrayed their promises of eternal friendship even before they had made them. But things were different this time. It was not that Albion had become less perfidious. Instead, Henry *needed* Francis. Indeed, thanks to the Great Matter, his need for Francis was rather greater than Francis's need for him. It was a good basis for assuming that Henry might keep to his promises.

The germ of the scheme for a personal meeting had been sown on Gardiner's Embassy to France. The language of the English King's despatches was unusually warm; he also expressed the desire for an up-to-date portrait of the French King. And he did so in terms which suggest that the mirror (or perhaps Anne) had been reminding Henry that time flies.

'Forasmuch,' Henry informed Gardiner, 'as it is long passed sith [since] we did see our said good brother's person, and being much desirous to have the portraiture of the same, in that form and favour that it now is, specially considering that few years do always change a man's countenance'. To satisfy this desire, Henry continued, the bishop, was 'to procure and get unto us, not only the same his portraiture and picture in the most like, best and curious fashion, but also the images and portraitures of our said good brother's children [that is, the recently released Princes]'. These would, Henry assured Gardiner, become treasured objects: 'which to behold shall always be unto us great rejoice and comfort'.[19]

Cromwell, who could spot a trend a mile off, had already anticipated part of this request in his New Year's gift to the King. It consisted of 'a ring with a ruby and a box with the images of the French King's children'. But then anticipating Henry's wishes was something that Cromwell was to become increasingly good at.[20]

By the summer, Henry's desire to behold Francis's portrait had openly turned into one to see his person. The desire was loudly and vehemently expressed – by Henry and still more perhaps by Anne. And once more, as so often previously, the Progress and the hunt provided her best opportunities.

The Progress began on 4 July. They stayed at Waltham Abbey for five days and then, on the 9th, continued to Hunsdon. The King, the Venetian ambassador reported, 'will proceed, hunting and amusing himself as far as "Nourgam" (Nottingham) ... and then return by another road, at the end of September'. 'He is accompanied solely by the French ambassador,' he added.[21]

The plan, it seems, was for another long Progress, in which one of the areas of the country least sympathetic to innovation – *any* innovation – would gradually get accustomed to Anne.

According to Chapuys's gleeful report, the plan backfired and the Progress had to be abandoned by the end of July. 'The King was on his way to the Northern parts', he wrote in his despatch of 29 July, 'when he suddenly changed his purpose and came back to town.' The reason was popular reaction. 'Wherever he went accompanied by the Lady, the people on the road so earnestly requested him to recall the Queen, his wife, and the women especially so insulted the Royal mistress, hooting and hissing on her passage, that he was actually obliged to retrace his steps.'

The story was of course just what Chapuys wanted to hear. But he had the grace to report, as hot news, another explanation. 'I heard yesterday, and again today . . . that the chief cause of the King's sudden return is that he wishes to be prepared for the interview, now in contemplation, between himself and the King of France, at Calais, on the last day of September.' The source, Chapuys added, was 'very authentic'.[22]

It was indeed.

We learn full details from De La Pommeraye who was on the Progress. Ever since they had left Greenwich, he reported on 21 July, the King had made him good cheer and used him familiarly. 'All day long', he wrote, 'I am alone with him in the chase.' During the hunt, 'he discusses with me all his [private] affairs' and he takes 'as much trouble to give me good sport as though I were some great personage'.

From Henry's point of view, of course, he *was* a great personage. As Francis's ambassador, he represented the King himself. And it was Francis whom Henry was trying to charm into agreeing to the proposed interview. The interview itself, as it happened, was conceded rather easily. But Henry would have preferred the world to think that it was Francis, not he, who had suggested the idea. He even tried to persuade

De La Pommeraye that Francis should appear to be the suppliant by coming first to visit him at Calais. But here Pommeraye drew the line. It was against his master's honour, he said flatly. Finally, after weeks of wheedling, Henry had to admit defeat. The terms of the interview were agreed and it was Henry who was to pay the first visit to Francis on his own territory at Boulogne.

But Henry also had another agendum. It was more secret and more important, and he did not trust himself as negotiator. Instead, he deliberately threw the ambassador into Anne's company. And she, if anything, outdid the King in her kind attentions.

'Sometimes', De La Pommeraye informed his correspondent, the French minister Montmorency, 'he puts my Lady Anne and me, each with our crossbow, to wait for the deer to cross our path, as you know this fashion of hunting.' 'On other occasions', he reported, 'she and I are together, quite alone, in some other place, to watch the deer run.' Anne had even supplied him with a brand-new set of hunting equipment, making 'me a present of a hunting frock, hat, horn and greyhound'.

According to De La Pommeraye, Anne was simply doing what Henry instructed her to do. From what we have seen of Anne's personality, this does not seem very likely. In fact, Anne wanted the interview with Francis at least as much as Henry. Above all, she wanted to be there herself. And getting her there was the object of *her* wooing of De La Pommeraye.

She was not so foolish, of course, as to ask directly. Instead, she would have chosen her moment and her point of attack with strategic care. It was, we can guess, one of those moments when she and De La Pommeraye were alone. There was, perhaps, a lull in the sport and maybe the quiet of the forest in the late summer afternoon seemed to invite confidence. She had something very secret to tell him, she whispered. But first he must promise never to reveal his source. He promised. She was, she continued, an ardent friend of France. But many of Henry's friends and councillors were not, and persisted in their hostility to the traditional enemy. Here she lowered her voice still further. Henry himself, she disclosed, wavered. But one thing would bind him to Francis forever. What was that, the ambassador asked eagerly. She hesitated before replying. Then she overwhelmed him in a burst of apparently artless confidence. Let Francis write to Henry to invite *her* to the meeting and all would be well. And it would be even better if Francis's sister, Marguerite of Angoulême, came too. She had such happy memories of her and so longed to see her again!

Those famous coal-black eyes smouldered and De La Pommeraye, gallant Frenchman that he was, did what they ordered.

'Monseigneur,' he wrote to Montmorency, 'I know reliably and from a good source that the greatest favour which the King [Francis] could do to the King his brother and to my Lady Anne, is that our Sovereign Lord should write to me that I should request King Henry to bring Lady Anne with him to Calais, in order that Francis could see her and entertain her.' In return, Francis must bring Marguerite of Angoulême to entertain Henry. 'I do not reveal my sources', Pommeraye explained, 'because I have sworn an oath.'

Anne had been equally open about whom Henry did *not* wish to see. Francis should not bring his wife, Queen Eleanor. She was Charles's sister and Catherine's niece and her very appearance would bring back bad memories. Artlessly, Anne explained that Henry 'hates Spanish dress since it makes him see a devil [in women's clothes]'.[23]

Anne, of course, had already said very similar things about Spaniards to the ladies of the English Court. They had been shocked. But Francis, she had reason to know, would appreciate the abuse. This was because her famously outspoken cousin, Sir Francis Bryan, who was then ambassador in France, had once more spilled the beans. King Francis had been forced to marry Eleanor in the aftermath of his defeat at Pavia, and he regarded her as his badge of servitude to the Emperor. He also found her personally unattractive, Bryan wrote. Even when they were in the same house, 'they lie not together once in four nights' and Francis continued to make open love to his mistress. Marguerite of Angoulême was even blunter. Francis found his Queen repellent, she told the Duke of Norfolk. And what made it worse was Eleanor's characteristic uxoriousness. 'She is very hot in bed and desireth to be too much embraced.' Francis could not get a wink of sleep next to her.[24]

Preparations for the meeting of the two Kings now went ahead. Time was short and even Cromwell's organizational abilities were stretched. He corresponded with Sir Edward Guildford, Sir Henry Guildford's elder half-brother, about shipping arrangements across the Channel. And he sorted out the all-important question of his-and-hers jewellery for Henry and Anne.[25]

Cromwell had taken over administrative responsibility for the royal jewels and plate when he was appointed Master of the King's Jewels on 14 April 1532. He found the paperwork of the office in some disorder. New inventories were drawn up and (as was then customary) he drafted in his own servants. These included Stephen Vaughan, who, like other of Cromwell's radical friends and dependants, now thought it safe to return to England. In the summer of 1532 Vaughan was acting as one of Cromwell's go-betweens, and he found himself kicking his heels. 'If you would come to Court', he wrote to Cromwell from Woodstock, where Henry and Anne were in residence from 7–18 August, 'the King would put me to some occupation'. He did not have long to wait.[26]

Probably in late August, he was despatched to Cromwell with the King's 'devices' (sketches) for the making and remaking of some important piece of jewellery, including his great State collar set with balas rubies and diamonds. Probably on Thursday, 5 September Vaughan returned with the worked-up designs from Cornelis Heyss, the royal Goldsmith, for Henry's approval.

On the Friday night he had audience with the King 'when he returned late from hunting'. Vaughan showed him the design for the collar (he calls it a 'chain'). At this point Henry called in Anne to have her advice. Luckily, they both approved – though Henry had feared that Cornelis would have put in more than seven balases, thus making the collar too large. Anne had a query, too: she wanted to know if Vaughan had brought her anything from Thomas Alvard, who had charge of the remains of Wolsey's plate and jewels at York Place. Her question was directed, almost certainly, at the eighteen diamonds set in troches of gold (that is, buttons set with three stones in a bunch) which Alvard eventually supplied to Heiss on 18 September.[27]

But not even Henry's vast store of jewels was enough for Anne: she decided she must have Catherine's too. Norfolk was sent to do the dirty work. But Catherine, so Chapuys heard, brushed aside his diplomatic feelers with scorn. She would never, she said, willingly give up her jewels to bedeck 'a person who is the scandal of Christendom'. However, if Henry sent her a direct personal command, she would submit as a good wife must. Swallowing the insult, Henry sent the required message by a Gentleman of his Privy Chamber.[28]

Anne had the Queen's jewels. She would not give them up easily.

Cromwell even dealt with matters of female dress. On 21 August, Norfolk wrote to him from the Court at Langley to countermand a previous order for crimson velvet robes for three countesses. 'The King's pleasure', he reported, 'now is that no robes of estate shall now be made but only for my wife. I send you the pattern.' Garter King of Arms, Norfolk ended, must also be at Abingdon on Saturday, 24 August.[29]

These were preparations, not for the forthcoming interview, but for another ceremony. For it had been decided that, before Anne met Francis as Henry's Queen- and Consort-to-be, she should be given appropriate rank by being created a peer in her own right. The title chosen was Marquess of Pembroke, which had strong royal associations, since the earldom of Pembroke had been held by Henry's great-uncle, Jasper Tudor, to whose lands he had succeeded as a boy.

Anne's creation took place in the grand and already historic setting of Windsor on Sunday, 1 September 1532. In the morning, Anne was conducted in procession to the King; she was accompanied by the peers, headed by the Dukes of Norfolk and Suffolk, by the French ambassador, De La Pommeraye, and by the heralds. Garter (who had been summoned to Abingdon to prepare for the ceremony) carried her Letters Patent of creation. Anne herself was magnificent. She wore a surcoat of crimson velvet, furred with ermine, and with straight sleeves. She was supported by two countesses, while her train was born by another great lady. And, according to the Venetian ambassador, she was 'completely covered with the most costly jewels'.

But here there had been a change of plan. The original intention, as Norfolk's letters show, was that Anne's train-bearer would be his wife, Elizabeth Stafford, daughter of the executed Duke of Buckingham. Formally, the task was an honour. But, for Elizabeth, it was an insult. For a Stafford to carry the train of a Boleyn was bad enough. Still worse was the fact that she was Catherine's oldest English friend and supporter. Her opposition to Anne had become increasingly blatant. Now Elizabeth refused the task point-blank and her daughter Mary had to be her substitute.

For Anne, however, nothing could detract from the moment as, 'in her hair', with her splendid auburn tresses hanging round her shoulders, she advanced towards Henry and knelt. Garter delivered her Patent to Gardiner, the royal Secretary, to read it out. Did he swallow as he pronounced the flowery Latin phrases setting out her lineage, merits and honour? Then Henry himself draped the mantle round her shoulders and put the coronet on her head. He also handed over her Patent of creation and another Patent settling lands on her worth £1,000 a year. Thomas Cromwell, inevitably, had organized these as well.

There followed 'a most solemn Mass' which Gardiner celebrated in the Chapel Royal, in his capacity this time as Bishop of Winchester. Then, in a deliberate pendant to Anne's creation, the Treaty of Mutual Aid with France, which had been agreed on 23 June, was ratified. Henry and the French ambassador advanced to the altar. The terms of the treaty were read. Then the King and De La Pommeraye signed the treaty and swore a solemn oath to observe it. The oath-taking was followed by a sermon delivered by Almoner Foxe. There was already a close alliance with France, he explained. But this treaty was 'for the purpose of uniting the two crowns more closely . . . to which effect the two Kings will employ their money, troops, their persons and all their forces'. 'For this purpose', he concluded, 'they will have an interview, to take counsel together and arrange what is necessary to be done.' 'After this the singers began to chant the *Te Deum Laudamus*, to the accompaniment of trumpets and other instruments.'[30]

Three days later, on 4 September, England's old friend, Guillaume du Bellay, sieur de Langey, arrived from France. He bore the eagerly awaited letters with Francis's formal request that Anne should be one of the party. Anne showed her gratitude by inviting the ambassador to a dinner which she gave for Henry at her new house at Hanworth.[31]

Henry and Anne sailed to France in the *Swallow*. At the last minute, Marguerite of Angoulême had declined the invitation on grounds of ill health. This was a disappointment for Anne and meant that, since there was no woman of the right rank to receive her, she could not accompany Henry to Boulogne on 21 October. But she made up for it when Francis paid his return visit to Henry at Calais on the 25th and stayed till the 29th. Francis began the mutual exchange of courtesies by sending her the gift of a magnificent diamond. Then, on the Sunday after supper, Anne led the party of seven masked English ladies who danced with the Kings and lords. Anne, naturally, partnered Francis. Henry, determined to show off Anne (and to show that she was dancing with Francis), snatched off the ladies' masks. They danced a little longer, and then Francis 'talked with [Anne] a space'. We do not, alas, know what they said.[32]

Henry and Anne took their time over the return journey. They lingered in Calais for a fortnight and spent almost ten days crossing Kent. And they did not arrive back at Greenwich till 27 November.[33]

Either in Calais or on the return journey, Anne allowed Henry to sleep with her for the first time. They were, at last, lovers in the physical sense.

But were they married?

59. Anne's marriage

There had been persistent rumours throughout the summer of 1532 that Anne and Henry would marry during the interview at Calais. At first, Anne had gone out of her way to encourage the gossip. 'Not later than a week ago', Chapuys reported in late August, 'she wrote a letter to her principal friend and favourite here, whom she holds as sister and companion, bidding her to get ready against this journey and interview, where, she says, that which she has been so long wishing for will be accomplished.' But, just before leaving England, she changed her tune. She 'assured a great personage', Chapuys discovered, 'that even if the King wished to marry her now she would never consent to it, for she wants the ceremony to take place here, in England, at the usual place appointed for the marriage and coronation of Queens'.[1]

Why the alteration?

The explanation, almost certainly, is that Anne had been doing her research. She had already, as we have seen, informed herself widely on the debate about the Divorce. Now she wanted to make sure that her own title as Queen would be unimpeachable. This meant that everything would have to be done in the proper form set out in the bible of ceremony known as *The Royal Book*.

The Royal Book devotes one of its longest and most detailed chapters to 'The Receiving of a Queen and her Coronation':

> Item [it provides] when a Queen shall be received out of a strange realm, the King must purvey certain lords and ladies of estate to meet with her at the seaside, and convey her to the palace where the King will be wedded . . . Also it must be understood whether the King will be wedded privily or openly . . . And that done, she must be conveyed unto her coronation to the City of London . . .

It was these stipulations, at least as much as the pressure of contemporary events, which governed Anne's and Henry's actions over the next few months.[2]

The Royal Book took for granted, as indeed had usually been the case in the Middle Ages, that the queen-to-be would be a foreign princess. Anne, on the other hand, was neither foreign nor royal. But she seems to have *imagined* that she was both. Her coats-of-arms, both as Marquess of Pembroke and later as Queen, proclaim her fictive royalty; and, clearly, her own self-identity was French rather than English.

The circumstances of the Calais interview reinforced all this. She had re-entered the world of the French Court; she had danced with the French King and talked privately with him. Now she was sailing to English soil where soon she would be crowned.

It was just as *The Royal Book* prescribed. What more natural therefore than to marry Henry as soon as they landed? And 'privily' – as *The Royal Book* permitted and the fact that Henry was still married to Catherine required?

And this, according to one generally well-informed source, is what actually happened. Anne and Henry landed at Dover on 14 November. This was St Erconwald's Day. And on this day, the chronicler Hall writes, 'the King after his return married privily the Lady Anne Boleyn ... which marriage was kept so secret that very few knew it'.[3]

The moment was psychologically right. Anne had lived with Henry in Calais openly as his consort. She had behaved and been treated as his Queen. And she had been given Francis's blessing. To have gone back to England and chastity must have seemed intolerable – both to her and to Henry. But equally Anne was not the woman to surrender without a marriage. Not even the promise of marriage would have done. Instead, there must have been the thing itself, with a priest, a ring and the exchange of vows.

Quite what such a secret marriage was worth, in view of Henry's now bigamous state, was another matter.

But, for the moment, neither Anne nor Henry cared. On their slow return journey through Kent, Henry was unusually generous with rewards and charitable gifts; and he threw money away on card-games. His partners were Anne herself, her cousin Francis Bryan, and Francis Weston, the handsome young page who was a favourite of both Henry and Anne.

It was, in short, a winter honeymoon.

As soon as they returned to Greenwich at the end of November, it seems, the couple had a single thought: to inspect the works at the Tower which had been begun in June 1532.

The works were preceded by a full structural survey and were on a scale large enough to attract the attention of foreign ambassadors. But none seem to have grasped their real purpose. For the Venetian ambassador, who was the first to notice that something was going on, it was simply a question of strengthening the defences: Henry 'has commenced inspecting the artillery and ammunition in the Tower, which he purposes fortifying', he reported. Chapuys, with his excellent sources of information, described the programme of works much more accurately: 'considerable repairs', he noted in September, 'have been made in the Tower of London, both inside and outside, refitting the apartments which were out of order'. Where his sources went wrong, however, was over the intended use of the refurbished rooms. 'Some people believe', he reported, 'that it is the King's intention to send the Queen thither.' Chapuys himself dismissed the story as 'highly improbable'. He was right to be dubious. For the apartments were destined, not for Queen Catherine, but for Queen Anne.[4]

Here once again we can see the results of Anne's reading of *The Royal Book*. It was the rule, the Book lays down, that the new Queen should go to the Tower two days before her coronation. She was to spend the night there, 'at her own leisure', before processing the following day in state through the City and along the Strand to Westminster.

But by 1532 the Tower was in no state to receive anybody, much less the woman for whom Henry had defied the world.

The reason lay in a radical change in the royal itinerary. Up to the reign of Henry's father, Henry VII, the Tower had been in frequent use as a royal residence. Henry had taken refuge there with his mother, Elizabeth of York, from the Cornish rebels in 1497 and Elizabeth had died there six years later in 1503. The newly-wedded Henry and Catherine had continued this pattern for the first two years of their reign. But after 1510 the King had visited the Tower only once, on 20 January 1520. And the building, unvisited by the King, had fallen into serious neglect.[5]

The state of disrepair is documented by the survey of 1532. It emerges even more vividly from the letters which John Whalley, the paymaster of the works, wrote during the absence of the Court at the Calais interview in October. The letters were addressed to Cromwell, who, as Lord High Everything Else, had been given charge of the Tower works as well. 'The house is wondrous foul,' Whalley reported. 'There is a thousand loads of rubbish to be taken out of the cellars and kitchen.' He had 'this day 400 persons at work, and all little enough'. Once the site was cleared, large numbers of masons and other craftsmen were impressed to rush through the actual work of rebuilding.[6]

By December, things were well advanced. On the 1st, Henry made a day trip by boat from Greenwich to see how they were coming along. He was pleased enough with what he saw to return twice, and on both occasions with company. On about the 5th, he was met at the Tower by the French ambassador, to whom he showed the Jewel House (Chapuys calls it 'the treasure room') – though without, according to Chapuys, 'giving him sight of its contents'. A few days later, Henry, with a small suite, took Anne herself to the Tower. Once again the French ambassador turned up with despatches hot from France. This time the ambassador accompanied the royal party on their inspection of the Jewel House. Its contents had just been reorganized and reinventoried under Cromwell's supervision and Henry showed them off with delight. He even gave the ambassador 'one of the finest gold cups' as a present. Chapuys could not discover whether the gift had been made to reward the ambassador for his news, which he had whispered privately to the King, or whether it had been 'to please the Lady [Anne]'.[7]

Anne herself, however, was not there only to act as Lady Bountiful to the French ambassador. Instead, almost certainly, she had come to make a personal choice of items of plate for her own use and that of her Household as Queen-in-waiting. The selection is recorded in a list headed 'parcels of plate given by the King's Highness to my Lady Marquess of Pembroke, in the month of December [1532]' and it numbered many dozens of cups, bowls, pots, chandeliers, and spoons. The total weight was over 5,000 ounces of gilt and parcel (partly) gilt plate and the total value was £1,200. Some of the items had previously belonged to Wolsey, while another large group formed part of the property of Anne's old enemy, Sir Henry Guildford, who had died so heavily in debt to the King that his personal goods had been forfeit.[8]

Even enemies, she might have reflected, came in useful when they were dead.

Henry would also have pointed out to her other objects on the shelves of the Jewel House, including the Queen's crown, sceptre and rod, which Anne would wear and carry after her coronation in the Abbey. Then he would have taken her to look at the work in progress on the Queen's apartments. These lay in the south-east corner of the Tower and they were still a building site. But already the skeleton of her new Great Chamber and Dining Chamber was clear. Here she would spend the night before going in procession to Westminster for her coronation.[9]

Now, at last, it must all have seemed very near.

And it all seemed near for another, even more pressing reason. Also in early December Anne became pregnant. The child, for whom Henry had longed for so many years, had to be a boy. And his birth had to be legitimate.

A new note of urgency was sounded in royal policy. And there was a new man of the moment: Thomas Cranmer.

60. Archbishop

Rumour has it that Anne had been Cranmer's pupil. He cannot have taught her during her youth, which had of course been spent in France. Instead, she would have been an adult student of his – in late 1529, when he had been lodged at her father's newly acquired town palace of Durham House, or again after his return from Italy in late 1530, when he had been part of the King's legal and theological team at Court. But however cloudy these details, one thing is certain: pupil and master developed a mutual regard, which survived throughout extraordinary swings of fortune. The first of these was about to occur. Cranmer would make Anne Queen. But first she had to make him Archbishop of Canterbury.[1]

The incumbent Archbishop of Canterbury was the aged, disillusioned and marginalized William Warham. Born in 1456, chosen as Archbishop and Chancellor by Henry VII, respected by the young Henry VIII and elbowed aside by Wolsey, Warham had seen it all. His face, as painted by Holbein, is as gnarled and wrinkled as an ancient oak tree. And he was as tough. He had skilfully obstructed Henry's wishes: first over the Divorce, and then over the royal headship of the Church. His strength was a masterly inactivity: he was a delayer and a survivor. But even he could not cheat death and he died on 22 August 1532 at the age of seventy-six.[2]

Henry could now appoint a more malleable primate – providing, that is, that he could persuade the Pope to agree to his choice. But he seemed to be in no hurry. News of Warham's death was reported by the Venetian ambassador, Carlo Capello, soon after the event on 26 August. 'Four days ago', he wrote, 'the Reverend Archbishop of Canterbury died. The King sent the Duke of Norfolk to take possession as usual; he will keep it for a year and then give it to Dom. Gramello or to Master [Reginald] Pole.'[3]

Assuming, as most scholars do, that by 'Gramello' the ambassador meant Cranmer, the prophecy is remarkable. Capello was also right about the immediate lack of urgency. Henry and Anne had one thing on their minds in late August and it was the planned meeting with Francis. Against this, the nomination of a new archbishop was a remote affair. But the postponement of the Calais/Boulogne interview from the beginning to the end of October gave a breathing space. Henry made use of it to clear the backlog of business which had built up during his exclusive concentration on the negotiation and planning of the interview.

There were two key items. The first was the timing of the next session of Parliament. In late September or early October, Sir Thomas Audley, More's successor as Keeper of the Great Seal, wrote to 'his loving and hearty friend' Cromwell to inform him that Henry, 'this afternoon', had decided to prorogue Parliament from its planned date of reassembly in November till 4 February 1533. Audley had lobbied hard for that particular date. He thought 'it a very good time, being about the middle of Hilary term, when the days will be improving' and the worst gloom of winter would be past.[4]

The other important policy decision was to summon Cranmer, who was on an Embassy to Chales V, back to England. This was decided on Tuesday, 1 October. Drafting, writing and despatching the various letters took at least twenty-four hours and it was not until 'Wednesday toward evening' that Dr Nicholas Hawkins, who was carrying the letters of recall, obtained 'licence' to leave, following an audience with Henry at Greenwich.

Interestingly, Hawkins also had another, apparently fuller, meeting with Anne before setting off. 'My Lady Marquess of Pembroke showed me', he reported back to Henry from Mantua, 'that it was your Highness's commandment that we should seek out such books, as be found here [concerning Papal power].' He was sending one which, he understood, 'treateth this matter very substantially'. But it was in German and Henry would have to 'command Master Cromwell to find an interpreter'.

This is incontrovertible evidence of Anne's direct involvement in the gathering of learned materials on the Divorce and Supremacy. It is also striking that, to judge from the actual language of the passage in Hawkins's letter, Anne had described the required books in Latin as *de potestate Papae*.[5]

Cranmer, it would seem, had done his tutoring well.

But his lessons had stopped early in 1532, when he had been sent on his Embassy to the Emperor Charles V. Bearing in mind later events, he seems a bizarre choice for such a mission. But, with his calm good manners, his outward reasonableness, and his careful reserve, he won golden opinions. This is the more surprising considering the range of his secret contacts: not only did Cranmer have formal dealings with the Emperor and his ministers, he was at the same time in semi-clandestine communication with some of the German reformers. And, most clandestine of all, he got married.

Cranmer had of course been married before. But that was before he joined the priesthood. His re-marriage now represented an extraordinary flouting of one of the basic rules of the clerical estate: even Henry, with all his future theological wanderings, was to remain committed to the necessity of clerical celibacy till the end.[6]

What drove Cranmer? Lust certainly, I suppose, and perhaps love. But the consequences were at least as important as the causes. Cranmer now had a personal investment, of the deepest sort, in the further progress of Reform. Similarly, the experience of his own frailty gave him a most untypical understanding, for a cleric, of the demands of human sexuality. This meant that he not only agreed with the *theological* arguments behind Henry's determination to end his first marriage (which, as we have seen, he did on first principles), he also sympathized with the *psychological* imperatives which drove the King ever onward on his extraordinary marital journey. Cranmer seems even to have sympathized with Anne.

Meanwhile, his marriage had to be a guilty secret which profoundly conditioned his behaviour over the next few months.

For his recall – the news of which was brought by Hawkins – came as no surprise. His friends in England (that is, the Boleyns and Cromwell) had already given him advance warning of Henry's intention to nominate him as Archbishop of Canterbury. According to Cranmer's enemies, the appointment was the result of a cynical deal between Cranmer and the

King. 'Give me the Archbishopric of Canterbury', Cranmer is supposed to
have promised Henry, 'and I will give you licence to live in adultery.' In
fact, the opposite seems to have been the case and, far from grasping at the
appointment, no man has said *nolo episcopari* (I am unwilling to be made a
bishop) more fervently than Cranmer.[7]

And it is easy to see why. To be a married priest was awkward
enough; to be an archbishop with a wife was unthinkable. Moreover,
Cranmer could become archbishop only by acknowledging, with the
most solemn oaths, the authority of the Pope, which he had already
rejected on grounds that were both conscientious and intellectual. These
barriers between himself and Canterbury were unavoidable; instead he
would have to slither over them by an unlovely combination of
hypocrisy and perjury. For a man who valued his integrity it was not a
happy prospect.

No wonder he made his journey home from Mantua, where Hawkins
finally caught up with him, last as long as possible. Twenty years later,
when his world had collapsed in ruins and he was on trial for his life, the
memory of those days was still vivid. 'I protest before you all', he told his
judges, 'there was never man who came more unwillingly to a bishopric,
than I did to that: in so much that when King Henry did send for me in
post, that I should come over, I prolonged my journey by seven weeks at
the least, thinking that he should be forgetful of me in the meantime.'[8]

There was little chance of that, since Anne and Henry were counting
the days to his arrival. But (as Cranmer intended) the weeks went by with
no news of him. Nothing had been heard from the man himself, of course.
Still worse, there had also been silence from Hawkins. Justifiably,
Hawkins was 'right pensive' when he imagined what Henry's reaction
might be and wisely he excused himself at length. The reason, he
explained in his despatch of 21 November, was 'that in all my journey I
never met with post, nor courier, or any other man of England', whom he
could trust to carry letters home.[9]

By early December, Henry and Anne were thoroughly alarmed.
They had now been sleeping together for almost a month; Anne may
even have had intimations of pregnancy. Something must be done! As

they tended to do at such moments, they turned to Cromwell. And Cromwell turned to the faithful Vaughan, who was sent to track down Cranmer and hurry him home.

Cromwell despatched Vaughan on Sunday, 1 December. He embarked at Dover at 10 a.m. on the Monday and made landfall at 10 p.m. at Whitesand Bay (that is, the modern Wissant) to the east of Boulogne. The weather was atrocious, with heavy snow that froze immediately it touched the ground. The result was that he 'could not get a horse for any money, the roads being so dangerous'. Not to be defeated, he walked the twelve miles to Boulogne, 'not [e]scaping more falls than I have fingers'. At Boulogne he took post-horses. But riding proved even more dangerous than walking. He and his horse fell near Abbéville and the injury to his leg 'was scantly eased by an application put on at Amiens'. The accident and its treatment cost him half a day. Nevertheless he arrived at Paris on the morning of the 5th.

But still there was silence about the whereabouts of his quarry. He 'has heard nothing of the man during his journey', Vaughan informed Cromwell in deliberately obscure language. 'A post who came from Lyon today had met with no such person.' On the 6th, Vaughan set out for Lyon himself.[10]

The bad weather continued, with 'the ways', he told Cromwell, 'being so perilous by the frost that I never expected to come home without a broken leg'. Nevertheless he arrived at Lyon only three days later and was rewarded with the information he wanted. 'I met an Englishman who had come from Mr Cranmer, who is ten leagues off, and is expected here.' 'The news', he added with nice understatement, 'will please the King.'

Vaughan was writing, he explained, at night. Early the next morning he would ride towards Cranmer. And, he swore, 'I will conduct him in safety, or die by the way.' It was a boast we should believe. But even Vaughan had to acknowledge that his youthful energy was up against a formidable obstacle in Cranmer himself: 'Mr Cranmer is disposed to make only small journeys', he reported. Nevertheless, 'I trust by Christmas we shall be in England'.[11]

It would be the best present that Henry and Anne could receive.

In fact, Cranmer managed to drag things out a fortnight further at least and it was not till the end of the second week of the New Year that he arrived at Greenwich, where Henry and Anne were spending the holidays. And it was there, amid the festivities (a hostile reporter claims that the audience took place at a bear-baiting), that Henry informed him formally of his decision to appoint him archbishop. Cranmer, who had been considering his position for the two months of his homeward journey, at first tried to refuse. When he was pressed by Henry, he invoked his conscientious scruples about taking an oath to the Papacy. And on this he proved immovable. The King consulted a panel of legal experts, led by Dr Oliver, who came up with a solution.[12]

Cranmer would enter a 'protestation' or disclaimer. This would assert that (as Cranmer himself put it): 'I did not acknowledge [the Pope's] authority any further than as it agreed with the express word of God, and that it might be lawful for me at all times to speak against him, and so to impugn his errors, when time and occasion should serve me'. The protestation would apply to two sets of oaths: to those which Cranmer's proctor would swear in Rome to secure his Bulls of appointment; and to those which Cranmer himself would, in the fullness of time, make at his consecration.

The procedures were explained to Cranmer thus: 'I might do it by way of protestation, and so one [his proctor] to be sent to Rome, who might take the oath and do everything in my name'. Cranmer's response had been to declare he was not his brother's keeper: 'Which, when I understood, I said he [his proctor] should do it *super animam suam* [on his own conscience]'.[13]

Cranmer, as he himself realized, had enough to do to look after his own.

Agreement on all this was not reached till 24 or 25 January. By a curious co-incidence, Henry's most effective agent in Rome, Dr Edmund Bonner, arrived home at the same time for further instructions. Bonner came from the same stable as Gardiner. Like Gardiner, to whom he was junior by about three years, he was a bright young canon lawyer, who had been recruited by Wolsey. He remained in the Cardinal's service after his fall and accompanied him on his fatal journey to the north. And it was from Wolsey's Household at Scrooby in Nottinghamshire on 4 September 1530 that he wrote to his fellow Wolseyian, Thomas Cromwell, in London. Cromwell, he reminded him, 'willing to make me a good Italian [had] promised unto me, long ago, the *Triumphs of Petrarch* in the Italian tongue'. Would he please send it now, by Dr Augustine's servant? And would he also supply other such works, especially 'the book called *Cortegiano* in Italian'? This last was Baldassare Castiglione's classic account of how to navigate the treacherous waters of the Renaissance Court. Bonner evidently learned more than the language from it and he made a seamless transition to the royal service.[14]

On Bonner's return from Italy Henry was at York Place. Bonner had an audience on the morning of 25 January 1533, and he found the King in an excellent mood – or, as he put it in full *Cortegiano* mode to his colleague in the Roman Embassy, Dr William Benet, 'I repaired to his Grace, which, being a Prince of most virtue, honour and goodness, gave me most gracious and benign audience'.

Henry had, as we shall see, good reason to be cheerful that morning.

Bonner reported to Benet that Henry was delighted with the signs of a softening in the Pope's position – for so the King chose to interpret recent developments. In return, the King promised to resume his accustomed loyalty to the Holy See. But first the Pope must back up his words with corresponding deeds. What would most please the King at the moment, Benet was to inform the Pope, was for the formalities of 'my Lord Elect of Canterbury, Mr Doctor Cranmer', to 'be . . . favourably handled, especially concerning the Annates, and charges of his Bulls'. If not, the suspension of Annates, 'which is in communication greatly and only stayed by the King's goodness', would be implemented forthwith. That was the stick. The carrot, as Bonner reported it, was equally clear: 'the good and favourable handling of this man shall stay, as me thinketh, many things, and cause diverse, and the King especially, to take it in good part'.[15]

Clement, in other words, was being offered a deal. There was also the further inducement, as Chapuys quickly discovered, that Henry was prepared to pay Cranmer's fees at the Papal Court upfront. Was there, the ambassador himself now wondered anxiously, 'some secret intelligence between the Pope and this King'? Certainly Henry was giving every impression that such an agreement had been reached: 'I know very well', Chapuys reported, 'that the King boasts of having gained the Pope to his side, or at least talks of having done so to the Gentlemen of his Privy Chamber.'[16]

From this moment, Cranmer's appointment was considered to be in the bag and the following day, 26 January, at about 3 p.m., after Henry had returned to Greenwich, 'Thomas Cranmer, elect of Canterbury', appeared as second in order of precedence of the witnesses of the investiture of Sir Thomas Audley with the office of Lord Chancellor.[17]

And indeed the signs, both in Rome and England, were that Clement was eager to grasp the proffered hand of friendship. Whether he would have been quite so eager if he had known of Henry's previous engagement, before he met Bonner on the 25th, is another matter.

For, earlier that day, Anne and Henry had been married for the second time. This marriage, like the first, was 'secret'. Unlike the first, however, the news leaked. Within the month, Chapuys was confidentially informed that the marriage had taken place. And the celebrant, naturally, was assumed to be Cranmer. But Cranmer hotly denied the charge. Far from having solemnized the marriage, he told Nicholas Hawkins, his friend and successor as ambassador at the Imperial Court: 'I myself knew not thereof a fortnight after it was done'.[18]

But if not Cranmer, who? Chapuys was informed two years later that the marriage was performed by an Augustinian friar, who was rewarded by being made head of his Order. The friar in question has been convincingly identified as George Brown, later Archbishop of Dublin. But a more likely candidate still is Dr Rowland Lee, who became Bishop of Coventry and Lichfield in 1534.[19]

Lee figures as celebrant in the account of the marriage given by

Nicholas Harpsfield in his *Treatise on the Pretended Divorce between Henry VIII and Catherine of Aragon*. The *Treatise* was written in the reign of Catherine's daughter Mary, and is a compendium of recusant tradition. It is, of course, bitterly hostile to Anne and Henry and, other things being equal, I would be inclined to discount its evidence. Harpsfield's account also contains one assertion which can be verified independently and which, at first sight, seems to be wrong.

Harpsfield claims that the marriage ceremony took place 'at Whitehall', as York Place soon became known. But the manuscript itinerary of Henry VIII in the Public Record Office shows the King to have remained at Greenwich for the whole of January 1533. However, on closer examination, it becomes clear that the compilers of the itinerary had failed to notice Bonner's letter to Benet. This shows, incontrovertibly, that Henry *was* at York Place overnight on Friday/Saturday, 24/25 January. It was, it is true, a brief visit. The King had not left Greenwich till late enough on the 24th to have signed a warrant before his departure, and he was back there soon enough on the 25th to sign another. But, brief though the visit was, it gave quite enough time for one of the most momentous acts of his life – and of Anne's.[20]

Bonner's evidence thus stands the argument on its head. Two independent witnesses (Cranmer and Chapuys) state that the marriage took place on the 25th. Harpsfield says that Henry was married at York Place. And indeed it now turns out that Henry was at York Place on the morning of the 25th – and, moreover, that this was (so far as we know) his *only* visit to York Place between Christmas 1532 and the opening of the new session of Parliament on 4 February 1533. The congruence of these facts is, surely, too much for mere coincidence. Harpsfield must be right about the place of Henry's marriage and he is likely to be correct about the other details also.

The marriage, Harpsfield says, took place 'very early before day'. The only witnesses were Henry Norris and Thomas Heneage, the two principal Gentlemen of Henry's Privy Chamber, and Anne Savage, later Lady Berkeley, who attended on Anne. And the celebrant, Harpsfield says, was Rowland Lee.

According to Harpsfield, Lee had been previously briefed by the King, who informed him that he had, 'gotten of the Pope a licence to marry another wife'. But 'to avoid business and tumult' the King felt that the ceremony must be performed 'very secretly'. The two agreed the time and place.

But when the party assembled, Lee was 'in a great dump and staggering'. For Henry had not produced the necessary documentation from the Pope. Lee pressed him once more: 'Sir, I trust you have the Pope's licence?' 'What else?' Henry replied lightly. Still Lee was not satisfied and, fully vested for mass, demanded that the licence be read. Henry was ready for this as well. The licence, he said, was 'in another, surer place whereunto no man resorteth but myself'. But if he were seen to go to get it so early in the morning, it would give the game away. 'Go forth in God's name, and do that which appertaineth to you!' the King ordered at last, 'and I will take upon me all other danger'.[21]

What (assuming that the words *were* said) was going on? Was Henry, as one historian has speculated, revealing even at this stage 'a psychological dependence on the papacy'? And how does the dithering, anxious Lee of Harpsfield's account square with the man we know elsewhere? For Lee's own correspondence presents a very different picture. He was the intimate friend of Cromwell, a shrewd and efficient administrator and, when necessary, as accomplished a bully as the great minister himself: later in 1533 he forced the Northern Convocation to accept the Divorce and, still more remarkably, he compelled the Welsh Marchers to submit to law and order when he was president of the Council of Wales.

So was he overcome by the moment on the 25th? Or was he acting? And how sincere, come to that, was Henry?[22]

The answer, surely, is that the whole ceremony was a carefully contrived performance. The first marriage in November had been designed to reassure Anne. This second, with its half-invocation of Papal authority, was intended to reassure Henry's subjects. When news of it leaked, which, as we have seen, it quickly did, it would suggest that Henry had received the nod from Rome.

The marriage thus forms part of the great game of 1533 in which

Henry decided to get his Divorce by deceiving everybody: Rome, his English subjects and even his French allies. The game was for the highest stakes and he played it well. So well indeed that, at moments, Anne seems to have wondered whether he might be deceiving her as well.

But she had ways of dealing with that.

61. Divorce Absolute

On 15 February 1533 or thereabouts, Anne informed the Duke of Norfolk, in front of many witnesses, that 'immediately after Easter, she was resolved to go on a pilgrimage to Our Lady [of Walsingham]in the event that she were not pregnant'. Chapuys reported the remark in shocked tones. But he also understood its significance: 'it seems that she wishes the world to understand that she is pregnant or that she is so indeed'.[1]

Amid the masculine games of diplomatic bluff and counter-bluff, Anne was playing a woman's card. And it was, she knew, the ace of trumps. She was also announcing a timetable, set by her own, insistent biology. By Easter, Catherine would be divorced. She, Anne, would be Henry's acknowledged wife and Queen. And she would be known to be pregnant with the heir-to-be.

The long game, which had begun on New Year's Day 1527 with Henry's pledge that he would marry her, would be over. And she would have won.

But the timetable was extraordinarily tight. Easter Day fell on 13 April, which left ten weeks at most to settle the Great Matter which had already dragged itself out over six years. Was it possible? Only two things might make it so: Cromwell's organizing genius and Cranmer's way with words.

The countdown began on 4 February. This was the date which Henry, in consultation with Audley, had fixed for the opening of the new session of Parliament. Little was done that day, other than to order the Commons to elect a new speaker to replace Audley who, as More's successor as Lord Chancellor, was now the presiding officer in the Lords. Four days later the new speaker was presented to the King in a ceremony which was grander than the opening itself: both the French ambassador and the Papal Nuncio were present and the Lords wore their crimson and miniver-trimmed Parliament robes. Henry had taken the Nuncio 'in his own barge and close to his person' from Greenwich to Westminster for the presentation; and, the ceremony over, De Burgo was shown round the buildings of the Palace of Westminster and entertained to dinner by the two Dukes of Norfolk and Suffolk.[2]

Chapuys concluded correctly that this extraordinary show of favour to the Papal representative in England was part of Henry's attempt to convince the world that he had done a deal with the Nuncio's master in Rome. And the Imperial ambassador railed at the folly which might lead Pope Clement to contemplate such a step. For the Divorce, Chapuys insisted to Charles V, was *already* decided on. Anne and her father were in charge. And, thanks to their patronage, Lutherans and heretics were on the threshold of power. Indeed, Cranmer himself had the reputation of 'belonging heart and soul' to the sect. Could not Clement be made to realize this? Could not Charles, who was staying with Clement in Bologna, get him to act before it was too late? And, above all, could not Rome be persuaded to block or at least postpone Cranmer's appointment as Archbishop of Canterbury? The Bulls, Chapuys suggested, could easily be delayed or a special clause could be inserted in the archbishop's oath 'forbidding himself to mix himself up with the Divorce case.'[3]

Chapuys's prophecies of doom proved all too accurate. But, Cassandra-like, he was ignored. Pope Clement, with his usual policy of giving with one hand what he took with another, felt that it was Henry's turn to enjoy a favour. The French were also applying heavy pressure on Henry's behalf: there was, they insinuated to the Pope, nothing that the English King wanted more than an amicable settlement with Rome. And

Charles, despite his ambassador's urgent warnings, did nothing either.

Instead, and conforming to the Reformers' worst stereotype, the Papal Curia haggled about money: it was not a question of *whether* Cranmer should get his Bulls, but only of how much he (or rather Henry VIII on his behalf) would have to pay. On 22 February, archdeacon Hawkins, Henry's agent in Rome, sent an interim report on the bargaining. Hitherto, he informed Henry, nothing had happened because 'they could not agree on the price'. But the previous day Campeggio (who, despite the debacle of the Blackfriars Trial, was still the Cardinal-Protector of England) had formally reported the vacancy at Canterbury in the Consistory and moved the grant of Bulls for Cranmer. Behind the scenes discussion of cost continued, however. If the annate, the principal Papal tax, were levied in full ('after the rigour') it would come to 10,000 ducats (that is, at the exchange rate of 4s and 6d to the ducat, £2,333). Campeggio himself was due a 'propina' (a *pourboire* or tip) of 1,500 ducats (£350) 'only for proponing the vacation in Consistory'. And the Pope's officials would expect 3,000 or 4,000 ducats (£700 or £933) 'for sundries' (*pro minutis servitiis*).

But when all these palms were appropriately greased, the way would be open for the next Consistory, due in nine days or so, to complete the formalities of Cranmer's appointment by approving the grant of the archbishop's pall or *pallium*. 'The Pall', Hawkins explained to Henry, 'is a piece of white cloth made of the wool of certain lambs, which the Pope halloweth [blesses], and consecrate by the Pope, and laid on St Peter's sepulchre.' It was thus the most sacred archiepiscopal vestment and symbolized the Primate's position as the Pope's direct representative. It was also expensive, and would cost yet another 1,000 ducats (£233).[4]

Happily, as Henry had already made clear, money was no object. Instead, the only hitch in the process came when Bonner arrived at the Papal Court hotfoot from England on 27 February, with Henry's new instructions to demand, once more, the delegation of the trial of the Great Matter to England. The English ambassadors had an audience with Clement on 2 March, and the Pope, for once, lost his temper. To press him further in the matter, the French Cardinal de Tournon warned his English colleagues, would 'so irritate and exasperate' him that it would 'destroy' the English and French positions in Rome and throw Clement unreservedly into the arms of the Emperor. There was also, Bonner reported to Henry, 'an evident peril and fear' that 'if we should have further pressed him, he would have denied my Lord Elect's Bulls'.[5]

Wisely, they laid off and the moment of danger passed. For, on 3 March, the day after the English ambassadors' stormy meeting with the Pope, the last two of the eleven Bulls conferring Canterbury on Cranmer were sealed: the one sending him the pall and the other ordering the Archbishop of York and the Bishop of London to invest him with it.[6]

These Bulls were the most traditional of overtures to the coming storm in the English Church. They also meant that the reality of revolution was covered (as though by Cranmer's pall) with the fig-leaf of tradition – to the fury of Henry's and Anne's conservative opponents and to the confusion of the people. For if Cranmer were so recently appointed by the Pope, how could the Pope disapprove of what Cranmer was doing?

While all this was going on in Rome, the Parliament in Westminster was left twiddling its thumbs and – as if to prove its harmlessness – on about 12 February De Burgo was taken to observe the Commons in session. He found them debating an insignificant bill against thieves. He did not stay long but went on to a sumptuous banquet at the lodgings of Treasurer Fitzwilliam.[7]

De Burgo should, of course, have eaten his supper with a long spoon. But he was by no means the only person, nor the most important, to be taken in by Henry's performance in the great game. The result was that by mid-February Henry and Anne were confident of success; they even felt free to indulge in a little careless talk. Twice Henry boasted to the inner circle of his Court that 'he would, immediately on the expedition of the Bulls, let people know what he was about, and what he himself intended doing'. And soon a more explicit version of his words became the common rumour. 'Well nigh everybody', the Venetian ambassador reported on 23 February, 'is of the opinion that immediately on the arrival of the Bulls . . . the Divorce case will be terminated, whether the Pope assents or not.'[8]

But, as usual, it was Anne who went the furthest. On 7 February, while dining in her own apartments, she said, in a vivid if ominous phrase, that she was 'as sure as her own death that she should be very soon married to the King'. A fortnight later, on the 22nd, she made her boast about her pregnancy public. Speaking, almost certainly, to her former flame, Thomas Wyatt, she said that she had 'a fearsome and unquenchable longing to eat apples', which she had never experienced before. The King, she added, had told her 'that it was a sign that she must be pregnant', But, she said, she had replied that 'she was sure she was not'. Then she burst out laughing and withdrew into her apartments.[9]

No one who heard her was in any doubt what she meant.

The upshot was that the King felt able to jump the gun. Cranmer's Bulls did not arrive in London till about 26 March. But already on 9 March there had been an officially sponsored sermon at Court, delivered in the presence of Henry and Anne themselves, which denounced the King's existing marriage as sinful and called on him to enter into a new and better union. No wonder, the preacher had continued, if Henry in such circumstances should take a wife who was of 'low rank' but eminent in 'virtues and secret merits . . . as happened in the cases of Kings Saul and David'.

When she heard about the sermon Catherine decided that it was 'a sign of her case being irretrievably lost'.[10]

Five days later, on the 14th, the Bill in Restraint of Appeals was introduced into the Commons. The Bill, painstakingly drafted and redrafted by Cromwell and Audley the previous autumn, was intended to do enough but no more. Extravagant and unnecessarily controversial schemes, like the transfer of matrimonial jurisdiction from the Spiritual to the Temporal law, were abandoned. Instead, the Bill left the Spiritual jurisdiction intact – up to a point. For appeals from Canterbury to Rome were forbidden. The Archbishop, as Chapuys put it, would now become Pope in England.[11]

But, as Henry and Anne had known all along, Cranmer intended to be a modest sort of Pontiff who would defer in almost all things to his royal master and mistress-to-be. And he made this clear from the moment of his consecration, which took place on Passion Sunday, 30 March, only four days after the arrival of his Bulls.[12]

First Cranmer went to the Chapter House of St Stephen's College in the Palace of Westminster. There, in the presence of a select group of witnesses – the King's prothonotary, the clerk of the Council and a handful of canon lawyers – Cranmer swore the required oaths to the Pope and then, as agreed, immediately undercut them by his Protestation. Nothing in the oaths, he affirmed, should oblige him to act 'against the Law of God, or against our illustrious King of England, his Commonwealth, Laws or Prerogative'. Nor should his oaths leave him 'any the less free to speak or less able to advise and assent to anything which might further the Reformation of the Christian religion, the government of the English Church, or the Prerogative of the Crown or the well-being of the Commonwealth'. Rather indeed, he promised to take the initiative in driving change: 'to reform wherever and whatever in the English Church that shall seem to me to require reformation'.[13]

Was it Cranmer himself who invoked 'Reformation'? Or Henry? Or Cromwell? Whoever it was chose well. For the clarion cry of 'Reformation' was one of the keys to the forthcoming revolution. It would be used to justify actions more dubious than the breaking of oaths and to quell consciences more sensitive than Cranmer's.

After making the Protestation, Cranmer processed south through the Cloister to St Stephen's chapel for his consecration.

Built by the first three Edwards, St Stephen's was the private royal chapel of Westminster Palace. And its lavish decoration and sculpture made it the symbol of the piety of the medieval English kings: there were images of King Edward III and Queen Philippa and their ten children, of the two sergeants-at-arms who attended them in procession, and of the Adoration of the Magi or Three Kings, on whose feast day of 6 January the King and Queen came to the chapel for the most splendid ceremony of the Court liturgical year.[14]

No one, however, who had worshipped in the chapel, not even the founder-kings, was a more devout believer in the religious role and authority of monarchs than Cranmer. But no one interpreted the role more radically either.

Before entering the chapel, Cranmer had been vested in his priestly robes and the ceremony he was to undergo would make him a priest of priests: Archbishop, Primate of All England, successor of St Augustine and the Apostles, and, through the laying-on of the *pallium*, the direct representative of the Pope and St Peter himself. But, throughout, Cranmer clutched the notarial copy of his Protestation like a royal talisman. And, at each crucial point, he referred himself to it: when he took his first oath to the Pope before his consecration, and, again, when he swore a second oath before he received the *pallium*. All that he did, swore and accepted, he insisted, was subject to the over-riding conditions made in his Protestation: the ceremony might seem to make him the Pope's but, to his mind at least, his Protestation kept him intact as God's and the King's.

Reginald Pole's brutal comment seems fair. 'Other perjurers', he told Cranmer, 'be wont to break their oath after they have sworn; you break it before.'[15]

The rights and wrongs of Cranmer's action were, finally, a matter between his conscience and his God. It was the *effect* of what he did that mattered. For Henry and Anne now had an Archbishop of Canterbury of their choice who would do their bidding. And he hastened to obey. He had to, because Easter, Anne's proclaimed deadline, was only a fortnight away.

The issue of the Divorce had already been submitted to Convocation on 26 March and, over the following days, the 'Determinations' of the universities, in the obtaining of which Anne's tutor, her father and her brother had played so prominent a role, were tabled and debated. But on 1 April Cranmer himself took the chair in the upper house of Convocation for the first time as Archbishop. He proved a ruthless business manager and, within a few days, secured large majorities for two key propositions: that there was proof that Arthur had 'carnally known' Catherine and that the Pope had no power to dispense the case. Fisher fought to the last and was silenced only by his arrest on the 6th. On the 8th, Convocation itself was prorogued. It had laid down the principles; it would be up to Cranmer to give them judicial effect.[16]

Parliament had also been prorogued for the Easter recess on 7 April. According to Chapuys, the Commons were still resisting the Bill in Restraint of Appeals on 31 March. But, within the week, opposition collapsed and the Bill cleared both Houses by the day of prorogation.[17]

Anne's deadline had been met.

On 9 April a high-ranking delegation of Councillors, headed by Norfolk, formally gave Catherine notice that Henry had already married Anne. But it was left to her Chamberlain, Mountjoy, to inform her of the corollary: that she was no longer Queen and must neither live nor be addressed as such. Indignantly, Catherine brushed the royal order aside.

'It is this Anne', Chapuys wrote, 'who has put [Henry] in this perverse and wicked temper . . . and we must believe that she will never cease until she has seen the end of the Queen, as she has done that of the Cardinal, whom she did not hate so much.'[18]

It is a harsh judgement. But events would prove it accurate.

Finally on 12 April, Easter Saturday, Anne, having vanquished her rival, appeared for the first time as Queen herself. 'Anne went', the Venetian ambassador reported, 'with the King to high mass, as Queen, and with all the pomp of a Queen, clad in cloth of gold, and loaded with the richest jewels.' During the service, she was prayed for as Queen and afterwards 'she dined in public' in state.

'All the world is astonished at it', Chapuys noted, 'and even those who take her part do not know whether to laugh or to cry.' But the incentive to keep a properly composed expression was great. 'The King', Chapuys continued, 'is very watchful of the countenance of the people, and begs the Lords to go and visit and make their court to the new

Queen.' Henry had also, the ambassador had discovered, done a deal with Cranmer to regularize his matrimonial position.[19]

That very day, in fact, Henry had replied to a letter from Cranmer, asking for permission to try his marriage. The request was an awkward one: Cranmer, who professed his submission to the King, had nevertheless to sit in judgement upon him. The irony of the situation had not disturbed Wolsey's serenely imperious confidence in either of the earlier trials of 1527 or 1529. But it concerned both the King and his Archbishop now, and it took two versions of Cranmer's letter before Henry was satisfied. In the first version, Cranmer had asked to know Henry's 'pleasure' before he proceeded. In the second version, this was formalized into a request for a royal 'licence' to judge the case, as specified by the Act in Restraint of Appeals. Nor was it sufficient for Cranmer to state that he sought such permission 'most humbly upon my knees'. Instead, he was coached into ending his second letter by proclaiming himself to be 'prostrate at the feet of your Majesty' and protesting that he had sued for the licence 'only for the zeal' he had to end the scandal of the Great Matter and to settle the succession 'and for none other intent and purpose'.[20]

Henry, clearly, was determined that the keys snatched from St Peter should not be handed over unconditionally to his English substitute. And Cranmer, out of conscience as well as expediency, was happy to acquiesce.

Armed with Henry's licence, Cranmer stepped, however improbably, into Wolsey's shoes and launched the third 'inquisition' into the marriage. And, as previously, the royal couple were summoned to appear before their ecclesiastical judge. According to Chapuys, the summons was served on Catherine on about 15 April. 'The Queen', he reported, 'has been cited to appear before the Archbishop of Canterbury on [1 May], at an Abbey 30 miles from here.' The Abbey was Dunstable Priory in Bedfordshire. It was near the royal hunting lodge of Ampthill, where Catherine had been ordered to take up residence – but, at a dozen miles to the south-west, it was not too near. Indeed, according to Chapuys, its remoteness was why it had been selected. 'This', he reported, 'being a solitary place [it] has been chosen for secrecy, as they fear that if the affair was managed [in London], the people would not refrain from speaking of it and perhaps from rioting.'[21]

Henry, clearly, had not forgotten his humiliation at the hands of the London crowd at the Blackfriars Trial. There must be no repetition, and Catherine must be given no opportunity to grandstand and milk sympathy.

Nevertheless, the King's preparations were strikingly disorganized. This is curious. Henry's arguments were hardly under-rehearsed (after all, he had been saying much the same thing for six years). And his leading counsel was the usually ferociously efficient Gardiner. What had gone wrong? Perhaps there were already tensions between Gardiner and Cromwell. Perhaps Henry's advisers had spread themselves too thin: after all, they had just coped with contentious sessions of both Parliament and Convocation and they were about to face a meeting of the Northern Convocation, which was even more rootedly hostile to the Great Matter than its southern equivalent. Perhaps Anne's own driving energy was absent, as her mind had already moved on from fighting for her new status to celebrating and enjoying it; if so, it proved a temporary aberration, albeit a dangerous one.

Whatever the reason, crucial documentation was missing. Where, Audley wrote to Cromwell, were the 'Determinations' of the universities? Cranmer had already been approached, but 'Wiltshire reports he hath them not'. If Cromwell did not have them, they must be at York Place or with Dr [Rowland] Lee. 'If at York Place the King says you may go thither; if not, send for Dr Lee, or, if he be not in town, search his chambers'. For the papers must be found! 'The King', Audley concluded, 'wishes them sent with speed to [Gardiner].'[22]

All this accounts for the fact that Cranmer did not open his court till Saturday, 10 May. Even then the King's case was not watertight: papers were still astray and crucial witnesses were missing.

Ironically, the day was saved for Henry only by Catherine's own behaviour. For Catherine was not for turning. Instead, she stuck rigidly to the strategy she had pursued since the Blackfriars Trial and refused either to recognize the court or to respond to the summons. This enabled Cranmer, like the Cardinal-Legates, to pronounce her 'contumacious' and proceed in her absence.

But it was still a close-run thing, as Thomas Bedell, the clerk to the Council, detailed in a letter to Cromwell written immediately after the end of the first day's session. The key witnesses to Catherine's response to the summons, Bedell reported, had not arrived at Dunstable; the two aged ladies who were to testify to the consummation of Catherine's marriage had not appeared either; the King's 'protestation' (in effect his witness statement) was not to hand nor, despite Henry's imperious command, had the 'Determinations' of the universities turned up. Oh, and they were still missing 'the instrument of the opinion of the Convocation', which Cranmer had secured with such effort the previous month.[23]

It is an extraordinary catalogue of ineptitude. But Catherine's own absence and, *a fortiori*, the absence of her lawyers, enabled Cranmer to keep the show on the road. Anne's cousin, Sir Francis Bryan, turned up like a bad penny for the second session on Monday, 12 May and his evidence of Catherine's response to the summons enabled her to be pronounced definitively contumacious (*vere et manifeste contumacem*). This, in turn, meant that the two elderly ladies, who had refused to imperil their bodies as well as their consciences by travelling to Dunstable, could depose in London without the need for a further summons to Catherine and the consequent delay while her response was awaited.[24]

But the most important advantage of the King's men was, as Chapuys had foreseen, Dunstable's rural isolation. 'Few or almost none were present at the place of judgement', Bedell reported, 'but such as came thither . . . with their lords and masters.' Not even Catherine, though she was only a few miles distant, bothered to send observers. 'There came', Bedell reported in his second letter to Cromwell, written after the Saturday session of the court, 'no servant of hers in Dunstable, sith our coming hither, but only such as this day be brought in as witness against her.'[25]

Practically *in camera*, therefore, the King's lawyers felt able to cut corners. Henry's counsel, Bedell noted in a revealing remark, 'studieth, as diligently as they possibly can, to cause everything to be handled, so as it may be most consonant to the law, *as far as the matter will suffer*'. Much the same went for Cranmer himself as judge, according to the same observer. 'And my Lord of Canterbury', he wrote, 'handleth himself very well, and very uprightly, without any evident cause of suspicion to be noted in him by the counsel of the said Lady Catherine, if she had any present here.'[26]

Indeed, so happy was the present state of affairs for the King's case that Cranmer did everything he could to prevent any further publicity. He had not, he explained to Cromwell on 17 May, 'even written to the Queen' (that is, Queen Anne, not Queen Catherine) but only to the King himself. His reason was the overwhelming need for discretion: 'I think it expedient that ... the process be kept secret for a time,' he insisted. And, above all, it must be kept secret from Catherine, lest 'a great bruit and voice of the people in this behalf might move her to do that thing herein which peradventure she would not do if she shall hear little of it'. For Cranmer's fear was that Catherine might think better of her position and appear in his court, which would throw the whole smoothly running machinery out of gear. Say nothing, he begged Cromwell, and beseech Henry himself to say nothing either.[27]

It is an unlovely picture. But the tactic worked. By the 17th Cranmer was able to advise Henry that, at last, 'your Grace's great matter is now brought to a final sentence, to be given on Friday now next ensuing [the 23rd]'. That was almost a week away. But the court, Cranmer explained to his impatient master, could not convene any earlier since all the intervening days were 'ferial' or holy days, on which an ecclesiastical court could not sit.[28]

On the 23rd Cranmer duly reported to Henry 'that I have given sentence in your Grace's great and weighty cause' and sent him a transcript. But immediately there arose another problem: Cranmer had been instructed that Henry's marriage with Anne was to be found good. But the details were lacking. So, Cranmer reminded Henry, was time: 'for the time of the Coronation is so instant and so near at hand, that the matter requireth good expedition to be had in the same'.[29]

This time, as Anne herself was directly involved, there were no hitches.

62. Coronation

According to Cranmer, writing to his friend ambassador Hawkins in Rome, the preparations for Anne's coronation began after 'our rejourneying home' from the trial at Dunstable: in other words, in the last week of May 1533. Cranmer's letter is important since it is, I think, the first account of a coronation by the officiating prelate. But, as so often, its writer was being economical with the truth. It would, no doubt, have been more decorous if the preparations *had* been delayed until Henry's Divorce was absolute. But Anne's timetable dictated otherwise. She had been recognized as Queen at Easter and she would be crowned at Whitsuntide, which fell on 1 June. This meant that, even as Cranmer was riding back from divorcing one Queen in Bedfordshire to crowning another in London, the preparations for the latter event had been going on for several weeks, even for a year, if the rebuilding of the Tower is counted (as it should be) as part of the operation.[1]

And the man in charge (as with the Tower works) was Cromwell – Anne's other right hand man. He takes the credit for the fact himself. In the list of 'things done by the King's Highness sithence I came into his service', he notes as the penultimate item: '[the King] has borne most costly charge at the coronation of Queen Anne'. Contemporaries also recognized Cromwell's role. He was glad, wrote Sir Anthony Browne, one of Henry's inner circle and ambassador in France, at the report that the Queen's coronation had been so honourably done – 'which was not a little to Cromwell's credit'. But the best testimony of all is Cromwell's own papers. These show that he planned the event; marshalled the personnel and paid for much of the finery from the secret funds under his direct control.[2]

The result was not only one of the best organized, but also one of the best documented coronations in English history. Here an insider view is useful. 'The Queen's coronation', Anne's Vice-chamberlain, Sir Edward Baynton, wrote to her brother, Lord Rochford, 'is honourably passed as ever was, if all old and ancient men say true.' Memory clearly was the issue: the last coronation was Henry's and Catherine's, twenty-four years previously in 1509. And the last royal entrée of a woman into London was Catherine's for her wedding to Arthur in 1501. These events were a bench-mark; they also introduced a note of direct comparison and competition between Anne and her displaced rival. To match them was not enough. Instead, Anne's coronation had to exceed anything that anyone could recall of any of the celebrations for Catherine – for the sake of Anne, for Henry and for their marriage.

It was Cromwell's task to provide this extra panache of pomp and circumstance. How well he performed it – in reality as well as in possibly prejudiced comment – remains to be seen.[3]

The coronation rituals were, of course, already ancient: the coronation *ordo* or order of service had changed relatively little since the coronation of King Edgar in AD 973. The crown and much of the regalia were likewise Anglo-Saxon and were ascribed, probably correctly, to Edward the Confessor (1042–66). It was also Edward the Confessor who had first determined on Westminster Abbey as the coronation church. But each succeeding age had added something, with the result that, round the central Anglo-Saxon stem, there clustered a thick ivy-growth of precedent and tradition.[4] 'To do things by the book' – that is, *The Royal Book* – was therefore the first test for each re-enactment of the ceremony.

The Court of Claims, which determined the right to perform various hereditary offices at the coronation, met on about 5 May under the presidency of the Duke of Suffolk. He was the Lord High Steward for the day of the coronation, and, as such, took charge of the honorifics of the secular side of the ceremony.[5]

Suffolk's acceptance of the appointment was, in itself, a triumph for Anne. Following the lead of his formidable Duchess, Mary Tudor, Suffolk had been one of Anne's leading opponents. Now, however, he led the way in paying her honour. Admittedly, he had always been politically supple. But his present conversion was probably helped by his wife's illness, which proved mortal. Mary wrote a pathetic letter to Henry, as 'my most dearest and best beloved brother'. 'I am rather worse than better,' she wrote of her sickness. Nevertheless she intended to come to London with her husband, 'because I would be glad to see your Grace'. 'I have been a great while out of your sight', she continued. This was a result of her self-exile from a Court dominated by the hated Anne. But now 'I trust I shall not be so long again; for the sight of your Grace is to me the greatest comfort to me that may be possible'. She never made the journey, however, dying at Westhorpe Hall, Suffolk, on 25 June, some three weeks after Anne's coronation.[6]

Meanwhile, Suffolk duly ratified the claims of his fellow peers to perform their honorific services. In one sense this was pure convention. But it was also a vindication for Anne. Chapuys's despatches had been full of the boasts of great nobles that they would have nothing to do with the upstart royal mistress who would be Queen. Instead they would prevent her from becoming Queen by refusing to exercise their ancient offices for so unworthy a candidate. Most outspoken of all, apparently, was the Earl of Shrewsbury. According to Chapuys, 'to his office in this kingdom belongs the right of holding the Queen's royal crown'. And, since neither he nor his family had ever incurred reproach, 'he now would take care not to fall into dishonour by placing [the crown] on any other head but that of the present Queen'.[7]

Chapuys admitted that he had got the story at second-hand. And he certainly got it wrong. For Shewsbury's coronation 'service' or function, which he claimed in right of his tenure by 'serjeanty' of the manor of Farnham Royal, Buckinghamshire, was not to carry the Queen's crown, but to support her right hand while it carried the sceptre. But, far from boldly refusing his charge, Shrewsbury petitioned the Court of Claims for the service. On the day itself the task was performed by his son and heir, Lord Talbot and Furnival. Perhaps this deputization was a concession to Shrewsbury's conscience; even so, it was a long way from his original boast and exposed it for the hot-air it was. Nor did his fellow nobles even make the gesture of dissent.[8]

And where the peerage led, the rest followed. The heralds performed their usual esoteric services, for which they billed the Keeper of the Privy Purse. Their charges included £50 for the crying of 'largesse', that is the proclamation of titles, at 'the most honourable and joyous marriage' and another £50 for the largesse at the coronation. The heralds, however, agreed to remit the former charge 'because they were not present'.[9]

This careful following of tradition led to episodes which, even then, struck observers as archaic. Cranmer, for example, was much taken by the creation of eighteen Knights of the Bath at the Tower on Friday night, 30 May. The ceremonial involved stripping and bathing the postulant knights, putting them to bed, rousing them in the small hours, cladding them in new robes of ancient form, and setting them to keep vigil in church. All of which was, Cranmer informed Hawkins, 'so strange to hear of, as also their garments stranger to behold or look on'. Clearly, Henry made sure that the rituals, which he himself had undergone at the age of three and a half at the hands of his father, on the occasion of his creation as Duke of York, were performed in their full, outlandish splendour.[10]

But equally Cromwell was not afraid to innovate. His most important change was in the processional route. In the traditional ritual, the Queen came to the Tower, rested the night, and then, the day before the coronation, processed through the City to Westminster in an open litter. Cromwell added to this a water procession which conveyed Anne in state from Greenwich to the Tower. The effect was to more-than-double the usual length of the processional route, to add another day to the ceremonies, which now stretched over four days, and to make the rebuilt Tower, sparkling in new stone and fresh paint, an important theatre of pageantry in its own right.

Anne thus had a larger stage and a longer performance. It was an opportunity to shine – or to fail in the most public fashion possible.

The ceremonies got underway on Thursday, 29 May at 1 o'clock, when the Lord Mayor, Sir Stephen Peacock, and the Aldermen in their scarlet and chains assembled at St Mary-at-Hill and, together with the Common Councillors, boarded the City barge at New Stairs by Billingsgate to lead the water pageant. The pageant was modelled on the annual river procession from the City to Westminster for the new Lord Mayor's swearing-in at Star Chamber. But the decoration of the barges was much more lavish, with royal escutcheons, and banners and pennants. First came a boat with a great dragon 'continually moving and casting wildfire', surrounded with monsters and wildmen, all likewise belching fire and making 'hideous noises'. Next, at 'a good distance', came the Lord Mayor's barge with, on the right hand, the gaily decorated bachelors' barge, with innumerable pennants tipped with bells, and on the left a barge with a pageant of Anne's badge of the white falcon, imperially crowned, on a golden tree stump which, made fertile by the bird's landing, sprouted red and white roses. Then followed, in order of precedence, the barges of the livery companies – dozens of them, all painted and gilded and hung with banners and tapestries.[11]

The procession made good order downstream, each barge two lengths behind the preceding one. They passed the river-front of Greenwich Palace, then, at Blackwall, in a carefully choreographed manoeuvre, the procession turned round and assumed a reverse order of precedence, with the Lord Mayor's barge coming last. In this order they rowed back to Greenwich, where they anchored. At 3 o'clock Queen Anne appeared. Clad in cloth of gold, she entered the Queen's barge. Actually, it was Catherine's barge, stripped of her emblems and redecorated with Anne's. Accompanying the Queen's barge were the lords and bishops, each in his own barge.[12]

Prominent among the bishops, of course, was Cranmer and his letter to Hawkins gives a vivid thumb-nail sketch of the return journey to the Tower: 'trumpets, shawms [a sort of oboe], and other diverse instruments all the ways playing, making great melody, which, as is reported, was as comely done as never was like in any time nigh to our remembrance'. The ships lining the river fired their guns, with particular heavy salvos at Limehouse and Ratcliff. Then, as the flotilla passed Wapping and came in sight of the Tower, the Tower's mighty guns, by a pre-arranged signal, joined in the salute, firing four at a time.[13]

Anne alighted at Tower wharf. There a 'long lane' or corridor had been cleared for her through crowds to the King's Bridge, which crossed the moat at the Byward Tower. She was greeted first by the Lieutenant and Constable of the Tower, then by the Lord Chamberlain, next by the Great Officers of State and finally, at the entrance to the Tower, by Henry himself, who publicly embraced her. It seemed a spontaneous gesture – like Catherine and Arthur turning to salute the crowd in St Paul's, thirty-two years previously in 1501. In fact, like that earlier gesture, Henry's greeting was written into the script. But this time it is certain that the couple kissed. The King, according to the clumsy prose of the recording herald, 'laid his hands on both [Anne's] sides, kissing her with great reverence and a joyful countenance'.[14]

Anne's face, we can imagine, was even more cheerful. For everything she had hoped for since 1527 – the King, the throne, the very kingdom itself – was now hers. But, before Henry swept her off into the Tower, she paused to give thanks to the Lord Mayor 'with many goodly words' for the water pageant. This was still anchored by the Tower, since only a small delegation had been permitted to land with the Lord Mayor. 'But for to speak of the people they stood on every shore to behold the sight,' wrote the chronicler, Edward Hall, who was another eye-witness. 'He that saw it would not believe it.'[15]

And a professed non-believer in the whole thing was, of course, Chapuys. Nevertheless even he acknowledged that 'innumerable people' were involved – though he claimed that they 'showed themselves as sorry as though it had been a funeral'.[16]

On the Thursday night Anne and Henry supped at the Tower and gave a splendid reception or 'void'. Late the following day, the pageantry recommenced with the ceremonial immersion of the postulant Knights of the Bath, which so excited Cranmer's curiosity. Eighteen baths were set up in the customary 'long chamber' in the White Tower, with rails for the hangings for the adjacent bedsteads. On the Saturday morning, the knights were dubbed by the King before taking part in Anne's procession, where they stood out (as Cranmer also noted) by virtue of their extra-ordinary costume of 'violet gowns with hoods purfled [bordered] with miniver, like doctors' – which more resembled the already antiquated forms of academic dress than normal fashionable male attire.[17]

Taking advantage of the long summer evenings, the procession left the Tower late, at about 5 o'clock. Anne's own equipage conformed precisely to the rules laid down in *The Royal Book*. Everything was white – her dress, her litter, and even the trappings of her horses. Also according to precedent, her head was uncovered, and, in Cranmer's vivid phrase, 'she [sat] in her hair' – that lustrous, dark hair that so contravened contemporary ideals of beauty. She wore a plain gold circlet, heavily jewelled, and her canopy was carried by the Barons of the Cinque Ports. Behind her came England's highest ranking peeresses, in chariots covered in cloth of gold and wearing robes of crimson velvet carefully differenced according to their rank. Cranmer, more sensitive to female beauty than to blood and position, dismissed these *grandes dames* as 'diverse ancient old ladies'. More youthful, though less dignified, women brought up the rear.[18]

There were also some innovations. Powerfully symbolizing Anne's francophilia, the procession was headed by twelve Frenchmen – merchants and servants of the French ambassador – all dressed in violet velvet with one sleeve in Anne's colours of violet and blue. Anne's own dress was in the French fashion, and an anonymous Frenchman who wrote an account of the event seems to have acted as a sort of style consultant – claiming credit, for instance, for the pennants hung with bells in the water procession, which he describes as being trimmed 'by my advice' with '*or clinquant*', to reflect the sun's rays as well as to make a noise. New groups were also invited to march in the procession, including the judges, who turned up in a body. They were headed by

FitzJames, the Chief Justice and included Sir John Spelman. And they wore their full judicial finery of scarlet gowns, hoods and tippets and gold collars of Ss. At the end of the procession, Anne bestowed kind words on the judges, saying to them: 'I thank you for all the honour you have done me this day'. The thanks were well repaid, for, over the next few years, the judges were to be very busy enforcing her title against the many who would deny it.[19]

The result of including such extra groups was that the procession was unusually long: 'from beginning to end', according to Cranmer, who rode next to the French ambassador, '[it] extended half a mile in length by estimation or thereabout'.[20]

The procession followed the usual route through the City, along streets which were freshly gravelled, railed on one side and hung with arras. At key points, the Queen paused to hear and applaud pageants. These, like the rest of the ceremonies, were a rather successful mixture of old and new.

The first was at Fenchurch Street, where children dressed as merchants welcomed the Queen to the City. This was an allusion to Anne's wide range of contacts with the merchant community – through the overlapping circles of Reform, book-sellers and the importers of French luxury goods. But there was also surely more than a nod to the fact that Anne was the first Queen of England who numbered a Mayor and citizen of London among her ancestors: when the citizens saluted Anne, they were hailing one of their own.

The next pageant, at Gracechurch Street, was mounted by the Hanseatic merchants of the Steelyard. These were another group heavily influenced by Reform. But it was the Renaissance, rather than the Reformation, which shaped their offering. It was designed by Holbein and it represented Mount Parnassus, with Apollo and the Nine Muses, who saluted Anne in appropriate verse. If the pageant as executed followed Holbein's surviving preparatory drawing at all faithfully, it was the most sophisticated piece of Renaissance theatrical design that London would see till the spectacular masque settings of Inigo Jones almost a century later.

Nor were the natives far behind in adopting the new fashions. The pageants laid on by the City included the Judgement of Paris, in which, predictably, Paris gave the prize to the Queen, not Venus, because Anne uniquely combined the attributes of the three rival goddesses:

> As peerless in riches, wit and beauty;
> Which are but sundry qualities in you three.

The theme of the Three Graces, performed at the Conduit in Cornhill, underwent a stranger transformation. The Graces were given their proper Greek names, which must have sounded mighty odd to English ears. But the translations changed them from the ethereal qualities of female beauty in the Greek into stolid badges of worldly prosperity in the English: Aglaia (*Brilliance*) became 'Hearty Gladness', Thaleia (*Bloom*) 'Stable Honour' and Euphrosyne (*Mirth*) 'Continual Success'.[21]

These translations were the result of deliberate choice and cultural difference, not ignorance. For the authors of the pageant-verses, Nicholas Udall and John Leland, were the cream of English scholarship. Udall, of Corpus Christi College, Oxford, had been caught up in the illicit book scandal of 1529, when Anne had tried to protect the miscreants whom Wolsey was seeking to root out, and he would go on to be an equally scandalous headmaster of Eton, whence he was dismissed after charges of pederasty with one pupil and complicity in a robbery committed by two others. Leland's life was scarcely less colourful. A student at both Oxford and Cambridge, he had in 1526–9 paid an extended visit to Paris, where he had been influenced by Lefèvre d'Étaples in religion and Guillaume Budé in scholarship and antiquarianism. Finally he went mad, after laying more-or-less single-handed the foundations of English historical scholarship on the wreckage of the monastic libraries. But what mattered in 1533 was that he was the most skilled Latin poet in England: 'Leland stands', it has been asserted, 'to the Latin poetry of sixteenth-century England as Wyatt and Surrey do to the English.'[22]

None but the best would do for Anne.

With authors like these, it was only to be expected that Anne's interests in Reform would also feature. They appeared in the great pageant at the Gate to St Paul's Churchyard. It showed an empty throne – Anne's throne – round which was written *Regina ANNA prospere! precede! et regna!* 'That is, in English, "Queen Anne prosper! proceed! and reign!"' Beneath were three ladies, each holding a gold or silver tablet inscribed with versions of the kind of Biblical texts that figured in Anne's own religious reading. The tablet of the Lady on the left read: *Confide in DOMINO* (from Psalm 11.1, 'In the Lord I put my trust'); and the tablet of the Lady on the right: *DOMINE! dirige gressos meos* (from Psalm 119.133, 'Order my steps in Thy word'). These two tablets were of silver. But the lady in the centre held a golden tablet with the words: *Veni amica coronaberis*: 'Come my love! thou shalt be crowned!' These words, which apply so neatly to Anne, are rather more difficult to track to their Biblical source. They *sound* like the ecstatic *Song of Songs*. But the precise quotation does not appear. Instead, it is almost certainly based on *Esther* 2.17:

> And the King loved Esther above all other women, and she
> obtained grace and favour in his sight more than all the virgins;
> so that he set the royal crown upon her head, and made her
> Queen instead of Vashti.

Vashti's offence had been to refuse to come when the King, Ahasuerus (Xerxes of Persia), had commanded. This was the crime of disobedience, for which that other displaced Queen, Catherine, could likewise be plausibly condemned.[23]

But all that was, for the moment, in the past. Instead, the principal message of the pageant looked firmly to the future and found it golden. For written at the feet of the ladies were Latin verses, of which the following is the contemporary translation:

> Queen Anne, when thou shalt bear a new son of the King's blood;
> there shall be a golden world unto thy people!

As Anne passed by, the ladies threw rose-petals and confetti ('wafers') over her head, with the verses written on the wafers in letters of gold.

The theme was continued in St Paul's' Churchyard, where she was greeted by a massed choir of children. 'Amen', she said, 'with a joyful smiling countenance', when their performance was over. Was it relief? Or appreciation?

She then passed through Ludgate, which was freshly painted and gilded, along Fleet Street and finally came to Westminster. The Hall was hung with tapestries and reglazed. In the middle of the Hall, she was helped out of her litter. She processed to the dais under the Cloth of Estate and took refreshments. By this time it must have been 8 or 9 at night. But still she was all graciousness. She sent the refreshments to her ladies, and thanked each group of participants in the procession.[24]

But now, it was over. She had, as *The Royal Book* required, showed herself to the people, going 'bareheaded and bare-visaged till she come to Westminster that all men may behold her'. Many, like Chapuys, had thought that she could not survive such exposure. She had proved them wrong. Still, it was with relief that she withdrew from the gaze of so many eyes – first to the Queen's Chamber, beyond the White Hall, where she changed, and then to the greater security of York Place itself and Henry's arms.[25]

Cranmer, privileged by both his position and his intimacy with the Queen to step behind the scenes, caught this moment of withdrawal from the public to the private with unique vividness. 'She was conveyed', he wrote to Hawkins, 'out of the backside of the palace to a barge and so unto York Place, where the King's Grace was before her coming.' 'For this you must ever presuppose', he continued, 'that his Grace came always before her secretly in a barge, as well from Greenwich to the Tower, as from the Tower to York Place.'[26]

Henry, as usual, was having his cake and eating it. It was Anne's day, not his, and he did not want to steal her thunder. But equally he wanted to savour Anne's triumph, for which they had both waited so long. In his barge on the Thames he was in earshot of the procession: he could follow its progresses, and hear the singing and cheers. He was also at hand to protect her with his powerful presence in case – God forbid – anything went wrong.

But it did not. His people acquiesced; some even rejoiced. A golden world had been promised by the poets; it must have seemed very near with Anne in the royal bedchamber at York Place.

The couple rose early the following morning, Whitsunday, 1 June, for the coronation itself. Between 8 and 9 o'clock Anne and her ladies entered Westminster Hall and stood on the dais. The Queen wore a royal surcoat and robe of purple velvet furred with ermine, with a high collar and tied with a lace with heavy gold tassels; while her ladies were dressed in their crimson robes, laced and furred according to rank. The Lord Mayor of London and the nobles who would take part in the coronation were already gathered in the Hall to greet her.[27]

Meanwhile, as Cranmer reported to Hawkins, 'there assembled with me at Westminster Church' the officiating clergy. They included the Archbishop of York, five bishops, one of whom was Gardiner of Winchester, the Abbot of Westminster and ten or twelve other abbots. '[We] all', Cranmer continued, 'revested ourselves in our *pontificalibus*, and, so furnished, with our Crosses and Crosiers, proceeded out of the Abbey in a procession to Westminster Hall, where we received the Queen.'[28]

There was now a pause, while the railed way from the Hall to the coronation stage or *theatre* in the crossing of the Abbey was covered over with blue cloth. Then the heralds marshalled the procession in order of precedence and, protected by the cloth, they marched to the Abbey. Anne was supported on her right hand by the Bishop of London and on her left by Gardiner, while her train, 'which was very long', was carried by the Dowager Duchess of Norfolk.[29]

Then came the coronation service. Disappointingly, Cranmer's report gives no details, referring simply to 'diverse ceremonies'. But it is clear that the usual ritual for a Queen consort was followed. There was no oath; instead the anointing was followed by the investiture with the ring, the crown, the sceptre and the ivory rod. 'I did set the Crown upon her head', wrote Cranmer, 'and then was sung *Te Deum*.'[30]

What Cranmer did not tell Hawkins, however, was that the crown used was St Edward's Crown itself. This was normally reserved for the coronation of the Sovereign and was very heavy. Immediately after the *Te Deum*, therefore, '[Cranmer] took off the Crown of St Edward, being heavy, and set on the crown made for her', which Anne wore for the ensuing coronation mass. After the mass, Anne went behind the high altar to offer at St Edward's shrine and to rest briefly. Meanwhile, all the peeresses had put on their coronets: 'every Duchess ... a coronal of gold wrought with flower'; 'every Marchioness . . . a demi-coronal of gold [and] every Countess a plain circlet of gold without flowers'.[31]

The procession now reassembled to conduct Anne back to Westminster Hall for the coronation feast. She wore her own crown and this time her right hand was supported by her father, the Earl of Wiltshire, and her left by Lord Talbot and Furnival, deputizing for his father, the absent Earl of Shrewsbury. The musicians struck up and 'the trumpets played marvellous freshly'.[32]

The banquet was described by Cranmer, who sat (though at a considerable distance) at Anne's right hand, 'as a great solemn feast [which lasted] all day'. Two ladies knelt at the Queen's feet, to attend to her private needs. On her right stood the Dowager Countess of Oxford and, on her left, the Countess of Worcester. Their task was to 'hold a fine cloth before the Queen's face when she list to spit or do otherwise at her pleasure'. To the sound of trumpets the Queen was served by great nobles who acted as her carver, sewer and butler, while her ewerer was Thomas Wyatt, deputizing for his aged father. And the Lords vied in their obsequiousness: 'these noblemen', as the official souvenir pamphlet noted, 'did their service in such humble sort and fashion, as it was a wonder to see the pain and diligence of them: being such noble persons'.[33]

The high table was protected by a kind of enclosure, while beneath it were four other tables running the length of the Hall, two against the walls and two free standing. The Barons of the Cinque Ports sat on the first table by the east wall; on the second, free-standing table, were the lords and bishops; on the third the peeresses and ladies; and on the fourth, by the west wall, the Lord Mayor and citizens. Before the feast started, the gentlemen removed their heavy outer robes and sat down to eat in comfort. Meanwhile Suffolk as Constable and Lord William Howard as Deputy Earl Marshal 'rode often times about the Hall, cheering the Lords, Ladies and the Mayor and his brethren'.

What struck Cranmer, like all other observers, was 'the good order' of the event. The service was so efficient 'that meat or drink nor anything else, needed not to be called for' – 'which', as the chronicler Hall noted, 'in so great a multitude was a marvel'. The food was likewise excellent – or at least expensive: 'there could be devised no more costly dishes nor subtleties'. Even more impressive, perhaps, was the discipline imposed on the company (especially after all that food and drink). For at the end of the meal everybody was required 'to rise and to stand still in their places' while the Queen washed: those seated with their backs to the wall stood on the benches, while the rest stood in front of the tables.[34]

Two people (apart from Anne herself) took particular satisfaction in all this: Cromwell, sitting below the lords in a specially designed crimson outfit furred with miniver, and Henry, who, accompanied by the French and Venetian ambassadors, watched the proceedings from a latticed viewing platform, built out from St Stephen's cloister. From the platform he had an excellent view of the ladies, who had all been seated facing him 'on the left side of the table along, and none on the right side'.[35]

After Anne had washed, there came a final round of ceremonies. The Lord Mayor offered her a gold cup of wine. She drank the wine and then gave the cup to the Mayor, with her thanks. Then, at the entry to her chamber, she presented the canopy, which the Barons of the Cinque Ports had borne over her during all the ceremonial processions, to the bearers, again 'with her great thanks'. As she was withdrawing the judges too knelt in a body to her and once more she said to them: 'I thank you for all the honour you have done me today'.[36]

The next time she spoke to the judges, it would be in the Tower, when she was on trial for her life.

By now it was 6 o'clock. She had been on show for ten hours and still there were the coronation jousts to sit through on the following day. It would have tested anyone's stamina and she, we must remember, was six months' pregnant.

*

Naturally, there were dissenters. And their feelings were brilliantly captured in a paper which may be Chapuys's report to Charles's minister, Granvelle. No one in the crowd would kneel, doff their caps and cry 'God Save the Queen'; the royal cipher 'HA', for Henry and Anne, was wilfully misinterpreted as 'Ha, ha!'; 'the crown became her very ill, and a wart disfigured her very much'. And so on. No doubt some people saw the event in this light and said such things. But at this stage they were a minority and probably a small one. For Anne was visibly, as Cranmer reported, 'somewhat big with child'. And if, as everybody confidently predicted, the child was a boy, it would be the heir of England and Anne would be impregnable.[37]

A few, like More, were conscientious (or fanatical) enough to ignore these calculations. Well-wishers (including Gardiner) sent More £20 to buy a new gown, but still he stayed away.[38]

The rest, however, knelt to the Queen and waited for the birth of her child.

63. Christening

The person who was most eager for Anne's child was, of course, Henry. He was forty-two. Mary, his only surviving child, had been born seventeen years previously. And Henry was desperate for another. Above all, he was desperate for a son. So Chapuys touched the rawest of nerves when, just after the coronation, he told the King that he should be content with Mary as his heir. 'I know better', Henry replied, 'I wish to have children.' But children could not be guaranteed, Chapuys coolly pointed out, even with a new wife. That was the last straw for the King. 'Am I not a man a man like any other? Am I not a man, a man like any other?' Henry burst out, repeating the question three times.[1]

Here indeed was the man behind the King. The King longed to give his kingdom an heir; the man was even more desperate to prove his continued virility.

And it rested on Anne, and Anne alone, to satisfy both King and man.

For the moment, however, Anne behaved as though she had not a care in the world. Her coronation had been a triumph, whatever her detractors might say. And she and her women were determined to celebrate, as Vice-chamberlain Baynton informed Rochford, who was on Embassy in France. 'As for pastime in the Queen's Chamber', Baynton wrote only a week after the ceremony, '[there] was never more'. 'If any of you', he continued with rough humour, 'that be now departed have any ladies that they thought favoured you, and somewhat would mourn at parting of their servants, I can no whit perceive the same by their dancing and pastime that they do use here.'[2]

Some six weeks later, however, preparations for the birth were underway in earnest. Anne and Henry had spent their post-coronation honeymoon at Greenwich, which, like the Tower and York Place, had been extensively refurbished for Anne. It had also been decided that Anne would 'take to her Chamber' there: Greenwich was Henry's own birthplace and his mother's favourite palace, and the omens were good.[3]

But first both Henry and Anne took a break. They left Greenwich at the end of June and moved by water, in slow stages and with lengthy pauses at York Place and Chertsey, to Windsor, where they arrived on 17 July. Then they went their separate ways. The new Queen remained at Windsor, while Henry, despite his ambitions for fatherhood, absented himself on a short Progress, staying with his courtier friends and hunting their parks. He was never very distant (Guildford was the furthest point he reached) and the Progress lasted only a month. But it was the first time that Henry and Anne had been apart since 1529 and the separation was enough to set tongues wagging. 'The long time the King has been away from the Lady', reported Chapuys hopefully, '[suggested] that he has begun to repent'.[4]

The rumours were moonshine, of course. Instead, all the couple's energies were focused on the forthcoming birth. On 24 July, Mountjoy, Catherine's Chamberlain, who had seen it all so many times before, wrote to Cromwell to hand over the baton. 'I send you', he wrote, 'certain remembrances of things to be provided against the Queen's taking her Chamber, of which I had experience when I occupied the room [position] . . . Please send it to [Anne's] Chamberlain.'[5]

In fact, Cromwell had matters in hand already and, soon after Anne vacated her apartments at Greenwich, the builders moved in to prepare them for her confinement. The workmen built 'a false roof in the Queen's Bedchamber for to seal it and hang it with cloth of arras'. They also constructed 'a cupboard of state . . . for the Queen's plate to stand on' in the Bedchamber, together with an altar, a platform and a stool where the Queen could sit during her devotions. Finally, they erected a 'great bed of state' in her Presence Chamber, or Throne Room.[6]

Meanwhile Anne was making her characteristic contribution to the preparations. Catherine, apparently, had brought with her from Spain 'a very rich triumphal cloth . . . to wrap up her children with at baptism'. Anne determined that the cloth, like Catherine's jewels and Catherine's barge, should be hers, and she got Henry to make the request. Catherine reacted with a predictable mixture of indignation and horror: 'It has not pleased God', she said, '[that] she should be so ill-advised as to grant any favour in a case so horrible and abominable.'

The source is Chapuys, and from what we know of both women, his story seems all too likely to be true. But it cannot be independently vouched for. On the other hand, Catherine certainly clung on to other tokens of her many unhappy encounters with childbed. Among her goods stored at Baynard's Castle, her principal London residence, were the 'Counterpanes [of state] of tissue [of cloth of gold], furred with powered ermine, provided for [the ex-Queen] what time she lay in childbed'. Similarly, she had kept the 'necessaries, provided for . . . child-bed'.

They included three smocks of fine Holland cloth, two petticoats and three breast cloths. There were also items for the baby, such as two rollers or swaddling bands and 'a lawn [fine linen or cambric cloth], to cover a child, fringed with gold'. The latter sounds like the 'very rich triumphal cloth' which Anne had coveted. But it can hardly be the same, since, when she had the opportunity, she did not bother to take it for herself.[7]

Henry, for his part, was thriving on the prospect of renewed fatherhood. 'The King's Highness is merry and in good health,' reported Sir John Russell on 6 August. Indeed, he continued, 'I never saw him merrier of a great while than he is now; and the best pastime in hunting of red deer that I have seen.' But, within a week, the party would return to Windsor, 'and soon after the Queen removeth from thence to Greenwich where her Grace taketh her chamber'. Once again, the river journey was done by easy stages. Henry rejoined the Queen at Windsor according to plan on the 17th. On the 21st they removed to York Place and on the 26th they went to Greenwich.[8]

Anne's confinement now began. Her Chamberlain, Lord Burgh, briefed by Mountjoy, offered the pledge, unheard at Court for over a dozen years, 'to the Queen's good hour'. The procession formed and accompanied Anne towards her Chamber. They passed the great bed of state. This Anne had turned into another triumph over her fallen rival. For hung on the frame constructed by the carpenters, were the ceiler, tester and counterpane, all 'richly embroidered upon crimson velvet', of the 'Bed of Alençon'.[9]

According to Chapuys, the bed had formed part of the ransom of the Duke of Alençon who had been captured at the Battle of Verneuil in 1424. And certainly a bed of this name was carefully kept among the royal treasures, with its precious stuff protected by '16 yards of old red cotton to fold the same in'. Now why should Anne so want this magnificent but ancient relic? For Chapuys its opulence was grounds enough. As well, Anne may have been interested in its French associations.[10]

But I would guess that there was a livelier motive. Was Anne confusing Alençon with that other French Duke captured by the English, Longueville? Longueville was the trophy of Henry's victory at the Battle of the Spurs in 1513 and the King had sent him back to England as a pledge of his love for Catherine. Meanwhile, Catherine's forces won the much greater victory of Flodden; and Catherine, as we have seen, was able to reply proudly to her husband that, for his French Duke, she sent him the coat of the dead King of Scots. It was Catherine's finest hour in England. Had Anne decided that the 'Bed of Alençon' was its symbol and that now, at the time of *her* finest hour, she would persuade Henry to let her appropriate it for herself?

It seems a real possibility.

At the Chamber door, the Chamberlain and other gentlemen stood aside. Anne entered. She had wanted Catherine's place and Catherine's possessions. Now she had them. Less desirably, she also faced Catherine's predicament. Would she, unlike Catherine, deliver?

What made the pressure worse, probably, was Henry's serene confidence. 'His physicians and astrologers', Chapuys reported, had told him that it was 'certain . . . that the Lady would bear a son'. The King clearly believed them and had made arrangements accordingly. He had already started planning the celebratory jousts. The French were approached to send a 'notable personage' to represent Francis I at the christening of the Prince. And the royal clerks prepared circular letters announcing the 'deliverance and bringing forth of a Prince' and requiring the addressees to 'pray for the good health, prosperity and continual preservation of the said Prince'. The letters were written in Anne's name and sealed with the Queen's signet, and they needed only the date to be filled in.[11]

Chapuys was writing on 3 September, a week after Anne had taken to her Chamber. But just before she stepped into this other, female world, Chapuys reported, Henry and Anne had their first quarrel. It was, needless to say, about another woman – perhaps indeed one of the Court beauties whom Henry had had such opportunity to scrutinize at Anne's coronation banquet. In response, Anne, 'full of jealousy . . . used some words to the King at which he was displeased'. And this time Henry did not swallow his displeasure. Instead, he told her 'that she must shut her eyes, and endure as her betters had done'. And he added a threat: 'she ought to know that it was in his power to humble her again in a moment more than he had exalted her'.

Anne was finding out the difference between being a mistress and a wife. And she did not like it. There was 'a grudge' (a sulk) and Henry did not speak to her for two or three days.

Chapuys, naturally, was gleeful. But he was wise enough in the ways of the world to warn the Emperor about taking the story too seriously. 'No doubt these things are lovers' quarrels,' he cautioned, which blow over almost as soon as they have begun.[12]

The Royal Book specified only that the Queen should take her Chamber 'when it pleaseth [her]'. But a confinement of some weeks was usual. However, after only twelve days, Anne's labour began. Either her doctors had miscalculated or the baby was premature. The former seems the more likely as the delivery was smooth and the baby, born between 3 and 4 p.m. on Sunday, 7 September, was 'fair' and healthy. Henry had everything he wanted.[13]

Except that the baby was a girl.

We know nothing of the immediate response of either Anne or Henry. But it is certain that the baby's gender was a heavy blow. On no account, however, could they give their opponents the satisfaction of showing their disappointment. So they carried on regardless. The pre-prepared letters announcing the birth were sent out, with the word 'Prince' altered to 'Princes[s]' with a stroke of the pen. And arrangements for a magnificent public christening were put into immediate effect. It would take place three days after the birth, on the afternoon of Wednesday, 10 September. Once more, the Lord Mayor, aldermen and common councillors of London were summoned in a body to Greenwich. The French ambassadors were invited. Only one thing – the planned celebratory jousts – was cancelled.[14]

A mere three days between the birth and the christening of course imposed a terrifyingly tight timetable. The ceremonial itself was not the issue: the leading nobility were already on standby at Court and the rituals they would perform were familiar and (for the older participants at least) well rehearsed. But getting the infrastructure ready was another matter, and the Office of Works at Greenwich moved into overdrive. The 7th, the day of the baby's birth, was a Sunday and the 8th was the Feast of the Nativity of the Blessed Virgin Mary. Nevertheless, one carpenter started work on the Sunday and by the Monday he was joined by twenty-eight others. They worked through the Feast day and were paid double on the Tuesday for overtime. They were still at it on the Wednesday morning. But, by the time the dignitaries started to arrive for the afternoon ceremonial, all was ready.[15]

The workmen had created a processional way from the Hall door of the palace to the Church of the Observant Friars. They had erected frames, which were hung with tapestry, and rails, to keep off the crowds. The inside of the Church had likewise been transformed into a *theatre*. The carpenters had built a large octagonal stage, three steps high. The centre was strengthened with a solid post to take the weight of the great silver font, which, following the practice of the last hundred years, was brought up specially from Canterbury. And the top of the stage, where the font stood, was also protected by rails. The rails were covered in red cloth; 'fine cloth' was laid over the stage and above hung a square canopy of crimson satin fringed with gold. There was an enclosure with a brazier, where the child could be undressed in comfort. And the font was lined with fine linen and filled with warmed water.[16]

When the preparations were complete, the procession was marshalled in the Hall. Nobles carried the basins, in which the god-parents would wash, the candle which would be thrust into the newly baptized child's hand, the salt which would exorcize her and the chrism cloth which would be bound over her anointed head. The baby herself was borne by the Dowager Duchess of Norfolk and wrapped (in default of Catherine's Spanish robe) in a royal mantle of purple velvet with a long train furred with ermine.

It was a Boleyn triumph: Anne's uncle, Norfolk, back hotfoot from France, officiated as Earl Marshal; her father, Wiltshire, supported the baby's train; her brother, Rochford, was the first of the four nobles who carried the portable canopy over the child; and her creature, Cranmer, was godfather.

Chapuys had heard that the baby would be named Mary. In fact, she was christened Elizabeth. This was the name of both her grandmothers: Henry's mother, Elizabeth of York, and Anne's mother, Elizabeth Boleyn née Howard. At the moment of the christening the Church was filled with a blaze of light: the candle in the child's hand was lit and, simultaneously, five hundred torches carried by yeomen of the guard and other servingmen were fired as well. Then Garter King of Arms proclaimed the child's name and titles 'with a loud voice':

> God, of his infinite goodness, send prosperous life and long to the
> high and mighty Princess of England, Elizabeth!

And the trumpets sounded.[17]

So Mary had been left with her name at least. But her title of Princess and her status of heir were transferred to the new royal child.

Mary, however, took after her mother. She was not the surrendering kind, and she would yield nothing, it quickly became clear, without a ferocious struggle.

64. Resistance

Even before she became Queen, Anne had Mary in her sights. 'She has boasted', Chapuys reported in April 1533, 'that she will have the Princess for her lady's maid.' Elizabeth's birth gave Anne the opportunity for an even more exquisite vengeance: she would make Mary, willy-nilly, a member of her baby daughter's Household and force the pretend Princess to serve the real one.[1]

But it proved easier said than done.

Elizabeth, preceded by her baptismal gifts, had been carried back to the Queen's Chamber to be presented to her mother and father after her christening. But then, as was usual with royal children, she was whisked away to a specially adapted nursery suite at Greenwich. In it, there was a newly-built screen to protect the royal baby from draughts, and a table to enable her nurse to roll the swaddling clothes in which she was wrapped to encourage her limbs to grow straight. She also had a substantial staff. At its head was the Lady Mistress of the Nursery, Margaret, Lady Bryan. She was the sister and heiress of Lord Bourchier and mother of Sir Francis Bryan. But she could not have been more different in character from her rake-hell son. She was sensible and warm and indiscriminately motherly, and she transferred her affections easily from Mary, over whose infancy she had also presided, to Elizabeth.[2]

The other key member of Elizabeth's staff was her wet-nurse, who suckled the child. The appointment was important. It was also eagerly sought for, and Anne would have received many nominations from interested parties. But the name of her final choice is unknown. There is also a story that Anne was eager to breast-feed her own baby, and was only prevented from doing so by Henry's selfish desire for a good, uninterrupted night's sleep! Refusing a wet-nurse would have been a characteristically unconventional gesture on Anne's part. But, alas, the tale is derived from Leti's fictionalized account and is without foundation.[3]

Nevertheless, it *is* clear that Anne was immensely proud of her daughter and took an unusually close interest in her upbringing and welfare. This was no mere maternal indulgence, of course. Until Anne had a son, Elizabeth was the prime symbol of Anne's marriage – and the child's position, honour and dignity were the guarantee of her own.

This is why Anne was so determined to enforce Elizabeth's status as Princess. It is also why others resisted her infant claims so vehemently.

The contest of wills began in December 1533. On the 2nd, there was an unusually large and important meeting of the Council. The last, but by no means the least, item on the agenda was to take 'a full conclusion and determination . . . for my Lady Princess's house'. 'House', in Tudor English, meant both the house, or physical building, where Elizabeth was to stay, and the Household, or staff of servants, who would run her not-so-little Court. Both were to change dramatically.[4]

Hitherto, Elizabeth had remained with her parents at Greenwich. But now, with the approaching Christmas season, the palace was felt to be unsuitable for the infant. Too many people came to pay court, and there was too much risk of infection. Instead, it was decided that she should be moved to a salubrious rural retreat. The area chosen was the agreeable, well-wooded and gently rolling countryside of Hertfordshire. It was close enough to London for ease of access and far enough away to be healthy. There was also a choice of suitable houses, all lying within a few miles of each other. The first thought was to send her to the small royal residence of Hertford Castle. But for some reason minds were changed and it was resolved instead that Elizabeth should take up residence at Hatfield, a few miles to the west.[5]

Hatfield was a country retreat of the bishops of Ely and it was Bishop John Morton, later Archbishop of Canterbury, who had rebuilt the house as a fine, modern red-brick palace in about 1480. Arguably, from the point of view of his politically less influential successors, Morton built *too* well. Henry VIII took to the house and used it as if it were his own – first for himself and later for his children. Indeed, in 1533 he paid out of his own pocket for the few minor repairs that were necessary to get the house ready for Elizabeth and her suite.[6]

And with Elizabeth's new house went a new, and much bigger, Household staff. Hitherto, her nursery, with its dozen or so women, headed by Lady Bryan, had been a semi-autonomous department within, and serviced by, the large, well-oiled machinery of the royal Household. But at Hatfield her entourage would have to be self-sufficient. This meant the appointment of a multitude of new, largely male, servants to run the hall, kitchens, buttery and the other multifarious departments of a great Tudor household. And that, in turn, according to sixteenth-century notions, required that a man be put in charge. The choice fell on a Norfolk gentleman, Sir John Shelton, who owed his appointment to the fact that he was married to Anne's aunt on her father's side.[7]

There was ample scope for dispute between Shelton as Steward and Lady Bryan, who had hitherto reigned supreme as Lady Mistress. And there was soon to be another, much greater source of discord.

The Council decided that Elizabeth should begin her move to her new home on 10 December, which was the day that her parents also vacated Greenwich for a few days so that the palace could be cleaned and got ready for the Christmas festivities.[8]

En route to Hatfield, the child was carried through London in what, at the age of three months, turned out to be her first Progress-cum-entrée. According to Chapuys, there was 'a shorter and better road' to Hertfordshire which did not touch the capital (though it is difficult to imagine what it was). But instead the deliberate decision was taken to parade Elizabeth through the City 'for greater solemnity and to insinuate to the people that she is the true Princess'. To this end, she was accompanied, not only by her new Household, but also by a distinguished escort of 'two Dukes and several lords and gentlemen'.[9]

But Norfolk and Suffolk were there not only for show. Instead, each had been given an important mission by the Council meeting on 2 December. For, following Anne's double triumph of her coronation and Elizabeth's birth, there were now *two* Queens in England – and *two* Princesses also. Chapuys proposed, half-seriously, that the situation should be allowed to continue. But for Anne and Henry it was intolerable: their conduct could only be right if Catherine and Mary were wrong and had no claim to their titles.

The first move had taken place five months earlier against Catherine. On 5 July 1533 a proclamation had been issued, stripping her of the title of

Queen and requiring that she be henceforth known only by the style of Princess Dowager of Wales, to which she was entitled by virtue of her position as Arthur's widow. Two days before the issuing of the proclamation, Catherine's Household officers, headed by her Chamberlain, Mountjoy, were ordered to inform her of her demotion. She played the resulting encounter like a scene from grand opera. All her servants were summoned to her Privy Chamber. There they found Catherine reclining on her pallet or day-bed because, she claimed, she had hurt her foot with a pin. She was also racked by a cough.[10]

The sympathies of an already favourable audience thus caught, she ordered Mountjoy and his fellows to read their instructions. They did so, thereby disclosing immediately that they were required to address themselves to her as the Princess Dowager. This gave Catherine her opening for a magnificent tirade. She rejected such a title and always would. She was the King's wife and his Queen and the mother of his legitimate child and heir. She did not recognize either Cranmer's court or its verdict. And if any of her servants addressed her as Princess Dowager, 'she would never answer to any that shall so call her'.

And she proved as good as her word. The following day, Mountjoy, as a courtesy, showed her his written report, in which she was of course referred to throughout as 'Princess Dowager'. Once again, she rose to the occasion with a grand gesture. 'She called for pen and ink, and in such places as she found the name "Princess Dowager", she, with her pen struck it out' – 'as is apparent', noted Mountjoy of his defaced report of their encounter, which still survives, crossings-out and all.[11]

After such a performance and encore, Catherine's servants had supported her to a man. And Mountjoy, whose heart was not in it, had backed off.

Meanwhile, Mary was left temporarily untouched. 'As to the Princess', Chapuys had reported in April 1533, 'her name is not yet changed, and I think they will wait until the Lady has a child.'[12]

But the child *was* now born and Mary's hour had come. She was more than equal to it. There had already been one, abortive attempt against her position. On 14 September, a week after Elizabeth's birth, Mary's Chamberlain, Lord Hussey, was given oral instructions from the Council 'concerning the diminishing of her high estate of the name and dignity of Princess'. Mary reacted with a magnificent disdain. How dare Hussey act alone, she asked him, without other councillors and without written instructions, in 'such an high enterprise'? She 'could not a little marvel' at his rashness.[13]

It was her father's phrase and her father's authentic voice, and it was this similarity of character that made the clash between Henry and his daughter so terribly destructive to Mary – and so exasperating to Anne.

But now, in early December 1533, Norfolk was on his way with the written instructions and the posse of fellow councillors that Mary had required. He found her at Beaulieu or New Hall in Essex. Brusquely, he informed her of his mission: 'her father desired her to go to the Court and service of [Elizabeth], whom he named Princess'. Mary replied that 'the title belonged to herself and no other' and started to give many reasons. Wisely, Norfolk refused to get into an argument. Instead, he said 'he had not come to dispute but to accomplish the King's will'.

He spoke like a soldier under orders and Mary, in turn, beat a tactical retreat. She asked for 'half an hour's respite to go to her Chamber'. There, instead of womanish tears or a frantic packing up of favourite possessions, she sat down to execute a 'protestation'. It followed a draft sent her by Chapuys, and declared that nothing she might do under compulsion or by fraud should be prejudicial to her rights. Then she was ready. She asked what company she should bring. The Duke replied that it was unnecessary to bring much, as she would find plenty where she was going. 'So she parted with a very small suite.'[14]

Norfolk, of course, acted in the King's name. But Chapuys was in no doubt about the real source of his orders. '[The King]', he reported, 'is bewitched by this cursed woman [Anne] in such a manner that he dares neither say nor do except as she commands him.' Chapuys, of course, exaggerated: Henry had his own motives for requiring his ex-wife and his elder daughter to submit. He was King and everyone, even the closest members of his family, were 'subjects' whose principal, God-given duty was to obey. But there is also a kernel of truth in Chapuys's over-statement. It was Anne, as so often in the Great Matter, who supplied the emotional drive and energy behind the attacks on Catherine and Mary. The ambassador understood this – which is why, as the attacks were stepped up, his language about Anne became correspondingly more extreme. Thus far, his usual term for her had been 'the Lady'; now he calls her 'the whore' (*la putaine*), while the three-month-old Elizabeth, sleeping contentedly in her cradle, is denounced as 'the bastard'.[15]

There is a shocking ferocity about all this – as there was to be in Anne's response to Mary's intransigence. The female, we are told, is more deadly than the male. So it proved. For, from this contest, between two mothers and their daughters, was born the religious passion and violence that inflamed England for centuries.

The journey from Beaulieu to Hatfield was only about thirty miles and Mary, feeding off her rage and affronted dignity, remained in high spirits. When they arrived, Norfolk asked her 'whether she would not go and pay her respects to the Princess'. Mary had her reply off pat. 'She knew no other Princess in England except herself', she said, 'and . . . the daughter of My Lady Pembroke had no such title.' Then she proffered a small, contemptuous olive-branch. Out of courtesy, she explained, she called her father's bastard son, the Duke of Richmond, 'brother'. On the same grounds, 'since the King her father acknowledged her to be his', she would be prepared to address Elizabeth as 'sister'.

Exasperated, Norfolk asked her what message he should carry from her to the King. 'Nothing', she said proudly, 'except that his daughter, the Princess, begged his blessing.' He dared not bear such a message, replied Norfolk. Then he might leave it, she snapped.

Then, suddenly, Mary's strength snapped too and 'she retired to weep in her Chamber' – which, Chapuys added, 'she does continuously'.[16]

And her Chamber now became her refuge. Elsewhere, in the public spaces of the house, her every action paid an involuntary tribute to the hated Elizabeth. When she dined or supped in the Hall, the place she sat in and the food she ate betokened her inferiority. So she played on medical advice to have a large, early breakfast served in her Chamber. That enabled her to cut dinner or at least to touch neither food nor drink if she did put in an appearance. Then, if she could, she pleaded sickness again to have her supper served in her Chamber as well.

That her behaviour inflicted added cost and inconvenience on her half-sister's Household officers was, no doubt, a bonus.

Anne of course quickly learned of Mary's tactics, and moved to block them. '[She] has now ordered that she shall not be served in her Chamber', Chapuys reported. Anne had also decided to visit Hatfield herself on 18 February and stay for two days: 'I pray this may not be to the injury of [Mary],' Chapuys wrote.

Indeed, it seems clear that Anne trusted nobody in the matter of Mary apart from herself. Her aunt, Lady Shelton, who had been put in formal charge of the girl, received a stream of orders of mounting severity. If Mary used the banned title of 'Princess', she was to have her ears boxed 'as the cursed bastard that she was'. And if she persisted in refusing to eat except in her Chamber she was to be starved back into the Hall. But Lady Shelton seems to have been reluctant to exercise the full rigour of her instructions, and was sharply criticized by both Norfolk and Rochford for her leniency.[17]

Even Henry might backslide – or so Anne feared. He was, as we have seen, outraged at Mary's disobedience. But he was still the proud father, who, in 1527, had shown off Mary's auburn hair. It would take little, his new wife knew, to ignite that pride again. Finally, and most dangerously, Henry had a sentimental streak. He was easily moved to tears, especially when he was feeling sorry for himself. And he was impulsive. Better, Anne decided, not to trust him alone with Mary. Accordingly, when Henry visited Hatfield in January, she contrived that he should not meet his elder daughter.[18]

Henry naturally presented his behaviour in a different light. 'He had not spoken to [Mary]', he informed the French ambassador, 'on account of her obstinacy, which came from her Spanish blood.' But the ambassador's emollient reply that 'she had been very well brought up' was enough for 'the tears to come into his eyes and he could not refrain from praising her'.[19]

Anne's doubts were vindicated.

But in fact she had little better luck herself on her flying visit to Hatfield. At first, she tried kindness. Mary was warmly invited 'to visit her and honour her as Queen'. 'It would be', she said, 'a means of reconciliation with the King.' Anne also offered to intercede with Henry for her. But Mary's response was intransigent: 'she knew no Queen in England except her mother'. Anne tried again, only to be rebuffed once more. Then she resorted to threats, which left Mary equally unmoved. Anne departed in a rage, vowing 'to bring down the pride of this unbridled Spanish blood'.

'She will do the worst she can,' added Chapuys.[20]

Perhaps it was in response to the news of Anne's impending visit that Catherine had written an extraordinary letter to Mary. 'Daughter', she began, 'I have such tidings today that I do perceive, if it be true, the time is come that Almighty God will prove you.' 'I am very glad of it,' she continued, 'for I trust he doth handle you with a good love.' She had heard that 'this Lady' was coming to her, some said with a letter from the King. 'Answer you with few words,' she enjoined her, 'obeying the King your father in everything, save only that you will not offend God and lose your own soul.'

But the rest of Catherine's letter, with its reference to Mary's loss of the servants 'of your acquaintance' and its commendations to her old governess, Lady Salisbury, suggests that it was written a few months earlier in December, when Mary's own Household was dissolved and she was first brought to Elizabeth's Court.

Be that as it may, Catherine's purpose was clear: she was welcoming her daughter to the ecstasy of shared martyrdom. 'And now you shall begin and by likelihood I shall follow. I set not a rush by it; for when they have done the uttermost they can, then I am sure of the amendment.'

And if things did not get better on earth, they would, she knew, in Heaven.[21]

Catherine's premonition was correct. On 17 December 1533, a few days after Norfolk carried Mary off to Hatfield, his fellow duke, Suffolk, turned up at Catherine's lodgings at Buckden in Huntingdonshire. The house was another episcopal mansion, belonging to the bishop of Lincoln. Like Hatfield, it was a modern, red-brick structure, with a handsome gate-house and fine lodgings. But it lay only a mile from the Great Ouse and Catherine, who was allergic to damp, found its situation detestable.

Suffolk's mission was twofold: first, to compel Catherine's servants to swear a new oath of office to her not as Queen but as Princess Dowager; and, second, to persuade Catherine herself to move to Somersham, a few miles to the north-east. After much bullying, the Duke enjoyed limited success with Catherine's servants; but he failed completely with their mistress. Somersham, like Buckden, was situated on the Great Ouse, but it lay a few miles downstream, on the edge of the Fens. Chapuys paints a nightmarish picture of it as a sort of watery grave, 'surrounded with deep water and marshes'. It was also, 'as [Catherine] is informed, the most unhealthy and pestilential house in England'. Catherine refused to go. They would, she told Suffolk and his colleagues, have to 'bind her with ropes and violently enforce her thereto'.

And that was a step too far. Suffolk was prepared to do almost anything for his King and former brother-in-law. But to use force against the woman he had called Queen for twenty-four years was too much, even for him. It was an 'extremity' and, he informed Henry, since such 'extremities' had not been foreseen in his instructions, he referred the matter back to him for further orders.[22]

Once again, apparently, Catherine had seen off her persecutors. But it was a victory dearly bought. For the first time, she had played to her weakness rather than her strength. Her former imperious dignity vanished and instead she became openly hysterical – with, Suffolk feared, worse to follow. 'She may feign herself sick, and keep to her bed; or keep her bed in health, and will not put on her clothes,' he informed Henry.[23]

Suffolk clearly thought that it was all an act. It may indeed have begun as such. But it quickly went further and, a month later, Catherine remained in self-imposed imprisonment in her Chamber. '[She] has not', Chapuys reported in mid-January, 'been out of her room since the Duke of Suffolk was with her, except to hear Mass in a Gallery. She will not eat or drink what her new servants provide. The little she eats in her anguish is prepared by her chamberwomen, and her room is used as her kitchen.'

'She is very badly lodged,' he concluded somewhat redundantly.[24]

This, then, is what Catherine was reduced to: the daughter of Spain and the sometime Queen of England, she who had had the Alhambra and Hampton Court at her command, was squatting in a squalid bed-sit. Chapuys, of course, contrived to make it sound as though it were Henry's fault – or rather Anne's, since, in his book, Anne was to blame for everything. In fact, however, the full indignity of Catherine's situation was self-inflicted. She had decided that Henry and Anne were out to poison her, or at least to destroy her constitution by forcing her into unhealthy lodgings. But the truth was that her counter-measures were more damaging than anything her enemies were prepared to do. Cooped-up in her Chamber, without air or exercise, she became really unwell, and her health, indifferent for several years, broke down entirely.

The terrible mental strain of the last half dozen years was also catching up with her. She was, she knew, in the right. But Henry refused to admit the fact and persevered in his sin. Indeed, he gloried in it and flaunted his new 'wife' and daughter in her face. The Pope, who owed her justice, had done nothing and still seemed more anxious to conciliate Henry than to vindicate her. And her nephew Charles (though she scarcely dared admit the fact to herself even now) had not lifted a finger to enforce her rights either. To whom then should she turn? Many English nobles offered their sympathy. But, despite their fine, brave words, they too did nothing. Her women were loyal. But they were as helpless as she. Only Chapuys was left. Brave, trustworthy and inde-fatigably active on her behalf, he ceased to be an ambassador and became instead 'My Special Friend' – as she addressed him in intimate letters written in Spanish.[25]

But even Chapuys at times thought of giving up. 'Considering that my words only serve to irritate [Henry]', he informed Charles, 'and make him more fierce and obstinate, I have resolved not again to address to him a single word [about the plight of Catherine and Mary] . . . without a command from [Catherine].'[26]

Catherine was indeed alone.

These frustrations and tensions all came to a head in the spring of 1534. On 23 March, Rome finally gave sentence in Catherine's favour. But the sentence was not couched in the form she wished. She had staked everything on her claim to have been a virgin when she married Henry. But the sentence did not even mention the issue. Instead, with admirable economy, it simply declared that Henry's first marriage 'was and is valid and canonical'. Nor, it is clear, was Catherine's plight of much concern in Rome. Instead, Pope Clement acted at last because of outrage against Cranmer's unilateral sentence and the Act in Restraint of Appeals. These were direct challenges to Papal power and they could not go unanswered.[27]

But, however disappointing the sentence and however demeaning its motive, at least Catherine had got the substance of what she wanted. Or at least she had in Rome.

In England, though, it was a very different matter.

For, on 23 March, the same day that sentence was given in Rome, the Act of Succession completed its final reading in the Lords. It cleared the Commons three days later and, on 30 March, in the ceremonies marking the end of the session, it received the royal assent.

And the Act was the mirror-image of the Papal sentence. It began by citing Cranmer's verdict on Henry's marriage to Catherine, and Henry's good and lawful union with Queen Anne. Then it drew the consequences. Catherine was to be styled the Princess Dowager. The succession was to be fixed in Henry's male heirs by Anne or by a subsequent wife. And, in default of such male issue, the succession was to pass to Elizabeth.

Mary was not mentioned at all in the final version of the Act. In an earlier version, she had paid the full penalty for her 'rebellious and disobedient' behaviour. But the King's legal counsel, cautious and conservative like most lawyers (and probably sympathetic to Mary as well), found fault with the drafting. Rebellion, they pointed out, was already treason, while disobedience, though no doubt deplorable, 'is no cause of forfeiture of inheritance'. Thanks to these quibbles, Mary's exclusion (like her bastardy) was left merely tacit.

Nevertheless, the Act was a crushing blow to Catherine and her daughter. Also, unlike the Pope's sentence, the Act had teeth. Anne's marriage to Henry and its issue were now protected by the full penalties of treason. And all Henry's subjects, noblemen and commoners alike, were required to take an oath 'truly, firmly and constantly without fraud or guile' to observe and maintain its provisions.[28]

A few weeks later, yet another delegation of councillors turned up at Buckden to try, once more, to get Catherine to accept these facts. There is, however, a sense of both sides going through the motions. Catherine barely bothered to listen to her husband's advisers; instead, 'in great choler and agony', she 'always interrupt[ed] our words'. For their part, the councillors were perfunctory, both in expounding their case and in writing down Catherine's answers, which 'for tediousness' they left to an oral report by their junior assistants.[29]

Already, that is to say, Catherine saw herself in another, juster world. Her husband and her adoptive country, misled by Anne and Anne's faction, had ruled against her. But what matter? Christendom, the Universal Church and the Vicar of Christ had endorsed her marriage. There, and in their sight, she was still Henry's wife, and Mary was his heir. And, what mattered most of all, her soul was unspotted by any hint of compromise.

But, unfortunately for Catherine, her body remained in England and in Henry's power.

So, more unfortunately still, did the bodies of her leading supporters. For they were not protected by the royal status and royal blood which, for the moment at least, spared Catherine and her daughter from a worse fate. Instead, the penalties of the Act of Succession were turned ruthlessly against them. And, when the Act (thanks again to the revisions of the King's legal counsel) proved inadequate to justify the death penalty, new, severer laws were passed in the autumn session of Parliament. The Act of Supremacy 'authorized' the King to assume the Supreme Headship of the Church, with all the annexed rights, and repudiated any 'foreign laws or foreign authority' to the contrary. Another Act established a definitive oath of obedience to the King. This now involved a renunciation of the power of any 'foreign authority or potentate' – that is the Pope – as well as the endorsement of the Boleyn marriage and succession. Finally, the Act of Treasons declared that it was treason, either by overt act or maliciously by 'wish, will or desire, by words or in writing', to do any harm to Henry, Anne and their heirs, or to deprive the King of his titles (including that of Supreme Head) or to call him heretic, tyrant or usurper.[30]

The argument of the Great Matter would now be settled by the axe and the knife.

And the first victims were chosen deliberately for their eminence and distinction: the monks of the Carthusian Order, Bishop Fisher of Rochester and Sir Thomas More himself. The Carthusians were the holiest monastic order in the country, Fisher the most saintly prelate and greatest theologian, while More was both Henry's intimate friend from boyhood and the Englishman with the widest European reputation. But none of this counted for anything against their support for Catherine and their disobedience to Henry.

In May 1535 four leading Carthusians were subjected to the full horrors of execution for treason. Still in their habits, they were dragged on hurdles (in a bizarre parody of Anne's coronation procession) from the Tower, through the City, to Tyburn near the present Marble Arch. There, in turn, as the others were forced to watch, each was half hanged, cut down while still alive and conscious, and then castrated, disembowelled, and finally, after his entrails had been burned before his face, quartered and beheaded.

In June, Fisher (his sentence commuted to a mere beheading) was executed on Tower Hill and More followed at the beginning of July.[31]

Anne undoubtedly rejoiced. They had been her enemies, and they were gone. But she wanted other, yet more distinguished victims too. 'She is incessantly crying after the King', Chapuys reported a few weeks later, 'that he does not act with prudence in suffering the Queen and the Princess to live, who deserved death more than all those who have been executed, and that they were the cause of all.'[32]

Would she get her way in this too?

65. Hearts and minds

The trials and executions of Fisher and More, which Henry supervised from Windsor, delayed the start of the summer Progress by a few days. The original intention had been to leave on 5 July but it was not until the 9th that the royal party set out. Despite the blood-letting and the unseasonably wet weather, the Court was in high spirits: Henry was 'more given to matters of dancing and of ladies than ever he was'; while Anne and her henchman Cromwell, 'who are omnipotent with [the King]', were in confident political control.[1]

It was time, this ruling clique had decided, to turn from lopping heads to winning hearts and minds, and the Progress was to be the means.

For Anne, despite her stridency and the divisiveness of her actions, was by no means indifferent to public opinion. Even Chapuys recognized the fact. 'This woman', he reported in May 1533, on the eve of her coronation procession, 'does all she can to gain the goodwill of Londoners'. Naturally, Chapuys was sure that she would fail: 'she deceives herself', he asserted. On the basis of a simple head-count he was right. For good Catholics, especially for good Catholic women, no name was too bad for her. And good, or at least conventional, Catholics were in the overwhelming majority. But revolutions are not made by majorities, and the views of Evangelicals and Reformers were very different. For them, Anne was a protector and a patron in the present and a beacon of hope for the future.[2]

There were, of course, far fewer Reformers than Catholics. But their numbers were increasing. Nor, in any case, were numbers everything. For the Reformers were in strategic positions. They had masterful preachers and the control of the printing-presses. They commanded, for the moment, the levers of power and patronage. And in parts of the country they had local roots. One of these areas was London, which Anne had wooed in 1533. Another was the west country, which was her destination on the Progress of 1535.[3]

Bristol, the regional capital, was second only to London as a trading city and economic centre – and, as in London, a significant number of both the merchant élite and the common citizens of Bristol were early converts to Reform. The remote valleys of the Cotswolds were also a stronghold of the pre-Reformation English heresy known as Lollardy, whose principal tenets, such as the importance of being able to read the Bible in English, merged easily with the 'New' developments in religion. Here, at West Kington, was Hugh Latimer's parish, whence he descended on nearby Bristol (so the conservative local clergy felt) like the wolf on the fold, doing 'much hurt among the people by his ... preaching, and soweth errors'. Equally, many local gentry in Gloucestershire and Wiltshire were sympathetic to Reform and a handful went further and became committed supporters. They included Richard Tracy, M.P. of Stanway in Gloucester, whose father William had acquired notoriety by his sensationally anticlerical Will; Sir Edward Baynton of Bromham, who was Vice-chamberlain of Anne's Household and Latimer's correspondent and protector; Sir John and Lady Walsh of Little Sodbury, who had been won over by their children's live-in tutor, William Tyndale, and Lady Walsh's nephew, Nicholas Poyntz of Iron Acton.[4]

The Progress was designed to fertilize these west country roots of Reform with the rich humus of Court favour. The local gentry who were favourable to Reform – including Poyntz at Iron Acton, Walsh at Little Sodbury and Baynton at Bromham – were singled out for the honour of a visit from the King and Queen. For Bristol a royal *entrée* was planned which would, it was hoped, emulate the success of Anne's coronation procession in London. Local clergy, like Latimer, who had the ear of the Court, were marked out for accelerated promotion. But what really showed that the Court meant business was that Cromwell was scheduled to join the Progress and remain with it for eight weeks. During this time, the government of England was wherever he happened to be. He used the opportunity to pilot daring schemes of Reform – and to disarm opposition with the magic of the royal presence. And, throughout, his most active coadjutor was Anne herself. She managed Henry; wrote to Cromwell on his absences from Court, and, where necessary, took the initiative on the ground.[5]

One of the pageants at Anne's coronation *entrée* had enjoined her to 'prosper, proceed, and reign'. She evidently took the injunction to heart, and the Progress of 1535 shows her putting it enthusiastically into practice.

As usual, the route of the Progress or 'gists' had been planned carefully in advance. From Windsor, it followed the valleys of the Thames and its tributary the Evenlode; skirted the northern edge of the Cotswolds to the Vale of Evesham; and then, turning south and still keeping to the foothills of the Cotswolds, it passed via Sudeley Castle to Tewkesbury. En route, there were the usual frequent stops – to rest, to hunt, and, it turned out, to view property.

Ewelme in Oxfordshire, where the Court stayed for a couple of days on the 12th and the 13th, was a splendid red-brick palace built in the mid-fifteenth century by the de la Poles, dukes of Suffolk. Henry had been conceived there during an extended visit by his parents in the autumn of 1490. But the de la Poles, cursed by their Yorkist blood, dabbled repeatedly in treason. Their property and titles had been forfeit and had been re-granted by Henry to his then great favourite, Charles Brandon, who had been created Duke of Suffolk in 1513. But now Suffolk himself had fallen out of favour, thanks to his less than whole-hearted commitment to the Boleyn marriage. It was time to pay the price, and in the course of the Progress Anne and Henry inspected some of Suffolk's properties which were ear-marked for surrender to the Crown.[6]

They included Ewelme and Hook Norton, where they probably hunted en route from Langley Castle to Sudeley. But they were not impressed with what they saw. Suffolk, trying to save what he could from the wreck, claimed to have spent £1,000 on Ewelme and £1,500 on a hunting lodge at Hook Norton. Henry, who rather liked bargaining, was brutally incredulous. He had recently visited Ewelme, his agent was instructed to inform Suffolk on 29 July, and had 'viewed' the property. He found it 'in great decay and great sums would not repair [it]'. As for Hook Norton, 'it will require no small sums of money to repair and build it after the King's mind'. Henry also hinted that he had seen little trace of the eighty red deer which the Keeper was supposed to maintain in the park. Let Suffolk stop quibbling, the King's instructions ended. Instead, he, 'of all men', should consider the 'manifold benefits' he had received from the King. Henry had 'advanced him to his honour and estate'; he could just as easily undo him.[7]

Anne, no doubt, had been irritated by the lack of sport at Hook Norton as well. But the hunting-down of another of her old enemies offered some compensation.

After this diversion, the Progress got down to its intended business at Sudeley Castle. The King and Queen and their immediate servants stayed in the Castle. But many of their entourage, including Cromwell, who arrived on about 23 July, were lodged in the nearby Winchcombe Abbey.

Rarely has hospitality been worse returned. Winchcombe itself survived till 1539. But by 1540 the last of England's monasteries would be gone, their land and buildings confiscated by the Crown, and a thousand years of religious life and ritual came to an end. And the process which led to all this – the Dissolution of the Monasteries – began here, at Winchcombe, while Cromwell was staying under the Abbey roof in 1535. Thence, he launched it and directed it. And he did so with Anne's eager, high-profile involvement.

Quite whether the full-scale Dissolution was envisaged from the beginning is another matter, however.

In January 1535 Cromwell had been appointed Henry's Vicegerent-in-Spirituals. The office, which was a new-fangled one, made him the King's deputy as Supreme Head of the Church, with full authority to exercise the vast powers which the Supremacy had conferred on the Crown. Among these was the power to 'visit' or inspect monasteries. The power, traditionally exercised by the local bishop, was an ancient one. But the purpose to which it was now put was almost wholly new.

The articles for the visitation were relatively innocuous. But the sting in the tail came in the form of the injunctions, or orders to reform, which were issued to the monks after the inspection was complete. These injunctions, drawn up in full consultation with Henry himself, required the abbot and brethren to enforce and obey the recent Oath of Obedience and the Acts 'made or to be made' for the 'extirpation . . . of the usurped and pretended jurisdiction of the Bishop of Rome' – as the Pope was now insultingly styled. Such of them as were priests were also 'everyday in [their] mass [to] pray for . . . the King and his most noble and lawful wife Queen Anne'. It was a prayer which would stick in the throat of any but the most compliant.[8]

Then came a Reforming attack on the religious ceremonies which were the *raison d'être* of monastic life. The abbot was to explain that 'true religion' was not a matter of observing the traditional rules and customs – 'apparel, manner of going, shaven heads . . . nor in silence, fasting, uprising at night, singing and such other kinds of ceremonies'. Instead, it was 'cleanness of mind, pureness of living, Christ's faith not feigned and brotherly charity'.

Another Reforming *bête noire* was the monasteries' central role in popular piety as places of pilgrimage to miracle-working images or relics. These images and relics offered comfort to the people, as well as providing nice little earners for the monks. But, the injunctions sternly required, all such displays were to stop. Instead, sober charity was to be substituted for the heady satisfactions of religious mysteries, and would-be pilgrims were to be told 'to give that to the poor that they thought to offer to their images or relics'.

Finally, despite their professed contempt for religious 'ceremonies', the injunctions proceeded to impose with unparalleled severity the traditional restrictions of monastic life: 'enclosure' (that is, the requirement to remain within the monastery), the exclusion of women, and simplicity of food, drink, dress and manner of life. Most problematic was enclosure. This was covered by the Injunction which required 'that no monk or [lay] brother . . . by any means go forth of the precincts of the same'. If enclosure were literally enforced, the economic infrastructure of monastic life would collapse. Rents could not be collected nor produce sold, and bankruptcy or starvation would quickly overwhelm the community.[9]

This Injunction, like the rest, was probably formulated in reasonably good faith. (Henry was always very keen that other people should observe their obligations.) But its potential to harm monastic life was soon spotted – and exploited.

Cromwell briefed his agents, known as visitors, at Winchcombe, and they sallied forth in different directions. Their subsequent reports concentrated on two areas: the sexual failings of the monks, on which subject (like today's Sunday-newspaper reporters) the visitors managed to combine intense disapproval with lip-smacking detail, and the false miracles and relics, of which they gave equally gloating accounts. One monastery, however, was spared the usual run of visitors, only to be subject to a more high-powered inquisition. This was Hailes, which lay a mere two miles to the north-east of Winchcombe.

Hailes owned a relic of the Holy Blood of Christ. This was not the mystic blood – the wine that was made blood by consecration in the mass – but, supposedly, the Saviour's actual blood which had been shed on Mount Calvary. It had even preserved a certain viscosity and the mere sight of it, so the faithful believed, would put them in a state of Grace. The presence of this relic had turned Hailes Abbey into one of the great pilgrimage centres of late medieval England. Now, it attracted Anne's disapproving attention. According to William Latymer's account, she, 'being in progress at Winchcombe', sent 'certain of her chaplains and others [to Hailes] . . . truly and faithfully to view, search and examine by all possible means the truth [of the relic]'. Their verdict was damning: partly by testing the relic and partly by questioning its custodians, they discovered it to be 'nothing else but the blood of some duck, or, as some say, red wax'.[10]

Latymer goes on to claim that Anne got Henry to order the immediate destruction of this irreligious fraud. This portion of his narrative, however, is mistaken since the relic survived until 1538, when it was formally investigated by Hugh Latimer and Richard Tracy, acting in their then capacity as royal commissioners. Following their discovery that, when removed from its outer casing, it was not blood at all but a yellowish, gum-like substance, it was sent up to London for public exposure and destruction.

Latimer, almost certainly, had been a member of the earlier investigation team sent by Anne; so too, probably, was John Hilsey, who delivered the sermon on the occasion of the relic's final exposure at St Paul's Cross, the great outdoor London pulpit, in November 1538. In 1535 Hilsey had been Prior of the Black Friars in Bristol and rising rapidly at Court. With his local knowledge, he had been the likely source of the story, accepted by Anne's investigators, that the relic was duck's blood. Certainly, he repeated this description in another sermon preached in February 1538. In the November sermon, however, he made a retraction of this earlier assertion and instead, drawing on the commissioner's recent report, showed the relic to be 'honey coloured with saffron and lying like a gum'. He then offered it up for general inspection![11]

After Sudeley, the 1535 Progress went to Tewkesbury and then, following the course of the Severn Valley, it continued to Gloucester, Berkeley Castle and Thornbury Castle – that magnificent monument to the ambitions of the Duke of Buckingham, which had been left half-finished at his fall. The next scheduled stop was Bristol, which was the goal of the whole Progress. But now there came bad news. Plague had struck in Bristol and it was unsafe for Henry and Anne to enter the town. Instead, the town fathers came to Thornbury to pay their homage there. They presented Henry with gifts of livestock, to feed his itinerant Household, while to Anne they gave a parcel-gilt cup and cover filled with 100 marks (£66 13s 4d) in cash. The Queen replied prettily that she desired 'to demand or have none other gift' but only that she should be able to return to Bristol in the future.[12]

The intended route now took the King and Queen to Nicholas Poyntz's house at Iron Acton. Poyntz had made lavish preparations to receive his sovereigns. Building very quickly, to judge from the non-existent foundations, he added a brand-new wing to his existing manor-house. On the first floor was a suite of three fine rooms, each over seventeen feet high, that replicated the King's or Queen's apartment in one of their own palaces. As in a royal palace, the rooms were arranged in an enfilade (that is to say, each opened directly into the other) and they were decorated in the latest style with tapestry, stucco and high-quality wall-paintings with roundels, grotesque work and other classical archi-tectural features. Poyntz also provided all mod-cons and each room had a large fireplace and, next to it, a garderobe or lavatory, opening into the moat. Additionally, since feasting was a feature of entertaining royalty, he bought the latest table-ware, including blue-and-white tin-glazed earthenware and hugely expensive Venetian glass.

But, after all that, it is impossible to be sure whether the planned visit took place. Perhaps it was a victim of the delayed start to the Progress, and Poyntz was left alone in his expensive new buildings to gnash his teeth in disappointment. But there are several indications to the contrary. Poyntz was knighted, almost certainly that year and in reward for his hospitality, and was drawn by Holbein wearing his new chain of knighthood and striking a Frenchified pose that accords well with the avant-garde style of his building works. Excavations of the moat have also come up with many broken fragments of his new earthenware and Venetian glass, suggesting that his royal guests had dined well, if not wisely.[13]

In any case, Anne would have found herself supremely at home at Iron Acton. The layout of the rooms was familiar. The combination of advanced, Frenchified taste with religious radicalism reflected perfectly the ethos of her own Court. Finally, there was the added satisfaction of knowing that Nicholas Poyntz was a convert: his grandfather, Sir Robert, had been Catherine's Vice-chamberlain; now the grandson was dancing attendance on her.[14]

But Anne would have been even more satisfied still if she had been able to read a despatch written by Chapuys on 10 August. For the Progress, he reported gloomily, was achieving its aim of 'gaining the people'. 'It is said', he continued, 'that many of the peasants where [Henry] has passed, hearing the preachers who follow the Court, are so much abused as to believe that God has inspired the King to separate himself from the wife of his brother.'[15]

Since, until his departure on urgent personal business, the Court preachers included Latimer, the result is scarcely surprising. Nor was it only the country folk, the 'bumpkins' (*idiotes*) as Chapuys contemptuously describes them, who were won over. Of a quite different calibre was Mr Scrope, 'a very worshipful gentleman'. Scrope had failed to swear the Oath of Obedience, not out of malice but only because of the slackness of the commissioners who were responsible for the imposition of the Oath. But, overwhelmed by Latimer's preaching, he confessed his sin to him and was sent back to Court as Latimer's 'prisoner', burning to serve Cromwell and the new regime. 'Perchance he can tell you of more as far behindhand as he', Latimer wrote to Cromwell, 'only for lack of calling-on hitherto slow.'[16]

Now, more than ever, Anne was in her element. She next stayed at Little Sodbury, which belonged to Poyntz's aunt and uncle, and after that at Bromham, the seat of her Vice-chamberlain Baynton. Baynton, as we have seen, was Latimer's patron, while the Walshes at Little Sodbury had given refuge to Tyndale in the awkward days before he had fled abroad to escape Wolsey's persecutions. Now, suddenly, Tyndale's name moved to the top of the agenda again.

After going into exile, Tyndale's main undertaking had been the translation of the Bible into English. He had completed his first version of the New Testament in 1526 and he was making good progress with the Old. He had also written important controversial works. One of these, the *Obedience of a Christian Man*, had been brought to Anne's attention by one of her maids and she in turn had shown it to Henry. Her motives were a characteristic mixture: she did so partly because she approved of the work and partly to spite and thwart Wolsey. Henry, for his part, was mightily impressed with the thrust of Tyndale's argument, which deduced from Scripture that the Christian had an absolute duty of obedience to the King, not to the Pope. 'This book is for me and all Kings to read,' he is supposed to have said.

But then Tyndale made the error – a fatal one as it turned out – of writing on the wrong side of the Great Matter. His *Practice of Prelates* spoke approvingly of Catherine; rubbished the King's vaunted Scriptural arguments; and presented him as being led by the nose by Wolsey to seek the Divorce. Henry was enraged and made serious, if unsuccessful, attempts to secure Tyndale's extradition.

Nevertheless, Anne, Cromwell and their friends continued, though discreetly, to try to bring about a reconciliation. Under their influence, Henry had announced a determination to make the Scriptures available to his people in an English translation. And Tyndale was incomparably the best translator. Anne had a fine copy of the revised 1534 edition of his New Testament, inscribed 'Anne the Queen' on the gilt fore-edge. And Cromwell's correspondents, including Stephen Vaughan, were busy trying to keep channels open.[17]

The gap proved unbridgeable, however. Then fate struck, in the form of an English double-agent and agent-provocateur called Henry Philips. Having got Tyndale's confidence and that of his host, the English merchant Thomas Poyntz, who came from the Essex branch of the family, Philips betrayed Tyndale to the Flemish authorities and he was arrested on 21 May 1535. The Council of the Emperor Charles V's sister Mary, who had succeeded his aunt Margaret as Regent of the Netherlands, had hitherto turned a blind eye to Tyndale. The Council had enough to do, dealing with native heresy, without bothering about an Englishman who kept himself to himself and wrote and published only in a foreign tongue.[18]

But Philips had energy, contacts and, somehow, money and he continued to press the case against Tyndale. 'I cannot perceive', wrote Thomas Theobald to Cranmer, 'by what [Philips] says, but that Tyndale shall die.' 'Which', Theobald continued, 'he procures with all diligent endeavour, rejoicing much thereat.' It has been speculated that the source of Theobald's money was the recently executed Sir Thomas More. In life, More had maintained a long and savage war of words with Tyndale, whom he regarded as an abominable heretic, fit only for the flames. Now, if the guess about Theobald's funding be correct, More was having his revenge from beyond the grave.[19]

Cromwell and Anne were in a quandary. They wished to intervene on Tyndale's behalf. But was it politic to do so? Finally Cromwell screwed up courage to speak to Henry. 'To know the King's pleasure touching Tyndale, and whether I shall write or not', he noted in his 'Remembrances' or memoranda for early August. The resulting conversation probably took place at Thornbury, shortly before 16 August. Anne, then riding high, probably lent her voice as well and Henry's consent was obtained. The necessary letters were written and forwarded to Stephen Vaughan in London. He received them on 4 September and sent them on promptly. And they reached their destination equally promptly.[20]

But the recipients on the Flemish Council were politely dismissive. 'It were good', Vaughan wrote to Cromwell, 'that the King had a man of reputation in Flanders.' That, however, was easier said than done. The Great Matter had led to an almost complete political breach between England and the Netherlands: trade – vital to both parties – continued, but that was all. In the circumstances, Philips, despite Thomas Poyntz's increasingly desperate appeals to England, had the field to himself. He also procured the arrest of Poyntz, who escaped back to England only with difficulty. 'If now you send but your letter to the [Flemish] Privy Council', Vaughan wrote to Cromwell from Antwerp on 13 April 1536,

'I could deliver Tyndale from the fire, so it came by time, for else it will be too late.'[21]

This letter was never sent. Anne, by then, was too worried about trying to save her own head. And Cromwell, from being her friend and ally, had become her deadliest enemy.

While the English Reformers feuded, Tyndale burned.

But during the Progress of 1535 the alliance between Queen and minister seemed closer than ever. It showed clearly in their co-operation in the rush of appointments to bishoprics, as four sees (or one fifth of the total) were filled in quick succession.

The vacancies had arisen for a variety of reasons. Rochester was freed by Fisher's conviction and execution, and Hereford by Charles Booth's death from natural causes in May 1535. At the same time, Parliament passed an Act seizing the English sees held by Henry's Italian agents at the Papal Court. This created vacancies at Salisbury, where Campeggio had been Bishop, and at Worcester, which Wolsey had procured for his friend Ghinucci. And in place of a fervent, upright Catholic, such as Fisher, and supple, time-serving ones, such as Campeggio and Ghinucci, it was decided to appoint thorough-going Reformers.[22]

Anne clearly took the lead and the first appointment was that of her Almoner, Nicholas Shaxton, to Salisbury. The decision to appoint him was known to Chapuys as early as January 1535. But it followed a long and tortuous course.

The particular sticking-point, as always, was fees. Once, these had gone to the Pope but with the Supremacy they were transferred to the King of England, and a new revenue department, the Office of First Fruits and Tenths, was set up to administer them. Its head, known as the Treasurer of First Fruits and Tenths, was John Gostwick. But, despite his new status, Gostwick's relationship with Cromwell was an ambiguous one. He was Cromwell's former servant and continued to act as a general treasurer for him. Moreover, he was also working in harness with Cromwell's personal financial agents, Henry Polsted and William Popley.[23]

The resulting confusion of roles was a recipe for crossed-wires and delay. Gostwick and his colleagues in London were trying to play by the rules and maximize returns for the King; Cromwell at Court, on the other hand, was alive to the realities of politics and patronage but was often too busy with bigger matters to give his proper attention to the to-and-fro of negotiations. Finally, and caught in the middle, were the newly appointed bishops, with Shaxton at their head.[24]

Shaxton was consecrated by Cranmer, again in St Stephen's Chapel, on 11 April 1535. By then all the formalities should have been over. But the issue of his 'temporalities', as the estates of the bishopric were known, was still in negotiation. By the end of May the outlines of a settlement were visible. Shaxton would give securities for the staged payments of his First Fruits, which amounted to one year's net revenue of his see. In return the King would tide him over with a grant of the previous half year's income of the bishopric, from September 1534 to March 1535. The agreement would be given effect in the formal instrument, known as the *Custodias Temporalium* or Restitution of Temporalities, which permitted the new Bishop of Salisbury to receive the income of his see. On 27 May, Shaxton wrote to Cromwell, asking him to order Popley to prepare the Restitution of Temporalities as agreed for the King's signature. He was still waiting for it a week later on 4 June. And it was only on 8 July – the last business day before the start of the Progress – that it was signed by the King.[25]

It is impossible to penetrate fully the workings in this instance of the Tudor 'Circumlocution Office'. But it seems probable that it was Anne who finally cut the Gordian Knot with a direct approach to Henry. She also helped Shaxton out with a loan of £200 from her own purse.

Despite the delays, Shaxton's settlement with the Office of First Fruits and Tenths came to be regarded as a model by the other new bishops, all of whom were closely associated with Anne. Edward Foxe, the great theoretician of the Divorce and Supremacy, got Hereford, Hugh Latimer Worcester and John Hilsey Rochester. All had formed part of the great caravanserai of the 1535 Progress, during which Latimer, as we have seen, was particularly active. Now, they, too, were sent off to cut a deal with Gostwick's office.

Foxe's experiences are unknown but Latimer and Hilsey acted as a team with the ebullient Latimer naturally taking the lead. They left Court for London on about 21 August, while the King and Queen were staying at Thornbury. Before leaving they had an interview with Cromwell, also at Thornbury, in which they requested that 'they may pay their First Fruits as the Bishop of Salisbury does'. Cromwell agreed and promised to write to Gostwick to this effect. But when Latimer and Hilsey met Gostwick on 29 August, the Treasurer informed them that he had received no such letter. They both continued to badger Gostwick and six days later, on 4 September, Latimer also tackled Polsted, but Polsted had heard nothing from Cromwell either.[26]

Latimer was now losing patience and, immediately after his frustrating meeting with Polsted, wrote Cromwell a characteristically blunt letter. Things would have been sorted out more quickly if he had remained at Court, he said. He also reminded Cromwell that he had other, even more powerful, friends. His first intention, he recalled, had been 'to have gone to the King's Grace myself'. 'But', he continued, 'the Queen's Grace, calling to remembrance what end my lord of Salisbury [Shaxton] was at, said I should not need to move the King, but that it should be enough to inform your mastership thereof.' Anne, characteristically, had put her money where her mouth was and had given Latimer, as well, a loan: £200 for which he entered into a bond on 18 August.[27]

Despite Latimer's near-ultimatum, another inconclusive meeting with Polsted followed on 11 September. It was now Hilsey's turn to write a despairing letter to Cromwell. 'Since I have come to London', he informed him, 'I have done nothing and can do nothing.' It was only on 15 September that the minister's instructions concerning Rochester finally reach Polsted.[28]

But by then, having fought their bruising encounter with bureaucracy to a draw, the bishops-elect were on their way back to Court.

*

The Progress had reached Winchester in Hampshire. Winchester was the old capital, with a noble cathedral to match. And the cathedral was now the setting for one of the most extraordinary scenes of the Reformation.

In mid-September, Jean de Dinteville, who had been painted by Holbein in *The Ambassadors* on an earlier mission to England, arrived at Winchester as a special envoy. At his first audience, either he or a member of his suite presented Marguerite of Navarre's compliments to Anne and Henry. 'The Queen', the report of the interview continued, 'said that her greatest wish, next to having a son, is to see you [Marguerite] again.'[29]

But Dinteville bore disturbing news. Clement VII had died in 1534 and had been succeeded as Pope by Alessandro Farnese who had taken the title Paul III. Despite Paul's luxurious Court, his artistic patronage and the 'unlimited nepotism' he used to advance his already-powerful family to still greater things, he took his religion more seriously than his predecessor. He was outraged by Henry's conduct, and the beheading of Fisher, whom he had made a Cardinal just before his execution, was the last straw. In late July, 'at the unanimous solicitation' of the College of Cardinals, Pope Paul III 'deprived [Henry] of his kingdom and royal dignity' and wrote a 'Brief' or letter to Francis to ask him to give effect to the sentence.[30]

Francis, of course, had no intention of doing any such thing. Instead he hoped to use the Brief as diplomatic blackmail to secure English support for renewed French intervention in Italy. But the plan backfired. Henry was far too concerned at the possible impact of the Brief on English domestic politics to have the inclination for foreign adventures and Dinteville left England empty-handed after only two weeks.

But how to respond to the Brief? Henry, according to Chapuys's informants, 'appeared sad and melancholy when he had read the letters [Dinteville] presented' and he summoned the leading bishops to Winchester for an emergency meeting. Those attending included Foxe, Cranmer and of course the Bishop of Winchester himself, Stephen Gardiner.[31]

But, before the consultations got under way, Henry and Anne

decided on a gesture of defiance. They would take advantage of the gathering of prelates in the city to stage a major ceremony. Since the break with Rome, the consecrations of English bishops had been hole-in-corner affairs – performed, like Cranmer's and Shaxton's, in the decent obscurity of St Stephen's Chapel. Now, to face down doubters at home and abroad, they would go public. Thus, on 19 September, in Winchester Cathedral, the three most recently appointed bishops, Foxe of Hereford, Latimer of Worcester and Hilsey of Rochester, were consecrated together. The consecration was performed by Cranmer himself; the cream of the English episcopate was present as, almost certainly, were Henry and Anne. Henry was there to defy the Pope; Anne to give her support to 'her' bishops. She had solicited their appointments and had worked vigorously to remove the bureaucratic obstacles thrown in their way by Gostwick and his colleagues.[32]

Now she had her reward as she started to shape an episcopate in the image of her own Reforming piety.

The bishops then got down to the task of countering the Papal Brief and, over the next ten days, they laboured furiously. The lead was taken by Gardiner. The last three years had not been kind to him. He had fallen badly foul of both Henry and Anne with his resistance to the Supremacy in the Convocation of 1532, and neither fully trusted him ever again. In April 1534 he had been rusticated to his diocese and told not to return to Court until summoned. He had also been stripped of the Secretaryship which – inevitably – was given to Cromwell. A year later he had come within a whisker of treason and Henry had ordered Cromwell to investigate him on suspicion of 'coloured doubleness' over the Supremacy.

But he survived. Now the crisis provoked by the Papal Brief gave him the opportunity to rehabilitate himself. According to Chapuys, the King's Council was in complete disarray: they were 'quite astonished without knowing where to begin'. And only Gardiner's intervention rescued the situation. He, among all the bishops, had the readiest pen and the most incisive mind. He also knew how to work fast.[33]

Within a few days he had completed drafts of two works. One was a direct answer to Paul's Brief. The Pope laments the death of bad men, like Fisher, and rejoices in those of the good, Gardiner wrote. Moreover he does so in extravagant words put in his mouth by a petty little orator (*rhetorculus*), his secretary Bloxius, who bemoans Fisher's death as monstrously cruel when in fact it was the gentlest that could be devised and he was 'killed with a sudden stroke of the sword'. And so on. Gardiner's answer is bitter and mocking and was obviously written in the heat of the moment. His other work, however, was longer and more reflective. It could, such was his facility, have been knocked out in the week or so following Dinteville's arrival. Or it might have been prepared earlier, during his months of exile at Winchester, and pulled out of the hat only now.

It was entitled *De Vera Obedientia* (Of True Obedience), and, like Tyndale's, similarly entitled *Obedience of a Christian Man*, it defended the Royal Supremacy on the grounds of Scripture and attacked the Papal Monarchy on the same basis. Gardiner concluded by acknowledging frankly that he had once sworn an oath to the Pope. He had done so in good faith. But, as he had subsequently discovered, he had been wrong. And the oath was wrong, too. Therefore, because it is a recognized principle of both civil and canon law 'that no man is bounden to perform an unlawful oath', he was released with no stain on his integrity. As were all other Englishmen who had done the same.

Both Gardiner's works were circulated for comment among a select group, including Cranmer, Foxe and Cromwell. Foxe was seriously worried by the passage in which Gardiner defended the breach of his oath and wrote in strict confidence to Cromwell about it. 'If this were taken for an example', he pointed out, 'the malice of men might elude such oaths [to the Boleyn succession] as we have now lately made.' 'I have turned down the leaf', he continued, 'and marked the place with a hand.'[34]

Foxe's point was a shrewd one. Nevertheless, the passage was left untouched. Cranmer, on the other hand, proposed a lengthy addition to the answer. At this point, Cromwell called for the text of the answer to read it himself. Gardiner was frustrated. He had intended, he wrote to

Cromwell, to sit up all night and polish it, as he had already done with his *De Vera Obedientia*. But this was now impossible as he was sending the only copy to Cromwell. If Cromwell would bring it up to London, where he was about to deliver *De Vera Obedientia* to the royal printer, Thomas Berthelet, he would finish it off too. 'I will in a day and a night put it *in mundum* [into the world],' he boasted.[35]

This was the old Gardiner. Power and favour were a tonic, and he was in his element again.

But, within a few weeks, he was sent away from Court once more as ambassador to France. Did Henry guess that his Council was not big enough for both Cromwell and Gardiner? Was Anne working to remove another enemy?

As it happened, Gardiner's Embassy lasted for three years. When he returned to England in 1538 it was to a new world. For three Queens had died in the interim.

66. The death of Catherine of Aragon

In May 1534, Catherine had been moved at last to a new house, Kimbolton in Huntingdonshire. It was only four miles from Buckden, but, despite its proximity, its situation was better as it lay to the west, on slightly higher ground and away from the hated Fen.[1]

There, her life settled into a kind of rhythm. In place of the extravagant scenes and direct confrontations of Buckden, she maintained a cold war with the men whom Henry had placed about her, treating the head officers of her Household – Sir Edmund Bedingfield, her Steward, and Sir Edward Chamberlain, her Chamberlain – as her gaolers and banishing them from her presence for months at a time. Instead, she spent her days with her women, her confessor, her doctor and her apothecaries. She continued with her needlework, and, when her health permitted, with her devotions. According to Catholic hagiography, these lasted for several hours a day, and were performed on the bare stones which she left so wet with her tears that it was 'as though it had rained upon them'.[2]

It was, in short, an existence little different from the nunnery which she had so indignantly refused. And, like the quiet life of the cloister, it had its own satisfactions. But there was a corresponding danger. In the fastnesses of Huntingdonshire and deliberately cut off from the outside world, it was a case of out of sight, out of mind. At best, the former Queen Catherine would be a fading memory, while Queen Anne rode from Reforming triumph to Reforming triumph, as Anne seemed to be doing in 1535. At worst, so Catherine and Chapuys both feared, she would be secretly done away with, with no one a jot the wiser.

But Chapuy was determined that Catherine should not be forgotten. He intrigued outrageously with her supporters and constantly badgered Henry and Cromwell about the conditions in which she was held. And, if they ignored him, he had his own ways of making his presence felt. Most dramatically, in July 1534, he decided to use a pilgrimage to Walsingham as a cover for a demonstration in Catherine's favour. He announced that he would visit her en route and, to gain maximum publicity, signalled his departure from London by riding through the City with a troop of sixty horse. Repeated messengers were sent to inform him that he would not be allowed access to the former Queen. Nevertheless, he persevered to within a few miles of Kimbolton. Then Catherine herself sent to say that she was well satisfied. Chapuys himself remained at a distance, but ordered a detachment of his followers to parade in front of the house, 'to the great satisfaction . . . of the ladies with the Queen, who spoke to them from the battlements and windows'.

Mission more or less accomplished, the pilgrimage to Walsingham was abandoned as ostentatiously as it had been begun, and Chapuys returned to London. He was shadowed all the way by Stephen Vaughan, Cromwell's usual agent in a crisis.[3]

*

In a sense, of course, Chapuys's efforts were redundant, as neither of the two people most affected could or would forget Catherine, or leave her in peace. Anne (at least according to Chapuys) continued to press, loudly, for her execution; while Henry never forgave her for not accepting his Divorce. Yet again, commissioners were instructed to upbraid her with her refusal to yield to his case. The world acknowledged that she had been 'known' by Arthur; why would not she? Once again, she reiterated her story, but with a fresh and strange twist. 'And furthermore', she said, 'whereas you do declare Prince Arthur to have sufficiency of age [for intercourse], I will briefly declare unto you his age. He was fifteen years, twenty-seven weeks and odd days when he died.'[4]

What was she trying to prove? That Arthur was too young for sex? That her memory was so good about his age that it could be trusted in all else? Her point remains unclear, as it seems to have done to her interlocutors.

But, finally, the point-scoring stopped and she appealed directly to Henry. She invoked 'the great love that hath been betwixt him and me ere this . . . the which love in me is as faithful and true to him . . . as ever it was'. And she begged him, for the sake of that love, 'that his Grace will not use such extremities with me'.[5]

She begged in vain. Henry's love for her was dead, long dead, and it was turned – not to hate, as with Anne – but to a cold irritation. She was in the way. And he did not tolerate obstacles willingly.

Catherine had fallen seriously ill in the early winter of 1535 but she seemed to make a good recovery. In late December, however, she had a relapse and her apothecary, Philip Greenacre, wrote a hasty note to the *maître d'hôtel* of Chapuys's Household. 'The Queen [as of course he persists in calling her] is very ill . . . She gets worse every hour', he wrote. For two days and nights she had been unable to keep down either solids or liquids. And she had not slept more than an hour and a half 'for the pain in her stomach'. Chapuys must come immediately, 'for she has lost all her strength'. Another, similar letter was written by her doctor, Miguel de la Sa.[6]

Chapuys received Dr de la Sa's letter on 29 December and immediately sent to Court for permission to visit Catherine. Cromwell agreed readily but said that Chapuys must first have an audience with the King.

The next day, Thursday, 30 December, Chapuys presented himself at the appointed time at Greenwich, where he was met on the Privy 'Bridge' or landing stage by Sir Thomas Cheyney. Cheyney had weathered the storms of his disputes with Sir John Russell to become the virtual kinglet of the Isle of Sheppey in east Kent, and one of the most influential of Henry's personal attendants. He took Chapuys through the palace to the tilt-yard on the south, or landward, side. The King, who was preparing for the forthcoming New Year's jousts, greeted the ambassador warmly. With a great bear-hug 'he ... embraced me still more cordially by the neck' and then got down to business.

First, he talked at length of England's relations with those two perennial rivals: Charles V, Chapuys's master, and Charles's enemy, Francis I. Henry's tone about his supposed ally, Francis I, was less than cordial; on the other hand, he spoke with regret about the tensions in the Anglo-Imperial relationship. Then, at the end of the interview, he came suddenly and brutally to the point: '*Madame* [Catherine]', he told Chapuys, who reported back to his master, 'would not live long and that if she died you [Charles] would have no cause to trouble yourself about the affairs of this kingdom and might refrain from stirring in the matter.' Shocked, Chapuys replied 'that the death of the Queen could do no possible good' and the audience was at an end.

As he went back to his boat through the palace, Chapuys was recalled to the King. News had just come, Henry told him with barely concealed delight, that Catherine was '*in extremis*' and that 'I should hardly find her alive'. Then the King returned to his essential point: 'moreover that this would take away all the difficulties between your Majesty [Charles] and him'.

Chapuys, on the basis of his own reports, thought that Henry exaggerated. Nevertheless, he took horse straight away for Kimbolton.[7]

*

Meanwhile, also on the Thursday, Maria de Salinas, Catherine's former lady-in-waiting and now the Dowager Lady Willoughby and mother-in-law of the Duke of Suffolk, sent urgently to Cromwell from her house at the Barbican. 'I heard that my mistress is very sore sick again,' she wrote. Cromwell had promised her a formal 'licence' or permission to visit Catherine 'before God did send for her, as there is no other likelihood'. Despite the holidays and his own business, the licence must, she implored, be obtained immediately. Otherwise it would be too late.[8]

Between 7 and 8 o'clock in the evening of the same day, a post arrived at Kimbolton with letters from the Court at Greenwich. In them, Cromwell passed on Chapuys's news that Catherine 'was in danger of life'. Sir Edmund Bedingfield, understandably, was chagrined that 'the ambassador should have knowledge before us that do daily continue in the house' but reported back the latest bulletin as he had it. He had spoken to Dr de la Sa, who resorted to the phrase which doctors have been using since the days of Hippocrates. She was 'not much worse than she was, nor much better' (*non multum peius quam erat, neque longe melius*). De la Sa also advised a second opinion. But Catherine had been adamant: 'she would in no wise have any other physician, but only commit herself to the pleasure of God'.[9]

The New Year feast, which was ordinarily a time of festivity in the Court and its associated Households, would have been a quiet one at Kimbolton. At about 6 p.m. on New Year's day, Lady Willoughby burst into the house. She was visibly agitated. She had, she claimed, 'a fall from her horse within a mile'. And she was desperate for the sight of Catherine, 'saying', Bedingfield reported, 'she thought never to have seen [Catherine] again by reason of such tidings as she had heard of her'.

Bedingfield and his colleague, Sir Edward Chamberlain, were moved. She was a great lady. And she was in distress. But, still, they had a job to do. Where was her licence? they demanded. 'It was ready to be showed next morning,' she replied. Meanwhile, in view of her shaken state following her fall, could she sit by the fire? They agreed.

They found out what happened later. Immediately, and evidently by prior arrangement, she had been smuggled in to see Catherine. Then, miraculously recovered from her fall, she had disappeared. 'Since that time', Bedingfield reported in proper policeman tones, 'we never saw her, neither any letters of her licence to repair hither.'[10]

The next day, Sunday 2 January, Chapuys arrived at the house 'before dinner' and was admitted to see Catherine immediately. Both Catherine and Chapuys were anxious to demonstrate that her illness was real and 'not feigned'. So the interview took place in front of a substantial company. Stephen Vaughan, who had been sent once more, as Chapuys reported, 'to accompany me or rather to spy' was there, as were the Steward, Bedingfield, and the Chamberlain, Sir Edward Chamberlain, both of whom 'had not seen her for more than a year'.

The interview was short and was conducted in Spanish. Catherine thanked Chapuys for his services, and for his trouble in coming to see her. It would do her good, she thought. If not, 'it would be a consolation to her to die in my arms, and not unprepared, like a beast'. In reply, Chapuys tried to keep her spirits up, speaking of the better houses and more generous funding which Henry had promised. Above all, he assured her, 'the King was very sorry for her illness'.[11]

This was a blatant lie. But, in the circumstances, it was a justifiable one.

Exhausted by the effort, Catherine asked to be left alone to sleep, which she did for a few hours. At 5 o'clock, Dr de la Sa summoned Chapuys who spent more than an hour with her, alone apart from the doctor and Catherine's 'old trusty women'. The latter were a safe audience, since they did not speak Spanish – or at least had convinced Bedingfield that they did not. And the interview was repeated, at the same time and with the same company, on the 3rd and the 4th.

In these conversations, Chapuys was worried about tiring Catherine. But she insisted on prolonging them, and their exchanges became more and more frank. Chapuys tried to justify Charles's failure to act decisively on her behalf. More importantly, he also addressed Catherine's mounting doubts about the effect of her actions. She was worried about More and Fisher – the 'good men [who] had suffered in persons and goods' – and about the mounting tide of heresy which threatened to engulf England. Such things were anathema to her. But they had arisen because of her steadfastness. Had she, she now asked herself, been right? Or was her behaviour a mere selfish intransigence, which God was punishing by visiting these horrors on her adoptive country?

Once again, though probably with more conviction this time, Chapuys said what she wanted to hear. God sent heresies, he explained, not because of her or any other human agency, but for His own purposes in the 'exaltation of the good and the confusion of the wicked'. Nor were the heresies deep-rooted, and there was hope that those who had lapsed would, like St Peter, return to the Faith with redoubled strength.

'At these words', he reported, 'she showed herself very glad, for she had previously had some scruple of conscience because the heresies had arisen from her affair'.[12]

Catherine's original doubts, however, were right. She had acted her part from the best of motives. And, bearing in mind her character, she could scarcely have behaved otherwise. Nevertheless, the awful truth remains that the Reformation, and all it entailed, was her work as much as Henry's and Anne's.

While Chapuys was at Kimbolton, Catherine's physical as well as her mental state seemed to improve. She began to sleep better. 'Her stomach also retain her food.' In view of these hopeful signs, Chapuys decided he should return to London. He took his leave on the Tuesday evening. Despite his forthcoming departure, Catherine was 'very cheerful' and actually laughed two or three times. She also had another good night, and Chapuys began his journey as planned the following morning in reasonable spirits. He travelled at leisure, lest he needed to be recalled.[13]

But this time it was Cromwell who received the intelligence first.

Catherine continued to do well on the 5th and, before going to sleep on the 6th, she was able to prepare herself for the night: when 'without any help, [she] combed and tied her hair and dressed her head'.

But she wakened in the small hours, and it was immediately clear that the hand of death was on her. Canonical rules, which Catherine insisted on obeying, discouraged the saying of mass before dawn. But, as first light broke, her Confessor, de Athequa the Bishop of Llandaff, sang the office and Catherine took the sacrament. Then she prayed and begged the bystanders to pray with her for her own soul and for Henry's: 'that God would pardon the King her husband for the wrong that he had done her, and that the divine goodness would lead him to the true road and give him good counsel'.[14]

One thing was omitted, however. It had been arranged between Chapuys and Dr de la Sa that 'whenever her life should be in danger, she should be reminded to affirm *in extremis* that she had never been [carnally] known by Prince Arthur'. But, 'in his grief and trouble', the doctor forgot to prompt. Nor did Catherine herself remember. Did she simply forget as well? Or, confronting her eternal judge, did she decide that the words which had baffled lesser, human tribunals were best left unsaid?[15]

At 10 o'clock, she received Extreme Unction which Bedingfield and Chamberlain were summoned to witness. Four hours later, at a little before 2 p.m., she died.[16]

Within the hour, Chamberlain and Bedingfield were writing to Cromwell for their instructions about the burial and the dissolution of the Household.

Meanwhile, the rituals of preparing a body that, whatever its exact earthly status, was certainly royal, were already underway. 'Sir', Chamberlain and Bedingfield informed Cromwell, 'the groom of the Chandlery [the department where candles were kept] here can cere her' – that is, disembowel and embalm the body. A plumber would be sent for, 'to close the body in lead'. 'The which', they added, 'must needs shortly be done, for that may not tarry.'[17]

Much has been read into this haste. For Chapuys and Catholic conspiracy theorists, it is evidence that Catherine had been poisoned and that her murderers were in a hurry to conceal the deed. But these notions seem far fetched. Chamberlain and Bedingfield were simply going by *The Royal Book* and the procedures it described. Moreover, Catherine's health had been poor even before the Divorce. And the Great Matter had imposed its own dreadful strains.[18]

In short, nature had taken its course and Catherine, in dying, had at last done what Henry wanted.

67. Reaction

The news reached the Court within twenty-four hours on 8 January. 'You could not conceive', reported Chapuys with distaste, 'the joy that this King and those who favour the concubinage have shown at [Catherine's] death.' Henry exclaimed: 'God be praised that we are free from all suspicion of war!' Anne's father and brother, Wiltshire and Rochford, focused on domestic concerns, saying 'that it was a pity [Mary] did not keep company with her [mother]'.

The following day was a Sunday, when the King's procession to hear mass in the Chapel Royal provided a ready-made setting for ceremonial. This Sunday it was turned into a carnival-like celebration of Catherine's death.

The King dressed flamboyantly: 'Henry was clad all over in yellow, from top to toe, except the white feather he had in his bonnet'. And Elizabeth, who was staying with her parents for the Christmas festivities, was paraded like a trophy, being 'conducted to Mass with trumpets and other great triumphs'. Then, after he had dined, Henry went to Anne's apartments and 'entered the room where the ladies danced and there did several things like one transported with joy'. He kissed, he embraced, he laughed. 'At last he sent for [Elizabeth] and, carrying her in his arms, he showed her first to one and then to another.' He put up similar performances on subsequent days. He also jousted.[1]

Henry, in short, was rejuvenated. The woman who had clung on to him, dragging him down and keeping him back, was dead. The future was his.

But with whom?

Recusant tradition preserves a different story. In this, it is Anne who wore the outrageous 'yellow for mourning', while Henry, smitten with conscience, wept over Catherine's last letter.

> My lord King Henry [she is supposed to have written], the love which I bear you makes me now, when the hour of my death is drawing nigh, put you in mind of your soul's salvation ... I forgive you myself, and I pray God to forgive you. I recommend to you our child.

It would be better for Henry's reputation if all this were true. But, alas, it is pious nonsense. Chapuys's contemporary report alone proves that. So does Henry's subsequent behaviour. For he showed only two concerns for Catherine after her death. The first was to exploit her funeral to drive home, irrefutably and for the last time, that she had never been his wife nor Queen of England; and the second was to get his hands on what was left of her property.[2]

Awkwardly, the two aims conflicted. For if Catherine were only Arthur's widow, then she was a 'woman sole' and, as such, had the right to dispose of her property as she wished. And she had already made her wishes clear in a Will. In this, she described herself, with characteristic neatness, as 'I, Catherine etc.' and divided her still considerable personal wealth (later estimated at £3,333) between her servants and her daughter. Henry did not get a look in.[3]

Luckily for Henry, the Solicitor-General, Richard Rich, was to hand. His economy with the truth had already provided the vital evidence which had sent Sir Thomas More to the block. Now, with equal legal ingenuity, he came up with the formula which enabled Henry to seize Catherine's property without conceding that she had ever been his wife.[4]

Rich was indeed a man to watch.

*

Anne's reaction to Catherine's death was, apparently, more complex. At first, like Henry, she showed unbounded joy at the news and gave a handsome present to the messenger who brought it. But then, so Chapuys learned later, she had second thoughts: 'she had frequently wept, fearing that they might do with her as with [Catherine]'. Chapuys had been inclined to be dismissive of his sources for this story, thinking them not to be 'very good authorities'. But the general thrust of the information was confirmed by the unimpeachable source of Gertrude Blount, Marchioness of Exeter, and her husband, the Marquess, whose place as the King's first cousin and honorific head of his Privy Chamber gave him unparalleled access to all Court gossip.[5]

They reported that Henry had shared with someone 'in great confidence, and as it were in confession' his doubts about Anne. 'He had made this marriage', he said, 'seduced by witchcraft and for this reason he considered it null.' 'This was evident', he continued, 'because God did not permit them to have any male issue, and that he believed he might take another wife.'

Indeed, he indicated that he was thinking of doing just that.

Despite its provenance, Chapuys was frankly incredulous of the story. But he resolved to exploit it by passing it on to Lady Shelton, Mary's governess, in order that, with an eye to her possibly uncertain future, she might treat Mary better.[6]

Anne, as it happened, had already made her own moves in the same direction. In mid-January she had written to Lady Shelton ordering her to suspend all pressure on Mary. So far, Anne claimed, she had been cruel to be kind and her efforts to get Mary to conform had been actuated 'more for charity than for anything [else]'. But now, considering the Word of God and its injunction 'to do good to one's enemy', she was advising Mary to submit to her father while she could still gain benefit from the act. For soon, Lady Shelton was to inform Mary, Catherine's daughter would have no choice, since Anne was pregnant again.

It was a bombshell, which Anne presented as only she knew how.

'[And] if I have a son as I hope shortly', she wrote menacingly, 'I know what will happen to her.'[7]

Anne was right: a son was a trump-card. His birth would guarantee her triumph and Mary's oblivion. But what if her confidence was misplaced?

Meanwhile, for all his supposed doubts about his second marriage, Henry continued to appear in infectious high spirits. And the most unlikely people were affected. Sir William Kingston was the sober, middle-aged Lieutenant of the Tower and Captain of the Guard, in which capacity he had arrested Wolsey. Nevertheless, he caught the prevailing spirit. 'My Lord', he wrote on 14 January from Court to his friend and Hampshire neighbour, Lord Lisle, the Deputy or Governor of Calais, 'here is much youth.' 'I am but in the middest of mine age,' he continued, '[nevertheless] I will be a' horseback among them.' Could Lisle 'help me to some good horse for my money'? It would have to be, he reminded his friend, 'a free horse and able to bear me'. For Kingston was a big man, who took after Henry's own build and had been unhorsed by him in a memorable jousting encounter in 1516.[8]

It is unclear whether Kingston wanted the horse for riding or the tilt. Henry, for his part, showed off his own youthfulness once more by preparing for the jousts on 24 January. But then disaster struck. He was 'mounted on a great horse to run at the lists', Chapuys reported, when 'both [horse and rider] fell so heavily that everyone thought it a miracle he was not killed'.[9]

Indeed, the King's escape was even greater. For, once he was unarmed, it was clear he was not even hurt.

Anne was not present when her husband had his accident. Perhaps she had absented herself because of their temporary estrangement. Or perhaps she was feeling the strain of her advancing pregnancy. At all events, she was spending the time quietly with her women when Norfolk broke the news. He told the story baldly, it was claimed later, and she was badly shocked.[10]

It was the eve of the third anniversary of her formal wedding on the Feast of the Conversion of St Paul, 1533.

*

Five days after the tilt-yard incident, Catherine was buried at Peter-borough Abbey. She had asked to be interred in a Carthusian monastery, but, as Cromwell pointed out, there were none left in the kingdom. He refrained from adding that this was because he had rooted them out as centres of resistance. The rest of her funeral ceremony would have been equally unwelcome to Catherine. She was buried as Princess Dowager, not as Queen. Still worse, in his sermon Hilsey, the Bishop of Rochester, claimed that 'in the hour of death she acknowledged she had not been Queen of England'. Chapuys, aware of what was coming, had boycotted the service and instead made his own private devotions for her in London.[11]

But Catherine had her revenge.

For, on the day of the funeral, Anne miscarried. The foetus, Chapuys reported, 'seemed to be a male child which she had not borne three and a half months'. The rumour mill of the Court came up with various reasons, including, most hurtfully, '[Anne's] incapacity to bear children'.[12]

But, despite the gloating of her enemies, the Queen recovered quickly. She even had the presence of mind to comfort 'her maids who wept'. 'It was for the best', she told them, 'because she would be the sooner with child again.' Moreover, she added, 'that the son she bore [then] would not be doubtful like this one, which had been conceived during [Catherine's] life'.[13]

Henry's reaction was far more extreme. Anne had been pregnant for a second time in 1534. That too had ended in a miscarriage or still birth. He had a new marriage. But, it seemed, the old pattern had reasserted itself.

'When she miscarried', Chapuys heard, '[Henry] scarcely said anything to her, except that he saw clearly that God did not wish to give him male children.' Anne, for her part, had protested that the disaster was due to her love for Henry. She had been distraught at his jousting accident. '*And her heart broke when she saw that he loved others.*'[14]

*

Anne's remark was pointed and Henry responded furiously. For, the same day that he reported Anne's miscarriage, Chapuys mentioned for the first time that Henry was making much of 'a lady of the Court, named Mistress Semel [Seymour], to whom, many say, [Henry] has lately made great presents'.[15]

This, indeed, is the first reference at all to Jane Seymour. The King had stayed at Wolf Hall, her father, Sir John Seymour's house near Marlborough during the 1535 Progress. The visit was a substantial one, lasting five days and romantic speculation naturally has Henry and Jane meeting and falling in love in a rural idyll. But there is not a scrap of contemporary evidence. Instead, Henry's new love seems to have been a product of New Year 1536. Death had liberated him from Catherine. His own mounting disillusionment was freeing him from Anne. And her miscarriage was the last straw.[16]

It was time to turn over a new leaf. Or, as Chapuys put it, time to exchange 'a thin, old and ugly ring' for a new one.[17]

68. Fall

By March, the breach between the Queen and the King had been followed by another, between the Queen and the minister. There has been much speculation about Cromwell's personal motives. He and Anne had come to disagree about foreign policy, where Cromwell, with his strong links to the London merchant community, was viscerally pro-Imperial just as much as Anne was instinctively pro-French. There was also, as we shall see, a widening rift over the direction that religious policy should take.

But, essentially, the question about Cromwell's motives is *mal posé*. It was not Cromwell's business to have motives of his own. Instead, it was his job to do what the King wanted. In breaking with Anne, therefore, Cromwell was acting as jackal to Henry's lion. Which is not to say that he did not extract the maximum personal advantage from his change of sides. And it is hard to blame him: he was merely earning high interest on a very high-risk investment.

For Anne might be tottering. But she had not fallen. And she was a brutal and effective politician who had been more than a match for Cromwell's old master, the great Cardinal Wolsey himself.

Chapuys was kept abreast of developments by his friends at Court, who were drawn from the highest, the most conservative and the most Catholic elements of the aristocracy. As well as the Exeters, they included Henry Pole, Lord Montague. He was the eldest son of Mary's old governess, the Countess of Salisbury, and the brother of Reginald Pole, who was then in Venice, half way through writing the book, *In Defence of the Unity of the Church*, which would turn him from Henry's protégé into his bitterest enemy. Additionally Montague, as he never forgot, was also the great-nephew of King Edward IV, and therefore, it could be argued, the person through whose veins coursed the purest Yorkist royal blood, free from the taint of illegitimacy, which, thanks to the slanders of Richard III, clung to Henry's own mother, Elizabeth of York.[1]

With these contacts, Chapuys found it easy to assemble an impressive guest-list at his London residence. But, even by his standards, the company that sat down to dinner one day in late March was spectacular: it included two peers of the blood royal, Exeter and Montague, as well as the Dowager Countess of Kildare, *née* Elizabeth Grey, who was also the King's cousin of the half blood. The conversation began with a general lament that the country was going to the dogs. Then Montague became interestingly specific. '[Anne] and Cromwell were on bad terms', he revealed, 'and ... some new marriage for the King was spoken of.'[2]

Chapuys made good use of the information in his next meeting with Cromwell. He had deliberately refrained from seeking him out, he informed Cromwell, so as to avoid arousing Anne's suspicions. Then he became even more confidential. He spoke 'for the love' he bore him. He wished him 'a more gracious mistress, and one more grateful for the inestimable services he had done the King'. Finally came the warning. 'He must beware of enraging her, else he must never expect perfect reconciliation.' She had destroyed Wolsey: Cromwell would have 'to see to it better than the Cardinal' if he were to survive.

In his reply, Cromwell, who, like many vulpine politicians, had a good line in sanctimoniousness when required, took the appropriate tone of resigned other-worldliness. 'Only now', he said, 'had [he] known the frailty of human affairs, especially those of the Court . . . and [he trusted] that if fate fell upon him as upon his predecessors, he would arm himself with patience, and leave the rest to God.'[3]

There would come a moment when Cromwell's resolution to 'leave [it] to God' would be put to the test. But it was not yet.

Nevertheless, Anne struck back forcefully.

Her instrument, unsurprisingly, was one of the many clergy she patronized, John Skip, who had succeeded Shaxton as her Almoner. Skip was the preacher for the day in the Chapel Royal at Greenwich on Passion Sunday, 2 April 1536. His congregation included the King and Queen and the cream of the Court and Council. And he spared none of them.

Henry was reminded of Solomon, who, 'in the latter end of his reign . . . became very unnoble and defamed himself sore by sensual and carnal appetite in taking of many wives and concubines'. Cromwell (for there could be no doubt that he was the target) was roundly compared to the evil councillor Haman. Members of the Council were warned against Reform for its own sake: '[they] have need to take good heed what counsel they give . . . in altering of any ancient things'. Finally the entire political establishment was the preacher's victim in his satirical picture of Parliament:

There is no unquietness, no tumultuous fashion; there is no checking or taunting of any man for showing his mind . . . there speaketh not past one at once . . . There no man speaketh for any carnal affection or lucre of the promotions of this world. But all thing is done for zeal of the Commonwealth.

'This think I', the preacher concluded with his tongue firmly in his cheek, 'and other men ought to think the same.'[4]

Just as striking was Skip's defence of the position of the clergy. His text was 'Which of you convicteth me of sin?' (*John* 8.46). Nowadays, he pointed out, it was fashionable to attack the clergy, and the fault of one was treated as though it were the fault of all: 'if they [the laity] may spy a great or notable vice or fault in one priest . . . then they will infame and rebuke all the whole clergy for the same'. This was the technique of Cromwell's visitors, and it had just been used to stampede Parliament into agreeing to the Act for the Dissolution of the Smaller Monasteries. The Bill had been passed on 18 March and it was even then awaiting the Royal Assent.[5]

But what, Skip wanted to know at this crucial juncture, was the motive? Was it really to reform the lives of the clergy? Or was it malice and covetousness: 'because they [the laity] would have from the clergy their possessions'?

Clearly, Skip's sermon was designed to put pure Holy Water between Cromwell and Anne on religious policy. Cromwell, he argued, was using Reform as a cloak for expropriation. Anne, on the other hand, meant it.

Latymer's *Life* offers precise corroboration. When Anne heard that the Dissolution of the Smaller Monasteries was mooted, he writes: 'she commanded that godly preacher of England, Mr Latimer, to take some occasion in his next sermon to be made before the King to dissuade the utter subversion of the said houses and to induce the King's Grace . . . to convert them to some better use'.[6]

And the 'better use' was education. Some houses could be turned into Bible-based educational foundations, like Stoke-by-Clare in Suffolk where she appointed her Chaplain, Matthew Parker, as Master with a mandate to carry out the Reform. And all could be required to direct part of their wealth to fund university bursaries and scholarships to train future clergymen to be more effective preachers of the 'Word of God'. Skip touched on this theme as well when he lamented 'the great decay of the Universities in this realm and how necessary the maintenance of them is for the continuance of Christ's faith and his religion'. And Anne had already made a major contribution to their revival, when she sued to Henry to exempt the universities from the payment of First Fruits and Tenths. If the charge had been levied, as the university of Cambridge explained in its letter of thanks to the Queen, '[it] would [have] greatly diminish[ed] the number of scholars in every College'.[7]

Anne's attitude naturally gave the smaller monasteries hope and, again according to Latymer, their heads petitioned Anne in a body. She sent them away with fleas in their ears, however. Their degenerate manner of living, which was so different from that of their founders, meant, she said, that the dissolution was God's judgement on them. Nevertheless, she dropped heavy hints that moves to increase their educational endowments would win her favour.[8]

Skip's boldest stroke was his treatment of the Haman story. In the *Book of Esther*, Haman, the councillor of King Ahasuerus, persuades his master to order a pogrom of the Jews, 'because their laws are diverse from all people, neither keep they the King's laws' (*Esther* 3.8). For Skip, as we have seen, Haman was Cromwell, while the persecuted Jews were the clergy and, more particularly, the about-to-be dispossessed monastic clergy, who had indeed been accused of obeying the Pope's laws and not Henry's. The parallels were clear enough. But Skip deliberately altered his text to drive the point home. In the original story, Haman offered Ahasuerus the gift of 10,000 talents of silver as an inducement to agree to the pogrom; in Skip's adaptation, Haman promised the King 10,000 talents to be taken from the Jews (just as Cromwell was proposing to fill the royal coffers from the dissolution).

But Haman met his come-uppance at the hands of Ahasuerus's Queen Esther, who was a secret Jewess and intervened to protect her people. We have already encountered the parallel between Anne and Esther, which had been alluded to in her coronation *entrée*. But that was in respect of her displacement of Catherine, who was identified with Ahasuerus's first Queen, the proud and unyielding Vashti. Now, in Skip's sermon, Anne/Esther appeared in her more heroic role as the destroyer of the evil and overweening minister.

It was a role, however, that dared not quite to speak its name. For not even Skip was rash enough to describe Esther as Queen or even to mention her name. Instead, overcome by an uncharacteristic fit of discretion, he referred to her as 'a good woman (which this gentle King Ahasuerus loved very well and put his trust in because he knew she was ever his friend) and she gave unto the King contrary counsel'. But, this necessary caution over, Skip returned with relish to the conclusion of his tale. Thanks to this 'good woman', he explained, the pogrom was can-celled; the Jews were saved and Haman, the evil councillor, was hanged on a gallows fifty cubits high.[9]

After such a performance, Skip inevitably found himself hauled before the Council on charges of slandering 'the King's Highness, his council-lors, his lords and nobles, and his whole Parliament'. Interrogatories were prepared. But he survived unscathed. Anne was still able to protect her own.

But was she able to protect herself?

Earlier, Cromwell had told Chapuys that Anne wanted his head. Now, before the whole Court, her Almoner had threatened him with being hanged as high as Haman. It is little wonder that he decided to strike first.

He may have made his first move too quickly, however. Over the Easter holidays, 14–17 April, Chapuys, with Cromwell's enthusiastic backing, made an overture for a settlement of the outstanding differences between Henry and Charles V and a renewal of their former friendship. He put forward four specific proposals, which Henry himself summarized as follows. First, that Charles would broker a reconciliation between him and the Pope. Second, that 'for as much as there is great likelihood and appearance that God will send unto Us heirs male to succeed Us ... We would vouchsafe, at his contemplation, to legitimate our daughter Mary, in such degree, as in default of issue by our most dear and most entirely beloved wife the Queen, she might not be reputed unable to some place in our succession.' Third, that Henry would help the Emperor against the Turk. And fourth, that he would also help him against the anticipated French attack on Milan.[10]

Henry apparently reacted favourably and Chapuys was summoned to Court on Tuesday, 18 April. He was asked if he would go and kiss Anne's hand. As usual, he refused. He was then conducted to mass in the Chapel Royal by Rochford. The ambassador, along with the rest of the Court, was below, in the body of the Chapel, while Henry and Anne, with their immediate suites, were above in their first-floor pews or 'Holiday Closets'. But, at the moment of the offering in the mass, the demarcation was broken down as the King and Queen descended from their pews by staircases on either side of the Chapel to make their way to the altar.

Anne and Chapuys would come face to face. This was the first personal confrontation between them since Anne had become Henry's wife and Queen. What would happen? The Court crowded round. 'There was a great concourse of people', Chapuys reported, 'to see how [Anne] and I behaved to each other.' 'She was courteous enough', he continued, 'for when I was behind the door by which she entered, she turned back, merely to do me reverence, *as I did to her*.'[11]

For the first time, whether he fully realized it or not, Chapuys had acknowledged Anne as Queen. Mary was furious when she heard.

With this gesture, one major achievement from Chapuys's visit had been notched up by Henry. But, typically, Henry saw no need to give anything in return. He had an acrimonious exchange with Cromwell and then turned to deal with Chapuys. One by one he dismissed his four proposals out of hand. He was at his most outrageous over the last. 'He was not a child', he said, 'and that they must not give him the stick, and then caress him.' Then, to drive home the point, he enacted a dumb-show, 'playing with his fingers on his knees, and doing as if he were calling a child to pacify it'.[12]

*

Many things have been read into the events of this day. It was, Cromwell later told Chapuys, the moment he decided Anne had to go. He would never again accept such a rebuff on foreign policy; it was either her or him.[13]

The remark comes from the horse's mouth and it is tempting to take it at face value. But the temptation should be resisted. Cromwell was an adept flatterer, and in this case he was trying to persuade Chapuys that the concerns of the Emperor and his ambassador had come first. In fact, the concerns of the King of England and his minister had come first. And, as we have seen, these concerns point to a different timetable, with wider areas of dispute and a significantly earlier breaking-point between Anne and Cromwell; if the events of 18 April mattered at all, it was as the last straw in their relationship.

The day has also been seen as victory for Anne. She had at last got Chapuys to bow and doff his cap. And Henry had made an emphatic restatement of his commitment to the Boleyn marriage. But this last is doubtful, also. In the circular report of his exchange with Chapuys which the King sent to his main ambassadors abroad, Henry mentions 'our most dear and most entirely beloved wife the Queen' only in his summary of Chapuys's proposals. She does not figure at all in his reply to the ambassador and nowhere is she referred to by name. If this is a ringing endorsement of his marriage, it would be difficult to think of a weaker one.

But most extraordinary of all is the interpretation foisted on the words 'for as much as there is great likelihood and appearance that God will send unto Us heirs male to succeed Us'. These words mean, it has recently been claimed, that Anne was pregnant again; and, furthermore, since Henry persuaded himself that the child was not his, that they offer a clue to the tragedy which was to follow.

If this were true, it would indeed be a major insight. But it is not. For the statement 'for as much as there is great likelihood and appearance that God will send unto Us heirs male to succeed Us' is followed immediately by the proviso: 'in default of issue by our most dear and most entirely beloved wife the Queen'. The statement refers to Henry's potency, not to Anne's fecundity, and the qualifying proviso indeed presumes her to be barren, at least of male issue. Finally, of course, the words are not Henry's own, but the King's summary of Chapuys's proposal.[14]

The notion of Anne's pregnancy and all that has been deduced from it is therefore, alas, a case of much ado about nothing. Whatever drove Henry forward, it was not this.

The Feast of Easter was followed by the Feast of St George. And on St George's Day, 23 April, a Chapter of the Order of the Garter was held at Greenwich, with Henry himself presiding.[15]

The Garter was the oldest and most prestigious Order of Chivalry in Christendom and there was hot competition for appointment to it. This year there were two front-runner candidates, Anne's brother Rochford and her cousin, Sir Nicholas Carew, the Master of the Horse. And one of them would have to be disappointed as there was a single vacancy. Both candidates had powerful support. There had been heavy French pressure, going back over a number of years, for Carew's election; while Anne herself was pushing equally strongly for her brother. The voting in the Chapter was inconclusive and Henry, 'having perused' the list of names, 'put it in his bosom' and, most unusually, postponed his decision to the following day.[16]

Then, before the requiem mass for the Knight who had died in the previous year, the King announced his choice. There were many of the nominees, he said, 'who were indeed most exceeding worthy'. 'But at that time', he continued, 'he thought good that Sir Nicholas Carew should be preferred in the election.' Carew was summoned, fell on his knees and delivered an oleaginous disabling speech. He owed his appointment, he protested, not to his own merits or actions, but only to Henry's 'most excellent goodness'.[17]

He also owed it, indirectly, to Anne since, in her decline, her opposition had become a recommendation to Henry.

Anne, naturally, was furious, especially since Henry's decision made

her fall from the King's favour public knowledge. '[She] has not ...
sufficient influence to get it for her brother,' Chapuys noted gleefully.
But Anne was also afraid, because Carew was the leading supporter of
her rival, Jane Seymour. Still worse, he made little effort to conceal the
fact. Indeed, Chapuys learned, he was boasting to anyone who would
listen that he would soon pitch Anne out of the saddle.[18]

Also on 24 April, as the drama and pageantry of the Garter was unrolling
at Greenwich, a judicial commission of 'Oyer and Terminer' was issued
at Westminster. Such commissions – 'to hear and to determine' a wide
list of offences, including treason and the misprision of treason – were
routine. But was this one intended for routine purposes?

And three days after that, on the 27th, writs were issued for a new
Parliament. The old Parliament, the 'Reformation', which had legislated
the break with Rome, enabled Anne's marriage and protected it with the
penalties of treason, had only been dissolved on 14 April. To summon
another so quickly was without precedent. What was it intended to do?[19]

Probably the truth is that no one, not even the ruling triumvirate of
Henry, Cromwell and Lord Chancellor Audley, quite knew. Meanwhile,
Carew and his friends were floating a variety of schemes. One would
divorce Anne on the grounds that her precontract with Northumberland
amounted to a valid marriage. And another would legitimate Mary
because she had been born *bona fide parentum*. *Bona fide parentum* (during
the good faith of her parents) was a technicality of canon law which
nicely squared the circle. By it, Henry's first marriage was acknowledged
to be null (for Henry would never accept anything else); but, equally,
because Catherine and Henry had *thought* that they were married, their
offspring, Mary, was presumed to be legitimate despite the invalidity of
her parents' marriage.

Stokesley, the Bishop of London, and a leading canonist, was
consulted on the legal situation. But, wisely, he declared 'that he would
not give any opinion to anyone but the King himself'.[20]

There is, in short, the powerful impression that Anne's opponents
were flailing around. They had her on the defensive. But they had not

come up with an open-and-shut case against her. She might easily escape and turn the tables.

But then, over the weekend of 29–30 April, there took place two incidents which delivered Anne into her enemies' hands. Or rather, perhaps, she delivered herself.

For Anne the religious Reformer was only one side of the Queen. The other is glimpsed in Baynton's description of the goings-on among the Queen's ladies in the weeks after her coronation. Absent lovers and husbands, he had said, were forgotten, as the women rejoiced in their new conquests. For life in the Queen's Chamber was not all Bibles, sermons and politics. There was dancing, singing and poetry. There were word-games and acrostics, gossip and jokes. Above all, there was love. Sometimes it was real. Sometimes it was a game. And often it was difficult to tell the two apart.[21]

Anne in her days as a maiden in the Queen's Chamber had been mistress of this game of Courtly Love: it was how she had attracted and won Henry in the first place. But now that she was Queen, her expected role changed from practitioner to president. As Queen, she was the focus of the sighs of musicians, poets and Court gallants. But the sighs were supposed to be ceremonious and chaste. As was she.

She was also expected to preserve discipline among her ladies and maids and their male suitors. This was a tall order. For the Court, as Kingston's wry remarks show, was the kingdom of youth. It was filled with young men and young women who were attractive, athletic and ambitious. They were on the make and had time on their hands. In the circumstances, constant virtue, on the part of either sex, must have been something of a miracle. And miracles were no more common in the sixteenth century than in the twenty-first. Nor was it only the young. For even the middle aged, as Kingston admits against himself, caught the prevailing ethos and behaved as though they too were young. Likewise the married were tempted to act as though they were not.[22]

Anne's relationship to all this was ambiguous. She had the character, intelligence and presence to keep control. But she also had a shrewish

Devout, aristocratic and grasping, Lady Margaret Beaufort *(left)* was devoted to her only son, Henry VII *(below left)*. As far as her daughter-in-law, Elizabeth of York *(below right)* was concerned, she was the mother-in-law from hell. Nevertheless, the marriage of Henry VII and Elizabeth was happy. Elizabeth brought up her second son, the future Henry VIII, along with her two daughters. Her early death in 1503, when Henry was eleven, deeply affected the boy. Henry's relations with his father were less happy, though he always respected him for ending the civil strife of the Wars of the Roses.

The marriage of Ferdinand of Aragon (*above left*) with Isabella of Castile (*above right*) unified Spain and led to the country's golden age. The Catholic Kings (as they were entitled by a grateful Pope in 1498) completed the Reconquest from Isla at home and laid the foundation of the Spanish Empire abroad.

Ferdinand, a master-politician, used Spain's new power to challenge France for the domination of Europ He was anxious to enlist the aid of England, a traditional enemy of France, so in 1489 Ferdinand and Isabella betrothed their youngest daughter, Catherine, to Arthur, Prince of Wales (*right*), the eldest so of Henry VII. The couple were married in 1501 in a magnificent ceremony in St Paul's but Arthur died the following Easter. To preser the alliance, Catherine was then betrothed to Arthur's younger brothe Henry (*left*), who was now heir.

Catherine (*left*) was the youngest daughter of Ferdinand and Isabella. She was given an excellent education to prepare her for her destiny as Queen of England. But her mother's death in 1503, which threatened the union of Aragon and Castile, damaged her prospects. Henry VII lost interest in her as a daughter-in-law and ordered his son Henry to repudiate his promise to marry her. But, when Henry became King in 1509, he went ahead with the marriage nonetheless. A son was born in January 1511 and Henry celebrated with a magnificent tournament at Westminster in which he rode as Catherine's 'Sir Loyal Heart' (*below*). But the boy died, as did all Catherine's other children, save for a single daughter. Thanks to her many pregnancies, Catherine lost her figure (*right*) and Henry's love; she devoted herself instead to religion and the upbringing of her daughter.

Bridewell (*above*), situated on the Thames near the present Blackfriars Bridge, was Henry's main London residence in the first half of his reign. And it was here that Henr and Catherine came in 1529 for the trial of their marriage. Henry met the Legate, Campeggio, who came to be one of the judges, at the foot of the Processional Staircas (to the left of the courtyard), while the trial itself took place in the Parliament Chambe of the adjacent Blackfriars Monastery. After the trial was aborted by Catherine's appea to Rome, Henry resorted to a series of other devices to persuade the Pope to annul hi marriage, including the Petition to the Pope, signed and sealed by the almost all the English nobility in 1530 (*below*). But, like all his other efforts in Rome, it failed.

The political power of the Emperor, Charles V (*right*), over the Pope, Clement VII (*left*), destroyed any hope that Henry might have had of receiving a favourable hearing in Rome. A diplomatic understanding with Francis I of France (*below left*) was vital when Henry decided to seek a solution by divorcing Catherine in England. Mary (*below right*), only child of Henry and Catherine, was the subject of a tug-of-love between her parents. She chose Catherine, with enormous consequences for herself and England.

CARDINAL WOLSEY

STEEVEN GARDNER

Henry's efforts to divorce Catherine became a parting of the ways for the English political elite. The King's Minister, Cardinal Wolsey (*above left*) fell because he failed to get the Divorce from Rome. Stephen Gardiner, Bishop of Winchester (*above right*), objected to the Royal Supremacy over the English Church, which was the necessary preliminary to getting the Divorce in England. John Fisher, Bishop of Rochester (*below left*), Catherine's eloquent partisan, was executed in 1535. Sir Thomas More (*below right*), Wolsey's successor as Chancellor, resigned when Henry was declared Supreme Head on Earth of the Church of England without qualification. More too was executed in 1535.

side, and was tempted to bandy words, which was undignified and could easily escalate. There was a fundamental issue as well. She was the most successful poacher of her age or any preceding one. This might make her an equally effective gamekeeper. On the other hand, her life story was a testament to the fact that, while virtue may be its own reward, vice really pays.

Anne, in short, might command: 'Do as I say.' But the temptation was to reply: 'Why? I am only doing what you did.' And, as we shall see, many found it hard to resist temptation.

The first incident of that fatal weekend took place on the Saturday. And it shows Anne in a proper, if rather snobbish, light. When she went into her Presence Chamber or Throne Room she found Mark Smeaton, a favourite young musician of the King's Privy Chamber, standing in the bay-window.

What happened next was a scene from tragi-comedy, which Anne later described in her own words. Smeaton was pensive, probably extravagantly so, in the manner of a romantic poet smitten with love. 'Why are you so sad?' she asked. He replied, 'It was no matter'. And then he sighed. Her patience snapped. Not only was Smeaton making an exhibition of himself, he was getting above himself as well. A cat may look at a Queen, but a mere musician should not make love to her.

So, ruthlessly, she slapped him down. 'You may not look to have me speak to you as I should do to a nobleman', she said, 'because you be an inferior person.'

'No, no, Madam,' he replied, 'a look sufficed me; and thus fare you well!'

He had swallowed the reproof. It was his place to do so. And he had the memory of those coal-black eyes, that had bewitched many a greater man.[23]

On the following day, Sunday, 30 April, Anne had another exchange. This time her interlocutor was indeed 'a nobleman' and the tone was strikingly different.

Henry Norris, the Groom of the Stool and Chief Gentleman of the Privy Chamber, was the head of the King's private service and Henry's principal personal favourite. He had also become close, personally and politically, to Anne. He had spent most of the spring away from Court on his estates in Oxfordshire, where he was a beneficiary of Suffolk's fall from grace the previous summer.

There was only one fly in the ointment. For it was a truth, universally acknowledged in the sixteenth as much as in the nineteenth century, that a single man, in possession of a good fortune, must be in want of a wife. And Norris was both rich and unmarried. Or rather, he was between marriages. His first wife, the daughter of Thomas Fiennes, Lord Dacre of the South, had died before 1530. He had subsequently had an on-off relationship with Anne's cousin, Margaret Shelton, the daughter of Mary's custodians, Sir John and Lady Shelton. But he had made no commitments.

'Madge' Shelton was a bit of a goer. She was vivacious and attractive and had for a time been the King's mistress. She also had a string of other conquests. Maybe Norris delayed tying the knot because she was shop-soiled goods. Maybe he was worried that her Boleyn blood was turning into a liability. Or, most likely, he hesitated because he was not sure he loved her.

Anne, however, was determined to force the issue. 'I asked him', she recalled later, 'why he went not through with his marriage?' He replied 'he would tarry a time'. Irritated by his prevarication Anne snapped back: 'You look for dead men's shoes. For if aught came to the King but good, you would look to have me.' Norris was appalled. 'If he should have any such thought', he said, 'he would his head were off.' Anne then became openly threatening: 'She could undo him if she would.' And the two had a violent quarrel.

Anne's words were unutterably foolish. And they can be explained only by the nervous strain she was under. Cromwell had deserted her. Now it seemed that Norris was abandoning her as well. In her fear, she lashed out.

Quickly, of course, both realized their folly and, that same day at

Anne's command, Norris informed Almoner Skip 'that he would swear for the Queen that she was a good woman'. But this was a remedy that was almost worse than the disease.[24]

And, in any case, the damage was done. For some of Anne's ladies had high-powered brothers and husbands and, in the echo-chamber of the Court, such an incident could not be kept quiet. By the afternoon, Henry himself knew. He confronted Anne directly. She said what she could. But her words seemed damning and Henry, in disgust, thrust her away and retreated to sulk alone in the bay-window.

In this extremity, the Queen played her trump card.

Elizabeth had spent the spring with her parents. Probably she had stayed at Eltham, Greenwich's satellite palace. Anne lavished attention on her. She bought her beautiful caps, made out of rich fabrics and exquisitely trimmed with gold nets and laces. She even paid for a crafts-man to come from London only 'to take measure of caps for my Lady Princess'.[25]

Henry, as his behaviour after Catherine's death shows, was fond of his pretty auburn-haired daughter. Would the child speak to Henry as Anne's words could not?

The resulting scene was witnessed by the Scottish Reformer, Alexander Alane ('Alesius'). And he claimed to remember it vividly – though it was by then over twenty years later, and the child was Queen herself.

> Never shall I forget [he wrote] the sorrow which I felt when I saw the most serene Queen your most religious mother, carrying you, still a little baby, in her arms and entreating the most serene King, your father, in Greenwich Palace, from the open window of which he was looking into the courtyard, when she brought you to him.

'I did not perfectly understand what had been going on', Alane con-tinued, 'but the faces and gestures of the speakers plainly showed that the

King was angry, although he could conceal his anger wonderfully well.'[26]

For the moment, however, Anne's gesture worked and Henry seemed pacified. Or perhaps he was merely biding his time. For the signals were mixed. The decision was taken that the May Day jousts should proceed as planned the next day. On the other hand, very late at night (at about 11 o'clock), the forthcoming Progress to inspect the new harbour and fortifications at Dover was cancelled.[27]

For a new front had opened up. Somehow, and again probably through Anne's ladies, Cromwell had heard about the Queen's conversation with Smeaton on Saturday. The young musician was seized and was taken to Cromwell's house at Stepney, where he was 'in examination on May Even'. Maybe it was the results of this preliminary examination, without the use of torture, which led to the last minute decision to cancel the Progress.[28]

Nevertheless, the tournament went ahead in the presence of the King and Queen. Both behaved as though nothing had happened. Henry, indeed, with that mastery of self-control to which Alane referred, went out of his way to be gracious and even lent Norris a horse when his own mount refused to charge. Anne, too, put up a good show and appeared as her radiant self, presiding over the jousts from her viewing-box hung with cloth of gold and encouraging the combatants with smiles and gestures.[29]

It was a final triumph in a familiar arena. For Henry and Anne never saw each other again. Just as he had done with Catherine, Henry slipped away without a word.

The moment the jousts were over, Henry returned to York Place. He was in such a hurry that he did not wait for the tide to turn. Instead, he rode. And riding at his side was Norris.

But instead of the usual easy banter between master and favourite attendant, Norris was talking for his life. 'All the way', George Constantine, Norris's servant, reported, '[the King] had Mr Norris in examination and promised him his pardon in case he would utter the truth.' The pressure was intense: 'but whatsoever could be said or done, Mr Norris would confess nothing to the King'.

Norris was held overnight at York Place and committed to the Tower at dawn the following morning. During this second journey, according to his own chaplain, a confession of sorts was wrung out of him by Treasurer Fitzwilliam. But Norris later claimed 'that he was deceived to do the same'.[30]

Meanwhile, Smeaton had been admitted to the Tower at 6 p.m. on May Day. Constantine later heard that 'he was . . . grievously racked'. Probably he was put to the torture as soon as he arrived. His ordeal lasted almost four hours, as 'it was 10 of the clock or he were well lodged [in his cell]'.[31]

The time taken shows that he put up impressive resistance. But finally the pain and Cromwell's brutal questions broke him, and he confessed to adultery with the Queen.

Cromwell had his first breakthrough.

69. The Tower

Anne spent the night after the jousts in her apartments as usual. But the following morning she, too, was interrogated by the Council at Greenwich. The questioning was harsh and Anne later complained that she was 'cruelly handled'. Her uncle Norfolk, anxious to distance himself from her fall, set the tone of high moral opprobrium. 'He said "Tut, tut, tut" and shaking his head three or four times.' Treasurer Fitzwilliam, fresh from his success with Norris, joined in the hunt from different motives. He had been Wolsey's 'Treasure'; now he relished destroying Anne, because she had been the Cardinal's nemesis. 'He was in the Forest of Windsor,' Anne said bitterly. On the other hand, Controller Paulet was 'a very gentleman'.

The examination over, Anne was taken by boat to the Tower. And neither in life nor in death would she ever leave it.[1]

It was not quite three years since she had travelled the same route on her pre-coronation river pageant. As then, the weather was fine. She had a distinguished escort, including Norfolk, Oxford, the Great Chamberlain, and Sandys, the Lord Chamberlain of the Household. And there were great crowds of spectators. But they had come to witness her shame, not her triumph.

And there was no Henry to greet her with a kiss when she landed. Instead, Kingston, the Lieutenant of the Tower, met her to conduct her to her prison. 'Mr Kingston,' she asked, 'shall I go into a dungeon?' 'No, Madam,' he replied, 'you shall go into your lodging that you lay in at your Coronation.'

So far, her courage had held up. But now she broke down. 'It is too good for me,' she cried. 'Jesu, have mercy on me,' she prayed, kneeling and weeping profusely. Then suddenly, the tears dried, 'and in the same sorrow [she] fell into a great laughing', Kingston reported, 'and she hath done so many times since.'[2]

Anne's hysteria proved as valuable to Cromwell as Smeaton's agony on the rack.

Also on the Tuesday, Anne's brother Rochford was arrested at the Court at York Place, where he had followed the King. He was examined on the spot before the Council and, like Norris, denied any impropriety. Nevertheless, he too was brought to the Tower, where he arrived some hours after Anne.[3]

The investigation now seemed to have hit a rock. Smeaton had indeed confessed under terrible torture. But neither Norris nor Rochford had admitted anything useful. Nor had Anne. 'There is much communication', Anne's former Vice-chamberlain Baynton wrote to Fitzwilliam, 'that no man will confess anything against her, but all only Mark of any actual thing.' 'Wherefore', he continued, 'in my foolish conceit, it should much touch the King's honour if it should no further appear.' Falling over himself to turn King's evidence, Baynton then recommended a trawl through Anne's ladies. 'Mrs Margery' Horsman, the Mistress of the Maids, had behaved 'strangely' to him. She must be in the know because 'there hath been great friendship between the Queen and her of late'. And so on.[4]

But all such endeavours were rendered redundant by Anne's own behaviour. The original intention had been to hold her incommunicado. She was given four unsympathetic women who were headed by the pious and disapproving Lady Kingston. And there were strict instructions that she should speak only in Lady Kingston's presence. But the arrangement turned out to be impracticable. Two of the women slept on a pallet mattress in Anne's chamber; while Kingston and his wife slept in the next room. Left unchaperoned, Anne talked uncontrollably. And it soon became clear that it was not in Cromwell's interest to silence her.

For, within twelve hours of her imprisonment, she had given full details of her conversation with Norris. Then she remembered another incident. 'She more feared Weston,' she said. 'For on Whitsunday Tuesday last [18 May 1535] Weston told her that Norris came more unto her Chamber for her than for Madge [Shelton].' 'Weston' was Sir Francis Weston, a young rake-hell and Henry's former favourite page. Oral reports of what Anne said were passed on to Kingston by the aptly named Mrs Coffin, while Kingston in turn made written reports to Cromwell.

On the morning of 3 May 1536, Anne again babbled. She had remembered further details about the Weston incident. 'She had spoke to him', she said, 'because he did love her kinswoman Mrs Shelton and that . . . he loved not his wife.' This was Anne acting properly in her role of censor of morals. But Weston had ready a tart reply. 'He loved one in her house better than them both,' he had said. The Queen had walked into the trap. 'Who is that?' she had said. 'It is yourself,' the insolent boy had replied.[5]

It had been a smart retort. But it would cost him his head, and within a few hours he too was in the Tower.

*

Weston's imprisonment marked a turning-point in the investigations. Hitherto, only Anne's closest circle had been involved. Now the arrests widened into a moral purge which picked up the most notable reprobates of the Court. By Monday, 8 May, Sir Richard Page, Richmond's indulgent guardian, and Sir Thomas Wyatt, the poet, lover and flagrant adulterer, were also in the Tower. And Anne's cousin, Sir Francis Bryan, who was an obvious target in view of his nickname of the 'Vicar of Hell', narrowly escaped the same fate.[6]

Rather apart from these was William Brereton. At Court, he held the relatively minor office of Groom of the Privy Chamber. But he was a mighty figure in the local administration of his native Chester and North Wales. Constantine had spoken with him on Thursday, 4 May at about 9 a.m. and found him resigned to his fate. 'There was no way but one with any matter,' he said. His premonitions proved correct and he was a prisoner in the Tower by 2 o'clock. 'What was laid against him', Constantine said a few years later, 'I know not nor never heard.' And posterity is little the wiser. Was he too close to Rochford? Had he trodden on toes in North Wales? We do not know.[7]

Anne's revelations in the Tower were not confessions, of course. Far from it. Instead, they were part of a desperate quest for meaning. 'She to be a Queen', she said, 'and [so] cruelly handled . . . was never seen [before]'. What could have brought it about? Was it the work of accusers, as she fancied Weston to be? Was Henry testing her? 'I think the King does it to prove me,' she said. 'And', Kingston added, 'she did laugh withal and was very merry.'[8]

These violent mood-swings continued. Sometimes she prophesied vengeance. There would be no rain till she came out of the Tower, she said on one occasion. And, on another: 'If I die, you shall see the greatest punishment for me within these seven years that ever came to England'. Then, in another frame of mind, she ate a hearty dinner and joked and punned. Would the male prisoners have anyone to make their beds? she asked. 'Nay, I warrant you,' Lady Kingston replied. Anne's exact answer is lost because of the damage sustained by the Kingston correspondence in the Cottonian Library fire. But it clearly involved a pun on the 'ballets' (ballads or poems), for which Rochford as well as Wyatt was famous, and the 'pallets' (beds), on which they would now have to exercise their skills as 'makers' (which also meant poets).[9]

This, for better or for worse, was the old Anne. 'Such desire as you have had to such tales has brought you to this,' one of her women brutally informed her. But there was also the old Anne in her religious obser-vances. Almost her first request was that she might have the sacrament in the closet or oratory next to her chamber, 'that she might pray for mercy'. A day or two later, she repeated the request. She also asked for Almoner Skip – 'whom', Kingston noted drily, 'she supposeth to be devout'. Clearly, Skip's Passion Sunday Sermon was unforgiven, by one of its victims at least.[10]

Also impressive is Anne's family feeling. The Boleyns were nothing if not a tight-knit clan. And it showed. Where was her father? Her brother? How would her mother cope? 'Oh my mother, thou wilt die for sorrow!' she lamented. When she finally discovered that her brother was also in the Tower, it came almost as a relief. 'I am very glad', she said, 'that we both be so nigh together.'[11]

Her attitude to her fate changed as swiftly as her mood. 'One hour she is determined to die', Kingston reported, 'and the next hour much contrary to that.' Even her religion was pressed into service. 'I would God I had my Bishops', she said on 4 or 5 May, 'for they would all go to the King for me.' Unfortunately for Anne, Cromwell had anticipated this manoeuvre and took care to block access to the King, by the bishops or anybody else.[12]

Cromwell's particular concern was Archbishop Cranmer. Cranmer was at his palace of Knole in Kent when the blow fell and it is unclear what, if anything, he knew of recent events at Court. On the 2nd, he received a letter from Cromwell, commanding him in the King's name to come to Lambeth but equally forbidding him to make any attempt to see the King. The letter gave no details, but 'open report' filled Cranmer in all too fully on the charges laid against his patroness.[13]

Once arrived at Lambeth Cranmer did what he could. He was forbidden to see the King. But he could try to send him a letter. It was, however, one of the most difficult compositions of his life. On the one hand, he had to soothe Henry's wounded pride. On the other, he wanted to plead for Anne to whom, as he frankly acknowledged, he owed everything 'next unto [the King]'. Yet he could not plead too hard, for that would be to doubt the King's justice.

'I am in such a perplexity', he wrote to Henry, 'that my mind is clean amazed.' 'For I never had better opinion in a woman', he continued, 'than I did in her, which maketh me to think that she should not be culpable. And again, I think your Highness would not have gone so far, except she surely had been culpable.'

But beyond Anne, and even beyond Henry, Cranmer had a higher duty still: to God's Word itself. Here, too, Cranmer confronted a paradox. 'As I loved her not a little, for the love which I judged her to bear towards God and his Gospel', so, he explained, 'if she be proved culpable, there is no one that loveth God and his Gospel that ever will favour her, but must hate her above all other.' Indeed, 'the more they favour the Gospel, the more they will hate her; for there was never creature in our time that so much slandered the Gospel'.

But what has happened? And what subconscious voice is it speaking through the writer's grammar? For in this last clause Cranmer has shifted from talking of Anne's guilt in the conditional, as something to be proved, and slipped into the indicative, as though it were already manifest.

He ends with a plea and an assertion: 'wherefore I trust that your Grace will bear no less entire favour unto the truth of the Gospel than you did before: *for as much as your Grace's favour to the Gospel was not led by affection unto her but by zeal unto the truth*'.[14]

Already, therefore – before trial, before even formal charges were laid – Anne's strongest supporter had leaped beyond her individual fate to the bigger question. For what mattered for Cranmer and his ilk was not Anne, nor the guilt or innocence of the men accused with her, but the future of Reform. She and they might go. But Reform must remain. It was bigger than them, bigger than them all. But it would survive, Cranmer acknowledged, only if Anne and her contribution were air-brushed out of history.

It was a price, finally, that he was prepared to pay.

Cranmer has been much criticized for the queasy tone of his letter, for its 'on the one hand this' and 'on the other hand that'. Why did he not defend his mistress and co-Reformer directly and courageously? And to the hilt? The answer, of course, is that he would have destroyed himself without saving her. And what would have been the point of that? Within the limits of prudence, he acted courageously. And certainly more courageously than anyone else.

But it is unlikely to have done much good. Indeed, the letter over which Cranmer had laboured may never have reached Henry. If it did, it would have been read cursorily. For Henry was not interested in defences of Anne. He had eyes and ears only for Jane Seymour.

But before Henry could have Jane, Anne had to be disposed of. On her first evening in the Tower, she questioned Kingston closely. 'Shall I die without justice?' she asked. Kingston answered gravely: 'The poorest subject the King hath had justice'. That was the official line. Anne, intelligent, perceptive Anne, had the sense to laugh at his reply. Nevertheless she returned to the theme. 'I shall have justice,' she said a day or two later. 'I have no doubt therein,' replied Kingston once more. 'If any man accuse me', she continued, 'I can say but "nay" and they can bring no witness.'[15]

Like the rest of Anne's comments, this remark was reported to Cromwell. And he did not forget it in his preparation of the case.

Normally, in cases of High Treason, the accused were subject to repeated examination before the Council. Detailed questionnaires, known as interrogatories, were prepared to guide the questioning, and verbatim transcripts were made of the answers. Nothing of the kind survives for Anne or her co-accused. The papers could, of course, have been abstracted from the records at a subsequent date – say when Anne's daughter Elizabeth was Queen – and destroyed. But it does not seem very likely. For Elizabeth, unlike her sister Mary, lived firmly in the present and showed no interest in rewriting history, much less in obliterating it.

Instead, it is probable that the records do not exist because the examinations never took place. Early in the second week of May, for instance, Rochford asked Kingston 'at what time he should come afore the King's Council'. 'For I think I shall not come forth till I come to my judgement,' he continued, 'weeping very [much]'. Anne had similar concerns. 'I much marvel', she told Kingston, 'that the King's Council comes not to me.'[16]

And the Council never came because its members knew they would get nothing to the purpose. The status of Anne and her brother put them beyond the use of torture. And their intelligence and strength of character meant that little would be got out of them any other way.

Instead, Cromwell, together probably with Audley and Rich, decided to make do with the materials they had to hand. These consisted of three distinct elements. First, there was Smeaton's extorted confession. Second, there was a mass of rumour and innuendo about Anne for which, paradoxically, her own heedless remarks in the Tower were the strongest evidence. And third, there was the already bad reputation of Weston, Wyatt and the rest. This last was particularly useful, since the manifest deficiencies of the concrete evidence could be concealed by invoking a wave of moral panic. And the higher the wave and the deeper the alleged depravity, the better.

In these circumstances the very extravagance of the accusations brought against Anne became an asset to the prosecution, rather than a liability. The initial charges, of adultery with Norris and Smeaton and incest with Rochford, excited incredulity. What sort of woman would do that? But increase the tally of Anne's lovers to five (for Page and Wyatt were quickly eliminated), and the accusation became almost believable. Add, too, the shocking details of Anne's unnatural seduction of her brother – 'alluring him with her tongue in [his] mouth, and his tongue in hers' – and right-minded people would agree that burning and quartering was too good for them.[17]

What all this makes clear, alas, is that the prosecution's strongest card was Anne. She had already done so much that people were prepared to believe that she was capable of anything. Hence the case's relentless, prurient focus on her:

> She [the Indictment read], following daily her frail and carnal lust, did falsely and traitorously procure by base conversations and kisses, touchings, gifts, and other infamous incitations, divers of the King's daily and familiar servants to be her adulterers and concubines.

It was Anne, in other words, who took the initiative. She was insatiable. She was jealous and domineering. Her lovers, on the other hand, were the mere creatures of a male harem, squabbling among themselves for her favours and living only to serve her lusts, which, nevertheless, they could not satisfy.[18]

For such a woman marriage was a restriction and a husband a nuisance. Hence the culminating charges that she had conspired Henry's death; had promised to marry one or other of her lovers when he was gone; and, in a sort of travesty of the marriage vows, had affirmed 'that she would never love the King in her heart'.

Through this fog of language – as through a glass darkly – it is possible to see the strange, distorted outlines of Anne's exchanges with Smeaton, Norris and Weston. But that is only the detail. Dominating everything, and lending verisimilitude to each several allegation, is a monstrous caricature of Anne herself.

This was the Anne who had defied convention; won Henry; broken his marriage; tongue-lashed dukes and earls; driven Catherine to her grave and More and Fisher to the block.

She had remade the political world in her own image. Why, the Indictment in effect asked, should she be any more respectful of the moral universe?

The difference of rank between the accused dictated two distinct modes of trial. The commoners were judicable before the Commission of Oyer

and Terminer, sitting in Westminster Hall and with a jury. Anne and
Rochford, on the other hand, were Peers and had to be tried by a special
tribunal known as the Court of the Lord High Steward. The Steward,
who held the office for a day, presided over a panel of Peers who served
as both judge and jury.

This convention, too, was turned to the government's advantage.

On Friday, 12 May, the four Gentlemen of the King's Privy
Chamber – Norris, Weston, Brereton and Smeaton – were brought to
Westminster Hall. Norris had probably last stood there when he
attended on Henry in his latticed viewing closet at Anne's coronation
banquet. Smeaton, who had been kept in irons in the Tower, to remind
him of what might befall if he changed his story, pleaded guilty and
admitted adultery with Anne three times. The rest pleaded not guilty
and protested their innocence. They were found guilty nonetheless.
Chapuys, deeply unsympathetic though he was, was dismissive of the
evidence against them. 'They were condemned', he reported, 'upon
presumption and certain indications, without valid ~~~ ~   9

But that was a sophisticate's reaction.
was the response of Lord Lisle's principa
Husey was overwhelmed by the horror of
and chronicles were totally revolved . . . an
hath been penned, contrived and written
same were, I think, verily nothing in compar
done and committed by Anne the Queen.'
everything with which she was charged. 'Ye
'that which hath been by her confessed, and ot
her own alluring, procurement and instigation,
ashamed that any good woman should give e
the contrary but she and all they shall suffer,' h

The prosecution strategy had worked. An   ~p~~~ssly
prejudiced by the prior condemnation of most of her fellow accused.

Probably for reasons of security, it was decided that Anne and her
brother should be tried inside the Tower. Special stands were built in the

Great Hall and, according to Chapuys, 2,000 spectators crowded in for the trial of the century. It took place on Saturday, 15 May. Anne's uncle, the Duke of Norfolk, presided as Lord High Steward for the day, and among the panel of Peers was her former suitor, Northumberland. He had been summoned to London to testify to the true status of his betrothal to Anne, and was in a state of high tension. He was also, as it turned out, mortally sick.[21]

As well as the panel of Peers, the judges were present in a body, to supply authoritative legal advice, if required. Anne had last had dealings with them at her coronation and, as on that occasion, the event was described by Sir John Spelman in his *Reports*. Finally, either Chapuys or an agent of his was there with the rest and his account is the fullest and probably the most accurate.[22]

Once again, the order of proceedings had been carefully considered. Anne was effectively already condemned by the verdicts of the previous Wednesday. Rochford was not. He was also felt to be the toughest nut to crack.

So Anne was tried first. And, despite the procedural rigging, she put up a good defence.

The Queen, Chapuys reported, 'was principally charged with ... having cohabited with her brother and other accomplices; that there was a promise between her and Norris to marry after the King's death, which it thus appeared they hoped for; ... [and] that she had poisoned [Catherine] and intrigued to do the same to [Mary]'. Anne, as was usual in treason trials, had no counsel, and it was probably the first time she had heard the detailed charges. But she stood her ground. 'These things,' Chapuys continued, 'she totally denied, and gave a plausible answer to each.' She admitted, on the other hand, to giving presents to Weston. But so she had often done, she said, to other young gentlemen.[23]

It was an impressive performance. But it made no difference. Norfolk called for the verdict. Starting with the most junior, each of the Peers said 'guilty'. What it cost Northumberland can only be guessed.

Norfolk now declared the sentence. The usual punishment for a traitoress was burning alive. But, 'because she was Queen, the Steward gave judgement that she should be burned or beheaded at the King's pleasure'.

At this point the judges 'murmured'. They had sat in silence through the trial, even though Spelman dismissed the evidence as 'all . . . bawdery and lechery, so that there was no such whore in the realm'. But at Norfolk's 'disjunctive' sentence, they registered their protest. That was not the law.[24]

Such was the concern of the professionals with justice.

Despite the verdict and sentence, Anne kept her composure. She was resigned to die, she told the court. But what she regretted was that so many others, who were innocent and loyal to the King, were to die with her.[25]

Anne was removed before her brother was brought in and the two did not have the consolation of seeing each other for the last time.

As predicted, Rochford put up a vigorous defence. No witnesses were brought against him and the betting was running ten to one that he would be acquitted.

He also had his revenge. One of the charges against him was that Anne had told his wife that the King 'was no good in bed with women, and that he had neither potency nor force'. Rochford was warned not to repeat this in open court. But, on pretext of protecting the King's issue, he did so, 'in great contempt of Cromwell'.

Once again, Norfolk called for the verdict. At this point, Northumberland 'was suddenly taken ill' and was excused. The rest said 'guilty'.[26]

In her speech to the court after sentence, Anne had asked 'a short space for shrift' – that is, to make confession and settle her account with God. Kingston discussed this question with Henry in person on the 16th and the King informed him that 'my lord of Canterbury should be her confessor'. Cranmer, Kingston reported to Cromwell, 'was here this day with the Queen, and not in that matter'.[27]

'And not in that matter'. This phrase has been either overlooked or misunderstood by historians. But it is crucial. For what other 'matter' could take precedence over the state of the Queen's immortal soul? The answer, I fear, is the divorce which Cranmer had been ordered to pronounce between Anne and Henry. Northumberland had been unco-operative and, as late as 13 May, had repeated his denial that 'there were ever any contract or promise of marriage between her and me'. And he had done so 'to his damnation' if he lied. Only Anne herself, therefore, could set Henry free. What she said to Cranmer we will never know. But it was enough for the Archbishop of Canterbury to pronounce her marriage dissolved the following day.[28]

And later on the 16th, it may be by coincidence, it may not, it was determined that Anne should die, not by the agony of the fire, but at the hands of the executioner of Calais. He used the sword rather than the axe and had a reputation for removing heads with an exquisite surgical skill.[29]

But, for the moment, Cranmer was too busy with preparing Henry's divorce to turn up at the Tower again to confess Anne, despite her desperate pleadings with Kingston. Presumably he did so eventually. But we do not know when.[30]

The men, including Rochford, were executed on Tower Hill on Monday, 17 May. The scaffold had been built especially high, to give a good view to the vast crowds who were certain to turn up. Weston, who had written a pathetic letter of apology to his father and mother and his poor neglected wife, spoke of his youthful folly and insouciance. 'I had thought', Constantine remembered him saying, 'to have lived in abomination yet this twenty or thirty years and then to have made amends.' 'I thought little', he added, 'it would have come to this.' Rochford apologized, too, for having slandered the Gospel. 'For if I had lived according to the Gospel as I loved it, and spake of it,' he said, 'I had never come to this.' The rest said almost nothing.[31]

Anne, it was decided, would die two days later, on the 19th. And she would be executed within the Tower, on Tower Green. Care was taken to remove all foreigners, including the servant that Chapuys had sent along. And, though the gates were left open, crowds were deliberately discouraged by the simple expedient of not announcing the time in advance and indeed postponing it beyond the usual hour. Kingston, writing to Cromwell that morning, was open about the motive. 'Sir,' he wrote, 'I think a reasonable number were best, for I suppose she will declare herself to be a good woman for all men but the King at the hour of her death.'

Indeed, he had just had confirmation of the fact, as Anne had summoned him to be present when she took her last sacrament. She received the host and swore 'as touching her innocency alway to be clear'.[32]

The device of postponing the execution was an excellent piece of crowd-control. But it played a final cruel trick on Anne. For executions normally took place first thing in the morning. Knowing this custom, Anne had been up praying with her Almoner since 2 o'clock. By mid-morning she summoned Kingston. 'Mr Kingston', she rebuked him, 'I hear say I shall not die afore noon, and I am very sorry therefore, for I thought then to be dead and past my pain.' Kingston ignored her complaint about the gratuitous delay but tried to console her on one thing at least. 'It should be no pain', he said, 'it was so subtle.'

The solemn obtuseness of the remark tickled Anne's sense of the absurd for the last time. 'I heard say the executioner was very good', she replied, 'and I have a little neck.' Then she put her hand round it and burst out laughing.

But Kingston, with much experience of executions, was not deceived. 'I have seen many men and also women executed', he wrote, 'and ... they have been in great sorrow.' But, he continued, 'to my knowledge this lady hath much joy and pleasure in death'.[33]

Eventually, Kingston conducted Anne to the scaffold. She was attended by the four women who had been with her throughout in the Tower. To one observer, she seemed 'very much exhausted and amazed'. She also looked frequently behind her. Was she trying to avoid looking at the scaffold? Or hoping against hope for a pardon?

None of course came. Instead, she sought and received permission to make a final speech. She chose her words carefully, so that they were neither the strident protestation of her innocence that Kingston feared, nor the confession of guilt that he would have hoped for. Instead, she cried 'mercy to God and to the King'. And she begged the people to pray for the King, 'for he was a good, gentle, gracious and amiable prince'.[34]

Knowing Anne, one might almost suspect satire. But the moment was too serious for that. Had she loved him as the man she described? And did she still?

Her mantle trimmed with ermine – she had worn a royal fur to the last – was removed. Then she took off her headdress herself. It was – another gesture this – in the ponderous English gable style and not the much more becoming French hood that she normally wore. She knelt and, for decency's sake, tucked her dress tight about her feet. Then one of her women blindfolded her.

Immediately, before she had time to register what was happening, the executioner swung his sword and her head was off.

It was wrapped in a cloth and the body was buried immediately in the adjacent Chapel of St Peter ad Vincula.

Anne had said, all those years ago, that she would fulfil the prophecy that a Queen would be burned. Save for the method of execution, she was right.

Jane Seymour

70. She stoops to conquer?

How a woman like Jane Seymour became Queen of England is a mystery. In Tudor terms she came from nowhere and was nothing.

Chapuys confronted the riddle in his despatch of 18 May 1536, which was addressed to Antoine Perrenot, the Emperor's minister, rather than to the Emperor Charles V himself. Freed from the decorum of writing to his sovereign, the ambassador expressed himself bluntly. 'She is the sister', he began, 'of a certain Edward Seymour, who has been in the service of his Majesty [Charles V]'; while 'she [herself] was formerly in the service of the good Queen [Catherine]'.

As for her appearance, it was literally colourless. 'She is of middle height, and nobody thinks she has much beauty. Her complexion is so whitish that she may be called rather pale.'

This is a neat pen-portrait of the woman whose mousy, peaked features and mean, pointed chin are rendered by Holbein with his characteristic, unsparing honesty.

So much Chapuys could see. But when he turned to her supposed moral character he gave his prejudices full rein. 'You may imagine', he wrote to Perrenot, man-to-man, 'whether, being an Englishwoman, and having been so long at Court, she would not hold it a sin to be *virgo intacta*.' 'She is not a woman of great wit,' he continued. 'But she may have' – and here he became frankly coarse – 'a fine *enigme*.' '*Enigme*' means 'riddle' or 'secret', as in 'secret place' or the female genitalia. 'It is said', he concluded, 'that she is rather proud and haughty.' 'She seems to bear great goodwill and respect to [Mary]. I am not sure whether later on the honours heaped on her will not make her change her mind.'[1]

What was there here – a woman of no family, no beauty, no talent and perhaps not much reputation (though there is no need to accept all of Chapuys's slanders) – to attract a man who had already been married to two such extraordinary women as Catherine and Anne?

But maybe Jane's very ordinariness was the point. Anne had been exciting as a mistress. But she was too demanding, too mercurial and tempestuous, to make a good wife. Like the Gospel which she patronized, she seemed to have come 'not to send peace but the sword' and to make 'a man's foes ... them of his own household' (*Matthew* 10.34–6). Henry was weary of scenes and squabbles, weary too of ruptures with his nearest and dearest and his oldest and closest friends. He wanted his family and friends back. He wanted domestic peace and the quiet life. He also, more disturbingly, wanted submission. For increasing age and the Supremacy's relentless elevation of the monarchy had made him ever more impatient of contradiction and disagreement. Only obedience, prompt, absolute and unconditional, would do.

And he could have none of this with Anne.

Jane, on the other hand, was everything that Anne was not. She was calm, quiet, soft-spoken (when she spoke at all) and profoundly submissive, at least to Henry. In short, after Anne's flagrant defiance of convention, Jane was the sixteenth-century's ideal woman (or at least the sixteenth-century *male*'s ideal woman).

And it was not only Henry who noticed the difference. Sir John Russell had been one of the many who had felt the repeated rough edge of Anne's tongue. Now he rejoiced at her successor: indeed, his gladness seems to have blinded him to the reality of her looks. 'I do assure you, my Lord', he wrote to his friend Lord Lisle, 'she is as gentle a lady as I ever knew, and as fair a Queen as any in Christendom.' 'The King', he continued, warming to his theme, 'hath come out of hell into heaven, for the gentleness in this, and the cursedness and the unhappiness in the other.'

Lisle, he advised, should write to congratulate Henry, saying 'you do rejoice that he is so well matched with so gracious a woman as she is' – 'wherein', Russell stated with his insider's knowledge, 'you shall content his Grace'.[2]

Everybody – Henry, Jane and the Court – was happy.

In his first audience with Jane, Chapuys played on this idea of happiness with a debonair gracefulness which contrasts gratingly with his private judgement. He kissed her and congratulated her. 'Her predecessor', he said, 'had borne the device "The Most Happy".' She, on the other hand, 'would bear the reality'. Then he continued to pile flattery on flattery. He was sure, he said, that '[Charles V] would be immeasurably pleased that the King had found so good and virtuous a wife, especially as her brother had been in [Charles's] service'.[3]

On the back of this reference to the Seymours' Imperial connexions, Chapuys smoothly shifted to politics. 'The satisfaction of the people ... was incredible', he said, 'especially at the restoration of Mary to the King's favour'. And it would be even greater, he hinted, if Mary were made heiress once more. Then indeed Jane would deserve the title that he hoped would be hers of 'the pacific' or peace-maker – abroad as well as at home.

This was getting into deep water. At this point Henry, who had been enjoying the company of the Queen's ladies without the reproving stares which had spoiled such pleasures under Anne, pricked up his ears, came over and interrupted the conversation. Jane, he said, was overwhelmed. Chapuys was the first ambassador who had spoken to her and she was not used to such attentions. However, he was sure she was eager for the title of 'pacific'. 'For, besides that her nature was gentle and inclined to peace, she would not for the world that he was engaged in war, that she might not be separated from him.'[4]

Henry's little woman was rescued. But from what? Chapuys had addressed her in French. Was she, unlike Anne, unable to reply easily in the same language? Was she simply bashful? Or was Henry afraid that she might disclose too much of her own opinions in her reply?

In other words, was Jane really quite such a doormat as at first appears? Or was there strategy in her submissiveness? Did she choose the extravagant humility of her motto 'Bound to obey and serve' because it represented her view of her position? Or because it would tickle Henry's patriarchal visions?

Even more interesting is the question of her badge or personal emblem. Her father, Sir John Seymour, had sported 'a peacock's head and neck couped Azure, between two wings erect Or'. But of course the peacock, then as now, symbolized pride. That was hardly suitable for the message Jane was supposed to convey. So she, or someone on her behalf, effected an ingenious substitution. Out of filial loyalty, she kept a bird as her badge. But a few deft strokes changed it from the peacock to the phoenix. This was the peacock's opposite. Instead of empty pride, it represented renewal through self-sacrifice. According to the legend, it lived for a thousand years. Then, feeling its end near, it built a nest-cum-pyre. This it ignited, and then burned itself to ashes from which there arose a new phoenix.[5]

And so, Jane's badge said, she would renew the Tudor dynasty. As indeed she did, and, as it happened, at the cost of her own life.

The extent of Jane's 'ordinariness' is therefore debatable. Moreover, why had this ordinary woman won the King's hand? Had Henry spotted her for himself? Or had she been chosen for him? And why?

These questions cannot be answered definitively because the obscurity, which veils the whole of Jane's early life, also masks the origins of her love affair with the King. We do not know when it began. Or where. Instead, she appears fully-fledged in February 1536 as 'the young lady ... whom [Henry] serves'. This is how Henry's relationship with Anne had begun also. It too had been an episode in the game of Courtly Love that had quickly turned serious.[6]

But, then, it was Anne herself who had brought about the transformation. In 1536, on the other hand, it is clear that Jane had many helping hands.

Her two principal patrons were Gertrude, Marchioness of Exeter, and Sir Nicholas Carew, the highly influential Master of the Horse who had won out in the struggle for the Garter with Rochford. Gertrude's activities were supported by her friends and relations in the conservative high nobility, such as Montague; while Carew had the enthusiastic backing of his colleagues of the Privy Chamber, such as Sir Anthony Browne and Sir John Russell. Even Carew's brother-in-law, Sir Francis Bryan, once so closely identified with Anne, had gone over to the enemy after his furious quarrel with Rochford in December 1534.[7]

But it is important to be clear about Jane's place in the scheme of things. For the Marchioness, Carew and the rest, she was a means, not an end. Their immediate goal was to restore Mary as heir to the throne, and, with Mary as a stalking-horse, to bring about a Catholic restoration also. Or, at the very least, to stop Reform in its tracks.

All of this, they knew, would happen only over Anne's dead body. And Anne's dead body was something they could contemplate with equanimity, if not enthusiasm.

For they had only ever paid the minimum lip-service to the Boleyn marriage. They detested Anne, and they detested the consequences of her marriage. And, from the beginning, they had sought for means to overthrow her. The obvious tactic was to turn her own weapons of bed-chamber politics against her. She had shown that a mistress could become Queen. Why should not another woman repeat the trick? And why should this other woman not overthrow Anne and all she stood for, as completely as Anne had toppled Catherine?

The problem, of course, was to find the right mistress. Each young woman who caught Henry's eye was nobbled by Anne's opponents and enthusiastically talked up as her nemesis. Things had reached a fever-pitch of excitement in late 1534. Henry had acquired a new 'young lady' who refused to pay court to Anne. And Henry refused to back Anne when she appealed to him to slap down the insolent new-comer. Instead, he brushed off his wife angrily, and complained loudly about her importunity. The Court seethed with rumour. Was this the beginning of the end of Queen Anne?

Chapuys at least kept a sense of proportion. 'Not much weight', he wrote, was to be attached to the report, 'unless the love of the King for the young lady ... should grow warm and continue for some time'. But, he warned, 'it is impossible to form a judgement [of this], considering the changeableness of [Henry]'. The ambassador was right to be sceptical. The 'young lady' disappeared and we do not even know her name.[8]

But of course the situation in early 1536 was very different. Catherine died, which meant that Henry could repudiate his second marriage without reaffirming his first. Anne miscarried. Cromwell turned against Anne. And, above all, Henry's love for Jane Seymour indeed 'grew warm and continued for some time'.

It is possible to pin-point the moment that the nature of Henry's feelings for Jane changed more or less exactly to mid-March. The last Session of the Reformation Parliament opened on 4 February. At first, Henry alternated between Greenwich and York Place, spending a few days at a time in each. But, when the Bill for the Dissolution of the Monasteries showed signs of sticking, he moved to York Place for the whole of March. Meanwhile Jane remained at Greenwich. And Henry, obviously fearing lest his dalliance prove out of sight, out of mind, sent her a valuable present. It consisted of 'a purse full of sovereigns' and a covering letter.[9]

Jane's response, however, was utterly unexpected. She kissed the letter and returned it unopened to the messenger. Then, 'throwing herself on her knees' before the messenger, she addressed the King through him:

[She] begged ... [Henry] to consider that she was a gentle-woman of good and honourable parents, without reproach, and that she had no greater riches in the world than her honour, which she would not injure for a thousand deaths, and that if he wished to make her some present in money she begged it might be when God enabled her to make some honourable match.

Jane, in other words, was playing the Boleyn card, and playing it rather well. She would not be Henry's mistress, but only his wife.

Was it her idea? Or had she been coached? We know certainly that she had had lessons. According to Chapuys, Carew 'continually counsels [Jane]'. More generally, she 'had been well taught by members of the King's Privy Chamber that she must by no means comply with the King's wishes except by way of marriage'. And she had learned her lessons well: 'she is quite firm [in the matter]', Chapuys reported.[10] Whether Jane had written her own script for the scene at Greenwich, or not, there can be no doubt about the effect. 'Henry's love and desire . . . was wonderfully increased,' the delighted Marchioness informed Chapuys. '[Jane] had behaved most honourably,' Henry said. 'To show that he only loved her honourably,' he continued, 'he did not intend henceforth to speak with her except on the presence of some of her kin.' Cromwell was moved out of his lodging, which was connected to the King's apartments by secret galleries. And Jane's eldest brother Edward and his wife Anne, née Stanhope, were moved in. With such sympathetic chaperones, Henry could still see Jane to his heart's content.[11]

From this moment, Jane was Henry's wife-in-waiting.

And, thanks to Cromwell's brutal efficiency and Anne's ill luck, she did not have to wait long.

Anne's arrest, however, brought about a temporary separation. Henry could hardly protest about Anne's supposed misconduct if he were seen to be paying open court to another woman. So, for decency's sake, Jane was removed from Court. The choice of her refuge has its own significance. She was sent to Beddington, Carew's luxurious house and garden near Croydon. And it was also Carew who was sent to bring her back to the neighbourhood of the capital on 14 May, the day before Anne's trial. She was lodged at Chelsea, Sir Thomas More's former house, which was on the river, only a short boat-ride from York Place.[12]

All this looks like a formal recognition of Carew's role as Jane's sponsor. He was Pygmalion. She was the statue to whom he had given life and speech. His reward would come when, as he hoped, she continued to deliver his lines after she was Queen.

Jane now had the throne in all but name. 'She is splendidly served by the King's cook and other officers,' Chapuys reported. 'She is [also] most splendidly dressed.' But the last hours of Anne's life still stood between Jane and her King. They could not wait to get Anne out of the way. On the morning of the 14th, Henry informed Jane that at 3 o'clock he would send her news of Anne's condemnation. At the appointed hour, Bryan turned up with the glad tidings. Other good news followed in quick succession. On the 17th Cranmer, as we have seen, pronounced Henry and Anne's marriage null and void. On the 19th, he issued a dispensation for Henry and Jane to marry, despite the fact that they were related in 'the third degree of affinity' – perhaps, as it has been guessed, through one of Henry's former mistresses. That same day came the best news of all: Anne was beheaded.[13]

According to Chapuys, 'the King, immediately on receiving news of the decapitation of [Anne], entered his barge and went to [Jane]' at Chelsea. We do not know how she reacted. But, at the least, she showed no compunction in stepping to the throne over the headless corpse of her rival. Anne might *talk* of killing Catherine; the gentle Jane went further and was an accessory-after-the-fact to the judicial murder of her predecessor.[14]

The following day, Saturday, 20 May, Henry and Jane were betrothed: at 9 a.m. at York Place, according to Chapuys, and 'secretly at Chelsea', according to the chronicler Wriothesley who, as both a herald and the cousin of Cromwell's right-hand man, Thomas Wriothesley, was very well informed.[15]

At this point, the breakneck speed of events was slowed – not because Henry had cooled but because the precipitance of his new union with Jane 'sounded ill in the ears of the people'. Jane probably remained in seclusion at Chelsea for another ten days. On Tuesday the 30th she was brought to York Place, where she was married 'in the Queen's Closet'. On Friday, 2 June, so Russell informed Lisle, 'the Queen sat abroad as Queen [at dinner], and was served with her own servants. And they were sworn that day.'[16]

In the afternoon, the King and his third wife took boat for

Greenwich. There, on Whitsunday, 4 June, Jane was formally proclaimed Queen, and processed with Henry to mass. '[She] went in
procession', Wriothesley reports, 'after the King, with a great train of
ladies following after her, and also offered at Mass as Queen.' Then she
dined in state 'in her Chamber of Presence'. She sat 'under the Cloth of
Estate' and in the chair which, only five weeks earlier, had been occupied
by Anne.[17]

Two days later, as the Seymour cup of honour ran over, Jane's
brother Edward was created a peer, taking, after personal consultation
between Henry and Garter King of Arms, the title of Viscount
Beauchamp.[18]

Henry's first divorce took seven years; his second, less than as many
weeks. This was Cromwell's work and, on 18 June, he had his reward.
Wiltshire, Anne's father, was stripped of the office of Lord Privy Seal,
which was given to Cromwell. Three weeks later, on 9 July, the
shearman's son was created Lord Cromwell of Wimbledon.[19]

It remained only to determine the nature of the new regime. The
Reformers feared the worst and, on 23 May, Shaxton added his urgent
voice to Cranmer's more measured pleading. 'I beseech you, Sir,' he
wrote to Cromwell, 'that ye will now be no less diligent in setting forth
the honour of God and his Holy Word, than when the late Queen was
alive, and often incited you thereto.' 'Leave not off, for God's sake,' he
continued, 'though she by her misconduct have sore slandered the
same.'[20]

The emphasis on Anne's role is striking – both for what it says about
her and also, indirectly, what it presumes about Jane. For Shaxton was
only too aware that Jane would not be 'inciting' Cromwell to Reform.
Indeed, he had every reason to fear that she would do the opposite.

And Shaxton's fears were complemented by the hopes of Carew, the
Exeters and the rest of the conservative high nobility. Anne, the
Reformer, was dead; Jane, the pious, as well as the pacific, was Queen –
their Queen.

*

As so often in the sixteenth century, ceremony told its own story. It had already been decided that the ultimate ceremony – Jane's coronation – would be postponed until the autumn when, it was hoped, she would be pregnant. Nevertheless, a series of events combined to launch the new reign in a blaze of pageantry. The first was the opening of the new Parliament, which had been summoned to undo the Boleyn marriage.[21]

The ceremonial began with a river procession from Greenwich to York Place on Wednesday, 7 June. It was modelled, of course, on Anne's pre-coronation river pageant. But its message was the opposite. Then, a Frenchman had acted as image-consultant. Now, Chapuys dominated the scene and gave the Emperor's benediction to the new marriage.

The ambassador had set up a ceremonial pavilion at Rotherhithe, where he had a house, conveniently mid-way between the City and Greenwich. The Emperor's arms were on top of the tent and banners hung on poles around it. Chapuys himself was dressed in a rich gown of purple satin, with a suite of gentlemen dressed in velvet. As the royal procession passed Limehouse and came into sight, he sent two boats of musicians to salute the King and Queen. There were trumpets in one boat and wind-instruments in the other. Then, on land, a forty-gun salute was fired.[22]

A few moments later, there came an even mightier sound when the Tower shot four hundred guns. Only a few weeks earlier, it had been a place of desolation, its scaffolds running with the blood of Anne and her alleged accomplices. Wyatt had watched the scene from his cell and it left an indelible impression.

These bloody days have broken my heart.
My lust, my youth did then depart,
And blind desire of estate.
Who hastes to climb seeks to revert.
Of truth, *circa regna tonat* [around the throne the lightning
    strikes].

The Bell Tower showed me such a sight
That in my head sticks day and night.
There did I learn out of a grate,
For all favour, glory or might,
That yet, *circa regna tonat.*

But now the mighty fortress presented its other face and 'all the Tower walls towards the water side were set with great streamers and banners'. The storm had passed; the sun shone and all was fair in the world:

So the King passed through London Bridge, with his trumpets blowing before him, and shawms and sackbuts and drumslades playing also in barges going before him. Which was a goodly sight.[23]

Did Jane, as she passed the Tower where her predecessor was barely cold in her grave, think that the weather could change again? That the spring of royal favour could turn into the bitter winter of indifference and contempt? Or did she somehow feel exempt?

The following day, Jane stood in the new Gate-house at York Place to watch her husband ride out in procession to open the Parliament that would give the succession to her children. But first, as was customary, the King and the Lords heard the Mass of the Holy Ghost. The mass was celebrated in the newly-completed Henry VII Chapel. Henry was met by the Abbot and the monks in copes of cloth of gold. The Abbot presented him with St Edward's sceptre and four monks held a canopy of cloth of gold over him.[24]

It was almost like a second coronation.

Then the King processed to the Parliament Chamber for the opening proper. Audley made the speech, 'which', Wriothesley noted with some surprise, 'continued half an hour large'. For there was, after all, a lot to explain. Since the last Parliament, Audley said, Anne's abominable treasons had come to light. Reluctantly, and only at the petition of the nobility, Henry had remarried a wife who was 'chaste, pure and fertile'.

Now, concerned as ever for the welfare of his subjects, he wished to provide for their security by re-establishing the succession. Finally, Audley offered up a prayer for the King.

> Let us pray God to send offspring to our most excellent Prince; let us give thanks that He has preserved him for us safe from so many and so great dangers ... and leave us thus to his posterity.[25]

Whether this prayer would be fulfilled depended largely, of course, on Jane.

A week later, on Corpus Christi Day, 15 June, Henry rode in procession once more from York Place to the Abbey. But this time he was accompanied by Jane and her ladies. In the Abbey, the King and Queen, with the Parliament and the Court, joined in procession to honour the Real Presence in the Sacrament.

For once, Henry was not the focus. Instead, four Grooms of the Privy Chamber bore the cloth of gold canopy over the monstrance with the consecrated wafer. The monstrance was carried by Richard Sampson, Bishop of Chichester and Dean of the Chapel Royal, who wore a rich cope and mitre and was supported by the sub-Dean. And another four Grooms walked round him, carrying flaring torches.[26]

It would be hard to think of a clearer signal of the limits of Reform. Other things might change. But Henry's belief in the miracle of the mass remained unshaken. And let any who denied it tremble.

Jane, by her presence and her known orthodox piety, lent her enthusiastic support.

Jane's smooth ascent produced near euphoria among Mary's supporters. 'The joy shown ... at the hope of [Mary's] restoration is inconceivable,' Chapuys reported. Mary's leading partisans were the new Queen's patrons and promoters. And Jane herself, quite unfeignedly, was a Mary loyalist. 'She bears great love and reverence to [Mary]', Chapuys had informed Perennot. Even before Anne's arrest, Chapuys heard, Jane had begged Henry for Mary's restoration. She got little thanks. 'She was a fool,' Henry snapped. '[She] ought to solicit the advancement of the children they would have between them, and not any others.' But Jane stood her ground. She was doing what Henry asked, she replied. '[For], in asking for the restoration of [Mary as] Princess, she conceived she was seeking the rest and tranquillity of the King, herself, her future children, and the whole realm'. 'For,' she dared to continue, without Mary's restoration 'neither [Charles V] nor this people would ever be content'.[27]

Chapuys naturally returned to the subject when he had his first audience with Jane on 6 June at Greenwich. 'It was not her least happiness', he informed her in his most courtly style, 'that, without having had the labour of giving birth to her, she had such a daughter as [Mary].' He begged her to favour Mary's interest. And she said she would.

It was at this sensitive point that Henry had intervened to cut the conversation short. But, as soon as Chapuys had gone, Cromwell informed the ambassador, Jane had returned to the attack. 'She had spoken to the King as warmly as possible in favour of [Mary].' She had also extolled the power and greatness of Mary's family connexions.

Chapuys had another important interview at Court that day with Jane's brother, Edward Seymour. A satisfactory solution to the question of Mary's status would do good both to the Seymours and Christendom, he explained. Seymour seemed convinced, and Chapuys left him 'sure he will use his good offices therein'.[28]

So far, despite Henry's initial slapping down of Jane, all seemed to be going to plan. And Mary, above all, dared to hope. Mary and Elizabeth were now staying at Hunsdon, an agreeable royal house a few miles to the south-west of Bishop's Stortford in Hertfordshire. And there, in the third week of May, Lady Kingston, fresh from accompanying Anne to the scaffold, had gone with the good news. Mary had immediately written to Cromwell. She would have asked him to intercede for her with Henry before, she wrote. 'But I perceived that nobody durst speak for me as long as *that woman* lived.'

But Anne was gone, 'whom I pray our Lord of his great mercy to forgive'. And the world looked brighter. Almost flippantly, Mary apologized for her 'evil writing'. 'For I have not done so much this two year and more, nor could have found the means to do it at this time but by my Lady Kingston's being here.'[29]

Cromwell, as usual, moved fast. Four days later, on the 30th, Mary thanked him for getting her Henry's blessing and permission to write to him. They were the highest comforts that ever came to her. In return, she would be as obedient to him 'as can reasonably be expected'.[30]

- The letter, despite its formal humility, breathes an easy confidence. 'That woman', who had destroyed Mary's mother's marriage and poisoned Mary's own life, was out of the way. Instead, Henry had a good Queen who longed, she knew, to welcome her as a daughter. And he was surrounded by courtiers and councillors who were her devoted servants and now dared to show it. Soon, and with the minimum of fuss, everything would be back to normal.

She had reckoned without Henry – and without Cromwell.

By 8 June, apparently, her reconciliation with her father was complete. Mary understood, she wrote, 'that he has forgiven all her offences and withdrawn his displeasure'. But her happiness would not be complete until she was allowed to see him. '[She] hopes God will preserve him and the Queen and send them a Prince'.[31]

Then, over the next two days something went wrong. More would be required of her, perhaps as much as Anne herself would have exacted. On the 10th she wrote to Cromwell in a state of desperate anxiety. 'I desire you, for Christ's passion,' she wrote, 'to find means that I be not moved to any further entry in this matter than I have done.' 'For I assure you,' she continued, 'I have done the utmost my conscience will suffer me.'[32]

But it was not enough and, within a few days, a delegation of the Council, headed once more by Norfolk, appeared at Hunsdon with a list of formal demands. Would she acknowledge Henry as her Sovereign Lord and accept all the Laws and Statutes of the Realm? Would she accept him as Supreme Head of the Church and repudiate the jurisdiction of the Bishop of Rome? And would she acknowledge that her mother's marriage was invalid by the laws of God and Man?

Anne could have done no more, and Mary responded as she had done previously. In return, the Councillors threatened her crudely. If she were their daughter, they said, 'they would knock her head so violently against the wall that they would make it as soft as baked apples'. She was a traitoress, and deserved to be punished as such. Finally, before leaving, they ordered Lady Shelton to hold her incommunicado.

Nevertheless, Mary managed to get in touch with Chapuys to ask for advice. Yield in the face of the threat of death, he advised. But yield as little as possible.[33]

Cromwell now wrote to her, disowning her and commanding her, in the King's name, to sign the articles required. Or else she would face the consequences. And he reminded her of her likely fate by launching a pre-emptive strike against her supporters. Lady Hussey, the wife of her former Chamberlain, was sent to the Tower. The Marquess of Exeter and Treasurer Fitzwilliam were suspended from the Council. Sir Anthony Browne and Sir Francis Bryan were interrogated on the 14th, and Browne for a second time on the 17th. Their answers pointed inescapably to Carew as the prime mover in the campaign for Mary's restoration. And Carew clearly knew that the game was up. He wrote to Mary advising her to submit and to follow Cromwell's advice. His wife Elizabeth, who was Sir Francis Bryan's sister, used her mother, Lady Bryan, to get a still more urgent message to Mary. '[She] desired her, for the Passion of Christ, in all things to follow the King's pleasure, otherwise she was utterly undone.'[34]

And Mary would not be the only one to be undone. For the new Bill of Succession, which Audley had promised, had not yet been submitted to Parliament. Until it was passed, the First Act of Succession remained in force. This, as we have seen, made it treason to impugn Elizabeth's status as heiress to the throne. The activities of Carew and the rest undoubtedly fell within its scope: they were traitors, as much as Mary was a traitoress. And, if she did not yield, they were likely to suffer together.

At this point, Jane tried to intervene in the crisis, praying Henry on her knees to forgive his daughter. But her influence counted for nothing and 'she was rudely repulsed'.

Only a day or two before she had taken part with Henry in the Corpus Christi Day celebrations in the Abbey. They made a magnificent couple. 'For as his Grace', Bryan recalled in his examination, 'stood above all those present in person, so [he] surpassed all in princely gesture and countenance'. Sir John Russell had been equally enthusiastic about Jane's appearance: 'The Queen was in likewise ... in apparel the fairest ... lady [there]'. They seemed made for each other, destined for 'long life together' and many children.[35]

But suddenly, out of this clear blue sky, storm clouds had gathered. When would lightning strike? And where?

Inevitably, faced with this threat to her supporters as well as to herself, Mary yielded and, late at night on the 22nd, she signed the formal 'confession' required of her. Even so, it seems to have taken more than one attempt to get her to concede everything. Easiest to allow, apparently, were the general issues raised by the Reformation. She acknowledged Henry's Sovereignty and Supremacy and repudiated the Bishop of Rome. Then she signed the paper, as though she had finished.

But she had not. For she had not yet brought herself to address the more personal question of the invalidity of her mother's marriage and her own bastardy. Finally this too was wrung from her. 'I do freely [and] frankly ... [ac]knowledge that the marriage, heretofore had between his Majesty, and my mother, the late Princess Dowager, was, by God's law and Man's law, incestuous and unlawful.'[36]

Each word was a poisoned arrow which pierced her heart, and she died a little with each. Then she signed a second time. She had signed away, she knew, everything that she had stood for.

'Incredible rejoicings' at Court greeted the news of her submission. Many, of course, were thanking God for their own escape. But Mary was racked with doubt. Chapuys was at hand with plausible justifications. But she sought relief from a higher authority and asked Chapuys to obtain a secret Papal absolution – 'otherwise her conscience could not be at perfect ease'.[37]

Nothing was now too good for Mary. Councillors knelt to her and sought her pardon. She was offered her choice of servants, and new and sumptuous clothes. The King sent her a horse. And, as the final mark of favour, he agreed to meet her for the first time in five years.[38]

Bearing in mind all that had happened, it was felt that this first encounter should be kept both secret and private. In the small hours of Thursday, 6 July, Mary was brought from Hunsdon to Hackney. Then, in the afternoon, the King and Queen, 'with a small and secret company', also left for the rendezvous. Henry, now that Mary had cast herself at his feet, was at his most expansive. He talked to her constantly and showered her with affection and promises. Jane gave her a beautiful diamond and Henry a present of 1,000 crowns 'for her little pleasures'. They parted on the Friday evening, with many expressions of mutual love.[39]

Henry last words were to promise that she would be brought to Court. She was, and took her place immediately after the Queen. But she did so solely on Henry's terms.

Mary was a trophy. And it is hard to think, after all this, that Jane was much more.

This was made even clearer by the Act of Succession as it was eventually passed. Chapuys had justified Mary's surrender on the grounds that it would open the way for Henry to recognize her as heir. But neither she nor her supporters were given any such consolation. The Act was introduced into the Lords on 30 June, eight days after Mary's capitulation. And it took full advantage of it. For the Act, like Henry, contrived to take with both hands. On the one hand, it stripped Elizabeth of her title of Princess and her status as heir. On the other, it failed to restore them to Mary. Instead the succession was given only to Henry's children by Jane or (lest she become too proud) by any subsequent wife.[40]

This decision, since no such child existed, created a dangerous vacuum. To fill it, Henry was given unprecedented powers to nominate such successor as he wished, from time to time, by his Will.

Henry had always guarded his power jealously. Now, like misers throughout the ages, he could use the Great Expectations of his Will to control the behaviour of his possible heirs while he was alive.

The handling of Carew and the rest of Mary's supporters was also an object lesson in political management. Cromwell had used them to help bring down Anne. But, when they demanded their share of the spoils, they were threatened with the same fate as the Boleyns. It was an extraordinary achievement and confirmed his absolute mastery of the political scene. Not even Wolsey had enjoyed such power.

Nor had he been so hated for it.

The weary catalogue of unfulfilled dreams and broken promises continued throughout the summer. The idea of a great Progress to the north, to match the one to the west country of 1535, had been abandoned even before Anne's fall and it was not reinstated. The Dissolution of the Monasteries gathered pace, despite Jane's rather pathetic attempt to save the admirably managed nunnery of Catesby in Northamptonshire. Finally, at the end of September, Henry decided to reconsider the plans for Jane's coronation. The date fixed on was Sunday, 29 October. But as Ralph Sadler, Cromwell's new fixer at Court, reported to his master on 27 September, the King was having second thoughts. Perhaps significantly, he gave voice to them after having supped with Jane in her Chamber.[41]

'The plague had reigned in Westminster and in the Abbey itself', Henry told Sadler. This meant, he continued, 'that he stood in a suspense, whether it were best to put off the time of the Coronation for a season'. Cromwell was to summon a full meeting of the Council to Windsor to debate the matter with the King.

The decision, inevitably, was 'to put off'. No doubt the excuse of plague was genuine. But there must also be the suspicion that Jane was being punished for her failure to conceive. Moreover, Henry's notorious eye had started to rove again. 'The King will not have the prize of those who do not repent in marriage,' Chapuys reported. A week after the publication of his marriage to Jane, Henry had met two beautiful young ladies. He had sighed and said '[he was] sorry that he had not seen them before he was married'.[42]

Jane's honeymoon was proving shorter than she expected.

And there was a price to pay for Cromwell's magnificent dishing of conservative hopes. For the three years of Anne's reign, Chapuys's correspondence had been filled with predictions of rebellion. Now, five months after her death, the predictions were fulfilled. First Lincolnshire and then the north rose in revolt. In Lincolnshire, Hussey offered feeble and temporising resistance to the rebels, while his formidable wife was openly sympathetic, giving them food and drink and offering money. The rebels found a charismatic leader in Robert Aske and they framed a coherent programme of thorough-going reaction. The monasteries were to be restored. Mary was to be declared heir. Cromwell, Rich and Audley were to be executed or at least exiled. And Anne's heretic bishops, Cranmer, Latimer, Shaxton and Hilsey, were to be burned.[43]

Faced with rebellion, the royal family closed ranks and both Mary and Elizabeth were brought to Court and treated with near-royal honours. 'The Lady Mary', a French agent reported, 'is now first after the Queen, and sits at table opposite her, a little lower down, after having first given the napkin for washing to the King and Queen.' 'The Lady Elizabeth', he noted, 'is not at that table, though the King is very affectionate to her. It is said he loves her much.'

But, behind the façade of unity, there were deep divisions over policy. Jane, undoubtedly, was sympathetic to the main thrust of the rebel demands. 'At the beginning of the insurrection', the French report continued, 'the Queen threw herself on her knees before the King and begged him to restore the Abbeys.' Henry repulsed her once more. 'Get up!' he said. 'He had often told her not to meddle with his affairs.' Then he added the terrible warning: remember Anne. '[It] was enough', the Frenchman concluded, 'to frighten a woman who is not very secure.'[44]

But, though Henry could rule his wife and his Court with a rod of iron, the provinces proved more recalcitrant. Norfolk, who, in his younger days, had played a crucial role in Catherine's great victory at

Flodden, was brought out of retirement to lead the King's armies. But the
north was too strong, Norfolk advised, for the King to defeat the rebels
in the field. Instead, he must negotiate. With profound reluctance, and
always in bad faith, Henry agreed. Finally, in tense negotiations at
Doncaster in early December, a settlement was reached. It was
understood differently by the two sides. But they at least agreed that
outstanding differences were to be referred to a Parliament.

The rebel armies were now disbanded, and on 15 December Henry
sent a personal message to Aske, carried by Peter Mewtis of the Privy
Chamber, to summon him to Court for the Christmas festivities at
Greenwich.[45]

These got off to a magnificent start. The Thames was frozen solid, which
made the usual journey downriver impossible. Instead, the Court
travelled by land. And, as with Jane's river pageant from Greenwich, the
journey was turned into a resounding reaffirmation of royal orthodoxy.

First, the new Lord Mayor of London was presented to the King and
knighted in the Presence Chamber at York Place. The palace itself was
now officially known as the Palace of Westminster. But popular usage
had already started to refer to it as Whitehall, to distinguish it from what
was left of the old medieval Palace of Westminster. And, as usual,
popular usage won.

Preceded by the newly-knighted Lord Mayor carrying the mace, the
King, the Queen and the Lady Mary then rode from Whitehall through
the City of London. The streets were freshly gravelled, from Temple Bar
to the Southwark end of London Bridge, and were hung with cloth of
gold and arras. The four orders of Friars stood in Fleet Street in cloth of
gold copes, 'with crosses and candlesticks and censers to cense the King
and Queen as they rode by'. At the West Door of St Paul's, where the
young Henry had led Catherine to her marriage with Arthur, there was
yet more incense, as the Bishop of London, two Abbots and the whole
choir greeted Henry and Jane. Thence, the sweet smoke, the rustle of
copes, and the glint of crosses and candlesticks continued the whole way
to London Bridge.[46]

The chronicler Wriothesley, who was both religiously conservative and a lover of ceremony, was delighted. '[It] was a goodly sight to behold', he concludes. Richard Lee, writing to the equally conservative Lady Lisle, was even more impressed. 'The like sight', he wrote, 'hath not been seen here since the Emperor's being here [in 1522].' He particularly noted the presence of Chapuys, 'the ambassador to the Emperor', with the royal party, and concluded, like Wriothesley, that 'it rejoiced every man wondrously'.[47]

Chapuys, at least, knew better. As early as 5 November he had reported his suspicions that Henry intended to double-cross the rebels. And he could only watch as, over the next few months, his gloomy prophecy was fulfilled.

Did Jane in her golden cage feel the same?

If she did, she was wise enough not to show it. According to Husey, she, like Henry, was 'never merrier' as they settled down to celebrate Christmas with 'as great mirth and triumph as ever was'. Aske arrived between the 25th and the 31st and was lionized. Henry gave him 'a jacket of crimson satin'. And he was even more prodigal with promises. He was Aske's gracious sovereign lord. He reaffirmed his liberal pardon to all the north. He intended to hold his next Parliament in the north at York and to have Jane crowned there. He 'tendereth the Commonwealth of his subjects and extends his mercy from his heart'.[48]

It was a consummate performance. And Aske swallowed it. On the 5th, he left the Court in haste and the utmost secrecy for the north. His mission was to broadcast Henry's message of forgiveness. Naturally, he placed heavy emphasis on its two most dramatic elements: the promised Parliament and coronation at York. Parliament had last met there over two centuries previously, in 1322. And no King or Queen had been crowned there since the Conquest.

Aske was not heard uncritically. But his mission had the desired effect of dividing and disarming opposition. In February, a few disgruntled elements launched a new revolt. Henry now had his opportunity. The revolt was crushed easily and the King regarded himself as being exonerated from his promises. The rebel leaders, headed by Aske, Hussey and Darcy, who had played the same ambiguous role in Yorkshire as Hussey in Lincolnshire, were arrested, tried and condemned, along with dozens of others. They included Sir Robert Constable, who trusted to his family relationship with Jane to obtain his pardon. He trusted in vain.[49]

Aske's last request was to be spared the full horror of execution for treason. 'Let me [be] full dead ere I be dismembered,' he begged. Henry, who, like the Mikado, had a bizarre taste in executions, granted his wish. Instead, Aske 'was hanged in the City of York in chains till he died'.[50]

Probably, as he twisted there in agony for hour after hour, he wished for the swifter death of the knife.

Jane had a final part to play in this 'pacification' of the north by fair words and deceit. On 23 May her pregnancy was known at Court, and on the 27th, as a welcome change from the executions which had disfigured the City for months, a *Te Deum* was celebrated in St Paul's. Audley and Cromwell attended and Latimer of all people preached the sermon.[51]

What, a quizzical observer must have wondered, had changed since the days of Queen Anne?

Henry took swift advantage of the Queen's pregnancy to put off, yet again, his planned Progress to the north. It was the only one of his plethora of promises to Aske to have survived. Now it, too, was broken.

Ungallantly, in his letter of justification to Norfolk, who was mopping up in the north, he blamed the cancellation on Jane's womanish fears. Normally, the King conceded, Jane was a good and obedient wife: 'of that loving inclination and reverend conformity, that she can in all things well content . . . herself with [what] we shall think expedient and determine'. Nevertheless, if he were so far from her, and in such an unsettled country, even she, in the condition that she was, might take fright, with disastrous consequences: '[to the] no little danger . . . to that wherewith she is now pregnant'.[52]

But at least in the narrow sphere of her own household, Jane was sovereign. Henry refused to interfere in the appointment of her women. And Jane was strict in what she required of them.

In mid-July, Jane, then six months pregnant, was eating quails for dinner. The quails had been sent by Lady Lisle, and the Countesses of Rutland and Sussex, who were serving the Queen, took advantage of the fact. They reminded her of Lady Lisle's suit for her daughters by her previous marriage, Anne and Catherine Basset, to be taken into the Queen's service. The birds were delicious and the Queen was disposed to be gracious. But not too much. Let both girls be sent for, she decreed, and she would take her pick of one of them.[53]

The girls arrived and Jane chose Anne. There was an immediate problem about what she should wear. Lady Lisle had equipped her in the latest French fashion. But that, with its associations with her predecessor, was anathema to Jane. However, as a special concession, she agreed that 'Mrs Anne shall wear out her French apparel'. But two things were non-negotiable. Anne had to have an English-style bonnet or headdress and a frontlet or bodice. Husey provided them for her, but was not happy with the results. 'Methought [the bonnet] became her nothing so well as the French hood,' he wrote to her mother. 'But the Queen's pleasure must needs be fulfilled.' A few weeks later, even the remnants of Anne's French attire were banished, at the Queen's express insistence.[54]

In one respect at least, she would be different from 'that woman'.

The day after Anne Basset had been sworn as one of Jane's servants, she accompanied her new mistress when she took to her Chamber at Hampton Court on Sunday, 16 September. But, despite the short time she had been at Court, Henry, with his keen eye for the ladies, had already spotted that she was 'far fairer' than her rejected sister.

Jane's confinement lasted over three weeks. Meanwhile, the plague struck in the vicinity and some courtiers were infected. Henry himself withdrew to Wolsey's old house at Esher for four days, 'so that [there should be] less resort' to Hampton Court. As the time went by the tension mounted. 'We look daily for a Prince,' Thomas Wriothesley wrote to his friend, Sir Thomas Wyatt, who was now ambassador in Spain. 'God send what shall please him.' Jane went into what turned out to be a prolonged labour. On Thursday, 11 October, a solemn general procession was made at St Paul's, 'to pray for the Queen that was then in labour of child'. At 2 a.m. on Friday morning she was safely delivered. It was the eve of the Feast of St Edward, England's royal saint. And the baby was a boy.[55]

Straight away, the pre-signed letters were sent out, in which 'Jane the Queen' proudly announced the birth of 'a Prince, conceived in most lawful matrimony between my lord the King's Majesty and us'.[56]

Cromwell received his copy early and wrote immediately to Wyatt. 'Here be no news', he began teasingly, 'but very good news, which for surety I have received this morning.' 'That it hath pleased Almighty God,' he continued, 'of his goodness, to send unto the Queen's Grace deliverance of a goodly Prince, to the great comfort, rejoice, and consolation of the King's Majesty, and of all us his most humble, loving and obedient subjects.'[57]

It would be interesting to know Wyatt's reactions.

Immediately, the celebrations began. By 8 o'clock, the *Te Deum* was being sung in every parish church in London. The bells were rung and there were bonfires in the street. At 9 a.m. a solemn *Te Deum* began in St Paul's, in the presence of the Council, the judges and the mayor and citizens. Then the King's waits and the City waits joined forces with a shrill display on the shawms, and the guns of the Tower fired a salute.

The celebration resumed in the evening, with more bonfires and music and free food and wine. Two thousand guns were shot off in the Tower and the ringing of church bells continued until 10 o'clock.[58]

On Monday, 15 October, the baby was christened in the Chapel Royal at Hampton Court. Cranmer officiated, Mary was his godmother and Elizabeth carried the chrisom-cloth. He was christened 'Edward', and Garter King of Arms proclaimed his titles: 'EDWARD, son and heir to the King of England, Duke of Cornwall and Earl of Chester'. Then, with Mary and Elizabeth supporting his train, he was carried back to the Queen's apartments, where his proud parents were waiting to greet him.[59]

Despite her lengthy labour, Jane seemed to make a good recovery and plans were put in hand for her churching, which would mark her return to ordinary life after the purdah of her confinement. Anne Basset, her mother was informed, would have to have a 'new satin gown' for the occasion. Meanwhile, in another splendid ceremony, Jane's brother Edward and Treasurer Fitzwilliam were both made earls. There was a rumour that Cromwell would be created an earl too. But he had to wait.[60]

A few days later, however, Jane's condition suddenly worsened. On Friday the 19th, there was another general procession at St Paul's for 'the health of the Queen'. By Tuesday the 23rd, 'the bruit [rumour] was her Grace was departed'. But Jane pulled round. 'If good prayers can save her life', Lady Lisle was informed, 'she is not like to die, for never lady was so much plained [lamented] with everyman, rich and poor.'[61]

At first, the prayers seemed to work. On the Tuesday afternoon, she had a natural 'lax' or discharge and she seemed to improve. But she was very ill all night, and, so her doctors reported, 'doth rather appair [worsen] than amend'. Her confessor was with her from dawn and, at 8 a.m., was preparing to administer Extreme Unction.[62]

Henry's reaction was curious. 'The King was determined', Russell informed Cromwell a little later on the 24th, 'as this day to have removed to Esher.' But because the Queen was very sick, he had stayed. However, he was determined to be in Esher on the 25th. 'If she amend, he will go,' Russell wrote, 'and if she amend not, he told me this day, he could not find it in his heart to tarry.'[63]

What was Henry doing? Was he grief-stricken and seeking solitude? Or did he find Jane's death, like other unpleasant things, distasteful and something to be avoided?

In any event, he did not have long to wait. By 8 p.m. on the 24th she was dying and Norfolk summoned Cromwell from London. 'I pray you', he wrote, 'to be here tomorrow early to comfort our good master, for as for our mistress there is no likelihood of her life, the more pity, and I fear she shall not be in life at the time ye shall read this.'

Jane died about midnight. We do not know whether Henry was present.[64]

PART THREE

The Later Queens

A conversation
Anne of Cleves
Catherine Howard
Interlude
Catherine Parr

71. A Conversation

For whatever reason, Henry was in no hurry to remarry after Jane's death. Perhaps he really was inconsolable. Perhaps it was the difficulty of finding another suitable wife. The most likely explanation, however, lies in a quirk in the King's amorous nature.

For Henry, as we have seen, being in love, or at least being able to imagine himself in love, was a prerequisite for marriage. But he tended to fall *in* love with a woman only when he was falling *out of* love with another one. It was thus that Anne had succeeded Catherine and thus in turn, as her own star waned, that Anne had been displaced by Jane. But Jane died while Henry was still in love with her – or, at least, not much out of it. Moreover, the fact that she died giving him a son meant that he came to love her more dead than alive. In these circumstances, the machinery of love on the rebound did not come into play and the post of Queen lay vacant.

But the vacancy was intended to be a short one only. This is shown by the fact that, despite Jane's death, the ladies of her Chamber were kept together. Henry provided for the young unmarried women, including Anne Basset, by boarding them out with the senior married ladies. He entertained the ladies, young and old, with splendid banquets at Court. And he even supplied them with holiday fun when he sent them off as a group, at his own expense, to view the fleet at Portsmouth. Henry was not being wholly altruistic, of course. He loved the company of women and, whether he had a wife or not, he could not live without it.[1]

And, who knows, one of the young ladies, like Anne Basset, might have kindled his sleeping fires.[2]

Nevertheless, as time went by, the King's continuing failure to wed became a subject of concern to the Tudor chattering classes.

Normally, their conversations – at Court, over the dinner-table or in the hunting field – are lost to us. But an extraordinary chance recorded one in the summer of 1539. Even more remarkably, the two main participants were men who have figured in our story. One was George Constantine, Henry Norris's former servant and priest. He was opinionated, talkative and an incorrigible gossip. He was also remarkably well informed. The other was John Barlow, Anne's former chaplain and factotum, who still held the Deanship of the College of Westbury-on-Trym which she had given him. Barlow was an altogether different character. He was a shrewd, taciturn red-head, given to sharp turns of phrase and quick, probing questions.[3]

In late August 1539 the two were riding together from Bristol to St David's, where John's brother, William, was bishop. And, as they rode, they talked. It seemed ordinary good-fellowship. But, though Constantine did not realize it at the time, Barlow was pumping him for information – perhaps with a view to entrapping him. At all events, their conversation attracted Cromwell's attention and was recorded from memory by Constantine in an effort to exonerate himself.[4]

'Hearest of no marriage toward?' Barlow asked. It was a sensitive subject and even Constantine at first tried to steer clear of it. 'I cannot tell what to say,' he replied, 'but methink it great pity that the King is so long without a Queen: his Grace might yet have many fair children.' Barlow returned to the attack: 'But hearest anything of any marriage?' The conversation now became a sort of truth game. 'There be two spoken of,' Constantine replied, with deliberate obscurity. 'Yea, marry! the Duchess of Milan and one of Cleves,' Barlow replied, showing that he too was up-to-date with the latest news.

Now that both men had put their cards on the table, Constantine became more confidential. 'Little Dr Wotton', the ambassador to Cleves, had sent home his companion, one of the Privy Chamber. 'I have forgotten his name,' said Constantine. Barlow prompted him: 'Marry! his name is Beard.' 'It is Beard indeed,' Constantine acknowledged. 'Now, Sir,' he continued, 'this Beard is come home and sent thitherward again with the King's Painter.' 'I pray you keep this gear secret,' he added.

Both agreed that the swift re-despatch of Beard was a good sign. For their attitude to Henry's two possible marriages was not neutral. They were strongly opposed to the marriage with the Duchess of Milan – which they, in any case, thought doomed since her Habsburg family was insisting on a Papal dispensation for the match. 'I pray God it be dashed,' said Constantine. 'For of this I am sure, that it is not possible that there can be faithful amity betwixt the King, the Emperor [who was the Duchess's uncle] and the French King, so long as the King receiveth not the Pope, who is their God in earth.'

In contrast, they were warm partisans of the Cleves match. Constantine, naturally, spoke the most plainly. 'I may tell you', he said, 'there is good hope, yet, that all shall be well enough if that marriage go forward.' 'For', he explained, 'the Duke of Cleves doth favour God's Word, and is a mighty Prince now; for he hath Guelderland in his hand too, and that against the Emperor.'[5]

Constantine's and Barlow's partisanship about Henry's next marriage was typical and reflected the wider divisions within the political élite. For the bitter politico-religious tensions of the earlier 1530s had intensified in the years after Jane's death.

On the one hand, people were more aware of the issues and cared about them more strongly. On the other, Henry himself, partly out of policy and partly out of a convinced belief in the *via media* or third way, swung now this way and now that. The result was that policy shifted, with dangerous unpredictability, from Reform to counter-Reform. In the summer of 1538 it seemed as though Cromwell would pull off the coup of an alliance between Henry and the Lutheran Princes of Germany who had formed themselves into the Schmalkaldic League. But the scheme was scotched by Bishop Tunstall of Durham, who, after years of internal exile in the north, came back to the Court and high favour during the Progress of 1538. Another more ambiguous gain for the conservatives was Gardiner's return from his prolonged French Embassy on 28 September.

Constantine and Barlow were fully alert to the threat presented by these two men. '[Gardiner]', Constantine conceded, 'is learned and, as I think, the wittiest, the boldest and the best learned in his faculty that is in England, and a great rhetorician.' But then came the qualification: '[he is] of very corrupt judgement'. 'He hath done much hurt, I promise you,' Barlow agreed. 'Nay,' Constantine dissented, 'there is not man hath done so much hurt in this matter as the Bishop of Durham.' 'For he,' he added, 'by his stillness, soberness and subtlety, worketh more than ten such as Winchester and he is a learned man too.'[6]

Despite the successes of Gardiner and Tunstall, Cromwell struck back at the end of 1538 by successfully pinning charges of treason on the Exeters, Montague and the rest of the Pole family, including its matriarch, the Countess of Salisbury. And in the New Year, Carew himself followed them to the block on charges of complicity in the Poles' treason. Past historians have seen these executions as the result of Henry's tyrannical hatred of the surviving members of the rival House of York. In fact, by contemporary standards, the victims deserved their fate, since, as we have seen, they had been root-and-branch opponents of Reform since the earliest days of the Boleyn marriage.

But then, in the Parliament which met in the early summer of 1539, Reform came a cropper. Led directly by Henry and by Norfolk as Henry's willing spokesman, Parliament passed the Act for the Abolishing of Diversity in Opinion, otherwise known as the Act of Six Articles. The principal Article reaffirmed belief in the Real Presence in the Sacrament, to which, as the Corpus Christi Day celebrations of 1536 showed, Henry was passionately committed. 'First', it declared, it was necessary to believe that 'in the most holy sacrament of the altar, by the strength and efficacy of Christ's mighty word, it being spoken by the priest, is present really, under the form of bread and wine, the natural body and blood of our Saviour Jesus Christ' and nothing else.[7]

The remaining five Articles ruled equally definitively on a whole range of currently disputed positions. Communion 'in both kinds' – that is, by partaking of both the bread and the wine – was not necessary. Priestly marriage was unlawful. Monastic vows should be kept. Masses for the dead were allowable. Confession to a priest was both necessary and desirable.

Only the most radical, known rather confusingly as 'Sacramentaries', disagreed with the doctrine of Transubstantiation as defined by the first Article. But the other five Articles outlawed what had become mainstream Reformed opinion.

The result was a disaster for Anne's bishops. Cranmer argued openly against the Bill in the Lords and was only 'persuaded', Constantine heard, by Cromwell. Hilsey of Rochester likewise compromised. But Latimer and Shaxton refused to bend and resigned their sees in return for pensions. Barlow expressed satisfaction at the news of the pensions, since Latimer owed him money. But his satisfaction was tempered by his awareness of Latimer's outspokenness. 'I am sure', Barlow said, '[Latimer] shall never receive a penny of his pension, for he shall be hanged, I warrant him, ere Christmas!'[8]

The defeat, then, for Reform was only just short of a rout and Constantine and Barlow were aware of belonging to a party under siege. They had to trust, Constantine said, to 'moderation'. This was not a very safe refuge in Henrician politics. Better to trust, instead, to the Cleves marriage and to the hope that a new wife would mean a new policy in religion.

But was Henry really able and willing to marry? 'His Grace *was* lusty', Constantine lamented, 'but it grieved me at the heart to see his Grace halt [limp] so much upon his sore leg.'[9]

For Henry had developed a severe ulceration on the calf of his left leg. The ulcer was not syphilitic as some have supposed. Instead, it was almost certainly the legacy of an old jousting or riding injury which had damaged the shin-bone. Splinters of bone remained in the muscle, which created a deep and ineradicable ulceration. It followed a cycle. The ulcer would discharge; heal over; re-infect; swell, burst and finally discharge. And so on. The swelling was agonizing; the discharge offered a deceptive and temporary relief.

The uncertainties of illness were now added to Henry's frighteningly unpredictable character. Still worse, at the age of forty-eight, he was suddenly aware of ageing and ageing fast.

He did not like it. Was Anne's supposed gibe that he was impotent becoming true?

Anne of Cleves

72. From Queen to sister

romwell had first floated the idea of a German marriage for Henry during the negotiations with the Schmalkaldic League in 1538. 'The Lord Cromwell', the principal ambassador wrote home after private discussions with the minister, 'is most favourably inclined to the German nation.' '[And he] wants very dearly', the ambassador continued, 'that the King should wed himself with the German Princes.'

Unfortunately, the ambassador could think of no suitable Protestant princess. But then he remembered the Duke of Cleves. The Duke ruled a powerful agglomeration of territories in north Germany with their capital at Dusseldorf and had two marriageable sisters, Anne and Amelia. From Cromwell's politico-religious point of view, the Cleves alliance was not ideal, since the Duke was neither Lutheran nor a member of the Schmalkaldic League. But he was closely connected by marriage to the Lutheran leader, Duke John Frederick of Saxony, who had married the Duke of Cleves's eldest sister, Sybilla.[1]

Early in 1539 the English took the first soundings in the Saxon court. The English ambassador, Christopher Mont, had two sets of instructions: his official ones from Henry, and another, secret set from Cromwell. The latter were addressed by Cromwell 'to his friend Christopher Mont', and ordered him to make discreet enquiries about 'the beauty and qualities of [Anne], the eldest of the two daughters of Cleves, her shape, stature and complexion'. If his enquiries led him to think that 'she might be likened unto his Majesty', he was to suggest the proposed marriage to the Saxon minister Burchard, though the formal initiative would have to come, it was made clear, from Cleves.[2]

Anne, Mont quickly discovered, had won golden opinions all round. 'Everyman', he reported to Cromwell, 'praiseth the beauty of the said Lady, as well for the face, as for the whole body, above all other ladies excellent.' Among the superlatives one struck home particularly with Henry. 'She excelleth', it was reported, 'as far the Duchess [of Milan], as the golden sun excelleth the silvern moon.'[3]

This was high praise indeed. Christina of Denmark, the youthful widowed Duchess of Milan, was, as we have seen, the rival candidate for Henry's hand. She had been closely observed by John Hutton, the English agent in the Netherlands, while she was staying at the viceregal court there. 'She is not so pure white', Hutton reported, 'as [Jane Seymour]. But she hath a singular good countenance, and, when she chanceth to smile, there appeareth two pits in her cheeks, and one in her chin, the which becometh her right excellently well.' She was only sixteen years old, 'but very high of stature for that age'. 'She [also]', Hutton concluded, 'resembleth much one Mistress Shelton, that sometime waited in Court upon Queen Anne [Boleyn]'.[4]

'Mistress Shelton' was Madge Shelton, Anne's cousin and Henry's old flame.

Hutton was careful to deprecate his taste in women. 'I knowledge myself of judgement herein very ignorant,' he wrote. But, clearly, he knew exactly what Henry liked.

Fired by Hutton's description, Henry sent Holbein to paint the Duchess of Milan. The resulting portrait confirmed all the details of her beauty, down to the dimpled cheeks and chin. It also confirmed that she was Henry's type. He fell in love with the woman, and, when the marriage failed to proceed, remained in love with the picture, which he kept in his collection to his dying day.[5]

If Anne were really so superior to Christina then she was beautiful indeed.

But Henry was wise enough at this stage not to trust to mere report. He wanted the testimony of his eyes – or at least of a painter's eyes. 'First', Cromwell informed Mont, 'it is expedient that they should send her picture hither.' Mont broached the matter directly with Duke John Frederick of Saxony. 'He should find some occasion to send it,' the Duke replied. But unfortunately, the Duke continued, 'his [own] painter, Lucas, was left sick behind him at home'.[6]

'Lucas' was Lucas Cranach the Elder, the Saxon court painter. Illness continued to disable Cranach, it seems, and the English had to try for an alternative.

By March 1539, direct negotiations had begun with the Cleves court. Top of the list for the English envoys, 'the little doctor', Nicholas Wotton and Richard Beard of the Privy Chamber, was the question of Anne's portrait. They had discussed the matter with the Cleves minister Olisleger, who was handling negotiations in the absence of the Duke. He offered them two recent portraits of Anne and her sister, probably by Barthel de Bruyn the Elder. But, as the ambassadors pointed out, there was no way they could vouch for the accuracy of the pictures, since they had only been able to catch a glimpse of the two ladies while they were attired in full German Court dress. And that, they said bluntly, was almost worse than useless. 'We had not seen them', they told Olisleger, 'for to see but a part of their faces, and that under such monstrous habit and apparel, was no sight, neither of the faces nor of their persons.'

'What,' Olisleger replied tartly, 'would you see them naked?'[7]

The result was stalemate. In early July, another English envoy, Dr William Petre, was sent with additional instructions to try to speed things up. If Beard had not already set out with the pictures, every effort was to be made to obtain them and to send them to England as soon as possible. They were also to demand a proper sight of the ladies, 'since one of them [was] to be their Queen'.

This last phrase has not received its proper weight. For it makes clear that already, long before he had seen any portrait, the Cleves marriage was a *fait accompli* for Henry. He had decided that he would marry one of the Cleves sisters, and, of the two, he much preferred Anne on grounds of her age. At twenty-four, he felt, she would make an ideal wife for a man in his late forties. Having made up his mind, he was cavalier about possible problems. He had heard that there had been previous negotiations to marry Anne to the son of the Duke of Lorraine. Did these constitute an obstacle to the proposed marriage with Henry? He hoped not, as he felt a strong preference for her rather than her younger sister. Similarly, the envoys were not to haggle about a dowry, 'for the King prefers virtue and friendship to money'.[8]

Beard arrived back in England in early July. He may have brought the De Bruyn portraits with him. But there is no firm evidence one way or another. Within a week or two, however, Beard was on his way back to Cleves, taking with him Hans Holbein, 'the King's painter'. The two were given a generous allowance of £40 to cover the costs of their journey; while Holbein received a separate payment of £13 6s 8d 'for such things as he is appointed to carry with him'. The wording is obscure, perhaps deliberately so. But it probably refers to the tools and materials of Holbein's craft.[9]

Constantine and Barlow had heard of Holbein's departure as the latest news. And they, too, took it as a sign that the Cleves marriage was virtually a done deal. The ensuing speed of events shows that they were right.[10]

Beard and Holbein reached the Castle of Düren, where the Cleves ladies were in residence, early in August. Holbein got to work immediately, and, with his usual facility, produced finished portraits of both sisters in little more than a week. 'Hans Holbein', Wotton wrote to Henry on 11 August, 'hath taken the effigies of my Lady Anne and the Lady Amelia and hath expressed their images very lively.'

Wotton also supplemented Holbein's paintings with his own vivid pen-portrait of Anne. He began with her relationship with her mother. 'She has been brought up', he wrote, 'with the [widowed] lady Duchess her mother and in manner never from her elbow.' 'The lady Duchess being,' he continued, 'a wise lady and one that very straitly looketh to her children'. Anne was also, so Wotton had gathered, the Duchess's favourite daughter: 'All report her to be of very lowly and gentle conditions, by the which she hath so much won her mother's favour that she is very loath to suffer her to depart from her.'

What the Duchess had *not* done, however, was to give her daughter any real education. Anne had become skilled 'with the needle', which employed most of her time. Otherwise, she had few accomplishments. 'She can read and write [her own language]', Wotton reported, '[but] French, Latin, or any other language she hath none, nor yet she cannot sing nor play upon any instrument'. 'For', he explained, 'they take it here in Germany for a rebuke and an occasion of lightness that great ladies should be learned or have any knowledge of music.'

Not, Wotton hastened to point out, that Anne was stupid. 'Her wit is so good', he insisted, 'that no doubt she will in a short space learn the English tongue, whenever she putteth her mind to it.' Finally, she was free from the excessive indulgence in food and drink – 'the good cheer' – for which, even then, Germans, men and women alike, were notorious.[11]

Anne's virtues, then, were of the passive, negative sort. She was gentle and obedient on the one hand, and neither stupid nor indulgent on the other. It was not an exciting list and the contrast with the learned Catherine of Aragon or the witty, accomplished Anne Boleyn was extreme. But perhaps Jane Seymour had lowered Henry's expectations in these matters. Time would tell.

Holbein made haste back to England. And on 1 September the French ambassador reported that the 'excellent painter, whom this King sent to Germany to bring the portrait of the sister of the Duke of Cleves, recently arrived in Court'. Soon after, there followed the news that an Embassy had set out from Cleves for England to conclude the marriage treaties.[12]

What we do not know, however, is Henry's reaction to Holbein's portrait. It cannot have been unfavourable. But there is no report of enthusiasm either. For Holbein, contrary to legend, does not appear to have flattered Anne. Instead, his painting and Wotton's pen-portrait are all of a piece. Both highlight the woman's gentle, passive character, which, as Mont had previously reported, 'appeareth plainly in the gravity of her face'.[13]

But, in any case, by this point Henry was almost beyond putting off. For he had fallen in love, not as previously with a face, but with an idea. And his feelings were fed, not with images, but with words. All over the summer, Cromwell and his agents had told him that Anne – the beautiful, the gentle, the good and the kind – was the woman for him. Finally he had come to believe them.

Only a sight of the woman herself might break the spell.

The joint Cleves-Saxon Embassy, headed by Burchard for Saxony and Olisleger for Cleves, arrived in England by 17 September. A few days earlier, Henry, who was drawing towards Windsor at the end of the summer Progress, had caught a chill. His physicians decided to treat it with a laxative and an enema and sent him early to bed. He slept until 2 in the morning, when, as a consequence of his medication, he 'rose to go to the stool' or lavatory. The stool 'had a very fair siege' and Henry felt much better, 'saving his Highness saith he hath a little soreness in his body'.

These intimate details, so vital for managing the King, were reported to Cromwell by Sir Thomas Heneage, who had replaced the executed Henry Norris as the King's chief body servant.[14]

With the news of the arrival of the Embassy, Henry's lingering malaise disappeared and his spirits soared. By this time, Heneage had temporarily handed over his duties of personal attendance on the King to his colleague, Anthony Denny. And it was Denny who reported Henry's delight to Cromwell. The task was an agreeable one, since Denny was a Reformer and an eager partisan of the Cleves marriage. 'The King is quiet and merry,' he wrote, 'considering God's goodness showed to him in his affairs, which by him and his ministers are so prudently handled as it passeth wishing.' The smugness of this sentiment is probably Henry's but the pious exhortation which follows is certainly Denny's own. 'God loving us', he solemnly adjured Cromwell, 'will force us or rather overcome us with heaped benefits.'[15]

For Denny and his like, the Cleves marriage was the answer to their prayers.

When the Embassy arrived, Cromwell was busy 'travail[ing] after his accustomed fashion in the examination of the prisoners in the Tower'. Henry immediately ordered him to cease 'to trouble his head' with such trivial matters as the rack and the vile dungeon known as Little Ease. Instead he was to concentrate wholly on the 'great weighty causes' of the Cleves marriage.

With Cromwell in charge, the negotiations lasted less than a fortnight and the marriage treaty was signed on 4 October.[16]

The only matter that now remained to be decided was Anne's route to England. There were two possibilities. One was to bring her overland to Calais. The other was to use the direct sea-route from the Cleves-ruled port of Harderwijk on the Zuiderzee to the Thames estuary. The former was much safer. But it required a safe-conduct from Charles V as the ruler of the Netherlands, through which Anne would have to pass. And this was in doubt in view of the ongoing dispute between the Emperor and Cleves over the Duchy of Guelderland.

The Cleves envoys were strongly in favour of the land-route. The long sea-voyage, they argued, was hazardous. It also risked harming Anne's appearance. '[She] is', they pointed out, 'young and beautiful, and if she should be transported by the seas they fear much how it might alter her complexion.' In particular, bearing in mind the approaching winter, 'she might . . . take such cold or other disease, considering she was never before upon the seas, as should be to her great peril and the King's Majesty's great displeasure'.

Henry's feelings were the opposite. The sea-voyage appealed to his (vicarious) sense of derring-do. It was also an opportunity to cock a snook at the Emperor and to show off the strength of the English navy and the quality of English seamanship. Probably before the treaties were signed, the King sent off two experienced ship-masters, John Aborough and Richard Couche, to the Zuiderzee to spy out the route.

They produced a written 'rutter' or route and a 'plat' or sketch-map.

Henry's imagination immediately took fire: he would snatch his bride from under the nose of his enemy and bring her safe to his arms. On 9 October he showed the Aborough and Couche sketch-map to Fitzwilliam, who was now Lord Admiral as well as Earl of Southampton. 'His Majesty is marvellously inflamed [with the "plat"],' the Admiral informed Cromwell, 'supposing many things to be done thereon.'

The Admiral and his staff got to work immediately and the King's ideas were worked up into another, finished map. It shows how Anne was to be smuggled out of the Zuiderzee to Henry's flag-ship, which is drawn proudly flying the royal standard and the pennant of St George. Meanwhile, other English ships are represented blockading the coast south of Zieriksee, enabling Anne to make her crossing in safety.[17]

But, alas for Henry's romanticism, the Cleves envoys vetoed the scheme and the Emperor's representatives proved surprisingly co-operative. By 19 October, Anne had been given a safe-conduct and by 25 October Henry had capitulated and agreed the land-route.[18]

Meanwhile, the Cleves envoys had returned home to conduct Anne to England. She left Dusseldorf in November and made a stately progress across the Netherlands, where, according to Wotton, she rarely travelled more than five miles a day. Her *entrée* into Antwerp excited huge popular interest. The Count of Buren, one of the leading Flemish nobles, told the English that 'he never saw so many people gathered in Antwerp at any *entrée*, even the Emperor's'.[19]

Was it curiosity that drew the crowds? Or pity?

On 11 December Anne arrived at the English stronghold of Calais. Lord Lisle, the Lord Deputy or Governor, had been instructed to make the town look its best to receive her. But it was hoped that her stay would be a short one. A detailed timetable of the state of the tides, starting on 12 December, was sent to Henry. And, before Anne even entered the walls, Admiral Fitzwilliam, who was in charge of the reception party, took her to look at the ship that would carry her to England. It was a fine sight. Just as in the Zuiderzee map, it was decked with streamers, banners and flags.

Seamen were on the tops, shrouds and yard-arms and the guns fired a salute.

But adverse winds made a quick departure impossible. In the hope that the weather would change soon, experienced captains, including Aborough and Couche, were sent 'to lie out side the walls and give immediate notice of fair weather'. They were to remain there rather a long time.[20]

Meanwhile, Admiral Fitzwilliam, as instructed, set himself to entertain Anne, while Anne, for her part, did her best to prepare herself for her new role. On the afternoon of the 13th, for instance, she sent Olisleger, who acted as her interpreter, to invite Fitzwilliam 'to go to cards [with her] at some game that [the King] used'. Fitzwilliam, who was one of Henry's oldest gaming cronies, decided that she should be taught 'cent', which resembled piquet. 'I played with her at cent,' Fitzwilliam reported to Henry, while three others, who spoke German, 'stood by and taught her the play'. 'And I assure your Majesty,' Fitzwilliam concluded, 'she played as pleasantly and with as good a grace and countenance as ever in all my life I saw any noblewoman.'[21]

This, if it were true, was high compliment. For Fitzwilliam had been at Court when Henry had played with Anne and Rochford.

Moreover, this was only one of a stream of letters that Fitzwilliam sent to the King. Indeed, he claimed to Cromwell, 'his two clerks are [so] fully occupied in writing to his Majesty' that he was scarcely able to write separately to the minister. Most of the correspondence has disappeared. But, according to Fitzwilliam himself, his comments were uniformly favourable and he did 'much praise her and set her forth'.[22]

Nor was Fitzwilliam the only one to do so. Lady Lisle wrote enthusiastically to her daughter, Anne Basset, who was ear-marked for the new Queen's Chamber. And Anne Basset, in turn, echoed her praises in her reply to her mother. 'I humbly thank your Ladyship', she wrote, 'of the news you write me of her Grace, that she is so good and gentle to serve and please.' 'It shall be no little rejoicement to us, her Grace's servants here', she continued, 'and most comfort to the King's Majesty, whose Highness is not a little desirous to have her Grace here.' Anne knew this because, as instructed, she had passed Lady Lisle's comments on to Henry himself.[23]

Better and better, it must have seemed to the King. Previously, he had had to rely on diplomats and agents of uncertain status. Now his own familiars and courtiers had seen Anne. And, to a man and a woman, their verdicts were favourable.

How soon before the weather allowed him to add his own praise to theirs?

In fact, it was not until 27 December that the winds turned and Anne was able to sail. She landed at the Downs between 6 and 7 p.m. and was received by the Duke and Duchess of Suffolk.[24]

She was in her new kingdom at last. And she would never leave it.

The weather continued to be as bad on land as at sea. 'The day', Suffolk reported to Cromwell, 'was foul and windy, with much hail [that blew] continually in her face.' There were also long delays in getting her cloth of gold covered chariot, in which she had travelled from Cleves, and her elaborate trousseau ashore.

Nevertheless, to the evident surprise of her escorts, she insisted on setting out after only a day's rest, 'so . . . desirous [was she] to make haste to the King's Highness'. Her first halt was at Canterbury. There Cranmer made a speech; the Mayor and citizens received her with torches and a peal of guns, and fifty ladies in velvet bonnets turned up to see her in her chamber. 'All of which', Suffolk's report continued, 'she took very joyously . . . that she forgot all the foul weather and was very merry at supper.'

She then continued to Sittingbourne and Rochester, where she arrived on New Year's Eve. The official programme envisaged that she would spend the New Year's holiday at Rochester and then travel via Dartford to her formal meeting with her bridegroom-to-be at Blackheath on 3 January.[25]

But Henry, burning with impatience to see the woman about whom he had heard so much, decided to give her a surprise New Year's Gift.

*

New Year's Day was already half-over and Anne of Cleves was standing in the window of her chamber at Rochester, watching a bull-fight which had been laid on for her entertainment. Then a party of six gentlemen came unannounced into the room. They were disguised in identical 'marbled' or multi-coloured cloaks and hoods. Suddenly, one of the group stepped forward and, without warning, kissed her and presented her with a 'token' or gift, which, he said, came from the King. Anne, taken by surprise, was 'abashed [and], not knowing who he was, thanked him'. The unknown gentleman continued to try to 'commune' with her – that is, to make love to her. 'But she regarded him little but always looked out of the window on the bull-baiting.'

Unused to being treated in this fashion, the gentleman lost patience and withdrew. A few moments later, he returned without his disguise and dressed in a coat of purple velvet.

It was the King.

Everyone bowed and Anne, embarrassed afresh, made him a deep courtesy.[26]

There are two accounts of what followed, one by the chronicler and herald, Charles Wriothesley, and the other by Sir Anthony Browne, Gentleman of the Privy Chamber and Carew's successor as Master of the Horse. Both were eye-witnesses, yet their accounts differ radically. According to Wriothesley, Henry raised Anne up, kissed her again, talked with her 'lovingly' and took her by the hand into another, more private chamber.

According to Browne, on the other hand, the King spoke barely twenty words to Anne and left her as quickly as possible without giving her the precious New Year's Gift of bejewelled sables which he had brought.[27]

The difference between the two accounts is, of course, the result of point of view. Wriothesley wrote as one of the audience, unable to go with Henry and Anne into the more private chamber. Browne, on the other hand, had the *entrée*, both to the King's private rooms and, it will become clear, to his most intimate thoughts.

And Browne knew, from the King's face alone, that the meeting had been a disaster.

Two things had gone wrong. The first was Anne's reaction to Henry – or rather her lack of reaction since she had failed to recognize him. This meant in turn that she had failed her first test as Henry's loved one. For, in visiting her in disguise, Henry was re-enacting a scene from chivalric romance. In the romances, and in the Courtly entertainments based on them, ladies encountered their lovers in a variety of disguises. But, no matter how fantastic the disguise, the second-sight of passion always penetrated it and the lady recognized her lover.

Any woman with even a little experience in the ways of the world would have known this and known what she was expected to do. But Anne, utterly unprepared by her strict and cloistered upbringing for such frivolities, did not. Instead, she behaved naturally, like a peasant, rather than artificially, like a lady.

Who was this strange man? she seems to have wondered. Why was he kissing her and making love to her? Was it some strange custom of the country? Better to ignore him and pretend to be interested in the bull-baiting in the courtyard below.

Put like this, Anne's behaviour can be interpreted as both sensible and decorous. From Henry's perspective, on the other hand, it was an unheard-of humiliation. Not to have recognized him – he who stood head and shoulders above his courtiers and exceeded them in all qualities, mental as well as physical . . . !

His New Year's romance had turned into a vulgar farce, with himself as the Fool.

It was not a part he relished.

All this was bad enough. What was worse was Henry's reaction to Anne. Everything he had been told about her led him to expect love at first sight. Instead, he was overwhelmed with disgust.

He brooded about his feelings overnight at Rochester. Then, the following day, during the return journey by barge to Greenwich, he shared them with two of his attendants. First he called Browne to sit beside him. 'I see nothing in this woman as men report of her,' he said, speaking 'very sadly and pensively'. 'And I marvel', he continued, 'that wise men would make such report as they have done.' At this point Browne fell silent, fearful for his half-brother, Admiral Fitzwilliam, who had written so enthusiastically in Anne's praise from Calais.

Dismissing Browne, Henry spoke next to Lord Russell, as he now was. 'How like you this woman?' he asked. 'Do you think her so fair and of such beauty as report hath been made unto me of her? I pray you tell me the truth.' Russell replied 'that he took her not for fair, but to be of a brown complexion'.

'Alas,' sighed Henry. 'Whom should men trust?'[28]

The King had the answer to his question when he got back to Greenwich. For, on cue, Cromwell, the man whom he trusted most, appeared. Henry had told Cromwell about his intention to visit Anne secretly at Rochester 'to nourish love'. And Cromwell was eager to know the result. 'How ye liked the Lady Anne?' he asked the King. 'Nothing so well as she was spoken of,' answered Henry, speaking 'heavily and not pleasantly'. Then he continued: 'if [he] had known as much before as [he] then knew, she should not have come within this realm'.

'What remedy?' he concluded. Cromwell took this as a 'lamentation'. It was not. It was a question. Cromwell had got him into this marriage. How, Henry wanted to know, would he get him out of it?

But Cromwell, for once, was stumped. 'I know none,' he replied, adding lamely that 'he was very sorry therefore'.[29]

On Saturday, 3 January Anne and Henry met for the second time in the formal public encounter at Blackheath. Both were dressed in cloth of gold and accompanied by a great procession of servants. They greeted each other and rode to Greenwich together through lines of courtiers, who were also finely turned out in velvet with gold chains.

Henry conducted Anne to her apartments and then returned to his own. Once more he found Cromwell in his Privy Chamber. 'My Lord,' he said, 'is it not as I told you? Say what they will, she is nothing as fair as she hath been reported.' 'Howbeit,' he conceded, 'she is well and seemly.'

Cromwell snatched at this straw. 'By my faith, Sir,' he replied, 'ye say truth.' 'I thought', he added, 'that she had a queenly manner.'[30]

The wedding should have taken place the following day, Sunday the 4th. Instead, it was postponed as Henry desperately sought a way out.

First, he ordered Cromwell to summon the Council to see if it were possible, even at this late stage, to find a legal pretext to break off the marriage. Immediately, the Council fixed on the issue of the possible precontract between Anne and the Duke of Lorraine's son, which Henry had dismissed so lightly a few months previously. The Cleves ambassadors, headed by Olisleger, were summoned to clarify the matter. Naturally, in view of Henry's previous attitude, they were unprepared and had brought none of the necessary documentation. But they solemnly assured the Council that the Lorraine match had never gone beyond an engagement, which could be, and had been, properly broken off. They also offered to remain as hostages in England until the documentation to prove this was produced.

It was a reply which would have satisfied any reasonable man. But Henry was not in a reasonable mood. 'I am not well handled,' he said to Cromwell, after the minister had returned from the Council meeting to the Privy Chamber by 'the privy way'. But equally he recognized the impasse he was in. 'If it were not', he added, '. . . for fear of making a ruffle in the world – that is, to be a mean to drive her brother into the hands of the Emperor – I would never have married her.'

The next day, he made a final attempt to escape. Anne must make a solemn, notarized declaration before the Council 'that she was free from all contracts'. But, alas for Henry, she did so promptly.

The trap had snapped shut. 'Is there none other remedy', Henry asked Cromwell when he brought the news of Anne's declaration, 'but that I must needs, against my will, put my neck in the yoke?'

Without even trying to reply, Cromwell fled.[31]

*

Cornered at last, Henry now recognized that he had to go through with the ceremony, which was rearranged for 8 o'clock in the morning on Tuesday, 6 January, the day of the Epiphany. But he acquiesced with the worst possible grace. 'If it were not to satisfy the world and my realm', he told Cromwell on their way to the service, 'I would not do that I must do this day for none earthly thing.'

But, curiously, the final delay was Anne's. Had the two-day post-ponement of the ceremony and the humiliation of the declaration made her have second thoughts? Or was she simply exercising a woman's prerogative to be late?

Whatever it was, it put Henry in an even worse mood. Like Macbeth, he had decided that 'if 'twere done, . . . 'twere well it were done quickly'. 'Therewith', Cromwell afterwards remembered, 'one brought your Grace word that she was coming; and thereupon your Grace repaired into the gallery towards the Closet, and there paused for her coming, being nothing content that she so long tarried, as I judged then.'[32]

But eventually she came, arrayed magnificently like a bride. She wore a gown of cloth of gold, embroidered with flowers of pearls. Her hair, 'which was fair, yellow and long', hung loose, while on her head was a coronet of gold, jewelled and fashioned with sprigs of rosemary, for remembrance. When she met Henry, whose gown of cloth of gold was also embroidered with flowers of silver, she made three low curtsies. Then they entered the Queen's Closet, where they were married by Cranmer. Henry said 'I will', and the wedding ring, engraved with the words, 'GOD SEND ME WELL TO KEEP', was set on Anne's finger.

They were man and wife.

They dined and supped together and spent the evening with 'Banquets, Masques and divers disports, till the time came that it pleased the King and her to take their rest'.[33]

What may be the bed-head made for the occasion survives. It is dated 1539 and is decorated with the royal cipher 'HA' and two lewd carvings that stand guard over the sleepers on either side. The one on the left shows a male cherub with an enormous erection, and the one on the right a female cherub with a fine, swollen belly.[34]

But, alas, the human figures below seem to have been less active.

The morning after, Cromwell came to the Privy Chamber. He saw immediately that the King was in a bad mood. Nevertheless, he persevered and asked him 'how [he] liked the Queen'. Henry replied 'soberly'. 'Surely, as ye know,' the King said, 'I liked her before not well, but now I like her much worse. For I have felt her belly and her breasts, and thereby, as I can judge, she should be no maid.' '[The] which', he continued, 'struck me so to the heart when I felt them that I had neither will nor courage to proceed any further in other matters.'

'I have left her', he concluded, 'as good a maid as I found her.'[35]

That same morning, Henry discussed his failure to consummate the marriage with his physicians, Dr John Chamber and Dr William Butts. 'He had not that night carnally known the Queen,' he said. Chamber, who was a wise old bird, advised the King 'not to enforce himself, for eschewing such inconveniences as by debility ensuing in that case were to be feared'. Henry took the advice and the 'second night he lay not with her'. But he tried again on the third and fourth nights – always with the same lack of success.

Other consultations with his doctors followed, in which Henry described the problem as he saw it. 'He found her body in such sort disordered and indisposed to excite and provoke any lust in him,' he explained. 'Yea,' he continued, '[it] rather minister[ed] matter of loathesomeness unto [him], that [he] could not in any wise overcome that loathesomeness, nor in her company be provoked or stirred to that act.'

On the other hand, he was not, God forbid, impotent. And he had evidence to prove it. 'He hath had', he confessed to Butts, 'two wet dreams [*duas pollutiones nocturnas in somno*].' He also told him that '[he] thought himself able to do the act with other, but not with her'.[36]

Nevertheless, Henry continued to go through the motions and, every other night at least, solemnly processed to the Queen's apartments to sleep with her.

But sleep was all he did.

What, however, of Anne in all this? It is difficult to be sure of her reaction. She was still escaping from her mother's shadow and found it hard to say what she wanted. Indeed, until she picked up some English, she found it difficult to say anything at all. But, as Wotton predicted, she proved a quick learner and, a few months after her marriage, she had a frank exchange with her ladies.

It began when 'they [all] wished her Grace with child'. 'She knew well', she replied, 'she was not with child.' 'How is it possible', asked one, 'for your Grace to know that and lie every night with the King?' 'I know it well I am not,' Anne insisted.

This was too much for Lady Rochford, George Boleyn's widow, who seems to have learned little from her late husband's fate. 'By Our Lady', she said, 'I think your Grace is a maid still indeed.' 'How can I be a maid', the Queen replied, 'and sleep every night with the King?' 'There must be more than that,' said Lady Rochford, with an insolent directness.

But instead of slapping her down, the long-suffering Anne entered into a patient explanation. 'Why,' she said, 'when he comes to bed, he kisses me and taketh me by the hand and biddeth me, "Goodnight, sweetheart"; and in the morning [he] kisses me and biddeth me, "Farewell, darling". Is this not enough?'

'Madam,' replied the Countess of Rutland, 'there must be more than this, or it will be long ere we have a Duke of York.'

'Nay,' said the Queen, 'I am content with this, for I know no more.'[37]

Was Anne really as naïve as this exchange suggests? Or was she trying to keep up appearances? Was she even, perhaps, trying to protect Henry?

For there is a clear indication that she knew that something was wrong from the start. 'The Queen [has] often desired to speak with me,' Cromwell told Henry on 7 January, during their post-mortem discussion on the disaster of the wedding night. 'But I durst not.' 'Why should [you]

634 THE QUEENS OF HENRY VIII

not?' Henry replied. 'Alleging', Cromwell remembered, 'that I might do much good in going to her, and to be plain with her in declaring my mind.'

Despite Henry's encouragement, however, Cromwell managed to avoid having the awkward conversation himself. Instead, he shuffled off the responsibility onto the Earl of Rutland, who was Anne's Lord Chamberlain. Cromwell had a private word with Rutland, in which he begged him 'to find some means that the Queen might be induced to order [her] Grace pleasantly in her behaviour towards [the King], thinking thereby for to have had some faults amended'. Cromwell also spoke more generally to the Queen's Council, 'to counsel their mistress to use all pleasantness to [the King]'.[38]

We have no means of knowing whether anyone acted on this advice. The suspicion must be that they did not. If, Rutland and the rest must have reasoned, Cromwell himself was afraid to speak to the Queen directly, why should they risk their necks on his behalf?

For Cromwell was only reaping what he had sown. He had instituted a reign of terror, in which careless talk cost lives. And no talk, of course, was more careless than talk which cast doubt on the succession. But none, in the present circumstances, was more vital either.

Somehow, the circle had to be squared. Anne had to be taught the facts of life. She had even, in the face of Henry's 'loathesomeness', to be taught to take the sexual initiative. But how to do this without offering the least hint of Henry's incapacity or outright impotence? After all, it was only three years since Rochford had gone to the block after doing just that.

It was an awkward but not impossible task and Cromwell, of all men, should have been able to do it. He had the King's direct authority to proceed. He also had the most powerful incentive, since, as he well knew, such a conversation with Anne was the best hope of rescuing the Cleves marriage. But, on his own admission, he lacked the courage even to try.

There was, of course, an alternative route. Rutland may not have spoken to the Queen, but it seems pretty clear that he spoke to his wife, the

Countess. For she, as a woman, could go where a man could not. She could tackle the Queen, woman to woman, in the secrecy of her private apartments. And she could raise the dreaded topic naturally, without an overt political context or agenda. That is the background, I think, to the conversation between Anne and her ladies which has already been described.

But, equally, this conversation shows the limitations of this approach. It did not take place till June, by which time the breakdown in the marriage was irretrievable. And, even then, it quickly encountered barriers of language and of trust. But the most important obstacle was Anne's own attitude. 'Did not your Grace tell Mother Loew this?' asked the Countess.

Mrs Loew was a German gentlewoman, who had accompanied Anne from Cleves. Unlike most of Anne's German entourage, who, as was the custom, were sent home soon after the marriage, she was allowed to remain in England. And she quickly established a pre-eminent position in the Queen's Household. She was the 'mother' of the German maids. She was also Anne's chief confidante. Apply to Mrs Loew, the Countess of Rutland advised her friend Lady Lisle, for she 'can do as much . . . as any woman' to secure the appointment of Anne Basset's younger, uglier sister, Catherine, as one of the Queen's maids.[39]

In view of all this, Mrs Loew should have been Anne's natural comforter and adviser in the problems of her marriage. She was a shoulder to weep on. She was also, as 'mother' of the maids, expected to be a fount of knowledge and woman's lore.

But Anne apparently was too embarrassed to invoke her. 'Fie, fie, for shame!' Anne said, when the Countess of Rutland asked if she had discussed Henry's behaviour in bed with Mrs Loew. 'God forbid!'

Between Cromwell's cowardice and Anne's shamefacedness, any hope of rescuing the marriage from Henry's initial disgust was lost.

But Henry's cup of sorrow was not yet full. For, little more than a month after the marriage, the latent toughness of Anne's character started to appear. The bone of contention seems to have been the treatment of

Henry's elder daughter, Mary. Mary was now fully restored to her father's good graces and marriage negotiations were in full swing for a match between her and the Duke of Bavaria. In Lent, which began on 11 February, Henry had some discussions with Anne about his daughter. But Anne, Henry complained bitterly to Cromwell, had begun 'to wax stubborn and wilful'.[40]

It was not what the King was used to after Jane Seymour.

The outside world, however, knew none of this. Nor, for that matter, did most of the King's intimates. They could, and did, draw their conclusions from the external signs of Henry's behaviour. But at first only Cromwell and the two doctors were in the King's full confidence.

Thereafter, however, the circle of those in the know steadily widened. A week after the wedding, Cromwell told Admiral Fitzwilliam. He also, Fitzwilliam claimed, tried to pin the blame on him for having over-praised Anne in his letters from Calais. Heneage seems to have learned the truth at about the same time. But even Denny remained in the dark for almost a month.

In Denny's case, it is true, it was probably a wilful blindness. As a partisan of Reform, he was desperately anxious for the marriage to succeed. So he stuck loyally to the script which Cromwell had given him, and continued to praise Anne 'at the first arrival of the Queen and long after'. Finally, just before Lent, Henry lost patience and decided to take Denny into his confidence as well, 'as . . . servant whom he used secretly about him'. Denny heard out the King's description of Anne's body and his own repulsion from it. Then he tried to comfort his master.

'The state of Princes . . . in matters of marriage', he said, '[was] far of worse sort than the condition of poor men.' 'For Princes', he continued, 'take as is brought them by others, and poor men be commonly at their own choice and liberty.'[41]

This was Job's comfort indeed.

Meanwhile, the machinery of ceremony ground on obliviously. On 4

February Anne and Henry removed from Greenwich to Whitehall in another great river pageant. The Lord Mayor and citizens gave their attendance. And the Tower shot off 'above a thousand chambers of ordnance, which made a noise like thunder'.[42]

On 18 April, Cromwell, the author of the Cleves marriage, had his reward. He was created Earl of Essex and Lord Great Chamberlain of England. After the ceremony, the King went to dine with the Queen in her Chamber, while the newly created Earl dined in the Council Chamber with his fellow magnates. There Garter King of Arms proclaimed his style: 'Earl of Essex, Vicegerent and High Chamberlain of England, Chancellor of the Exchequer, and Justice of the Forests beyond Trent'. Short of a dukedom, he could rise no higher.[43]

May Day, too, was celebrated with the accustomed pageantry. Henry, increasingly lame as he was, was no longer able to ride as Anne's knight. But a new generation of coming young men, including Sir Thomas Seymour, the late Queen's younger brother, and Richard Cromwell, the minister's nephew, showed off their jousting skills before the new Queen in the tilt-yard at Whitehall. After the tournament, the jousters kept open house at Durham Place, 'where they feasted the King's Majesty [and] the Queen's Grace and her ladies'.

There were rumours, which Anne sought eagerly to turn into reality, that she would be crowned round Whitsuntide.[44]

It was just like old times.

But it was all a façade. Soon, rumours were circulating of another sort of entertainment. Henry was seen crossing the Thames in a little boat, often in broad daylight and occasionally even at midnight. His destination was either the Dowager Duchess of Norfolk's house in Lambeth or Winchester Palace in Southwark, where Gardiner was providing 'feasts and entertainments'.

For Henry had fallen in love again, with a 'young lady of diminutive stature'. Her name was Catherine Howard. She was one of the Queen's ladies and, like Anne Boleyn, was niece to the Duke of Norfolk.[45]

However the relationship began (and its origins are unknown), it soon became as political as the Cleves marriage, to which it was the perfect counterpoise. For all year the political pendulum had swung wildly from one extreme to the other. First Reforming friends and clients of Cromwell, such as Robert Barnes, were humiliated and arrested. Then Cromwell struck back in May with the arrest of leading conservatives, including Lord Lisle, the Deputy of Calais, and Bishop Sampson of Chichester who was also Dean of the Chapel Royal.

The moment of crisis had been reached. On 1 June the French ambassador, Marillac, reported that 'things are brought to such a pass that either Cromwell's party or that of the Bishop of Winchester must succumb'. And his money, he made clear, was on Cromwell to emerge as the victor.[46]

It is easy to see why. For Cromwell, despite his fatal lack of courage in speaking to Anne, was the bolder and better politician. But the failure of the Cleves marriage proved the chink in his armour and on 10 June he was arrested at the Council Board, insulted by his fellow-councillors, whom he had terrorized and humiliated for so long, and taken straight to the Tower.

Only Cranmer dared to speak up for him, in the sort of ambiguous phrases he had once used about Cromwell's earlier victim, Anne Boleyn. 'I loved him as my friend,' the Archbishop wrote to Henry. 'But now, if he be a traitor, I am sorry that I ever loved him or trusted him.' 'I am very glad his treason is discovered in time', he continued, 'but again I am very sorrowful. For who shall your Grace trust hereafter, if you might not trust him?'

'Alas, whom should men trust?' Henry had asked Russell.

Not Cromwell, he had decided at last.[47]

The fallen minister was not even given the dignity of a trial. Instead, he was condemned by a Parliamentary process known as an Act of Attainder. The charges were a fantastic mixture of treason, heresy and *scandalum magnatum*, or being rude and oppressive to nobles. Only the last had any vestige of truth. But truth, as Cromwell had fatally taught Henry, was not important.[48]

Only Henry's convenience was.

With the Act of Attainder, Cromwell was legally dead. And he was kept alive for a few weeks only to facilitate the now inevitable divorce from Anne of Cleves.

His co-operation was not in doubt. He would do and say anything to avoid the full, horrible penalties for treason or heresy, which, in view of his humble birth, were likely to be his hideous fate. He also had the temperament of a bully: strong and bold when he was in the ascendant, but craven in defeat. 'Most gracious prince, I cry for mercy, mercy, mercy!' he wrote at the end of one of the letters in which he supplied the required circumstantial detail about the Cleves marriage and its debacle.[49]

Anne herself probably understood little of the political storm which raged round her and of which she was the all-too passive cause. She was shrewd enough, however, to notice the King's attentions to Catherine Howard, and, on 20 June, she complained vigorously about them to the Cleves agent in London, Karl Harst. Two days later, she was in better spirits, because Henry had spoken to her kindly.[50]

It was the last time she saw him as her husband.

On 24 June, like Catherine of Aragon before her, Anne was ordered to leave the Court. In her case, the move was to Richmond Palace, because, it was claimed, it enjoyed a better climate. Anne was not deceived. She knew about the precedent of Henry's first Queen and feared she would share the same fate. Harst did his best to comfort her, but without much conviction.[51]

On 6 July, the anticipated blow fell, as, in two separate meetings, Harst and Anne were informed of the King's intention to have the Cleves marriage reconsidered. In his meeting with the Council and his own subsequent investigations, Harst discovered the range of conservative Councillors arrayed against his mistress. Tunstall took the lead in explaining Henry's case; Gardiner had found a German in Henry's employ to translate, from German into Latin, the key document concerning the marriage contract between Anne and the son of the Duke of Lorraine, and Norfolk was also seeking information about the tense of a crucial word in the document.[52]

At the same time as Harst was seeing the Council in London, a powerful delegation of Councillors, which included Suffolk and Gardiner together with two interpreters, waited on Anne at Richmond. They handed her a paper, which gave notice that Henry intended to submit their marriage to the judgement of Convocation. Did she agree? According to the Councillors' report to the King, Anne, 'without alteration of countenance' gave her immediate oral consent, saying 'that she is content always with your Majesty's [desires]'. According to Harst, however, Anne, far from giving her informed agreement, paid no attention to the paper.[53]

Was it a genuine misunderstanding? Or was the delegation simply reporting what Henry wanted to hear?

Whatever the genuineness of Anne's consent, however, it was enough for Convocation to proceed. This it did at speed. It met early on Wednesday the 7th. The morning session considered the case against the marriage. This was presented 'in a lucid speech' by Gardiner, who had returned post-haste from Richmond the previous night. Cranmer then adjourned the full session till the following day. Meanwhile, in the afternoon, from 1 to 6 p.m., depositions were taken from a wide range of witnesses. It is these which, together with Cromwell's two written confessions, provide the intimate details about the failure of the marriage. On the Thursday the depositions were tabled and agreed to present a *prima facie* case against the marriage. Finally, on Friday the 9th, the judgement was drawn up in proper form and assented to by all present.[54]

From first to last the proceedings had taken three days.

Harst was taken by surprise at the speed of events and on the 9th he went to Court to complain about the lack of consultation. He was told that, because the matter concerned the validity of the King's marriage, it was up to the bishops and clergy to decide it. He was also informed that another delegation of Councillors had already left to inform Anne of the decision of Convocation. Harst followed this delegation at speed; indeed, he seems to have overtaken it.

He arrived at Richmond at 4 o'clock on the Saturday morning and found Anne in a pitiable state. She had just received another message from Henry by Richard Beard. Beard had been Holbein's escort to Cleves when he painted her portrait. Now he bore Henry's demand that she should give her consent to the divorce proceedings, not orally as before, but formally in writing.

This seems to have been the moment that the reality of her situation dawned. Henry really intended divorce. And she, like two of his previous wives, would be discarded.

Anne was heartbroken. She was also in a quandary about how to reply.

She discussed the situation first with Harst. Then she summoned Rutland, who, since he claimed to understand neither the Queen nor the ambassador, turned up with an interpreter.

Seeing her distress, the Earl tried to comfort her. Henry was a good and gracious King, he said. He would proceed by law and conscience, and Anne had nothing to fear. This seems to have calmed her. At any rate, Anne heard his explanation in silence 'and said nothing to it'.

Harst paints a more dramatic and probably more accurate picture. When her consent to the divorce proceedings was required, he wrote, she broke down. 'She knew nothing other', she protested, 'than that she had been granted [by God] the King as her husband, and thus she took him to be her true lord and husband.' Then the tears flowed. 'Good Lord,' Harst reported, 'she made such tears and bitter cries, it would break a heart of stone.'

She also had the courage to refuse Henry's demand for her written consent and instead sent Beard with a message only by word of mouth, as before.

Harst left her in this state of mingled distress and obstinacy and returned to London to send off his despatch to her brother, the Duke. But he promised to return later that day.[55]

Over the next twenty-four hours, however, Anne's initial hysteria subsided. So did her resistance. Instead, she heard out the formal report from the delegation of Councillors, and considered carefully their advice. Henry, it seems, was offering a deal. She would cease to be his wife, of course. But he was willing to honour her as his 'sister'. He would also, it was hinted, pay her as such.[56]

It did not take her long to weigh the alternatives. She would accept the offer.

On the Sunday, Anne wrote to Henry on the lines suggested. She began by repeating in unambiguous terms her previous oral agreement that the marriage should be tried by Convocation. Next she accepted their judgement that it was invalid. Finally, she submitted herself, 'for her [future] state and condition', wholly to the King 'goodness and pleasure', begging only that she might 'sometimes have the fruition of your most noble presence'.

The letter was signed 'Your Majesty's most humble sister and servant, Anne, Dochtter the Cleyffys'.[57]

Henry seems to have been rather surprised by Anne's sudden 'conformity'. He had not expected it. And Anne, as we have seen, had given him some grounds for his fears by her initial resistance.

But, with her submission, the King set himself to be both generous and agreeable. He replied to Anne's letter on the 12th, addressing her as 'sister' and outlining the terms of the financial settlement he proposed. She would have an income of £4,000 a year. She would be given Richmond and Bletchingley as her residences. And these, the King explained, were both near the Court, which she would be welcome to visit, 'as we shall repair unto you'.[58]

Never, after Anne's initial tantrum, had a divorce been more amicable.

The usual body of Councillors turned up with Henry's letter on the 14th. Anne asked Secretary Wriothesley to read it. But, since he knew the contents of the letter to be 'sweet and pleasant', he felt it better to leave Anne to digest it at leisure with her own interpreter. After a while, she summoned the Councillors back and questioned them closely.

Where was Bletchingley? What men servants would she have? And what women?

They did their best to satisfy her and exhorted her to continue her 'conformity'. She promised she would. She also let slip what may have been the over-riding motive in her behaviour. If she returned to Germany, she seems to have said, she feared that someone, presumably her brother, 'would slay me'.[59]

Did she think that her humiliation had injured her family's honour so much that she would be safe only in England?

It now remained only to tie up a few loose ends. On the 17th she undertook to 'receive no letters nor messages from her brother, her mother, nor none of her kin or friends, but she would send them to [Henry]'. On the 21st, she wrote to her brother the Duke, to inform him of her satisfaction at her treatment and to insist that, 'God willing, I purpose to lead my life in this realm'. Finally, on the same day, after having made a good dinner, she sent Henry 'the ring delivered unto her at their pretensed marriage, desiring that it might be broken in pieces as a thing which she knew of no force nor value'.[60]

And that, it seemed, was that.

Catherine Howard

73. 'Virtuous and good behaviour'?

Catherine Howard was the opposite in every way from Anne of Cleves. She was English, and she was petite, plump, pretty and accomplished in the Courtly graces. She had an easy charm and an abundant store of good nature. And she knew how to attract men with a skill beyond her teenage years – perhaps indeed beyond her supposedly virginal state when she met Henry.

Catherine belonged to the mighty Howard clan. Her father, Lord Edmund, was the third son of the second Duke of Norfolk. The third Duke of Norfolk was her uncle and Anne Boleyn was her cousin. But, in Catherine's case, mighty connexions did not lead to an easy upbringing.

Her father Edmund, like most Howards, enjoyed fighting. But, unlike his own father and his elder brother Thomas, he was a brawler rather than a general. He spent his youth hanging about the Court with no very obvious employment and it was not until 1531 that his niece, Anne Boleyn, helped find him a position as Controller of Calais. Even so, the salary was barely enough for a man of his status to live on, much less to pay off his debts.

Catherine's mother, Jocasta Culpepper, was Edmund's first wife. She was co-heiress of the Culpeppers of Aylesford, Kent, and widow of Ralph Legh, by whom she already had several children. She had about ten more by Edmund in some fifteen years of marriage. She was dead by the late 1520s and Edmund went on to marry two other wives, both widows, by whom he was childless. He was dismissed from his post in Calais in 1539 and died shortly afterwards.[1]

Lord Edmund Howard, in short, was a man of no importance – save for the fact that he had a daughter who happened to become Queen of England.

Catherine was one of the younger members of his brood, which suggests that she was born in about 1520. But it is impossible to be sure. Her place of birth is also unknown, as are the places where she spent her childhood. It seems certain, however, that her mother, who brought considerable assets to the marriage, managed to keep some sort of establishment together – though Catherine's father must often have been away. In 1527, for example, Edmund complained to Wolsey that his debts were such that he dared not 'go abroad, nor come at my own house, and am fain to absent me from my wife and poor children'.

The suggestion, then, is of a scrabbled childhood, with a dominant, providing mother and a weak, debt-ridden and (to judge by the evidence of one of his later marriages) hen-pecked father. But, whatever its nature, Catherine's childhood was a short one, even by Tudor standards. Its end was marked by her mother's death, and her father's remarriage and appointment to Calais which followed each other in quick succession. Catherine, at the age of ten or twelve, was now considered a young woman and was sent off to finish her upbringing in the Household of her step-grandmother, the Dowager Duchess of Norfolk.[2]

Agnes Howard *née* Tilney was the second wife and widow of the second Duke of Norfolk. As a Dowager Duchess, she was one of the highest ranking women in England outside the royal family. She was also, thanks to her dower-rights and her tight-fistedness, one of the richest. As was customary, she kept a great Household, which was lodged, depending on her movements, in either of her main residences: at Horsham in Sussex, or at Lambeth on the south bank of the Thames opposite the King's new palace of Whitehall.[3]

When Catherine joined her step-grandmother's Household, she was placed in the Maidens' Chamber. This was a large dormitory, in which the inmates generally slept two to a bed. There, Catherine found herself among other young unmarried women of gentle or noble birth. They were connected by blood or marriage to the Howards or came from lesser families which had hitched their stars to the ducal clan. They acted as the Duchess's waiting women; they were also there, like Catherine herself, to complete their education. A music master was employed and the Duchess had clerks and secretaries who could teach them reading and writing. Also in the Household were many young gentlemen who were eager to teach the maidens other things as well.

The Duchess's Household, in short, had something of the atmosphere of a slackly run mixed boarding school. The Duchess was an imperious but ineffectual headmistress; the boys spent their time trying to get into the girls' dormitory; and there was excessive fraternization between pupils and staff.[4]

Here, at last, Catherine found herself in her element. She was a quick developer, both physically and mentally. She also showed all the drive her father lacked. The result was that she became the leader in every escapade and act of domestic rebellion. And, because she was related to the Duchess, she got away with almost all of it.

She began, as is often the way with such girls, by attracting the attentions of one of her masters. Henry Manox had been employed by the Duchess in about 1536 'to teach . . . Mrs Catherine Howard to play on the virginals'. According to Manox's admission, he 'fell in love with her' and she with him. But Catherine kept the relationship within bounds. This was not out of virtue, but rather a fierce sense of Howard pride. 'I will never be nought with you', she told him, 'and able to marry me ye be not.' But she permitted him consolatory favours which were, on more than one occasion, interrupted by the Duchess. Once, 'it chanced . . . the Duchess . . . to find them alone talking in a Chamber'. As usual, the old lady struck first and remonstrated afterwards. 'She gave . . . Mrs Catherine two or three blows and gave straight charge both to her and to

... Manox that they should never be alone together.'[5]

But a better antidote to Manox's attentions appeared in the form of Francis Dereham. Dereham was a Howard cousin and gentleman-servitor. He was of some independent means and so was able to give Catherine trinkets and lovers' tokens, such as 'a heart's-ease of silk for a New Year's gift'. He cut an altogether more dashing figure than Manox, whom he soon displaced in Catherine's affections. She also permitted him attentions denied to the socially inferior music master. These included admission to the Holy of Holies, the Maidens' Chamber.[6]

In theory, the Maidens' Chamber was out of bounds to all men. And, to enforce the rule, the Duchess 'every night ... would cause the keys of the [Maidens'] Chamber to be brought to her Chamber'. But Catherine quickly saw a way round the problem and suborned the Duchess's chamberer or maid, Mary Lascelles, 'to steal the key and bring it to her'. The door was unlocked and Dereham and other favoured gentlemen were admitted to enjoy the delights within.[7]

'They would', the excluded Manox bitterly observed, 'commonly banquet and be merry there till two or three of the clock in the morning.' 'Wine, strawberries, apples and other things to make good cheer' were served and an escape route for the intruders was carefully spied out 'into the little gallery' next door.[8]

Jealous, angry and frustrated, Manox decided to inform the Duchess of these midnight feasts by an anonymous letter:

Your Grace

It shall be meet you take good heed to your gentlewomen for if it shall like you half an hour after you shall be a-bed to rise suddenly and visit their Chamber you shall see that which shall displease you. But if you make anybody of counsel you shall be deceived. Make then fewer your secretary.

The letter was laid in the Duchess's pew, where she found it and read it. 'When she came home [she] stormed with her women and declared how she was advertised ... of their misrule.'[9]

*

Catherine was determined to get to the bottom of the plot against her. Employing her already developed skills in larceny, '[she] stole the letter out of my Lady's gilt coffer and showed it to Dereham who copied it and thereupon it was laid in the coffer again'. Dereham immediately guessed the authorship of the letter and tackled Manox, calling him 'Knave' and saying 'that he neither loved [Catherine] nor him'.[10]

But Dereham need hardly have worried. For, despite the Duchess's occasional outbursts, neither she nor the other senior members of the Household, including Catherine's aunt, the Countess of Bridgewater, and her uncle, Lord William Howard, took her goings-on very seriously. The Countess indeed reproved Catherine for her 'banqueting by night'. But that was because she feared 'it would hurt her beauty', not her morals. Lord William made even lighter of it all, saying 'What mad wenches! Can you not be merry amongst yourselves but you must thus fall out?'[11]

Catherine Howard was, therefore, already a woman with a past when, in late 1539 and in anticipation of Henry's forthcoming marriage, she was appointed one of Queen Anne of Cleves's maidens.

Dereham was distraught, since he knew he would lose her. 'If I were gone', she remembered him saying, 'he would not tarry long in the [Duchess's] house.' Her reply was brutal: 'he might do as he list'.

For she would let nothing and no one stop her promotion. 'All that knew me, and kept my company, know how glad and desirous I was to come to the Court,' she insisted.[12]

Catherine's instincts were right, for she took to the Court like a duck to water. Whitehall and Greenwich, after all, were only Horsham and Lambeth writ large. There were the same preening, predatory young men. There was the same jockeying and rivalry. There were the same fish to catch, only they were bigger.

Catherine's name was soon linked with one of the hotter properties in the Court: Thomas Culpepper, a Gentleman of the Privy Chamber and her relative. He was a handsome, delinquent boy and a favourite of men and women alike. As Henry's former Page, he had sometimes slept in his master's bed, and, when he got older, he had a queue of female admirers. But with Catherine, it seems, it was different. She was his female equivalent and there was an instant, powerful attraction between them. Soon, it was rumoured, they would marry. But there were quarrels and they drifted apart. 'If you heard such a report [that she should marry Culpepper]', Catherine dismissively assured a former admirer, 'you heard more than I do know'.[13]

For meantime Catherine had landed a bigger catch – indeed the biggest of all.

It was love at first sight. Or, as the old Duchess heard, 'the King's Highness did cast a fantasy to Catherine Howard the first time that ever his Grace saw her'. When this was is not clear. It might even have been in the autumn of 1539, in the run-up to Anne of Cleves's arrival in England. But, certainly, by the late spring of 1540 a fully developed love affair was under way. It was public knowledge by June, and everyone assumed that the couple had consummated their relationship long before their marriage was celebrated on 8 August 1540 at Hampton Court.[14]

There were even strong rumours that Catherine went pregnant to the altar.

It is easy to read Henry's motives. Physically repelled by Anne of Cleves, and humiliated by his sexual failure with her, he sought and found consolation from Catherine. We can also guess that sex, which had been impossible with Anne, was easy with her. And it was easy because she made it easy. Henry, lost in pleasure, never seems to have asked himself how she obtained such skill.

Instead, he attributed it all to love and his own recovered youth.

Of course, other, less innocent, forces were at work. Norfolk sang his niece's praises. Gardiner, who had something of an eye for the ladies himself, made his episcopal palace available for midnight banquets which far outdid the impromptu entertainments in the Maidens' Chamber at

Horsham or Lambeth. And the old Duchess gave Catherine new and fashionable clothes and the benefit of her advice on how to handle Henry.[15]

Henry, however, was indifferent or oblivious to such manipulation. Indeed, in so far as it smoothed the path of his relationship with Catherine, he probably welcomed it. For he had eyes, ears and time only for her. Kingship was put on hold, foreign policy stalled, and the block and the stake stood idle as life at Court became one long honeymoon.

Even the weather conspired to help. The summer of 1540 was unusually 'hot and dry'. 'No rain', the chronicler Wriothesley reported, fell from June till eight days after Michaelmas (that is, till 7 October). This summer-long drought inflicted terrible suffering on many of Henry's subjects. Cattle died of thirst, and men and women of plague. But, for the King and Queen, it created a perfect, prolonged hunting season. In August 1540, when Henry was at Windsor, the French ambassador, Marillac, reported that nothing had happened because the King had 'gone to the chase with a small company'. A month later, the Court had moved to Ampthill in Bedfordshire. Otherwise it was the same. 'Nothing being spoken of here,' Marillac noted, 'but the chase and the banquets to the new Queen.'[16]

In September, Marillac visited the Court, probably at Grafton, and had an opportunity to form his own opinion of Catherine. He thought she was graceful, rather than the great beauty he had been led to expect. She dressed herself and her ladies in the French fashion. And she had chosen as her motto *'Non autre volonté que la sienne* [No other wish but his]'.[17]

Now, this may be no more than Catherine doing what came naturally. On the other hand, it could be interpreted as an ingenious combination of two of the most successful management techniques of her predecessors: Anne Boleyn's deployment of seductive French fashions in behaviour and dress, and Jane Seymour's carefully calculated submissiveness.

Whatever its origins, however, the result gave Catherine (and her husband) the best of both worlds and Henry was more demonstratively in love with her than with any previous wife. 'The King', Marillac reported, 'is so amorous of her that he cannot treat her well enough and caresses her more than he did the others.'[18]

Marillac's picture of an infatuated King is borne out by the inventory of Catherine's jewels, which shows that Henry lavished an Aladdin's cave of precious stones on her. Most formed part of his wedding gift to his new Queen. The gift included an 'upper biliment' or trimming for the top of a French hood, 'of goldsmith work enamelled and garnished with 7 fair diamonds, 7 fair rubies and 7 fair pearls'; a 'square' or shaped necklace 'containing 29 rubies and 29 clusters of pearls being 4 pearls in every cluster', and an 'ouch' or pendant 'of gold having a very fair table diamond and a very fair ruby with a long pearl hanging at the same'.

And these same jewels, minutely depicted, appear in Holbein's miniature of the Queen. Dispute has raged as to whether its subject really is Catherine. But the identification of the jewels settles the issue once and for all. It also establishes, for the first time, her exact appearance. She had auburn hair, pale skin, dark eyes and brows, the rather fetching beginnings of a double chin, and an expression that was at once quizzical and come-hither.

It is easy, in short, to understand what Henry saw in her and why the rain of gifts continued. He gave her others, at The More in October 1540, perhaps on the occasion of the anniversary of their first meeting; while Christmas and New Year 1540–1 provided an excuse for yet more lavish presents, including a 'square' set with thirty-three diamonds and sixty rubies and bordered with pearls, and a jewelled sable muffler.

Henry was caught. And nothing, save Catherine's own mistakes, could ever release him. 'The new Queen', Marillac informed his government in November, 'has completely acquired the King's Grace and the other [Anne] is no more spoken of than if she were dead.'[19]

The ambassador's exaggeration is a pardonable one. Nevertheless, Anne of Cleves was very much alive and her presence as a sort of ghost from the past continued to be an embarrassment – for Henry, for Anne herself and, perhaps above all, for Catherine. For, despite her short reign, Anne had become remarkably popular. Her divorce, Marillac reported, had been 'to the great regret of this people, who loved and esteemed her as the sweetest, most gracious and kindest Queen they ever had or would desire'. This assessment might be dismissed as ambassadorial gossip. But Marillac's judgement is confirmed by the English chronicler Wriothesley. '[It] was great pity', he commented, 'that so good a lady as she should have lost her great joy.' And Wriothesley's verdict carries the more weight, since, as a religious conservative, he had no reason to be committed to the Cleves marriage. Instead, it must have been Anne's own personal qualities of modesty and goodness which had won his regard.[20]

Modesty and goodness, on the other hand, were not, perhaps, Catherine's strongest suits. Nevertheless, Anne had to be fitted into a world in which she, as the King's adoptive sister, could play a comfortable second fiddle to Catherine, as Henry's wife and Queen.

As part of the divorce settlement, Henry had assured Anne of a welcome at Court. But, wisely, the offer was neither extended nor taken up for the first few months of the King's new marriage. At New Year 1541, however, the ice was broken. Chapuys's account, on which we largely depend, makes Anne take the initiative. But equally she must have received permission for her planned visit to Court.[21]

Anne began by sending Henry a magnificent New Year's gift of two fine horses caparisoned in mauve velvet. Then, on 3 January, she presented herself at Hampton Court. There was a delay while Chancellor Audley and the Earl of Sussex, who, as Cromwell's successor as Lord Great Chamberlain, was ceremonial head of the royal Household, briefed Queen Catherine on the delicate question of etiquette presented by her meeting with ex-Queen Anne. There were no precedents and they must have resorted to a mixture of common sense and invention.

Finally, Catherine was ready and Anne was admitted to the Queen's presence. Only a few months before, Catherine had been one of Anne's women. She had knelt in her presence and spoken to her only when spoken to. How, everyone must have wondered, would Anne cope with the role reversal?

She did so by giving a virtuoso performance of humility. 'Having entered the room', Chapuys reported, 'Lady Anne approached the Queen with as much reverence and punctilious ceremony as if she herself were the most insignificant damsel about Court.' 'All the time', he continued, 'addressing the Queen on her knees'.

But Catherine was not to be outdone. Her schoolgirlish humour must have tempted her to laugh. But her sense of decorum and her coaching carried the day and she was all graciousness. She asked Anne, nay begged her, to rise and 'received her most kindly, showing her great favour and courtesy'.

So far, Henry was not to be seen. Instead, he left it to the two women in his life to establish the appropriate relationship between them – of submission, on Anne's part, and gracious acceptance, on Catherine's. But, once it was safely accomplished, he appeared and, if anything, outdid Catherine in his courtesy to Anne.

'The King', Chapuys reported, 'entered the room, and, after making a very low bow to [the] Lady Anne, embraced and kissed her.' Then all three sat down to supper at the same table. Throughout the meal, they kept 'as good a mien and countenance and look[ed] as unconcerned as if there had been nothing between them'. The conversation continued a while after supper until Henry withdrew, leaving the two women once more to themselves. They passed the time in dancing: first with each other and then with two Gentlemen of the King's Household.

Was Catherine's partner perhaps her old flame, Thomas Culpepper?

The next day, the show of Happy Families continued 'with conversation, amusement and mirth'. Catherine gave a present of a ring and two lap dogs to Anne, who, after dinner on the 5th, left Court for her own house at Richmond.[22]

The visit had been a triumphant success all round. Anne had established a place in the English royal family which she was to keep across three reigns, while Catherine had shown herself to be a model consort: gracious, forgiving and willing to let bygones be bygones.

These were, of course, the traditional qualities of a Queen. But, under Henry, their display had been the exception rather than the rule. For all of Catherine's predecessors, one way or another, had been partisan, political Queens: each had had her own axe to grind, and each had ground her axe with a will. Catherine of Aragon represented the Spanish alliance. Anne Boleyn fought for Reform, and Jane Seymour against it. And even Anne of Cleves was intended to be Cromwell's stalking-horse in the final push for Reform.

The natural thing was for Catherine to follow in their footsteps and become the figurehead for a revived anti-Reform policy. This, it seems certain, was the part which Gardiner and Catherine's Howard backers had assigned to her. But would she do as they wished? Or would she strike out on her own?

Here a fresh look is needed. Catherine's behaviour in her step-grandmother's Household has often been seen to indicate that she was a crass, self-indulgent teenager, without a thought in her head, unless others had put it there. But a different reading is possible. Catherine, like many teenagers, certainly showed herself to be wilful and sensual. But she also displayed leadership, resourcefulness and independence, which are qualities less commonly found in headstrong young girls.

At Horsham and Lambeth, of course, she was a rebel without a cause, other than her own pleasure. But at Court, and as Queen, her independence of mind could be put to better use.

But would it be? As it happens, there *are* early indications that Catherine was prepared to think for herself. For example, she quickly established good relations with Cranmer, Gardiner's *bête noire*. Similarly, as we have just seen, she responded enthusiastically to Anne of Cleves's attempt to bury the hatchet. All this suggests at least a reluctance to toe the factional line, if not a positive commitment to reconciliation and healing.[23]

Then there is the question of her sensuality. The long, withdrawing roar of Victorian morality inhibited generations of historians from treating this with anything other than disapproval and distaste. But we are past that now. We can confront sex as a fact, not as a sin. We can even, if pushed, see a sort of virtue in promiscuity.

Catherine benefits enormously from this shift in moral values. True, she was a good-time girl. But, like many good-time girls, she was also warm, loving and good-natured. She wanted to have a good time. But she wanted other people to have a good time, too. And she was prepared to make some effort to see that they did.

Nor, refreshingly in that God-infested century, does she seem to have had much truck with religion. If she thought of God at all, it was, perhaps, as a sort of superior Duchess of Norfolk: like her step-grandmother, He was haphazardly tyrannical and a kill-joy. But, with a little ingenuity, His strictures, too, could be avoided.

This was not the stuff of martyrs. But nor was it the stuff that made martyrs of others. And that, in the reign of Henry VIII, was something.

Catherine, in short, had begun rather well. She had a good heart, and a less bad head than most of her chroniclers have assumed. But would the pressure of politics and kin let her keep to her path of live and let live? And would she be able to carry Henry with her?

The first test came quickly. On 3 January, as Catherine was entertaining Anne of Cleves at the start of her visit to Court, the Council was interrogating Thomas Smith, the Clerk of Catherine's Council. His fellow-examinee was William Grey, 'sometime servant to the late Lord Cromwell', and the two were charged with writing and publishing invectives against each other. Also in trouble was the leading printer-publisher, Richard Grafton, who was accused of printing and distributing the offending material.

At first sight it is difficult to see why the Council bothered to get itself involved in a private quarrel of literary men. Such quarrels were as frequent, intractable and insignificant then as now. Today, they take the form of 'debates' in learned journals, or leak and counter-leak in gossip columns. Then, a 'flytyng', or ritual public exchange of insults in verse, was the established device.

Smith's and Grey's exchanges followed the traditional form. But they gave them a new and dangerous twist by using them to take opposite sides on the burning political issues of the day. Smith struck the first blow by attacking Grey's fallen master Cromwell:

> Both man and child is glad to tell
> Of that false traitor Thomas Cromwell
> Now that he is set to learn to spell
> Sing troll-a-way

Grey replied in kind and in equally bad verse. It was, he began, unChristian to rail on the dead. Then he went on to suggest that, though Cromwell was a traitor,

> Yet dare I say that the King of his grace
> Hath forgiven him that great trespass.

Finally, he went fully on the offensive, and accused Smith of being Popish. Smith upheld, he claimed:

> . . . both monks and friars
> Nuns and naughty packs and lewd lousy liars,
> The Bishop of Rome with all his rotten squires.
> To build such a church thou art much to blame.

Smith responded hotly to the charge of Papistry and threatened to seek redress 'before the highest powers'. He did not name them. But since he described himself in print as 'servant to the King's Royal Majesty and Clerk of the Queen's Grace's Council', there was not much doubt who was intended.[24]

It all threatened to get out of hand, and justified the Council's intervention. On the 3rd, Smith and Grey were subject to 'long examination'. The intention, clearly, was to discover whether they had written on their own initiative or whether they were acting as a front for other, more powerful figures. The results seem to have been inconclusive and they were ordered to reappear before the Council the following morning at 7 a.m.

Bearing in mind Smith's status as a royal servant, Henry must have been consulted overnight about his treatment. As, surely, must Catherine. But neither lifted a finger to protect him and on the 4th he joined Grey and Grafton in being 'committed to the Fleet [Prison] during the King's pleasure'.[25]

Catherine, Smith's imprisonment made clear, had no intention of following Anne Boleyn as the patroness of religious controversy.

The tensions which led to the clash between Smith and Grey – between Reformer and anti-Reformer – of course operated at the highest political levels as well. The fact had been obscured by Catherine's marriage and the prolonged Progress of 1540, which imposed a kind of truce. But, with the New Year, politics began to return to their normal state of vicious in-fighting. On 17 January, Sir Thomas Wyatt, Anne Boleyn's former suitor and Cromwell's protégé, was led bound to the Tower. And Sir Ralph Sadler, another Cromwell client, who had succeeded him as joint Secretary, was also arrested. These, evidently, were victims of Cromwell's enemies. A few weeks later, on 5 February, Cromwell's friends struck back by getting Sir John Wallop, the highly conservative former ambassador to France, sent to the Tower as well.[26]

It was tit for tat. And where and when would it stop?

Marillac, the French ambassador who had correctly predicted the crisis of 1540, took the gloomiest view. 'There could be', he wrote home immediately after Wyatt's arrest, 'no worse war than the English carry on against each other.' 'For', he continued, 'after Cromwell had brought down the greatest of the realm, from the Marquess [of Exeter] to the Master of the Horse [Carew], now others have arisen who will never rest till they have done as much to all Cromwell's adherents.' 'And God knows,' he concluded, 'whether after them others will not recommence the feast.'[27]

But this time Marillac's prediction was wrong. Wyatt, Sadler and

Wallop were not executed. Indeed, they not only survived but were restored to favour and office as well.

Saturn, it seemed, had stopped eating his children.

What had happened? Were the rival groupings at Court and on the Council so evenly balanced that neither was able seriously to harm the other? Was Henry, freed from Cromwell's malign influence, now consciously pursuing a policy of moderation and balance? Or was he simply too happy in his new marriage to bother with treason and vengeance?

All seem likely.

But the official explanation was different again. According to the Council's letter to the new English ambassador in France, Henry had been predisposed to pardon Wyatt and Wallop because of their ready acknowledgement of their faults. But what had been decisive were 'the most humble suits and intercessions made unto [the King], both for [Wallop] and for Wyatt, by the Queen's Highness'.[28]

For once, bearing in mind what we know about both Henry and Catherine, there seems no reason to disbelieve a government handout.

Chapuys's account adds an interesting twist to the story, since he links the pardon with Catherine's inauguration ceremonies as Queen. These, following the precedents of her immediate predecessors, took the form, not of a coronation, but of a river pageant.[29]

The peculiarity lay in their delay. Anne Boleyn, Jane Seymour and Anne of Cleves had all made their river *entrée* into the City within a few weeks of their marriage to Henry. But the long, hot summer of 1540, the extended Progress, the plague and the pleasures of marriage combined to postpone Catherine's inaugural visit to the City, and it was not until 19 March 1541, more than seven months after her wedding, that she passed for the first time under London Bridge.

But the City made up for the delay with the warmth of its welcome. The Mayor and Livery Companies in their gaily trimmed barges waited to receive the King and Queen between London Bridge and the Tower. At 3 o'clock, the royal barge, in which, most unusually, Henry and

Catherine travelled together, shot the bridge. The City barges then formed an escort for the King and Queen as they were rowed downstream. The Tower 'shot a great shot of guns' and the ships lining the river fired salutes all the way to Greenwich.[30]

Chapuys, who could be dismissive about English ceremonial, was impressed. 'The people of this City', he reported, 'honoured her with a most splendid reception.' As for Catherine, she struck while the iron was hot. 'From this triumphal march', the ambassador continued, 'the Queen took courage to beg and entreat the King for the release of Mr Wyatt, a prisoner in the Tower.'[31]

This showed a shrewd sense of priorities. To have sued first for Wallop, who was one of her own, would have savoured of *parti pris*. But to begin with Wyatt, whose affiliations were all with the enemies of her house, established that her gesture was disinterested. Only once Wyatt was restored to the King's good graces (though on the hard condition of taking back his hated estranged wife) did she kneel once more for Wallop. And, once more, she was successful.

There was scope also for Catherine's emollient talents nearer home, among Henry's strange, fractious brood of half-siblings.

With Mary, the eldest and most difficult, she got off to an awkward start. Mary, who was at least four years older than her new stepmother, had failed (on Chapuys's own admission) 'to treat her with the same respect as her two predecessors'. Catherine, in revenge, moved to cut back her establishment of maids. But a chastened Mary, Chapuys reported, had 'found means to conciliate her and thinks her maids will remain'.[32]

The storm in a tea-cup over, the two established cordial relations, though the serious Mary and the pleasure-loving Catherine were too different in character ever to become real friends. Nevertheless, they were able to co-operate in bringing about the most important gesture of family solidarity since the Divorce from Catherine of Aragon.

Chapuys's account makes clear that he recognized its significance. 'A week ago', he reported on 17 May, 'the King and the Queen went . . . to

visit the Prince [at Waltham Holy Cross in Essex] at the request of the
[Lady Mary], but chiefly at the intercession of the Queen herself.' The
visit went well and 'upon that occasion', Chapuys continued, 'the King
granted [Mary] full permission to reside at Court, and the Queen has
countenanced it with good grace'.[33]

Naturally, the ambassador's narrative omits Elizabeth, who was still
unforgiven by Imperialists on account of her position as Anne Boleyn's
daughter. But Catherine made sure that she, too, had some sort of part in
the family get-together. On 4 May, a day or two before the visit to
Waltham, Catherine travelled by river from Chelsea to her town-house
at Baynard's Castle. The next day, 'my Lady Elizabeth' was taken by
water from Suffolk House in Southwark to Chelsea and on the 6th, the
Queen made the return journey from Baynard's Castle to Chelsea as
well.[34]

Quite what these journeys signify is unclear. Catherine could have
been supervising the preparation of Chelsea as Elizabeth's residence on
the 4th and making sure that she was settled in with her second visit on
the 6th. Or she could have been collecting her to take her to join the
family party at Waltham.

At any rate, she was showing an appropriate concern for her younger
step-daughter, which she also expressed by giving Elizabeth little
presents of jewellery alongside her more substantial gifts to Mary.[35]

Catherine's intervention had the desired effect of fully normalizing
relations among Henry's offspring and at New Year 1543 all three of his
children, apparently for the first time, exchanged New Year's gifts.[36]

But Catherine's indiscriminate good nature had other, less desirable,
consequences. She might be indifferent to the broader Howard political
agenda. But she felt strong loyalty to those who had brought her up. She
was also eager to do what she could for her former fellow inmates in the
Duchess's Household.

The result was that the plums of patronage fell in some otherwise
unlikely places. Lord William Howard replaced Wallop as ambassador
to France, on her nomination. Katherine Tilney, who had shared her bed

at Horsham, was made one of her women. And she even gave a position in her Household to Francis Dereham, who had returned some time previously from a short, self-imposed exile in Ireland and was in London kicking his heels once more.

Now, it is important here to be clear about Catherine's behaviour. It was *not*, as almost all modern historians agree, improper and irresponsible to the point of lunacy. On the contrary. Looking after one's own was a moral imperative in the sixteenth century and long remained so. Which is why other powerful figures in the Dowager's entourage also involved themselves in fixing Dereham's Court appointment. 'Lady Bridgewater and Lady Howard [Lord William's wife]', the Dowager recalled, 'sued to her to speak to the Queen for Dereham.' And, though the evidence is unclear, the Duchess herself may have given her blessing to the arrangement by bringing Dereham to Court and formally presenting him to the Queen.[37]

There *was* a danger nonetheless.

For Catherine's whole position as Queen depended on drawing a veil of decent obscurity over her days at Horsham and Lambeth. This does not seem to have been too difficult. Many, even most, Tudor girls (if we believe Chapuys's jaundiced verdict on English womanhood) had similarly murky pasts. So it was in no one's interest to dig too deep. Least of all was it in Henry's. Wildly in love, he had, it seems, asked no questions and had been told no lies.[38]

It was a happy arrangement.

Nevertheless, it depended on everybody observing certain rules. The first and most important was to distinguish sharply time past from time present. For in the Tudor Court, as in the future Soviet Union, individuals and moments were air-brushed out of history. In the past Catherine had been a maid and Anne of Cleves a Queen. In the past, too, Catherine and Dereham had been lovers, perhaps, as it would appear, consummated lovers. But the present required them all to forget these earlier selves. Anne of Cleves survived because she showed herself willing to do so. Catherine had a fair stab at it. But would Dereham?

The signs were not good. He quickly quarrelled, for instance, with

Mr Johns, one of the Queen's Gentlemen Ushers. The occasion was Dereham's habit of lingering over his dinner or supper. This was a privilege reserved for the Queen's Council, as the senior members of the Household were known, and not for riffraff like Dereham. Outraged by his presumption, Johns sent him a messenger to know 'whether he were of the Queen's Council?' Dereham was unabashed. 'Go to Mr Johns', he ordered the messenger, 'and tell him I was of the Queen's Council before he knew her and shall be when she hath forgotten him.'[39]

The reply was magnificent. But it was not wise. For it provoked a whole series of questions. What did Dereham mean when he said he had been 'of Council' with the Queen? Did he really mean that he had been a friend and advisor of 'Mrs Catherine Howard' *before* she married Henry? If so, just what relationship between them did this suggest?

The proper answer to any of these questions would have destroyed Catherine. But still her luck held, and thoughts turned to the summer Progress.

The Progress to the north, first planned in 1536, had been postponed on one ground or another ever since. But now Henry resolved to make it a reality. He had a mixture of motives. Another abortive Yorkshire rising had been nipped in the bud in the spring. There was the prospect of meeting at York with his nephew, James V of Scotland. But, above all, he would make the Progress with a Howard Queen at his side. And the name of Howard counted for as much in the north as that of Tudor.

The planning got seriously underway in May 1541. And Chapuys was clearly surprised by the scale of the preparations. Henry intended, he reported, 'to repair to the Northern counties in pompous array, followed by at least 5,000 horse'.[40]

The King and Queen left London, according to plan, at the end of June. But then the problems began. James of Scotland played hard to get. The weather was as unseasonably wet that summer as it had been dry the previous one with the result, Marillac reported, that 'the roads leading to the North . . . have been flooded and the carts and baggage could not proceed without great difficulty'. And Catherine herself fell ill.[41]

In the face of these accumulated difficulties, the Court lingered damply in Bedfordshire and Northamptonshire for most of July and the whole thing, Marillac heard, was nearly called off once more. But this time too much had been invested in the preparations and too many hopes had been raised for cancellation to be a feasible option. Finally, in the third week of July, and about a month late, the Court left Northampton on the first leg of its journey to the north of England – that third of his kingdom which Henry had never previously visited and which he knew much less well than his titular realm of France.

The Progress was to be the crowning glory of Catherine's reign – and its undoing.

After spending four or five days at Collyweston, the great country palace of Henry's grandmother, Lady Margaret Beaufort, the King and Queen crossed into Lincolnshire. The county had been the seat of the first of the northern rebellions of 1536. Both the rebellion and its suppression had been traumatic, and relations between the locality and the crown had not yet recovered. The Progress was intended to be the moment of healing. It would bury the lingering resentment, on one side, and the mistrust, on the other, and knit up King and subjects into a unity once more.[42]

By and large, it was successful. There were processional *entrées* into Stamford and Boston and, on 9 August, into Lincoln, the regional capital. The royal tents were set up at Temple Bruer, seven miles to the south-east of the city, where Henry and Catherine had a picnic dinner. Then they were greeted by three distinct groups: the gentry and their servants of the Parts of Lindsey (one of the three administrative divisions of the county), the mayor and citizens of Lincoln, and the clergy of the Cathedral. Each group had played a part in the revolt and each now made amends. First, a representative of the clergy made a speech and offered a gift, to be followed in turn by spokesmen for the gentry and citizens who did likewise. The King handed the copy of the Recorder's speech to the Duke of Norfolk and gentlemen and citizens knelt and cried: 'Jesus save your Grace'.

By this time Henry and Catherine had changed into more

sumptuous dress: his of cloth of gold, hers of cloth of silver. The heralds put on their tabards, the Gentlemen Pensioners presented their battle axes, Lord Hastings carried the sword of state, and the Masters of the Horse led the two magnificently caparisoned 'horses of estate' after the King and Queen. In this order, and preceded by the gentry and citizens, Henry and Catherine made their entry into the city. At the west doors of Lincoln Cathedral there was a carpet with cushions and faldstools. The King and Queen knelt down, and kissed the crucifix, which was presented to them by the bishop in cope and mitre. He 'censed' them and, through the clouds of incense, they entered the Cathedral to pray at the reserved sacrament while the choir sang the *Te Deum*.

Then, at the end of a long day, the couple withdrew to their lodgings at Lincoln Castle.[43]

Henry was quickly asleep. But there were light and movement in the Queen's apartments till far into the small hours. Even more strangely, the door to the backstairs, which led directly to Catherine's bedchamber, was left ajar. The watchman, doing his rounds with his light, noticed the open door. He pulled it to, locked it from the outside and continued on his way. Shortly after, two figures approached and, after fumbling with the lock, somehow got the door opened. One remained on guard outside; the other entered.[44]

Was he a thief? Or was he aiming to steal something more precious even than the Queen's jewels?

From Lincoln, the route of the Progress turned inland towards Yorkshire. Just across the border lay the teeming hunting grounds of Hatfield Chase. Here Henry took an extended holiday from the political side of the Progress. He and Catherine stayed in magnificent tents and pavilions which were, in reality, fully equipped portable palaces. And they spent their days in hunting and their nights in feasting.

The French ambassador, Marillac, who accompanied the Court on the Progress, described one such day. A large area of the Chase was enclosed; it contained ponds and marshes as well as scrub and woodland. The latter was rich in game, the former in fish and wild fowl. Hunters and fishers in boats went on to the water, while bowmen stood on the land. The result was an extraordinary mixed bag of flesh, fish and fowl: two hundred stags and deer, 'a great quantity of young swans, two boats full of river birds and as much of great pikes and other fish'.

It was a scene of pastoral bliss from a hunting tapestry. Almost, indeed, the Garden of Eden. Nature gave with a prodigal hand, and deer grazed near the tents as tame 'as if they had been domestic cattle'. Proudly, Henry pointed them out to Marillac who was supping with him in his tent.[45]

In this Garden of Eden, there was also an Eve. For it was at Hatfield that '[Catherine] looked out of her Privy Chamber window on Mr Culpepper'. It was a look of desire and her woman remembered it.[46]

Henry then moved to Pontefract, which was 'one of the finest castles in England', as Marillac admiringly noted, for another extended visit. Here the King received the submission of Yorkshire. The ceremonies were almost as curious as the hunt at Hatfield Chase and they were described by Marillac with the same minute interest. The gentry and other notables were divided into two groups: the sheep and the goats. 'Those who in the rebellion remained faithful were ranked apart', the ambassador reported, 'and graciously received by the King and praised for their fidelity.' 'The others', he continued, 'who were of the conspiracy, among whom appeared the Archbishop of York, were a little further off on their knees.' As in Lincolnshire, a spokesman then made their submission. 'One of them', Marillac wrote, 'speaking for all, made a long harangue confessing their treason in marching against their sovereign and his Council, thanking him for pardoning so great an offence and begging that if any relics of indignation remained he would dismiss them.' 'They then', Marillac concluded, 'delivered several bulky submissions in writing.'[47]

One survives. 'We your humble servants, the inhabitants of this your Grace's county of York', it begins, 'confess that we wretches ... have most grievously, heinously and wantonly offended your . . . Majesty.' They promise henceforward to be good subjects and to pray for the preservation of King Henry, Queen Catherine and Prince Edward.

And no doubt Catherine lent her prayers to theirs. They received 'a benign answer'. It was like the pardons of Wyatt and Wallop writ large.[48]

At Pontefract, there was another odd incident. Denny, sent as usual from the King to the Queen, 'one night found [her bedchamber door] bolted'.[49]

But, with his usual discretion, he said nothing about it. At the time.

From Pontefract the Progress moved to York, by easy stages and with a major detour to inspect the fortifications at Hull. At York, Henry lingered much longer than the pre-published programme of the Progress envisaged. Marillac was puzzled. Twelve hundred or a thousand workmen were labouring night and day to complete the refurbishment of the dissolved Abbey of St Mary's into a new northern palace for the King. Henry had also, the ambassador noted, 'brought from London his richest tapestry, plate and dress, both for himself and his archers, pages and gentlemen, with marvellous provision of victuals from all parts'.[50]

Were the preparations, the ambassador wondered, for the meeting with James V of Scotland? Or were they for Catherine's coronation in the Minster which would follow the birth of the Duke of York?[51]

In the event, neither the King of Scots nor the Duke of York appeared, and the Court began its slow return journey southwards.

The Court arrived at Hampton Court on 29 October, just in time for the celebrations of the great Feasts of All Saints Day on 1 November and All Souls Day on the 2nd. Henry, who had noticed nothing of the strange goings-on in the Queen's apartments during his visit to the north, and had not been told about them either, was in a genial and expansive mood. The Progress, despite James V's failure to keep the rendezvous at York, had been a political success. The King had enjoyed himself and was happy.

For at last, he thought, he had found the right wife.

His feelings were reported a little later in a letter from the Council.

'Now in his old days', the King felt, 'after sundry troubles of mind which have happened unto him by marriages, [he had] obtained . . . a jewel [in Catherine]'. 'For womanhood and very perfect love towards him' she would be 'to his quietness'; she was also likely to '[bring] forth the desired fruits of marriage'. And in conduct, above all, she was perfect, showing outwardly all 'virtue and good behaviour'.[52]

All Saints Day was one of the Days of Estate when the King took communion publicly in the Chapel Royal. There at Hampton Court, under the splendours of the blue and gold roof of Wolsey's Chapel which depicts the angelic host blowing on trumpets in triumph, Henry offered up his grateful prayers for his new-found marital happiness with Catherine. 'He gave [God] most humble and hearty thanks for the good life he led and trusted to lead with [the Queen].' He also ordered Bishop Longland of Lincoln, his confessor, 'to make like prayer and give like thanks with him'.

The following day, however, the Chapel witnessed a very different scene. Henry arrived in his Closet for the mass for All Souls Day. But on his seat he found a letter. He opened it and read it. It was from Cranmer and it made sensational charges against his 'jewel' of womanhood. During her time in the Duchess's Household, the letter claimed, Francis Dereham 'hath lied in bed with her in his doublet and hose between the sheets a hundred nights'. And Henry Manox also 'knew a privy mark of her body'.[53]

Knowledge of Catherine's relationships with both Manox and Dereham was, as we have seen, an open secret in the Duchess's Household. But the allegations in this letter went much further than anything the Duchess or Lady Bridgewater or Lord William Howard had allowed themselves to see.

Clearly, the information was the result of an inside job. Its source was Mary Hall *née* Lascelles, who had been a serving woman in the Duchess's Household at the same time as Catherine. She had spoken to her brother, John Lascelles, and Lascelles, in turn, had spoken to Cranmer. Lascelles claimed that the information had emerged innocently. But the fact that he was later burned as a Protestant heretic strongly suggests that he had a factional motive in denouncing the Howard Queen.[54]

Similarly, Cranmer's behaviour in the affair was complex – as Cranmer's behaviour usually was. Once the information had come to his hands, his oath as a Councillor, as well as his personal concern for Henry's honour and happiness, required him to disclose it to the King. But how unhappy was he with his task?

One thing is clear. Cranmer was not, as used to be thought, simply pursuing a Reforming vendetta against a 'Catholic' consort. Instead, as we have seen, he had got on surprisingly well with Catherine. According to some reports, in the dark days of June and July 1540, she had protected him when it seemed likely that he would share the fate of Cromwell. Nor, thanks in part to her indifference to the Howard political agenda, was the persecution of Reformers in the wake of the Act of Six Articles anything like as fierce as might have been expected. On the other hand, Catherine was also indifferent to Cranmer's concerns. She had no interest in Reform. And, so long as she was Queen, there was always the possibility that her 'Catholic' relatives, the Howards, and their allies, including Gardiner, might be able to use her to initiate a fresh persecution of Reformers.[55]

So, Cranmer decided, Catherine should go. His decision was reached with some regret. But, as so often in his career, he did not let regrets get in the way of stern necessity.

But even Cranmer, well as he knew Henry, must have been disconcerted by the King's reaction. For Henry at first flatly refused to believe the allegations. He, who had been willing to magnify every scrap of gossip against Anne Boleyn, loftily dismissed the denunciations against Catherine Howard as 'rather a forged matter than of truth'.

The King did agree, however, that the charges should be investigated. But, to protect Catherine, whose reputation, he was sure, would be vindicated, from 'any spark of scandal', he ordered the investigation to be conducted in the utmost secrecy.

It was entrusted to four confidential Councillors: Fitzwilliam, who had succeeded Cromwell as Lord Privy Seal; Russell, who was now a Baron and Lord Admiral; the Master of the Horse, Sir Anthony Browne; and Secretary Wriothesley. As instructed, they proceeded in the strictest confidentiality. Elaborate subterfuges were used to summon witnesses and suspects. And the Councillors wrote the transcripts of the examinations themselves. This resulted in some documents of rare illegibility. Which is one reason why they have been so little used by historians. The other is the sensational nature of their contents, which I reproduce here in unexpurgated form for the first time.[56]

On 5 November Fitzwilliam began with Mary Hall *née* Lascelles. She not only stuck to her story but provided shocking corroborative detail. When she had learned of the extent of Manox's affair with Catherine, she testified, she had reproached the music teacher for his folly and presumption. But he had laughed in her face. 'I know her well enough', Manox had boasted, 'for I have had her by the cunt, and I know it among a hundred.' 'And she loves me', he had continued, 'and I love her, and she hath said to me that I shall have her maidenhead, though it be painful to her, and not doubting but I will be good to her hereafter.'[57]

Meanwhile, that same day, Manox himself was being interrogated at Lambeth by Wriothesley. Under the Secretary's cold questioning, the music teacher's boasts shrank to a more complex and credible story. Catherine, as we have seen, had refused him full intercourse. Manox accepted this, but demanded a token of her affection. 'Yet', he said to her, 'let me feel your secret (naming the thing plainly) and then I shall think that indeed you love me.' 'I am content', Catherine replied, 'so as you will desire no more but that.' Manox gave his word as she had required.

A day or two later Manox and Catherine met in 'my Lady's Chapel Chamber at Horsham'. The room, dark and deserted, was a fine and secret place, and Manox took the opportunity to beg Catherine to fulfil her promise. She agreed. '[And] I', Manox testified, 'felt more than was convenient.'

It was more than convenient indeed. But that, he insisted desperately, was as far as he had gone. 'Upon his damnation', he swore, 'and most extreme punishment of his body, he never knew her carnally.'[58]

And, despite brutal pressure, he refused to budge from this.

But Dereham, whom Wriothesley examined later on the 5th, could offer no such defence. 'He hath had carnal knowledge with the Queen', he admitted, 'lying in bed by her in his doublet and hosen divers times and six or seven times in naked bed with her.'

Other ladies of the Duchess's Household, who were subsequently examined, glossed Dereham's bald account with lascivious details. Mary Lascelles testified that 'she hath seen them kiss after a wonderful manner, for they would kiss and hang by their bills [that is, lips] together and [as if] they were two sparrows'. Alice Restwood, who was legitimately sharing Catherine's bed, said that there was 'such puffing and blowing between [Dereham and Catherine] that [she] was weary of the same'. Indeed, Dereham's heavy breathing and other noises had become a running joke in the Maidens' Chamber. 'Hark to Dereham broken winded!' exclaimed another frequent gentleman-visitor after a particularly strenuous display.[59]

But it was Margaret Benet who contrived to witness the most. '[She] looked out at a hole of a door', she stated, 'and there saw Dereham pluck up [Catherine's] clothes above her navel so that [she] might well discern her body.' And Benet's ears had been as busy as her eyes. 'She heard', she told her interrogator, 'Dereham say that although he used the company of a woman ... yet he would get no child except he listed.' And Catherine, according to Benet, had replied in a similar vein. 'A woman', she had said, 'might meddle with a man and yet conceive no child unless she would herself.'[60]

Was this confident contraceptive knowledge? Or merely old-wives' tales? In either case, it explains why Catherine was prepared to have frequent sex with no apparent heed to the risks of pregnancy.

The examinations of Manox and Dereham established, beyond doubt, the truth of Mary Lascelles's charges against Catherine. Henry was badly shaken. He had believed. And he had been proved wrong. 'His heart was so pierced with pensiveness', the Council reported, 'that long it was before his Majesty could speak and utter the sorrow of his heart unto us.' And when he did so, he wept freely 'which was strange in one of his courage'.[61]

Were his tears for Catherine? Or the loss of his own illusions?

Whatever his state of mind, Henry acted quickly. A summons was sent to the senior members of the Council, including Catherine's uncle, Norfolk, at about midnight on Saturday the 5th. The following day, Henry 'on the pretext of hunting', dined in a little pleasure-house in one of the parks around Hampton Court. Then, under the cover of night, he left secretly for London.

Catherine never saw him again. As always with Henry, the break with an about-to-be-discarded wife was clean and clinical. There was no time for hysterics or for her supposed last, desperate attempt to see him in the Chapel Gallery. Indeed, when her husband left the palace, she was aware neither of his departure nor that anything was wrong.

The King arrived at Whitehall late at night. Soon after his arrival, the Council met at midnight and remained in session till 4 or 5 a.m. on Monday morning. 'These lords have been ever since in Council morning and evening', Marillac reported, 'the King assisting, which he is not wont to do.' 'They show themselves very troubled', the ambassador added, 'especially Norfolk, who is esteemed very resolute, and not easily moved to show by his face what his heart conceives.'

While these urgent debates continued, Catherine, the occasion of them all, remained at Hampton Court with her women. She was in a sort of limbo. No one had yet told her anything officially. But the King's unexplained absence made clear that something was amiss. Confused and unsure, she abandoned her usual round of pleasure. 'She has taken no kind of pastime', the very well-informed Marillac reported, 'but kept in her Chambers.' 'Before', he added, 'she did nothing but dance and rejoice [but] now when the musicians come, they are told there is no more time to dance.'[62]

The blow fell on Monday the 7th. In the evening, a powerful delegation of Councillors, headed by Cranmer, was despatched to Hampton Court, to confront Catherine with her misdeeds. Her first reaction was to brazen it out. But, as the evidence against her was rehearsed, her resistance collapsed. She had another interview with Cranmer that night and made, it was thought, a full written confession. She begged the King's mercy, which she had so often procured for others; she pleaded her youthful frailty and the wicked ways of young men; and she acknowledged that she had been so 'blinded with desire of worldly glory that I could not, nor had grace, to consider how great a fault it was to conceal my former faults from your Majesty'.[63]

Cranmer handled her with tact and real kindness. For her condition was pitiable. 'I found her', he reported to Henry, 'in such lamentation and heaviness as I never saw no creature, so that it would have pitied any man's heart to have looked upon her.' Indeed, her 'vehement rage' was such that he really feared for her sanity. Fortunately, he was able, when he saw her next, to give her the news that Henry, softened by her confession, had decided to show her mercy. This quietened her. But then her paroxysms resumed, worse even than before. Gently, Cranmer questioned her to discover their cause. It was the King's mercy, she said through sobs, which more brought home to her the enormity of her conduct than her previous fear of death.

After that, she continued in a calmer state till about 6 o'clock (probably on the 8th or 9th) when she had 'another like pang, but not so outrageous as the first was'. The explanation was, she told Cranmer, 'for remembrance of the time'. For six was the hour when 'Mr Heneage was wont to bring her knowledge of your Grace'.[64]

It was the prettiest picture of female repentance which could be desired. But was it real? Or the work of a quick-witted actress?

Whatever their nature, Catherine's agonies of grief were enough to win Henry's mercy. Probably, he was inclined to extenuate her misbehaviour as the result of a poor education, and to blame those who had brought her up more than Catherine herself. Moreover, it was far from clear whether Catherine and Dereham had committed any offence. The fall of

Catherine's predecessor, Anne Boleyn, had established that adultery by a Queen was certainly treason – both for the Queen and her paramour(s). But Dereham and Catherine had enjoyed their nights of passion *before* Catherine became Queen. Neither had been married then; and, while fornication was a sin, it was not a crime.

Catherine had been shameless. She had been deceitful. But that was all.

The Duchess, who had a sharp forensic brain, was quick to grasp all this. She had spoken to her stepson, Norfolk, on the night of Sunday 6 November, on his return to Lambeth from Hampton Court, and again after the marathon session of the Council in the small hours of the Monday morning. And the upshot of these conversations was that she was confident Catherine would escape. 'The Duchess', one of her servants testified, 'said that if it were done while [Catherine and Dereham] were here [at Lambeth], neither the Queen nor Dereham should die for it.' 'But', she added, 'I am sorry for the King, for he taketh the matter very heavily.'

The Duchess's optimistic reading of events seemed to be vindicated when, on 11 November, the Council at Court wrote to inform Cranmer at Hampton Court of Henry's decision about the Queen's immediate fate. She was to be moved to the former nunnery of Syon, 'there to remain, till the matter be further resolved ... [and] furnished moderately, as her life and conditions hath deserved'. She would have the use of three Chambers, 'hanged with mean stuff, without any cloth of state', and the services of four gentlewomen and two chamberers.

It was hardly the luxury she had been used to. Nevertheless, she had kept the essentials, for she was still to be treated 'in the state of a Queen'.[65]

But Catherine was aware of the fragility of her position. For she had another, much more dangerous, secret.

'The Queen', Lady Rochford later testified, 'three or four times every day since she was in this trouble, would ask [her]: what she heard of Culpepper?' According to Lady Rochford, Catherine added: 'If that matter came not out, she feared not for no thing and said she would never confess it and willed [Lady Rochford] to deny it utterly.' Catherine was to admit that these conversations had taken place. But she turned them round. According to her, it was Lady Rochford who had encouraged her to be steadfast, and she claimed that Lady Rochford had said: 'I will never confess it, to be torn with wild horses'.[66]

The truth, probably, is that each egged on the other. Catherine had behaved like the love-sick Juliet and Lady Rochford like Juliet's pandering Nurse.

Some of the Council, meanwhile, were convinced that they were not yet to the bottom of their investigations. But their suspicions were not directed at Thomas Culpepper. Instead, they were convinced that Catherine's appointment of Dereham to her Household meant that this love affair had continued *after* her marriage to Henry. That, of course, *would* have been treason and Dereham was pressed brutally on the point, almost certainly with the use of torture. Finally, Marillac heard, that 'Dereham, to show his innocence since the marriage, said that Culpepper had succeeded him in the Queen's affections'.[67]

Dereham's revelation was made on Saturday, the 11th. That day, Culpepper, oblivious to the disaster which was about to overtake him, 'was . . . merry ahawking'. On the Sunday, Catherine was questioned on the new allegations by Russell and Browne. She admitted three secret interviews with Culpepper at Lincoln, Pontefract and York, and that she had given him gifts of a cap, a chain and a cramp-ring. But she threw all the blame on Culpepper's own persistence and Lady Rochford's encouragement of it. 'Yet must you give men leave to look', Lady Rochford had said, 'for they will look upon you.'

Lady Rochford's motives are hard to understand. She was the widow of George Boleyn, Lord Rochford, and, as such, had seen her husband and her sister-in-law, Queen Anne, destroyed by charges of adultery and incest. Those charges were a fabrication. But now she was encouraging her new mistress, Queen Catherine, to act out such follies indeed. Had Lady Rochford's been a life starved of affection? Was she living out in Catherine the romantic fantasies that she had never known?[68]

We can only guess. But her indulgence proved fatal: to her mistress, to herself and to Catherine's lover.

The mysterious comings and goings in the Queen's apartments during the northern Progress were now explained. But had Catherine admitted everything? 'As for the act', Russell and Browne reported, 'she denieth upon her oath, or touching any bare of her but her hand.' The Councillors' suspicion, clearly, was that she was being economical with the truth as before.[69]

What Catherine had said already, however, was quite enough to undo her. Henry's projected mercy was abandoned, and the terms of her confinement were notably tightened.

The King, in a letter written by Secretary Sadler late at night on the 12th, showed himself especially anxious about Catherine's jewels. They were the tokens of his besotted love for her. Now that she had forfeited his love, she should go unadorned. She was to be given, Sadler instructed Cranmer, six French hoods 'with edges of goldsmiths' work, so that there be no stone nor pearl in the same'. She was also to have six gowns, 'with such things as belong to the same, except always stone and pearl'.[70]

Culpepper was arrested on the 12th or at the latest on the 13th. He was taken straight to the Tower and on the 14th his goods were inventoried for confiscation. He was examined soon after his arrival in the Tower, and, protected by his rank and favour from the kind of duress that was freely applied to Dereham, he told a balanced and nuanced tale. He stressed that Catherine had taken the initiative. But he also admitted the strength of his own feelings, and the eagerness with which he had responded. He is, in short, to be believed.

The result reads like a piece of romantic fiction. The predominant tone is tender and wistful. But it is enlivened with flashes of humour and coarse directness and moments of unintended bedroom farce. It is also a story that, again because of the illegibility of the original, has lain largely untold for four and a half centuries.[71]

It was 'on Maunday Thursday last [14 April 1541] at Greenwich',

Culpepper recalled, that Catherine had renewed their acquaintance. He was summoned by her servant, 'Henry Webb, [who] brought him to the entry between her Privy Chamber and the Chamber of Presence'. There he found the Queen herself, who 'gave him by her own hands a fair cap of velvet garnished with a brooch and three dozen pairs of aglets (decorative pins) and a chain'. 'Put this under your cloak,' she said, '[and let] nobody see it!' 'Alas, Madam,' he replied, 'why did not you this when you were a maid?'

This was not at all the response that Catherine had intended to provoke and at their next meeting she made her dissatisfaction plain. 'Is this all the thanks ye give me for the cap?' she demanded. 'If I had known ye would have [said] these words you should never have had it.'[72]

Nevertheless, her attentions continued and 'at Greenwich [she] sent to him, being sick, at diverse times flesh or the fish dinner by Morres the Page'. Perhaps it is to this period that Catherine's only surviving letter belongs. 'Master Culpepper', it begins, 'I have heard you are sick ... the which thing troubled me very much till such time that ... you ... send me word how that you do, for I have never longed so much for [a] thing as I do to see you and speak with you, the which I trust shall be shortly now ... It makes my heart to die to think what fortune I have that I cannot always be in your company ... Yours as long as life endures – CATHERINE.'[73]

Despite the passionate tone of this letter, the relationship seems to have stalled till the start of the Progress in July. Once again, a gift was used to get things under way. 'In the Progress time', Culpepper testified, he 'took a cramp-ring (a preventative against rheumatism) off my Lady Rochford's finger, which, she said, was the Queen's'. Lady Rochford then told the Queen of Culpepper's pretty theft. In response, Catherine 'took another cramp-ring off her own finger and bade the Lady Rochford carry it to Culpepper' with a message. The message was that 'it was an ill sight to see him wear but one cramp-ring and therefore she did send him another'.

Nevertheless, and despite Catherine's best endeavours, it was not until the beginning of August, at Lincoln, that the first of their clandestine meetings took place. Lady Rochford, as usual, acted as inter-mediary and 'appointed him to come into a place under her Chamber being, as he thinketh, the Queen's stool house (that is, her lavatory)'.

The assignation nearly turned into a disaster. As we have seen, one of the watch, noticing the open door of the backstairs, had locked it shut. But Culpepper and his servant managed to pick the lock.

When Culpepper finally arrived in the stool house, he found the Queen and Lady Rochford 'and no other body'. It was about 11 o'clock at night and he and Catherine talked till three in the morning. 'They had there', he said, 'fond communication of themselves and of their loves before time and of Bess Harvey.'

Elizabeth ('Bess') Harvey was a well-known, even perhaps a notorious, figure at the Tudor Court, where she had been in and out of employment in the Queen's Household. She had been in service to Anne Boleyn, during which time she got on friendly terms with Sir Francis Bryan. But in 1536 she was dismissed in circumstances which, she claimed, were a mystery to her. By 1539, however, she was once more a member of the 'shadow' Queen's Privy Chamber, and, as such, accompanied Anne Basset and the rest on the outing to view the fleet at Portsmouth. But she was not appointed to Catherine's own Household and in March 1541 was retired with a life annuity of £10 a year.

Had Culpepper broken Bess's heart, as he broke so many others? At any event, Catherine felt that he had treated her badly and left her shabbily dressed. So, after the conversation at Lincoln, she 'gave a damask gown [to Bess]' and sent Culpepper a message of reproof by the ubiquitous Lady Rochford. 'He did ill', the message went, 'to suffer his tenement to be so ill repaired and that she, for to save his honesty, had done some cost over it.'

The remark, which characterizes Bess as a rented building ('tene-ment'), ill-maintained by Culpepper as its lessee, is saucy and mocks both Culpepper and his former mistress. But, typically, Catherine made up for the hurt by the kindly gesture of the gift of the gown.

*

But, now, in the stool house at Lincoln, Catherine had been thoroughly unsettled by the incident with the watch. '[She] always at that time', Culpepper recalled, 'started away and returned again as one in fear lest somebody should come.'

Nevertheless, as the hours went by, and they talked of old times, their love returned. 'Now she must indeed love him,' Catherine said. 'She had bound him', Culpepper gallantly replied, 'both then and now and ever that he both must and did love her again above all other creatures.'

When he finally left, he kissed her hand, 'saying he would presume no further'.[74]

On another occasion, the Queen's worst fears were fulfilled and 'Lovekyn, one of her Chamberers, came down when he was with the Queen, and the Queen put her out'. Catherine never forgave the woman for her tactlessness and threatened to dismiss her from her service.[75]

These problems with her servants and the lack of suitable retreats in the little houses where she and Henry were staying on the Progress meant that it was almost a fortnight before Culpepper and Catherine were able to have another nocturnal tryst. Even then, it was postponed for a night as 'the Queen feared lest the King had set watch' on the door to the backstairs. But the coast turned out to be clear and on 31 August Culpepper was summoned once more 'and talked with her till the King went to bed'.

At this meeting, in Pontefract Castle, Catherine began by reproaching him for his previous unfeeling conduct in abandoning her. 'I marvel', she said, 'that ye could so much dissemble as to say ye loved me so earnestly and yet would and did so soon lie with another.' Culpepper's reply was unanswerable. Catherine, he retorted, 'was married [to Henry] afore he loved the other'. Moreover, he continued, she had only herself to blame. 'He found so little favour at her hands at that time', he said, 'that he was rather moved to set by other.'

Catherine now changed tack and became frankly vampish. 'If I listed [wished]', she said, 'I could bring you into as good a trade as Bray hath my Lord Parr in.' Culpepper replied indignantly. 'He thought her no such woman as Bray.' 'Well', answered Catherine, 'if I had tarried still in the Maidens' Chamber I would have tried you.'[76]

All this casts light on another unhappy Tudor aristocratic marriage. Sir William Parr, ennobled in 1539 as Lord Parr of Kendal, had married Anne Bourchier, daughter of the Earl of Essex. The marriage was a great catch, as Anne was her father's only child and heiress, but it turned into a personal disaster and both parties sought comfort elsewhere. Anne 'eloped' from her husband and refused to return, while Parr, Catherine's reference makes clear, had taken a mistress called Bray. She was, almost certainly, Dorothy Bray, the next to the youngest of the six sisters of John, Lord Bray and Catherine's colleague as one of Anne of Cleves's maids. Parr clearly developed a taste for women of the Bray family and in 1548 went on to marry Elizabeth Brooke, who was Dorothy's niece as the child of her eldest sister Anne. As Parr was separated but not divorced from his first wife at the time, this second marriage was bigamous. Subsequently, it became a plaything of religious politics: its validity was asserted by Protestants and rejected by Catholics.[77]

Stories like this, in which both men and women of Catherine's acquaintance flouted conventional morality to pursue their own sexual happiness, make her own behaviour seem almost commonplace.

But these other women were not married to the King.

It was also at Pontefract that Catherine sent Culpepper a note to make another assignation. 'As ye find the door', she wrote, 'so to come.'

By York, she was confident enough to make a joke about their clandestine meetings. 'She had store of other lovers at other doors as well as he,' she said. 'It is like enough,' he replied in the same spirit. But then she became more serious. 'She had communication with him how well she loved him.' She also 'showed him how when she was a maiden how many times her grief was such that she could not but weep in the presence of her fellows'.

And, it is clear, she had a similar 'grief' about the promiscuous and popular Culpepper. At Sheriff Hutton, he testified, he sent a ring by Lady Rochford and, in return, the Queen sent him two bracelets. They were accompanied with the message that 'they were sent him to keep his arms warm' – for normally, she knew, he kept them snug in the embraces of other women.

Her other fear, of course, was of the mighty monarch who was her husband. 'She doubted not', she told Culpepper, 'that he knew the King was Supreme Head of the Church and therefore the Queen bade him beware that whensoever he went to confession he should never shrive him of any such things as should pass betwixt her and him.' 'For, if he did', she added, 'surely the King, being Supreme Head of the Church, should have knowledge of it.'

'No, Madam, I warrant you,' Culpepper replied.

Catherine's meaning is not entirely clear. Did she suspect that the priest would betray such sensational revelations to the King? Or that God would somehow communicate them to his deputy on earth? Or did she even confuse her husband with God himself?

After all, at times, that was an easy enough mistake to make.

But, really, there was so little to confess. It was all talk, talk, talk. Nevertheless, as Culpepper admitted, the intention was there. 'He intended', he admitted, 'and meant to do ill with the Queen and that likewise the Queen so minded with him.'[78]

It was little. But it proved enough for the law.

Dereham and Culpepper were tried for treason at Guildhall on 1 December and found guilty. Their execution was postponed for several days as the Council made final frantic efforts to extract from them the admission that they had actually committed the act with Catherine as Queen. But, despite 'serious examination', the efforts failed.

There was now no reason to delay the process of law. Dereham's final request was for Henry to spare him the full penalty of treason. But Henry, the Council reported, 'thinketh he hath deserved no such mercy at his hands and therefore hath determined that he shall suffer the whole execution'. On 10 December, therefore, he was dragged on a hurdle to Tyburn and hanged, castrated, disemboweled, beheaded and quartered.

And all for sleeping a few times with an attractive and willing teenage girl who at the time was not married.

Culpepper was luckier. Benefiting from Henry's former favour and his powerful friends he was, despite the fact that his crimes were 'very heinous', only beheaded.[79]

On 22 December, it was the turn of the Duchess, Lord William, the Countess of Bridgewater and the women of the Duchess's Household. They were tried for 'misprision of treason', for concealing and abetting Catherine's offences, and they were sentenced to imprisonment at the King's pleasure and forfeiture of goods.[80]

The rumour was that Norfolk himself would share their fate. But on 12 December he wrote Henry an abject letter. He distanced himself from 'mine ungracious mother-in-law, mine unhappy brother . . . with my lewd sister of Bridgewater'. And he denounced 'the most abominable deeds done by two of my nieces', Queen Anne and Queen Catherine. In view of that toll of disasters inflicted by his family, the Duke conceded, it would be reasonable for Henry 'to conceive a displeasure in your heart' against him and his whole Howard kindred. But, in extenuation, Norfolk pleaded that it was he who had first pointed the finger of suspicion at the Duchess; moreover, Anne Boleyn and Catherine, his 'two false, traitorous nieces', had borne him 'small love'.[81]

The letter proved excuse enough. Norfolk was quickly restored to favour and even the convicted members of his family were soon pardoned.

Only against Catherine and Lady Rochford was Henry implacable. They were condemned by an Act of Attainder. The Bill was introduced on 21 January 1542 and completed all its Parliamentary stages three weeks later. The key clauses of the Act were flagrantly retrospective. If any loose-living woman dare marry the King 'without plain declaration before of her unchaste life unto his Majesty', it was treason. Adultery by or with the Queen or the wife of the Prince of Wales was treason. And failure on the part of the witnesses to disclose such offences was misprision of treason. Finally, with all the loop-holes closed, Catherine and Lady Rochford were declared convicted of high treason.

On 11 February the Act received the royal assent *in absentia* by letters patent, to spare Henry the grief of hearing, once again, a recital of the 'wicked facts' of the case.[82]

Catherine was now legally dead. It remained only to inflict the actual penalty.

All this time, Catherine had remained in her easy confinement at Syon House. 'She is', Chapuys reported at the beginning of 1542, 'making good cheer, fatter and handsomer than ever she was, taking great care of her person, well dressed and much adorned; more imperious and commanding, and more difficult to please than ever she was when living with the King her husband.'

Was this stupid indifference, as most modern accounts have supposed? Or merely making the best of a bad job? Chapuys himself seems to incline to the latter. Notwithstanding her apparent pleasure in life's luxuries, he reported, 'she believes that her end will be on the scaffold, for she owns she has deserved death'.[83]

And it was this responsible, dignified Catherine who confronted a delegation of Lords at Syon. There had been some nervousness about using an Act of Attainder against the Queen and condemning her unheard. '[The] Queen', Lord Chancellor Audley informed the House, 'was in no sense a mean and private person but an illustrious and public one.' 'Therefore', he continued, 'her case had to be judged with . . . integrity.' To remove any suspicion of injustice, he recommended the despatch of a delegation to hear her speak in her own defence, for it was 'but just that a princess should be tried by equal laws'.

The delegation duly waited on the Queen. But Catherine refused the opportunity to defend herself, either with the delegates or before a more public assembly. Instead, she 'openly confessed and acknowledged to them the great crime of which she had been guilty against the most High God and a kind prince'. She had only two requests to make: that Henry 'would not impute her crime to her whole kindred and family' and that the King would also give some of her fine clothes to her attendants, 'since she had nothing now to recompense them as they deserved'.[84]

Catherine the rebel, it seemed, was tamed at last. For she was here acknowledging her submission to the core values of the sixteenth century: God, King, Family and Dependants.

She was now ready for the final submission: to the Good Death.

There were still a few flashes of the old Catherine, however. On 10 February, she was removed from Syon to the Tower by water. According to Chapuys, she did not go without a struggle: '[there was] some difficulty and resistance'. As with the fallen Anne Boleyn, the procession to the Tower was like a black parody of her inauguration river pageant. Lord Privy Seal Southampton went first in a large barge. Then followed the Queen and her ladies in a small covered boat. While at the rear was Suffolk in another large barge, filled with armed men. Catherine landed at the water gate and stepped ashore. She was dressed in black velvet and was 'received with the same honours and ceremonies' as if she were still Queen.[85]

Two days later, on Sunday the 12th, she was told to prepare herself for death on the morrow. Marillac heard that, since 'she weeps, cries and torments herself miserably, without ceasing', her execution had been postponed to give her time to compose herself. But his chronology is wrong and so too, probably, is his picture of Catherine's state.

For Chapuys tells a very different story: not only was Catherine prepared for death, she even went through a form of rehearsal to make sure she got things right. Later on the Sunday evening, the ambassador reported, 'she asked to see the block, pretending that she wanted to know how she was to place her head on it'. Her request was granted and the block was brought into her Chamber. Once it was in place, 'she herself tried and placed her head on it by way of experiment'.

Like so much in Catherine's life, her preparation for death was curiously materialistic.[86]

The execution was scheduled for early the following morning. Soon after

7 o'clock, the Council and other dignitaries arrived to act as witnesses. Norfolk was absent, but his son and heir, the Earl of Surrey, was present to watch his cousin beheaded. He was a poet and man of action. Did he imagine that one day he might be in her place?

According to Marillac, Catherine was 'so weak that she could hardly speak'. But he was not an eye-witness. The merchant Ottwell Johnson was – and he gives a very different account. 'I see the Queen and the Lady Rochford', he wrote to his brother John on the 15th, 'suffer within the Tower.' 'Whose souls', he continued, 'be with God, for they made the most godly and Christian end.'[87]

Catherine, according to Johnson, 'uttered [her] lively faith in the blood of Christ only'. She 'desired all Christian people to take regard unto [her] worthy and just punishment'. She had offended 'God heinously from [her] youth upward, in breaking all his commandments'. And she had offended 'against the King's royal Majesty very dangerously'. She was 'justly condemned ... by the Laws of the realm and Parliament to die'. And she 'required the people (I say) to take example at [her], for amendment of their ungodly lives and gladly to obey the King in all things'. Then she prayed 'heartily' for '[the King's] preservation, and willed all people so to do'. Finally, she commended her soul to God and earnestly called for mercy on Him.

That is what Johnson heard and what Catherine must have said. God knows what, if any of it, she believed. The reference, in particular, to her faith in 'the blood of Christ only' sounds more like Cranmer than anything that Catherine would say of her own accord. Had he coached her? Had she undergone some form of conversion in the Tower?

We cannot know.

After she had finished speaking she knelt at the block, in her carefully rehearsed gesture, and her head was struck off.

Lady Rochford's turn was next. According to Chapuys, she 'had shown symptoms of madness until the very moment when they announced to her that she must die'. But she, too, made a good end.

The strange, delinquent partnership of mistress and servant was over.[88]

74. *Interlude*

Would Henry marry again after his bitter disappointment and humiliation over Catherine Howard? It seemed a moot point to intelligent observers, including Chapuys.

For by the winter of 1541–2, the ambassador had known Henry for a dozen years. He had seen him change from a fit, if florid, forty-year old to the prematurely-aged and bloated monster he had become a decade later. He had witnessed his reaction to Anne Boleyn's execution and to Jane Seymour's death. But he had never seen him behave as he did over Catherine Howard. 'This King', he reported on 3 December 1541, 'has wonderfully felt the case of the Queen, his wife.' 'He has certainly shown', he continued, 'greater sorrow and regret at her loss than at the faults, loss or divorce of his preceding wives.'

Indeed, the contrast was so great that Chapuys felt the need to offer what we might call a little psychology to explain it. He did so by means of a homely comparison. 'I should say', he wrote, 'that this King's case resembles very much that of the woman who cried more bitterly at the loss of her tenth husband than she had cried on the death of the other nine put together, though all of them had been equally worthy people and good husbands to her.' 'The reason', Chapuys's tale continued, '[was] that she had never buried one of them without being sure of the next. But after the tenth husband she had no other one in view: hence her sorrow and her lamentation.'

'Such', Chapuys concluded, 'is the case with this King, who does not seem to have any plan or female friend to fall back upon.'[1]

It can be put more simply. Previously, with the exception of the ever-sainted Jane Seymour, Henry had abandoned his wives. Now, he felt, a wife had abandoned him.

He did not like it.

But Henry's loss was, Anne of Cleves thought and hoped, her gain. As we have seen, Anne had handled her demotion from wife to 'sister' with dignity and aplomb. But that does not mean that she was reconciled to it – or, much less, that she welcomed it. On the contrary. Instead of rejoicing in her escape, as we might imagine, she was eager to put her head in the lion's mouth once more. 'I hear also', Chapuys reported on 19 November 1541, 'that the Lady Anne of Cleves has greatly rejoiced at [Catherine's fall], and that in order to be nearer the King she is coming to, if she is not already at, Richmond.'[2]

A formal diplomatic initiative to restore the Cleves marriage followed from her brother, the Duke. Harst delivered letters from the ducal minister Olisleger to Privy Seal Fitzwilliam and Archbishop Cranmer, to ask for their good offices. But, knowing Henry's sensitivity on the subject, both refused to have anything to do with the matter and informed the King of the approach. Harst next tried for a personal audience with the King. This, too, was refused on the grounds of his 'grief' about Catherine Howard's betrayals. Finally, Harst presented his case to the Privy Council on 15 December, when it was politely but firmly rejected. '[The King intended]', the Councillors explained, 'that the Lady [Anne] should be graciously entertained and her estate rather increased than diminished.' 'But the separation', they continued, 'had been made for such just cause that [Henry] prayed the Duke never to make such a request [again].'

Unwisely, Harst tried to press the matter. At this point, things turned nasty and Gardiner, speaking 'with every appearance of anger', told him the blunt truth. 'The King', he said, 'would never take back the . . . Lady [Anne].'[3]

It was a truth that Anne still found difficult to accept. And it is easy to understand why. She had her slighted honour to avenge. She found her position of Henry's 'sister', despite its comfort, both awkward and anomalous. And she had positive reasons for wanting Henry back. As we too easily forget, Henry had been kind and generous to her as he was to all his wives. For he was a good husband – as long as the marriage lasted. Nevertheless, Anne's attempt to renew the marriage led only to a fresh rejection. But, once again, she had the wisdom to swallow the slight and to submit.

Her situation aroused widespread sympathy. According to Marillac, 'all regret her more than they did the late Queen Catherine [of Aragon]'. More particularly, another royal lady took a sisterly interest in her plight. Francis I's sister, Marguerite – who was now Queen of the little Pyrenean kingdom of Navarre after marrying its King, Henri d'Albret, as her second husband – used Marillac to send Anne good advice and her portrait. Anne, the ambassador reported, had no real need of the advice, 'as she wants neither prudence nor patience' while her conduct had been above reproach. But he knew, he continued, that Anne would be delighted with Marguerite's portrait as she had often asked for it. He had already requested hers in return.[4]

Marguerite's kindness was not disinterested of course. The renewal of the Cleves marriage would serve French interests by tying England to an enemy of Charles V. It would also, she thought, encourage Henry along the path of moderate religious Reform which she favoured. But such considerations were secondary. Above all, she wanted to express the solidarity of royal women in the face of the frequently monstrous conduct of royal men.

Anne's enthusiastic response raises questions of its own. At first sight it would be hard to think of two more different figures or more ill-assorted friends. Anne was ill-educated and abused; whereas Marguerite, thanks to her own intelligence and her brother's indulgence, was conspicuous for her independence of thought and action. These had secured her a European-wide reputation and made her a role-model for royal women everywhere.

As we have seen, Henry's second wife, Anne Boleyn, had sought Marguerite's acquaintance and endorsement. Now, it seemed, Anne of Cleves, despite her apparent submissiveness, was eager to copy Marguerite's example as well. Or did she see her only as a friendly shoulder to cry on?

Meanwhile, Henry's black mood continued for several weeks. 'The King', Marillac reported from London on 16 December, 'has left his Privy Council here, and is, with a small company, in the neighbourhood, seeking in pastimes to forget his grief, until it is time to come to Greenwich, where he spends Christmas.' Henry moved restlessly between the small royal residences of north Surrey – Beddington, Esher, Oatlands, Woking, Horsley and back to Beddington – and hunted their deer parks. He listened to the Council's reports on their mopping-up of the Catherine Howard affair and issued astringent instructions. Otherwise, Chapuys learned, '[he] will not hear of business'. And he delayed his return to Greenwich, for a Christmas which he did not wish to celebrate, until the evening of 23 December.[5]

Only with Catherine's formal condemnation did he begin – in the language of psychotherapy – to find 'closure'. Ever since the discovery of his wife's affair, Chapuys reported, 'the King had shown no alacrity or joy'. But on 29 January, as the Parliamentary process against Catherine entered its final stages, the clouds started to lift and Henry 'gave a grand supper'. 'There were no less than 26 at his table', Chapuys continued, 'and at another table close by 35'. Even his eye for the ladies seemed to have come back. 'The lady for whom he showed the greatest regard', Chapuys heard, was Wyatt's repudiated wife, Elizabeth née Brooke, the sister of Lord Cobham. 'She is a pretty young creature', the ambassador noted, 'with wit enough to do as badly as the others if she were to try.' 'The King is also said to have a fancy', he concluded, for two other ladies: a niece of Sir Anthony Browne and Anne Basset. Anne Basset, as we have seen, had first caught Henry's attention six years previously when she made her debut at Court as one of Jane Seymour's maids. And he had continued to show a rather avuncular interest in her ever since.[6]

Anne was fair, modest and charming. But somehow the spark failed to strike.

Henry's spirits rose even further with Catherine's execution: now that the headsman's axe had drawn the clearest of lines under his fifth marriage, the quest for his sixth wife could begin. But it would prove neither quick nor easy.

Catherine was executed on 12 February. Henry spent the days surrounding the execution privately at Hackney and Waltham. But on the

14th he returned to Whitehall for the feasts that marked the beginning of Lent. In contrast with his miserable Christmas, he decided to celebrate them in fine style. There were three successive days of feasting, with a different group of guests on each day. He entertained the Lords and Privy Councillors on Sunday, 19 February, the Lawyers on the Monday and the Ladies on Shrove Tuesday itself, 21 February. Ever the good host, Henry supervised the arrangements for his female guests in person. 'The King', Chapuys reported, 'did nothing else on the [Tuesday] morning . . . than go from one chamber to another to inspect the lodgings prepared for the ladies.'

At the party itself he was universally charming: 'he received [them all] with much gaiety', Chapuys continued, 'without, however, showing particular affection for any of them'.[7] This behaviour led Chapuys to wonder whether Henry would ever take another wife. More importantly, he speculated, would any woman wish – or dare – to take him?

For, as Chapuys pointed out, the new treasons created by Catherine's Act of Attainder raised formidable obstacles for any would-be successor. Who was so chaste that no breath of scandal could ever touch her? Or who was so bold, and so confident of Henry's love, that she would risk confessing her indiscretions beforehand?

The list, it would seem, was not long.

A year later, however, in the early summer of 1543, Henry had chosen. And the woman, after much soul-searching, had accepted. Her name was Catherine Parr.

Catherine Parr

75. A courtier's daughter

C atherine Parr is usually seen as the Queen who came from nowhere. Actually, she was the daughter of a substantial northern knightly family that – like the Boleyns – had gone up in the world as a result of royal favour and successful marriages. She was not sent to France, to acquire a courtly polish, like Anne Boleyn. But she was probably better educated overall. And her family certainly had the better lineage and was more securely based at Court.

The foundations of the family fortunes had been laid by Catherine's grandfather, Sir William Parr, in the later fifteenth century. Parr gave his support to Edward IV at the crucial moment in 1471 when Edward returned to reclaim his kingdom from the 'Kingmaker' Earl of Warwick. Parr never looked back. Edward made him Controller of the Household and Knight of the Garter and, no doubt, assisted his second marriage to the wealthy heiress, Elizabeth Fitzhugh.[1]

The career of Parr's eldest son and Catherine's father, Thomas, promised to be even more spectacular. Soon after his father's death in 1484, his widowed mother, Elizabeth, married again, this time Sir Nicholas Vaux of Harrowden in Northamptonshire. The Vauxs were as committed Lancastrians as the Parrs were Yorkists and they benefited accordingly from the accession of Henry VII. Young Thomas Parr shared in their success and became very close to his stepfather, Sir Nicholas Vaux. This led, after Elizabeth's death in 1507, to a double marriage between Vaux and Parr and the sisters Anne and Maud Green, who were the daughters and co-heiresses of another leading

Northamptonshire landowner, Sir Thomas Green. The resulting pattern of relationships was tangled even by sixteenth-century standards since, for example, Lady Vaux (Anne Green) was Parr's stepmother as well as his sister-in-law.[2]

Parr's marriage to Maud Green also changed the Parrs' territorial interests. The family's ancestral lands centred on Kendal in Westmorland. But these were dwarfed by the Northamptonshire properties Parr acquired in the right of his wife as her share of the Green inheritance, and that county now became his main residence – though his Westmorland connexions were far from forgotten.

But a more important sphere of activity for Parr than either Westmorland or Northamptonshire was the Court.

Parr had the Court in his blood: as we have seen, his father, Sir William, had been a great figure in the Yorkist Court, while Catherine Vaux (the mother of his stepfather, Sir Nicholas Vaux) had been equally prominent in the Lancastrian Court as the devoted lady-in-waiting to Queen Margaret of Anjou. These ancestral ties mattered (which is why service at Court tended to run in certain families) and they explain why Parr became an Esquire of the Body to Henry VII. He was in post at the latest by 1500 when he attended on the King to his meeting at Calais with the Archduke Philip, father of the Emperor Charles V.

The position of Esquire of the Body was an ambiguous one: it could mean very little, or it could mean a lot. On the one hand, the title was given as a reward to trusted local gentlemen. They received no fee and attended Court only on special occasions. But they enjoyed the increased status that belonged to all royal servants, whatever their rank. There were dozens of these supernumerary Esquires and their importance was purely local. On the other hand, there was a much smaller group of Esquires with the Fee who were in regular attendance at Court. They were paid a fee of 50 marks (£33 6s 8d) and they held a position of real importance. Parr belonged to this latter, select group.

Under Edward IV, the Esquires with the Fee had been the King's principal body servants, whose 'business is many secrets'. They dressed and undressed the King, waited on him at table and attended to his other private wants and instructions. Under the Tudors, the Esquires lost this privileged place with the transfer of the King's private service to the new, inner department of the Privy Chamber. So it is the Gentlemen of the Privy Chamber, not the Esquires, who figure so prominently in our story as the favourites of Henry VIII and the alleged lovers of his Queens.

But the Esquires with the Fee nevertheless retained a dignified (and much safer) role. They were the leading regular servants of the outer group of royal apartments known collectively as 'the Chamber'. These apartments were the scene of most public ceremonial, in which the Esquires played a leading part. They also deputized for the frequently absentee noblemen who acted as the head officers of the Chamber. The Esquires, therefore, were well placed to catch the King's eye and to move on, if they also caught his fancy, to higher things.[3]

Parr, with his wealth and his family connexions, was better placed than most to succeed. He was given the Esquire's fee of 50 marks by Henry VIII soon after his accession. But he surrendered it within a year to his younger brother William. For already Thomas Parr was on the way up. He was knighted, and in 1513 raised and captained a hundred troops for the war with France. Like other leading courtiers, his detachment at first formed part of the Middleward under the immediate command of the King himself. But, at some point, he was assigned to the Vanguard, which was led by Charles Brandon. The following year he was nominated for the Garter. He received the support of many knights but was not elected. He was also considered for a peerage, though there were objections to giving him the title of 'Lord Fitzhugh' since his mother had been the younger and not the elder daughter of the fifth Baron. At an unknown date he was made joint Master of the Wards with Sir Thomas Lovell. This – since it was responsible for controlling the lands and persons of minors who had inherited their estates while under age – was an immensely lucrative and influential post. Finally, probably in 1516, he became Vice-chamberlain of Queen Catherine of Aragon's Household.[4]

He now enjoyed the rank of knight banneret, which occupied a debatable ground between baron and knight. He was given a 'great chain of gold, which is worth £140 ... [by] the King's Grace', and he figured prominently in royal ceremonial. In 1515, he took part in the ceremonies for the reception of Wolsey's Cardinal's Hat, and the following year he was one of the four bannerets who carried the canopy over the infant Princess Mary at her christening. On both occasions, his stepfather/ brother-in-law, Sir Nicholas Vaux, figured as one of his colleagues, as did Sir Thomas Boleyn.[5]

Boleyn, it is now clear, was a man of similar background and aspirations to Parr. Boleyns's daughter would become Queen first. But, at this stage, Parr was ahead of the game.

This was made clear when, in April 1516, Parr was sent to meet Henry's elder sister Margaret at Newcastle and conduct her to London. It was her first visit to England since she had left to become Queen of Scots in 1503. Now she was returning as a widow after Henry's forces had killed her husband, James IV, at Flodden. Henry met her at Tottenham on 3 May. 'The same day', the Earl of Shrewsbury's Court agent informed him, 'her Grace did ride behind Sir Thomas Parr through Cheapside, about 6 o'clock, and so to Baynard's Castle, and there remains yet.' Parr was paid £100 'for the expenses of the Queen of Scots'.[6]

Parr's family life was equally successful. His marriage to Maud Green seems to have been happy and it was certainly fruitful. Their first child, born in 1512, was a girl. She was christened Catherine, almost certainly because Catherine of Aragon stood as her godmother. A son, William, was born the next year, followed by another daughter, Anne.

Quite where this growing brood was based is not clear. Parr, like many courtiers, seems to have had a London house in or near the precinct of Blackfriars monastery. This was convenient for the King's new London residence at Bridewell, which lay next door to Blackfriars to the west. It was also in easy reach by water of Greenwich, which was much the most frequently used palace at this time. Probably the Parr Household stayed at Blackfriars in the winter, with extended sojourns in the summer on the Northamptonshire estates Parr had acquired in right of his wife.

Catherine was, in short, the daughter of a coming man. Her father was well born, rich and well connected. He was blessed with children. And, above all, he enjoyed the royal favour. In the sixteenth century such men were magnets, who attracted the service of others. And Parr was sufficiently powerful to number the young Francis Bryan among his clients. Bryan was a cousin of the Howards and the Boleyns. His maternal grandfather was a baron and his own father a knight and Parr's predecessor as the Queen's Vice-chamberlain. Nevertheless it was Parr, Bryan wrote, 'whom I took as a special patron'. Years later he registered his gratitude to Parr's son William, who was by then a great man himself. Bryan fondly recollected 'the great goodness showed unto me by your most wise father', and offered his services to William in turn.[7]

But in 1517 disaster struck. The 'great plague', as the royal Secretary Pace called it, continued its ravages far into the year and in November Parr fell victim. At the time of his death, Catherine was five and her widowed mother twenty-two. Parr left £800 between Catherine and her sister for their marriages and he gave his wife a life-interest in his whole paternal inheritance to provide an income during her widowhood.[8]

With her youth and wealth, Maud Parr was, once more, a highly desirable bride. But she never remarried. Instead, she continued as one of the Queen's ladies and devoted herself to the upbringing of her children.[9]

Indeed, it seems clear that her Household soon established something of a reputation as a finishing school for the young – male as well as female. In 1523, for instance, Lord Dacre advised his son-in-law, Lord Scrope, that his son should live with Lady Parr for the remaining three years of his nonage. 'For I assure you', Dacre continued, 'he might learn with her, as well as in any place that I know, as well nurture, as French and other language, which me seems were a commodious thing for him.' We can see the results in Maud's own son, William. In about 1546, Bryan reminded him, 'I found you looking in a little book called in the French language *Méprise de la Cour* [*An Invective against the Court*]'. Parr had lent

Bryan the book and eventually got him to translate it, to help it become more generally known.

Catherine also seems to have been an able pupil. Like her brother, she certainly acquired a good knowledge of French. But her skills in the 'other language[s]' that might have been on offer in her mother's Household, in particular in Latin, have been much debated. On balance, however, the evidence would suggest that she got at least an elementary grasp of Latin as well.

Finally, she acquired the wide range of social skills comprised in Dacre's word 'nurture'. These included a knowledge of etiquette and good manners, an easy conversational style, the ability to sing and play music and, above all, the polish that made a gentleman or gentlewoman. Another word for these skills was 'courtesy' (that is, courtly behaviour) and, in the fullness of time, Catherine would prove herself an adept courtier.[10]

Maud's widowed status provided no obstacle to any of this. On the contrary. Only 'if [Lady Parr] keep her widowhood', Dacre recommended, should young Scrope remain with her. This proviso reflected the fact that any future husband was an unknown quantity. But it was also a positive endorsement of the lady herself. For Maud had a formidable character, and was a hands-on manager of her family and her fortune. She also had a right hand man in the shape of her 'cousin' and 'steward of my house', Thomas Pickering. 'My ... mother', William later informed Cromwell, 'trusted him implicitly, and admonished me implicitly to follow his advice.'[11]

This, then, was the world of Catherine's girlhood. Apart from the death of one parent (which, after all, was then the rule rather than the exception), it was as secure, prosperous and loving a childhood as anything the sixteenth century could offer. But, as again was the rule in Tudor England, her childhood was destined to be a short one. Already by 1523, when she was scarcely in her teens, the negotiations for her marriage had begun. And the prospective bridegroom was the son of Lord Scrope, whom, as we have already seen, Dacre wished to place with Lady Parr.[12]

There was, Dacre told Scrope, much in favour of Catherine as a bride for his son and heir. 'I cannot see', Dacre wrote, 'that ye can marry him to so good a stock as my Lady Parr, for divers considerations.' He then enumerated them: 'First, in remembering the wisdom of my said Lady, and the good wise stock of the Greens, whereof she is coming, and also of the wise stock of the Parrs of Kendal.' Second, there were the material advantages. For Catherine, Dacre noted, was a potential heiress, since she 'has but [the life of] one child [her brother, William] between her and 800 marks yearly to inherit thereof'.[13]

Despite Catherine's advantages of heredity and fortune, however, the marriage negotiations proved difficult. Scrope was relatively poor and his son's marriage was his only realizable cash-asset, for which he was determined to exact a premium price. But Maud Parr would have none of it. She knew the price, as well as the value, of everything and she would pay not a penny more than the going rate. By December 1523 Dacre was starting to despair of his role as honest broker: 'My Lord', he informed Scrope at last, 'the demands you have and my Lady's demands are so far asunder that it is impossible ye can ever agree'.[14]

But the warning was ignored and neither Scrope nor Maud would budge an inch. Finally, in March 1524, it was the latter who broke off negotiations in a letter addressed to Dacre 'From the Court at Greenwich'.[15]

Her marriage plans for her daughter thwarted, Maud now turned her attentions to her only son, William. In 1526 she bought back her son's marriage, control of which belonged to the King during William's minority, for the enormous sum of £1,000. She also paid other 'great sums' to Henry Bourchier, Earl of Essex, for the marriage of his daughter and heiress, Anne. William and Anne were married in February 1527, in the Chapel of the Earl's country residence, Stansted Hall in Halstead, Essex. And they continued to reside there during the first six years of the marriage.[16]

Maud was clearly delighted – though the sums she had paid to Henry and Essex were beyond even her resources and she had put herself heavily, though not imprudently, in debt. But it seemed well worth it. Not only was her 'well beloved son, William' married to a great heiress; he was also in line for the Earldom of Essex itself. Noble titles could not of course, except in the most special circumstances, be directly inherited in the female line. Nevertheless, there was a custom, known as 'the courtesy of England', by which an extinct title might be revived for the husband in right of his heiress-wife. If this custom were to be followed, William, after his father-in-law's death, would become Earl of Essex.

It was a glittering prospect. But it was bought at a price that went far beyond his mother's cash. For William was 'my Lord Parr', the man whose marital unhappiness and whose goings-on with his mistress, Dorothy Bray, were, as we have seen, regarded as an object lesson by the not very choosy Catherine Howard and her would-be lover, Thomas Culpepper.

Would his sister Catherine's marital history turn out any better?

At all events, Catherine was launched into matrimony by 1529, when she was seventeen. Fresh from her triumph with William, Maud – once more with borrowed money – had secured for Catherine the hand of Sir Edward Burgh. Burgh was not in the league of Anne Bourchier as a match. But he was a coup nonetheless. He was son and heir to Thomas, Lord Burgh of Gainsborough in Lincolnshire, and he numbered among his ancestors Beauchamps and Staffords. But, as a less fortunate aspect of his genealogy, there was a streak of hereditary insanity in the family. Edward's grandfather, also called Edward, had never been summoned to the Lords, being 'distracted of memory'. And Edward himself seems to have suffered from poor health and died in about 1533 after only four years of marriage.[17]

Catherine was now a childless widow at the age of twenty-one. She was also an orphan, since her formidable mother had died two years previously, in 1531. Catherine's share of her parents' fortune had already been used to buy her marriage. Nevertheless, she figured prominently in her mother's will. Maud left her 'my bed of purple satin, paned [panelled] with cloth of gold' and 'my beads [rosary] of lignum [a kind of hardwood] always dressed with gold, which the ... Queen's Grace [Catherine of Aragon] gave me', as well as a third of her ample collection of jewels. These included, in addition to several hundred pearls, eighteen substantial pieces, ranging from 'a ring with a table diamond, set with black anneal [enamel], meet for my little finger', to a 'tablet with pictures of the King and the Queen'. This latter was, almost certainly, another royal gift either from Henry or from Catherine's namesake and likely godmother, Catherine of Aragon.[18]

It is a set of legacies that speaks of the wealth and luxury of Catherine's upbringing, and of her family's proximity to the Court.

Within a few months, Catherine had married again. Her husband, John Neville, Lord Latimer, was twenty years older than she, twice widowed and with two children, a boy and a girl.[19]

The principal broker of the marriage was, most likely, Cuthbert Tunstall, Bishop of Durham, and the bastard son of Thomas Tunstall, who was a cousin of the Parrs. He was an executor of Maud's will as well as that of her late husband; he was also Latimer's senior colleague as President of the Council in the North, of which Latimer too was a member. Tunstall even had a remote cousinship with the Nevilles. All this fitted him perfectly for the role of intermediary.[20]

The other likely key figure in arranging the marriage was Catherine's uncle, Sir William Parr. Sir William, as we have seen, had stepped into his brother Thomas's Court office of Esquire of the Body. Subsequently, after Thomas's death, he had also stepped into his shoes as the acting head of the family during the minority of his nephew and namesake, Catherine's brother William. He acted as intermediary for young William with Cromwell and there is every reason to suppose that he played a similar role for Catherine. Certainly, when she was in a position to do so, she showed herself eager to reward him.[21]

As Lady Latimer, Catherine was the wife of a rich and substantial peer. She was the mistress of a large Household which divided its time between Latimer's magnificent country seat at Snape Castle, in the

North Riding of Yorkshire, and the Charterhouse, by Smithfield in London, where Latimer had acquired a town-house. She was also the stepmother to her husband's two children by his first wife: John, aged thirteen, and Margaret, who was much younger. Catherine never seems to have become close to her stepson, who was a tearaway, like so many Nevilles. But with Margaret her relations were warm and affectionate.

After only three years of marriage, however, the couple were engulfed in the great northern rising of the Pilgrimage of Grace. Their reactions seem to have been very different.

John Neville, Lord Latimer was one of the first peers to join the rebellion. And his defection, in view of the strategic location of his lands, was one of the most important. Snape Castle lies mid-way between Richmond to the north and Ripon to the south. To the west is the valley of the River Ure while that of the Swale is to the east. The Great North Road, known at this point as Dere Street, follows the line of the two river valleys and is commanded by Snape Castle. If Latimer remained loyal, communications between Durham and York would be difficult; if he joined the rebels, the whole strength of the north could be mustered against the King.

Archbishop Lee of York realized this. So, in early October, as news of the Lincolnshire revolt began to trigger sympathetic risings across the north, he wrote to Latimer, who was also steward of his estates in and around Ripon, to 'stay' (control) the Archbishop's tenants. Latimer obeyed but was quickly overwhelmed by the popular feeling in favour of the Pilgrimage. By 14 or 15 October he was captured; required to swear the Pilgrims' oath; and – like all captured gentry and noble leaders – compelled to assume the command of his local sector of the revolt.[22]

The idea of 'being compelled to lead' is a strange one. Were the gentle and noble Pilgrims really coerced? Or did they connive? The question has been much debated, by contemporaries and historians alike. After the event, Latimer protested that his role in the revolt was 'a very painful and dangerous time to me'. And his fellow rebels and the Duke of Norfolk, who suppressed the rebellion, both concurred. John Dakyn, the

Vicar General of York, had also found himself at Richmond on 14 or 15 October. He was intimidated by the grim determination of the rebel rank and file and guessed that Latimer was too. 'No man', Norfolk agreed, 'was in more danger of his life.'[23]

On the other hand, once he had thrown in his lot with the Pilgrimage, Latimer showed every sign of committed and active leadership. On 20 October, riding under the banner of St Cuthbert of Durham, he entered York at the head of the rebels. Then he marched to Pontefract. There he joined Lord Darcy, who, after another charade of coercion, had assumed joint leadership of the revolt. Latimer joined in the subsequent council of war, and was assigned to the van of the rebel host. On 27 October he was one of the rebel leaders who met Norfolk on Doncaster Bridge, to present the Pilgrims' terms. He took part in the Great Council of the Pilgrims which met at York on 21 November and in the subsequent, more important, meeting at Pontefract on 2–4 December. In the latter he was responsible for one of the most striking initiatives, when he asked Archbishop Lee and the other clergy to 'show their learning whether subjects might lawfully move war in any case against their prince'.[24]

This is the doctrine of resistance, which was anathema to the Tudors and to Henry above all. Indeed, the implications of Latimer's remark are *so* radical that it seems doubtful that he was the sole author of it. Instead, there must be a suggestion of discussion with a stronger, more questioning intelligence than Latimer ever showed himself to be.

And, as we shall see, his likely interlocutor, and the key to much that is puzzling about Latimer's behaviour, is Sir Francis Bigod.

So much, for the moment, for Lord Latimer. But what of Lady Latimer? For the Pilgrimage was a movement in which women showed themselves at least as active as their menfolk. Indeed, it was often the wife who took the lead, and the husband who vacillated prudentially – as with Mr and Mrs Christopher Stapleton. Stapleton, an elderly and valetudinarian gentleman, was in the habit of spending his summers in the Grey Friars at Beverley for a change of air. This meant that he was caught in the town when Beverley declared for the rebels on 8 October. Stapleton ordered his people to remain within the Friary. But his wife defied him and went outside to greet the crowds: 'God's blessing have ye', she cried, 'and speed you well in your good purpose.' Still worse, she betrayed the hiding place of her husband and his servants. 'They be in the Friars', she volunteered, 'go pull them out by the heads!' 'What do you mean', the wretched Stapleton exclaimed when the virago returned indoors, 'except ye would have me, my son and heir, and my brother cast away?' 'It was God's quarrel', she replied simply.[25]

Lady Hussey, the Dowager Countess of Northumberland, and Margaret Cheyney, the mistress-cum-wife of Sir John Bulmer, both behaved similarly. But not, apparently, Lady Latimer. Not one scrap of evidence was produced against her and her name appears in none of the multitude of depositions which were gathered after the event.[26]

At first sight, this is surprising. As we have seen, Catherine's mother, born Maud Green, had been one of Catherine of Aragon's ladies-in-waiting and had left her elder daughter a rosary of the Queen's gift as an heirloom. Catherine herself was probably the old Queen's god-daughter. And Catherine Parr was, or soon became, close to Catherine of Aragon's daughter Mary. It was ties of this kind which turned Lady Hussey into a more-or-less open partisan of the Pilgrims. And nothing, not even an earlier spell in the Tower for continuing to refer to Mary as 'Princess' after she had been stripped of her title, seemed to deter her.

But somehow Lady Latimer remained immune. Was it the combined 'wisdom' of the Greens and the Parrs, to which Lord Dacre referred so appreciatively, which led her to keep her distance? Or had she already begun to lose sympathy with the 'old religion', which provided the driving force of the Pilgrimage?[27]

Here we enter a minefield. We know, because Catherine herself later lamented the fact, that she had once been an enthusiastic Papist. 'I sought', she confessed, 'for such riffraff as the Bishop of Rome had planted in his tyranny and kingdom, trusting with great confidence by the virtue and holiness of them to receive full remission of sins.'[28]

That she underwent conversion, as all the first generation of Reformers did, is therefore clear. The question is when?

Recent fashionable academic opinion has tended to place the moment as late as 1544, when she was in her mid-thirties. I followed this, without much thinking about it, in my *Elizabeth*. But what if her conversion was much earlier, while she was in her twenties? It was, after all, the young who were most susceptible to Reform, as the young always tend to be to extravagant new doctrines. But, it will be objected, she spent her twenties in the north, which was Catholic and conservative. Actually, Yorkshire in the mid-1530s was far from this caricature of homogeneous conventionality. There *were* passionate Reformers and outstanding preachers and Catherine, as we shall see, had close family ties with the most radical of them.[29]

What if she had begun to listen to them? What if she had begun to believe them?

But, despite Catherine's caution and whatever the nature of her religious belief, the Pilgrimage finally caught up with her. It did so in a particularly ugly way.

Like the other chief leaders of the Pilgrimage, Latimer had been summoned to Court at New Year 1537. But when he reached Buntingford in Hertfordshire on his journey south, he was informed that he had been countermanded because, on 16 January, Norfolk had been redespatched to the north with orders to pacify the countryside and punish offenders. Latimer was to return home and assist him. He can only have been away a week or two at most. But the damage had been done. The common people were now suspicious that the gentry and nobility were preparing to double-cross them with a covert deal with the King. Latimer's sudden departure for the Court seemed to confirm these fears, and his home and family became a target. 'The Commons in coming forward', Darcy heard on about 18 January, 'have been at the houses . . . of . . . the Lord Latimer and other gentlemen who have been with your Highness in London and taken inventories of all their goods'.[30]

Latimer himself learned the news two days later at Stamford on his return journey and he poured out his distress in a letter to Admiral Fitzwilliam. 'I learn', he wrote, 'that the commons of Richmondshire, grieved at my coming up, have entered my house at Snape, and will destroy it if I come not home shortly.' 'If I do not please them', he continued, 'I know not what they will do with my body and goods, wife and children.'

Latimer was now caught between the King and the common people. He was mistrusted by both and whatever he did would give offence to both. Faced with this impossible situation, he desperately sought a way out. 'If it were the King's pleasure that I might live upon such small lands as I have in the South', he concluded, 'I would little care of my lands in the North.'[31]

But he was to be allowed no such easy escape. Nor was Catherine. She had already faced the fury of the commons, who had burst into her house and (taking a leaf out of the King's book) had listed its contents for seizure. They had also, or so Latimer believed, threatened her and her stepchildren. All that was bad enough. But worse was to come since she would now have to try to protect her husband from the slower, but more terrible, wrath of the King.

Henry, as we have often seen, was capable of dissimulating his anger until the moment was ripe to strike. By June 1537, Latimer's turn had come, and he seemed particularly exposed. For in 1534, the year after his marriage to Catherine, he had entered into an agreement for the marriage of his daughter and Catherine's favourite, Margaret Neville, with Ralph, the son and heir of Sir Francis Bigod. Bigod was a substantial knight of the East Riding, with his seat some forty-five miles to the east of Snape at Mulgrave Castle, on the coast near Whitby.[32]

A marriage agreement between neighbouring county families was of the most commonplace. But Bigod was not. Instead, though aged only thirty, he had already emerged as one of the most singular men of his age. He was a scholar and a gentleman, an MP and a published author, an Henrician loyalist and – at the last – a rebel. But, above all, he was an ardent believer in Reform. This he worked for, at every level: in Parliament, where he was an activist MP; at Court, where he lobbied Cromwell; in his Household, where he maintained distinguished (and very radical) chaplains; and in his 'country' of Yorkshire, where he mounted a one-man campaign 'in setting forth the word of God, having there preachers of my own cost, and rode all over the country with them'.[33]

He even, he told Cromwell, who was his friend and confidant since their days together in Wolsey's Household, aspired to be a priest himself. 'Specially, afore anything', he begged the minister, 'help me to be a priest, that I may preach the Word of God, or else dispense with me, that being no priest I may do it.'[34]

A priest – especially perhaps a priest *manqué* like Bigod – requires a congregation: to move, to convert and eventually to answer and echo his certainties with their own. And it seems likely that Bigod found a willing listener in Catherine and probably in her husband too. For connexions between the two families were close. Apart from the marriage agreement, for which 'Mr Parr' (probably Catherine's uncle, Sir William) acted as a trustee, Latimer had helped out the perpetually indebted Bigod by buying a large chunk of his lands for £600 cash, payable in instalments. Latimer's servants evidently frequented Bigod's house and Latimer's brother William Neville and his wife spent Christmas 1536 with the Bigods at Mulgrave.[35]

The result of this intercourse was that the Latimers' Household borrowed some of the features of Reform. Robert Plumpton of Knaresborough, about twenty miles to the south-west of Snape, who had been won over to Reform by Tyndale's translation of the New Testament, was eager 'not only to be [Latimer's] servant, but of his household and attending unto him'. And Margaret Neville, Catherine's step-daughter and Bigod's intended daughter-in-law, received a 'godly education' at Catherine's hands, for which, as she later acknowledged, 'I am never able to render to her . . . sufficient thanks'.[36]

The mystery of Catherine's refusal to endorse the Pilgrimage is now on the way to a solution. She held aloof because she was already converted to Reform – perhaps by Bigod or perhaps by one of his chaplains, such as the charismatic Thomas Garrett. It was Garrett, then a missionary-cum-bookseller, who had 'infected' Oxford with heresy in 1527. One of his converts, then or soon after, was Bigod, who had studied at Oxford though without taking a degree. Was Catherine, as now seems possible, another of Garrett's conquests for Reform?[37]

But the strange saga of Bigod's life was not yet complete. As a convinced Reformer, his first reaction to the Pilgrimage had been to try to flee. He took ship at Mulgrave and set sail for London. But the treacherous winds of the North Sea in autumn drove him back to land. Eventually, he was captured by the rebels and, like others of his class, forced to swear the Pilgrims' oath-and to 'lead' a detachment of the rebellion.[38]

There is no doubt that the process was even more fraught in Bigod's case than most: he was contemptuous of the rebels as Papist reactionaries; they were suspicious of him as a meddling Reformer. But the chemistry of revolt wrought a remarkable change in Bigod's opinions. He, unlike Henry and Cromwell, had never seen the Supremacy as an end in itself. Instead, he acclaimed it as an historic moment, in which 'we be delivered from the hard, sharp and ten thousand times more than judicial captivity of that Babylonical man of Rome, to the sweet and soft service, yea, rather liberty, of the Gospel'.[39]

But what had happened to these extravagant, almost Millennarian, hopes? They had been dashed. Indeed, as Bigod was one of the first to see, the Supremacy, as interpreted by Henry and enforced by Cromwell, was leading, not to liberty, of the Gospel or anything else, but to servitude and tyranny.

By the time of the Pontefract Council of 2–4 December, Bigod's fluent pen had expressed these doubts in a thesis. It examined, from first principles, 'what authority belonged to the Pope, what to a Bishop, and what to a King'. And it concluded that 'the Head of the Church of England might be a spiritual man, as the Archbishop of Canterbury or such'. 'In no wise', however, might the Headship belong to the King, 'for he should with the sword defend all spiritual men in their right'.[40]

*

Bigod, though starting from the opposite religious position, had now reached the same conclusion about the Royal Supremacy as Aske and Darcy. It was wrong and illegitimate, and Henry must be made to give it up. But having come to agree on ends, they now differed on tactics. Aske and Darcy were confident that their demonstration and Henry's apparent surrender to it were enough. Bigod was shrewder. Only force, he argued, would compel Henry to give up what he had acquired. The common people in the north felt the same and Bigod, with a series of bold and impassioned speeches, put himself at their head in a new uprising in January 1537.[41]

The uprising fizzled out quickly, largely because Aske and Darcy refused their support. Instead, they persisted in trusting to Henry's promises, and acting as good subjects meanwhile. In vain. Henry used Bigod's rising as an excuse comprehensively to break his word with the Pilgrims. His lawyers twisted Aske and Darcy's careful distancing of themselves from Bigod into evidence of treasonable intent and they and the rest were executed.

Would Latimer meet the same fate?

It seemed very likely. On 2 June Norfolk thanked Cromwell 'for his information that the King does not much favour Lord Latimer'. But what if Latimer made the short journey from Snape to consult Norfolk at his headquarters at Sheriff Hutton? How, the Duke of Norfolk wanted to know, should he deal with him? Cromwell's instructions were that the Duke should trick Latimer into coming to London. Norfolk obeyed. He had 'contrived', he wrote to Cromwell on 16 June, 'to make him go to London as a suitor on his own affairs'.[42]

Latimer, aware that it might be his last journey, travelled at a fairly leisurely pace and stopped off en route to visit his brother Thomas, who lived at Aldham near Colchester in Essex. There Latimer was arrested by the neighbouring magnate, the Earl of Oxford, and sent to London. He arrived by the end of the month and was promptly clapped in the Tower.[43]

Latimer had, semi-voluntarily, placed himself in the King's power.

Was this suicide? His brother Thomas Neville certainly thought so. 'Alas, Mary', he said to his wife, 'my brother is cast away.' 'By God's Blood', he added, 'if I had the King here I would make him that he should never take man into the Tower!' Thomas was also sure that it was Latimer's great wealth that made him such tempting prey. Would her master, the Parson of Aldham, who had been arrested on suspicion of treason, be put to death? Margaret Towler asked Thomas on 4 July. 'No, Margaret', he replied, 'he shall not be put to death, for he hath no lands nor goods to lose.' 'But', he added bitterly, 'if he were either a knight or a lord that had lands or goods to lose, then he should lose his life.' Surely, Margaret remonstrated, 'the King's Grace will put no man to death neither for goods nor lands?' 'Yes, by God, Margaret', Thomas Neville countered, 'but he would.'[44]

Thus Latimer's brother. But what of Latimer's wife?

Once again, as six months earlier in the Pilgrimage, Catherine was silent. And once more the silence is eloquent. For Catherine never wavered in her judgment of Henry. She followed neither Bigod nor her brother-in-law into a cynical reading of Henry's motives. Always, for her, whatever the King did was for the best. He was just. He was virtuous.

But being just and virtuous are merely human qualities. The Henry she saw was more than that. He was God's chosen instrument. He was 'our Moses', as she put it in her posthumously published *Lamentations of a Sinner*, '[who] hath delivered us out of the captivity and spiritual bondage of Pharaoh (that is, the Pope)'. He was even, she seemed to suggest, a Messiah, who 'hath taken away the veils and mists of errors, and brought us to the knowledge of the truth by the light of God's Word'.

One Messiah had been King of the Jews; the other was King of England, sent 'in these latter days to reign over us' – by God and for God's purposes.[45]

It was a conviction which stood Catherine in good stead in her first brush with royal power on the arrest of her husband. And it would be her rock in her relations with Henry thereafter.

*

Catherine's unimpeachable loyalty and her steadying influence were, no doubt, part of the reason that Latimer, contrary to his brother's expectations, survived his sojourn in the Tower. But other things came into play as well. Latimer used some of his wealth to bribe Cromwell: with an annual fee, with the lease of his London house, and with the sale, doubtless on advantageous terms, of one of his southern manors. He also re-invented himself as a model citizen: loyal and dependable, yet never pushing himself forward. But the most important reason for his survival, I would guess, was the increasing political weight of his wife's family.[46]

For this, the Parrs had, in the first instance at least, to thank the Pilgrimage. In the case of most of the northern élite, of course, the Pilgrimage was a disaster. For the Parrs, on the other hand, it was an opportunity. They were a leading northern family. But, having followed the high road to London, their absenteeism in the south preserved them from the local pressure which had turned even Reformers, including Bigod, into potential traitors. Instead, the Parrs could be loyal without risk and they took advantage of their good fortune by a display of conspicuous activism on the King's behalf. Catherine's uncle, Sir William, was the right hand man of the Duke of Suffolk in suppressing the Lincolnshire revolt; while her brother, young William, gained his first practical experience as a member of the suite of the Duke of Norfolk on the mopping-up operation in the north in 1537.

William's assiduity caught the eye of the Duke of Norfolk, who recommended him to Cromwell for having 'wisely handled himself in this business'. Nothing seems to have come of the Duke's hint. Nor did Cromwell take up Sir William's suggestion in January 1539 that, 'considering the late change' (that is, the fall and execution of Exeter and Sir Nicholas Carew), the minister should 'procure a place in the King's Privy Chamber for his nephew'. But William did not have long to wait for even better things. Two months later, on Sunday, 9 March 1539, he was created Baron Parr in a splendid ceremony in the Presence Chamber at Whitehall. And four years later still in 1543, he was made Lord Warden of the West Marches and a Knight of the Garter.[47]

He was barely thirty and already most of his mother's ambitions for him were fulfilled.

Meanwhile, it fell to Catherine's young sister, Anne, to step into her mother's place as one of the Queen's ladies. By 1537, as 'Mrs Parr', Anne had become one of Jane Seymour's maidens. She was barely sixteen, sweet and, thanks to her mother's foresight, eminently marriageable. As we have seen, her father had left her a substantial marriage portion, to which her mother's will added 400 marks in plate and a third share of her jewels. The whole fortune, Lady Parr had directed, was to be securely chested up 'in coffers locked with divers locks, whereof every one of them my executors and my . . . daughter Anne to have every of them a key'. 'And there', Lady Parr's will continued, 'it to remain till it ought to be delivered unto her' on her marriage.[48]

And the marriage, everyone thought, would not be long delayed and there were repeated rumours of its imminence in the summer of 1537. 'I think Mrs Parr shall shortly fall [into marriage]', John Husey reported to Lady Lisle in June. 'Men thinketh Mrs Parr shall shortly marry', he wrote again in August. In the event, Anne was still unmarried at the time of Jane's funeral in October and she may have remained so for another year or more. But by January 1539 she had married the up-and-coming courtier, William Herbert. She had also become the Chief Gentlewoman of the Privy Chamber to the new Queen, Anne of Cleves. And she was to retain the office when Anne of Cleves in turn gave way to Catherine Howard.[49]

As her siblings were launched on glittering careers of their own, Catherine almost disappears from view. Historians, indeed, imagine they glimpse her and write vivid accounts of her Protestant salon in her husband's house in the Charterhouse. It became, they claim, a centre of advanced doctrine and was frequented by such luminaries as John Parkhurst, Hugh Latimer and Miles Coverdale. But, alas, it is all a mirage. In the early 1540s, Parkhurst was at Oxford; Latimer was in disgrace and Coverdale was in exile, where he remained till 1547. If

Catherine ever hosted such a salon, which I rather doubt, she could not have done so till the reign of Henry VIII's son, Edward VI.[50]

But on 2 March 1543 her husband, Lord Latimer, died, having made his will the previous 12 September. There is nothing in his will to suggest (as some historians have guessed) that there had been any open rupture or disagreement with Catherine. On the contrary, he left his wife two manors in her own right as well as money for four years, 'for the bringing up of my daughter (Margaret)'. This bequest must only have regularized the existing position, as a tailor's bill addressed to Catherine on 16 February (a fortnight before her husband's death) charges her for a 'kirtle' (a dress) provided 'for your daughter'.[51]

Catherine was now a widow for the second time: still pretty, still unblemished by child-bearing, and well-off. She was desirable, and, it is clear, she desired in return.

The individual on whom she had set her heart was Sir Thomas Seymour, the late Queen Jane's younger brother and uncle to Prince Edward. Seymour was dashing and rather dangerous. That Catherine found him so attractive suggests hidden emotional depths. Or rather, perhaps, very human shallows: after a lifetime of doing what she ought, as a daughter and a wife, a little of what she fancied might have seemed irresistibly appealing. 'My mind', she wrote to Seymour some years later, 'was fully bent . . . to marry you before any man I know.'[52]

We do not know when they met, or when their evidently mutual attraction began. Probably it was before Latimer's death. If so, she handled her feelings with her usual 'wisdom' and discretion.

The feelings were strong nevertheless. 'I was at liberty to marry you', she reminded Seymour. And it is evident that she revelled in her freedom.

But a force more powerful still intervened: the King himself.

76. Queen Catherine

Sometime in the late spring of 1543 Henry VIII offered Catherine Parr his hand. As with her simultaneous courtship with Sir Thomas Seymour, the background to the relationship is obscure. Perhaps Catherine and Henry were introduced by Catherine's brother or sister, both of whom were now well placed and high in favour. Perhaps Catherine at some stage had petitioned the King in person on behalf of the disgraced Latimer and had caught the royal eye.

However it occurred, it is clear that Henry's offer was unwelcome to Catherine. She was already in love with Seymour. And she was not, unlike Henry's previous English wives, in the least infatuated with the idea of being Queen. Instead, she seems to have been aware of the pitfalls and dangers of the position and properly doubtful of her capacity to fulfil it. But equally, for a subject, a royal request to marry was the equivalent of a command. It was almost unthinkable to say no.

In this dilemma, Catherine, like a true believer, turned to God for guidance. An answer came. But it was not the one she wanted. She prayed again. The answer remained the same. Still she resisted; still God was implacable. And so the struggle continued: 'God', she wrote to Seymour, 'withstood my will therein most vehemently for a time.'

But finally her resistance was overcome. 'Through His grace and goodness', she remembered, '[He] made that possible which seemed to me impossible: that was, made me renounce utterly mine own will and to follow His most willingly.'

And His will, she now accepted, was that she should marry Henry.[1]

Her submission, which was as ecstatic as her resistance had been fierce, had the effect of a revelation. Henceforward Catherine was a woman with a mission. She was marrying Henry at God's command and for His purpose. And that purpose was no less than to complete the conversion of England to Reform.

So the last and apparently the most unassuming of Henry's Queens was, in fact, the most dedicated and determined. She had known the passions of both earthly and heavenly love and she had emerged with her character formidably annealed in the flames.

How would the ever more irrascible and self-willed King cope? And would she survive?

It may be that God had another auxiliary in the struggle to persuade Catherine to choose to marry Henry.

The man she really loved, Sir Thomas Seymour, had spent most of 1542 on a mission to Charles V's brother Ferdinand, King of the Romans, during which he had witnessed Ferdinand's unsuccessful attempt to recapture Pest from the Turks. He returned home in the New Year, only to be redespatched almost immediately as ambassador to Mary of Hungary, Regent of the Netherlands. Chapuys had first caught wind of the intention to send Seymour to the Netherlands on 10 March 1543; a week later, on the 17th, Henry informed the ambassador that the decision had been taken.[2]

What has excited historians' attention, of course, is that Latimer had died only a few days earlier on 2 March. Was Henry moving quickly to get an inconvenient rival out of the way?[3]

It is possible. But, on closer examination, the King's manoeuvres turn out to have been less than decisive. In the same letter that Chapuys announced Seymour's official nomination as ambassador, he also noted that it was unlikely that Seymour would leave until after Easter (25 March). In the event, his departure was delayed a further six weeks until the beginning of May. If Henry really had feared Seymour's hold over Catherine, it is inconceivable that he would have left him kicking his heels at Court for two full months after Latimer's death. For these weeks, surely, were the time when the crucial struggle between Catherine's will and God's declared intention took place. Had Seymour had the power to alter the outcome, Henry's dilatoriness gave him every opportunity to try.[4]

Instead, it seems almost certain that Catherine's own subsequent account of her choice is correct. In it, she made no mention of Seymour's temporary exile as a factor in her decision. Rather she attributed it solely to God and to her own struggle with her inner voices.

By June the struggle was over. One of the first to be told the way the wind was blowing was Catherine's brother, William, Lord Parr, who had been appointed Lord Warden of the Western March in April 1543. Other news 'is none', John Dudley, who was now Lord Admiral and Viscount Lisle, wrote to him from Greenwich on 20 June, 'but that my Lady Latimer, your sister, and Mrs Herbert [Parr's other sister Anne] be both here at Court with my Lady Mary's Grace and my Lady Elizabeth'.[5]

The movements of the royal family would suggest that Dudley's letter marks the actual moment of Catherine's decision. For during June its members had been unusually scattered. Henry had spent most of the month journeying to and from Harwich, 'where he perused and saw two notable havens but liked Colne Water best'. Mary had taken advantage of her father's absence to pay a visit to her ex-stepmother, Anne of Cleves, at Richmond. While Catherine, presumably, had pondered her fate at the Charterhouse.[6]

When, therefore, Catherine rejoined the Court at Greenwich, where Henry arrived on the 19th, it can only have been to inform the King that she had accepted him. Plans for the wedding then moved forward swiftly. On 10 July Cranmer issued his licence to permit the marriage to be solemnized 'in any church, chapel or oratory without the issue of banns'. And two days later, on the 12th, the ceremony itself took place in the Queen's Privy Closet at Hampton Court.[7]

This was the more private of the Queen's two oratories. Similarly, the wedding itself, as might be expected in the case of an already much-married, middle-aged couple, was a quiet, almost private affair. But it was by no means a hole-in-corner one. The celebrant was Stephen Gardiner, Bishop of Winchester. And the congregation, which numbered about twenty, was made up of the Gentlemen of the King's Privy Chamber, as well as close family members of the bride and groom. Both Henry's daughters, Mary and Elizabeth, were present, as was Lady Margaret Douglas, his niece by his elder sister Margaret's second but divorced husband, Archibald Douglas, Earl of Angus. Catherine's family was represented only by her sister and brother-in-law, Anne and William Herbert. But the three aristocratic ladies who were then closest to her – Catherine, Duchess of Suffolk (*née* Willoughby), Anne, Countess of Hertford (*née* Stanhope) and Joan, Viscountess Lisle (*née* Guildford) – were also present.

Inevitably, in the close-knit world of the Tudor Court, there were many reminders of the past. Only a few dozen yards away from where he then stood, Henry had found Cranmer's letter denouncing Catherine Howard. The celebrant, Gardiner, had already helped make or unmake four of the King's previous marriages. And many other members of the congregation had been almost as actively involved. Russell had been abused by Anne Boleyn; had rejoiced at her fall and had been confided in by Henry over Anne of Cleves. Browne, Heneage and Denny had likewise shared the King's confidences in the Cleves affair. But it was of course his daughters, Mary and Elizabeth, who bore the heaviest scars.

If Henry was aware of any of this he showed no sign. Instead, he made the marriage vows '*hilari vultu*' – 'with a joyful countenance'.[8]

Catherine's expression is not noted.

Four days later, Secretary Wriothesley, who had done well out of the fall of his master Cromwell, wrote to Henry's former brother-in-law, the Duke of Suffolk. He enclosed a letter from the Duchess of Suffolk, who had of course been a witness of the wedding. But he also added his own comments on the bride. Catherine was 'a woman, in my judgment', Wriothesley wrote, 'for virtue, wisdom, and gentleness, most meet for his Highness and I am sure his Majesty had never a wife more agreeable to his heart than she is'. 'Our Lord', he ended piously, 'send them long life and much joy together.'[9]

Four days later still, on the 20th, Wriothesley forwarded another letter, from Catherine herself to her brother William. Naturally, there is no mention of her own doubts about the marriage. Instead she expresses a simple, heart-felt happiness: 'It [hath] pleased God to incline the King to take her as his wife', she writes, 'which is the greatest joy and comfort that could happen to her.' And she is eager for William to share in her delight, 'as the person who has most cause to rejoice thereat'.

Some historians have detected a note of cynicism in this last remark, as though Catherine should hint that she had been sacrificed on the altar of her brother's family ambition. But this is to strain both Catherine's language and the facts. William may have (re)introduced Henry and Catherine. But there is no evidence that he played a decisive part in the marriage. And certainly, far away in the north, he can have exercised no direct pressure on his sister. Moreover, Catherine had a straightforward Tudor sense of family honour, and, it is clear, a real affection for her brother. 'Let her sometimes hear of his health', she begs him, 'as friendly as if she had not been called to this honour.' In other words: write to me just as you used to, and forget that I am Queen.[10]

Wriothesley glossed this letter, too, in a covering note. 'Your good lordship', he wrote, 'shall herewith receive a letter from the Queen's Highness, who is a most gracious lady and to your lordship a most kind sister.' 'I doubt not', he continued, 'but you will earnestly thank God of His goodness, and also frame yourself to be every day more and more an ornament to her Majesty.'[11]

Perhaps, in view of these effusions and his earlier Judas-record, it is not surprising that Wriothesley turned into one of Catherine's most dangerous enemies.

The welcome, real or simulated, for Catherine's marriage was not universal of course. Indeed, for that other relic of the past, Anne of Cleves, it represented the last straw. 'She is', Chapuys was informed, 'in despair and much afflicted in consequence of this late marriage.' For Catherine, so Anne proudly felt, was her 'inferior ... in beauty and gives no hope of posterity to the King, for she had no children by her two first husbands'. Now that Henry was definitively lost, as even Anne was forced to admit, her estates, palaces and possessions had lost their charm as well. 'She would rather', Chapuys heard from 'an authentic quarter', 'be stripped to her petticoat and return to her mother than remain longer in England.'[12]

Perhaps. But we should remember that Chapuys, in view of the hostility between the Empire and Anne's brother, the Duke of Cleves, was not an impartial witness: he was eager to bring about a final rupture between England and Cleves and eager, too, to get Anne out of the way. But, in any case, Anne's desperate mood did not last. She was not the despairing sort and England, finally, was her destiny.

The coolest reaction of all to Catherine's wedding came from the radical English merchant, Richard Hilles, self-exiled in Strasbourg. 'Our King has, within these two months', he reported in September to Henry Bullinger, 'burned three godly men in one day.' But then, Hilles added, Henry had got married at the same time, 'and he is always wont to celebrate his nuptials by some wickedness of this kind'. Hilles's letter shows that Catherine's own Reformist leanings were as yet unknown outside the Court; indeed, they may even have been unknown to Henry himself.[13]

For the moment, perhaps, it was better that way.

Catherine was proclaimed Queen at Hampton Court on the day of her wedding. It was the barest of formalities. Otherwise, there was no *entrée* into London, or river procession, or any other kind of inauguration ceremony. And the idea of a coronation was not even mentioned, either then or subsequently.

A few days later, the King and Queen left on what turned out to be a protracted honeymoon that kept them away from the capital for the rest of the year. It began, however, as an ordinary Progress. First they travelled into Surrey, with visits to some of Henry's favourite hunting parks at Oatlands, Woking, Guildford and Sunninghill. Then, in mid-August, the royal party crossed the Thames on their way north. They stayed a few days in Catherine's own house as Queen at Hanworth, near Twickenham, before skirting London to the west on their way to Hertfordshire and

Bedfordshire. There they spent the high summer, going from Wolsey's old house at The More, to Ashridge, Dunstable and Ampthill.

Ampthill, where Henry was a frequent visitor because of the excellence of the sport and 'the cleanness of air', had its usual rejuvenating effect. Or perhaps it was his new marriage. For, during the royal visit, carpenters were set to work on a new spiral staircase to give Henry access from his Privy Chamber to the gardens and park, while in the park itself they erected three new standings from which the King could view the hunt and shoot at the game.

After Ampthill, the King and Queen turned west into Buckingham-shire and Oxfordshire. They reached Woodstock in the middle of September, and they remained there till the end of the month.[14]

Usually, the Progress would have ended about then. But the plague, which had been particularly virulent in London in the summer, raged all the autumn and interrupted the ordinary routines of public life. The sessions of the Law Courts were moved from London to St Albans while the King and Queen returned to safety at Ampthill, where they spent much of October and November. Henry paid a flying visit to Whitehall on 20–21 December, but then withdrew once more to spend Christmas at Hampton Court.[15]

The effect of all this was to throw Catherine together with her new husband almost uninterruptedly for six months. It also gave Henry his most prolonged taste of family life for almost two decades.

He seems rather to have enjoyed it.

It had all begun in the run-up to Catherine's marriage. As we have seen, Catherine seems to have told Henry of her decision to accept him at Greenwich on about 20 June. Mary and Elizabeth were at Court as well and the assumption must be that they had been summoned to meet their new stepmother. Was this Henry's doing? Or Catherine's?

Catherine's predecessor, Catherine Howard, had made a similar attempt at bringing Henry's children together. But it took place several months after her marriage and followed a sticky patch with her difficult eldest stepchild, Mary. Between them, Catherine and Henry were contriving to get matters off to a much smoother start. Mary and Elizabeth were honoured guests at their wedding, and, on the wedding day itself, Catherine gave Mary a very substantial present of £20 and no doubt made a similar gift to Elizabeth as well. The two half-sisters then continued at Court with their parents for the first leg of the Progress. After that, they went their separate ways.[16]

The fact was reported with glee by Chapuys. 'The King continues to treat [Mary] kindly', he wrote on 13 August, 'and has made her stay with the new Queen, who behaves affectionately towards her.' 'As to Anne Boleyn's daughter', he continued disparagingly, 'the King has sent her back again to stay with the Prince, his son.'[17]

Here, however, it is Chapuys's own prejudices that speak. In reality, there was a perfectly proper reason for the contrasting treatment of Catherine's two step-daughters. Mary was in her mid-twenties: gracious, as attractive as she ever would be, and an ornament to the Court. Elizabeth, on the other hand, was just ten. She was growing up quickly. But she was still more suited to the schoolroom than the Court and it was to her schooling that she returned.

There would be plenty of other opportunities for Catherine to get to know her better.

For the moment, then, it was Catherine's relationship with Mary that flourished. Her own mother's long years of service to Mary's mother, Catherine of Aragon, would have provided the key bond. Probably indeed Catherine still had Maud Parr's bequest of the 'beads of lignum always dressed with gold, which the ... Queen's Grace gave me'. The rosary was not something to be shown to Henry. But, with Mary, it would have been an instant passport to her affection and trust. Besides, with only a four-year gap between them, stepmother and daughter were almost of an age. And they shared the same interests, from scholarship to dancing.[18]

As the Progress continued, however, circumstances would also have brought Henry's other children to Catherine's attention. Probably this was planned as well. Their nursery-houses were located in and around

Hertfordshire, which was the destination of the second half of the Progress. Here Henry was killing several birds with one stone: he was eager to inspect his houses at Dunstable, where he was converting the nunnery in which Cranmer had granted his first divorce, and at Ampthill, which he planned to turn into a palace. But the royal couple also visited Ashridge, where Elizabeth and Edward seem to have been staying. And the unexpected return of the Court to the area in the autumn brought fresh opportunities. Mary's accounts for these months show that messengers were sent to and from the other royal Households in the vicinity and servants exchanged. Almost certainly, family meetings and visits took place as well – though just who met whom is impossible to establish.[19]

By Christmas, Henry's new-found domesticity was becoming a subject of speculation in foreign Courts. In the Netherlands, for example, the Lady Regent, Mary of Hungary, asked the English ambassador 'how the Queen's Grace, my Lord Prince, my Lady Mary and my Lady Elizabeth did, and whether [the King] and they continued still in one household?'[20]

It made a change from deaths and divorces.

But we must not sentimentalize too much, or exaggerate Catherine's own role. No doubt she facilitated. But the accommodation with Henry's children took place because he, Henry, wanted it. And it was a prelude to a much more momentous decision: on 16 January 1544 the Court returned to Whitehall for a new session of Parliament whose principal item of business would be to legislate a new, radical settlement of the Succession.[21]

The existing law had been laid down by the Second Succession Act, which was passed in 1536 after the Seymour marriage. This Act determined the order of succession as Henry's heirs male by Queen Jane; his heirs male 'by any other lawful wife'; his female heirs by Queen Jane, and his female heirs by any future wife. At the time, these provisions seemed to cater for any forseeable eventuality. But, eight years later, time and dynastic luck were, it appeared, threatening to run out.[22]

Henry was fifty-two. He remained capable of extraordinary bursts of energy, as on the Progress of 1543. But, in general, he was ageing visibly and rapidly. On the other hand, Prince Edward, his heir and sole legitimate offspring, was only a boy of six. He was a healthy and vigorous child. Even so, sixteenth-century mortality rates made it an open question whether he would live to marry and have children.

Equally open to doubt was the fertility of the new Queen, on which rested the possibility of any further legitimate children, male or female. For contemporaries, as we have seen in the case of Chapuys, looked at Catherine's two previous marriages, which were childless, and drew the conclusion that she was sterile. The conclusion, as it turned out, was wrong and when she married a husband who was potent she conceived almost immediately, despite being in her mid-thirties. But that lay in the unknown future and, meanwhile, the doubt remained.

The result was that a real and pressing uncertainty now bedevilled the whole future descent of the Tudor crown. This the new Succession Act frankly admitted. 'It standeth', it acknowledged, 'in the only pleasure and will of Almighty God whether the King's Majesty shall have any heirs begotten and procreated between his Highness and his ... most entirely beloved wife Queen Catherine.' 'Or whether', it continued, 'the said Prince Edward shall have issue of his body lawfully begotten.'[23]

If, God forbid, the worst happened and both these lines of descent failed, then an alternative was necessary. The solution proffered in the Act was to restore Catherine's step-daughters, Mary and Elizabeth, in that order, to the succession. They remained bastardized. And the Act envisaged that special conditions would be imposed on them by the King. Nevertheless, they were now acknowledged heirs presumptive to the crown.

Thus the 'one Household', in which Henry had lived with his new wife and his three children for much of the time since his marriage to Catherine, had found its legal expression. And there is every reason to believe that Catherine had encouraged Henry in this decision, which, for better and for worse, shaped the future of England for the rest of the sixteenth-century and beyond.

*

The other principal concern of the 1544 Session of Parliament was religion. And here again Catherine's influence was strong, although historians have been slow to recognize the fact. But they are hardly to be blamed, in view of the intractability of the sources. These consist of a series of stories and reminiscences, to be found either in Foxe's *Book of Martyrs* or in Foxe's working papers. The stories, as usual with Foxe, are more or less undated. But, it turns out, the prolonged Progress of 1543, which I have just documented for the first time, provides the clues which both pin-down and validate the incidents narrated by Foxe.[24]

And their (admittedly off-stage) heroine is Catherine.

The previous Session of Parliament, which had ended on 12 May 1543, a couple of months before Catherine's wedding, marked the high point of the conservative reaction in religion. Its chief target and intended victim was Archbishop Cranmer and its architect and presiding genius was Bishop Gardiner of Winchester.

It had been clear ever since Thomas Garrett's book-selling trip to Oxford in 1528 that printed books, especially in English, were the prime source for innovations in religion. But the conservative response, with book-burnings, like Wolsey's, or printed counter-propaganda, like More's, had been patchy. Gardiner, on the other hand, was that rarest of things, a reactionary with a clear sense of strategy, and the will and boldness to carry it out. Not for him, therefore, the piecemeal approach of his predecessors. Instead, under his guidance, the Lords launched a frontal attack on the whole new print culture.

The Act, 'concerning printing of books', was drawn in the widest of terms, banning not only erroneous printed books but also 'printed ballads, plays, rimes, songs and other fantasies'. Indeed, its terms were *so* wide that almost anything on sale could be caught by them and a series of hastily added provisos were necessary to define what was still acceptable in the vernacular. The resulting list was not long. The Lord's Prayer, Ave Maria and Creed in English were permissible, as were the *Chronicles*, Chaucer's books and Gower's writings. Songs and plays on purely secular themes were allowed as well, as were translations of the Bible other than Tyndale's or Coverdale's.

But these approved translations were hedged around with a series of fierce restrictions. Only the bare text of the Scriptures was permissible: all prefaces and glosses had to be blotted out. And, even with this bowdlerization, only upper-class males – the 'highest and most honest sort of men' – were allowed to read them. In contrast, all 'artificers, prentices, journeymen, serving men ... husbandmen [and] labourers' were forbidden to read the Bible in English, either publicly or privately, on the pain of a month's imprisonment.

And so were all women.[25]

This blanket restriction on the whole female sex evidently caused some outrage. Religion, as we have seen, was a recognized sphere of activity for women and in the course of debate a further proviso was added to the Bill which allowed ladies of noble and gentle status to join their menfolk in reading the English Bible. But they were to do so 'to themselves alone, and not to others'.

They were not, in other words, to lead Bible readings with their children or female servants or to encourage public readings of the Scripture in their chambers. But such readings had become common-place features of life in Godly households and Anne Boleyn, for instance, had encouraged them over a decade previously.

Would Catherine Parr quietly forego them now?

There were further defeats for Reform in Convocation (held as usual at the same time as Parliament), where Cranmer meekly submitted to a new and very conservative formulary of faith. Known as the *King's Book*, it reflected Henry's own traditionalist opinions on disputed points. The King made detailed corrections to the exposition of the Creed in his own hand and made sure also that Luther's doctrines on the key questions of faith – justification, free will and good works – were emphatically rejected.[26]

Finally, and most important of all, religious persecution struck into the very heart of the royal Household.

The information had been gathered by Dr John London, Dean of Oxford and Canon of Windsor. He found several heterodox clergy and musicians among his colleagues in St George's Chapel; he also discovered that they had powerful supporters among the courtiers who frequented the Castle. Dr London, who had been active as a heresy-hunter since his involvement in the prosecution of Garrett in 1528, began by acting on his own initiative. But, quite soon, he presented his findings to Gardiner, who took over the strategic management of the affair. The Bishop fitted the Windsor denunciations into his broader attack on Reform; he also made sure that his fellow Councillors were primed and sympathetic to what they were about to hear.

By the week starting on Passion Sunday (11 March) 1543 all was ready and, over the next few days, London appeared before the Council at Whitehall to lay his accusations. Gardiner passed on a sensational summary of them to the King: '[heretics]', Gardiner explained to Henry, 'were not only crept into every corner of the Court but even into his Privy Chamber'. Thoroughly alarmed, Henry authorized a commission for a 'privy search' in the town, but not the Castle, of Windsor. Late at night on Thursday, 15 March, at about 11 o'clock, the commissioners struck. They sought out Anthony Pearson, a radical and charismatic priest, Henry Filmer, a tailor and churchwarden, and two 'singing men' in St George's Chapel choir, Robert Testwood and John Marbeck, the latter of whom was also a composer and organist of distinction. The men were arrested and their papers seized, including the biblical concordance (or word index) – the first in English – on which Marbeck was working. With the possible exception of Marbeck, all the men seized at Windsor were flamboyantly unorthodox and, in the event, would almost embrace martyrdom.[27]

The scene then shifted to London, where, in a wave of arrests, the socially more distinguished supporters of the Windsor radicals were picked up: Dr Simon Haynes, Dean of Exeter and Canon of Windsor, was imprisoned on 16 March; Thomas Weldon, a Master (that is, a high administrative official) of the Household, on 17 March; Thomas Sternold, Groom of the Wardrobe of the Robes and versifier of the *Psalms*, and Philip Hoby, diplomatist, scholar and Gentleman Usher of the Privy Chamber, on Palm Sunday, 18 March. On Monday the 19th, the Windsor men were sent up to London where they too were imprisoned.[28]

Over the Palm Sunday weekend, John London, delighted with the success of the Windsor operation (which, with characteristic boastfulness, he called a 'spectacle'), launched the second stage of the plot. This consisted of a further series of revelations of heresy, equally sensational and this time concerning the spiritual centre of the English Church at Canterbury. Senior members of the Cathedral clergy were among those accused and the finger was pointed at Cranmer himself.[29]

Reform was now thoroughly on the defensive and remained so till late June, when a series of events began to swing the balance in the other direction. On 19 June, as we have seen, Henry returned from his flying visit to inspect the naval facilities at Harwich; on about the 20th he was joined at Greenwich by Catherine Parr, who had just accepted his proffered hand; and on 12 July they were married at Hampton Court by the apparently triumphant Gardiner.

Meantime, however, Henry, together presumably with Catherine, spent a few days at Whitehall to catch up on business. He did so to striking effect. On 5 July Dean Haynes, the first of the Windsor ringleaders to be arrested, was set at liberty, 'after a good lesson and exhortation, with a declaration of the King's mercy and goodness towards him'. And Henry was even more merciful to Cranmer. Or perhaps, in a famously ambiguous encounter, he merely played with his timorous Archbishop, like a big cat with a mouse.[30]

The incident cannot be dated precisely. But, since it took place on the Thames between Lambeth and Westminster, it must have occurred during the six days from 2 to 8 July, which, because of the plague, were to be the King's last visit to Whitehall for six months. Henry, 'on an evening', was 'rowing in the Thames in his barge' and paused at the 'bridge' or landing stage at Lambeth. There he summoned Cranmer to join him in his recreation. 'Ah, my chaplain!' the King said 'merily', 'I have news for you: I know now who is the greatest heretic in Kent.'

Thereupon he took out Dr London's list of charges against the Canterbury clergy and their Archbishop, and appointed Cranmer, despite his protests, head of the commission to investigate them.[31]

It was a deliberately poisoned chalice. What would have been even worse, from Cranmer's point of view, was if Henry had given the job to Gardiner, who was eagerly angling for it.

Was Cranmer to wriggle free yet again? The sense that the tide was turning against him probably led Gardiner, who was usually so aware of the importance of timing in politics, to overreach himself in his effort to make sure that his Windsor victims did not escape.

The result was justice that was summary even by Tudor standards. On Thursday, 26 July, Pearson, Filmer, Testwood and Marbeck were tried before a commission at Windsor headed by Bishop Capon of Salisbury. They were all found guilty under the Act of Six Articles and sentenced to be burned. On the 27th, Capon, probably by pre-arrangement, wrote to Gardiner at the Court, which was conveniently to hand at Woking, to recommend that he petition the King for Marbeck's pardon. Gardiner did so and the pardon was granted immediately. The following day, Saturday the 28th, Marbeck's less fortunate co-accused were paraded through Windsor to the place of execution. They were in a state of exaltation that seemed like a kind of spiritual inebriation. More earthly intoxicants were involved as well as they pledged each other in ale before the fires were lit. Pearson even put straw on his head so that he would die with a burning crown of martyrdom.[32]

That marked the end of the public business at Windsor. But there was also a secret process, as advantage was taken of the sessions to get courtier-supporters of Reform 'privily indicted' before the commissioners. Fortunately for them, one of Catherine's servants had been an observer of the trial. He 'had lain at Windsor all the time of the business and had got knowledge what number were privily indicted'. Immediately the trial was over, he made haste to Court to inform one of the accused, Thomas Cawarden, Gentleman of the Privy Chamber, of

the danger. We do not know the full name of this servant as Foxe refers
to him only as 'Fulke', which was probably his Christian name (but its
popularity among the Greville family suggests that he belonged to it, or
else was of its kin). Nor do we know whether he acted on his own
initiative, or on the Queen's orders.[33]

But his actions cannot have been displeasing to her. And they were
decisive. For, alerted by Fulke, Cawarden had the Clerk of the Peace, the
official messenger from the commissioners at Windsor, waylaid at
Guildford before he could deliver the trial reports to Gardiner. His
papers were seized by Cawarden and William Paget, the newly
appointed King's Secretary, and examined by the Council. Among them
they found the 'privy indictments'.[34]

These were fatal to Gardiner's scheme as the men listed in them
were all intimate personal attendants of the King: Cawarden himself,
Hoby, Weldon, Sternold, Edmund Harman, another Groom of the Privy
Chamber, and William Snowball, one of the King's cooks. Also indicted
were the men's wives: Mrs Cawarden, Mrs Hoby (known, in right of her
previous husband as Lady Compton), Mrs Harman and Mrs Snowball.
This may well explain Fulke's presence at Windsor since the wives of
the Gentlemen of the King's Privy Chamber also served as part of the
Queen's establishment at Court. By intervening through her servant,
Catherine was protecting her own.

As, of course, would Henry. The King reacted with outrage to the
fact that someone had dared to launch legal process against his own
servants without express permission and on 31 August at Ampthill he
issued them with a comprehensive pardon.[35]

Who, however, was to blame for this act of *lèse-majesté*? Gardiner was
obviously under suspicion. But he had covered his tracks well enough to
escape – for the moment at least.

The collapse of the Windsor scheme also jeopardized the Canterbury
end of the plot. This had previously been going badly for Cranmer. As
ordered by Henry, the Archbishop had launched an on-ground
investigation into the charge and counter-charge of popery as well as

heresy among his Cathedral clergy. But the conservative party, suppliers of the original information to Dr London and Bishop Gardiner, remained insubordinate while Cranmer himself felt obliged to proceed with kid gloves. The reason, as he told his secretary Ralph Morice, was 'that it is put into the King's head that he [Cranmer] is the supporter and maintainer of all the heretics within the realm'.[36]

This was even more frightening: in July, Henry had 'merily' told him only that he was the biggest heretic in Kent; now, Cranmer feared, the King thought that he was the heresiarch of all England.

But help was already on the way. It was on 2 November that Ralph Morice reported Cranmer's fears and inhibitions to his friends at Court. Two days previously, as it happened, on Hallow E'en, 31 October, the leading canon lawyer, Dr Thomas Leigh, had arrived at Canterbury. He came armed with the King's ring, as a symbol of authority, and with orders to act as Cranmer's lieutenant in the investigations. As a former visitor of the monasteries, and trained in the school of Thomas Cromwell, Leigh brooked no nonsense. Lay commissioners were sworn in and were directed to seize the papers of Cranmer's accusers.[37]

It was now the conservatives' turn to panic. On 1 November, the day after Leigh's arrival, a messenger was sent post-haste to Gardiner at Court. The distance and the difficulty of locating Ampthill meant that he did not arrive till the 3rd. But he got small comfort from Gardiner, who was now desperately trying to backtrack. 'Get you home again', the Bishop said, 'what need you come so far for such a matter?'[38]

Gardiner could not escape so easily, however. The searches ordered by Leigh in Canterbury turned up letters between the conservative clergy there and John London and Bishop Gardiner himself. John London was condemned for perjury and false witness; paraded with his face to the tail of a horse through Windsor, Reading and Newbury, and exhibited in the pillory in each town wearing a paper declaring his offences on his forehead. For one who had always been so proud and highly-strung the humiliation was bitter. Almost certainly, too, John London was injured in more than his dignity. The pillory was not a pleasant place and, especially if you were unpopular, people threw worse things than insults at you. The result was that London died, still in prison, in December. And Gardiner himself only avoided a worse fate at Henry's hands by a timely and prostrate submission.[39]

But the pendulum was to swing one more time. On 20 December, Cranmer, whose palace at Canterbury had just burned down and whose brother-in-law had been killed in the flames, was summoned to Court in a letter signed by Norfolk and Lord Privy Seal Russell. The letter was apparently routine. But it was marked by Secretary Paget: 'Haste, post, haste'. Why? The explanation, almost certainly, is that the conservative majority on the Council had now made their final push against the Archbishop. They had asked Henry for permission to arrest him and send him to the Tower, and the King had agreed.[40]

Henry, however, was playing a double game. On 12 January the Court returned to Whitehall at the end of the Christmas festivities which had been spent at Hampton Court. Within the next day or two, and late at night, Henry sent Anthony Denny, Cranmer's friend and the leading Reformer in the Privy Chamber, to summon the Archbishop to his presence. The King told Cranmer that he was to be sent to the Tower on the morrow, and, when the Archbishop protested his willingness to submit to the King's justice, upbraided his folly. 'Think you to have better luck that way than your master Christ had?' he asked brutally. But Cranmer was not left to the tender mercies of his fellow councillors. Instead, Henry gave him his ring, to use as a talisman when the Council tried to arrest him.

The summons came next day. Cranmer showed the ring and the Council, led by Norfolk and Russell, tumbled into the King's apartments to abase and exonerate themselves.[41]

Thereafter, while Henry lived, Cranmer was untouchable.

There was a postscript to the affair. When Cranmer journeyed from Canterbury to London in the last days of 1543, to meet whatever fate awaited him, he brought with him in a chest the great cache of papers that had been accumulated by his and Leigh's investigations. The intention was that Henry should peruse the papers himself. Whether he did so remains unclear. But the information they contained undoubtedly played a part in the forthcoming Parliamentary session.

First, there was an unusually generous General Pardon, which was tagged to the Act making the 1542 forced loan to the King an outright gift. Foxe suggests that the Pardon was the work of the conservatives, who were eager to avoid their impending punishment for perjury or conspiracy. But it was equally useful to the Reformers, since religious offences were not excluded. Of even more benefit to the Reforming party, however, was the Act which tightened up judicial procedure under the Act of Six Articles. This was designed to rule out the 'secret and untrue accusations and presentments', which had been 'maliciously conspired against the King's subjects' in 1543. The Lords, with its inbuilt conservative majority, was unenthusiastic about the Bill, and insisted that 'certain words be put in and out'. But they had to acquiesce in its passage. Gardiner's worst fangs were now drawn.[42]

It would, of course, be absurd to attribute Gardiner's defeat in 1543–4 solely to Catherine. But to ignore her entirely, as most recent historians have done, is equally mistaken. For it is clear, on grounds of chronology alone, that Henry's sixth marriage marks a watershed in religious policy. Catherine's own personal role in the change was almost invisible at the time and will remain forever opaque. But we are probably right to guess that her servant Fulke's crucial part in thwarting the second stage of the Windsor plot was only the tip of an iceberg.

For who else was there? Cranmer was too insecure to defend himself, much less to challenge policy. Denny and Sir William Butts, the King's doctor, brought all their backstairs and behind-the-scenes influence to bear on the side of Reform. But, since they had been unable to prevent the conservative excesses of the first half of 1543, it seems unlikely that they alone could have reversed them in the last quarter of the year.[43]

The only new factor, in short, in the delicate balance of forces round Henry was Catherine herself. Shrewd, tactful and patient she might be. But she was also, as we have seen, a woman with a mission – and, in the circumstances of 1543, an opportunity as well. For the extended Progress meant that she had the King pretty much to herself for the first six months of her marriage, when her influence was at its freshest and most appealing.

The resulting religious turnaround suggests that she used her moment well.

We can go further. Save for the all-important fact that she had not become pregnant, Catherine had made the most successful debut of any of Henry's wives.

She, and her family, had their reward at Christmas 1543.

Probably on 22 December the Court took up residence at Hampton Court for the Christmas holidays. The following day was a Sunday, when the King went in solemn procession to hear mass in the Holiday Closet of the Chapel Royal. While he was there, Catherine's brother William, Lord Parr of Kendal, and her uncle and Lord Chamberlain, Sir William Parr, took up their places in the Pages' Chamber next to the royal apartments. Normally, the Chamber was fairly unsalubrious, as such service rooms tend to be. But it was cleaned up for the occasion and its floor strewn with fresh rushes. After mass the King returned to his apartments and stood under the throne canopy in the Presence Chamber. Thither, in turn, Catherine's brother and uncle were led by peers of appropriate rank. The former was created Earl of Essex (in right of his already estranged wife), while the latter was made a baron as Lord Parr of Horton.[44]

The double ceremony was unique and it marked the Parrs' arrival in the front rank of the English aristocracy. Moreover, their promotion was exceedingly rapid. Anne Boleyn had had to wait for some three years before her father was made Earl of Wiltshire; Edward Seymour had not been created Earl of Hertford till his sister Jane had given birth to Prince Edward. But the Parrs got their titles less than six months after Catherine's wedding.

Why?

The formal decision on the promotions and their timing was of course Henry's. Likewise, it was Catherine's mother, Maud Parr, who had laid the ground-work by her shrewd matrimonial strategy for her children. But Catherine, it seems certain, played her part as well, since, more even than most sixteenth-century women, she displayed a fierce family pride. The badge she chose as Queen, of a maiden's head, was the Parr family badge. Her signature was also a tribute to her family. For, uniquely among Henry's Queens, she incorporated the initials of her maiden name, 'K[atherine] P[arr]', into her royal sign manual by always signing herself thus: 'CATHERINE THE QUEEN: KP'. Finally, there were those words in which she had informed her brother of her wedding. 'He was', she had told him back in July, 'the person who has most cause to rejoice [at her marriage].' Written by her, the words had the effect of a promise.[45]

The events of December show that she had moved swiftly to fulfil it.

77. *Queen Regent*

The other main event of the 1543–4 Christmas season was the arrival and entertainment at Court of Fernando de Gonzaga, Duke of Ariano, Prince of Malfeta and Viceroy of Sicily. He came to agree a timetable and strategy between Henry VIII and his master Charles V for a joint invasion of France. For Henry, having more-or-less weathered the storms of the Reformation, had resolved to return to his first love: war. Once more, as in 1513, he would invade France and see off Scotland. And, once more, as in those early years of his reign, he had at his side a Queen whom he trusted as his co-adjutor in power.[1]

She was even called Catherine, after her namesake Catherine of Aragon.

That earlier Catherine had war with France in her blood; she was a daughter of Spain, and Henry would be fighting alongside her father, Ferdinand of Aragon (or at least he would be if Ferdinand could have been persuaded to fight). But for Catherine Parr, it would seem, the issue was more complex. And it was complicated, above all, by the question of religion. Charles V was the great hope for Catholicism in Europe and the Imperial alliance was the great hope also for religious conservatives in England. The alliance had been argued for strenuously by Gardiner, and its signature, in February 1543, had coincided with the triumph, likewise engineered by Gardiner, of orthodoxy and the apparent defeat of Reform in England.

But if Catherine experienced any doubts about the alliance between the English Moses and the Protector of the Roman Church, she showed no sign of it. Her already excellent relations with Mary, who was Charles's cousin as well as Henry's daughter, were a help. But Catherine, whether out of policy or conviction, also went out of her way to charm the succession of Imperial grandees who now came to England. The Viceroy left in early January but was succeeded by Manriquez de Lara, Duke of Najera, who arrived on 6 February on his way back to Spain. The Duke was denied an audience for several days – officially because the King had pressing business at Greenwich, but really, so he learned, because Henry wanted time to assemble a sufficently impressive Court to receive so distinguished a visitor.[2]

The audience finally took place on Sunday, 17 February, when the Duke was '*assez bien recueilli*' ('well enough received') by the King. It sounds as though Henry was in a less expansive mood than usual. But any lack of warmth on the King's part was more than made up for by Catherine's behaviour. According to Chapuys, who escorted the Duke, the Queen was 'slightly indisposed'. Nevertheless, 'she would come out of her room to dance for the honour of the company'.[3]

Chapuys's was an insider view. In contrast, the Duke's Secretary, who wrote his own account of his master's visit, knew nothing of the Queen's illness and saw only the splendid show she put on for her visitors. She first received the Duke in her Privy Chamber. She was accompanied by Mary, while the Duke was escorted by the Queen's brother, Essex. 'The Duke kissed the Queen's hand, by whom he was received in an animated manner.' There followed a more general entertainment for the Spanish party in the Queen's Presence Chamber. The Queen entered; sat on her throne and bade the Duke himself to sit. Then the royal band of violins, who had only arrived from Venice in 1540 and thus represented the latest fashion, struck up. The Queen had the first dance with her brother, 'very gracefully'. Next it was Mary's turn, followed by other ladies, until the entertainment culminated in a display by a professional dancer, who was also a Venetian. He danced 'so lightly', the Secretary noted, 'that he appeared to have wings on his feet'. 'Never did I witness such agility in any man', he added.

He was equally impressed by Queen Catherine. She 'has a lively and pleasing appearance', he wrote, 'and is praised as a virtuous woman'. She was certainly a magnificently dressed one, as he could see for himself.

> She was dressed in a robe of cloth of gold, and a petticoat of brocade with sleeves lined with crimson satin, and trimmed with three-piled crimson velvet; her train was more than two yards long. Suspended from her neck were two crosses, and a jewel of very rich diamonds, and in her head-dress were many and beautiful ones. Her girdle was of gold, with very large pendants.

The description is instantly recognisable. For its principal features – the elaborate underskirt, the exaggerated width of the lower sleeves and the length of the girdle with its gorgeous tasselled ends – are all to be found in the costume worn by Catherine in the portrait which has been recently reidentified as hers.[4]

In March Najera was succeeded at the English Court by another Spanish grandee, the Duke of Alburquerque. According to the Imperial minister, Granvelle, the Duke was 'somewhat too full of ceremonies'. Despite this (or perhaps because of it), he hit it off well with Henry, who, perceiving his 'gravity, wisdom, knowledge and experience', requested his company in the forthcoming expedition to France and 'made him the best cheer in the world'. But, once again, Catherine went one better and gave the Duke 'an even greater [welcome]'.

The result was that the Duke became virtually a member of the extended royal family: he was lodged near the palace; encouraged to behave like one of Henry's own leading courtiers, and even invited to attend meetings of the Privy Council.[5]

Meanwhile, preparations for the war proceeded rapidly. As in 1513, it was to be fought on three fronts: France, Scotland, and, not least, the home front.

This last would be Catherine's own responsibility and it is clear that Henry kept her informed in detail of the arrangements as they evolved. In early June, for instance, she wrote to Anne Seymour *née* Stanhope, the Countess of Hertford, about her husband Edward's movements. Hertford had been sent north to harry the Scots, and it is clear that his wife feared that he would be ordered to remain there. Catherine was able to reassure her. 'Madam', she wrote, 'my Lord your husband's coming hither is not altered, for he shall come home before the King's Majesty take his journey overseas.' She knew this, she added, 'as it pleasith his Majesty to declare it me of late'.[6]

This was Catherine's first involvement in Scottish affairs, which were to absorb so much of her time and energy in the coming months. For Hertford's return was the result of yet another shift in the bloody kaleidescope of Scottish politics.

The country had been plunged into chaos once more following the shattering English victory at Solway Moss on 23 November 1542. But, unlike his father James IV, King James V had not been killed gloriously, fighting in the field at the head of his troops. Instead he died, of grief as it was said, two weeks later. It may equally have been of exhaustion. He had fathered at least seven bastard sons in an adventurous amorous career. But his sole surviving legitimate issue by his wife, Queen Marie of Lorraine, was a week-old daughter, Mary, who was proclaimed Queen of Scots.[7]

'It came with a lass', James is supposed to have said on his deathbed, 'it will pass with a lass.' And so it seemed six months later, with the signature of the Treaty of Greenwich on 1 July 1543. Mary Queen of Scots was betrothed to Prince Edward, and Scotland was delivered up to Edward's father, Henry VIII.[8]

But, as had happened so often before, Scotland escaped. Henry's interests lay elsewhere, in France. And he tried to clinch his victory in Scotland, not by English arms but by Scottish proxies, who were happy to take English gold, but almost invariably betrayed English interests. Henry's first white hope was the Earl of Arran, the Regent and Heir Presumptive. But, despite the offer of Elizabeth's hand for his son, he threw Henry over and joined with the Franco-Catholic party in Scotland that was led by David Beaton, the Cardinal-Archbishop of St Andrew's. Hertford's sack of Edinburgh and Leith was Henry's revenge.[9]

Then fate offered the English King another instrument: Matthew Stuart, Earl of Lennox, and the next in line to the throne after Arran. Lennox had spent over a decade in France, in the service of Francis I, and had been naturalized along with his brother, James, Seigneur d'Aubigny and Captain of the French Scots Guard. Lennox returned to Scotland in 1543, but, denied the Regency, rejected the French, cast the dust of Scotland off his feet and entered the service of Henry VIII.[10]

Lennox cut a striking figure when he arrived at the English Court in May 1544. Chapuys described him straightforwardly as 'young and good-looking'. But Sir James Melville, though writing over twenty years later, probably got nearer the mark when he painted him in more ambiguous colours: as 'liker a woman than a man, for he was very lusty, beardless and lady-faced'.[11]

Catherine, whose feelings for Seymour show that she was susceptible to male beauty, was probably struck. But there was another, more important, point of contact between them. For Lennox, like many of the Scots nobility, flirted with the Reformation. And Reform was to be the touchstone of the Treaties that were signed between Henry and Lennox on 26 June 1544.[12]

By these, the King gave the Earl of Lennox the hand of his niece, Lady Margaret Douglas, in marriage. Margaret was the daughter of Henry's elder sister, Margaret, by her second, scandalous marriage to

Archibald Douglas, Earl of Angus. Margaret Douglas herself was no better than she should be and, when caught up in the moral panic which followed the Catherine Howard affair, had been warned by Henry (that rigorous censor of other people's behaviour) to 'beware the third time'. But, through her mother, she had a possible claim to the English throne and she was endowed by Henry with enough lands to compensate Lennox for the income he had forfeited by renouncing his French allegiance. And that was enough.[13]

In return, Lennox promised to be ruled by Henry when he became Governor of the puppet-kingdom of Scotland. He would also, he agreed, 'cause the Word of God to be taught and preached in his country, as the only source of truth and means of judging who proceeds justly with him and who abuses him for their own private glory, lucre and purpose'. To help Lennox forward, Henry was to supply him with a small expeditionary force, with the hint of a greater army to follow once France had been dealt with.[14]

The signature of the treaties was celebrated the same day with a formal dinner at Whitehall for Henry, Edward, Mary, Elizabeth and Lennox himself. There followed (almost certainly) a hunting expedition to Hyde Park, the great new park which Henry had acquired from the Abbot of Westminster. And the entertainment was rounded off by 'a supper at Hyde Park'.[15]

Queen Catherine was a notable absentee from the celebrations. Perhaps, as I have suggested previously, it was felt inappropriate for the childless Catherine to be present at a feast which, in effect, introduced Henry's heirs to the nobility of his two kingdoms of England and Scotland. More probably, it was a question of bridal etiquette. Lady Margaret Douglas, despite the cloud over her reputation, had been one of the great ladies of the Court, figuring prominently, for instance, in the reception of the Duke of Najera. But Lennox could hardly dine with his prospective bride. Instead, she was entrusted to the care of the absent Queen, who kept her in temporary purdah.

Her seclusion did not last long, however, and three days later, on 29 June, Chapuys reported that 'the marriage of the Earl of Lennox and

Lady Margaret Douglas took place this morning at Mass, the King and Queen being present'.[16]

The treaties with Lennox and Lennox's marriage to Margaret Douglas gave Henry a half-plausible policy towards Scotland. With that in place, the last remaining obstacle to his own departure for France was removed and on Monday, 7 July the Council met at Whitehall to hear and endorse the King's arrangements for the government of the realm in his absence. The arrangements centred on two figures: his wife and his son.

'The King's Majesty hath resolved', the agenda-cum-minute began, 'that the Queen's Highness shall be Regent in his absence and that His Highness's process [that is, legal and governmental business] shall pass . . . in her name.' To assist her, she was given a five-man Council. It was formally headed by Cranmer. But Wriothesley, now Lord Chancellor and a baron, and the Earl of Hertford were to be its key members and (subject to business) to give their continuous attendance on the Queen Regent at Court. Hertford was also to be Lieutenant of the Realm 'in case' – that is to say, if a sudden deterioration of the Scottish situation required the raising of a large army, as in 1513. Finally, Catherine and her Council were empowered to issue warrants for the payment of money.[17]

Catherine was yet to celebrate her first wedding anniversary. But already she had been given more public authority than any of her predecessors, apart from her namesake, Catherine of Aragon. And the earlier Catherine had been royal by birth and by upbringing as well as by marriage.

It is a striking testimony to Henry's respect for his new wife, and to his judgment of her loyalty and capacity.

The arrangements for his son were equally dramatic. Two days later, on Wednesday, 9 July, Prince Edward was to remove from Whitehall to Hampton Court. This was his birthplace; it also contained a large, specially built Prince's Side for his occupation. The next day, Wriothesley and Hertford were to go to Hampton Court and dismiss the women of his Household, headed by his Lady Mistress, Margaret, Lady Bryan, and appoint a male Household of gentlemen and tutors instead. Years later, when the boy began his journal or 'Chronicle', he remembered this as one of the liminal days of his short life. 'He was brought up', he recorded, 'till he came to six years old, among the women. [Then] at the sixth year of his age, he was brought up in learning by . . . two well-learned men.'[18]

For Edward, the change signalled that his infancy was over, and that the harsh business of training him to be a man and a King had begun. The world outside was intended to read a variant of this message. Henry could safely go abroad, it was implied, because his heir was no longer a mere child but a youth on the threshold of the age of discretion.

On Friday, 11 July, Henry left Whitehall by water to begin his journey to France. From Gravesend he travelled overland to Dover and arrived at Calais at 9 p.m. on the 14th.[19]

For the first time in thirty years the King was at the head of his troops. He was rejuvenated, almost indeed a boy again.

We know nothing of Catherine's parting from Henry and nothing of their farewells, whether public or private. But we can guess at Catherine's feelings from the letter she wrote to Henry soon after. It is dated from Greenwich, which suggests that the Queen had accompanied him there on the first leg of his journey. 'Although the discourse of time and account of days neither is long nor many of your Majesty's absence', it begins, 'yet the want of your presence so much beloved and desired of me, maketh me that I cannot quietly pleasure in anything until I hear from your Majesty.' She longed for his presence. But she knew that his absence was necessary. She knew also that she should submit her will to his. 'And thus love', she continued, 'maketh me in all things to set apart mine own commodity and pleasure and to embrace most joyfully his will and pleasure whom I love.'

Did she *really* love Henry? And are the words sincere? Or are they courtly posturing?

Almost as though she could hear the query, Catherine then offers an impassioned reassurance – to Henry and to us. 'God, the knower of secrets', she writes, 'can judge these words not only to be written with ink, but most truly impressed in the heart.' Thus she wrote, and thus, I think, we should believe her.

But this is not mere artlessness. On the contrary, Catherine's letter is a supreme example both of the epistolary art and of the art of managing a King who was difficult, imperious and unpredictable and yet, for all that, was a man, and a man, moreover, who was peculiarly susceptible to a woman's charms.

Catherine, however, had not yet reached the limits of her quiet audacity. For in the last lines of her letter she ventures to compare her love for Henry with her love for God. 'I do make', she wrote, 'like account with your Majesty, as I do with God for his benefits and gifts heaped upon me daily.' She was hopelessly in debt to God and unable to repay his least benefit. And she was certain to die in this unregenerate condition. Nevertheless she hoped that God would accept her good will and save her in spite of her sinfulness and ingratitude. 'And even such confidence', she continued, 'I have in your Majesty's gentleness.' She could never repay his love, any more than she could her debt to God. Yet Henry, divine in his forgiveness, loved her, she knew, in spite of her inadequacies.[20]

This was daring indeed. Not because of the extravagance of the comparison between Henry and the Almighty, which so grates on the modern sensibility. But rather because of the theology. For Catherine, the theologically literate Henry would have realized immediately, was explaining her relationship with him in terms of the doctrine of Justification by Faith.

Man (and Woman too) the doctrine held, was wholly sinful. This meant that Humankind could never fulfil the commandments which God had laid down as necessary for salvation. By God's justice therefore all were condemned. The only hope was in God's charity: 'in his gracious acceptation of [human] good will', as Catherine put it. And this good will was shown, not by actions or 'works', but only by faith. The doctrine of Justification by Faith was the cornerstone of Lutheranism and ordinarily it was anathema to Henry. But when Catherine used it as an analogy to explain her own absolute, submissive love for him, even he found it acceptable.

If this was a woman's preaching, he seems to have felt, long let it continue. At least, that was his reaction for the moment.

In fact, despite her heartfelt pleas, Catherine had to wait some time before she heard from her husband, who had thrown himself all-absorbingly into the business of war. Her own life, too, as Queen Regent was scarcely less busy. She managed the rump Council which Henry had left with her as a kind of Cabinet for domestic affairs. She oversaw the supplies – of men, *matériel*, and, above all, of money – for the war. She took immediate decisions on northern and Scottish affairs. These were invariably reported to Henry. But, by then, action – and actions decided by Catherine – had already taken place. Finally, in the absence of Henry as *paterfamilias*, she became acting head of the royal family.

In the immediate aftermath of Henry's departure, this last task, which was probably the most congenial to Catherine, loomed largest. Continuing business had kept her at Whitehall until 20 July. But on the 21st she joined Edward and his reconstructed Household at Hampton Court. Mary, who, together with her entourage, now formed a sub-department of the Queen's Household, accompanied her. The result was that two of the royal children and their stepmother were, once more, under one roof.[21]

But Elizabeth was not. Clearly she felt somewhat left out and on 31 July she wrote to Catherine from her temporary residence at St James's. The letter is written in Italian, which was Elizabeth's latest linguistic acquisition. Was this a language which Catherine had learned as well in her own mother's Household? Or would she have needed a translator? In view of the highly personal tone of the letter, it seems likely that Elizabeth assumed that Catherine could read and understand it unaided.

It was 'a whole year', Elizabeth began, since she had seen Catherine. We know that she had left Court soon after her stepmother's marriage. But this must also mean that their paths had failed to cross in the autumn, when the royal Court and the little Courts of the King's younger children were in such close proximity. And Elizabeth had no better luck after she returned to Court on the eve of her father's departure for the French war. Catherine herself, as we have seen, was absent from the reception for Lennox, at which the rest of the royal family were present; while Elizabeth, in turn, must have missed Lennox's wedding a few days later.

Well, therefore, might Catherine's younger step-daughter exclaim against 'Unkind fortune, envious of all good and always turning human affairs upside down, [which] has deprived me for a whole year of your most illustrious presence, and not thus content, has again robbed me of the same good!' 'Which thing', she continued, 'would be intolerable to me, did I not hope to enjoy it very soon.' But she further consoled herself with the reflexion that, though she was out of Catherine's sight, she was not out of her thoughts: 'I well know', she wrote, 'that the clemency of your Highness has had as much care and solicitude for my health as the King's Majesty himself.' She was grateful to Catherine for mentioning her in her letters to Henry in France and she ended by looking forward to the day when her father and Catherine's husband came back a conqueror, 'so that your Highness and I may, as soon as possible, rejoice together with him on his happy return'.[22]

It is difficult to know which to admire more – the eleven-year-old Elizabeth's linguistic talents and courtly skills, or the speed and completeness with which Catherine had won her trust and affection.

How Elizabeth was to repay it was another matter, however.

Elizabeth had written to Catherine that she 'hope[d] to enjoy [her presence] very soon'. Indeed, a letter from Secretary Paget, dated 29 July and written at the King's camp, took for granted that they were *already* together, since it informed Lord Russell 'the Queen, my lord Prince and the rest of the King's children now at Hampton Court' were in prosperous health. But Paget's remark is impossible to reconcile with Elizabeth's own Italian letter. Probably he anticipates a decision which had been taken but not yet implemented back in England. Nevertheless, Elizabeth did not have long to wait and, shortly after the date of the

Italian letter, she had her wish and rejoined Catherine and her half-siblings at Hampton Court.[23]

But it was Catherine's influence that mattered. Her younger step-daughter remained with her for most of the summer and autumn and the effect was profound. Elizabeth imbibed the religious life of Catherine's Household. She witnessed Catherine's masterful conduct of business and the effortless ease with which she, a mere woman, imposed her authority in and on a masculine world. She established relationships among the Queen's servants, men and women, and, in the fullness of time, would recruit many of them into her own Household.

In short, if Catherine had a legacy, it was Elizabeth herself.

Catherine seems first to have had formal word from Henry in a letter dated 23 July, almost a fortnight after his departure from London. There were probably earlier word-of-mouth messages, but evidence of them does not survive. And even the letter of 23 July was from the King's Council, not from Henry himself. But Catherine was undeterred. Two days later, on 25 July, she wrote a brief acknowledgement to the Council with the King. It is signed at the head in royal style – 'CATHERINE THE QUEEN, KP' – and it is couched in the lofty, first-person-plural language of sovereignty: 'Right trusty and right well beloved cousins and trusty and right well beloved', it begins, 'we greet you well.' It thanks them for their letter and their good news, and then refers them for further details to Catherine's letter to Henry of the same date, 'not doubting but that his Highness will communicate the same unto you accordingly'.[24]

For it was to her husband, not to his Council, that Catherine wrote her substantive reply.

And this letter was very different. The combined signature-cipher, 'CATHERINE THE QUEEN, KP', is the same. But it is at the foot of the letter, not at the head and the writer has undergone a corresponding role-reversal. Writing to her husband's Council she was every inch the imperious Queen Regent; to her husband himself she was, as she signed herself, 'Your Grace's most obedient, loving wife and servant'. This is the same language she had employed in the intensely personal Greenwich letter. There is also the same religiosity, shaping itself this time into Catherine's certainty of Henry's divine calling.[25]

The Council's letter had begun by informing her of 'the prosperous beginning in your Highness's affairs and proceedings against your enemies'. It would have mentioned Suffolk's laying siege to Boulogne on the 19th; the fall of the lower town on the 21st and the commencement, the following day, of the bombardment of the fortifications of the upper town, whither the French had retreated.

Catherine was ecstatic. It was 'so joyful news unto me', she wrote to Henry, 'that giving unto Almighty God upon my knees most humble thanks, I assuredly trust that it shall please Him, by whose only goodness this good commencement and beginning hath taken good effect, to grant such an end and perfection in all your Majesty's most noble enterprises, as shall redound to His glory, to the common benefit of Christendom, and especially of your Majesty's realms'.[26]

At first sight, Catherine's words seem much the same as the proud boasts of her predecessor, Catherine of Aragon, in the wake of the English victory at Flodden. In fact, there is a notable difference of tone.

First, Catherine Parr is much less blood-thirsty. Catherine of Aragon had crowed openly over James IV's corpse and his spoils. In contrast, Catherine Parr, in the prayer she wrote specially for the wars, prayed God 'so to turn the hearts of our enemies to the desire of peace, that no Christian blood be spilt'. Or, if that were impossible, her petition continued, she begged that Henry's victories should be bought 'with small effusion of blood and little damage of innocents'. She also had much more of a sense of England's manifest destiny, casting her country as the plucky underdog – David against Goliath – which, nevertheless, was destined to triumph because its cause was just and its King was chosen of God.[27]

The difference is partly a product of the contrasting personalities of the two women; it is also a result of their different times – the one writing as a crusading Catholic, the other as an evangelical, even, though the word hardly yet dared speak its name in England, as a Protestant.

But, of course, neither Henry's first wife nor his sixth, let religious enthusiasm in the least get in the way of common sense and a sound practical grasp of realities. Instead, after the effusions of her first paragraphs, Catherine's letter to her husband reports briskly on the despatch of business. The £40,000 in cash Henry had ordered to be sent would be shipped 'on Monday next'. And Henry, his wife recommended, should take appropriate security precautions on his side of the Channel as she had done on hers. Similarly, musters were already in hand to raise the required standing reserve of 4,000 troops, ready to be sent off 'upon one hour's warning'. And so on. Finally, she added a paragraph in her own hand which assured Henry 'of the good diligence of your councillors here, who taketh much pain in the setting forth of your Highness's affairs'.[28]

The praise must have been deserved, for Catherine's own standards of efficiency were high.

Next to attract Catherine's attention were the affairs of Scotland. 'This afternoon [31 July]', as Catherine informed Henry, 'were brought unto me letters from your Majesty's Lieutenant of the North [the Earl of Shrewsbury].' The letters reported the chance capture of a Scottish ship. This had turned out to be carrying French and Scottish envoys with highly confidential despatches, which Shrewsbury had sent to Court along with his letter. Catherine quickly assessed their contents and decided that they merited immediate action.

'Because I thought this taking of them', she wrote later the same day to Henry, 'with the interception of the said letters, to be of much importance for the advancement of your Majesty's affairs ... I have presently sent such of the said letters as, upon view of the same, appeared of most importance to your Majesty.' Meanwhile, she also advised him, the principal envoys had been summoned by her Council for further 'examination'.

That was the practical Catherine. But the chance event, with its potential to make such a powerful contribution to Henry's northern policy, also fitted with Catherine's providential view of the world. It was 'ordained, I doubt not, of God', she wrote to Henry, 'to the intent your

Highness might thereby certainly understand the crafty dealings and juggling of that nation [the Scots]'.[29]

Once again, she was sure, her God had intervened actively to assist her husband.

On 4 August, the Council replied to Catherine's letters on Henry's behalf, thanking her for her diligence and reporting the success of the bombardment of the fortifications of upper Boulogne. 'Yesterday', they wrote, 'the battery began, and goeth lustily forward, and the wall beginneth to tumble apace, and the loops [loopholes] of the defences of the town so well laid to by our artillery, as a man dare not once look out for his life'. The result, they reported, optimistically as it turned out, was that the town must surrender 'shortly'.[30]

Ordinarily, the triumphant militarism of the language might have grated with Catherine. But, in a good cause, she swallowed it and, in her reply written on the 6th, she thanked them for their news of 'the good health and prosperous success of my Lord the King's Majesty'. 'Which', she continued, 'we doubt not in the goodness of God, Whose Almighty hand directeth and governeth his Highness, shall long continue and increase more and more'.[31]

Catherine's providentialism proved infectious. Indeed, it became the language of the moment and was picked up, for instance, by Lennox in the letter which he wrote to Catherine's Council on 8 August from Chester en route to Scotland. He acknowledged their report of the capture of the Scottish ship and the incriminating Scots correspondence, and went on to attribute it (in broad Scots) to 'the provision of God, who ever works with the King's Majesty our master'. Nor was Catherine, for her own part, in doubt about the reasons for the initial success of Lennox's own mission. For when, on 9 August, she forwarded some of the Earl's earlier letters to Henry, she added a postscript. 'She imputes', she wrote, 'the good speed which Lennox has had to his serving a Master whom God aids.' 'He might have served the French King, his old master', she added, 'many years without attaining such a victory.'[32]

*

To this stream of letters from Catherine Henry had, as yet, made no direct reply. But he used other means to keep in touch. On 2 September, for instance, he ordered Hertford, who had left for the French front as soon as it became clear that the Scots were incapable of launching any serious attack on England during the King's absence, to 'bring the Queen's Highness good news of this town'. Accordingly, Hertford wrote a note to the English Council 'from the King's Majesty's camp before Boulogne'. He informed them of the capture of the strategically important 'bray' or outwork of the castle, as well as giving them assurances about the King's own state of health. 'Thanks be to God', he wrote, 'his Highness is merry and in as good health as I have seen his Grace at any time this seven years.' '[All of] which', he ended, 'I pray you show her Grace.'[33]

Finally, on 8 September, Henry at last found a moment to write to Catherine himself. It had taken him almost eight weeks. But, he did his best to make clear, it was not for want of affection, but of time. 'Most dearly and entirely beloved wife', he began. Then he thanked her for her most recent letters and messages, as well as for the boat-load of venison she had sent him (for the royal parks, freed from Henry's usual depredations, teemed with deer that summer). In return, he explained, he had wished to 'have written unto you a letter with our own hand'. 'But', he continued, 'we be so occupied, and have so much to do in foreseeing and caring for everything ourself, as we have almost no manner rest or leisure to do any other thing.' Hence his resort to a secretary.[34]

There was some truth in Henry's excuses. But, equally, he had always hated writing, and grasped at any straw to free himself from the disagreeable task – as with his present claim to being overwhelmingly busy.

But Henry then made up for his failure with the vivid immediacy of his dictated prose. In quick, deft phrases, he described the current state of the siege, the first French feelers for a peace and the manoeuvrings between himself and his ill-yoked ally, the Emperor, to claim the credit. Throughout he is straightforward and matter-of-fact and, in sharp contrast to Catherine's own side of the correspondence, makes only a single mention of the Almighty and that a cursory one to 'the grace of God'. On the other hand, his boast that the winning of the 'bray' (which had been mentioned in Hertford's earlier letter) had been done 'without any loss of men', *may* show the influence of Catherine's humanitarianism. More likely, however, the King is slapping himself on the back at the success of his own generalship.

Towards the end of his letter, Henry turns away from the great questions of war and peace and the fate of nations to the membership of Catherine's Household. In theory, this was in the gift of the Queen; in practice, Catherine, like her wiser predecessors, consulted Henry every step of the way. She had asked, Henry noted, 'to know our pleasure for the accepting into your chamber of certain ladies in places of others that cannot well give their attendance by reason of sickness'. Henry's reply made clear that he thought little of Catherine's nominees: they were, he wrote, almost as unfit as those they were supposed to replace and they were quite unsuited to the often physically demanding role of body-service. Nevertheless, he conceded, Catherine might have her way and 'take them into your Chamber' as companions rather than body-servants: 'to pass the time sometime with you at play or otherwise to accompany you for your recreation'.[35]

The incident, as it stands, is insignificant and it is not possible even to identify the names of the women in question. But it is a pointer to something of real importance, since Catherine's advent marked a turning-point in the history of the Queen's Household.

Hitherto, while Henry's Queens had come and gone, their servants had been a remarkably stable body. Not so with Catherine. No doubt the accident of mortality played a part. Thomas Manners, Earl of Rutland, who had served as Lord Chamberlain successively to Queens Jane Seymour, Anne of Cleves and Catherine Howard, died on 20 September 1543 and was followed to the grave just over a year later, on 27 November 1544, by his even longer-serving deputy, Sir Edward Baynton, who had been Vice-chamberlain to all of the last five of Henry's Queens, including, briefly, Catherine herself.[36]

These two deaths allowed for a clean sweep at the senior levels of the Queen's male Household. Catherine's uncle, William, Lord Parr of Horton, became Chamberlain; Sir Edmund Walsingham, Vice-chamberlain; Sir Thomas Arundell, Chancellor; Sir Robert Tyrwhit, Comptroller and later Master of the Horse; and Walter Bucler, Secretary. The result, once again, could have come from the pages of R. H. Tawney's *Religion and the Rise of Capitalism*, as these men introduced a distinct, though by no means exclusive, Evangelical flavour in religion and combined it with a marked tightening-up in the running of the Queen's lands and the administration of her Household.[37]

The change among her women was even more striking. Once more, the decline and death of the Earl of Rutland was crucial, as his wife, Eleanor, had exercised a parallel sway over the ladies of the Queen's Household for almost a decade. Born a Paston, and daughter of the great Norfolk family, she was a grande dame of the old school, being kindly, level-headed and generous. She was also catholic in her friendships and mainstream in her religion. But she took advantage of her husband's death to retire from the Court and she was replaced as the dominant force in the Queen's Household by Catherine's sister, Anne Herbert, who became Chief Lady of the Queen's Privy Chamber. Anne, as we have seen, was well established in the Household of Henry's Queens, with a record of service going back to Jane Seymour. But Catherine's other leading attendants were the new-comers, Lady Lane and Lady Tyrwhit. Both were related to Catherine: Lady Lane was born Maud Parr and, as Parr of Horton's eldest daughter, was Catherine's first cousin, while Elizabeth Tyrwhit *née* Oxenbridge, was, as wife of Sir Robert, a member of Catherine's more remote cousinage.

Most importantly of all, however, all three women shared Catherine's religious inclinations. Elizabeth Tyrwhit, indeed, went too far even for her puritanically inclined husband, who remarked a little later to Sir Thomas Seymour that she was 'not sane [sound] in divinity, but she was half a Scripture woman'.[38]

The result was that the change of personnel in Catherine's House-hold went hand in hand with an even more radical change of tone. This

was well described by Francis Goldsmith, who was recruited into Catherine's Household from Peterhouse, Cambridge at some time after 1543 and was agreeably surprised with what he found there. 'Every day [is] like a Sunday', he wrote in his letter of thanks to Catherine, '[which is] a thing hitherto unheard of, especially in a royal palace.' For though '[Reformed] religion [was] long since introduced, not without great labour, to the palace' – not least, though Goldsmith is too tactful to say so, by Catherine's predecessor, Anne Boleyn – it had been left to Catherine to cherish and perfect it.[39]

The fact was obvious to everybody – apart from Henry. Wrapped up in his boy-games of war, he was oblivious and, as we have seen, referred soothingly in his letter to Catherine's recruiting her women 'to pass the time with you at play or otherwise accompany you for your recreation'. This was the old role of royal ladies in waiting. Their new one was to be agents of radical religious change.

When would Henry wake up to the transformation brought about by his new wife? And what would he do when he noticed?

For the moment, the war-games were all-absorbing and when Henry snatched the pen from his secretary to add a final paragraph to his letter, it was to give Catherine the latest blow-by-blow account of the bombardment. 'As this day', he wrote, 'which is the eighth day of September, we begin three batteries and have three mines going, besides one which hath done his execution in shaking and tearing off one of their greatest bulwarks.'

No more to you at this time, sweetheart [he concluded] both for lack of time and great occupation of business, saving that we pray you to give in our name our hearty blessing to all our children, and recommendations to our cousin Margaret [Countess of Lennox] and the rest of the ladies and gentlewomen, and to our Council also.

Written with the hand of your loving husband
HENRY R[40]

The mining, which Henry described so enthusiastically, was almost immediately effective. On 11 September, three days after the date of Henry's letter, a mine was exploded under the castle and on the 14th the town surrendered. One of Henry's first actions after receiving the surrender was to despatch the newly knighted Sir William Herbert 'to declare at length his Majesty's good success and conquest of Boulogne to the Queen's most noble Grace'. The messenger was carefully chosen, being both Henry's favourite Gentleman of the Privy Chamber and Catherine's brother-in-law. Partly, presumably, because of adverse weather conditions in the Channel, and partly because of the remoteness of Woking, where the Court then was, Herbert took some five days before he was able to give the tidings to Catherine 'this night' on the 19th.[41]

This was her great opportunity to put *her* spin on events and the Council's letter announcing the fall of Boulogne to their colleagues in the Council of the North is heavy with the providential language the Queen had made her own. The Queen, the letter informed them, had just heard of the conquest, which had taken place 'without effusion of blood'. She was sure that the news would be joyful to them and that they would order appropriate thanks-givings 'in all the towns and villages of those Northern parts' for 'this great benefit of God'.

No doubt Catherine had offered such a prayer herself and I think we can hear its actual words embedded in the Council's letter. Henry's triumph was, the letter continued, a benefit 'heaped upon us in such sort as we all are most bounden to render most humble thanks to Him, and pray for the long continuance of our most puissant [powerful] master, whom Almighty God long preserve'.[42]

But Catherine's thanks for victory came too soon. For that same day, unbeknown to the English, Charles V signed a separate peace with the French at Crépy. Fighting now on one front rather than two, the French armies were free to turn on the English and the Dauphin immediately marched against the second English force under the Duke of Norfolk which was besieging Montreuil. It was panic stations and on the 23rd the Council with the King wrote home to order the despatch of the 4,000 reinforcements, 'which so often hath been demanded and counter-manded', and 50,000 marks (that is £33,333). The letters reached Lord Chancellor Wriothesley, who was holding the fort in London, at 9 o'clock on the 25th. He opened them and, in view of the emergency, ordered the immediate despatch of letters – in the Queen's name – to summon the troops and raise the cash without losing more valuable time by consulting the Queen herself.

But this is the exception that proves the rule about the reality of Catherine's regency powers. For Wriothesley was profuse in his apologies and pleas of urgent necessity. 'Thus, my Lords', he concluded his report to his colleagues in the Council at Court, 'I have passed a piece of the storm, wherein, if I have not taken the best ways, I shall beseech the Queen's Highness most humbly to pardon me.' 'And for that in our letters', he continued, 'we use her Grace's name and authority, before the letters came to her hands, surely, me thought, it was not mete to lose so much time, as to send to Woking and tarry the answer back again, before the doing of anything.'[43]

The reasoning was unanswerable – which, no doubt, was well for Wriothesley, for Catherine's, it is clear, was not a name to be taken lightly in vain.

The emergency proved shortlived. Henry ordered a protective retreat from Montreuil and on 30 September, convinced that Boulogne itself was safe, he set sail for England and landed at midnight at Dover. Meanwhile Catherine, who had moved to Eltham, set out to meet him. She travelled in slow stages, dining at Mereworth, the Master of the Rolls' house, Allington Castle, the seat of Sir Thomas Wyatt, and Foot's Cray. Finally, she met Henry at Otford, the former great palace of the archbishops of Canterbury near Sevenoaks, which Henry had seized for himself in 1537.[44]

Her regency was over; she was a Queen Consort again – with a Queen Consort's vulnerability.

78. The test

The aftermath of war was demanding and it was not till Christmas Eve that Henry and Catherine were able to get away from Whitehall to Greenwich for the 1544–5 holidays. And it was there that Catherine received (rather late I would guess) her New Year's Gift from her step-daughter Elizabeth. It survives and it is eloquent testimony to the change which Catherine had brought over the royal family – and hoped to bring over England.

Elizabeth had left Court in September 1544, just before her parents' reunion, and had returned to the schoolroom with her brother Edward. But the memory of that summer spent with Catherine was strong and she resolved to mark it with a new kind of present. Instead of the expensive trinkets, to which royalty then as now was prone, she would give something of and by herself: a book. It was not an original composition, of course. Instead it was a translation of the French religious poem, *Miroir de l'âme pécheresse* (*Mirror or Glass of the Sinful Soul*) by Marguerite of Angoulême.

The choice was predictable. Marguerite was, as we have seen, the archetypical royal female author and her work was a favourite of Catherine's. Probably she had introduced Elizabeth to it over the summer; perhaps she had even read parts of it with her. But, otherwise, she seems to have intervened little and the translation was all Elizabeth's own work, being made, written and perhaps bound by her.[1]

Naturally, historians have concentrated on what the work tells us about its remarkable eleven-year-old author. But its insights into Catherine are just as striking. For Elizabeth's dedicatory letter to Catherine makes it clear that her stepmother would be no passive recipient. Instead, Elizabeth expected she would edit and correct her text. 'I do trust', she wrote, 'that the file of your most excellent wit and godly learning ... shall rub out, polish and mend ... the words or rather the order of my writing.' She also rather took for granted that Catherine would circulate the work and begged her not to – or, at least, that she would refrain until she had corrected it, 'lest my faults be known of many'.[2]

Here, then, is a glimpse of another Catherine: the queen bee of a literary circle, who inspired, edited and circulated improving religious works among a coterie of women and like-minded men. It remained only for the Queen herself to emerge as an author. There was not long to wait and in June 1545 Thomas Berthelet, the royal printer, published her *Prayers Stirring the Mind unto Heavenly Meditations*. The work was an immediate success. There was a second, augmented edition as early as November and it went through at least another five editions by 1548.

Obviously, its tone caught the moment. But its authorship undoubtedly helped: then, as now, royals sell books. This was realized by the publisher, who plugged Catherine's position heavily on the title page. 'Prayers or Meditations', this read in the November 1545 edition, 'wherein the mind is stirred patiently to suffer all afflictions here, to set at naught the vain prosperity of this world, and alway to long for the everlasting felicity. Collected out of holy works by the most virtuous and gracious Princess CATHERINE, Queen of England, France and Ireland'.[3]

And Catherine evidently was an easy author to sell. She commissioned multiple copies of her book, in luxury bindings, to use in her Household devotions. She also seems to have given other such copies away as presents to friends. This was royal product-endorsement at the highest level and would certainly have helped sales outside the élite.

But it was not mere vanity publishing. On the contrary, in her writing as in her marriage, she was using her royal status as a means to an end: the promotion of the Gospel.

Nor was Catherine under any illusions about the extent of her talents. Affecting prayers, she knew, she could do very well. But serious scholarship was best left to others who were better qualified. This meant that for her next project, the translation into English of Erasmus's

Paraphrases of the Gospels, her role reverted from authorship to commissioning and financing. The *Paraphrases* were one of the key texts of Reformed scholarship, but, like all Erasmus's works, they were written in a sophisticated and idiomatic Latin. Catherine picked an excellent managing-editor for the project in Nicholas Udall. He organized a team of translators, one for each Gospel, and produced a finished manuscript of his own share, the *Paraphrase* of St Luke, by October 1545. The Preface, naturally, was dedicated to Catherine and it incorporated her own view of the importance of publication. The King, Udall ventured to hope,

> will not suffer it to lie buried in silence, but will one day . . . cause the same to be published and set abroad in print, to the same use that your Highness [Catherine] had meant it, that is to say, to the public commodity and benefits of good English people now a long time sore thirsting and hungering the sincere and plain knowledge of God's word.[4]

But here, too, Catherine was aware of the benefits of royal participation and she managed to persuade Mary, with her superior Latinity, to undertake the translation of the *Paraphrase* of St John. Mary began the work and made good progress. But her chronic ill health prevented her from finishing it, and it was eventually completed by her chaplain, Francis Mallet. Mary, however, was less forthcoming as an author than Catherine, and the Queen wrote her a robust letter to remonstrate. It will serve as a model for any publisher who is faced with similar circumstances.[5]

Catherine's first aim, naturally, was to get hold of the manuscript, 'that it may be committed to the press in due time'. Her second was to discover Mary's line on authorship. Did she 'wish it to go forth to the world (most auspiciously) under your name'? Or did she prefer anonymity?

The latter, Catherine insisted, was thoroughly undesirable. 'To which work', she wrote, 'you will, in my opinion, do a real injury if you refuse to let it go down to posterity under the auspices of your own name.' Mary, after all, had done most of the work (and had *intended* to do it all) and she deserved the credit. 'And . . . I do not see why you should repudiate that praise which all men justly confer on you'.

But, Catherine concluded, 'I leave the whole matter to your discretion'.[6]

Catherine was, in short, a natural. Not until Victoria would there be another royal author who was as successful and as at home in the world of books and publishing. But Henry failed lamentably to play the part of Disraeli. Instead of murmuring quietly (on the basis of his own *Assertio*), 'we authors', as Victoria's Prime Minister was to do, he showed a disagreeable jealousy.

Was it the envy of a less successful writer for a bestseller? Or a man's reluctance to be bested by a woman? Or just the customary tension within any literary couple?

Such emotions were, I think, involved. But the age meant that far larger issues were at stake as well. For instance, on 10 November 1545, four days after the publication of the augmented edition of Catherine's *Prayers or Meditations*, a shocking incident took place at Ely Place, the town-palace of the new Lord Chancellor, Wriothesley. 'As I was going to Mass', Wriothesley informed Secretary Paget, 'a bill . . . was let fall . . . in my dining chamber.' The 'bill' or paper denounced his activities in reporting to Henry the discovery of forbidden religious books and (almost certainly) threatened him in crude and highly personal terms. 'You know', Wriothesley's report to Paget continued, 'that when those naughty [wicked] books were brought unto me, I could do no less than send them to his Highness, and also travail, as much as I could, to find out the author.' 'Wherein', he reflected ruefully, 'though I have not much prevailed, yet some be angry with my doing.'

Paget was to report the incident to Henry; show him the bill and find out what the King wished to be done in the matter.[7]

The incident cast a long shadow over the first Session of the new

Parliament, which opened two weeks later on 23 November. For the swash-buckling Member for Tavistock, Sir Peter Carew, 'was found to have had one of [the offending bills] in his custody' and was arrested and detained. He was released fairly promptly, on 13 December. But the arrest of an MP proved counter-productive in the Lower House, with fatal result for the Bill against illicit books. 'The bill of books', Secretary Petre reported to his colleague Secretary Paget at the end of the Session, 'albeit it was at the beginning set earnestly forward, is finally dashed in the Common House.'

According to Petre, Henry took the failure in his stride. 'Whereat I hear not', Petre reported, 'that his Majesty is much miscontented.' This would suggest that Catherine's policy, which tolerated and even encouraged the publication of works of the 'new learning', was still in the ascendant. She was still in high favour at New Year, when Henry, despite having almost bankrupted himself in the war, gave her an extraordinarily extravagant New Year's Gift of 1000 marks (£666 13s 4d).[8]

On the back of all this Cranmer was riding high, too, and in the first half of January 1546 he manoeuvred Henry into agreeing to abolish a whole series of traditional observancies as 'superstitious'. First the ringing of bells on Hallow E'en, the covering of images in Lent and the kneeling to the uncovered cross on Palm Sunday were to go. But having got so far, why stop? In collusion with Paget, it was decided that Henry should endorse more radical measures: there was to be no kneeling to the cross at any time and the yet 'greater abuse' of 'creeping to the cross' on Good Friday should 'cease from henceforth and be abolished'.

But suddenly, as Denny was presenting the final papers to the King for signature, he brushed them aside saying, 'I am now otherways resolved'.[9]

What had happened?

The conventional answer is that Gardiner, who was in Brussels negotiating with the Emperor, pulled off a coup by warning Henry that further religious Reformation in England would jeopardize the renewal of the Imperial alliance. Henry listened and Gardiner, able now to conclude the treaty, returned in triumph to England on 21 March.[10]

There is some truth in this. But I am sure that other, more intimate forces moved Henry as well.

For Elizabeth had decided to repeat the success of her last New Year's Gift to Catherine by producing a similar present this year for her father. As with the *Mirror*, it would be a translation of a religious work by a leading royal authoress. But instead of Queen Margaret of Navarre, the writer would be Queen Catherine of England and the work her recently published *Prayers or Meditations*. This Elizabeth turned into Latin, French and Italian and topped with an elegant Latin epistle dedicating the whole to 'my matchless and most kind father'.

Historians, including the present writer, have fallen over themselves to praise Elizabeth's tact and subtlety in sending him the gift of a book 'compiled by the Queen your wife . . . [and] translated by your daughter'. But was it really such a clever choice after all?

For though the dedication emphasized that theology was the proper study of Kings, 'whom philosophers regard as Gods on earth', it went on, rather awkwardly, to sing the praises of the *Prayers or Meditations* and its author, who was, of course, not a King at all but a woman and a Queen. 'A work of such piety', Elizabeth innocently enthused, 'a work compiled in English by the pious industry of a glorious Queen and for that reason a work sought out by all!'

For all those reasons, Elizabeth concluded, *Prayers or Meditations* 'was by your Majesty highly esteemed'.[11]

But was it?

It is, in fact, unlikely that Henry had bothered to read Catherine's work in the original English. For Henry was not interested in vernacular religion, which he thought of either as a woman's world or (in its less innocent form) as a dangerously heterodox nuisance. Instead, his concerns (as Elizabeth mentioned) were with theology and religious controversy. These took place in Latin and were properly royal and masculine.

But Elizabeth's Latin translation would have brought home to Henry just how far his wife was trespassing into this realm. She had also got his daughter Elizabeth at it. And, he would soon have discovered, she had set his other daughter Mary's pen to work as well. Indeed, I wonder if the illness which stopped Mary from finishing her translation of the Erasmus *Paraphrase* was not a diplomatic one that followed an explosion from her father.

All this is speculation, of course. But it is borne out by the great speech which Henry gave at the prorogation of Parliament on Christmas Eve 1545.

Normally the task was performed by the Chancellor. But, on this occasion, aware perhaps of the bad odour in which Wriothesley was held by many members, Henry delivered the speech himself. The mere fact caused a sensation. But its content was still more impressive. For Henry, that most extreme of men, uttered a heartfelt plea for moderation. And central to it was the proper use of Scripture.

It had been given to his people 'in your mother tongue', Henry explained, as a concession, 'only to inform your own consciences and to instruct your children and family'. But the concession had been abused and God's Holy Word was 'disputed, rimed, sung and jangled in every alehouse and tavern'.[12]

Henry, according to Petre, spoke 'so sententiously, so kingly, or rather fatherly', that even many who were used to hearing him talk wept. As for Petre himself, he wrote, it gave him 'such a joy and marvellous comfort as I reckon this day one of the happiest of my life'.[13]

With such applause ringing in his ears, Henry had begun the holidays in expansive mood. But, as Christmas turned into New Year, he discovered that the 'jangling' of Scripture had spread from the alehouse into the palace and that the jangler-in-chief was none other than his own wife.

There is one final piece to be fitted into the jigsaw. One of the most contentious matters debated in the 1545 Parliament was the Act to dissolve the remaining religious foundations known as Chantries, which existed primarily to pray for souls in Purgatory. The doctrine of

Purgatory was now in dispute and the King was desperate for the cash. But the Bill was fought to the last. 'The book of colleges etc.', Petre noted in his end-of-session report, 'escaped narrowly and was driven over to the last hour, and yet then passed only by division of the House.'[14]

As Petre's description of the Act implies, it could also be construed to threaten the endowments of the Colleges of Oxford and Cambridge with confiscation as well. Cambridge knew instantly where to turn and appealed to Catherine in a sonorous Latin letter.

On 26 February the Queen replied, pointedly, in English and in a letter drafted in her own hand. After drawing attention to her use of the vernacular, she turned to the learning which they had called on her to defend. She understood, she said, 'that all kind of learning doth flourish amongst you in this age, as it did amongst the Greeks at Athens long ago'. But, she warned them, they were 'not so to hunger for the exquisite knowledge of profane learning' that it might be thought that 'the Greeks' university was but transposed or now in England revived'. For that would be to forget the great difference between now and then: Christianity. Learning, she emphasized, existed only to serve the true doctrine of the Gospel; all else was vanity. This should define their activities, so 'that Cambridge may be accounted rather a university of divine philosphy, than of natural or moral, as Athens was'.

Finally, she informed them, she had put their suit to 'my lord, the King's Majesty'. And he in turn had assured her that not only would he forgo their existing possession but also found new Colleges.[15]

The confidence and assurance of this letter is astonishing. And its contents, no doubt relayed to Henry in Catherine's interview with him, probably astonished – and troubled – Henry. For here was a woman who not only strayed into the territories of sacred and profane learning but presumed to redefine their respective frontiers as well. Where would it stop? Or rather, when would it stop?

Henry decided to answer his own question and the result was that Catherine lost favour, suddenly and, it seemed, catastrophically.

On 27 February 1546, the day after Catherine had written to Cambridge, the Imperial ambassador Van der Delft, to whom the Queen had, as usual, gone out of her way to be agreeable, wrote home in some agitation. 'Sire', he informed Charles V, 'I am confused and apprehensive to have to inform your Majesty that there are rumours here of a new Queen, although I do not know why, or how true it may [be].'[16]

These rumours were linked, almost certainly, with Foxe's 'story' of the plot against Catherine, 'wherein appeareth in what danger she was for the Gospel by means of Stephen Gardiner and others of his conspiracy'. The 'story' has been dismissed as a fiction by some historians, most notably by Glyn Redworth, Gardiner's most recent biographer. Others have been impressed by the wealth of accurate circumstantial detail, including, in particular, the names of Catherine's women.[17]

But no one has managed quite to pin the 'story' down. In part, this is because of Foxe's characteristic vagueness over the chronology of the incident, which at one point he dates to 'about the year after the King returned from Boulogne' (October 1544) and at another to the period 'after these stormy stories' of the trial and execution of the Lincolnshire woman Anne Askew (18 June–16 July 1546) for denying that the bread and wine in the mass became the body and blood of Jesus Christ. It is also because historians have missed an important clue about the King's physicians, Drs Owen and Wendy, who figure crucially in the 'story'.

Foxe begins by describing Catherine's public profession of the Gospel. He notes her reading and study of the Scriptures, and her employment of learned chaplains, both for her own private instruction and also to give expositions of the Gospel in her Privy Chamber 'every day in the afternoon, for the space of an hour'. The 'conferences', as Foxe calls them, were a regular feature of life in her Court, but they were 'especially [prominent] in Lent'. They were intended primarily for the ladies and gentlemen of her own Household. But they were also available to 'others that were disposed to hear'.

'As these things', Foxe emphasizes, 'were not secretly done, so neither were their preachings unknown to the King.' 'Whereof at first', he adds, 'and for a great time [after], he seemed very well to like.'

But Catherine, Foxe allows, grew too bold and started 'frankly to debate with the King touching religion, and therein frankly to discover herself'. She was, in short, treading the same path as Anne Boleyn, and Henry came similarly to detest it. And, as with Anne, there were many who were prepared to take advantage of Henry's growing irritation with his wife.[18]

The breaking-point came probably in the last week of March. Henry moved from Greenwich back to Whitehall on the 28th while Gardiner had returned from his embassy on the 21st and immediately resumed a leading role in the Council and the Court. Catherine, who now had to visit her increasingly immobile husband in his own apartments, rather than waiting, as had previously been the custom, for him to come to hers, had spent some time with the King. And, as usual, she had turned the conversation to religion. Henry, never the most patient of men, had grown increasingly irritable with the painful disability of his ulcerated leg, and it was as much as he could do to keep his temper. So he deflected the conversation to other topics. But he kept up appearances and bade her a hearty 'Farewell sweetheart' as she left.

As soon as she had gone, however, he gave vent to his real feelings. ' "A good hearing", quoth he, "it is when women become such clerks; and a thing much to my comfort, to come in mine old days to be taught by my wife".' Gardiner, then and subsequently, played on Henry's feelings and 'marvellously whetted the King both to anger and displeasure towards the Queen, and also to be jealous and mistrustful of his own estate (power and position)'. 'For the assurance whereof', Foxe adds meaningfully, 'princes use not to be scrupulous to do anything.'

The result was that Gardiner and his new ally Wriothesley got Henry's agreement to a coup against the Queen. Her leading women, Ladies Herbert, Lane and Tyrwhit, would be arrested; their illegal books seized as evidence; and the Queen herself sent 'by barge' to the Tower.[19]

But Henry, after another contretemps with Catherine, unburdened himself to one of his physicians, 'either Dr Wendy, or else Owen, but rather Wendy, as is supposed'. The King told this physician that he was determined to be rid of such a 'doctress' as Catherine was. He also outlined the means he had chosen to do it.

Naturally, the King swore his physician to secrecy 'on peril of his life'. Equally naturally, he must have expected the story to leak. Was it to add to Catherine's terror? Or had he begun to have second thoughts?[20]

And why did Foxe highlight his uncertainty about the identity of the physician in question?

Foxe did so, I think, because he knew that there had been a recent change in the King's long-standing medical establishment. For in his letter of 17 December 1545, Petre had also reported to Paget that 'the long sickness of Dr Butts makes it necessary that another physician should be appointed'. As it happens, Butts had died on 22 November 1545, a day or two after Paget's departure on Embassy to France and his successor, Dr George Owen, had been appointed on the 24th, with the accustomed high fee of £100 a year. But Owen was not the only doctor in attendance on Henry in March 1546, for on the 8th a messenger was paid 'for posting to Cambridge to Dr Wendy for his repair to the Court'. The messenger had received the very large sum of £4, which suggests that the summons was urgent.[21]

So *both* Owen and Wendy were present at Court when the plot against the Queen broke. And both had powerful connexions with her. Owen, for instance, had acted as her personal physician on her becoming Queen, and had authorized her apothecary's bills for medicines which, no doubt, he had prescribed. There were also close ties between Owen and Catherine's religiously radical Secretary, Walter Bucler, who was then on Embassy to the German Protestants. But Owen's ties related primarily to the past. Wendy's, more interestingly, belonged to the future. For on 24 October 1546, as 'the Queen's [newly-appointed] physician', he was to receive the grant of a valuable manor and rectory. Was this the result of services rendered – and more, much more, than medical ones?[22]

It seems likely.

In which case it was Wendy whom Henry sent to his wife after her sudden collapse with shock. For the bill of articles against the Queen had been mislaid and brought to Catherine. Faced with the same terrible fate as her predecessor, she had broken down. Wendy now told her of the plot and also advised her what to do. She should, he counselled, 'somewhat... frame and conform herself to the King's mind'. 'If she would do so', he added, 'and show her humble submission unto him ... she should find him gracious and favourable unto her.'

Catherine accepted the advice and, accompanied by her three faithful ladies, took once more the road to her Canossa of the King's bedchamber.

Henry deliberately turned the subject of conversation to religion. But Catherine did not bite. Instead, she protested her weakness as a woman and the God-given superiority of men. Therefore, she said, she had no opinion worth having, since 'must I, and will I, refer my judgment in this, and all other cases, to your Majesty's wisdom, as my only anchor, Supreme Head and Governor here in earth, next under God'.

'Not so by St Mary', replied the King. 'You are become a doctor, Kate, to instruct us (as we take it) and not to be instructed or directed by us.'

Catherine had an answer for that too. She had disputed with Henry in religion, she said, principally to divert his mind from the pain of his leg but also to profit from her husband's own excellent learning as displayed in his replies.

'Is it even so, sweetheart?' Henry answered. 'And tended your arguments to no worse end? Then perfect friends we are now again, as ever at any time heretofore.'

And they kissed and made up.[23]

The next day her arrest was to have taken place. At the time fixed she was walking in the garden with Henry when Chancellor Wriothesley turned up with a detachment of the Guard. The King took him aside; Wriothesley fell to his knees and Henry berated him, 'Knave! arrant knave, beast! and fool!' After Wriothesley had fled, Catherine completed her victory by sweetly interceding with the King on his behalf.[24]

No doubt Foxe's 'story' was improved in the telling. But the fact that Dr Wendy received his reward from her would seem to clinch its essential truthfulness. Catherine's survival, however, had been bought at a price. She had forgone her independence as a woman. And there could be no going back.

Moreover, circumstances were now turning against her. The decline in Henry's health, which is the background to Foxe's 'story', now became precipitate. And, as it did so, all thoughts turned to the future. But it was a future in which the childless Catherine could have little role to play. As if to symbolize her isolation, the couple spent Christmas 1546–7 apart. 'The King', the Imperial ambassador reported, 'is here in London; the Queen being at Greenwich.' 'It is', he added, 'an innovation for them to be thus separated during the festivities.'

While they were apart, Henry, though mortally sick, had supervised the drawing up of charges of treason against the Duke of Norfolk and his son, the Earl of Surrey. Both were condemned and Surrey was executed on 19 January. Meanwhile, Henry had also drafted his will. The destruction of the Howards guaranteed the future of Reform, which meant so much to Catherine. But Henry's will, though it gave Catherine honour and wealth after her husband's death, excluded her from all part in government. She would be Queen Dowager, not Queen Regent.[25].

On 11 January 1547, Catherine's lodgings at Whitehall were got ready for her arrival. But it is unclear whether or not she was allowed to see the King. Certainly she was not present when Henry died on the night of 28 January 1547.

She did not take part in his funeral either, but watched it instead, high up, from her closet.[26]

By then her mind, like everybody else's, was on the future after Henry.

For Catherine at least, it was a future that seemed rosy. True, she would lose the political power and public role which had become second nature to her. But, in return, she would enjoy, perhaps for the first time in her life, full personal happiness. She would marry Thomas Seymour. She would have Elizabeth to live with her. Who knows, she might even have children.

And it all came to pass. She set up house with Elizabeth. With barely decent speed she married Seymour. And she became pregnant with a foetus that kicked so vigorously that mother and father were sure that it was a boy.

But it all went sour. Seymour made open love to Elizabeth. The baby turned out to be a girl. And Catherine, like Jane Seymour before her, caught puerperal fever after the birth. In her delirium, Lady Tyrwhit noted, she sometimes railed against Seymour and his betrayal of her with Elizabeth. She died on 7 September 1548, after four days illness.[27]

Perhaps marriage to Henry had been the better part after all.

Notes

Abbreviations

APC	*Acts of the Privy Council*, ed. J.R. Dasent *et al.*, 46 vols. (London, 1890–1964)
AR	*The Antiquarian Repertory*, ed. F. Grose, 4 vols. (London, 1807–9)
BIHR	*Bulletin of the Institute of Historical Research*
BL	British Library
Commons	*The House of Commons 1509–1558*, ed. S.T. Bindoff, 3 vols. (1982)
CPR	*Calendar of Patent Rolls*
CS	Camden Society
CSP Dom.	*Calendar of State Papers, Domestic*
CSP For.	*Calendar of State Papers, Foreign*
CSP Mil.	*Calendar of State Papers, Milanese*
CSP Sp.	*Calendar of State Papers, Spanish*
CSP Ven.	*Calendar of State Papers, Venetian*
DNB	*Dictionary of National Biography*
DKR	*Report of the Deputy Keeper of the Public Records*
EETS	Early English Text Society
EHR	*The English Historical Review*
Foedera	*Foedera, Conventiones, Litterae*, ed. T. Rymer, 15 vols. (London, 1704–35)
GEC	G.E. Cokayne, *Complete Peerage of England, Scotland, Ireland, etc., Extant, Extinct, or Dormant*, rev. ed. V. Gibbs and later H.A. Doubleday, 13 vols. (London, 1910–49)
HJ	*The Historical Journal*
HKW	*The History of the King's Works*, ed. H.M. Colvin *et al.*, 6 vols. (London, 1963–82)
HMC	*Historical Manuscripts Commission*
HO	*A Collection of Ordinances and Regulations for the Government of the Royal Household* (Society of Antiquaries, London, 1790)

HR	*Historical Research*
HS	Harleian Society
LJ	*Journals of the House of Lords*, 12 vols. (London 1817–1910)
LP	*Letters and Papers, Foreign and Domestic, of the Reign of Henry VIII, 1509–47*, ed. J.S. Brewer *et al.*, 21 vols. and addenda (London, 1862–1932)
LP Hen. VII	*Letters and Papers Illustrative of the Reigns of Richard III and Henry VII*, ed. J. Gairdner, 2 vols. (Rolls Series, 1861, 1863)
Materials	*Materials for a History of the Reign of Henry VII*, ed. W. Campbell, 2 vols. (Rolls Series, 1873, 1877)
Memorials	*Memorials of King Henry the Seventh*, ed. J. Gairdner (Rolls Series, 1858)
PPC	*Proceedings and Ordinances of the Privy Council of England, 1386–1542*, ed. N.H. Nicolas, 7 vols. (London, 1834–7)
PPE Elizabeth of York	*The Privy Purse Expenses of Elizabeth of York: Wardrobe Accounts of Edward the Fourth*, ed. N.H. Nicolas (London, 1830)
PPE Henry VIII	*The Privy Purse Expenses of King Henry the Eighth from November MDXXIX to December MDXXXII*, ed. N.H. Nicolas (London, 1827)
PPE Princess Mary	*Privy Purse Expenses of the Princess Mary from December MDXXXVI to December MDXLIV,* ed. F. Madden (London, 1831)
PRO	Public Record Office
Statutes	*Statutes of the Realm*, ed. A. Luders *et al.*, 10 vols. (London, 1810–1828)
St. P.	*State Papers of King Henry the Eighth*, 11 vols. (London, 1830–52)

References

Introduction
1. Edward, Lord Herbert of Cherbury, *The Life and Raigne of King Henry the Eighth* (London, 1649), p. 497; G. Burnet, *The History of the Reformation*, ed. N. Pocock, 7 vols. (Oxford, 1865), I, p. 514; A. Strickland, *Lives of the Queens of England*, 6 vols. (London, 1854) III, p. 234.
2. PRO, E315/161, fos. 22–34; N. Williams, *Henry VIII and his Court* (London, 1971), pp. 246–7. Williams does not cite his source; nevertheless, he is relied on by A. Fraser, *The Six Wives of Henry VIII* (London, 1992), p. 373 and n. 43.

Henry's Weddings
1. *AR* II, pp. 284–90; *The Receyt of the Ladie Kateryne*, ed. G. Kipling, (EETS 296, 1990), pp. 39–44.

2. *AR* II, p. 302; *Receyt of the Ladie Kateryne*, p. 73; *The Epistles of Erasmus*, ed. F.M. Nichols, 2 vols. (London, 1904), I, p. 201.
3. *LP* IV iii, 5774/5/ii.
4. S. Thurley, *The Royal Palaces of Tudor England: Architecture and Court Life 1460–1547* (London, 1993), pp. 125–7, 199.
5. Thurley, *Royal Palaces*, p. 199.
6. *LP* IV iii, 5774/1, 5774/5/ii.
7. *LP* IV iii, 5774/1; *CSP Sp.* II (1509–1525), p. 19.
8. *PPC* VII, pp. 352–3.
9. E.W. Ives, *Anne Boleyn* (Oxford, 1989), p. 210 n. 97; *A Treatise of the Pretended Divorce between Henry VIII and Catherine of Aragon by Nicholas Harpsfield*, ed. N. Pocock (CS new series 21, 1878) [hereafter Harpsfield, *Pretended Divorce*], pp. 234–5; D. MacCulloch, *Thomas Cranmer: a Life* (London, 1996), pp. 261, 637–8; *LP* X, 1000; XVIII i, 873; *A Chronicle of England . . . by Charles Wriothesley, Windsor Herald*, ed. W.D. Hamilton, 2 vols. (CS new series 11, 1875) [hereafter *Wriothesley's Chronicle*] I, p. 111.
10. E. Hall, *The Union of the Two Noble and Illustre Famelies of York and Lancaster* [hereafter Hall, *Chronicle*], ed. H. Ellis (London, 1809), p. 836; *LP* XV, 925.
11. *AR* I, pp. 296–341. The text is discussed and dated in D. Starkey, 'Henry VI's Old Blue Gown', *The Court Historian* 4 (1999), pp. 1–28.
12. *AR* I, p. 302; B. Wolffe, *Henry VI* (London, 1981), pp. 180–2.
13. *Wriothesley's Chronicle* I, pp. 43–4, 112, 124, 143.

Part One: Queen Catherine of Aragon
Chapter 1
1. G. Mattingly, *Catherine of Aragon* (London, 1942), p. 15. And see the List of Illustrations.
2. N. Macchiavelli, *The Prince*, trans. G. Bull (Harmondsworth, 1995), p. 70.
3. *CSP Sp.* I (1485–1509), pp. xxxiv–vii; Mattingly, *Catherine of Aragon*, pp. 14–15, 19.

Chapter 2
1. *Memorials*, p. 351; Mattingly, *Catherine of Aragon*, p. 16; *CSP Sp.* I (1485–1509), p. 404; II (1509–1525), p. 18.
2. Mattingly, *Catherine of Aragon*, pp. 16–18, 21; M. Dowling, *Humanism in the Age of Henry VIII* (London, 1986), p. 17; *CSP Sp.* I (1485–1509), p. 156.

Chapter 3
1. Mattingly, *Catherine of Aragon*, p. 20.
2. *CSP Sp.* I (1485–1509), p. 124; Mattingly, *Catherine of Aragon*, p. 21–2.
3. Mattingly, *Catherine of Aragon*, p. 22.
4. Ibid., p. 23.

Chapter 4
1. *Memorials*, pp. 350–1.
2. M.K. Jones and M.G. Underwood, *The King's Mother: Lady Margaret*

Beaufort, Countess of Richmond and Derby (Cambridge, 1992), chs. 1–2.
3. *Joannis Lelandi Antiquari de Rebus Britannicis Collectanea*, ed. T. Hearne, 6 vols. (2nd ed., London, 1770) [hereafter Leland, *Collectanea*], pp. 403–7; *PPE Elizabeth of York*, p. lxix; F. Bacon, *The History of the Reign of King Henry VII*, ed. B. Vickers (Cambridge, 1998), p. 22.

Chapter 5
1. *CSP Sp.* I (1485–1509), p. 23.
2. I. Arthurson, *The Perkin Warbeck Conspiracy 1491–1499* (Stroud, 1994), pp. 60, 81, 121–5; *LP Hen. VII* I, pp. 388–404.
3. *CSP Sp.* I (1485–1509), pp. 161–3.
4. *The Great Chronicle of London*, ed. A.H. Thomas and I.D. Thornley (London, 1938), pp. 275–6, 443 n.
5. S. Bentley, *Excerpta Historica* (London, 1833), p. 114; *CSP Sp.* I (1485–1509), pp. 145–6.

Chapter 6
1. *CSP Sp.* I (1485–1509), p. 11.
2. F. Hepburn, 'Arthur, Prince of Wales and his Training for Kingship', *Historian* 55 (1977), pp. 8–9; *Memorials*, p. 43.
3. *CSP Sp.* I (1485–1509), pp. 131, 143–4, 160.
4. W. Busch, *England under the Tudors I: King Henry VII*, ed. J. Gairdner (London, 1895), p. 132; *CSP Mil.* I (1359–1618), p. 539.

Chapter 7
1. *CSP Sp.* I (1485–1509), p. 164.
2. Ibid., pp. 145, 191–2.
3. Ibid., pp. 156, 255, 386; *Memorials*, pp. 350–1.
4. *CSP Sp.* I (1485–1509), pp. 218, 226.
5. Ibid., pp. 209–10, 240, 249–50.
6. Arthurson, *Perkin Warbeck*, pp. 16, 69, 212–15; R. Horrox, *Richard III: a Study of Service* (Cambridge, 1989), pp. 115, 215, 299; GEC XII ii, pp. 394–7; Mattingly, *Catherine of Aragon*, p. 27; *CSP Sp.* I (1485–1509), p. 213.

Chapter 8
1. *CSP Sp.* I (1485–1509), pp. 129, 214, 217.
2. Mattingly, *Catherine of Aragon*, p. 23. *CSP Sp.* I (1485–1509), p. 214.
3. *CSP Sp.* I (1485–1509), p. 218; Mattingly, *Catherine of Aragon*, p. 25.

Chapter 9
1. Mattingly, *Catherine of Aragon*, p. 15.
2. *The Catholic Encyclopedia*, 17 vols. (New York, c. 1907–1918), VIII, pp. 36–7; XIV, p. 783.
3. *CSP Sp.* I (1485–1509), pp. xlv, xlvii–viii, 164.

Chapter 10
1. *CSP Sp.* I (1485–1509), pp. 203, 214, 257, 258.
2. Ibid., p. 258.
3. Ibid., pp. 258–9; Mattingly, *Catherine of Aragon*, p. 26.
4. *CSP Sp.* I (1485–1509), pp. 261–2; *The Anglica Historia of Polydore Vergil A.D. 1485–1537*, ed. D. Hay (CS 3rd series 74, 1950) [hereafter Vergil, *Anglica Historia*], p. 122.
5. *CSP Sp.* I (1485–1509), pp. 254, 262, 264; *Receyt of the Ladie Kateryne*, p. 4; Hall, *Chronicle*, p. 493; *Chronicle of the Grey Friars of London*, ed. J.G. Nichols (CS old series 53, 1852), p. 27; Jones and Underwood, *The King's Mother*, p. 77; Leland, *Collectanea* V, p. 352; Bacon, *Henry VII*, p. 169.

Chapter 11
1. *CSP Sp.* I (1485–1509), p. 262.
2. Ibid., pp. 129, 226, 252, 255; J. Leland, *Itinerary*, ed. L.T. Smith, 5 vols. (London, 1906–8), I, pp. 212–13.
3. *Receyt of the Ladie Kateryne*, p. 5; *LP Hen. VII* I, pp. 406–11; II, pp. 103–5.
4. GEC XII ii, pp. 683–6; *LP Hen. VII* I, pp. 406–11.
5. *LP Hen. VII* I, p. 406; Leland, *Itinerary* I, p. 160.
6. *LP Hen. VII* I, p. 406.
7. Ibid., pp. 406–7.
8. Ibid., pp. 407–8; *Receyt of the Ladie Kateryne*, p. 5.
9. GEC IX, pp. 609–15; *LP Hen. VII* I, pp. 407–8; *Heraldry of Suffolk Churches I: Long Melford* (Suffolk Heraldry Society, 1979), p. 9.
10. *LP Hen. VII* I, pp. 407–8; *Receyt of the Ladie Kateryne*, p. 5.
11. *LP Hen. VII* I, pp. 407–8; *CPR Hen. VII* II (1500–1509), p. 343; *CSP Sp.* I (1485–1509), p. 327.
12. *Receyt of the Ladie Kateryne*, p. 7; P. Hembry, 'Episcopal Palaces, 1535 to 1660', in E.W. Ives, R.J. Knecht and J.J. Scarisbrick (eds.), *Wealth and Power in Tudor England: Essays presented to S.T. Bindoff* (London, 1978), pp. 150, 157.

Chapter 12
1. *AR* II, pp. 249–55.
2. *HKW* IV, pp. 222–8; *AR* II, pp. 253–4; *Receyt of the Ladie Kateryne*, pp. 5–6.
3. *AR* II, p. 254; *Receyt of the Ladie Kateryne*, p. 6.
4. *AR* II, p. 254; *Receyt of the Ladie Kateryne*, p. 6; Vergil, *Anglica Historia*, pp. 122–3.
5. *AR* II, p. 255; *Receyt of the Ladie Kateryne*, pp. 7, 8.
6. C.L. Schofield, *The Life and Reign of Edward IV*, 2 vols. (London, 1923), I, p. 585; II, pp. 23, 159; *LP* I iii, p. xl; III i, 228.

Chapter 13
1. *AR* II, p. 256; *Receyt of the Ladie Kateryne*, p. 8; B.J. Harris, *Edward Stafford: Third Duke of Buckingham* (Stanford, 1986).
2. *CSP Sp.* I (1485–1509), p. 253.

3. *AR* I, pp. 302–5; *LP Hen. VII* I, pp. 404–17; II, pp. 103–5.
4. S. Anglo, *Spectacle, Pageantry and Early Tudor Policy* (Oxford, 1967), pp. 57–8.

Chapter 14
1. *LP Hen. VII* I, p. 409.
2. *AR* II, p. 259; *Receyt of the Ladie Kateryne*, p. 12.
3. *AR* II, p. 260; *The Panorama of London c. 1544 by Anthonis van den Wyngaerde*, ed. H. Colvin and S. Foister (London Topographical Society 151, 1996).
4. *AR* II, pp. 260–2, 278–9; Anglo, *Spectacle, Pageantry and Early Tudor Policy*, pp. 58–94. But see D. Starkey, 'King Henry and King Arthur', *Arthurian Literature* 16 (1998), p. 193.
5. *AR* II, pp. 263–76; *Receyt of the Ladie Kateryne*, pp. 30, 31.
6. *AR* II, pp. 276–81; *Receyt of the Ladie Kateryne*, pp. 31–6. The topography of the City and Catherine's route through it are reconstructed from A. Prockter and R. Taylor, *The A to Z of Elizabethan London* (London Topographical Society 122, 1979).

Chapter 15
1. *LP Hen. VII* I, p. 412; *AR* II, p. 283; *Receyt of the Ladie Kateryne*, pp. 37, 38.
2. *AR* II, pp. 284–7, *Receyt of the Ladie Kateryne*, pp. 39, 42.
3. *AR* II, pp. 287–8; *Receyt of the Ladie Kateryne*, pp. 42–4.
4. *AR* II, p. 287; Bentley, *Excerpta Historica*, p. 126.
5. *AR* II, pp. 284–90; *Receyt of the Ladie Kateryne*, p. 44; *LP Hen. VII* I, pp. 414–15.
6. *AR* II, pp. 289–91; *Receyt of the Ladie Kateryne*, pp. 44, 46–7.
7. *CSP Sp.* I (1485–1509), p. 246; *AR* I, pp. 301–2; II, p. 278; *Materials* II, pp. 349, 359.
8. *AR* I, pp. 301–2; II, p. 291.
9. *AR* II, pp. 291–2; *Manuale et Processionale ad Usum Insignis Ecclesiae Eboracensis* (1875, issued as Surtees Society 63, 1874), pp. 24–5; *Receyt of the Ladie Kateryne*, p. 47.
10. *LP* IV iii, 5774/1, 2.

Chapter 16
1. *LP* IV iii, 5774/3, 13.
2. *AR* II, pp. 292–5; *Receyt of the Ladie Kateryne*, pp. 48–50.
3. *AR* II, pp. 295–302; *Receyt of the Ladie Kateryne*, pp. 50–68.
4. *AR* II, pp. 302–19; *Receyt of the Ladie Kateryne*, pp. 68–76; *CSP Sp.* I (1485–1509), pp. 264–5.
5. F.M. Nichols, *The Hall of Lawford Hall* (London, 1891), p. 196; *AR* II, p. 320; *Receyt of the Ladie Kateryne*, p. 77.
6. *Receyt of the Ladie Kateryne*, pp. 77–8.
7. W.C. Richardson, *Mary Tudor: the White Queen* (London, 1970), pp. 108–11.
8. *CSP Sp.* I (1485–1509), pp. 237, 245–7, 251–2, 255, 272; *Memorials*, p. 409.

9. *CSP Sp.* I (1485–1509), pp. 246–7.
10. Ibid., p. 265; Supplement to vols. I & II, p. 12.
11. *CSP Sp.* I (1485–1509), p. 237.
12. Ibid., p. 234.
13. *CSP Sp.* Supp. to vols. I and II, p. 6, and see n. 17 below.
14. Ibid., pp. 6–7.
15. Ibid., pp. 7–12.
16. *CSP Sp.* I (1485–1509), pp. 23, 129, 220–2, 244, 252.
17. *CSP Sp.* Supp. to vols. I and II, pp. 2–5, 8–11; W.D. Montagu, *Court and Society from Elizabeth to Anne* (London, 1864), pp. 60–1. I owe this reference, along with much else in my account of Arthur, to the kindness of Frederick Hepburn.
18. *CSP Sp.* Supp. to vols. I and II, p. 8.

Chapter 17
1. *HKW* II, p. 732; III, pp. 174–6.
2. A.B. Emden, *A Biographical Register of the University of Oxford to A.D. 1500*, 3 vols. (Oxford, 1957–8), II, pp. 1147–8; III, pp. 1721–2; Hepburn, 'Arthur', p. 7.
3. Hepburn, 'Arthur', p. 8; H. Pierce, 'The King's Cousin: the Life, Career and Welsh Connection of Sir Richard Pole', *Welsh Historical Review*, 19 (1998), pp. 187–8, 204–9, 214–25.
4. A.B. Emden, *A Biographical Register of the University of Oxford A.D. 1501 to 1540* (Oxford, 1974), pp. 453–5; *CSP Ven.* V (1534–54), pp. 257–8.
5. *AR* II, p. 321; *Receyt of the Ladie Kateryne*, pp. 78–9; Hepburn, 'Arthur', p. 8; W.R.B. Robinson, 'Prince Arthur in the Marches of Wales', *Studia Celtica* 36 (2002).
6. BL, Cotton MS Vitellius B XII, fos. 113–113v (*LP* IV iii, 5774/5ii); *LP* IV iii, 5774/13.
7. *AR* II, pp. 321–2; *Receyt of the Ladie Kateryne*, pp. 79–80; Dr Thomas Stuttaford, *The Times*, 4 June 1998.
8. *AR* II, pp. 322–3; *Receyt of the Ladie Kateryne*, pp. 80–1.
9. *AR* II, pp. 323–31; *Receyt of the Ladie Kateryne*, pp. 81–93.
10. E. McClure, 'Some Remarks on Prince Arthur's Chantry in Worcester Cathedral', *Worcestershire Archaeological Society*; N. Pevsner, *Worcestershire* (London, 1968), p. 311.

Chapter 18
1. *CSP Sp.* I (1485–1509), p. 269; *PPE Elizabeth of York*, pp. xc, 14, 103.
2. *CPR Henry VII* II (1494–1509), p. 258.
3. *CSP Sp.* I (1485–1509), pp. 268–9, 272, 354.
4. Ibid., p. 268.
5. BL, Add Ms 59899, fo. 18; Bentley, *Excerpta Historica*, pp. 127, 129; *CSP Sp.* I (1485–1509), pp. 327, 432. The first of these letters is dated 1 July at 'Eyton' (i.e. Eydon, Northamptonshire) and the second 7 September at Ashby-de-la-Zouche, Warwickshire. Margaret Condon's typescript Itinerary of Henry VII shows that both belong to 1503, *not* to 1504 and

1507, as in the Calendar.

6. *CSP Sp.* I (1485–1509), p. 335.
7. Ibid., pp. 267, 269–70.
8. Ibid., pp. 271–2.
9. Ibid., pp. 295–302, 306–8; *Great Chronicle*, ed. Thomas and Thornley, p. 323.
10. *CSP Sp.* I (1485–1509), p. 309.
11. Ibid., pp. 328, 330, 341; Emden, *Biographical Register... Oxford to 1500*, pp. 1685–7.
12. *CSP Sp.* I (1485–1509), pp. 322, 328, 330, 349–50.
13. Ibid., p. 322.
14. H.A. Kelly, *The Matrimonial Trials of Henry VIII* (Stanford, 1976), p. 72; *Memorials*, pp. 416–17 (*CSP Sp.* I [1485–1509], pp. 338–9).

Chapter 19
1. *CSP Sp.* I (1485–1509), pp. 339, 340.
2. Ibid., pp. 345–6.
3. Mattingly, *Catherine of Aragon*, pp. 60–1.
4. Bentley, *Excerpta Historica*, p. 132.
5. *CSP Sp.* I (1485–1509), pp. 371–2.
6. Ibid., pp. 339–40, 371–3.
7. *Letters of Royal and Illustrious Ladies*, ed. M.A.E. Wood, 3 vols. (London, 1846), II, pp. 131–3; *Letters of the Queens of England 1100–1547*, ed. A. Crawford (Stroud, 1994), p. 166 (*CSP Sp.* I [1485–1509], p. 376); *CSP Sp.* I (1485–1509), p. 425.
8. Bentley, *Excerpta Historica*, p. 133; L.P. Gachard, *Collection des Voyages des Souverains des Pays-Bas* I (Brussels, 1876), pp. 408–29; *CSP Ven.* I (1202–1509), pp. 311–3; *Memorials*, pp. 282–3; Mattingly, *Catherine of Aragon*, pp. 65–6.
9. *Memorials*, pp. 283–300, particularly pp. 287–8.
10. *CSP Ven.* I (1202–1509), p. 313; *Memorials*, pp. 300–3.
11. *CSP Sp.* Supp. to vols. I and II, pp. 132–3.

Chapter 20
1. Burnet, *History of the Reformation* IV, pp. 17–18 (*CSP Sp.* I [1485–1509], pp. 358–9).
2. A.B. Emden, *A Biographical Register of the University of Cambridge to 1500* (Cambridge, 1963), p. 629.
3. Burnet, *History of the Reformation* IV, pp. 17–18 (*CSP Sp.* I [1485–1509], pp. 358–9).
4. *CSP Sp.* Supp. to vols. I and II, pp. 88; *CSP Sp.* I (1485–1509), p. 412.
5. *Letters of Royal and Illustrious Ladies*, ed. Wood, I, pp. 131–4 (*CSP Sp.* I [1485–1509], pp. 376–7).
6. Ibid, pp. 339–40, 371–3.
7. *Letters of Royal and Illustrious Ladies*, ed. Wood, I, pp. 138–40 (*CSP Sp.* I [1485–1509], p. 386); *Letters of the Queens*, ed. Crawford, p. 168.
8. Ibid.

9. *Memorials*, p. 247; *Letters of Royal and Illustrious Ladies*, ed. Wood, I, pp. 138–40 (*CSP Sp.* I [1485–1509], p. 386); *Letters of the Queens*, ed. Crawford, p. 168.
10. *CSP Sp.* I (1485–1509), pp. 403–5.
11. Ibid., pp. 407, 408.
12. Ibid., p. 411.
13. *Epistle of Erasmus*, ed. Nichols, I, p. 425.
14. 19 Hen. VII, c. 26; *Statutes* II, p. 667; Bentley, *Excerpta Historica*, p. 131; *CSP Sp.* I (1485–1509), p. 329.
15. *CSP Sp.* I (1485–1509), p. 439; *Memorials*, pp. 116, 120, 124; A. Young, *Tudor and Jacobean Tournaments* (London, 1987), p. 194.
16. *CSP Sp.* I (1485–1509), pp. 412, 413.
17. Ibid.
18. Ibid., pp. 376, 410–11.

Chapter 21
1. *CSP Sp.* I (1485–1509), pp. 411, 413, 428.
2. Ibid., pp. 407, 415, 417, 419–20, 427, 467.
3. Ibid., pp. 411, 413, 427–8.
4. Ibid., pp. 405, 412, 427, 452.
5. Ibid., pp. 435–6.
6. Mattingly, *Catherine of Aragon*, p. 79; *CSP Sp.* I (1485–1509), pp. 421–2, 423–5, 457–65.
7. *CSP Sp.* I (1485–1509), pp. 461, 463–4.
8. Richardson, *Mary Tudor*, pp. 41–3; '"The Spousells" of Princess Mary, 1506', ed. J. Gairdner, *Camden Miscellany* 9 (CS new series 53, 1895), particularly pp. 17, 18, 26; Mattingly, *Catherine of Aragon*, p. 88.
9. *Letters of Royal and Illustrious Ladies*, ed. Wood, I, pp. 138–40 (*CSP Sp.* I [1485–1509], p. 386); *CSP Sp.* II (1509–1525), p. 6; Supp. to vols. I and II, pp. 14–15; Mattingly, *Catherine of Aragon*, pp. 88–9.
10. Mattingly, *Catherine of Aragon*, pp. 89–90; *CSP Sp.* Supp. to vols. I and II, pp. 19–29.
11. Mattingly, *Catherine of Aragon*, pp. 78–91; *Correspondencia de Gutierre Gomez de Fuensalida*, ed. Duque de Berwick y de Alba (Madrid, 1907), p. 194; *CSP Sp.* I (1485–1509), p. 469; II (1509–1525), pp. 3, 4.
12. *CSP Sp.* I (1485–1509), p. 469; Supp. to vols. I and II, p. 20.
13. *CSP Sp.* Supp. to vols. I and II, pp. 21–2.

Chapter 22
1. Mattingly, *Catherine of Aragon*, p. 92; *Correspondencia de . . . Fuensalida*, ed. Alba, p. 484.
2. Mattingly, *Catherine of Aragon*, pp. 102, 137.
3. Nichols, *Hall of Lawford Hall*, p. 196; *Epistles of Erasmus*, ed. Nichols, I, p. 201.
4. Starkey, 'King Henry and King Arthur', pp. 191–3.
5. S.J. Gunn, 'The Accession of Henry VIII', *HJ* 64 (1991) pp. 278–88; Mattingly, *Catherine of Aragon*, pp. 93–4; *CSP Sp.* II (1509–25), pp. 16–20.

6. Hall, *Chronicle*, pp. 507–10; *AR* I, pp. 302–4; *Great Chronicle*, ed. Thomas and Thornley, p. 340; Sir Thomas More, *Latin Poems*, ed. C.H. Miller *et al.* (The Yale Edition of the Complete Works of St Thomas More III ii, London, 1984), pp. 112–13; *LP* I i, 82 (pp. 41–2); *The Manner of the Coronation of King Charles the First of England*, ed. C. Wordsworth (Henry Bradshaw Society 2, London, 1892), pp. 134–5.
7. *LP* I i, 84.
8. Ibid., 119.
9. *Letters of Royal and Illustrious Ladies*, ed. Wood, I, pp. 158–161; *Letters of the Queens*, ed. Crawford, pp. 169–70 (*LP* I i, 127).

Chapter 23
1. *LP* I i, 112, 127; PRO, OBS 1419.
2. Hall, *Chronicle*, p. 513.
3. Ibid.
4. *AR* I, pp. 304–5; *LP* I i, 394; *CSP Sp.* Supp. to vols. I and II, pp. 34, 42.
5. Hall, *Chronicle*, p. 513.
6. *AR* I, pp. 304–5; *LP* I i, 394; *CSP Sp.* Supp. to vols. I and II, pp. 34–5, 42–4.
7. *CSP Sp.* Supp. to vols. I and II, pp. 39–41; GEC VI, p. 655; XII i, p. 519.
8. *CSP Sp.* Supp. to vols. I and II, p. 43; *LP* I i, 394; *CSP Sp.* II (1509–1525), p. 38.
9. *CSP Sp.* II (1509–1525), p. 38; Supp. to vols. I and II, pp. 34–6.

Chapter 24
1. PRO, OBS 1419; *LP* I i, 670; II ii, 1448; *CSP Ven.* II (1509–1519), p. 43; Hall, *Chronicle*, p. 516; Vergil, *Anglica Historia*, p. 152.
2. *LP* I i, 670, 673, p. 670/v; II ii, p. 1449.
3. *Commons* III, p. 147; *LP* I i, 674, g. 885(8); II ii, p. 1449.
4. PRO, OBS 1419; *LP* II ii, p. 1449.
5. *LP* I i, 671, 698; *The Great Tournament Roll of Westminster: a Collotype Reproduction of the Manuscript*, ed. S. Anglo (Oxford, 1968); Hall, *Chronicle*, pp. 517–19.
6. *LP* I i, 707 (pp. 381–2), 734; Hall, *Chronicle*, p. 519.

Chapter 25
1. *CSP Sp.* II (1509–1525), pp. 21–2, 25–9.
2. Ibid., pp. 30 (*LP* I i, 254), 52.
3. *CSP Ven.* II (1509–1519), p. 5; *LP* I i, 406; *CSP Sp.* II (1509–1525), pp. 33–5, 43.
4. *CSP Sp.* II (1509–1525), p. 45; Hall, *Chronicle*, pp. 514, 533–4, *LP* II ii, pp. 1498–9.
5. Hall, *Chronicle*, pp. 521–2; *LP* I i, 725, 727–8, 730.
6. Hall, *Chronicle*, p. 522; *CSP Sp.* II (1509–1525), p. 54.
7. GEC IX, pp. 614–15; Hall, *Chronicle*, p. 525; *CSP Ven.* II (1509–1519), 119; *Letters and Papers relating to the War with France in 1512–13*, ed. A. Spont (Navy Records Society 10, 1897), pp. viii–ix.

8.   Hall, *Chronicle*, p. 525; *LP* I i, 880, 974.
9.   R. Fiddes, *The Life of Cardinal Wolsey*, 2 vols. (London, 1724, 1726) II, pp. 8–9 (*LP* I i, 880).
10. Emden, *Biographical Register . . . Oxford to 1500*, pp. 2136–7; *LP* I i, 880.
11. *LP* I i, 939; *CSP Sp.* II (1509–1525), pp. 54–9; D.S. Chambers, *Cardinal Bainbridge in the Court of Rome 1509 to 1514* (Oxford, 1965), pp. 38–9.
12. Hall, *Chronicle*, pp. 527–32; *CSP Sp.* II (1509–1525), pp. 64–75.
13. *CSP Sp.* II (1509–1525), pp. 75–8.
14. Fiddes, *Life of Wolsey* II, pp. 10–11 (*LP* I i, 1356); *CSP Ven.* II (1509–1519), p. 83.
15. *LP* I i, 1735 (p. 791), 1775; I ii, 2077; *CSP Ven.* II (1509–1519), p. 87; D.S. Chambers, *Cardinal Bainbridge*, p. 40.
16. Hall, *Chronicle*, pp. 534–5; Fiddes, *Life of Wolsey* II, pp. 10–11 (*LP* I i, 1356); *Letters and Papers relating to the War with France in 1512–13*, pp. xxx–li; *CSP Ven.* II (1509–1519), p. 87.
17. Hall, *Chronicle*, p. 515; *Letters and Papers relating to the War with France in 1512–13*, pp. 103–7.
18. *Letters and Papers relating to the War with France in 1512–13*, pp. xxxvi–ix, 132–9, 147–8; Hall, *Chronicle*, pp. 534–7.
19. *Letters and Papers relating to the War with France in 1512–13*, pp. 132–9.

Chapter 26
1.   *CSP Ven.* II (1509–1519), p. 87.
2.   *CSP Sp.* I (1509–1525), pp. 115–16, 121–2, 143–4; *LP* I i, 1751.
3.   Hall, *Chronicle*, pp. 537–9; *LP* I ii, g. 2055 (46, 47, 60), 2065, 2295, 2391; II ii, p. 1461.
4.   Hall, *Chronicle*, p. 555.
5.   *House of Commons*, ed. Bindoff, II, pp. 548–9; S.J. Gunn, 'Sir Thomas Lovell (c. 1499–1524)', in J.L. Watts, ed., *The End of the Middle Ages? England in the Fifteenth and Sixteenth Centuries* (Stroud, 1998), pp. 117–53; R.C. Strong, *Tudor and Jacobean Portraits*, 2 vols. (London, 1969), I, p. 202; Hall, *Chronicle*, p. 539.
6.   Hall, *Chronicle*, pp. 540, 555–6; *LP* I ii, 2651; II ii, p. 1462; *Original Letters, Illustrative of English History . . . from Autographs in the British Museum and . . . Other Collections*, ed. H. Ellis, 11 vols. (1824–46), 1st series I, pp. 80–3 (*LP* I ii, 2120, 2162); *Letters of the Queens*, ed. Crawford, 171.
7.   *Original Letters*, ed. Ellis, 1st series I, p. 82; *CSP Mil.* I (1389–1618), p. 660; *LP* I ii, 2138, 2175; C.G. Cruickshank, *Army Royal: an Account of Henry VIII's Invasion of France 1513* (Oxford, 1969), pp. 92–3.
8.   *LP* I ii, 2019, 2098, 2143, 2163, 2312; *Original Letters*, ed. Ellis, 1st series I, pp. 90–1 (*LP* I ii, 2269).
9.   Hall, *Chronicle*, pp. 544–8; *Original Letters*, ed. Ellis, 1st series I, p. 83 (*LP* I ii, 2162); Cruickshank, *Army Royal*, pp. 114–16, 125; *CSP Ven.* II (1509–1519), p. 118 (where Longueville appears under his other title of Rothelin).
10. Cruickshank, *Army Royal*, pp. 116–17; R.V. Knecht, *Francis I* (Cambridge, 1982), p. 47; *CSP Ven.* II (1509–1519), pp. 140–1.

11. *Original Letters*, ed. Ellis, 1st series I, pp. 84–5 (LP I ii 2200); Hall, *Chronicle*, pp. 544–5; *LP* I ii, p. 1061; II ii, p. 1461.
12. Hall, *Chronicle*, pp. 555–7; *LP* I ii, 2330(3); *CSP Ven.* II (1509–1519), p. 134.
13. *Letters of Royal and Illustrious Ladies*, ed. Wood, I, pp. 163–5 (*LP* I ii, 2226); *LP* I ii, 2243, 2299; II ii, p. 1462; Hall, *Chronicle*, p. 564; *CSP Ven.* II (1509–1519), pp. 145–7.
14. *Letters of Royal and Illustrious Ladies*, ed. Wood, I, pp. 163–5 (*LP* I ii, 2226).
15. Hall, *Chronicle*, pp. 560–4; W.A. Sessions, *Henry Howard: the Poet Earl of Surrey: a Life* (Oxford, 1999), pp. 38–40.
16. *CSP Mil.* I (1389–1618), p. 396 (*LP* I ii, 2261); *Original Letters*, ed. Ellis, 1st series I, pp. 88–9 (*LP* I ii, 2268); Hall, *Chronicle*, p. 564.
17. *Original Letters*, ed. Ellis, 1st series I, pp. 88–9 (*LP* I ii, 2268); Hall, *Chronicle*, p. 564; Chambers, *Cardinal Bainbridge*, pp. 40, 52.
18. James IV's body was brought to the Observant Friars at Sheen, and (with papal permission) buried there. At the Reformation, the House was dissolved and the body, encased in lead, removed as a souvenir. It was dumped in a lumber room, where 'workmen there for their foolish pleasure hewed off his head': *A Survey of London by John Stow*, ed. C.L. Kingsford, 2 vols. (Oxford, 1908), I, p. 298. *Original Letters*, ed. Ellis, 1st series I, pp. 80–2, 88–9 (*LP* I ii, 2120, 2268); *LP* I ii, 2422 (2); *CSP Mil.* I (1389–1618), p. 408.

Chapter 27
1. *CSP Ven.* II (1509–1519), p. 188.
2. *LP* I ii, 2724, 2768; R.B. Wernham, *Before the Armada: the Growth of English Foreign Policy, 1485–1588* (London, 1966), pp. 86–7; *CSP Ven.* II (1509–1519), p. 201.
3. *CSP Sp.* II (1509–1525), p. 42.
4. *LP* II ii, 4071.
5. *CSP Ven.* II (1509–1519), pp. 198–9; *LP* I ii, 3136, 3146.
6. *CSP Ven.* II (1509–1519), p. 190.
7. Ibid., pp. 190, 199–200; *LP* II ii, p. 1465.
8. *CSP Ven.* II (1509–1519), p. 188; Mattingly, *Catherine of Aragon*, pp. 320–1.
9. *CSP Ven.* II (1509–1519), p. 200; *LP* I ii, 3041 (p. 1307), 3074 (p. 1317).
10. *LP* I ii, 3332–3, 3416, 3440.
11. Ibid., 3440; 3581; *CSP Sp.* II (1509–1525), p. 248.
12. *LP* I ii, 3581; *CSP Ven.* II (1509–1519), p. 223.

Chapter 28
1. *CSP Sp.* Supp. to vols. I and II, pp. xxii–iii, 44–6. *LP* I i, 20 (p. 15) shows that the individuals Diego named were indeed members of Catherine's household.
2. *CSP Sp.* II (1509–1525), p. 273; Mattingly, *Catherine of Aragon*, p. 201.
3. Knecht, *Francis I*, pp. 41–8.
4. *CSP Sp.* II (1509–1525), pp. 270–3.

5. Ibid., p. 273; *LP* I ii, 3482; *CSP Ven.* II (1509–1519), 690.
6. *CSP Ven.* II (1509–1519), 691.
7. *LP* II ii, 4074; *CSP Ven.* II (1509–1519), 1038.
8. *St. P.* I, p. 1 (*LP* II ii, 4279).
9. *LP* II ii, 4276; *St. P.* I, p. 2 (*LP* II ii, 4288).
10. PRO, OBS 1419; *LP* II ii, 4398, p. 1479; *CSP Ven.* II (1509–1519), 1093.
11. *CSP Ven.* II (1509–1519), 1103.

Chapter 29
1. *LP* I ii, 3041; *CSP Ven.* II (1509–1519), pp. 248, 529, 560.
2. *CSP Ven.* II (1509–1519), p. 560.
3. Ibid., pp. 242, 562.
4. *Original Letters*, ed. Ellis, 1st series I, pp. 88–91 (*LP* I ii, 2268–9); *CSP Ven.* II (1509–1519), p. 560.
5. Hall, *Chronicle*, pp. 590–1; *CSP Ven.* II (1509–1519), p. 385.

Chapter 30
1. *CSP Ven.* II (1509–1519), p. 434.
2. *LP* VIII, 200; *CSP Sp.* V i (1534–1535), p. 134. I have substituted the more vivid 'sit up with her' as in *CSP Sp.* for the lamer 'watch her' in *LP*.
3. *HO*, pp. 27–33; N. Orme, 'The Education of Edward V', *BIHR* 57 (1984), pp. 119–30.
4. *LP* II ii, 4326; *Original Letters*, ed. Ellis, 1st series I, p. 175 (*LP* III i, 873).
5. *LP* II i, 1573.
6. GEC XI, pp. 399–402; *LP* II ii, 3429, 3802, pp. 1473–4; *Original Letters*, ed. Ellis, 2nd series II, pp. 78–83 (*LP* XI, 203).
7. *AR* I, p. 306; *LP* III i, 491, 528, 577, 579; III ii, Appendix 20; *PPE Princess Mary*, p. xxi.
8. *LP* Addenda I i, 259; *LP* III i, 970; *PPE Princess Mary*, p. xxii; *LP* II ii, p. 1477; Thurley, *Royal Palaces*, pp. 78, 80.
9. *PPE Princess Mary*, p. xxii; *LP* II ii, p. 1477.
10. *LP* II ii, 4326.
11. *LP* II ii, 4326/ii; N. Samman, 'The Henrician Court during Cardinal Wolsey's Ascendancy' (University of Wales Ph.D. thesis, 1989), p. 351; D. Starkey, 'The King's Privy Chamber, 1485–1547 (University of Cambridge Ph.D. thesis, 1973), pp. 372–3; *LP* III ii, pp. 1539–43.
12. *LP* II ii, p. 1477; III i, 805; D. Erasmus, *De immensa dei misericordia*, trans. G. Hervet, Berthelet, 1526: STC 10474.
13. *LP* III i, 895–6, 970; VIII, 263 (p. 101).
14. Harris, *Buckingham*, pp. 55–6.
15. Samman, 'The Henrician Court', p. 359; *LP* III ii, 2585 (p. 1099); *CSP Ven.* III (1520–1526), 167; *HKW* IV, pp. 172–5; Thurley, *Royal Palaces*, pp. 44–5, 49–50.
16. Hall, *Chronicle*, pp. 622–3; *LP* III i, 1204, 1233; III ii, 1437, 1439, 1673.
17. *St. P.* I, p. 19 (*LP* III ii, 1437); *LP* III ii, 1669, 2585 (p. 1099), 3375 (p. 1409); Samman, 'The Henrician Court', pp. 361–3.

18. *LP* I ii, 1849; III ii, 3375 (pp. 1405, 1409); Nichols, *Hall of Lawford Hall*, pp. 174–7.
19. Dowling, *Humanism in the Age of Henry VIII*, pp. 221–3.
20. F. Watson, *Tudor School-boy Life: the Dialogues of Juan Luis Vives* (London, 1908), pp. vii–xiv; Dowling, *Humanism*, p. 149.
21. Watson, *Tudor School-boy Life*, pp. xiv–xvii; Dowling, *Humanism*, pp. 149–50, 223.
22. F. Watson, *Vives and the Renascence Education of Women* (London, 1912), pp. 32–8, 58–9, 62–3, 71–84, 102–4, 117–18, 130–1, 137, 139–47, 151–8; Dowling, *Humanism*, pp. 223–6, Samman, 'The Henrician Court', p. 365; *PPE Princess Mary*, pp. cxxviii–ix, cxxxiv–v.

Chapter 31
1. *LP* II ii, 4480, 4693, p. 1479; *CSP Ven.* II (1509–1519), p. 463; Hall, *Chronicle*, pp. 594–5.
2. *LP* III i, 514.
3. Ibid., 721.
4. Ibid., 728.
5. Ibid., 689.
6. Hall, *Chronicle*, pp. 604–5; *CSP Ven.* III (1520–1526), pp. 14–19.
7. Hall, *Chronicle*, pp. 603–20; *LP* III i, 861; M. Dowling, *Fisher of Men: a Life of John Fisher, 1469–1535* (Basingstoke, 1999), pp. 52–3, 76.
8. Hall, *Chronicle*, p. 620.
9. *LP* III ii, 1443/8, 1462, 2333/3.
10. *CSP Sp.* Further Supp. (1513–1542), p. 71; Starkey, *European Court*, p. 91; Hall, *Chronicle*, p. 692.
11. *CSP Sp.* Further Supp. (1513–1542), p. 138.
12. Ibid., p. 74.
13. Hall, *Chronicle*, pp. 635–41; *CSP Sp.* II (1509–1525), pp. 430, 432.
14. *CSP Sp.* II (1509–1525), p. 448; Hall, *Chronicle*, p. 641.
15. *CSP Sp.* II (1509–1525), pp. 432, 444, 448.
16. Hall, *Chronicle*, pp. 642–3.
17. *CSP Sp.* Further Supp. (1513–1542), p. 185.
18. Hall, *Chronicle*, pp. 661–2.
19. Ibid., pp. 661–2, 667–72.
20. *CSP Sp.* Further Supp. (1513–1542), pp. 325, 411.
21. *St. P.* I, pp. 151–3 (*LP* IV i, 882); Knecht, *Francis I*, p. 127; *CSP Sp.* III i (1525–1526), pp. 174–9.
22. J.J. Scarisbrick, *Henry VIII* (London, 1968), pp. 136–7; *St. P.* VI, pp. 412–36 (*LP* IV i, 1212); *CSP Sp.* III i (1525–1526), p. 114.
23. *CSP Sp.* III i (1525–1526), p. 108.
24. Ibid., pp. 174–9.
25. Ibid., pp. 1018–19.

Part Two: Rival Queens
Divorcing Catherine

Chapter 32

1. *CSP Ven.* II (1509–1519), 479 (p. 188); *LP* III i, 1284 (p. 491).
2. *CSP Sp.* III ii (1527–1529), pp. 842–3.
3. Hall, *Chronicle*, p. 703.
4. *CSP Ven.* III (1520–1526), 1053.
5. Nichols, *Hall of Lawford Hall*, p. 196; *Chronicles of London*, ed. Kingsford, p. 213.
6. *CSP Ven.* III (1520–1526), 1053.
7. *PPE Princess Mary*, pp. xxxix, xli–xlii, xliv.
8. W.R.B. Robinson, 'Princess Mary's Itinerary in the Marches of Wales, 1525–1527: a Provisional Record', *HR* 52 (1998), pp. 235–7, 240–2; *LP* Addenda I i, 458; IV i, 1940/1; Hall, *Chronicle*, p. 703; *PPE Princess Mary*, p. xxxix.
9. *Original Letters*, ed. Ellis, 1st series II, pp. 19–20 (dated at Woburn, probably on 26 October 1525); *Letters of the Queens*, ed. Crawford, p. 177.
10. *St. P.* I, pp. 161–2 (*LP* IV ii, 2452).
11. *CSP Sp.* III ii (1527–1529), pp. 109–11, 116–17.

Chapter 33

1. *CSP Sp.* III ii (1527–1529), pp. 193–4.
2. *LP* IV ii, 3140.
3. *Letters of Richard Fox 1486–1527*, ed. P.S. and H.M. Allen (Oxford, 1929), pp. 156–7; *LP* IV ii, 3140 (p. 1429); IV iii 5792 (p. 2588); Kelly, *Matrimonial Trials*, pp. 25–9.
4. *LP* IV ii, 3148; Dowling, *Fisher*, p. 133.
5. *St. P.* I, pp. 189–90 (*LP* IV ii, 3147).
6. *CSP Sp.* III ii (1527–1529), p. 276.
7. *St. P.* I, pp. 194–5 (*LP* IV ii, 3217).
8. *St. P.* I, pp. 194–5; N. Pocock, *Records of the Reformation, the Divorce 1527–1533*, 2 vols. (Oxford, 1870), I, p. 11 (*LP* IV ii, 3302).
9. *CSP Sp.* III ii (1527–1529), pp. 276–7.
10. Ibid., p. 277; *LP* I i, 20 (p. 15).
11. *St. P.* I, pp. 215–16 (*LP* IV ii, 3265); *LP* IV ii, 3283.
12. *CSP Sp.* III ii (1527–1529), pp. 300–3.

Chapter 34

1. *Letters of Royal and Illustrious Ladies*, ed. Wood, II, pp. 201–3 (*LP* IV ii, 4990).
2. Ibid.
3. *CSP Sp.* III ii (1527–1529), p. 443.
4. Ibid., p. 822 (misdated to 1528 by the Calendar); V. Murphy, 'The Literature and Propaganda of Henry VIII's First Divorce' in D. MacCulloch, ed., *The Reign of Henry VIII: Politics, Policy and Piety* (London, 1995), pp. 143–4.
5. Emden, *Biographical Register . . . Oxford to 1500*, III, p. 1417; *Biographical*

Register ... Oxford 1501–1540, pp. 599–600; J. Wegg, *Richard Pace; a Tudor Diplomatist* (London, 1932), pp. 274–7; *LP* IV ii, 3233–6.

6. Wegg, Richard Pace, pp. 279–81; *CSP Sp.* III ii (1527–1529), pp. 440–1.
7. *CSP Sp.* III ii (1527–1529), pp. 587–8.
8. *LP* IV ii, 3943, 4990.
9. *LP* IV ii, 5038.
10. *CSP Sp.* III ii (1527–1529), pp. 822–3 (my translation from the Spanish).
11. Scarisbrick, *Henry VIII*, pp. 212–13, 215.
12. Ibid., p. 212.
13. Emden, *Biographical Register ... Cambridge to 1500*, pp. 525–6; Fiddes, *Life of Wolsey* II, pp. 212–15 (*LP* IV ii, 4685).
14. *LP* IV ii, 4857, 4858, 4879; *CSP Sp.* III ii (1527–1529), p. 839.

Chapter 35
1. W.E. Wilkie, *The Cardinal Protectors of England: Rome and the Tudors before the Reformation* (Cambridge, 1974), pp. 104–5.
2. *LP* IV ii, 4858.
3. Ibid., 4875.

Chapter 36
1. *LP* IV ii, 4875; *CSP Sp.* III ii (1527–1529), p. 842.
2. Kelly, *Matrimonial Trials*, pp. 57–8, 62. G. de C. Parmiter, *The King's Great Matter* (London, 1967), pp. 76–8.
3. N. Pocock, *Records of the Reformation, the Divorce 1527–1533*, 2 vols. (Oxford, 1870), I, pp. 212–15; *CSP Sp.* III ii (1527–1529), pp. 789, 845.
4. *CSP Sp.* III ii (1527–1529), p. 854. This refers to the person Henry proposed to send as 'someone'; he is identified as Fitzwilliam by *CSP Sp.* III ii (1527–1529), p. 860 which describes him as 'King's treasurer' (i.e. Treasurer of the Household).
5. *LP* IV ii, 5053; iii, 5154, 5163, 5470; V, pp. 306, 308; *CSP Sp.* III ii (1527–1529), pp. 860, 877, 882, 884; Emden, *Biographical Register ... Oxford 1501–1540*, p. 1.
6. *LP* IV iii, 5283.
7. Ibid., 5154/ii, 5468.
8. Ibid., 5470 (*St. P.* VII, p. 161).
9. Ibid., 5423 (pp. 2383–4), 5425, 5470 (*St. P.* VII, pp. 158–64).
10. Ibid., 5469, 5470 (*St. P.* VII, pp. 161), 5471 (p. 2411).

Chapter 37
1. *CSP Sp.* IV i (1529–1530), p. 600; *The Inventory of King Henry VIII: the Transcript*, ed. D. Starkey (Society of Antiquaries, London, 1999), p. 259 (nos. 11591, 11594); *CSP Sp.* IV ii (1531–1533), pp. 222–4.
2. F. Kisby, '"When the King Goeth a Procession": Chapel Ceremonies and Services, the Ritual Year and Religous Reforms at the Early-Tudor Court, 1485–1547', forthcoming.
3. Samman, 'The Henrician Court', pp. 383–4; *LP* IV ii, 5016.
4. *CSP Sp.* III ii (1527–1529), pp. 861, 989–91; *LP* IV ii 5063; V, p. 304.

5. *LP* IV ii, 5072.
6. *CSP Sp.* III ii (1527–1529), p. 990; III iii (1529–1530), p. 95; Pocock, *Records* I, p. 252 (*LP* IV iii, 5762 [p.2566]).
7. *LP* IV iii, 5519, 5611, 5613/5, 5636, 5694/2; J. Gairdner, 'New Lights on the Divorce of Henry VIII', *EHR* 11–12 (1896–7), 12, p. 246.
8. *LP* IV iii, 5679, 5681, 5700; Gairdner, 'New Lights', 12, p. 250.
9. Pocock, *Records* II, p. 609; *CSP Sp.* IV i (1529–1530), p. 133.
10. A.W. Clapham, 'On the Topography of the Dominican Priory of London', *Archaeologia* 63 (1912), pp. 57–84, particularly pp. 78–80; E.K. Chambers, *The Elizabethan Stage*, 4 vols. (London, 1923) II, pp. 480–91.
11. *HKW* IV, pp. 53–7; Thurley, *Royal Palaces*, pp. 40–1; *LP* III ii, 2956.
12. *LP* V, p. 311; Hall, *Chronicle*, p. 756; *The Life and Death of Cardinal Wolsey by George Cavendish*, ed. R.S. Sylvester (EETS 242, 1959) [hereafter Cavendish, *Wolsey*], p. 79.
13. Pocock, *Records* I, pp. 216–22; *CSP Ven.* IV (1527–1533), p. 219; *LP* IV iii, 5694, 5695/2–3, 5702; Parmiter, *Great Matter*, p. 98 n. 1; Hall, *Chronicle*, p. 757.
14. Cavendish, *Wolsey*, pp. 78, 80–1; Hall, *Chronicle*, pp. 756–7; *CSP Ven.* IV (1527–1529), pp. 219–20; *LP* IV iii, 5702; Gairdner, 'New Lights', 12, p. 251.
15. *CSP Sp.* IV i (1529–1530), p. 352.
16. R. Scheurer, *Correspondance du Cardinal Jean du Bellay*, 2 vols. (Paris, 1969), I, p. 47 (*LP* IV iii, 5702); Gairdner, 'New Lights', 12, p. 251.
17. Cavendish, *Wolsey*, p. 82.
18. *LP* IV iii, 5702.
19. *CSP Sp.* III ii (1527–1529), pp. 845–6.
20. Gairdner, 'New Lights', 12, pp. 249–52; *LP* IV iii, 5572 (p. 2462), 5584 (p. 2470), 5775 (p. 2581).
21. Cavendish, *Wolsey*, p. 89.
22. *CSP Sp.* IV i (1529–1530), pp. 134, 154, 158.
23. *CSP Sp.* IV i (1529–1530), pp. 155–6.
24. Ibid., pp. 156–8. There are useful discussions of the technical terms in Parmiter, *Great Matter*, p. 108 n. 3 (*signatura*) and *LP* IV Introduction, p. div (advocation).
25. *CSP Sp.* IV i (1529–1530), pp. 158–60.
26. Ibid., pp. 158–9.
27. *LP* IV iii, 5791 (p. 2589); Hall, *Chronicle*, p. 758; Kelly, *Matrimonial Trials*, pp. 127–80.
28. Hall, *Chronicle*, p. 758; Cavendish, *Wolsey*, p. 90.
29. *LP* IV iii, 5789.

Chapter 38
1. *St. P.* VII, pp. 194–5.
2. Pocock, *Records* I, pp. 266–7.
3. Cavendish, *Wolsey*, p. 58.
4. *LP* IV iii, 5780, 5785.
5. *LP* IV iii, 5802, 5820.

6. Ibid., 5819, 5821 (Pocock, *Records* I, pp. 266–7).
7. *LP* IV iii, 5821; *St. P.* VII, pp. 194–5.
8. *LP* IV iii, 5865; *St. P.* I, p. 336.
9. *St. P.* I, p. 336.
10. *LP* IV iii, 5867, 5923; *St. P.* I, p. 347.
11. *LP* IV iii, 5866.
12. *CSP Sp.* IV i (1529–1530), pp. 214–15; *LP* IV iii, 5995.
13. *St. P.* I, p. 343; *CSP Sp.* IV i (1529–1530), p. 237.
14. *LP* IV iii, 6121 (p. 2732).
15. *CSP Sp.* IV i (1529–1530), p. 133 (*LP* IV iii, 5803); Cavendish, *Wolsey*, pp. 92–3.
16. *LP* IV iii, 6000, 6025, 6035, 6043; Cavendish, *Wolsey*, pp. 96–8; Hall, *Chronicle*, p. 760.
17. *CSP Sp.* IV i (1529–1530), pp. 303–4; Thurley, *Royal Palaces*, p. 51; S. Thurley, *Whitehall Palace: an Architectural History of the Royal Apartments, 1240–1690* (London, 1999), p. 37; Ives, *Anne Boleyn*, p. 151; Samman, 'The Henrician Court', p. 387.

Anne Boleyn

Chapter 39

1. E.W. Ives, *Anne Boleyn*, pp. 3–5; Howard de Walden, *Banners, Standards and Badges from a Tudor Manuscript...* (London, 1904), p. 17.
2. Ives, *Anne Boleyn*, pp. 4–7, 11, 17–21.
3. H. Paget, 'The Youth of Anne Boleyn', *BIHR* 54 (1981), pp. 165.
4. Ibid., pp. 164–5, 169.
5. Ibid., pp. 163–4, 166–67.
6. Ibid., pp. 163, 166, 167, 168; G. Ascoli, *La Grande-Bretagne devant L'Opinion Française depuis la Guerre de Cents Ans jusqu'à la Fin du XVIe Siècle* (Paris, 1927), p. 233; Richardson, *Mary Tudor*, chs. 3–6.
7. Paget, 'Youth', p. 168; Ascoli, *La Grande-Bretagne*, p. 234; Richardson, *Mary Tudor*, pp. 88, 108–11; S.J. Gunn, *Charles Brandon, Duke of Suffolk 1484–1545* (Oxford, 1988), pp. 35–7.
8. *LP* III i, 808.
9. Paget, 'Youth', pp. 168–9; Ascoli, *La Grande-Bretagne*, p. 234.
10. *LP* III ii, 1994; *CSP Sp.* Further Supp. (1513–1542), pp. 30–1.

Chapter 40

1. Cavendish, *Wolsey*, p. 29; *The Papers of George Wyatt, Esquire*, ed. D.M. Loades (CS 4th series 5, 1968), p. 143.
2. Hall, *Chronicle*, pp. 630–1; R.G. Siemens, 'New Evidence on Wyatt's "A Robyn" in British Library Additional Ms 31, 922', *Notes and Queries* ns 46, p. 190 n. 5; *CSP Sp.* Further Supp. (1513–1542), p. 71; *LP* III ii, pp. 1557–9.
3. Ives, *Anne Boleyn*, pp. 43–6; *St. P.* II, pp. 50–1 (*LP* III i, 1011); *St. P.* I, p. 92 (*LP* III ii, 1762); *Holbein and the Court of Henry VIII* (The Queen's Gallery, Buckingham Palace exhibition catalogue 1978–1979), pp. 67–8 (where the subject 'Ormond' is mistakenly identified as Anne Boleyn's

father, the Earl of Wiltshire and Ormond); D. Starkey, 'Holbein's Irish Sitter?', *The Burlington Magazine* 123 (1981), pp. 300–1.

4. Cavendish, *Wolsey*, pp. 30, 34; G.W. Bernard, *The Power of the Early Tudor Nobility: a Study of the Fourth and Fifth Earls of Shrewsbury* (Brighton, 1985), p. 154; E. Lodge, *Illustrations of British History, Biography and Manners*, 3 vols. (London, 1838), I, pp. 20–1 (*LP* II i, 1935); *LP* III ii, 3648.

5. Ives, *Anne Boleyn*, p. 83; *Commons* III, p. 669; Papers of George Wyatt, pp. 6–7; *LP* IV i, 214 (p. 85); K. Muir, *Life and Letters of Sir Thomas Wyatt* (Liverpool, 1963), p. 41; *CSP Sp.* VI i (1538–42), p. 314; P. Thomson, *Sir Thomas Wyatt and his Background* (London, 1964), p. 19.

6. Muir, *Life and Letters*, p. 206; R.A. Rebholz, *Sir Thomas Wyatt: the Complete Poems* (Harmondsworth, 1978), pp. 77, 85, 96; *The Life of Cardinal Wolsey by George Cavendish*, ed. S.W. Singer (London, 1827) [hereafter Cavendish, *Wolsey*, ed. Singer], p. 425.

7. Hall, *Chronicle*, pp. 688–91; 'The Letters of the Clifford Lords Clifford and Earls of Northumberland', ed. R.W. Hoyle, *Camden Miscellany 31* (CS 4th series 44, 1992), pp. 95–6; *LP* IV i, 965 (p. 419); Hall, *Chronicle*, p. 911; *Commons* I, pp. 518–21.

8. Cavendish, *Wolsey*, p. 29.

9. P. Friedmann, *Anne Boleyn, a Chapter in English History*, 2 vols. (London, 1884), I, p. 43; GEC XII i, pp. 602–3; *Commons* I, pp. 582–3; III, p. 419; *LP* III ii, p. 1939; IV i, 2972; VII, 1655; *CSP Sp.* IV ii (1531–1533), p. 473.

10. Cavendish, *Wolsey*, p. 30.

11. Ibid., pp. 30–4.

12. *LP* IV i, 1201; IV ii 2523, 3378.

13. Cavendish, *Wolsey*, pp. 34–5.

14. Bernard, *Power of the Early Tudor Nobility*, p. 153.

15. Cavendish, *Wolsey*, pp. 34–5.

Chapter 41

1. *The Love Letters of Henry VIII*, ed. H. Savage (London, 1949). My ordering of the Letters, which broadly agrees with M.St.C. Byrne, ed., *The Letters of King Henry VIII*, (London, 1936), would put the following as the earliest in the sequence: *Love Letters of Henry VIII*, ed. Savage, pp. 27–8, 29–30, 40–1, 38.

2. *Love Letters of Henry VIII*, ed. Savage, pp. 27–8; *Letters of King Henry VIII*, ed. Byrne, p. 54.

3. J. Rowlands, *The Age of Durer and Holbein: German Drawings 1400–1550* (London, 1988), pp. 245, 246.

4. *Love Letters of Henry VIII*, ed. Savage, pp. 29–30; *Letters of King Henry VIII*, ed. Byrne, pp. 55–6.

5. *Love Letters of Henry VIII*, ed. Savage, pp. 40–1; *Letters of King Henry VIII*, ed. Byrne, pp. 57–8.

6. *Love Letters of Henry VIII*, ed. Savage, p. 38; *Letters of King Henry VIII*, ed. Byrne, p. 58.

7. *Love Letters of Henry VIII*, ed. Savage, pp. 32–3; *Letters of King Henry VIII*, ed. Byrne, pp. 56–7.

8. *Love Letters of Henry VIII*, ed. Savage, pp. 34–6; *Letters of King Henry VIII*, ed. Byrne, pp. 54–5.
9. *Love Letters of Henry VIII*, ed. Savage, pp. 34–6; *Letters of King Henry VIII*, ed. Byrne, pp. 54–5.

Chapter 42
1. *Love Letters of Henry VIII*, ed. Savage, pp. 41–3; *Letters of King Henry VIII*, ed. Byrne, p. 59.
2. J. Lingard, *The History of England*, 10 vols. (London, 1854), IV, p. 237 n. 3; *CSP Ven.* IV (1527–1533), p. 61.

Chapter 43
1. Lingard, *History of England*, IV, p. 237 n. 3; *LP* IV ii, 3140.
2. Parmiter, *Great Matter*, pp. 3–4; Lingard, *History of England*, IV, p. 234 n. 6; T.F. Mayer, Reginald Pole: Prince and Prophet (Cambridge, 2000), ch. 1, p. 378; 'A Fate worse than Death: Reginald Pole and the Paris Theologians', *EHR* 103 (1988), pp. 883–7; Emden, *Biographical Register... Oxford 1501–1540*, pp. 454–5.
3. Emden, *Biographical Register... Oxford 1501–1540*, p. 635; *HO*, pp. 159, 160; *Select Cases in the Court of Requests A.D. 1497–1569* (Selden Society XII, 1898), pp. cv–vl, cviii, cxv.
4. *LP* IV iii, 5791 (pp. 2588–9); *Letters of Richard Fox*, ed. Allen, pp. 156–7.
5. *LP* IV ii, 3140; Cavendish, *Wolsey*, p. 179.
6. For example, *Letters of King Henry VIII*, ed. Byrne, pp. 78, 80, 81.
7. *St. P.* I, p. 189 (*LP* IV ii, 3147). The Pope understood the consequences of this takeover: he was clear that it was Wolsey who had persuaded Henry that the Divorce must be settled in Rome, not England. He did not thank Wolsey for it: *LP* IV ii, 5072.
8. *St. P.* I, pp. 194–5 (*LP* IV ii, 3217); Emden, *Biographical Register . . . Cambridge to 1501*, pp. 505–6.
9. Scarisbrick, *Henry VIII*, pp. 163–97.
10. *St. P.* I, pp. 194–5 (*LP* IV ii, 3217).
11. Ibid.

Chapter 44
1. Cavendish, *Wolsey*, pp. 35–6, 43–4.
2. *St. P.* I, p. 197.
3. *St. P.* I, pp. 230–3, 254–6 (*LP* IV ii, 3311, 3340).
4. *LP* IV ii, 3263.
5. *HKW* IV, p. 172; Thurley, *Royal Palaces*, pp. 44–5, 49–50.
6. Samman, 'The Henrician Court', p. 379; *LP* IV ii, 3318.
7. *LP* IV ii, 3335 (p. 1511).
8. J.A. Muller, *Stephen Gardiner and the Tudor Reaction* (New York, 1926), pp. 1–12.
9. *St. P.* I, p. 255; *LP* IV ii, 3167/2.
10. *St. P.* I, pp. 254–6.
11. *LP* IV ii, 3354.

12. *St. P.* I, p. 261 (*LP* IV ii, 3360).
13. *St. P.* I, p. 267 (*LP* IV ii, 3382).
14. Samman, 'The Henrician Court', p. 379; *CSP Sp.* III ii (1527–1529), p. 327.
15. *St. P.* I, p. 268 (*LP* IV ii, 3400).
16. *St. P.* I, pp. 267–77; Cavendish, *Wolsey*, pp. 58–9.
17. *LP* IV ii, 2828, 2830, 2864, 2871, 2914, g. 2927(4).
18. Cavendish, *Wolsey*, p. 63; *St. P.* VII, pp. 1–3 (*LP* IV ii, 3420, 3422).
19. Samman, 'The Henrician Court'. pp. 360, 379–80; *CSP Sp.* III ii (1527–1529), p. 432. Cavendish's memory seems to fail, for once, when he reports that the King and Wolsey met at 'Sir Harry Wyatt's house in Kent' (p. 67).

Chapter 45
1. Emden, *Biographical Register . . . Oxford 1501–1540*, p. 26.
2. *LP* X, 1182; *CSP Sp.* IV ii (1531–1533), p. 471; Gairdner, 'New Lights', p. 685.
3. *St. P.* VII, p. 3; Gairdner, 'New Lights', p. 685.
4. Gairdner, 'New Lights', pp. 685–6.
5. Ibid., p. 686; *St. P.* VII, pp. 13–14, 16 (Barlow is the 'chaplain of my lord of Rochford', whom Knight mentions, not Cranmer as *LP* IV ii, 3638 speculates); Emden, *Biographical Register . . . Oxford to 1500*, p. 1063.
6. Gairdner, 'New Lights', pp. 686–7; *SP* VII, pp. 16–17.
7. Burnet, *History of the Reformation* IV, pp. 34–35 (*LP* IV ii, 3751); Gairdner, 'New Lights', pp. 686–7.
8. Burnet, *History of the Reformation* IV, pp. 35, 37–9 (*LP* IV ii, 3749); *LP* IV ii, 3686; Kelly, *Matrimonial Trials*, pp. 41–2.
9. Burnet, *History of the Reformation* IV, p. 35.
10. Ibid., pp. 36, 39; *LP* IV ii, 3749; *St. P.* VII, p. 36 (*LP* IV ii, 3750).
11. *St. P.* VII, p. 36 (*LP* IV ii, 3750); Burnet, *History of the Reformation* IV, pp. 37–9 (*LP* IV ii, 3749); *LP* IV ii, 3851.
12. Pocock, *Records of the Reformation* I, pp. 22–7; Gairdner, 'New Lights', p. 691; Kelly, *Matrimonial Trials*, pp. 41 n. 6, which corrects Scarisbrick, *Henry VIII*, pp. 203–4 on the nature and possible authorship of the annotated copy of the Dispensation.
13. *LP* IV ii, 3913 (p. 1741); Pocock, *Records* I, p. 160 (*LP* IV ii, 4185).
14. *LP* IV ii, 4647; Fiddes, *Life of Wolsey*, II, pp. 255–6 (*LP* IV iii, App. 197).

Chapter 46
1. *Love Letters of Henry VIII*, ed. Savage, p. 46; *Letters of King Henry VIII*, ed. Byrne, p. 75.
2. Pocock, *Records* I, pp. 22–7; *LP* IV ii, 3913 (p. 1741); *CSP Ven.* VI iii (1557–1558), p. 1607.
3. *DNB sub 'Foxe'*; Gairdner, 'New Lights', p. 691; *LP* IV ii, 3913, 3932; Pocock, *Records* I, pp. 73–4, 115 (*LP* IV ii, 3925, 4120).
4. *CSP Sp.* III ii (1527–1529), pp. 587; *CSP Ven.* VI iii (1557–1558), p. 1607; Samman, 'The Henrician Court', p. 381; Hall, *Chronicle*, pp. 742–3.

5. Hall, *Chronicle*, pp. 742–3.
6. *Love Letters of Henry VIII*, ed. Savage, p. 46; *Letters of King Henry VIII*, ed. Byrne, p. 61.
7. Ibid.
8. *Love Letters of Henry VIII*, ed. Savage, pp. 46; *Letters of King Henry VIII*, ed. Byrne, p. 61; *LP* IV ii, 3910, 3932.
9. *Love Letters of Henry VIII*, ed. Savage, pp. 46–7; *Letters of King Henry VIII*, ed. Byrne, p. 80.

Chapter 47
1. *Original Letters*, ed. Ellis, 3rd series II, pp. 132–4 (*LP* IV ii, 4005).
2. PRO, SP1/47, fo. 120 (*LP* IV ii, 4081).
3. *Commons* III, p. 234; D. Willen, *John Russell, First Earl of Bedford: One of the King's Men* (London, 1981), pp. 16–17; PRO, SP1/47, fos. 64–5 (*LP* IV ii, 4456).
4. Starkey, 'The King's Privy Chamber, 1485–1547', pp. 133–81; *Commons* I, pp. 57–8.
5. *LP* IV ii, 3691 (Wallop was marshal of Calais; 'remys' should be rendered as 'reappointed', not 'replaced' as in *LP*), g. 3869(29).
6. *Commons* I, pp. 634–8; *LP* III ii, 2326, IV i, 2032; T. Fuller, *Worthies of England*, 3 vols. (London, 1840) II, p. 179; GEC V, p. 80; PRO, SP1/47, fo. 120 (*LP* IV ii, 4081).
7. *LP* IV ii, 3930, 4190.
8. *St. P.* I, pp. 284, 286 (*LP* IV ii, 4080) *LP* IV ii, 4147; *Tudor Royal Proclamations*, eds. P.L. Hughes and J.F. Larkin, 3 vols. (1963–1969), I, pp. 175–6.
9. *LP* IV ii, 3682.
10. Knecht, *Francis I*, pp. 215, 217; R.B. Wernham, *Before the Armada: the Emergence of the English Nation 1485–1588* (London, 1966), pp. 118–19.
11. Pocock, *Records* I, pp. 75–7, 84–5 (*LP* IV ii, 3932, 4077); *St. P.* VII, pp. 54–6 (*LP* IV ii, 3954).
12. Pocock, *Records* I, pp. 88–9 (*LP* IV ii, 4090).
13. Ibid.
14. Ibid., pp. 95–135 (*LP* IV, 4120, 4167).
15. Ibid., p. 141 (*LP* IV ii, 4251).

Chapter 48
1. Pocock, *Records* I, pp. 141–55 (*LP* IV ii, 4251). J. Gairdner, 'The Draft Commission', *EHR* 5 (1890), pp. 544–550; *LP* IV ii, 3643/1; Kelly, *Matrimonial Trials*, p. 43 n. 10. Gairdner, for once, is wrong to argue that the endorsement on the draft of the second dispensation (*Minuta dispensationis missae Thadeum cursorem*) means that it was the dispensation Wolsey sent to Knight the previous December. As we have seen, Thaddeus was also the courier for Foxe and Gardiner's mission; moreover, this draft of the second dispensation reflects the criticisms made of the first in London in February 1528.
2. A.F. Pollard, *Wolsey* (London, 1929), p. 232.

3. Pocock, *Records* I, pp. 156–8 (*LP* IV ii, 4290).
4. *LP* IV ii, 4355, 4430.

Chapter 49
1. Samman, 'The Henrician Court', p. 382; *LP* IV ii, 4391 (p. 1924); Ives, *Anne Boleyn*, p. 120.
2. *Love Letters of Henry VIII*, ed. Savage, pp. 30–2; *Letters of King Henry VIII*, ed. Byrne, pp. 88–9.
3. *Love Letters of Henry VIII*, ed. Savage, pp. 43–4; *Letters of King Henry VIII*, ed. Byrne, p. 70; *LP* IV ii, 4409.
4. G. Clark, *A History of the Royal College of Physicians of London*, 3 vols. (1964–6), I, p. 72; *Athenae Cantabrigienses*, ed. C.H. and T. Cooper, 2 vols. (Cambridge, 1858), I, p. 87; *LP* IV ii, 4277.
5. *St. P.* I, pp. 298–9 (*LP* IV ii, 4409).
6. *Love Letters of Henry VIII*, ed. Savage, pp. 43–4; *Letters of King Henry VIII*, ed. Byrne, p. 70; *LP* V, p. 305.
7. *LP* IV ii, 4392 (p. 1924); Cavendish, *Wolsey*, p. 35.
8. M.D. Knowles, '"The Matter of Wilton" in 1528', *BIHR* 31(1958), pp. 93–5; *Love Letters of Henry VIII*, ed. Savage, pp. 44–5; *Letters of King Henry VIII*, ed. Byrne, pp. 74–5.
9. *LP* IV ii, 4440, 4456, 4463, 4649.
10. *St. P.* I, pp. 309–12 (*LP* IV ii, 4468).
11. Ibid., p. 312 (*LP* IV, 4476).
12. Knowles, 'The Matter of Wilton', pp. 95–6; *SP* I, pp. 313–16 (*LP* IV ii, 4488, 4497).

Chapter 50
1. *St. P.* I, p. 316–17 (*LP* IV ii, 4508).
2. Friedmann, *Anne Boleyn* I, p. 63.
3. Fiddes, *Life of Cardinal Wolsey*, pp. 174–6 (*LP* IV ii, 4507).
4. Herbert, *The Life and Raigne of King Henry the Eighth*, p. 174 (*LP* IV ii, 4509).
5. *LP* IV ii, 4584.
6. Burnet, *History of the Reformation* I, p. 104 (*LP* IV ii, 4480; *Letters of the Queens*, ed. Crawford, 187).
7. Burnet, *History of the Reformation* I, p. 103 (*LP* IV ii, 4360; *Letters of the Queens*, ed. Crawford, p. 188).
8. *Love Letters of Henry VIII*, ed. Savage, pp. 37, 48; *Letters of Henry VIII*, ed. Byrne, p. 84–5; *CSP Sp.* III ii (1527–29), p. 789; Knecht, *Francis I*, pp. 217–18.
9. *LP* IV ii, 3682.

Chapter 51
1. *Love Letters of Henry VIII*, ed. Savage, p. 47; *Letters of King Henry VIII*, ed. Byrne, p. 82; 'The Romaunt of the Rose', 11. 7401–4 in The Works of Geoffrey Chaucer, ed. F.N. Robinson (Oxford, 1966), p. 634.
2. *Love Letters of Henry VIII*, ed. Savage, p. 47; *Letters of Henry VIII*, ed. Byrne,

p. 82; Murphy, 'Literature and Propaganda', pp. 146–8.

3. Fuller, *Worthies* II, pp. 234–5.

4. *CSP Sp.* III ii (1527–1529), p. 846.

5. Samman, 'Henrician Court', p. 383; *Commons* I, p. 527; *LP* IV ii, 4422; D. Starkey, 'The Court: Castiglione's Ideal and Tudor Reality – being a discussion of Sir Thomas Wyatt's *Satire addressed to Sir Francis Bryan*', Journal of the Warburg and Courtauld Institutes 45 (1982), pp. 232–9, espec. pp. 235–7.

6. *LP* IV ii, 4978, 5008, 5013–14.

7. *Love Letters of Henry VIII*, ed. Savage, p. 37; *Letters of Henry VIII*, ed. Byrne, p. 82–3.

8. *Ambassades en Angleterre de Jean du Bellay: la Première Ambassade*, ed. V.-L. Bourrilly et P. de Vaisserie (Paris, 1905), p. 481 (*LP* IV ii, 5016 [p. 2177]).

9. *LP* IV ii, 5063; Hall, *Chronicle*, p. 756.

10. *LP* IV ii, 5023, 5028; IV iii, 5148, 5150.

11. *Ambassades*, ed. Bourrilly et de Vaisserie, p. 527 (*LP* IV iii, 5163); *LP* IV iii, 5179.

12. *Ambassades*, ed. Bourrilly et de Vaisserie, p. 543 (*LP* IV iii, 5209, 5210); *LP* IV iii, 5572 (pp. 2463, 2464).

13. *The Letters of Stephen Gardiner*, ed. J.A. Muller (Cambridge, 1933), p. 7 (*LP* IV iii, 5184).

14. Burnet, *History of the Reformation* V, p. 444 (*LP* IV iii, 5422).

15. *St. P.* I, pp. 329–31 (*LP* IV iii, 5393); *LP* IV iii, 5375.

16. Samman, 'The Henrician Court', pp. 385, 433; *LP* IV iii, 5416.

17. Burnet, *History of the Reformation* IV, pp. 115–17 (*LP* IV iii, 5427); *LP* IV iii, 5428 (p. 2836).

18. *St. P.* VII, pp. 166–9 (*LP* IV iii, 5481).

19. Burnet, *History of the Reformation* IV, pp. 92–102 (*LP* IV iii, 5523); *LP* IV iii, 5535 (pp. 2449–50). The despatch of the couriers from England can be followed in *LP* V, p. 311.

20. *St. P.* VII, pp. 169–70 (*LP* IV iii, 5519).

21. *Correspondance du Cardinal du Bellay*, ed. Scheurer, I, p. 14; *LP* IV iii, 5541.

22. *Correspondance du Cardinal du Bellay*, ed. Scheurer, I, pp. 15–16, 109 (*LP* IV iii, 5547, 6011 [p. 2676]).

23. *LP* IV iii, 5572 (pp. 2463, 2464).

24. *St. P.* VII, p. 183 (*LP* IV iii, 5635).

Chapter 52

1. Samman, 'The Henrician Court', p. 386; *CSP Sp.* IV i (1529–1530), p. 235; *St. P.* I, p. 34 (*LP* IV iii, 5936).

2. *Letters of Gardiner*, ed. Muller, p. 21 (*LP* IV iii, 5798).

3. Ibid., pp. 21–2 (*LP* IV iii, 5819).

4. Ibid., pp. 20, 29 (*LP* IV iii, 5821, 5844).

5. F. Heal, *Of Prelates and Princes: a Study of the Economic and Social Position of the Tudor Episcopate* (Cambridge, 1980), p. 61.

6. Heal, *Of Prelates and Princes*, p. 113.

7.   *Letters of Gardiner*, ed. Muller, pp. 22–3 (*LP* IV iii, 5816).
8.   Richardson, *Mary Tudor*, pp. 245, 253; *CSP Sp.* IV i (1529–1530), pp. 189, 195.
9.   Mattingly, *Catherine of Aragon*, pp. 215–17; *CSP Sp.* IV i (1529–1530), p. 221.
10. *CSP Sp.* IV i (1529–1530), pp. 189–190.
11. Ibid., pp. 195, 196.
12. Ibid., p. 234.
13. Rebholz, *Wyatt: Complete Poems*, p. 77.
14. *CSP Sp.* IV i (1529–1530), pp. 213, 234.
15. Samman, 'The Henrician Court', p. 386.
16. Cavendish, *Wolsey*, 92–7.
17. *Commons* I, pp. 315–16; *Original Letters*, ed. Ellis, 1st series I, pp. 307–10 (*LP* IV iii, 5953).
18. Cf. Ives, *Anne Boleyn*, p. 150.
19. Samman, 'The Henrician Court', pp. 386, 434–5; Hall, *Chronicle*, p. 760; *Correspondance du Cardinal du Bellay*, ed. Scheurer, I, pp. 108, 110 (*LP* IV iii, 6011); *St. P.* I, p. 352 (*LP* IV iii, 6114).
20. *LP* IV iii, 6076 (p. 2715).
21. *LP* IV iii, 6083, 6085; *CSP Sp.* IV i (1529–1530), p. 366.
22. C. Sturge, *Cuthbert Tunstal: Churchman, Scholar, Statesman, Administrator* (London, 1938), p. 110; Heal, *Of Prelates and Princes*, p. 113; *LP* IV iii, 6286.

Chapter 53
1.   *St. P.* VII, p. 106; (*LP* IV ii, 4897 [p. 2120]).
2.   Knecht, *Francis I*, pp. 139–45, 180–1.
3.   E.E. Lowinsky, 'A Music Book for Anne Boleyn', in J.G. Rowe and W.H. Stockdale (eds.), *Florilegium Historiale: Essays presented to Wallace K. Ferguson* (Toronto, 1971), pp. 188–9; Dowling, *Humanism*, p. 231.
4.   'William Latymer's Cronickille of Anne Buleyn', ed. M. Dowling, *Camden Miscellany 30* (CS 4th series 39, 1990), p. 63; BL, Add. Ms. 43, 827, fos. 3–3v; J. Shakespeare and M. Dowling, 'Religion and Politics in Mid-Tudor England through the Eyes of an English Protestant Woman: the Recollections of Rose Hickman', *BIHR* 55 (1982), p. 97; Sotheby's Sales Catalogue, 7 December 1982, p. 71; *Henry VIII: a European Court in England*, ed. D. Starkey (London, 1991), p. 107–11; Ives, *Anne Boleyn*, p. 317.
5.   J.P. Carley, 'Her moost lovyng and fryndely brother sendeth gretyng', in M.P. Brown and S. McKendrick (eds.), *Illuminating the Book Makers and Interpreters: Essays in Honour of Janet Backhouse* (London, 1998), pp. 261–272.
6.   Fiddes, *Life of Wolsey* II, p. 256 (*LP* IV iii, App. 197).
7.   C.H. and T. Cooper, *Athenae Cantabrigiensis*, 2 vols. (Cambridge and London, 1858), I, p. 37.
8.   J. Foxe, *The Acts and Monuments*, ed. J. Pratt, 8 vols. (London, 1874), V, pp. 421–9; App. to V, no. 6; (*LP* IV ii, 4073); Sturge, *Cuthbert Tunstal*, pp. 140–1.

9. P. Gwyn, *The King's Cardinal: the Rise and Fall of Thomas Wolsey* (London, 1990), pp. 480, 486, 488.
10. *St. P.* VII, p. 106; (*LP* IV ii, 4897 [p. 2120]); Fiddes, *Life of Wolsey* II, p. 256 (*LP* IV iii, App. 197); *LP* IV ii, 4647.
11. *LP* IV iii, 5416.
12. Foxe, *Acts* IV, pp. 656–8; *LP* IV ii, 4030.
13. Foxe, *Acts* IV, pp. 659–64.
14. Foxe, *Acts* IV, p. 657; T.S. Freeman, 'Research, Rumour and Propaganda: Anne Boleyn in Foxe's "Book of Martyrs"', *HJ* 38 (1995), p. 809; Emden, *Biographical Register . . . Oxford to 1500* I, pp. 20–1.
15. Gwyn, *King's Cardinal*, p. 486; Dowling, *Fisher*, pp. 89–113.
16. J.A. Guy, *The Public Career of Sir Thomas More* (Brighton, 1980), p. 107; Sturge, *Tunstal*, pp. 363–4; P. Ackroyd, *The Life of Sir Thomas More* (London, 1998), p. 273; Gwyn, *King's Cardinal*, p. 486.
17. *The Complete Works of St Thomas More* VII: *A Supplication of Souls*, ed. F.O. Manley, G. Marc'hadour, R. Marius and C.H. Miller (London, 1990), pp. 127–8.
18. *Complete Works of St Thomas More* VII, pp. lxv–vi; Hall, *Chronicle*, p. 764.
19. *CSP Sp.* IV i (1529–1530), p. 326; Guy, *More*, pp. 106, 206–7. Gunn, *Charles Brandon*, p. 106–7 displays a proper scepticism about Suffolk's supposed role but even he leaves the views attributed to Darcy unquestioned.
20. GEC IV, pp. 73–4.
21. *LP* IV iii, 5749 (p. 2554).
22. *LP* IV iii, 5749 (p. 2550); *CSP Sp.* IV i (1529–1530), p. 235.
23. *LP* IV iii, 5749 (p. 2551).
24. Hall, *Chronicle*, pp. 764–6.
25. Hall, *Chronicle*, p. 766; S.E. Lehmberg, *The Reformation Parliament, 1529-36* (Cambridge, 1970), p. 88.

Chapter 54

1. Samman, 'The Henrician Court', p. 386.
2. *Narratives of the Days of the Reformation*, ed. J.G. Nichols (CS old series 77, 1859), pp. 240–2.
3. MacCulloch, *Cranmer*, pp. 16–22.
4. *Narratives of the Reformation*, ed. Nichols, pp. 241–2; Foxe, *Acts* VIII, pp. 6–7; MacCulloch, *Cranmer*, p. 45.
5. Samman, 'The Henrician Court', p. 386–7; *Narratives of the Reformation*, ed. Nichols, p. 242.
6. MacCulloch, *Cranmer*, p. 46; Foxe, *Acts* VIII, p. 7.
7. Foxe, *Acts* VIII, 8–9; *Narratives of the Reformation*, ed. Nichols, p. 242.
8. *Correspondance du Cardinal du Bellay*, ed. Scheurer, I, p. 105. This important despatch of 12 October 1529 has been overlooked since it is not calendared in *LP*.
9. *The Correspondence of Sir Thomas More*, ed. E.F. Rogers (Princeton, 1947), pp. 495–6.

10. Foxe, *Acts* VIII, 8–9; Burnet, *History of the Reformation* IV, pp. 130–3 (*LP* IV iii, 6247).

11. *Correspondance du Cardinal du Bellay*, ed. Scheurer, I, pp. 65, 82 (*LP* IV iii, 5862, 5945).

12. *CSP Sp.* IV i (1529–1530), p. 238; Emden, *Biographical Register . . . Oxford to 1500* III, pp. 1785–6; *St. P.* VII, p. 223 (*LP* IV iii, 6073).

13. *CSP Sp.* IV i (1529–1530), p. 238; *Correspondance du Cardinal du Bellay*, ed. Scheurer, I, p. 105; *St. P.* VII, p. 227 (*LP* IV iii, 6147).

14. *Narratives of the Reformation*, ed. Nichols, p. 242. I have inferred Cranmer's role in formulating the questions from the fact that his 'book' was the key text when the matter was submitted first to Cambridge.

15. *CSP Mil.* I (1385–1618), p. 533.

16. *CSP Sp.* IV i (1529–1530), pp. 351–2.

17. *Athenae Cantabrigienses* I, pp. 130–2; Foxe, *Acts* IV, p. 642; *Sermons of Hugh Latimer*, ed. G.E. Corrie (Parker Society, Cambridge, 1844), pp. 1–24.

18. *LP* IV iii, 6162; Dowling, *Fisher*, pp. 7–13, 144–5.

19. *LP* IV iii, 6176.

20. *Athenae Cantabrigienses* I, pp. 86–7; Burnet, *History of the Reformation* IV, pp. 130–3 (*LP* IV iii, 6247).

21. *LP* IV iii, 6259, 6325; V, p. 317; *PPE Henry VIII*, p. 30.

22. Foxe, *Acts* V, p. 135; Ives, *Anne Boleyn*, p. 327.

23. *Athenae Cantabrigienses* I, pp. 86–7; *LP* IV iii, 6259, 6325; *PPE Henry VIII*, p. 30.

24. Burnet, *History of the Reformation* IV, p. 132 (*LP* IV iii, 6247); M. Dowling, 'Anne Boleyn and Reform', *Journal of Ecclesiastical History* 35 (1984), pp. 38–9.

25. *Letters of Royal and Illustrious Ladies*, ed. Wood, II, p. 189 (*LP* VII, 693).

26. *LP* IV iii, 6111, 6163; V, p. 317; *CSP Sp.* IV i (1529–1530), pp. 432, 437; *PPE Henry VIII*, p. 19.

27. *St. P.* VII, p. 227–9 (*LP* IV iii, 6147).

28. *Correspondance du Cardinal du Bellay*, ed. Scheurer, I, p. 123.

29. Ibid., p. 125.

30. *LP* IV, 6111 (p. 2729), 6290; Friedmann, *Anne Boleyn*, I, pp. 106–7; *CSP Sp.* IV i (1529–1530), pp. 480–1; MacCulloch, *Cranmer*, p. 48.

31. *LP* IV iii, 6290 (pp. 2826–7).

32. Ibid., 6307; *St. P.* VII, p. 234 (*LP* IV iii, 6355); Friedmann, *Anne Boleyn*, I, pp. 108–9; *CSP Sp.* IV i (1529–1530), pp. 620–1.

33. *LP* IV iii, 6592; Pocock, *Records of the Reformation* II, pp. 13, 14 (*LP* IV iii 6669); MacCulloch, *Cranmer*, pp. 51–3; Hall, pp. 775–80.

34. *LP* IV iii, 6449. This letter is calendared as anonymous, but it is certainly from De Langes.

35. *LP* IV iii, 6455. This is a letter *to* Wiltshire, not *from* him as *LP* states.

36. *LP* IV iii, 6497, 6505; Knecht, *Francis I*, pp. 223, 239–40. Garay's reaction to the verdict and means by which it was obtained is *CSP Sp.* IV i (1529–1530), pp. 621–3.

37. *CSP Sp.* IV i (1529–1530), p. 634.

Chapter 55

1. *HKW* IV, pp. 76–7; Samman, 'The Henrician Court', p. 390; *CSP Sp.* IV i (1529–1530), p. 691.
2. *CSP Sp.* IV i (1529–1530), p. 690; *LP* V, p. 321.
3. *LP* IV iii, 6667 (*St. P.* VII, p. 261); Scarisbrick, *Henry VIII*, p. 261 especially n. 3. Scarisbrick dates the letter from Henry announcing the new doctrine to 'late August'; as I show, the proper date is 16/17 August.
4. A. Ogle, *The Tragedy of the Lollard's Tower* (Oxford, 1949), p. 153.
5. *LP* IV iii, 6293.
6. *Correspondance du Cardinal du Bellay*, ed. Scheurer, I, pp. 147, 150, 172.
7. Ibid., pp. 176–81. *LP* IV iii, 5790, as Scheurer points out on p. 176 n. 3, misdates these instructions to 1529.
8. *LP* IV iii, 6562, 6563; *Correspondance du Cardinal du Bellay*, ed. Scheurer, I, pp. 183–94; *CSP Sp.* IV i (1529–1530), p. 690.
9. *LP* IV iii, Appendix 256.
10. Samman, 'The Henrician Court', p. 389; *CSP Sp.* IV i (1529–1530), pp. 535–6.
11. *PPE Henry VIII*, pp. 47, 50, 74; *CSP Sp.* IV i (1529–1530), p. 691.
12. *CSP Sp.* IV i (1529–1530), p. 710.
13. *CSP Ven.* IV (1527–1533), p. 258; *CSP Sp.* IV i (1529–1530), p. 621.
14. *CSP Sp.* IV i (1529–1530), pp. 722–3.
15. *Tudor Royal Proclamations*, eds Hughes and Larkin, I, pp. 197–8.
16. *CSP Sp.* IV i (1529–1530), p. 734.
17. Ibid., p. 804.
18. Ibid., p. 790.
19. Ibid., p. 758–9.
20. *The Libraries of King Henry VIII*, ed. J.P. Carley (London, 2000), p. lxv; *PPE Henry VIII*, pp. 85, 89.
21. *Libraries of King Henry VIII*, pp. xxxiii, xxxvi–vii.
22. PRO, OBS 1419: Index; *PPE Henry VIII*, pp. 65, 153, 158, 248 (this last gift was made to Henry when he was actually staying in the Abbey); D. Knowles, *The Religious Orders in England: III The Tudor Age* (Cambridge, 1959), pp. 378–9; *Original Letters*, ed. Ellis, 3rd series II, pp. 77–80 (*LP* IV ii, 4004).
23. *Letters of Gardiner*, ed. Muller, p. 39 (*LP* IV, 5935); *Libraries of King Henry VIII*, ed. J.P. Carley, pp. xxxvii–ix.
24. *CSP Sp.* IV i (1529–1530), p. 803.
25. Ibid., p. 852.
26. Lehmberg, *Reformation Parliament*, pp. 109–116; Ives, *Anne Boleyn*, pp. 168–9.
27. *CSP Sp.* IV ii (1531–1533), p. 63.

Chapter 56

1. *CSP Ven.* IV (1527–1533), p. 263.
2. *St. P.* I, pp. 346–9 (*LP* IV iii, 6024); *LP* IV iii, 6035, 6059.
3. Lehmberg, *Reformation Parliament*, pp. 102–4; Fiddes, *Wolsey* II, p. 223

(*LP* IV iii, 6075).

4. *Original Letters*, ed. Ellis, 1st series II, pp. 7–9, 10–14 (*LP* IV iii, 6182, 6224).
5. *LP* IV iii, 6112.
6. *Commons* I, pp. 728–9.
7. P.J. Ward, 'The Origins of Thomas Cromwell's Public Career: Service under Cardinal Wolsey and Henry VIII, 1524–1530' (University of London Ph.D. thesis, 1999); *St. P.* I, p. 261 (*LP* IV ii, 3360).
8. *Original Letters*, ed. Ellis, 3rd series II, pp. 171–2 (*LP* IV iii, 6036).
9. Cavendish, *Wolsey*, pp. 104–5.
10. *St. P.* I, p. 355 (*LP* IV iii, 6181).
11. *LP* IV iii, 6115; X, 878.
12. *LP* IV iii, 6210, 6213, 6214, 6220.
13. Samman, 'The Henrician Court', pp. 436–7; Cavendish, *Wolsey*, pp. 130, 133, 138, 144; R.B. Merriman, *Life and Letters of Thomas Cromwell*, 2 vols. (London, 1902), I, p. 332 (*LP* IV iii, 6571).
14. *CSP Sp.* IV i (1529–1530), p. 368.
15. Ibid., pp. 514–15, 600–1, 619.
16. Ibid., pp. 647–8; Cavendish, *Wolsey*, p. 137.
17. *CSP Sp.* IV i (1529–1530), p. 486.
18. Merriman, *Cromwell* I, p. 327 (*LP* IV iii, 6076); *CSP Sp.* IV i, p. 630.
19. *CSP Sp.* IV i, pp. 707, 711–12.
20. *LP* IV iii, 6688; *Commons* I, pp. 337–9.
21. *CSP Ven.* IV (1527–1533), p. 267.
22. Cavendish, *Wolsey*, p. 137; *CSP Sp.* IV i (1529–1530), p. 819.
23. Cavendish, *Wolsey*, pp. 150–1.
24. Ibid., pp. 155–6.
25. Ibid., pp. 155–7.
26. Ibid., p. 152.
27. *CSP Ven.* IV (1527–1533), pp. 263, 267; *CSP Sp.* IV i, pp. 805, 819.
28. BL, Add. MS 48066, fos. 184–7; *CSP Sp.* IV i (1529–1530), p. 820.
29. Cavendish, *Wolsey*, pp. 167–81.
30. Ibid., pp. 178–9, 185; *Commons* II, pp. 470–1.
31. *CSP Ven.* IV (1527–1533), p. 267.

Chapter 57
1. *CSP Sp.* IV i (1529–1530), p. 600.
2. *LP* V, g. 220(18), p. 751; *PPE Henry VIII*, pp. 17, 72, 78, 84, 122, 197.
3. Friedmann, *Anne Boleyn* I, p. 130.
4. *CSP Sp.* IV ii (1531–1533), p. 3.
5. *CSP Sp.* IV ii (1531–1533), p. 112.
6. Ibid., pp. 169–70.
7. Ibid., pp. 171–6.
8. *CSP Sp.* IV ii (1531–1533), pp. 176–7; *Commons* II, p. 264; Gunn, *Charles Brandon*, pp. 115, 118.
9. PRO, OBS 1419; *PPE Henry VIII*, pp. 139–42; *CSP Sp.* IV ii (1531–1533), p. 198; J. Strype, *Memorials of the Most Reverend Father in God Thomas*

Cranmer, 2 vols. (Oxford, 1812), II, p. 679.

10.   *CSP Sp.* IV ii (1531–1533), p. 212.

11.   Hall, *Chronicle*, p. 781.

12.   *PPE Henry VIII*, pp. xiii–xv.

13.   Ibid., pp. xiii–xv, 147–52; *LP* V, g. 364(36–7); PRO, OBS 1419.

14.   *CSP Sp.* IV ii (1531–1533), p. 212.

15.   N. Pevsner and D. Lloyd, *Hampshire and the Isle of Wight* (1967), p. 638; W.R.D. Harrison and Viscount Chandos, *Oak Gallery, The Vyne, Hampshire* (Basingstoke, 1979); *Commons* III, pp. 72–5.

16.   *CSP Sp.* IV ii (1531–1533), pp. 222–4.

17.   *CSP Sp.* IV ii (1531–1533), p. 228.

18.   *CSP Ven.* IV (1527–1533), pp. 287–8.

Chapter 58

1.   *LP* V, 628; G.R. Elton, *Policy and Police: the Enforcement of the Reformation in the Age of Thomas Cromwell* (Cambridge, 1972), p. 384.

2.   A. Hawkyard, 'From Painted Chamber to St Stephen's Chapel; the Meeting Places of the House of Commons until 1603', *Parliamentary History* 21 (2002), p. 69.

3.   Lehmberg, *Reformation Parliament*, pp. 114–15; *CSP Sp.* IV ii (1531–1533), p. 63.

4.   *CSP Sp.* IV ii (1531–1533), p. 384; Lehmberg, *Reformation Parliament*, pp. 131–4.

5.   *The Debellation of Salem and Bizance*, ed. J.A. Guy, R. Kean and C.H. Miller (*The Complete Works of St Thomas More* X, London, 1987), pp. xxxiii–v.

6.   *CSP Sp.* IV ii (1531–1533), p. 384; Lehmberg, *Reformation Parliament*, p. 134.

7.   *CSP Sp.* IV ii (1531–1533), p. 405; Lehmberg, *Reformation Parliament*, pp. 134–5.

8.   Lehmberg, *Reformation Parliament*, pp. 135–8; *CSP Sp.* IV ii (1531–1533), p. 411–12; *LP* V, 886.

9.   Hall, *Chronicle*, p. 784; *Commons* II, pp. 280–1; III. pp. 471–2; Lehmberg, *Reformation Parliament*, pp. 117, 138–9.

10.   Foxe, *Acts* IV, pp. 659–64; *Complete Works of St Thomas More* VII, p. lxv; PRO, OBS 1419.

11.   Lehmberg, *Reformation Parliament*, pp. 84–6, 138–9.

12.   Ibid., pp. 145–53, 159.

13.   Merriman, *Cromwell* I, pp. 343–4 (*LP* V, 723).

14.   *CSP Sp.* IV ii (1531–1533), pp. 175, 446, 450–1.

15.   *LP* IV iii, g. 6542(23); V, g. 1139(32), g. 1207(7); *CSP Sp.* IV ii (1531–1533), p. 525; *HKW* IV, p. 148; B. Cherry and N. Pevsner, *London 3: North West* (1991), pp. 421–2.

16.   *CSP Sp.* IV ii (1531–1533), pp. 444, 463; *LP* V, 614, 1117; *Foedera* XIV, p. 435.

17.   Foedera XIV, p. 435.

18.   *CSP Sp.* IV ii (1531–1533), p. 508.

19. Pocock, *Records of the Reformation* II, pp. 188–9 (*LP* V, 791).
20. G.J. Richardson, 'Anglo-French Political and Cultural Relations during the Reign of Henry VIII' (University of London Ph.D. thesis, 1996), p. 210.
21. PRO, OBS 1419; *CSP Ven.* IV (1527–1533), pp. 342, 343.
22. *CSP Sp.* IV ii (1531–1533), pp. 487–9.
23. P.A. Hamy, *Entrevue de François Premier avec Henry VIII à Boulogne sur Mer en 1532* (Paris, 1898), pp. ix–xii (*LP* V, 1187). The writer of this letter is identified by *Correspondance du Cardinal du Bellay*, ed. Scheurer, I, p. 280 n. 4.
24. Knecht, *Francis I*, pp. 237–8; *LP* VI, 692 (pp. 309–10).
25. *LP* V, 1231.
26. Ibid., 1220.
27. Ibid., 1229, 1376.
28. *CSP Sp.* IV ii (1531–1533), pp. 524–5.
29. *LP* V, 1239.
30. *LP* V, 1271; *CSP Sp.* IV ii (1531–1533), p. 508, *CSP Ven.* IV (1527–1533), p. 351.
31. *CSP Sp.* IV ii (1531–1533), pp. 508, 511–12.
32. *LP* V, 1484; Hall, *Chronicle*, pp. 793–4.
33. PRO, OBS 1419.

Chapter 59
1. *CSP Sp.* IV ii (1531–1533), pp. 495, 527.
2. *AR* I, p. 302.
3. PRO, OBS 1419; Hall, *Chronicle*, p. 794; MacCulloch, *Cranmer*, pp. 637–8.
4. *PPE Henry VIII*, pp. 273–77; *CSP Ven.* IV (1527–1533), p. 340; *CSP Sp.* IV ii (1531–1533), p. 509.
5. PRO, OBS 1419: Index; Thurley, *Royal Palaces*, pp. 32–4.
6. *HKW* III, pp. 264–7; *LP* V, 1467.
7. *CSP Sp.* IV ii (1531–1533), pp. 566–7.
8. *LP* V, 1685.
9. *HKW* III, pp. 264–7; Thurley, *Royal Palaces*, p. 51; *Inventory of King Henry VIII*, ed. Starkey, I, p. 5 (nos. 6–8).

Chapter 60
1. *CSP Ven.* IV (1527–1533), p. 376; MacCulloch, *Cranmer*, p. 82.
2. J. Rowlands, *Holbein: the Paintings of Hans Holbein the Younger* (Oxford, 1985), pp. 133–4; Strong, *Tudor and Jacobean Portraits* I, pp. 323–4.
3. *CSP Ven.* IV (1527–1533), p. 349.
4. *LP* V, 1514.
5. *St. P.* VII, pp. 386, 390 (*LP* V, 1564); *LP* V, 1380–1.
6. MacCulloch, *Cranmer*, pp. 69–77.
7. Foxe, *Acts* VIII, pp. 55–6.
8. Ibid.
9. *St. P.* VII, p. 386 (*LP* V, 1564).
10. *LP* V, 1609.

11. Ibid., 1620.
12. Harpsfield, *Pretended Divorce*, p. 290; MacCulloch, *Cranmer*, p. 84.
13. Foxe, *Acts* VIII, p. 66.
14. Emden, *Biographical Register . . . Oxford 1501–1540*, pp. 57–9; *Original Letters*, ed. Ellis, 3rd series II, p. 178 – dated by Samman, 'The Henrician Court', p. 437.
15. *St. P.* VII, pp. 410–11 (*LP* VI, 101).
16. *CSP Sp.* IV ii (1531–1533), p. 585.
17. *LP* VI, 73.
18. *CSP Sp.* IV ii (1531–1533), p. 609; *LP* VI, 661 (p. 300).
19. Friedmann, *Anne Boleyn*, I, pp. 183–4.
20. Harpsfield, *Pretended Divorce*, pp. 234–5; PRO, OBS 1419; *St. P.* VII, p. 410; warrants dated 24 and 25 January 1533 (*LP* VI, 196 (3, 17)).
21. Harpsfield, *Pretended Divorce*, p. 235.
22. Ives, *Anne Boleyn*, p. 209.

Chapter 61
1. Friedman, *Anne Boleyn* I, pp. 189 n. 2. This despatch is not calendared.
2. *CSP Sp.* IV ii (1531–1533), pp. 593–4; Lehmberg, *Reformation Parliament*, p. 171.
3. *CSP Sp.* IV ii (1531–1533), pp. 597–9.
4. *St. P.* VII, p. 425 (*LP* VI, 177).
5. *St. P.* VII, pp. 442–3 (*LP* VI, 226).
6. Burnet, *History of the Reformation* I, p. 215 – dates corrected from MacCulloch, *Cranmer*, p. 87.
7. *CSP Sp.* IV ii (1531–1533), pp. 600–1 (*LP* VI, 160).
8. *CSP Sp.* IV ii (1531–1533), pp. 598–9; *CSP Ven.* IV (1527–1533), p. 383.
9. *CSP Sp.* IV ii (1531–1533), p. 602 (*LP* VI, 160); Friedmann, *Anne Boleyn* I, p. 190 n. 1. This latter despatch is not calendared.
10. *CSP Sp.* IV ii (1531–1533), p. 618; *LP* VI, 296.
11. Lehmberg, *Reformation Parliament*, pp. 174–5.
12. MacCulloch, *Cranmer*, pp. 88–9.
13. Strype, *Cranmer* II, p. 683; Lingard, *History of England*, V, p. 4.
14. *HKW* I, pp. 519–21.
15. Lingard, *History of England* V, p. 4 n. 2.
16. MacCulloch, *Cranmer*, p. 89.
17. Lehmberg, *Reformation Parliament*, p. 175.
18. *LP* VI, 351 (p. 167).
19. Ibid., (pp. 167–8); *CSP Ven.* IV (1527–1533), p. 393.
20. Lingard, *History of England* V, pp. 265–6; MacCulloch, *Cranmer*, pp. 90–1.
21. *LP* VI, 391 (p. 179).
22. Ibid., 366; *HKW* IV, p. 40; Thurley, *Royal Palaces*, p. 68.
23. Pocock, *Records of the Reformation* II, pp. 473–4 (*LP* VI, 461).
24. *St. P.* I, p. 94 (*LP* VI, 470).
25. Pocock, *Records of the Reformation* II, pp. 473–4 (*LP* VI, 461); *St. P.* I, p. 395 (*LP* VI, 469).
26. *St. P.* I, p. 395 (*LP* VI, 469).

27. *LP* VI, 496.
28. *St. P.* I, p. 396 (*LP* VI, 495).
29. *St. P.* I, pp. 396–7 (*LP* VI, 528).

Chapter 62
1. *Original Letters*, ed. Ellis, 1st series II, p. 36 (*LP* VI, 661).
2. *LP* VI, 396, 631; X, 1231.
3. *LP* VI, 613.
4. See P.E. Schramm, *A History of the English Coronation* (Oxford, 1937); *The Coronation of Richard III: the Extant Documents*, ed. A.F. Sutton and P.W. Hammond (Gloucester, 1983), pp. 228–44; *The Crown Jewels. The History of the Coronation Regalia in the Jewel House of the Tower of London*, ed. C. Blair, 2 vols. (London, 1998), ch. III.
5. Hall, *Chronicle*, p. 798.
6. *Original Letters*, ed. Ellis, 1st series, p. 304 (*LP* VI, 693): Gunn, *Charles Brandon*, p. 118; M. Perry, *Sisters to the King* (London, 1998), p. 212.
7. *CSP Sp.* IV ii (1531–1533), p. 80.
8. *LP* VI, 701; J.H. Round, *The King's Serjeants and Officers of State with their Coronation Services* (London, 1911), p. 375.
9. *LP* VI, 560.
10. *Original Letters*, ed. Ellis, 1st series II, p. 37.
11. Hall, *Chronicle*, pp. 798–9.
12. *LP* VI 556 (pp. 240–1, 244).
13. *Original Letters*, ed. Ellis, 1st series II, p. 37; *LP* VI, 563.
14. *LP* VI, 396 (p. 182), 563; Hall, *Chronicle*, p. 799.
15. Hall, *Chronicle*, pp. 799–800.
16. *LP* VI 556 (p. 244).
17. Hall, *Chronicle*, p. 800; A. Keay, *The Elizabethan Tower of London: the Haiward and Gascoyne Plan of 1597* (London Topographical Society 158, 2001), p. 41.
18. *Original Letters*, ed. Ellis, 1st series II, p. 37; Hall, *Chronicle*, pp. 800–1.
19. *LP* VI, 583, 584 (pp. 264–5); Hall, *Chronicle*, p. 800.
20. *Original Letters*, ed. Ellis, 1st series II, pp. 37–8.
21. J. Rowlands and D. Starkey, 'An old tradition reassessed: Holbein's portrait of Queen Anne Boleyn', *The Burlington Magazine* 125 (1983), p. 92; Hall, *Chronicle*, pp. 801–2; *An English Garner: Tudor Tracts*, ed. A.F. Pollard (London, 1903), pp. 24–6; *Everyman Encyclopaedia*, 1978 edn. *sub* 'Charites'.
22. Dowling, *Humanism*, p. 134; J.P. Carley, 'John Leland in Paris: the Evidence of the Poetry', *Studies in Philology* 83 (1986), p. 19.
23. *An English Garner*, ed. Pollard, p. 17.
24. Hall, *Chronicle*, pp. 799–800, 802.
25. *AR* I, pp. 302–3; Hall, *Chronicle*, p. 802.
26. *Original Letters*, ed. Ellis, 1st series II, p. 38.
27. Hall, *Chronicle*, p. 802.
28. *Original Letters*, ed. Ellis, 1st series II, p. 38.
29. Hall, *Chronicle*, p. 803.

30. *Original Letters*, ed. Ellis, 1st series, II, p. 39.
31. Hall, *Chronicle*, p. 803.
32. Ibid.
33. *Original Letters*, ed. Ellis, 1st series II, p. 39; Hall, *Chronicle*, p. 804; *An English Garner*, ed. Pollard, p. 19; *LP* VI, 701.
34. Hall, *Chronicle*, pp. 804–5.
35. Ibid., pp. 803–5.
36. Ibid., p. 805; *LP* VI, 583.
37. *LP* VI, 585; *Original Letters*, ed. Ellis, 1st series II, p. 39.
38. R. Marius, *Thomas More* (London, 1984), pp. 438–40.

Chapter 63
1. *LP* VI, 351 (p. 164). I have transposed Henry's words into direct speech.
2. Ibid., 613.
3. *HKW* IV, pp. 102–6; Thurley, *Royal Palaces*, pp. 49, 50.
4. PRO, OBS 1419; *LP* VI, 975 (p. 421).
5. *LP* VI, 890.
6. J.W. Kirby, 'Building Work at Placentia 1532–1533', *Transactions of the Greenwich and Lewisham Antiquarian Society* 5 (1957), p. 49.
7. *LP* VI, 918 (p. 397); 'Inventories of the Wardrobes, Plate, Chapel Stuff, Etc. of Henry Fitzroy, Duke of Richmond and the Wardrobe Stuff at Baynard's Castle of Katherine, Princess Dowager', ed. J.G. Nichols, *The Camden Miscellany* 3 (CS old series 61, 1855), pp. 30, 40.
8. *The Lisle Letters*, ed. M.St.C. Byrne, 6 vols. (Chicago and London, 1981), I, pp. 515, 518 (*LP* VI, 948, 1004).
9. *LP* VI, 1069 (p. 453).
10. *Inventory of King Henry VIII*, ed. Starkey, p. 182 (no. 9035); *The Bedford Inventories: the Worldly Goods of John, Duke of Bedford, Regent of France (1389–1435)*, ed. J. Stratford (Society of Antiquaries, London, 1993), pp. 85–6, 355.
11. *LP* VI, 1069 (p. 453), 1135; *St. P.* I, p. 407.
12. *LP* VI, 1069 (p. 453).
13. *AR* I, p. 304; *LP* VI, 1111.
14. *St. P.* I, p. 407; *LP* VI, 1112.
15. Kirby, 'Building Work at Placentia', p. 50.
16. Hall, *Chronicle*, p. 805.
17. *LP* VI, 1111, 1112; Hall, *Chronicle*, pp. 805–6.

Chapter 64
1. *LP* VI, 324 (p. 150).
2. *LP* VIII, 440; Kirby, 'Building Work at Placentia', p. 50.
3. Strickland, *Lives of the Queens of England* II, pp. 652–3.
4. *St. P.* I, p. 414.
5. Ibid., p. 415 and n. 3; *HKW* IV, p. 149.
6. N. Pevsner and B. Cherry, *Hertfordshire* (London, 1977), pp. 164–5; A. Emery, *The Greater Medieval Houses of England and Wales*, 2 vols. (1996, 2000), II, pp. 253–5; Hembry, 'Episcopal Palaces', p. 154; *HKW* IV,

p. 149. 'Prince Edward' in *HKW* is an error for 'Princess Elizabeth'.
7. *Commons* III, p. 312.
8. *St. P.* I, p. 415; PRO, OBS 1419.
9. *LP* VI, 1528.
10. *Tudor Royal Proclamations* I, pp. 209–11; *St. P.* I, p. 397 (*LP* VI, 760).
11. *St. P.* I, pp. 397 and n. 2, 402 (*LP* VI, 760, 765).
12. *LP* VI, 351 (p. 168).
13. Strype, *Ecclesiastical Memorials* I, pp. 230–1 (*LP* VI, 1139).
14. *LP* VI, 1528 (p. 617).
15. Ibid., 1528 (p. 618).
16. *LP* VI, 1558 (p. 629).
17. *LP* VII, 171 (p. 69), 214 (pp. 84–5); *LP* VIII, 440 (misdated).
18. Ibid., 83 (p. 31).
19. Ibid., 171 (p. 68).
20. Ibid., 296.
21. Ibid., 1126; *Letters of the Queens*, ed. Crawford, pp. 177–8.
22. N. Pevsner, *Bedfordshire, Huntingdon and Peterborough* (London, 1968), p. 215; Emery, *Greater Medieval Houses* II, pp. 229–33; Hembry, 'Episcopal Palaces', pp. 147, 153; *LP* VI, 1558 (p. 628); *St. P.*, p. 417.
23. *St. P.* I, p. 417.
24. *LP* VII, 83 (p. 33).
25. For example *Letters of the Queens*, ed. Crawford, pp. 178–9.
26. *LP* VI, 1528 (p. 618).
27. Kelly, *Matrimonial Trials*, p. 169.
28. Lehmberg, *Reformation Parliament*, pp. 198–9; 25 Hen. VIII, c. 25; *Statutes* III, pp. 471–4; *LP* VII, 51/3; G.R. Elton, *The Tudor Constitution: Documents and Commentary* (Cambridge, 1960), p. 12.
29. *St. P.* I, pp. 420–1 (*LP* VII, 695).
30. 26 Hen. VIII, cc. 1, 2, 13; *Statutes* III, pp. 492–3, 508–9; Lehmberg, *Reformation Parliament*, pp. 202–5.
31. *Wriothesley's Chronicle* I, pp. 27–29.
32. *LP* VIII, 1105.

Chapter 65
1. *LP* VIII, 683, 989, 1018; PRO, OBS 1419.
2. Ibid., 465 (p. 211).
3. *LP* VIII, 989; PRO, OBS 1419.
4. Strype, *Ecclesiastical Memorials* I, p. 255; *Commons* I, pp. 400–3; III, pp. 471–2; *Henry VIII: a European Court*, ed. Starkey, pp. 118–23; *LP* VIII, 989.
5. *Henry VIII: a European Court*, ed. Starkey, pp. 118–23.
6. J. Sherwood and N. Pevsner, *Oxfordshire*, (London, 1974), p. 600; J.A.A. Goodall, *God's House at Ewelme: Life, Devotion and Architecture in a Fifteenth-Century Almshouse* (Aldershot, 2001) pp. 13–14, 18; Gunn, *Charles Brandon*, pp. 44–5.
7. *LP* VIII, 1101, 1130; *HKW* IV, pp. 90–1.
8. J. Youings, *The Dissolution of the Monasteries* (London, 1971), pp. 149, 151, 152.

9. Youings, *Dissolution*, p. 149.
10. *Sermons and Remains of Hugh Latimer*, ed. G.E. Corrie (Parker Society, 1845), p. 364; 'William Latymer's Cronickille', pp. 60–1.
11. *Sermons and Remains of Latimer*, ed. Corrie, pp. 407–8; *Wriothesley's Chronicle* I, pp. 76, 90.
12. A. Hawkyard, 'Thornbury Castle', *Transactions of the Bristol and Gloucestershire Archaeological Society*, 95 (1977), pp. 51–8; *Commons*, I, p. 93; *The Maire of Bristowe is Kalendar*, ed. L.T. Smith (CS new series 5, 1872), pp. 53–4.
13. *Henry VIII: a European Court*, ed. Starkey, pp. 118–23; *Holbein and the Court of Henry VIII*, pp. 92–3.
14. *Commons* III, pp. 148–50.
15. *LP* IX, 58 (p. 18).
16. *Sermons and Remains of Latimer*, ed. Corrie, p. 367 (*LP* IX, 231).
17. Tyndale's career is well summarized in D. Daniell, *Let There Be Light: William Tyndale and the Making of the English Bible* (London, 1994); Ives, *Anne Boleyn*, pp. 314–15.
18. *LP* IX, 182, 405.
19. *LP* VIII, 1151; B. Moynahan, *If God Spare My Life: William Tyndale, the English Bible and Sir Thomas More – A Story of Martyrdom and Betrayal* (New York, 2002), especially pp. 313–54, speculates on More as the source of Philips's funding.
20. *LP* IX, 275, 409, 498. Cromwell's remembrances are dated to August by the reference to 'the royal assent and *congé d'élire* for Hereford'. This was granted on the 20th of the month.
21. *LP* IX, 275; X, 663.
22. 25 Hen. VIII, c. 27; *Statutes* III, pp. 483–4.
23. *LP* VIII, 48; G.R. Elton, *The Tudor Revolution in Government* (Cambridge, 1953), pp. 190–201; *Commons* II, pp. 238–9; III, pp. 124–6.
24. *LP* VIII, 290.
25. MacCulloch, *Cranmer*, p. 137; *St. P.* I, pp. 428–9 and n. 1 (*LP* VIII, 766); Strype, *Ecclesiastical Memorials* V, p. 527 (*LP* VIII, 821); *LP* VIII, 1158 (8).
26. *LP* IX, 203, 273; XI, 117; *Sermons and Remains of Latimer*, ed. Corrie, pp. 368–9 (*LP* IX, 272).
27. *Sermons and Remains of Latimer*, ed. Corrie, pp. 368–9 (*LP* IX, 272); *LP* XI, 117.
28. *LP* IX, 342, 360, 372.
29. Rowlands, *Holbein*, pp. 85, 139–40; *LP* IX, 378.
30. *LP* VIII, 1117; Muller, *Stephen Gardiner*, p. 60; W. Schenk, *Reginald Pole, Cardinal of England* (London, 1950), pp. 59–60, 109.
31. *LP* IX, 434 (p. 140), 741.
32. MacCulloch, *Cranmer*, p. 139.
33. Muller, *Stephen Gardiner*, pp. 55, 57–8, 60; *LP* IX, 594 (p. 198).
34. *LP* VIII, 1118; IX, 403; Muller, *Stephen Gardiner*, pp. 60–78.
35. *Letters of Gardiner*, ed. Muller, pp. 67–8 (*LP* IX, 442).

Chapter 66

1. Emery, *Greater Medieval Houses* II, p. 264; *LP* VII, 662.
2. N. Sanders, *Rise and Growth of the Anglican Schism*, ed. D. Lewis (London, 1877), pp. 7 n. 1, 131 n. 4.
3. *LP* VII, 1013 (pp. 386–8).
4. *PPC* VII, pp. 344, 345 (*LP* VII, 786).
5. *PPC* VII, p. 347.
6. *LP* VII, 135; IX, 1036 (p. 356), 1037.
7. *LP* IX, 1036 (pp. 356–8).
8. *LP* IX, 1040.
9. *St. P.* I, p. 451 (*LP* IX, 1050).
10. *LP* X, 28; Strype, *Ecclesiastical Memorials* I, p. 386.
11. *LP* X, 28, 59 (pp. 20–1); Strype, *Ecclesiastical Memorials* I, p.386.
12. *LP* X, 59 (p. 21).
13. Ibid.
14. *LP* X, 141 (pp. 49–50).
15. *LP* X, 142.
16. *St. P.* I, p. 452 (*LP* X, 37).
17. *St. P.* I, p. 452; *LP* X, 37, 41, 141 (p. 51).
18. *AR* I, pp. 310–11.

Chapter 67

1. *LP* X, 141 (p. 51).
2. Sanders, *Anglican Schism*, pp. 131–2.
3. Strype, *Ecclesiastical Memorials* V, pp. 578–80 (*LP* X, 40); *LP* X, 141 (p. 50), 351 (p. 134), 484 (p. 284).
4. Strype, *Ecclesiastical Memorials* V, pp. 580–2 (*LP* X, 128).
5. *LP* X, 199 (p. 69).
6. Ibid., 199 (p. 70).
7. Ibid., 141 (p. 48), 307/ii (p. 117).
8. *Lisle Letters*, ed. Byrne, III, p. 265 (*LP* X, 100); Hall, *Chronicle*, pp. 584–5.
9. *LP* X, 200 (p. 71).
10. Ibid., 282 (p. 102).
11. Ibid., 39, 141 (pp. 50, 53), 284.
12. Ibid., 282 (pp. 102–3).
13. Ibid., 352.
14. Ibid., 351 (p. 134).
15. Sanders, *Anglican Schism*, p. 132 n. 4; *LP* X, 282 (p. 103).
16. PRO, OBS 1419.
17. *LP* X, 908, p. 378.

Chapter 68

1. Schenk, *Reginald Pole*, pp. 49–69; GEC IX, pp. 94–7.
2. *LP* X, 601 (p. 243).
3. Ibid., 601 (pp. 243–4).
4. Ibid., 615; G.W. Bernard, 'Anne Boleyn's Religion', *HJ* 36 (1993), p. 13; MacCulloch, *Cranmer*, pp. 154–5; Lehmberg, *Reformation Parliament*, p.

245. Lehmberg fails to spot the preacher's irony.

5. Bernard, 'Anne Boleyn's Religion', p. 14; 27 Hen. VIII, c. 28; *Statutes* III, pp. 575–8; Lehmberg, *Reformation Parliament*, p. 227.

6. 'William Latymer's Cronickille', p. 57.

7. 'William Latymer's Cronickille', p. 57; E.W. Ives, 'Anne Boleyn and the Early Reformation in England: the Contemporary Evidence', *HJ* 37 (1994), p. 397; *LP* X, 345.

8. 'William Latymer's Cronickille', pp. 57–8.

9. MacCulloch, *Cranmer*, p. 155; Ives, 'Anne Boleyn and the Early Reformation', p. 398.

10. *LP* X, 351, 615/5; 699 (pp. 287–9, 292); *St. P.* VII, p. 684 (*LP* X, 726).

11. *LP* X, 699 (pp. 289–91); *CSP Sp.* V ii (1536–1538), pp. 91–3.

12. *LP* X, 699 (pp. 291–2); *CSP Sp.* V ii (1536–1538), pp. 94–6.

13. *LP* X, 1069 (pp. 440–1); *CSP Sp.* V ii (1536–1538), p. 137.

14. *St. P.* VII, p. 684 (*LP* X, 726).

15. *LP* X, 715.

16. *The Register of the Most Noble Order of the Garter*, ed. J. Anstis, 2 vols. (London, 1724), I, pp. 400–1 (*LP* X, 715); P.J. Begent and H. Chesshyre, *The Most Noble Order of the Garter: 650 Years* (London, 1991), particularly ch. 1; M.E.L. Collins, *The Order of the Garter 1348–1461: Chivalry and Politics in Late Medieval England* (Oxford, 2000), passim.

17. *The Register of the Most Noble Order of the Garter*, ed. J. Anstis, 2 vols. (London, 1724), I, pp. 400–1 (*LP* X, 715).

18. *LP* X, 752.

19. *Wriothesley's Chronicle* I, pp. 189–91; *LP* X, 736; S.E. Lehmberg, *The Later Parliaments of Henry VIII 1536–1547* (Cambridge, 1977), p. 1.

20. *LP* X, 752, 1134.

21. E.W. Ives, 'Faction at the Court of Henry VIII: the Fall of Anne Boleyn', *History* 57 (1972), pp. 172, 174.

22. *Lisle Letters*, ed. Byrne, III, p. 265 (*LP* X, 100).

23. Cavendish, *Wolsey*, ed. Singer, p. 455; *Original Letters*, ed. Ellis, 1st series II, p. 58 (*LP* X, 798).

24. *Commons* III, p. 19; *DNB sub* 'Norris'; Cavendish, *Wolsey*, ed. Singer, p. 452; *Original Letters*, ed. Ellis, 1st series II, p. 55 (*LP* X, 793).

25. *LP* X, 913.

26. *CSP For. Elizabeth* I, p. 527.

27. *Lisle Letters*, ed. Byrne, III, p. 352 (*LP* X, 789).

28. T. Amyot, 'Transcript of an Original Manuscript, containing a Memorial from George Constantyne to Thomas Lord Cromwell', *Archaeologia* 23 (1831), p. 64.

29. *Lettres de Henry VIII à Anne Boleyn*, ed. G.-A. Crapelet (Paris, 1835), p. 185.

30. Amyot, 'Memorial from George Constantyne', pp. 64–5; Hall, *Chronicle*, p. 819.

31. Amyot, 'Memorial from George Constantyne', p. 64; Cavendish, *Wolsey*, ed. Singer, p. 457; *Original Letters*, ed. Ellis, 1st series II, p. 60 (*LP* X, 797).

Chapter 69

1. Hall, *Chronicle*, p. 819; Cavendish, *Wolsey*, ed. Singer, pp. 256–7; *Original Letters*, ed. Ellis, 1st series II, pp. 59–60 (*LP* X, 797); *Commons* II, 142–5.
2. Cavendish, *Wolsey*, ed. Singer, p. 451; *Original Letters*, ed. Ellis, 1st series II, pp. 53–4 (*LP* X, 793); *LP* X, 782.
3. *LP* X, 782.
4. Cavendish, *Wolsey*, ed. Singer, p. 458; *Original Letters*, ed. Ellis, 1st series II, p. 61 (*LP* X, 799).
5. Cavendish, *Wolsey*, ed. Singer, pp. 452–3; *Original Letters*, ed. Ellis, 1st series II, pp. 55, 57–8 (*LP* X, 793).
6. Cavendish, *Wolsey*, ed. Singer, p. 454; *Original Letters*, ed. Ellis, 1st series II, pp. 53–4, 57 (*LP* X, 798); *LP* XIII I, 981/2 (14).
7. E.W. Ives, 'Court and County Palatine in the Reign of Henry VIII: the Career of William Brereton of Malpas', *Transactions in the Historic Society of Lancashire and Cheshire* 123 (1971), pp. 1–38; Amyot, 'Memorial from George Constantyne', p. 65.
8. Cavendish, *Wolsey*, ed. Singer, pp. 456–7; *Original Letters*, ed. Ellis, 1st series II, p. 60; *LP* X, 797.
9. Cavendish, *Wolsey*, ed. Singer, pp. 454–7; *Original Letters*, ed. Ellis, 1st series II, pp. 58–60 (*LP* X, 797–8).
10. Cavendish, *Wolsey*, ed. Singer, pp. 451, 454, 456; *Original Letters*, ed. Ellis, 1st series II, pp. 54, 59 (*LP* X, 793, 797, 798).
11. Cavendish, *Wolsey*, ed. Singer, pp. 451–2, 454; *Original Letters*, ed. Ellis, 1st series II, pp. 54–5 (*LP* X, 793, 798).
12. Cavendish, *Wolsey*, ed. Singer, pp. 456–7; *Original Letters*, ed. Ellis, 1st series II, p. 60; *LP* X, 797.
13. MacCulloch, *Cranmer*, pp. 156–7.
14. Burnet, *History of Reformation* I, pp. 320–1; MacCulloch, *Cranmer*, pp. 157–8.
15. Cavendish, *Wolsey*, ed. Singer, pp. 452, 457; *Original Letters*, ed. Ellis, 1st series II, p. 60 (*LP* X, 793, 797).
16. Cavendish, *Wolsey*, ed. Singer, p. 454; *Original Letters*, ed. Ellis, 1st series II, p. 57 (*LP* X, 798).
17. *LP* X, 876, particularly p. 362; *Wriothesley's Chronicle* I, pp. 189–226, particularly p. 192.
18. *LP* X, 876 (p. 361); *Wriothesley's Chronicle* I, p. 191.
19. *DKR*, 3rd report (1842), pp. 242–3; *LP* X, 908 (p. 377).
20. *Lisle Letters*, ed. Byrne, IV, p. 46 (*LP* X, 866).
21. *DKR*, 3rd report (1842), pp. 243–5; Keay, *The Elizabethan Tower of London*, p. 44; *LP* X, 908 (p. 377).
22. *The Reports of Sir John Spelman*, ed. J.H. Baker (Selden Society 93, 1977), p. 71; *Wriothesley's Chronicle* I, pp. 37–8; *LP* X, 876, 908; Ives, 'Faction', p. 187.
23. *LP* X, 908 (pp. 377–8).
24. *LP* X, 908 (p. 378); *Reports of Spelman*, p. 71; *Wriothesley's Chronicle* I, p. 38; Ives, 'Faction', p. 187.
25. *LP* X, 908 (p. 378).

26. *Wriothesley's Chronicle* I, p. 39; *LP* X, 876, 908 (p. 378).
27. Cavendish, *Wolsey*, ed. Singer, pp. 459–60; *Original Letters*, ed. Ellis, 1st series II, p. 63 (*LP* X, 890).
28. Burnet, *History of the Reformation* VI, p. 167 (*LP* X, 868); *LP* X, 896, 909 (p. 380).
29. *LP* X, 902.
30. *LP* X, 902; *Wriothesley's Chronicle* I, pp. 40–1.
31. *Wriothesley's Chronicle* I, pp. 39–40; Amyot, 'Memorial from George Constantyne', p. 65; *LP* X, 869, 908 (p. 379).
32. Cavendish, *Wolsey*, ed. Singer, pp. 460–1; *Original Letters*, ed. Ellis, 1st series II, pp. 64–5 (*LP* X, 910).
33. Cavendish, *Wolsey*, ed. Singer, pp. 460–1; *Original Letters*, ed. Ellis, 1st series II, pp. 64–5 (*LP* X, 910).
34. *LP* X, 911. For slightly different versions of Anne Boleyn's scaffold speech see Bentley, *Excerpta Historica*, p. 264 and Hall, *Chronicle*, p. 819.

Jane Seymour

Chapter 70

1. *LP* X, 901; Friedmann, *Anne Boleyn* II, p. 200; Rowlands, *Holbein*, p. 144, plates 99, 100; *Holbein and the Court of Henry VIII*, p. 81.
2. *Lisle Letters*, ed. Byrne, III, p. 306 (*LP* X, 1047).
3. *LP* X, 1069 (p. 450). Edward Seymour, who had earlier been in the employ of Cardinal Wolsey, had entered the Emperor's service early in 1521 on the recommendation of the King and Cardinal. This information, given in a letter of Cuthbert Tunstal's written at Worms (*LP* III i, 1201), testifies to Chapuys's accuracy and throws light on Seymour's pro-Imperial sympathies throughout his career.
4. *LP* X, 1069 (p. 450); *CSP Sp.* V ii (1536–1538), pp. 157–8.
5. *Banners, Standards and Badges from a Tudor Manuscript in the College of Arms* (The De Walden Library, 1994), pp. 19, 118.
6. *LP* X, 282 (p. 103), 601 (p. 245); *CSP Sp.* V ii (1536–1538), pp. 39–40, 84.
7. *Commons* I, pp. 375–8; *LP* VII, 1554.
8. *LP* VII, 1554 (p. 579).
9. PRO, OBS 1419.
10. *LP* X, 601 (p. 245); *CSP Sp.* V ii (1536–1538), p. 84.
11. *LP* X, 601 (p. 245).
12. *LP* X, 908 (pp. 377, 379); *Wriothesley's Chronicle* I, p. 43; *Inventory of King Henry VIII*, pp. 346–9; *HKW* IV, p. 64.
13. *LP* X, 908 (p. 379), 915; Kelly, *Matrimonial Trials*, pp. 259–60.
14. *LP* X, 926.
15. Ibid.; *Wriothesley's Chronicle* I, p. 43; *Commons* I, pp. 663–6.
16. *LP* X, 908 (p. 378), 926, *Lisle Letters*, ed. Byrne, III, p. 396 (*LP* X, 1047); IV, p. 52 (*LP* X, 1000); Hall, *Chronicle*, p. 819.
17. *Wriothesley's Chronicle* I, pp. 43–4.
18. *LP* X, 1017; *Wriothesley's Chronicle* I, p. 47.
19. *Wriothesley's Chronicle* I, p. 49; *Commons* I, pp. 728–34.
20. *LP* X, 942.

21. Lehmberg, *Later Parliaments*, pp. 15–16.
22. *Wriothesley's Chronicle* I, p. 44.
23. Rebholz, *Wyatt: Complete Poems*, p. 155; *Wriothesley's Chronicle* I, p. 44.
24. *Wriothesley's Chronicle* I, pp. 44–6.
25. *Wriothesley's Chronicle* I, pp. 46–7; Lehmberg, *Later Parliaments*, pp. 15–16; *LJ* I, p. 84.
26. *Wriothesley's Chronicle* I, pp. 47–8.
27. *LP* X, 901, 908 (p. 377).
28. *LP* X, 1069 (pp. 450–2); *CSP Sp.* V ii (1536–1538), p. 157.
29. *HKW* IV, pp. 154–6; *LP* X, 968.
30. *LP* X, 991.
31. Ibid., 1083.
32. Ibid., 1108.
33. Ibid., 1021; XI, 7 (p. 7).
34. *LP* VII, 1172 (misdated by the Calendar); X, 1110, 1134/1, 4, 1150.
35. *LP* X, 1134/4; XI, 7 (pp. 7–8).
36. *St. P.* I, pp. 457–9 and no. 2 on p. 458 (*LP* X, 1136–7).
37. *LP* X, 7 (p. 8).
38. *LP* X, 1186–7; XI, 6.
39. *Wriothesley's Chronicle* I, p. 51; *LP* XI, 40 (pp. 23–4).
40. 28 Hen. VIII, c. 7; *Statutes* III, pp. 655–62; *LJ* I, p. 92; Lehmberg, *Later Parliaments*, pp. 20–2.
41. *Lisle Letters*, ed. Byrne, III, p. 265 (*LP* X, 100); D. Knowles, *The Religious Orders in England*, 3 vols. (Cambridge, 1955–1959), III, p. 308; *Original Letters*, ed. Ellis, 3rd series III, p. 39 (*LP* IX, 457); *LP* X, 383 (the 'Queen' in this letter is Jane, not Anne, as the Calendar supposes), 858; Add I i, 1262 (misdated in the Calendar).
42. *Wriothesley's Chronicle* I, pp. 55–6; *St. P.* I, pp. 460–1 (*LP* XI, 501); *LP* XI, 8 (p. 9).
43. *Commons* II, pp. 423–4; *LP* XI, 854; A. Fletcher, *Tudor Rebellions* (London, 1968), pp. 120–1, 128–30.
44. *LP* XI, 860.
45. *St. P.* I, pp. 523–4 (*LP* XI, 1306).
46. *Wriothesley's Chronicle* I, pp. 59–60.
47. *Lisle Letters*, ed. Byrne, III, pp. 576–7 (*LP* XI, 1358).
48. *CSP Sp.* V ii (1536–1538), p. 280; *Lisle Letters*, ed. Byrne, III, pp. 577–8, 818 (*LP* XI, 1397; Addenda I i, 1154); *LP* XII i, 43, 44, 1224.
49. *Lisle Letters*, ed. Byrne, IV, 910 (*LP* XII i, 23); *LP* XII i, 43, 44, 1225.
50. *LP* XII i, 1224; *Wriothesley's Chronicle* I, p. 65.
51. *LP* XII i, 1267; *Wriothesley's Chronicle* I, p. 64.
52. *St. P.* I, pp. 551–2 (*LP* XII ii, 77).
53. *Lisle Letters*, ed. Byrne, IV, pp. 151, 162 (*LP* XII ii, 271, 626).
54. *Lisle Letters*, ed. Byrne, IV, pp. 163–4, 167 (*LP* XII ii, 711, 808).
55. *Lisle Letters*, ed. Byrne, IV, p. 172 (*LP* XII ii, 861); *LP* XII ii, 680, 839, 911; *The Works of Henry Howard Earl of Surrey and Sir Thomas Wyatt the Elder*, ed. G.F. Nott, 2 vols. (London, 1815–16), II, p. 423 (*LP* XII ii, 871); *Wriothesley's Chronicle* I, p. 65.

56. *Letters of the Queens*, ed. Crawford, p. 199 (*LP* XII ii, 889).
57. *Works of . . . Wyatt*, ed. Nott, II, pp. 320–1 (*LP* XII ii, 890).
58. *Wriothesley's Chronicle* I, pp. 65–7.
59. *Wriothesley's Chronicle* I, p. 68; *LP* XII ii, 911.
60. *Lisle Letters*, ed. Byrne, IV, p. 174; (*LP* XII ii, 923); *LP* XII ii, 939.
61. *Wriothesley's Chronicle* I, p. 69; *Lisle Letters*, ed. Byrne, IV, p. 428 (*LP* XII ii, 988).
62. *St. P.* I, p. 572 (*LP* XII ii, 970).
63. *St. P.* I, p. 573 (*LP* XII ii, 977).
64. *LP* XII ii, 971; 1060.

Part Three: The Later Queens
Chapter 71

1. *Lisle Letters*, ed. Byrne, V, pp. 491, 615–16, 665 (*LP* XIV i, 1014; XIV ii, 22, 284).
2. *Lisle Letters*, ed. Byrne, V, p. 666; *CSP Sp.* VI i (1538–1542), p. 468.
3. Emden, *Biographical Register . . . Oxford 1501–1540*, pp. 26–7.
4. Amyot, 'Memorial from George Constantyne', pp. 56–78.
5. Ibid., pp. 59–61.
6. R. McEntegart, 'England and the League of Schmalkalden, 1531–1547', (University of Cambridge Ph.D. dissertation, 1992), pp. 259–79, 288; *LP* XIII ii, 444; Amyot, 'Memorial from George Constantyne', pp. 62–3.
7. Lehmberg, *Later Parliaments*, pp. 65–6, 68–74, 82–3; 31 Hen. VIII, c. 14; *Statutes* III, pp. 739–43.
8. McEntegart, 'England and the League of Schmalkalden', pp. 319–45; Amyot, 'Memorial from George Constantyne', pp. 56, 58.
9. Amyot, 'Memorial from George Constantyne', pp. 58, 75.

Anne of Cleves
Chapter 72

1. R. McEntegart, 'Fatal Matrimony: Henry VIII and the Marriage of Anne of Cleves' in Starkey, ed., *Henry VIII: a European Court*, p. 140.
2. *LP* XIV i, 103, 103/2.
3. *St. P.* I, pp. 604–5 (*LP* XIV i, 552).
4. *St. P.* VIII, pp. 6–7 and note 1 (*LP* XII ii, 1187).
5. Rowlands, *Holbein*, pp. 116–17, 145; *Inventory of King Henry VIII*, ed. Starkey, pp. 237 (no. 10580), 240 (no. 10706), 384 (no. 15391).
6. *LP* XIV, i, 103/2; *St. P.* I, pp. 604–5 (*LP* XIV i, 552).
7. *LP* XIV i 490; A.B. Chamberlain, *Hans Holbein the Younger*, 2 vols. (London, 1913), II, pp. 174–5; McEntegart, 'Fatal Matrimony', pp. 140, 142 (plate XI.2).
8. *Commons* III, pp. 92–6; F.G. Emmison, *Tudor Secretary: Sir William Petre at Court and Home* (London, 1961), p. 43; *LP* XIV i. 1193.
9. Chamberlain, *Holbein* II, pp. 175–6; *LP* XIV ii, 781 (p. 312).
10. Amyot, 'Memorial from George Constantyne', pp. 60–1.
11. Chamberlain, *Holbein*, p. 176; Strickland, *Lives of the Queens*, III, pp. 35–60 (*LP* XIV ii, 33).

12. *LP* XIV ii, 117.
13. *St. P.* I, p. 605.
14. *LP* XIV ii, 153, 187; PRO, OBS 1419.
15. *House of Commons*, ed. Bindoff, II, pp. 27–9; *LP* XIV ii, 201.
16. *LP* XIV ii, 187, 200, 286.
17. *LP* XIV ii, 258, 309; Starkey (ed.), *Henry VIII*, p. 149.
18. *LP* XIV ii, 356, 388.
19. Ibid., 634.
20. Ibid., 347, 674; XV, 14 (p. 4); *St. P.* VII, pp. 208–9 (*LP* XIV ii, 677).
21. *St. P.* VII, pp. 212–13.
22. *LP* XIV ii, 685; Strype, *Ecclesiastical Memorials* VI, p. 213.
23. *LP* XIV ii, 718.
24. *LP* XV, 14 (p. 4).
25. *LP* XIV ii, 754; XV, 10; MacCulloch, *Cranmer*, 261.
26. *Wriothesley's Chronicle* I, pp. 109–10.
27. Ibid.; Strype, *Ecclesiastical Memorials* VI, pp. 215–16.
28. Strype, *Ecclesiastical Memorials* VI, pp. 214–16.
29. Burnet, *History of the Reformation* IV, pp. 424–5 (*LP* XV, 823).
30. *Wriothesley's Chronicle* I, pp. 110–11; Burnet, *History of the Reformation* IV, p. 425.
31. Burnet, *History of the Reformation* IV, pp. 425–6; *LP* XV, 861/2(ii).
32. Burnet, *History of the Reformation* IV, pp. 427.
33. Hall, *Chronicle*, pp. 836–7.
34. Thurley, *Royal Palaces*, pp. 236–7.
35. Burnet, *History of the Reformation* IV, p. 427.
36. Strype, *Ecclesiastical Memorials* VI, pp. 220–1; Burnet, *History of the Reformation* IV, p. 430.
37. Strype, *Ecclesiastical Memorials* VI, pp. 221–2.
38. *Original Letters*, ed. Ellis, 2nd series II, p. 166 (*LP* XV, 776).
39. *LP* XIV ii, 634; XV, 215–16.
40. Burnet, *History of the Reformation* IV, p. 428.
41. Strype, *Ecclesiastical Memorials* VI, pp. 213, 217–8.
42. *Wriothesley's Chronicle* I, pp. 112.
43. *LP* XV, 541.
44. *Wriothesley's Chronicle* I, pp. 116–17; *Commons*, I, pp. 734–5; III, pp. 297–301; R.M. Warnecke, *The Marrying of Anne of Cleves* (Cambridge, 2000), pp. 183–4.
45. *Original Letters relative to the English Reformation*, ed. H. Robinson, 2 vols. (Parker Society, Cambridge, 1846–7), I, pp. 201–2.
46. *LP* XV, 737.
47. Ibid., 766, 804, 770; MacCulloch, *Cranmer*, p. 270.
48. 32 Hen. VIII, no. 52 (*LP* XV, 498/60).
49. Burnet, *History of the Reformation* IV, p. 429.
50. *LP* XVI, 578; *Original Letters*, ed. Robinson, I, pp. 201–2; Warnecke, *Anne of Cleves*, pp. 184–5.
51. Warnecke, *Anne of Cleves*, pp. 184–5; *LP* XV, 848.
52. A.W. Bouterwek, 'Anna von Cleve', *Zeitschrift des Bergischen*

Geschichteverein 54 (Bonn, 1869), pp. 170–2; Kelly, *Matrimonial Trials*, pp. 268–9. I owe the translation of the documents printed in *Zeitschrift* to Dr Rory McEntegart.

53. *Original Letters*, ed. Ellis, 2nd series II, p. 159 (*LP* XV, 845); A.W. Bouterwek, 'Anna von Cleve', pp. 172–75.

54. *Original Letters*, ed. Ellis, 2nd series II, p. 159; *LP* XV, 823–4, 860–1; Strype, *Ecclesiastical Memorials* VI, pp. 210–222; Burnet, *History of the Reformation* IV, pp. 431–9; Kelly, *Matrimonial Trials*, pp. 268–9.

55. Bouterwek, 'Anna von Cleve', pp. 172–75; *HMC Rutland*, 4 vols. (1888–1905), I, p. 27 (*LP* XV, 844). *LP* XV, 844 is undated. It cannot belong to the 6th as *LP* followed by Warnecke assumes (p. 231) – though Warnecke also reuses it, unawares, in her account (p. 238) of the events of the 8th (*recte* the 9th and 10th)! Instead, I have assigned it to the night of the 9th–10th which fits with Harst's account. An annotation on the extant copy at Belvoir (*HMC Rutland* I, p. 27) also dates the encounter as occurring on the night of the 9th, the letter itself being written the following ('the present') morning by Rutland.

56. *St. P.* VIII, p. 405 (*LP* XV, 908); *LP* XV, 925.

57. *St. P.* I, pp. 637–8 (*LP* XV, 872); *Letters of the Queens*, ed. Crawford, pp. 204–5.

58. *LP* XV, 908, 925.

59. Ibid., 874 dated to 14 July by *LP* XV, 925/ii.

60. *St. P.* I, 643–5; *LP* XV, 925.

Catherine Howard

Chapter 73

1. L.B. Smith, *A Tudor Tragedy: the Life and Times of Catherine Howard* (New York, 1961), pp. 37, 39–41, 43–4.

2. Smith, *Tudor Tragedy*, pp. 44–5.

3. GEC IX, p. 615; Smith, *Tudor Tragedy*, pp. 44–5.

4. Smith, *Tudor Tragedy*, p. 45.

5. PRO, SP 1/167, fos. 135, 135v, 138v (*LP* XVI, 1321).

6. Burnet, *History of the Reformation* IV, p. 249.

7. PRO, SP 1/167, fo. 130 (*LP* XVI, 1320).

8. Burnet, *History of the Reformation* IV, p. 251; PRO, SP 1/167, fo. 136 (*LP* XVI, 1321).

9. PRO, SP 1/167, fos. 136v–137; (*LP* XVI, 1321). This letter is several times referred to in sworn depositions; e.g. *LP* XVI, 1400.

10. PRO, SP 1/167, fo. 137 (*LP* XVI, 1321).

11. *LP* XVI, 1469.

12. *LP* XIV ii, 572 (p. 203); Burnet, *History of the Reformation* IV, p. 252.

13. *LP* XVI, 625, 632, 1359; XVII, app. 10; Burnet, *History of the Reformation* IV, p. 252.

14. *LP* XVI, 901, 1409/1; *Letters*, ed. Robinson, I, pp. 201–2 (*LP* XVI, 578); *Wriothesley's Chronicle* I, pp. 121–2.

15. *Zurich Letters*, ed. Robinson, I, pp. 201–2 (*LP* XVI, 578); *LP* XVI, 1409/3.

16. *Wriothesley's Chronicle* I, p. 123; *Correspondance Politique de Mm. de Castillon*

et de Marillac, ed. J. Kaulek (Paris, 1885), pp. 213, 223 (*LP* XV, 976; XVI, 60).

17. *Correspondance Politique*, ed. Kaulek, p. 218 (*LP* XVI, 12); PRO, OBS 1419. But the motto was not, contrary to widespread opinion, complemented by the badge of a 'rose without a thorn'. Like so many entrenched errors about Henry's Queens, the story originates with Agnes Strickland (*Lives of the Queens* III, p. 122) and it has been repeated, with less excuse, by her many successors (e.g. Fraser, *Six Wives*, pp. 331–3).
     Strickland's authority is a coin, supposedly issued in Catherine's honour. She describes it as having the crowned royal arms and the cipher 'HR' for 'Henricus Rex' on the one side, and, on the other, a crowned rose with the motto: 'Rutilans rosa sine spina' (the dazzling rose without a thorn) and the cipher 'KR' 'Katerina Regina'. In fact, such coins, known as Crowns of the Double Rose, and worth five shillings, had been issued since Wolsey's recoinage of 1526. They indeed bore ciphers in honour of Henry's first three Queens: 'HK' for Henry and Catherine (of Aragon); 'HA' for Henry and Anne Boleyn and 'HI' for Henry and Jane Seymour. But after Jane's death, and in the absence of a Queen for over two years, the cipher became simply 'HR', which it remained till the end of the reign.
     Probably the coin described by Strickland is in fact one of those struck in honour of Catherine of Aragon (capital 'H', 'K' and 'R' are very similar in form in Tudor lettering and it is easy to confuse them). And, at any event, the rose badge and motto: 'Rutilans rosa sine spina' (the dazzling rose without a thorn) refer to Henry himself, and not to any of his Queens. C.A. Whitton, 'The Coinage of Henry VIII and Edward VI in Henry's name: Part 2', *British Numismatic Journal*, 26 (1949–51), pp. 171–212, esp. pp. 172–3.
     Thus the rose has nothing to do with Catherine and the motto has nothing to do with her supposed blemishlessness either. This reading of the evidence is confirmed by M. Siddons, *Heraldic Badges of England and Wales* (forthcoming). Dr Siddons finds that Catherine, unlike Henry's other wives, seems to have displayed no personal badge.

18. *Correspondance Politique*, ed. Kaulek, 218 (*LP* XVI, 12).

19. *LP* XVI, 223; BL, Stowe MS 559, fos. 55–58v (*LP* XVI, 1389); G. Reynolds, *The Sixteenth and Seventeenth-Century Miniatures in the Collection of Her Majesty The Queen* (London, 1999), no. 6.

20. *LP* XV, 901; *Wriothesley's Chronicle* I, pp. 119–20.

21. *CSP Sp.* VI i (1538–1542), p. 305 (*LP* XVI, 436).

22. *LP* XVI, 449; *CSP Sp.* VI i (1538–1542), pp. 305–6.

23. MacCulloch, *Cranmer*, pp. 272–4.

24. *PPC* VII, pp. 105–7 (*LP* XVI, 422, 424); *LP* XVI, 423; *Commons* II, pp. 105–7, 240–1.

25. *PPC* VII, pp. 105, 107.

26. *LP* XVI, 466, 515, 516; *Commons* III, pp. 249–52.

27. *Correspondance Politique*, ed. Kaulek, pp. 262–3 (*LP* XVI, 467).

28. *St. P.* VIII, p. 546 (*LP* XVI, 660).

29. *CSP Sp.* VI i (1538–1542), p. 314 (*LP* XVI, 662).

30. *Wriothesley's Chronicle* I, p. 124.

31. *CSP Sp.* VI i (1538–1542), p. 314 (*LP* XVI, 662).

32. *LP* XVI, 314.

33. *CSP Sp.* VI i (1538–1542), p. 324 (*LP* XVI, 835); *HKW* IV, pp. 14–15.

34. *LP* XVI, 804.

35. *LP* XVI, 1389.

36. *PPE Princess Mary*, p. 96.

37. *LP* XV, 21 (as Strickland asserts [Lives of the Queens of England III, pp. 122–3], this is a list of Catherine Howard's household, not of Anne of Cleves's, as *LP* seems to assume); XVI, 449, 1416; *PPC* VII, p. 354.

38. *LP* X, 901.

39. PRO, SP 1/167, fo. 161 (*LP* XVI, 1339).

40. *CSP Sp.* VI i (1538–1542), p. 327 (*LP* XVI, 864).

41. *LP* XVI, 1011.

42. PRO, OBS 1419; *HKW* IV, p. 47.

43. Hall, *Chronicle*, p. 842; *LP* XVI, 1088.

44. PRO, SP 1/167, fo. 160 (*LP* XVI, 1339).

45. *LP* XVI, 1130.

46. PRO, SP 1/167, fo. 153 (*LP* XVI, 1338).

47. *LP* XVI, 1130; Hall, *Chronicle*, p. 842.

48. *LP* XVI, 1131.

49. PRO, SP 1/167, fo. 154 (*LP* XVI, 1338).

50. *HKW* IV, pp. 355–6, 477; Thurley, *Royal Palaces*, p. 70; *LP* XVI, 1183.

51. *LP* XVI, 1183.

52. *PPC* VII, p. 352 (*LP* XVI, 1334).

53. *PPC* VII, pp. 352–3 (*LP* XVI, 1334); MacCulloch, *Cranmer*, p. 287.

54. *PPC* VII, p. 353 (*LP* XVI, 1334); *Select Works of John Bale*, ed. H. Christmas (Parker Society, Cambridge, 1849), pp. 138, 142, 243; *The Writings of John Bradford*, ed. A. Townsend (Parker Society, Cambridge, 1853), pp. 283, 288.

55. MacCulloch, *Cranmer*, p. 274.

56. *PPC* VII, pp. 354–5 (*LP* XVI, 1334); PRO, SP 1/167, fos. 128–31, 135–138v, 149–51, 155–67.

57. PRO, SP 1/167, fo. 129 (*LP* XVI, 1320).

58. PRO, SP 1/167, fos. 138–138v (*LP* XVI, 1320).

59. PRO, SP 1/167, fos. 129v, 157, 161; *LP* XVI, 1320, 1339.

60. PRO, SP 1/167, fo. 155 (*LP* XVI, 1339).

61. *PPC* VII, p. 355 (*LP* XVI, 1334).

62. *LP* XVI, 1332; *Correspondance Politique*, ed. Kaulek, pp. 352–4. I have followed Marillac's chronology (*LP* XVI, 1332). It fits with the time of the first interrogations on the 5th; it is also confirmed by the later testimonies of the Duchess of Norfolk and Robert Davenport about the Duke of Norfolk's movements on the Sunday and Monday (*LP* XVI, 1398, 1400). Chapuys gives another, quite different timetable (*LP* XVI, 1328; *CSP Sp.* VI i (1538–1542), p. 384). Since this is incompatible with both Marillac and the English evidence, I have ignored it.

63. *HMC Bath*, 5 vols. (London, 1904–1980), II, pp. 8–9.

64. *St. P.* I, pp. 689–90 (*LP* XVI, 1325); MacCulloch, *Cranmer*, p. 288.

65. *LP* XVI, 1398, 1400; *St. P.* I, p. 691 (*LP* XVI, 1331).

66. PRO, SP 1/167, fo. 159 (*LP* XVI, 1339); *HMC Bath* II, pp. 9–10.

67. *LP* XVI, 1334, 1366.

68. *HMC Bath* II, pp. 9–10; GEC X, pp. 141–2.

69. *HMC Bath* II, pp. 9–10.

70. *St. P.* I, p. 695 (*LP* XVI, 1333).

71. *LP* XVI, 1342–3; PRO, SP 1/167, fos. 157–9 (*LP* XVI, 1339).

72. PRO, SP 1/167, fo. 157 (*LP* XVI, 1339).

73. *LP* XVI, 1134; *Letters of the Queens*, ed. Crawford, p. 210; PRO, SP 1/167, fo. 158 (*LP* XVI, 1339).

74. PRO, SP 1/167, fos. 158–9; *Lisle Letters*, ed. Byrne, V, p. 616; *LP* X, 1134/4; XVI, g. 678 (13).

75. PRO, SP 1/167, fos. 153–4; (*LP* XVI, 1338); fos. 158–9.

76. PRO SP 1/167, fos. 158–9 (*LP* XVI, 1339).

77. GEC II, p. 288; III, pp. 699–73; IX, pp. 671–2; *LP* XIV ii, 572/4.

78. PRO, SP 1/167, fo. 159; (*LP* XVI, 1339).

79. *DKR*, 3rd report (1842), pp. 261–4 (*LP* XVI, 1395); *St. P.* I, pp. 701, 707 (*LP* XVI, 1425, 1434); *LP* XVI, 1430, 1432; *Wriothesley's Chronicle* I, pp. 131–2.

80. *DKR*, 3rd report (1842), pp. 264–6 (*LP* XVI, 1470); GEC II, p. 311.

81. *LP* XVI, 1457; *St. P.* I, p. 721 (*LP* XVI, 1454).

82. Lehmberg, *Later Parliaments*, pp. 144–6; Smith, *Tudor Tragedy*, pp. 201–2; *LJ*, I, pp. 168, 171, 172, 174–6; 33 Hen. VIII, c. 21; *Statutes of the Realm* III pp. 857–60; Hall, *Chronicle*, p. 843.

83. *CSP Sp.* VI i (1538–1542), p. 465 (*LP* XVII, 63).

84. Smith, *Tudor Tragedy*, pp. 201, 203; Lehmberg, *Later Parliaments*, pp. 144–5; *LJ* I, p. 176.

85. *CSP Sp.* VI i (1538–1542), p. 472 (*LP* XVII, 124 [p.50]).

86. *LP* XVII, 100; *CSP Sp.* VI i (1538–1542), p. 472 (*LP* XVII, 124 [p. 50]).

87. *LP* XVII, 100; *CSP Sp.* VI i (1538–1542), p. 472 (*LP* XVII, 124 [p. 50]); *Original Letters*, ed. Ellis, 1st series II, pp. 128–9 (*LP* XVII, 106).

88. Sessions, *Henry Howard*, p. 150; *Original Letters*, ed. Ellis, 1st series II, pp. 128–9 (*LP* XVII, 106); B. Winchester, *Tudor Family Portrait* (London, 1955), pp. 38–9; Hall, *Chronicle*, p. 543; *CSP Sp.* VI i (1538–1542), p. 472 (*LP* XVII, 124 [p. 50]).

Chapter 74

1. *CSP Sp.* VI i (1538–1542), pp. 410–11 (*LP* XVI, 1403).

2. *CSP Sp.* VI i (1538–1542), p. 396 (*LP* XVI, 1359 [p. 628]).

3. *St. P.* I, pp. 714, 716–18 (*LP* XVI, 1445, 1449, 1453); *LP* XVI, 1457.

4. *LP* XVII, 35.

5. *LP* XVI, 1457, 1459; PRO OBS 1419.

6. *CSP Sp.* VI i (1538–1542), p. 468 (*LP* XVII, 92).

7. *CSP Sp.* VI i (1538–1542), p. 473 (*LP* XVII, 124 [p. 51]).

Catherine Parr

Chapter 75

1. *DNB sub* Parr.
2. GEC XII i, pp. 218–19; *Commons* III, p. 521; *LP* I i, 1123/15; A.R. Myers, *The Household of Edward IV: the Black Book and the Ordinances of 1478* (Manchester, 1959), p. 289.
3. C.L. Schofield, *The Life and Reign of Edward IV*, 2 vols. (London, 1923) I, pp. 585, 589; II, pp. 23, 159; *LP Hen. VII* II, p. 89; Myers, *Household of Edward IV*, pp. 111–12; *HO*, pp. 11, 12, 14–16; D. Starkey, *The English Court: from the Wars of the Roses to the Civil War* (London, 1987), ch. 3.
4. *LP* I i, g. 257 (1), g. 604 (14); I ii, 2053/1–5, 2838; II ii, 3807.
5. N.H. Nicolas, *Testamenta Vetusta*, 2 vols. (London, 1826) II, p. 549; *LP* II i, 1153, 1573.
6. *LP* II i, 1759, 1861; II ii, p. 1472.
7. *Wills from Doctors' Commons*, ed. J.G. Nicols and J. Bruce (CS old series 83, 1863), p. 9; *A dispraise of the life of a courtier, and a commendation of the life of the labouryng man*, trans. by Sir F. Bryan, 1548: STC 12431, foreword.
8. *LP* II ii, 3747, 3807; *Testamenta Vetusta*, II, pp. 548–9.
9. *LP* III i, 528, 577; III ii, app. 20.
10. T.D. Whitaker, *A History of Richmondshire; in the North Riding of Yorkshire*, 2 vols. (London, 1823), II, p. 281 (*LP* III ii, 3649); *A dispraise of the life of a courtier*, foreword.
11. Whitaker, *Richmondshire* II, p. 281 (*LP* III ii, 3649); *Wills from Doctors' Commons*, pp. 14, 18; *LP* VII, 861.
12. GEC XI, pp. 546–7.
13. Whitaker, *Richmondshire* II, p. 281 (*LP* III ii, 3649).
14. *LP* III ii, 3178, 3210, 3264; Whitaker, *Richmondshire* II, p. 281 (*LP* III ii, 3649).
15. *LP* IV i, 162.
16. *LP* IV iii, 5508/2 (p. 2433); *Wills from Doctors' Commons*, p. 10; GEC IX, pp. 671–2; *Allegations for Marriage Licences issued by the Bishop of London 1520 to 1610*, ed. G.J. Armitage (HS 25, 1887), p. 5.
17. *Wills from Doctors' Commons*, p. 10; GEC II, pp. 422–3.
18. *Wills from Doctors' Commons*, pp. 13, 14, 18.
19. *Commons*, III, pp. 8–9; GEC VII, pp. 482–3.
20. *Testamenta Vetusta*, II, pp. 548–9; *Wills from Doctors' Commons*, p. 18; Sturge, *Tunstal*, table I, p. 148 n. 5.
21. *Commons*, III, pp. 60–2; *LP* Addenda I ii, 1297.
22. M.H. and R. Dodds, *The Pilgrimage of Grace 1536–1537 and the Exeter Conspiracy 1538* (Cambridge, 1915), I, pp. 201–2; M.L. Bush, *The Pilgrimage of Grace; a Study of the Rebel Armies of October 1536* (Manchester, 1996), pp. 143–4.
23. *LP* XII i, 101, 131, 789 (p. 345).
24. Dodds, *Pilgrimage* I, pp. 205, 237–8, 265, 345, 377; Bush, *Pilgrimage*, pp. 175, 376, 392.
25. *LP* XII i, 392(ii); Bush, *Pilgrimage*, pp. 29–30; M. Bush and D. Bownes, *The Defeat of the Pilgrimage of Grace* (Hull, 1999), p. 186.

26. Dodds, *Pilgrimage* I, 113, 131, 147; II, p. 81; *LP* XII i, 1084 (p. 492), 1087 (pp. 495, 501).
27. *LP* VI, 1199; VII, 1437.
28. Cited in B. Kemeys and J. Raggatt, *The Queen Who Survived: the Life of Katherine Parr* (London, 1993), p. 55.
29. MacCulloch, *Cranmer*, p. 326; D. Starkey, *Elizabeth: the Struggle for the Throne* (London, 2000), pp. 45–6.
30. *LP* XII i, 96, 131, 169, 173; Bush and Bownes, *Defeat of the Pilgrimage*, p. 43.
31. *LP* XII i, 173; Bush and Bownes, *Defeat of the Pilgrimage*, pp. 97–9.
32. *LP* XII ii, app. 28; A.G. Dickens, *Lollards and Protestants in the Diocese of York* (Oxford, 1959), pp. 61–2, 68; *Commons* I, pp. 432–4.
33. Dickens, *Lollards and Protestants*, ch. 3; *LP* X, 742.
34. *LP* X, 742.
35. Dickens, *Lollards and Protestants*, pp. 61, 68; *LP* XII i, 578.
36. *Plumpton Correspondence*, ed. T. Stapleton (CS old series 4, 1839), p. 232; Dickens, *Lollards and Protestants*, pp. 62–3; GEC VII, p. 484 note a.
37. Dickens, *Lollards and Protestants*, pp. 58–9, 76.
38. *LP* XII i, 578.
39. *Tudor Treatises*, ed. A.G. Dickens (Yorkshire Archaeological Society Record Series 125, 1959), p. 42.
40. *LP* XII i, 201 (pp. 91–2).
41. Dickens, *Lollards and Protestants*, pp. 96–102.
42. *LP* XII ii, 14, 101.
43. *LP* XII ii, 166, 665(ii).
44. *LP* XII ii, 665(ii); G.R. Elton, *Policy and Police, the Enforcement of the Reformation in the Age of Thomas Cromwell* (Cambridge, 1972), pp. 56 n. 4, 371–2. In p. 56 n. 4 Elton confuses Lord Latimer with another of his brothers, William Nevill, who had been arrested earlier on another matter.
45. Cited by Strickland, *Lives of the Queens* III, p. 212.
46. *LP* XII i, 913; XII ii, 784; XIII i, 312, 812; XIV ii, 782 (p. 334).
47. *Commons* III, pp. 60–61; *LP* XII i, 713; XIV i, 477; Add I ii, 1297 (which is misdated 16 January 1538); GEC IX, p. 669.
48. *LP* XII ii, 1060 (p. 374); *Testamenta Vetusta* II, p. 548; *Wills from Doctors' Commons*, p. 17.
49. *Lisle Letters*, ed. Byrne, IV, pp. 147, 157; VI, p. 18 (*LP* XII ii, 167, 424; XV, 135); *LP* XIV ii, 572 (p. 202); XV, 21 (p. 9): GEC X, pp. 405–9. In some of these documents Anne is referred to as Mrs Fitzherbert. I think this is probably a reflection of her husband's descent from a bastard line.
50. Strickland, *Lives of the Queens* III, p. 198; Emden, *Biographical Register . . . Oxford 1501–1540*, pp. 433–4; *DNB sub* 'Latimer' and 'Coverdale'.
51. PRO, PROB 11/29, fos. 134v–136v (*Testamenta Vetusta*, II, pp. 704–6); GEC VII, p. 483; PRO, SP 1/177, fos. 123–125v (*LP* XVIII i, 443). Since PRO, SP 1/177, fos. 123–125v calendared as *LP* XVIII i. 443 has been extraordinarily misused by Catherine's historians, it is important to get

the basic facts right. It is, as we have seen in the text, a tailor's bill which was addressed to Catherine while she was still Lady Latimer. But, as she seems to have been a late payer, it was only settled after she became Queen, when payment was authorised by the signature of her Chancellor, Sir Thomas Arundell. It does *not* therefore record gifts to Catherine by Henry. It does *not* mean that the King's relationship with her antedated her husband's death. And it does *not* show her taking pity on Princess Mary by providing her with clothes, as the (step)daughter referred to is Margaret Neville not Mary Tudor. Nor, finally, does it suggest that Catherine ever 'sought and obtained a position in Mary's household as one of her ladies' (S.E. James, *Katheryn Parr: the Making of a Queen* (Aldershot, 1999), p. 90).

52. *Commons* III, pp. 297–301; Sudeley MS; *Letters of the Queens*, ed. Crawford, p. 222.

Chapter 76

1. Sudeley MS; *Letters of the Queens*, ed. Crawford, p. 222.
2. *Commons* III, pp. 297–8; *LP* XVIII i, 42, 259 (p. 148), 288.
3. *Commons* III, p. 9; GEC VII, p. 483.
4. *LP* XVIII i, 288, 491–2.
5. *LP* XVIII i, 468, 740.
6. PRO, OBS 1419; *LP* XVIII i, 675, 676, 740; *PPE Princess Mary*, p. 118.
7. *LP* XVIII i, 854, 873; Hall, *Chronicle*, p. 858.
8. *LP* XVIII i, 873.
9. Ibid., 894.
10. Ibid., 918.
11. Ibid., 919.
12. *CSP Sp.* VI ii (1542–1543), p. 444 (*LP* XVIII i, 954). My translation of the phrase 'être en chemise'.
13. *Original Letters* II, pp. 240–1.
14. *Wriothesley's Chronicle* I, p. 143; PRO, OBS 1419; *HKW* IV, p. 44.
15. PRO, OBS 1419; *Wriothesley's Chronicle* I, p. 145.
16. *PPE Princess Mary*, p. 91.
17. *CSP Sp.* VI ii (1544), p. 459 (*LP* XVIII ii, 39).
18. *Wills from Doctors' Commons*, p. 14.
19. *PPE Princess Mary*, pp. 123–4; *HKW* IV, pp. 43–4, 47–8, 75–6.
20. *LP* XVIII ii, p. 501.
21. PRO, OBS 1419.
22. M. Levine, *Tudor Dynastic Problems, 1460–1571* (London, 1973), pp. 155–6.
23. Lehmberg, *Later Parliaments*, p. 194; 35 Hen. VIII, c. 1; *Statutes* III, pp. 955–8.
24. Lehmberg, *Later Parliaments*, pp. 195–6; Foxe, *Acts* V, pp. 475–97.
25. Lehmberg, *Later Parliaments*, pp. 186–8; 34 and 35 Hen. VIII, c. 1; *Statutes* III, pp. 894–7.
26. Lehmberg, *Later Parliaments*, pp. 184–5; MacCulloch, *Cranmer*, pp. 311–13, 313.
27. Foxe, *Acts* V, pp. 473–4.

28. *APC* I, pp. 96–8; *Commons* II, pp. 366–7; III, pp. 383, 571.
29. *LP* XVIII ii, 546/xix.i (p. 324).
30. *APC* I, pp. 150–1.
31. PRO, OBS 1419; *Narratives of the Reformation*, ed. Nichols, p. 352. MacCulloch's identification of other supposed royal visits to Westminster in this period (*Cranmer*, p. 315) is based on a misunderstanding of the procedures of the Great Seal.
32. Foxe, *Acts* V, pp. 490–97.
33. PRO, OBS 1419; *Commons* I, p. 599; Foxe, *Acts* V, p. 494.
34. Foxe, *Acts* V, p. 495.
35. Ibid.; *LP* XVIII ii, g. 241 (6).
36. Foxe, *Acts* VIII, p. 33–4; MacCulloch, *Cranmer*, pp. 302–5, 308, 311, 314–17, 319–20.
37. Foxe, *Acts* VIII, p. 29; MacCulloch, *Cranmer*, pp. 317–18; *Commons* II, pp. 513–15.
38. *LP* XVIII ii, 546 (p. 370).
39. Foxe, Acts V, p. 496.
40. *LP* XVIII ii, 504, 526; PRO, OBS 1419; MacCulloch, *Cranmer*, pp. 250, 320–1. Cranmer's summons to Court has not been noted in the attempt to date Foxe's story. It seems to be crucial, as does the evidence of the presence at Court of Norfolk and Russell, who figure prominently in Foxe and Morice's narratives.
41. Foxe, *Acts* VIII, p. 25; *Narratives of the Reformation*, p. 354–8. MacCulloch, *Cranmer*, pp. 320–1 offers a dating for this incident which Henry's itinerary makes impossible.
42. Foxe, *Acts* VIII, pp. 30–1. Lehmberg, *Later Parliaments*, pp. 196, 198; 35 Hen. VIII, cc. 5, 12, 18; *Statutes* III, pp. 960–2, 970–1, 981.
43. Emden, *Biographical Register . . . Oxford 1501–1540*, p. 90; MacCulloch, *Cranmer*, p. 320; *Narratives of the Reformation*, ed. Nichols, pp. 254–8.
44. PRO, OBS 1419; *LP* XVIII ii, 516.
45. Siddons, *Heraldic Badges* (forthcoming); *LP* XVIII i, 918.

Chapter 77
1. Hall, *Chronicle*, p. 859.
2. *LP* XIX I, 7, 9; 'Narrative of the Visit of the Duke of Najera to England, in the Year 1543–4; Written by his Secretary, Pedro de Gente', ed. F. Madden, *Archaeologia* 23 (1831), pp. 350–1.
3. *CSP Sp.* VII (1544), p. 55 (*LP* XIX i, 118).
4. 'Visit of the Duke of Najera', ed. Madden, pp. 352–3; P. Holman, *Four and Twenty Fiddlers: The Violin at the English Court, 1540–1690* (Oxford, 1993), pp. 78–80; S.E. James, 'Lady Jane Grey or Kateryn Parr?', *Burlington Magazine* 108 (1996), p. 204.
5. *LP* XIX i, 323; *St. P.* IX, p. 661 (*LP* XIX i, 392); *CSP Sp.* VII (1544), p. 182 (*LP* XIX i, 591).
6. *LP* XIX i, 620/ii.
7. M. Merriman, *The Rough Wooings: Mary, Queen of Scots, 1542–1551* (East Linton, 2000), pp. 77, 81, 83.

8. Merriman, *Rough Wooings*, pp. 111–13, 118–21.
9. Ibid., pp. 116–18, 144–9.
10. GEC VII, pp. 597–8; Merriman, *Rough Wooings*, pp. 48–9, 89, 97, 100, 103.
11. *CSP Sp.* VII (1544), p. 266 (*LP* XIX i, 730); GEC VII, p. 599 notes b and c.
12. *LP* XIX i, 779 (pp. 476–7).
13. *LP* XVI, 1333.
14. *LP* XIX i, 779; G. Donaldson, *Scotland: James V to James VII* (Edinburgh, 1965), p. 76; Merriman, *Rough Wooings*, pp. 141–2.
15. *LP* XIX, i, 780; *HMC Rutland* I, p. 30.
16. *CSP Sp.* VII (1544), p. 244 (*LP* XIX i, 799).
17. *St. P.* I, pp. 763–5 (*LP* XIX i, 864).
18. *St. P.* I, p. 764 (*LP* XIX i, 864); Thurley, *Royal Palaces*, p. 80; *The Chronicle and Political Papers of King Edward VI*, ed. W.K. Jordan (London, 1966), p. 3.
19. *LP* XIX ii, 424.
20. Strype, *Ecclesiastical Memorials* VI, pp. 312–13 (*LP* XIX i, 1029).
21. *LP* XIX i, 943, 954.
22. *LP* XIX i, 1020; *Letters of Royal and Illustrious Ladies*, ed. Wood, pp. 176–7; M. Perry, *The Word of a Prince: a Life of Elizabeth I from Contemporary Sources* (Woodbridge, 1990), pp. 30–1.
23. *LP* XIX ii, 4.
24. *LP* XIX i, 979, 980; *Letters of Royal and Illustrious Ladies*, ed. Wood, III, p. 172 (*LP* XIX i, 980).
25. *St. P.* X, pp. 12–14 (*LP* XIX i, 979).
26. *St. P.* X, pp. 12–14 (*LP* XIX i, 979); *LP* XIX ii, 424.
27. Strickland, *Lives of the Queens* III, p. 216.
28. *St. P.* X, pp. 12–14 (*LP* XIX i, 979).
29. *Letters of Royal and Illustrious Ladies*, ed. Wood, III, 173–4 (*LP* XIX i, 1019).
30. *St. P.* X, p. 23 (*LP* XIX ii, 35).
31. *St. P.* X, pp. 28–9 (*LP* XIX ii, 39).
32. *St. P.* V, p. 396 (*LP* XIX ii, 48); *LP* XIX ii, 58.
33. *LP* XIX ii, 174.
34. Ibid., 688 (p. 406).
35. *Letters of King Henry VIII*, ed. Byrne, pp. 365–7 (*LP* XIX ii, 201).
36. GEC XI, p. 255; *Commons* I, pp. 400–3.
37. *Commons* I, p. 337; III, pp. 60, 501, 539.
38. *Commons* II, p. 491; III, pp. 501–2.
39. *The House of Commons 1558–1603*, ed. P. W. Hasler, 3 vols. (1981) II, pp. 201–2; *LP* XVII ii, 531.
40. *Letters of King Henry VIII*, ed. Byrne, p. 368 (*LP* XIX ii, 201).
41. *St. P.* X, p. 69 (*LP* XIX ii, 228); *LP* XIX ii, 251.
42. Lodge, *Illustrations* I, pp. 55–6 (*LP* XIX ii, 251).
43. *St. P.* I, p. 768; X, pp. 82–3 (*LP* XIX ii, 292, 280).
44. *LP* XIX ii, 424 (p. 242), 688 (p. 407); *Wriothesley's Chronicle* I, p. 149.

Chapter 78

1. M. Shell, *Elizabeth's Glass* (Lincoln and London, 1993); J.K.M. McConica, *English Humanists and Reformation Politics under Henry VIII and Edward VI* (Oxford, 1965), p. 231.
2. Perry, *Word of a Prince*, pp. 31–35.
3. McConica, *English Humanists*, p. 228.
4. Ibid., pp. 230, 236–7, 241–2.
5. Ibid., pp. 231–2; Dowling, *Humanism*, pp. 236–7.
6. *Letters of Royal and Illustrious Ladies*, ed. Wood, III, pp. 181–2; *Letters of the Queens*, ed. Crawford, p. 219.
7. *St. P.* I, p. 840 (*LP* XX ii, 769).
8. *Commons* I, p. 579; *LP* XX ii, 995 (p. 490), 1030; XXI i, 643, p. 318 (fo. 85).
9. Scarisbrick, *Henry VIII*, p. 472; Foxe, *Acts* V, p. 562.
10. Muller, *Stephen Gardiner*, pp. 118–19, 135.
11. Perry, *Word of a Prince*, pp. 45–6.
12. *Letters of King Henry VIII*, ed. Byrne, pp. 418–22.
13. *LP* XX ii, 1030.
14. Ibid.
15. Strype, *Ecclesiatical Memorials* VI, pp. 318–20; *LP* XXI i, 279/2.
16. *CSP Sp.* VIII (1545–6), pp. 111, 232, 310, 318 (*LP* XXI i, 289).
17. Foxe, *Acts* V, pp. 553–61; G. Redworth, *In Defences of the Church Catholic: The Life of Stephen Gardiner* (Oxford, 1990), pp. 233–4.
18. Foxe, *Acts* V, pp. 553–4.
19. PRO, OBS 1419; Foxe, *Acts* V, pp. 554–7.
20. Foxe, *Acts* V, pp. 557–8.
21. *LP* XX ii, g. 910(55), 995 (p. 493); *APC* I p. 470–1.
22. PRO, E 315/161, fos. 22–34; *LP* XVII, g. 1154(49); XX i, 650(70); XXI ii, 331(71), g. 332 (73); *CSP Sp.* VIII (1545), pp. 130, 163.
23. Foxe, *Acts* V, pp. 558–60.
24. Foxe, *Acts* V, pp. 560–1.
25. *CSP Sp.* VIII (1545–1546), p. 535; XXI ii, 684; H. Miller, 'Henry VIII's Unwritten Will: Grants of Lands and Honours in 1547', in Ives, Knecht and Scarisbrick, eds., *Wealth and Power*, pp. 87–105; Sessions, *Henry Howard*, ch. 15.
26. PRO, E 101/424/12, fo. 76; Starkey, *Elizabeth*, pp. 63–4.
27. Starkey, *Elizabeth*, pp. 67, 69–71.

Index

The names of Henry's six wives are abbreviated wherever they occur within the entries:

CA Catherine of Aragon
AB Anne Boleyn
JS Jane Seymour
AC Anne of Cleves
CH Catherine Howard
CP Catherine Parr

The places included in this index are restricted largely to the cities, towns, villages and properties visited by Henry and his wives. Those actually in Henry's possession are comprehensively listed under 'palaces, royal houses and hunting lodges'. With the most favoured royal residences (Greenwich and Westminster/Whitehall), repeatedly visited by Henry and his wives, only the most significant entries, or ones of special interest, have been noted.

For the convenience of the reader 'Acts', 'battles', 'Bible, Holy', 'Household, royal', 'houses, religious', 'London and Westminster', 'treaties' and 'ships' are listed under these headings.

104–5, 108–9; proxy weddings to Arthur 29–30; Spanish Household 29, 66–7, 80, 104, 113, 154; religious piety 36–8, 70, 162, 198, 370, 541–2; journey to and arrival in England 38–48; appearance 47, 122, 444; wedding ceremony and arrangements with Arthur 50–7, 59–60; meets Elizabeth of York 58; marital relations with Arthur and consummation dispute 61–3, 68–70, 72, 76, 82–4, 86–7, 206, 209, 220, 224, 231, 291–3, 484, 521, 543, 548; homesickness 65; concern for protocol and status 68; accompanies Arthur to Wales 72–4, 83–4; and Arthur's death 77–8; illness and return to London 79–80; finances and maintenance as young widow 80–2, 95–7, 169; and negotiations for second marriage (to Henry) 82–5, 93–4, 104–5, 108; and mother's death 87–8; rebels against Dona Elvira 87–8, 90; supports father for Castile succession 90, 92; meets Juana in England 92; Henry renounces betrothal to (1505) 93–4, 98–9; Henry VII's stringent treatment of 95; Ferdinand appoints as envoy in England 100, 113; negotiates marriage between Henry VII and sister Juana 100–1; and proposed marriage of Charles V and Mary Tudor 102–3; influenced by Fray Diego Fernandez 103–4; and Henry VII's death 106, 108; coronation 109, 111; honeymoon with Henry 114–15; pregnancy and miscarriage 114–15, 119; false confinement (1510) 116–18; quarrel with Henry over dismissal of Elizabeth Fitzwalter 118; second pregnancy and birth of son 119–22; and death of son 123; and Ferdinand's war against France 123–4; role in war against France 127–32, 135–6, 139, 731; writes to Bainbridge 131–2;

patronizes tournaments 133; and Edward Howard's death in battle 135; as Regent during Henry's absence in France 137–91, 141–2, 149, 162, 736; anxiety over Henry's campaigning in France 139–40; in war against Scots 143–8, 393, 507, 743; masters English language 145–6; popularity in England 146, 163–4, 227, 243, 341, 455; later pregnancies and miscarriages 149, 153–4, 158, 160; pilgrimages to Walsingham 149, 171; at Mary Tudor's proxy marriage to Louis XII 152; and rumours of Henry's repudiation of marriage 153; embraces Englishness in conflict between husband and father 154; and Fray Diego's disgrace and return to Spain 156; letters to father on Henry 157–8; birth of daughter Mary 158, 197; fails to produce male heir 159–60, 162; loses looks and figure 160–3; marriage relations with Henry 160, 162, 232–4, 392–3; wins pardon for Mayday rioters 163–4; and upbringing of daughter Mary 165–9, 172–4; Progresses 168, 172–3; and Vives's education guidance of Mary 176–8; and Anglo-French alliance 181–2; Louise of Savoy's suspicions of 182; entertains Charles V 183–4, 187–8; at Field of the Cloth of Gold 184; and Mary's prospective marriage to Charles V 187; negotiates with Archduke Ferdinand 188–9; and Spanish alliance under Charles V 190; intervenes with Charles V 191; congratulates Charles V on Pavia victory 192–3; Charles V's antipathy to 193; contests Henry's divorce proceedings 197, 203–5, 208–15, 218–20, 222–9, 233–6, 248–50, 252–4, 292–3, 327, 341, 390, 393, 443; and question of succession to Henry 198–207; and

execution 581; removed from
lodgings 590; ennobled 592; and
Princess Mary's attempted return
to favour 596–8; and JS's
coronation 601; and JS's pregnancy
and birth of son 605, 607; and
Barlow-Constantine conversation
612; favours German marriage for
Henry 617; and Henry's reaction
to AC 629–31; and AC's marriage
relations with Henry 633–4, 636,
640; made earl and Lord Great
Chamberlain 636–7; arrests
opponents 637; arrested and
confined to Tower 638; in Smith-
Grey dispute 655–7; and Sir
William Parr 698, 708; Bigod
lobbies 703; enforces Act of
Supremacy 705; and Latimer in
Pilgrimage of Grace 706; Latimer
bribes 708; Leigh works with 727
Croy, William de, Cardinal-
Archbishop of Toledo 174
Croydon, Surrey 79
Cuero, Juan de 67, 71–2, 80, 110, 113
Culpepper, Jocasta, mother of CH
644
Culpepper, Thomas: at Court 648–9,
653; early relations with CH
648–9; CH's infatuation with 665,
674, 679–80; interrogation and
confession 675–8; tried for treason
and beheaded 680–1; and William
Parr's affair with Dorothy Bray 697
Curzon, a royal courier 230

Dacre, William, 4th Baron 694–6,
701
Dakyn, John 699
Darcy, Lady Elizabeth 60
Darcy, Thomas, Baron: leads
abortive expedition against Moors
125, 127, 381; and Henry's
residence at Windsor 172; articles
against Wolsey 381–2, 422;
executed for participation in
Pilgrimage of Grace 381, 605, 700,
702, 705–6; Memorandum on
status of Church and dissolution of

monasteries 381–4, 447–8;
supports CA in divorce 381
Darrell, Elizabeth 269–70
Daunce, Sir John 315
Deane, Henry, Archbishop of
Canterbury 57
Denny, Anthony 623, 636, 666, 714,
728, 729, 756
Denton, Elizabeth 116, 121
Dereham, Francis: relations with CH
646–8, 660–1, 667, 672–4;
interrogated 670–1, 675; executed
680
Devon, Princess Catherine
Plantagenet, Countess of 166
Devon, Gertrude, Countess of see
Exeter, Marchioness of
Diana, Princess of Wales 228n
Dinteville, Jean de 538, 540
Dogmersfield, Hants 44–5, 48, 251
Doria, Andrea 322, 338
Dorset, Thomas Grey, 2nd Marquess
of 62, 128–30
Douglas, Lady Margaret see Lennox,
Margaret, Countess of
Dudley, Edmund 108
Duque, Ferdinando 82–3
Durham: bishopric and temporalities
236, 356–8, 367

Easton Neston, Northants 364
Eden, Thomas or Richard 299
Edmunds, John 397–8
Edward III, King 22
Edward IV, King 22–4, 53, 165,
690–1
Edward VI, King: birth 607, 730; at
Ashridge 719; and succession
719–20; betrothed to Mary Queen
of Scots 735; celebrates Scottish
treaties 736; installed at Hampton
Court 737, 740; schooling with
Elizabeth 752
Edward the Confessor, King 490
Eleanor, Queen of Francis I of
France 457–8
Elizabeth, Princess, later Queen
Elizabeth I: birth and christening
508–10; babyhood and upbringing

Charles V 402, 407, 454; Henry
seeks good relations with 452–8,
460–1, 468; dances with AB 461,
463; Henry disparages 544; Lennox
serves 733
Francis, Dauphin of France; proxy
marriage to Princess Mary Tudor
180–2, 186
Fuensalida, Don Gutier Gomez de
66, 68, 99, 102, 103–6, 108
Fulke, servant of CP 726, 729

Gairdner, James 312
Gambara, Uberto de 310, 313–14,
316, 328
Garay, Pedro 401
Gardiner, Stephen, Bishop of
Winchester: officiates at Henry-
CP wedding 6, 713–14, 724; as
Wolsey's secretary 252, 299,
347–8; summoned to Henry on
1527 Progress 298–300; and
Henry's divorce proceedings
against CA 299, 384, 386–7, 486;
on missions to Clement VII
314–16, 322–5, 328–9, 334, 347–9,
352; character 347–8, 385; serves
AB 348, 356; as royal secretary
356–7, 384–5; and Durham
temporalities 357–8; at Waltham
Abbey 385; rivalry with Cranmer
385, 721, 725; and universities'
views on divorce 394–6, 397–9,
401; on imprisonment of Shirburn
418; and Wolsey's downfall 423,
425; defends Church privileges
450; surrenders Hanworth manor
to AB 451; diplomatic negotiations
with France 452, 454, 541; and
AB's elevation to Marquessate 460;
differences with Cromwell 486,
637; at AB's coronation 500;
contributes to gown for More 503;
answers Paul III's Brief against
Henry 538–41; fall from favour
539; returns to England 614;
entertains in London palace 637,
649; and dissolution of Henry's
marriage to AC 639–40; and CH's

role as Queen 654, 668; rebuffs
Harst's attempt to reinstate AC
686; acts against religious
reformers 721–3, 725–8, 732;
submits to Henry 727–9; supports
Imperial alliance 732; warns Henry
against religious reforms 756; and
plot against CP 760–1; *De Vera
Obedientia* 540–1
Garrett (or Gerard), Thomas 372–4,
376, 378–9, 418, 705, 721
Garter, Order of 562
Garton, Thomas 239
Gattinara, Mercurin de 232, 405
Gaunt, John of *see* John of Gaunt
Geraldini, Alessandro 16, 29, 70,
72–3, 82–4
Geraldini, Antonio 16
Ghinucci, Jerome, Bishop of
Worcester 535
Giustiniani, Sebastiano, Venetian
ambassador 152, 158–9, 161–2,
164–5
Gloucester 530
Goldsmith, Francis 749
Gonzaga, Fernando de, Duke of
Ariano 731
Goodrich, Thomas 399
Gordon, Lady Catherine 25
Gostwick, John 535–7, 539
Grafton, Richard 655–7
Grammont, Gabriel, Bishop of
Tarbes 404, 411
Granada 11, 13–14, 33; siege of
(1491) 15
Granvelle, Nicholas Perronet,
seigneur de 503, 733
Gravara, Maria de 110
'Great Enterprise' (against France)
190
Green, Sir Thomas 691
Greenacre, Philip 543
Grey, William 655–7
Grimaldi, Francesco 104
Guildford, Sir Edward 458
Guildford, Sir Henry 125, 425, 437,
438, 442, 448, 466
Guildford, Joan, Lady 47, 66, 70, 262,
439

brother of JS 637, 710–12, 719, 748,
765
Shaxton, Nicholas, Bishop of
Salisbury 399, 535–7, 539, 592, 615
Sheffield, Yorks 431
Shelton, Anne, Lady, née Boleyn 517,
551, 571, 598
Shelton, Sir John 513
Shelton, Margaret (Madge) 566,
618
Sherbourne, Robert, Dean of Chapel
Royal 86
ships:
Cordeliere 132
Mary Rose 134
Regent 132
Swallow 461
Shirburn, John, Prior of Reading
418–19
Shorton, Robert 219–20, 251
Shrewsbury, Francis Talbot, 5th Earl
of 492, 501, 744
Shrewsbury, George Talbot, 4th Earl
of: witnesses Henry's wedding with
CA 5; attends Arthur and CA at
wedding chamber 62; command in
France 136, 138–9; in daughter's
marriage negotiations 268; opposes
Henry's actions against CA 437;
absence from AB's coronation
491–2, 501
Sittingbourne, Kent 744
Skip, John 399, 556–9, 567, 573
Smeaton, Mark 434, 565, 568–70,
576–8
Smith, Thomas 654–6
Smith, William, Bishop of Coventry
and Lichfield, and later of Lincoln
74
Snape Castle, Yorks 699, 706
Snowball, William 726
Somerset, Anne, Duchess of see
Hertford, Anne, Countess of
Somerset, Edward Seymour, Duke of
see Hertford, 1st Earl of
Somersham, Hunts, 519
Southampton, Hants 39, 41, 159, 188
Southampton, William Fitzwilliam,
Earl of: and Papal Spanish Brief

229; loyalty to Wolsey 297–8, 300,
303, 319; as Wolsey's Treasurer
297; on Henry's 1527 Progress 298;
Knight on 300; Wolsey offers post
to 425; de Burgo visits 480;
interrogates Norris 568; questions
AB 569; suspended from Council
598; earldom 608; and AC's
journey to England 624–5, 629;
and Henry's relations with AC
636; investigates CH's infidelities
669; and CH's removal to Tower
683; and AC's attempt at
reinstatement 686
Southwark, Surrey 54; Suffolk Place
660; Winchester House 647
Spain: religious diversity and
suppression in 34–6; war with
France 123; renews treaty with
France (1514) 150; Henry's
hostility to 153; treaty with
England (1515) 157; rivalry with
France under Francis I 181–6;
Charles V accedes to throne 185;
England's alliance with under
Charles V 189–90; war with
France in Italy 192; and CA's
Papal Bull and Brief 226–9, 231–2,
341
Speke, Sir John 42
Spelman, Sir John 496, 579
Stafford, Lady Elizabeth see
Fitzwalter, Lady Elizabeth
Stafford, Henry, 1st Baron 171
Stafford, Ursula, Lady 171
Stapleton, Mr and Mrs Christopher
700
Sternold, Thomas 722, 724
Stokesley, John 390–1, 401–2, 410,
420, 563
Suffolk, Catherine, Duchess of, née
Willoughby 714
Suffolk, Charles Brandon, 1st Duke
of: clandestine marriage to Mary of
France 190, 262; command in
France (1523) 190–1; and verdict
of Legate's Court 247; jousting
264, 272–3; on Henry's 1527
Progress 297–8, 300; appointed